SOCIOLOGY

·THE CORE·

James W. Vander Zanden
Ohio State University

Alfred A. Knopf
New York

To my sons, Nels and Brad

THIS IS A BORZOI BOOK
PUBLISHED BY ALFRED A. KNOPF, INC.

First Edition

987654

Library of Congress Cataloging in Publication Data

Vander Zanden, James Wilfrid.
   Sociology: the core.

   Bibliography: p. i
   Includes indexes.
   1. Sociology. I. Title.
HM51.V354   1986   301   85-24011
ISBN 0-394-34109-0

Cover photo: George A. Dillon/Stock, Boston
Cover design: John Lennard

Manufactured in the United States of America

TO THE STUDENT

Alfred A. Knopf, Inc., publishes a Study Guide to accom-
pany *Sociology: The Core*. Your campus bookstore has copies on sale or can order a copy for you from Knopf.

Preface

Sociology illuminates the human experience. It affords a unique perspective that allows us to look behind the outer edifice of social life and discern its inner structure. Thus the discipline encourages us to scrutinize aspects of our social environment that we often ignore, neglect, or take for granted. As Peter Berger has observed, sociology equips us with a special form of consciousness. This consciousness not only provides us with a better understanding of society but also gives us new insights into ourselves. We come to appreciate the relationship between our private experiences and the larger social world, that C. Wright Mills has aptly labeled "the sociological imagination." In sum, sociology is a liberating science.

The Need for a Core Text

A course in sociology should broaden the horizons of students, sharpen their observational skills, and strengthen their analytical capabilities. Yet in recent years, as the store of sociological knowledge has grown, many instructors have felt it necessary to transmit more and more material to their students. This trend is reflected in many mainline introductory sociology textbooks that are little more than information catalogs. Unhappily, students are finding themselves overwhelmed with concepts, principles, and data, and the first course in sociology is becoming unmanageable.

I have written this text in the conviction that our central task remains one of communicating to students the uniqueness of sociological perspective and the sociological imagination. These components constitute the essence of sociology—the core of the discipline. Accordingly, this text strips away many peripheral concerns that preoccupy many textbooks and presents the essentials of sociology. In so doing, it does not neglect or compromise key topics—theory, culture, socialization, groups, formal organization, deviance, social stratification, race and gender, power, the family, religion, and social change. Indeed, the coverage of these topics is equal to—and in many cases, excels—that found in most other introductory textbooks.

A core approach has the advantage of giving greater latitude to instructors. They can supplement the text with papers, readers, or monographs that meet their unique teaching needs. It would be presumptuous for any sociologist to attempt to program another sociologist's course. Accordingly, I have attempted to provide a solid resource with the hope that each instructor will find it a useful foundation and go on his or her own way from there.

The Need for an Issue-Oriented Text

It is also amply clear that the study of social interaction and group life does not take place in a social vacuum. The stuff of sociology is everyday life and, even more significantly, is the issues that confront us as we endeavor to lead fuller, richer, and more fruitful lives. Knowledge offers us the opportunity to improve the human condition by helping us to achieve self-identity, freedom, and self-fulfillment. Accordingly, the text is issue-oriented. It deals with many of the timely matters that concern us as we approach the late 1980s. For instance, Chapter 3 considers life-span roles, changes, and death; Chapter 4, humanizing bureaucracy; Chapter 5, the criminal justice system; Chapter 6, poverty, the middle class, and prospects for social mobility; Chapter 7, social problems associated with race and gender; Chapter 8, issues of economic and political justice; Chapter 9, family violence, employed mothers, divorce, and alternative life styles; Chapter 10, the revival of religious fundamentalism, state-church issues, and the effectiveness of the schools; Chapter 11, environmental concerns, population policies, health care systems, and urban problems; and Chapter 12, the computer revolution, high technology and jobs, terrorism, and social revolution.

The Need for a Relevant Text

In my introductory classes at Ohio State University, I attempt to foster and encourage a sociological consciousness through student projects and journals. I ask my students to observe particular events and then interpret them with sociological concepts and principles. In so doing, students begin to think like sociologists. And they gain a more visceral understanding of sociology. The insights supplied by the students are frequently quite interesting. A sampling of this material is provided in boxes labeled "Doing Sociology." The boxes allow student to teach student by bringing the full drama, color, and richness of the human experience to the learning process.

Pedagogical Aids

In choosing which pedagogical aids to include, I decided to use those that provide the most guidance with the least clutter. Each chapter opens with an outline of its major headings, which allows students to review at a glance the material to be covered. Each chapter concludes with a numbered summary, which recapitulates the central points and allows students to review what they have read in a systematic manner, and with a list of key terms and their definitions, which provides students with a convenient means of reviewing key con-

cepts. The terms most essential to the core of sociology are set in **boldface** type and defined as they are presented in the text.

Ancillary Materials

The complete package of learning and teaching aids for *Sociology: The Core* represents the combined efforts of a number of outstanding teachers of the introductory course.

The student *Study Guide*, prepared by Mary Margaret Wilkes Karraker, offers major learning objectives for each chapter; chapter summaries; multiple-choice items that review key concepts; questions for review; and current-events exercises.

The *Instructor's Manual*, prepared by Sally Rogers, includes learning objectives and techniques for reinforcing them; chapter outlines that highlight key concepts; five student projects for each chapter; annotated lists of films and supplemental readings; and an outline of assignments for book and journal reviews.

The *Test Bank*, prepared by Sally Rogers, provides seventy-five multiple-choice items and five essay questions for each chapter.

Acknowledgments

One never writes a textbook by oneself. I recall with gratitude those countless individuals who over the generations have contributed to the knowledge we now have concerning social interaction and group life. Moreover, I am indebted to those instructors who prepared critical reviews of the manuscript at various stages. They appraised the clarity of expression, technical accuracy, and completeness of coverage. Their comments were invaluable, and I am most grateful to them. They include:

Benigno Aguirre, Texas A&M University
William R. Arnold, University of Kansas
Philip Berg, University of Wisconsin at La
   Crosse

Davita Silfen Glasberg, Southern Illinois University

Barbara Entwisle, Dartmouth College

William Feigelman, Nassau Community College

Norman Goodman, State University of New York

Ronald A. Hardert, Arizona State University

Charles S. Henderson, Memphis State University

Richard Juliani, Villanova University

Ronald Neff, Mississippi State University

Margaret Patton, Morehead State University

Eric D. Poole, Auburn University

Robert Schafer, Iowa State University

David A. Snow, University of Texas

Brad Lowell Stone, Oglethorpe University

Kenrick Thompson, Northern Michigan University

William Thompson, Emporia State University

Michael Timberlake, Memphis State University

Carol Tucker, Southwest Missouri State University

I have also had the opportunity to work with some very able and wonderful people at Random House/Alfred A. Knopf in preparing *Sociology: The Core.* I greatly appreciate their help. I was delighted when Cecilia Gardner was assigned to the book as project editor. I had worked with her previously on *Human Development* and found her once more a most competent and resourceful person. A number of skillful people, including editor Kathy Bendo, photo researcher Charlotte Green, and designer John Lennard joined with Cele in fashioning the design of the text. Lisa Moore coordinated the reviews and was responsible for developing the ancillary materials, tasks that consume much time and vision and make for a sound and well-rounded package. Finally, my thanks go to Bert Lummus (sponsoring editor), who also worked with me on *American Minority Relations* and *Social Psychology* and has been an invaluable partner. He offered patience, wisdom, and enthusiasm. This text, then, is the collective product of a great many individuals.

James W. Vander Zanden

Contents

PREFACE   iii

1   DEVELOPING A SOCIOLOGICAL CONSCIOUSNESS   1

The Sociological Perspective   2
    New Levels of Reality   3
    *Doing Sociology: Navigating Across
       Campus*   4
    The Sociological Imagination   6

The Development of Sociology   7
    Auguste Comte   7
    Herbert Spencer   8
    Karl Marx   9
    Emile Durkheim   11
    Max Weber   13
    American Sociology   14

Conducting Research   15
    The Logic of Science   15
    Steps in the Scientific Method   16
    Research Methods   19
    Research Ethics   23

Summary   24
Glossary   25

2   CULTURE AND SOCIAL STRUCTURE   27

Components of Culture   29
    Norms   30
    Values   31
    Symbols and Language   32

Cultural Unity and Diversity   34
    Cultural Universals   35
    Cultural Integration   35
    Ethnocentrism   36
    Cultural Relativism   37
    Subcultures and Countercultures   37

Social Structure   39
    Statuses   40
    Roles   41
    Groups   43

    Institutions   44
    Societies   44

Perspectives in Sociology   46
    The Functionalist Perspective   47
    The Conflict Perspective   49
    The Interactionist Perspective   51
    *Doing Sociology: Applying the Sociological
       Perspectives*   53
    Using the Three Perspectives   54

Summary   54
Glossary   56

3   SOCIALIZATION   59

Foundations for Socialization   61
    Nature and Nurture   61
    Social Communication   62
    Definition of the Situation   66

The Self   67
    *Charles Horton Cooley: The Looking-Glass
       Self*   68
    *George Herbert Mead: The Generalized
       Other*   69
    Doing Sociology: The Selfhood Process   71
    Erving Goffman: Impression Management   72

Socialization Across the Life Span   73
    Childhood   74
    Adolescence   75
    Young Adulthood   77
    Middle Adulthood   81
    Later Adulthood   82
    Death   84

Summary   85
Glossary   88

4   SOCIAL GROUPS AND FORMAL ORGANIZATIONS   89

Group Relationships   91
    Primary Groups and Secondary Groups   91
    In-Groups and Out-Groups   93
    Reference Groups   94

Group Dynamics   95
  Group Size   95
  Leadership   96
  Social Loafing   97
  Social Dilemmas   97
  Groupthink   98
  Conformity   99
Formal Organizations   99
  Types of Formal Organization   100
  Bureaucracy   101
  Weber's Analysis of Bureaucracies   101
  Disadvantages of Bureaucracy   104
  Informal Organization   106
  Doing Sociology: Informal Organization   107
  Alternative Perspectives   108
  Humanizing Bureaucracies   112
Summary   114
Glossary   116

5 DEVIANCE   119
The Nature of Deviance   120
  Social Properties of Deviance   120
  Doing Sociology: The Social Nature of
    Deviance   122
  Social Control and Deviance   124
  The Social Effects of Deviance   125
Sociological Perspectives on Deviance   127
  The Anomie Perspective   129
  The Cultural Transmission Perspective   131
  The Conflict Perspective   133
  The Labeling Perspective   135
Crime and the Criminal Justice System   138
  The Criminal Justice System   139
  Forms of Crime   140
  Measuring Crime   143
  Differing Conceptions of the Purposes of
    Imprisonment   144
Summary   148
Glossary   150

6 SOCIAL STRATIFICATION   151
Patterns of Social Stratification   152
  Open and Closed Systems   152
  Doing Sociology: Stratification in Campus
    Life   154

  Dimensions of Stratification   155
  Israeli Kibbutzim: Classless
    Communities?   161
  Identifying Social Classes   162
Explanations of Social Stratification   167
  The Functionalist Theory of Stratification   168
  The Conflict Theory of Stratification   169
  A Synthesis   172
The American Class System   172
  The Significance of Social Classes   173
  What Is Happening to the Middle Class?   174
  Poverty in the United States   175
Social Mobility   179
  Forms of Social Mobility   180
  Social Mobility in the United States   180
  Social Mobility in Industrialized Societies   181
  Status Attainment Processes   182
Summary   183
Glossary   185

7 INEQUALITIES OF RACE,
ETHNICITY, AND GENDER   187
Racial and Ethnic Stratification   188
  Minorities   189
  Prejudice and Discrimination   191
  Doing Sociology: Institutional
    Discrimination   193
  Dominant Group Policies   194
  The Functionalist and Conflict
    Perspectives   195
  Racial and Ethnic Groups in the United
    States   198
Gender Stratification   204
  Gender Roles and Culture   204
  Gender Roles and Biology   206
  Acquiring Gender Identities   207
  The Functionalist and Conflict Perspectives on
    Gender Stratification   208
  Gender Roles in the United States   209
Summary   214
Glossary   216

8 POLITICAL AND ECONOMIC
POWER   219
Power, Authority, and the State   220
  The State   220

The Functionalist Perspective on the
   State   221
The Conflict Perspective on the State   223
Legitimacy and Authority   224

Economic Power   226
  Comparative Economic Systems   227
  Corporate Capitalism   228
  Work and the Workplace   236

Political Power   238
  Types of Government   239
  Political Power in the United States   242
  Models of Power in the United States   246

Summary   248
Glossary   251

9   THE FAMILY   **253**
Structure of the Family   254
  Forms of the Family   255
  Forms of Marriage   257
  The Functionalist Perspective on the
     Family   259
  The Conflict Perspective on the Family   261
  The Interactionist Perspective on the
     Family   262

Marriage and the Family in
the United States   263
  Choosing a Marriage Partner   263
  Married Couples   265
  Doing Sociology: The Intimate Life   266
  Parenthood   268
  Employed Mothers   269
  Two-Income Families   271
  Family Violence, Child Abuse, and
     Incest   272
  Divorce   273
  Stepfamilies   274
  Care for the Elderly   275

Alternate Life Styles   276
  Singlehood   276
  Unmarried Cohabitation   278
  Childless Marriages   279
  Single Parenthood   280
  Gay Couples   281
  Communes   282

Summary   283
Glossary   285

10   RELIGION AND EDUCATION   **287**
Religion   288
  Varieties of Religious Behavior   288
  Religious Organizations   290
  The Functionalist Perspective on Religion   293
  Doing Sociology: Intercollegiate Rivalries   295
  The Conflict Perspective on Religion   297
  Reaffirming Tradition: The Iranian Islamic
     Revolution   299
  Promoting Secular Change: The Protestant
     Ethic   300
  Adapting Tradition: The Fundamentalist
     Revival   302
  Mainline Religious Groups   305
  State–Church Issues   309

Education   310
  The Functionalist Perspective on
     Education   310
  The Conflict Perspective on Education   313
  The Bureaucratic Structure of Schools   316
  The Effectiveness of the Schools   317
  The Availability of Education   319

Summary   321
Glossary   323

11   THE HUMAN ENVIRONMENT   **325**
The Ecological Environment   326
  The Functionalist Perspective on the
     Environment   327
  The Conflict Perspective on the
     Environment   328
  Environmental Concerns   328
  The Effects of Crowding   334

Population   336
  Elements in Population Change   336
  Population Composition   341
  Malthus and Marx   344
  Demographic Transition   345
  Population Policies   347
  The American Health Care System   348

The Urban Environment   350
  The Origin and Evolution of Cities   350
  Patterns of City Growth   352
  Ecological Processes   355

Urban Crisis and the Future of American Cities   *356*

Summary   358

Glossary   360

12 SOCIAL CHANGE   **363**

A World of Change   364

Sources of Social Change   *365*

Perspectives on Social Change   *368*

Social Change in the United States   *371*

Doing Sociology: Patterns of Social Change   *372*

Utopian Visions of Earlier Technological Periods   *375*

Social Change in Third World Nations   *377*

Collective Behavior   378

Varieties of Collective Behavior   *378*

Preconditions for Collective Behavior   *382*

Explanations of Crowd Behavior   *385*

Social Movements   387

Types of Social Movements   *387*

Social Revolution   *389*

Terrorism   *390*

Causes of Social Movements   *391*

Looking to the Future   394

Summary   395

Glossary   397

References   i

Name Index   xxv

Subject Index   xxxiii

1

Developing a Sociological Consciousness

THE SOCIOLOGICAL PERSPECTIVE

New Levels of Reality
The Sociological Imagination

THE DEVELOPMENT OF
SOCIOLOGY

Auguste Comte
Herbert Spencer
Karl Marx
Emile Durkheim
Max Weber
American Sociology

CONDUCTING RESEARCH

The Logic of Science
Steps in the Scientific Method
Research Methods
Research Ethics

"No man is an island, entire of itself," wrote the English poet John Donne some four centuries ago. He was drawing our attention to the fact that every person may be many things, but above all each of us is a social being. As infants we are born into a social environment; we become genuinely human only in this environment; and we take our places within the human enterprise in such an environment. Indeed, we cannot be human all by ourselves. What we think, how we feel, and what we say and do is shaped by our interaction with other people in group settings. It is the web of meanings, expectations, behavior, and structural arrangements that result when people interact with one another in society that is the stuff of sociology. Thus we may define **sociology** as the scientific study of social interaction and group life.

Judged by ancient folklore, myths, and archeological remains, human beings have had a long interest in understanding themselves and their social arrangements. They have pondered why people of other societies order their lives in ways that differ from theirs. They have reflected on the reasons that members of their society violate social rules. They have wondered why some people should be wealthy while others experience abject poverty. They have been bewildered by episodes of mass hysteria, revolution, and war. Yet it has been only in the past 150 years or so that human beings have sought answers to these and related questions through science. This science—sociology—pursues the study of social interaction and group behavior through research governed by the rigorous and disciplined collection and analysis of facts.

But many of us are not simply interested in understanding society and human behavior. We would also like to improve the human condition so that we and others might lead fuller, richer, and more fruitful lives. To do this, we need knowledge about the basic structures and processes involved in the social enterprise. Sociology, through its emphasis on observation and measurement, allows us to bring systematic information to bear on difficult questions associated with social policies and choices. Thus sociological findings often find application in practical matters. For instance, the U. S. Supreme Court placed heavy reliance on social science findings regarding the effects of segregation on children in reaching its historic 1954 decision declaring mandatory school segregation unconstitutional (Vander Zanden, 1983). Social science research has also dramatically changed our ideas about child development, aging, mental illness, alcoholism, foreigners, foreign cultures, and behavioral differences in men and women. As the result of this and other research, Americans today have a quite different view of human behavior and social institutions than their parents did only a generation ago (Sterba, 1982).

Sociologists may also deliberately design studies to evaluate public policies or to inform us about social conditions, such as those that assess the effects of various criminal justice programs (Feldman et al., 1983) and the social consequences of mass unemployment (Buss and Redburn, 1983). Further, the collection of census and other national statistical data, which is the foundation of many federal and state policies in health, education, housing, and welfare, is based on sample survey and statistical techniques developed by sociologists and other social scientists (Prewitt, 1982). Sociology, then, is a powerful tool both for acquiring knowledge about ourselves and for intervening in social affairs to realize various goals.

The Sociological Perspective

The sociological perspective invites us to look beyond the often neglected and taken-for-granted aspects of our social environment and examine them in fresh and creative ways (Berger, 1963). We find that there are many layers of meaning in the human experience and that things are not always what they seem. Networks of invisible rules and institutional arrangements guide our behavior. And we continually evolve, negotiate, and rework tacit bargains with family members, friends, lovers, and work associates as we steer our lives across the paths of everyday activity. Many of these understandings are beneath the usual threshold of our awareness (Collins and Makowsky, 1984), so as we look behind the outer edifice of the world and scrutinize the hidden fabric, we encounter new levels of reality. This approach to reality—a special form of consciousness—is the core of the sociological perspective.

NEW LEVELS OF REALITY

We can gain an appreciation for the sociological perspective by considering a classic study carried out by the social scientist Elliot Liebow (1967) in Washington, D.C. He spent eighteen months studying the lives of some twenty black men who "hung out" on the streetcorner in front of the New Deal Carry-out Shop. The shop is located a short distance from the White House in a blighted section of the city. It is open seven days a week, serving a diverse clientele coffee, hamburgers, french fries, hot dogs, and submarine sandwiches. The men come to the corner to eat, to enjoy easy talk, to banter with women who pass by, to "horse around," to see "what's happening," and in general to pass the time. Some of the men are close friends, some do not like others, and some think of others as enemies.

The following scene is typical of a weekday morning in this Washington neighborhood (Liebow, 1967:29):

A pickup truck drives slowly down the street. The truck stops as it comes abreast of a man sitting on a cast-iron porch and the white driver calls out, asking if the man wants a day's work. The man shakes his head and the truck moves on up the block, stopping again whenever idling men come within calling distance of the driver. At the Carry-out corner, five men debate the question briefly and shake their heads no to the truck. The truck turns the corner and repeats the same performance up the next street. In the distance, one can see one man, then another climb into the back of the truck and sit down. In starts and stops, the truck finally disappears.

The white truckdriver views the black streetcorner men as lazy and irresponsible, unwilling "to take a job even if it were handed to them on a platter." But Liebow discovered quite a different picture. Indeed, most of the men on the corner that morning had jobs. Boley had a weekday off because he worked Saturdays as a member of a trash collection crew. Sweets worked nights mopping floors and cleaning up trash in an office building. Tally had come back from his job after his employer had concluded that the weather was not suitable for pouring concrete. And Clarence had to attend a funeral at eleven o'clock.

Also on the corner that morning were a few men who had been laid off and who were drawing unemployment compensation. They had nothing to gain by accepting work that paid little more, and frequently less, than they received in unemployment benefits. And there were a small number like Arthur, able-bodied men who had no visible means of support but who did not want a job. The truckdriver had assumed that the Arthurs were representative of all the streetcorner men. Finally, not to be forgotten, the man on the porch turned out to be severely crippled by arthritis.

The truckdriver thought that able-bodied men like Arthur do not work because they are lazy and undependable. Like many middle-class Americans, he believed that black

Doing Sociology: Navigating Across Campus

Consider what happens as you navigate crowded campus sidewalks and intersections. If you and your classmates were to move like two sets of robots, each set maintaining its line of march, you would constantly knock one another down. Yet somehow you manage to minimize collisions. What crash-avoidance devices do you employ in routing your movement across campus? Students in introductory sociology classes at Ohio State University have examined this matter and have identified a number of social mechanisms.

In the photo on the left, notice the step-and-slide maneuver the man is making to effect a "clean pass." In the photo on the right, notice how the woman communicates through eye contact with the man her intention of crossing in front of him. Both parties must take account of each other in devising their movements if they are to avoid a collision. (Don McCarthy)

- Cultural rules assist us by providing guidelines for navigating walkways. They dictate that we use the right side of the walk. They define for us the "first come, first through" principle at crowded intersections. And they provide that men should defer to women, the young to the elderly, and the able-bodied to the handicapped. We need not invent a new solution for each sidewalk encounter. Instead, we employ common understandings or ready-made answers that were devised by earlier generations of Americans. Accordingly, we do not cross the campus in a haphazard or random fashion, but in accordance with established cultural formulas or recipes.

ghetto men live only for the moment, indulging their whims and satisfying their current appetites with little thought for long-term consequences. Rather than providing for a wife and children, saving their money, and investing in a future, the men appear to squander their limited resources in a life style consumed by gambling, alcohol, drugs, and "high living."

But Liebow found these stereotyped im-

ages to be wrong. He discovered that street-corner men and middle-class men differ not so much in their attitudes toward the future as in the different futures they see ahead of them. Middle-class men command sufficient financial resources to justify the long-term commitment of resources to money-market funds, savings accounts, mutual funds, stocks, and bonds. They hold jobs that offer the promise of upward mobility

- Even were we to computerize robots to remain on the right side of the walk, the robots would collide at intersections. So in crossing the campus, we need to communicate our intentions. For the most part, we accomplish this task on the nonverbal level. At about 15 to 20 feet, we ordinarily size up the situation by glancing at pedestrians we are likely to encounter at an intersection and occasionally establish fleeting eye contact with them. We then shut down eye contact until we are about 3 to 5 feet apart. At this distance we establish brief eye contact, signaling to others that we recognize their presence. However, we usually do not hold the visual contact unless we wish to take an assertive or aggressive stance. Simultaneously, we mentally calculate our own and the other person's pace, and make appropriate adjustments to avoid a collision. In doing so, we may "negotiate" with the other individuals—we slow our pace to signal to them that we would like them to increase their pace, or we quicken our pace to ask them to slow their pace. Additionally, we mutually inform one another of our anticipated route through body language. We may incline our heads, shoulders, or bodies and dart our eyes in the direction we are headed.

- Numbers make a difference. The lone individual is at a disadvantage and groups at an advantage. A lone individual is likely to give way or detour around a group of people (even stepping off the sidewalk), whereas a group is likely to ignore a lone individual and continue on course in an assertive fashion.

- Pedestrians "compress" themselves in crowded settings. For instance, individuals cooperate to effect a "clean pass." When they are about 5 to 6 feet apart, each person slightly angles his or her body, turns the shoulder, and takes a slight step to the side; hands are pulled inward or away to avoid hand-to-hand contact; bodies are twisted backward to maximize face-to-face distance. Likewise, students often pull their backpack or books toward a more central and less exposed position.

- In the course of navigating campus sidewalks, people are constantly sizing one another up, especially in terms of their basic roles and physical attractiveness. Men tend to hold their gaze longer when looking at women than when looking at men. Likewise, men seem to be permitted greater leeway in "looking over" women than women are permitted in "looking over" men. If individuals are interested in one another, after a few paces they follow with a backward glance.

in corporate or professional careers. And they can reasonably expect their children to pursue a higher education. But it is otherwise for streetcorner men, who are obliged to expend all their resources maintaining themselves in the present. Thus when streetcorner men squander a week's pay in two days it is not because, like animals or children, they are unconcerned with the future. They do so precisely because they are aware of the future and the hopelessness of their prospects.

Like many privileged Americans, the white truckdriver had located the job problems of ghetto men in the men themselves—or, more precisely, in their lack of willingness to work. Given this interpretation, social policy might best be directed toward changing the motivations of streetcorner men and encouraging them to develop those values and goals that lead to occupational achievement. But Liebow's research revealed a quite different state of affairs. The streetcorner men and other American men did *not* differ in their fundamental values or goals. The men on the corner also wanted stable jobs and marriages. However, they had continually discovered that jobs are only intermittently available, almost always menial, often hard, and invariably low-paying. Jobs as dishwashers, janitors, store clerks, and unskilled laborers lie outside those tracks that typically lead to advancement in the United States, and thus the jobs offer no more in the future than they do in the present. Moreover, armed with models of other men in their community who have failed, streetcorner men are uncertain of their ability to carry out their responsibilities as husbands and fathers.

In seeking an explanation for their behavior, Liebow looked beyond the individual men to the social fabric in which the men were enmeshed. He turned his investigative eye upon the social arrangements that are external to individuals but that nonetheless structure their experiences and place constraints on their behavior. In sum, society—and more particularly its groups and institutions—provides the framework for sociology, not the individual. The sociological perspective allows us to bring previously inaccessible aspects of human life to social awareness and gain a window on the social landscape that we often overlook or misunderstand.

THE SOCIOLOGICAL IMAGINATION

We have stressed that a basic premise underlying sociology is the notion that only by understanding the society in which we live can we gain a fuller insight into ourselves. C. Wright Mills (1959) termed this quality of the discipline the **sociological imagination**—the ability to see our private experiences and personal difficulties as entwined with the structural arrangements of our society and the historical times in which we live. We usually go about our daily activities bounded by our own narrow orbit. Our viewpoint is limited to our school, job, family, and neighborhood. The sociological imagination allows us to break out of this contracted vision and discern the relationship between our personal experiences and broader social and historical events.

Mills, an influential but controversial sociologist, pointed out that our personal troubles and public issues "overlap and interpenetrate to form the larger structure of social and historical life." Take, for instance, the job difficulties experienced by the streetcorner men studied by Liebow. In 1984, a year of "economic recovery" in the United States, nearly one out of five black adults and one of two black teenagers were unemployed (in contrast to one out of fifteen white adults and one of five white teenagers). Mills (1959:9) contended that we cannot look to the "personal character" of individuals to explain their employment problems under these sorts of circumstances:

The very structure of opportunities has collapsed. Both the correct statement of the problem and the range of possible solutions require us to consider the economic and political institutions of the society, and not merely the personal situation and character of a scatter of individuals.

Social and historical forces will also provide the external constraints governing the career opportunities of many students currently enrolled in the nation's colleges and universities. Shifts in the age structure of the population are reshaping the social, economic, and political landscape. The graying of American society is posing particularly thorny problems in the workplace as younger and middle-aged workers jockey for advancement. A nearly 60 percent increase in the number of 35- to 44-year-olds is expected in the decade between 1985 and 1995. A good many people will be lining up for promotions, but there will be fewer slots open than there will be people hoping to fill them. Thus the developing private job frustrations of many younger Americans must be understood within the context of the structural factors operating in the larger society and the workplace (see Chapter 12).

We see the operation of the sociological imagination in other spheres of life as well. Mills (1959:9) was especially concerned with issues of war and peace:

The personal problem of war, when it occurs, may be how to survive it or how to die in it with honor; how to make money out of it; how to climb into the higher safety of the military apparatus; or how to contribute to the war's termination. . . . But the structural issues of war have to do with its causes; with what types of men it throws up into command; with its effects upon economic and political, family and religious institutions, with the unorganized irresponsibility of a world of nation-states.

In sum, the sociological imagination allows us to penetrate our social world and identify the links between our personal biographies and the larger social forces of life—to see that what is happening to us immediately is a minute point at which our personal lives and society intersect.

The Development of Sociology

Just as we must seek an understanding of our private experiences and personal difficulties in the structural arrangements and the historical times in which we live, so we must locate the origins of sociology in the social milieu of the period in which it developed. The political revolutions ushered in by the French Revolution in Europe in 1789 and continuing through the nineteenth century provided a major impetus to sociological work. Many individuals were troubled by the chaos and disorder that characterized Europe, and they longed for the more peaceful and relatively orderly days of the Middle Ages. But more sophisticated thinkers recognized that the clock could not be turned back, and that they would have to seek new foundations of order in society (Ritzer, 1983).

Simultaneously, an additional force was at work. The Industrial Revolution that swept many Western nations resulted in large numbers of people leaving a predominantly agricultural setting for work in the factories. New social and economic arrangements arose to provide the many services required by emergent capitalism. The excesses of the industrial system led some thinkers like Karl Marx to scrutinize the operation of social and economic institutions and to propose alternatives to them. Let us turn, then, to a brief consideration of the contributions of five particularly influential sociologists and to the emergence of sociology in the United States.

AUGUSTE COMTE

Auguste Comte (1798–1857) is commonly credited with being the founder of sociology and as having coined the name "sociology" for the new science. He emphasized that the study of society must be scientific, and he urged sociologists to use systematic observation, experimentation, and comparative historical analysis as their methods. Indeed, he went so far as to construct a "hierarchy of the sciences," with sociology as the "queen" science. Although this hierarchy allowed Comte to assert the importance of his new science and to separate it from social philosophy, his grandiose image of sociology is not shared by contemporary sociologists (Turner, 1982: Ritzer, 1983).

Vast social changes during the nineteenth century drew the attention of a number of intellectuals to the study of society and institutional life. Political turmoil and revolutions, the distribution of traditional social patterns, and the new technology and capitalist arrangements of the Industrial Revolution provided a rich milieu for the emergence of sociology. (The Bettmann Archive)

Comte divided the study of society into social statics and social dynamics. **Social statics** involves those aspects of social life that have to do with order and stability and that allow societies to hold together and endure. **Social dynamics** refers to those aspects of social life that have to do with social change and that pattern institutional development. Although the specifics of his work no longer direct contemporary sociology, Comte exerted enormous influence on the thinking of other sociologists, particularly Herbert Spencer and Emile Durkheim.

HERBERT SPENCER

Herbert Spencer (1820–1903), an English sociologist called by some the "second foun-

der" of sociology, shared Comte's concern with social statics and social dynamics. He viewed society as having important similarities with a biological organism and depicted it as a *system*, a whole made up of interrelated parts. Just as the human body is made up of organs like the kidneys, lungs, and heart, so society is made up of institutions like the family, religion, education, the state, and the economy. Like biologists who portray an organism in terms of its structures and the functional contributions these structures make to its survival, Spencer described society in similar terms. This image of society is in line with what sociologists now call structural-functional theory, a perspective about which we will have more to say in Chapter 2.

Spencer handled social statics by means of the organic analogy. But he had an even greater interest in social dynamics. He proposed an evolutionary theory of historical development, one that depicted the world as growing progressively better. Intrigued by the Darwinian view of natural selection, Spencer applied the concept of the survival of the fittest to the social world. He sought to demonstrate that government should not interfere with the natural processes going on in a society. Only in this manner would people who were "fit" survive and those who were "unfit" die out. If this principle were allowed to operate freely, human beings and their institutions, like plants and animals, would progressively adapt themselves to their environment and reach higher and higher levels of historical development.

Spencer's Social Darwinist outlook shows that the ideas we hold about ourselves and the universe are shaped by the social age in which we live. Spencer did much of his serious writing at the height of laissez-faire capitalism, so it is hardly surprising that he should have embraced the doctrine that rugged individualism, unbridled competition, and governmental restraint achieve the greatest positive good. Spencer's Social Darwinist ideas were used extensively within England and the United States to justify unrestrained capitalism. John D. Rockefeller, the American oil tycoon, would echo Spencer and observe: "The growth of a large business is merely a survival of the fittest. . . . This is not an evil tendency in business. It is merely the working out of a law of nature" (quoted by Lewontin, Rose, and Kamin, 1984:26).

KARL MARX

Although Karl Marx (1818–1883) considered himself a political activist and not a sociol-

Karl Marx did more than devise a distinctive theoretical approach for analyzing social life. His sharp critique of capitalist institutions and his program of political activism provided a powerful impetus to the work of sociologists like Max Weber, who responded with alternative interpretations of institutional arrangements. Today significant sociological research is being conducted by American sociologists who have taken inspiration from the writings of Marx and his associates. (Culver Pictures)

ogist, in truth he was both—and a philosopher, historian, economist, and political scientist as well. He viewed science not only as a vehicle for understanding society, but also as a tool for transforming it. Marx was especially anxious to change the structure of capitalist institutions and to establish new institutions in the service of humanity.

Although born in Germany, Marx was compelled to spend much of his adult life as a political exile in London. Through the years his theories have come to be accepted by millions of people. Today governments claiming to be run on Marxist principles rule more than a third of the world's population. It should be stressed, however, that Marxism is not synonymous with modern-day communist movements or states. Indeed, it is quite likely that Marx would be greatly troubled by many aspects of life in the Soviet Union and Eastern European nations. As Mills (1962:25) points out regarding Marx: "A positive image of man [humankind], of what might come to be, lies under every line of his analysis of what he held to be an inhuman society." Marx anticipated a more humane society, and saw his task as fostering an objective understanding of institutional life that could be used to bring about social change.

Marx has influenced sociological thinking both by his penetrating insights and by the fact that some sociologists have constructed their work specifically *against* his theory (Gurney, 1981). Prior to the 1960s, most American theorists dismissed Marx as an ideologue whose partisan sympathies barred him from producing serious scientific work. But as young American sociologists were drawn into the civil rights and antiwar movements of the 1960s and early 1970s, they began to give serious attention to Marx's ideas. In the intervening two decades, American sociologists have come to accord Marx his rightful place among the giants of sociological thought (Ritzer, 1983).

Marx tried to discover the basic principles of history. He focused his search on the economic environments in which societies develop, particularly the current state of their technology and their method of organizing production (such as hunting and gathering, agriculture, or industry). At each stage of history, these factors dictate the group that will dominate society and the groups that will be subjugated. He believed that society is divided into those who own the means of producing wealth and those who do not, which gives rise to **class conflict** (see Chapters 6 and 8). All history, he said, is composed of struggles between classes. In ancient Rome, it was a conflict between patricians and plebeians and be-

tween masters and slaves. In the Middle Ages, it was a struggle between guildmasters and journeymen and between lords and serfs. And in contemporary Western societies that sprouted from the ruins of the feudal order, class antagonisms revolve about the struggle between the oppressing capitalist class or bourgeoisie and the oppressed working class or proletariat. The former derive their income through their ownership of the means of production, primarily factories, which allows them to exploit the labor of workers. The latter own nothing except their labor power and, because they are dependent for a living upon the jobs provided by capitalists, must sell their labor power in order to exist.

Marx was strongly influenced by the work of the German philosopher Georg Hegel (1770–1831), and especially by Hegel's notion of the **dialectic**. In Hegelian philosophy the term denoted an approach to logic or reasoning. The dialectic held that any idea, termed a *thesis*, takes on meaning only when it is related to its opposite or contradictory idea, called an *antithesis*. The interaction between the two ideas forms a new idea, termed a *synthesis*. The dialectic process, through its *reconciliation of opposites*, served as a method for interpreting history. For instance, in the development of art, one "period" interacts with and is succeeded by another, but higher form. The dialectic depicts the world as made up not of static structures, but of dynamic processes—a world of *becoming* rather than *being*.

Hegel applied the dialectic primarily to ideas; Marx adapted the approach to the study of social relations in the material world. His perspective is called **dialectical materialism**. Marx was more interested in the study of real relationships, especially the conflicts between classes, than in the highly abstract Hegelian notions of thesis-antithesis-synthesis. In the Marxian view of history, every economic order grows to a state of maximum efficiency, while it develops internal contradictions or weaknesses that contribute to its decay. The roots of an opposing order already begin to take hold in an old order. In time, the new order displaces the old order, while simultaneously absorbing its most useful features. In this manner society is propelled from one historical stage to another as each new order triumphs over the old. Marx depicted slavery as being displaced by feudalism, feudalism by capitalism, capitalism by socialism, and ultimately socialism by communism (the highest stage of society).

Marx portrayed political ideologies, religion, family organization, education, and government as making up the **superstructure** of society. The economic base of society—its mode of producing goods and its class structure—influences the forms that other institutions take. When one class controls the critical means whereby people derive their livelihood, they gain the leverage necessary to fashion other aspects of institutional life—the superstructure—in ways that favor their class interests. However, the economic structure does not shape the superstructure only in a one-way direction (see Chapters 8, 10, and 12). Aspects of the superstructure act upon the economic base and modify it in a reciprocal relationship. For this reason, as we shall see in Chapters 6 and 8, Marx thought that when the working class became armed with a revolutionary ideology that fostered its class consciousness, it would overturn the existing social order and establish one that would pursue humane goals.

We will have a good deal more to say about Marx in the chapters that follow, particularly in our consideration of social stratification in Chapter 6 and power in Chapter 8. For our purposes here, suffice it to note that Marx is now recognized by most sociologists as a major figure in sociological theory. Today he is better known and understood, and more widely studied, than at any time since he began his career in the 1840s. Much of what is valuable in his work has now been incorporated in mainstream sociology, particularly as it finds expression in the conflict perspective we will consider in Chapter 2.

EMILE DURKHEIM

Whereas Marx saw society as a stage upon which classes with conflicting interests contested with one another, the French sociologist Emile Durkheim (1858–1916) focused his sociological eye on the question of how societies hold together and endure. The principal objection Durkheim had to Marx's work was that Marx attributed too much importance to economic factors and class struggle and not enough to social solidarity (Bottomore, 1981). Central to Durkheim's (1897/1951) sociology is the notion that social integration is necessary for the maintenance of the social order and for the happiness of individuals. In particular, he suggested that happiness depends upon individuals finding a sense of meaning outside themselves that occurs within the context of group involvement. Durkheim sought to demonstrate that the destruction of social bonds has negative consequences, and under some circumstances can lead individuals to commit suicide. Other sociologists have picked up on this central idea and have shown how the breakdown of group bonds can contribute to deviant behavior (Merton, 1968) and participation in social movements (Kornhauser, 1959).

In *The Division of Labor in Society* (1893/1964), Durkheim examined social solidarity. He distinguished between the solidarity found in early and modern societies. In early societies the social structure was relatively simple, with little division of labor. People were knitted together by the fact that they engaged in essentially similar tasks as jacks-of-all-trades. They derived a sense of oneness because they were so much alike, what Durkheim termed **mechanical solidarity**. Modern societies, in contrast, are characterized by complex social structures and a sophisticated division of labor. People perform specialized tasks in factories, offices, and schools. Since each person performs a relatively narrow range of tasks, no one person can be self-sufficient and all must depend upon others in order to survive. Under these circumstances, society is held together by the interdependence fostered by the differences among people, what Durkheim labeled **organic solidarity**.

In examining social solidarity and other sociological questions, Durkheim ascribed ultimate social reality to the group, not to the individual. He contended that the distinctive subject matter of sociology should be the study of social facts. **Social facts** are aspects of social life that cannot be explained in terms of the biological or mental characteristics of the individual. People experience the social fact as external to themselves in the sense that it has an independent reality and forms a part of their objective environment. As such, the social fact serves to *constrain* their behavior. Illustrations include social rules, maxims of public morality, patterns of family living, and religious observances.

Viewed in this manner, the social fact takes on the qualities of a "thing," a reality in its own right that is independent of its manifestation in particular individuals. Since the social fact is real and external, like the physical and biological aspects of the human environment, it has implications for individuals and their behavior. The hallmark of this independent reality is the resistance it poses to our inclinations and the counterpressure it places on our actions. For instance, individuals cannot flout moral and legal rules without tangible evidence of social disapproval (Benoit-Smullyan, 1948).

Durkheim insisted that the explanation of social life must be sought in society itself. Society, he said, is more than the sum of its parts; it is a system formed by the association of individuals that comes to constitute a reality, with its own distinctive characteristics.

Durkheim convincingly demonstrated the critical part social facts play in human behavior in his book *Suicide* (1897/1951), a landmark study in the history of sociology. Whereas earlier sociologists were given to armchair speculation, Durkheim undertook the painstaking collection and analysis of data in order to test his theory. Moreover, he used statistical techniques for studying human populations. In doing so, he was the first major sociologist to face up to the complex problems associated with the disciplined and rigorous study of social life.

In his study of suicide, Durkheim used population data gained from government records statistically to refute theories that explained suicide in terms of climatic, geographic, biological, or psychological factors. As an alternative, he proposed that suicide is a social fact—a product of the meanings, expectations, and structural arrangements that evolve as people interact with one another. As such, suicide is explainable by social factors. Durkheim investigated suicide rates among various groups of Europeans and found that some groups had higher rates than others. Protestants had higher rates than did Catholics; the unmarried, higher rates than the married; and soldiers, higher rates than civilians. Moreover, suicide rates were higher in times of peace than in times of war and revolution, and in times of economic prosperity and recession than in times of economic stability. On the basis of these findings, he concluded that different suicide rates (as distinct from the individual case, which is a matter for psychology) are the consequence of variations in social solidarity. Individuals who are enmeshed in a web of social bonds are less inclined to suicide than individuals who are weakly integrated into group life.

MAX WEBER

No sociologist other than Marx has had a greater impact on sociology than the German sociologist Max Weber (1864–1920). Significantly, as we will see in later chapters, a good deal of Weber's work represented a debate with the ghost of Marx. Although finding much of value in Marx's writings, Weber disagreed with Marx on a number of important matters. Over the course of his career, Weber left a legacy of rich insights for a variety of disciplines, including economics, political science, and history. Among sociologists, he is known not only for his theoretical contributions, but for a number of specific ideas that in their own right have generated considerable interest and research. His sociological work covered a wide range of topics, including politics, bureaucracies, social stratification, law, religion, capitalism, music, the city, and cross-cultural comparison.

Weber believed that sociologists can derive an *understanding* of their subject matter in a manner that is unavailable to chemists and physicists. In investigating human behavior, sociologists are not limited to such objective criteria as weight and temperature; they can examine the "meanings" individuals bring to their interactions with one another. Consequently, Weber contended that a critical aspect of the sociological enterprise is the study of the intentions, values, beliefs, and attitudes that underlie people's behavior. Weber employed the German word **verstehen**—meaning "understanding" or "insight"—in describing this approach for learning about the subjective meanings people attach to their actions. In using this method, sociologists mentally attempt to place themselves in the shoes of other people and identify what they think and how they feel. Whereas Durkheim argued that sociologists should direct their investigations primarily to social facts that lie beyond the individual, Weber thought it also essential that sociologists examine the definitions people use in shaping their behavior.

Another notable sociological contribution made by Weber is his concept of the ideal type. An **ideal type** is a concept constructed by a sociologist to portray the principal characteristics of a phenomenon. The term has nothing to do with evaluations of any sort. Rather, it is a tool that allows sociologists to generalize and simplify data by ignoring minor differences in order to accentuate major similarities. In Chapter 4 we will see how Weber employed the notion of the ideal type to devise his model of bureaucracy, and in Chapter 10 how he used it to examine the connection between Calvinism (the Protestant ethic) and capitalism. Weber contended that if sociologists are to establish cause-and-effect relationships, they must have concepts that are defined in a precise and unambiguous manner. The ideal type affords such a standard, especially in the study of concrete historical events and situations. It serves as a measuring rod against which sociologists can evaluate actual cases.

In his writings, Weber stressed the importance of a **value-free sociology**. He insisted that sociologists must not allow their personal biases to affect the conduct of their scientific research. Weber recognized that sociologists, like everyone else, have individual biases and moral convictions regarding behavior. But he insisted that sociologists must cultivate a disciplined approach to the phenomena they study so that they may see facts as they are, and not as they might wish them to be. By the same token, Weber recognized that objectivity is not neutrality. *Neutrality* implies that a person does not takes sides on an issue; *objectivity* has to do with the pursuit of scientifically verifiable knowledge. Weber saw a role for values in certain specific aspects of the research process—namely, in selecting a topic for study and in determining the uses to which the knowledge is put. Clearly, data do not speak for themselves; they must be interpreted by scientists. For his part, Weber was led to study bureaucracy because it was an important part of the Germany in which he lived. Moreover, Weber was not afraid to express a value judgment or to tackle important issues of the day (Ritzer, 1983).

AMERICAN SOCIOLOGY

The sociologists we have considered thus far have been of European origin. Were sociologists to establish a sociological Hall of Fame, Comte, Spencer, Marx, Durkheim, and Weber would unquestionably be among its first inductees. Yet as sociology entered the twentieth century, Americans assumed a critical role in its development. In the period preceding World War I, an array of factors provided a favorable climate for sociology in the United States (Hinkle, 1980). As in Europe, the Industrial Revolution and urbanization gave a major impetus to sociological study. An added factor was the massive immigration of foreigners to the United States and the problems their absorption and assimilation posed for American life. Further, both sociology and the modern university system arose together. In Europe, by contrast, sociology had a more difficult time becoming established, because it had to break into an established system of academic disciplines.

A number of individuals like Lester F. Ward (1841–1913) played an important part in the development of sociology in the United States. Ward was influenced by Spencer's ideas, but unlike Spencer he was an advocate of social reform. He thought

that sociologists should identify the basic laws that underlie social life, and then use this knowledge to improve human society. However, contributions of more lasting significance to sociology were made by sociologists at the University of Chicago, where the first department of sociology in the United States was established in 1893. Until 1940, Chicago sociologists dominated the discipline, as did the study of Chicago itself. Chicago was viewed as a "social laboratory," and it was subjected to intense and systematic study. Included in this research were investigations of juvenile gangs, immigrant ghettos, wealthy Gold Coast and slum life, taxi-dance halls, prostitution, and mental disorders.

During the 1940s and until the mid-1960s, sociologists at Columbia, Harvard, and the University of California at Berkeley took the lead and established the major directions for sociological research and theory. Paul L. Lazarsfeld and his colleagues crafted techniques for surveying public attitudes, while Talcott Parsons, Robert K. Merton, and Kingsley Davis refined models that portrayed society as a system made up of parts with interrelated functions. The leaders of American sociology insisted that the discipline should remain outside social problems and concern itself strictly with the enlargement of sociological knowledge.

The social turmoil of the 1960s and early 1970s brought to sociology many students who were student power, civil rights, and peace activists. These "new breed" sociologists contended that the doctrine of sociological neutrality was a cloak concealing moral insensitivity—a crass disregard for such things as the suffering of the poor and minorities, the destructiveness of war, and the high social costs of crime. These sociologists looked to the writings of C. Wright Mills and other proponents of the sociological imagination for their inspiration. They also broke with established sociological theory and sought new directions in theory and research. Thus sociology today is a much more diverse, and many would say richer, discipline than it was a few decades ago.

Conducting Research

The sociologists we have considered have provided us with important theoretical insights regarding the nature and workings of social life. However, theory that is not confirmed by facts is merely speculation that has little solid value. We require both theoretical understanding and facts, and for this reason both theory and research are essential components of the sociological enterprise (see Chapter 2). Theory inspires research that can verify or disprove it. Research provides findings that permit us to accept, reject, or modify our theoretical formulations, while simultaneously challenging us to craft new and better theories.

Sociologist William B. Sanders (1974) points out that sociological research resembles detective work. Both entail initial perplexity and conjecture, the search for evidence, perceptive reasoning, false leads, and, ideally, a final sense of triumph. For example, consider how the great fictional detective Sherlock Holmes went about sizing up situations. Here is Holmes's account of how he figured out that Dr. Watson had recently returned from Afghanistan (Doyle, 1927:24):

Here is a gentleman of medical type, but with the air of a military man. Clearly an army doctor, then. He has just come from the tropics, for his face is dark, and that is not the natural tint of skin, for his wrists are fair. He has undergone hardship and sickness, as his haggard face says clearly. His left arm has been injured. He holds it in a stiff and unnatural manner. Where in the tropics could an English army doctor have seen such hardship and got his arm wounded? Clearly in Afghanistan.

Underlying both sociology and detective work is the notion of *causality,* an idea that merits closer examination.

THE LOGIC OF SCIENCE

As we go about our daily lives, we typically assume that when one event occurs, another event, one that ordinarily follows the first, will do so again. Science makes a similar assumption—namely, that every event or action results from an antecedent cause. Indeed, a primary objective of science is to decide what causes what. Sociologists assume that crime, racism, social inequality, and marriages do not simply "happen," but that they have causes. Moreover, they assume that under identical conditions, the same cause will always produce the same effect. So sociologists, like other scientists, proceed on the assumption that cause-and-effect relationships prevail in the universe. Otherwise social life would be unintelligible, because events would occur in a random or haphazard manner and be utterly unpredictable.

Viewed in a scientific context, truth is not a matter of belief, but of objective reality that can be *empirically* tested—that is, data can be gathered and analyzed by means of careful observation and meticulous measurement. Thus the reality established by science is assumed to be the same for all people regardless of their value judgments regarding it. This scientific reality derives from the way scientists go about testing for linkages among variables. A **variable** is the term scientists apply to something that they think influences (or is influenced) by something else. It usually occurs in different amounts, degrees, or forms. For example, heat is one variable that causes water to boil; atmospheric pressure is another. The variables sociologists typically study have to do with social conditions, attitudes, and behaviors. In studying political behavior, for example, sociologists commonly examine such variables as differences in race, sex, age, religion, and socioeconomic standing. They also frequently appraise the social climate of the times as it finds expression in such variables as the state of international tensions and the rates of unemployment, interest, and inflation.

In investigating cause-and-effect relationships, scientists distinguish between the independent and the dependent variable. The **independent variable** is the variable that causes an effect. The **dependent variable** is the variable that is affected. The causal variable (the independent variable) precedes in time the phenomenon it causes (the dependent variable). For example, as the temperature gets warmer, air can hold more water. The temperature—a measure of heat—is the independent variable and the amount of water suspended in the air is the dependent variable. Similarly, as the socioeconomic level of women (independent variable) increases, the mortality rate of their infants decreases (the dependent variable). In their research, scientists typically attempt to hypothesize the relationship they expect to find between the independent and dependent variables. Such a statement—or **hypothesis**—is a proposition that can then be tested to determine its validity.

Scientists spend a good deal of their time attempting to figure out how one thing relates to another. They seek to determine the degree of association that exists between an independent and a dependent variable. If the variables are causally related, then they must be correlated with one another. A **correlation** exists if a change in one variable is associated with a change in the other variable. Since the mortality rate of infants decreases as the socioeconomic level of women increases, the two variables are said to be correlated.

Correlation, however, does not establish causation (Cole, 1972). For instance, the death rate is considerably higher among hospitalized individuals than among non-hospitalized individuals. Yet we would be wrong to conclude on the basis of this correlation that hospitals cause death. Likewise, the amount of damage resulting from a fire is closely associated with the number of fire engines that are on the scene. Again, we would be wrong to conclude that fire engines cause greater fire damage. In these latter cases the correlation is *spurious*—the apparent relationship between the two variables is produced by a third variable that influences the original variables (severe sickness is associated both with admission to hospitals and with death; similarly, a large, uncontrolled fire is associated both with extensive damage and the mobilization of multiple firefighting units). In order to combat the likelihood that their research will be contaminated by third variables, scientists employ controls, a matter we will consider at greater length a little later in the chapter when we deal with experimentation.

STEPS IN THE SCIENTIFIC METHOD

The scientific method is a way of finding out about the world that relies on the rigorous and disciplined collection of facts and a logical explanation of them. It finds expression in a systematic series of steps that seek to ensure maximum objectivity in investigating a problem. Ideally sociological research follows this step-by-step procedure, although in practice it is not always possible. Even so, the following steps provide useful guidelines for conducting research (see Figure 1.1).

1. *Selecting a researchable problem.* The range of topics available for social research is as broad as the range of human behavior. Thus we need to find a problem that merits study and that can be investigated by the methods of science. For instance,

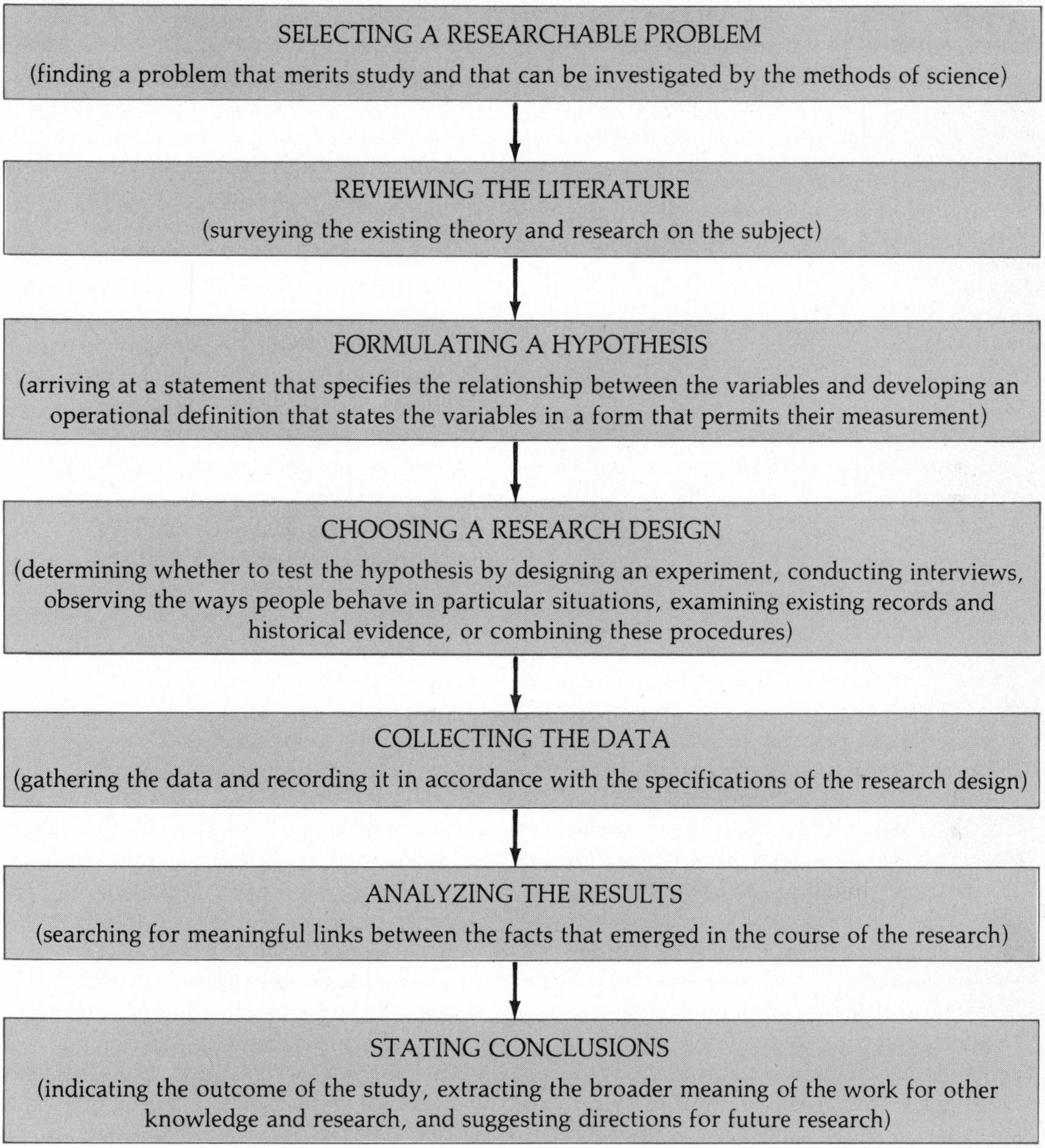

SELECTING A RESEARCHABLE PROBLEM

(finding a problem that merits study and that can be investigated by the methods of science)

↓

REVIEWING THE LITERATURE

(surveying the existing theory and research on the subject)

↓

FORMULATING A HYPOTHESIS

(arriving at a statement that specifies the relationship between the variables and developing an operational definition that states the variables in a form that permits their measurement)

↓

CHOOSING A RESEARCH DESIGN

(determining whether to test the hypothesis by designing an experiment, conducting interviews, observing the ways people behave in particular situations, examining existing records and historical evidence, or combining these procedures)

↓

COLLECTING THE DATA

(gathering the data and recording it in accordance with the specifications of the research design)

↓

ANALYZING THE RESULTS

(searching for meaningful links between the facts that emerged in the course of the research)

↓

STATING CONCLUSIONS

(indicating the outcome of the study, extracting the broader meaning of the work for other knowledge and research, and suggesting directions for future research)

FIGURE 1.1   THE STEPS IN THE SCIENTIFIC METHOD
The chart shows the steps researchers commonly follow in investigating a problem.

two social scientists, Donald O. Dutton and Arthur P. Aron (1974), were intrigued by the seeming connection between states of high anxiety and sexual attraction, a link first noted by the first-century Roman poet Ovid. Ovid had advised men that an excellent time to arouse romantic passion in women was while watching gladiators disembowel one another in the arena. Presumably the emotions of fear and repulsion excited by the grisly scene somehow translated themselves into romantic interest.

2. *Reviewing the literature.* Rather than plunging hastily into a research venture, Dutton and Aron surveyed the literature dealing with sexual attraction and states of strong emotion. This review told them about other research that had been undertaken, suggested a variety of leads, and saved them from duplicating work others had already done. For instance, ethologist Niko Tinbergen (1954) had found a connection between "aggression" and courting behaviors in some animal species, and a number of psychologists had experimentally documented the existence of similar linkages in human behavior (Clark, 1952; Barclay and Haber, 1965).

3. *Formulating a hypothesis.* After reviewing the literature, researchers commonly arrive at a tentative guess regarding the relationship they believe exists between two variables. They state this relationship in the form of a hypothesis. For instance, Dutton and Aron sought to test the hypothesis that a state of high anxiety (the independent variable) heightens sexual attraction (the dependent variable). But before undertaking their research, they had to develop operational definitions of their variables. In developing an **operational definition**, scientists take abstract concepts and put them in a form that permits their measurement. Dutton and Aron (1974:511) operationized their hypothesis as follows: "An attractive female is seen as more attractive by males who encounter her while they experience a strong emotion (fear) than by males not experiencing a strong emotion."

4. *Choosing a research design.* Once researchers have formulated and operationalized their hypothesis, they have to determine how they will collect the data that will provide a test of it. Depending on the nature of their hypothesis, they might design an experiment, conduct interviews, observe the way people behave in particular situations, examine existing records and historical evidence, or combine these procedures. Dutton and Aron undertook a field experiment in which they used the real world as their laboratory. They introduced the independent variable into a natural setting to determine its impact on behavior.

5. *Collecting the data.* The actual collection of the data plays a critical part in the research enterprise. Dutton and Aron collected their data near two footbridges hikers use to cross the Capilano River in North Vancouver, Canada. The first or "experimental" bridge is a 450-foot-long structure suspended 230 feet above a rock canyon and a rushing stream; it has a tendency to tilt, sway, and wobble, creating the impression that one could easily fall over the side. The second or "control" bridge is a wide, solid wood bridge farther upriver that is only 10 feet above a small, shallow stream. An attractive female interviewer approached male hikers who had crossed either of the bridges and explained that she was doing a project for her psychology class. The men were asked to complete a brief questionnaire and write a short dramatic story based on a picture of a young woman from the Thematic Apperception Test (TAT). When the men (termed *subjects*) completed their questionnaires, the woman gave each man her name and telephone number in the event that he "desired more information about the study."

6. *Analyzing the results.* Once researchers have their data, they must analyze them to find answers to the questions posed by their research project. Analysis involves a search for meaningful links between the facts that have emerged in the course of the research. As revealed by the content of the stories, Dutton and Aron found that the men who had crossed the wobbly suspension bridge were more sexually aroused than the men who had crossed the solid bridge. Additionally, half of the men on the high-fear bridge called the young woman, whereas only 13 percent of those on the low-fear bridge called her.

7. *Stating conclusions.* After completing their analysis of the data, researchers are ready to state their conclusions. They typically accept, reject, or modify their hypothesis. Additionally, researchers usually seek to extract broader meaning from their work by linking it to other knowledge and theory. In this case, Dutton and Aron accepted the hypothesis that strong emotion increases sexual arousal. And they suggested that their findings offer support in favor of the labeling theory of emotions, a perspective that parallels the symbolic interactionist approach we will discuss in Chapter 2. The two researchers concluded that love is a combination of physiological arousal and the application of the appropriate label to the feelings. Presumably, the men on the high, wobbly bridge had defined their inner stirrings of fear as romantic attraction. This labeling is encouraged by the popular stereotype that depicts a pounding heart, shortness of breath, and trembling hands (also the physical symptoms of fear) with falling in love. Viewed in this manner, love, or at least infatuation, arises when we define our inner feelings of arousal as love.

So in their daily lives people find it easy to pick up on the romantic cues that abound in their environment and decide that they are "in love."

RESEARCH METHODS

We have emphasized that the scientific method allows researchers to pursue answers to their questions by gathering evidence in a systematic manner. Although no single method can eliminate uncertainty, the steps embodied in the scientific method maximize the chances for deriving information that is relevant, unbiased, and economical. Four major techniques of data collection are available to sociologists: experiments, surveys, observation, and archival research. Let us examine each of these research designs in turn.

Experiments. The ideal design for scientific research is one that allows researchers either to accept or reject a hypothesis. In order to do so, scientists attempt to control all the relevant variables to eliminate other explanations for their findings. The **experiment** best meets this requirement. In the experiment, researchers work with two groups that are identical in all relevant respects. They introduce a change in one group—the **experimental group**—but not in the other group—the **control group**. The two groups are identical except for the variable that the researchers introduce in the experimental group. The control group affords a neutral standard against which the changes in the experimental group can then be measured. This procedure allows sociologists to test the effects of an independent variable on a dependent variable.

We commonly think of experiments as being performed in a laboratory setting, and this is the case for much medical research and for a good deal of the research done by psychologists and social psychologists.

However, sociologists are much more likely to perform field experiments of the sort conducted by Dutton and Aron than they are to undertake laboratory experiments. Sociologists usually wish to maximize the natural quality of the setting in which people interact. They want to observe various forms of social behavior under the conditions where they normally occur. Further, sociologists can use more representative subject populations than college students. And finally, in contrast to laboratory settings, where some subjects inhibit their behavior because they are afraid to appear incompetent or unattractive, the subjects of field experiments are unlikely to be "on guard" or seek the experimenter's goodwill by doing what is "expected" of them.

Although the field experiment seems to provide an ideal combination of the strict rules of experimentation with the realism of natural settings, it does have disadvantages (Deaux and Wrightsman, 1984). For one thing, it is difficult to control the independent variable and to get a good "fix" on the dependent variable. And, in contrast to laboratory scientists, researchers in the field have no control over unexpected intrusions that may reduce or destroy the effectiveness of the changes they make in the independent variable. Then too, there is an ethical question. Is it reasonable for sociologists to involve people in an experiment without their knowledge or consent? Most social scientists believe that such research is permissible so long as it does not disrupt a person's daily life, the setting is a public one, and the independent variable does not harm them. We will return to the matter of ethics later in the chapter.

Surveys. Methods that rely on observation attempt to describe and portray behavior as it occurs. But some aspects of behavior are not directly accessible to observation, particularly those having to do with people's values, beliefs, attitudes, perceptions, motivations, and feelings. Further, individuals may be willing to report but not permit researchers to observe some of their private

The survey is a particularly valuable tool for gaining information from people regarding aspects of their behavior that cannot be directly observed. Here a researcher interviews Native Americans on the Pine Ridge Reservation in South Dakota. (Owen Franken/Stock, Boston)

behaviors, particularly their sexual activity, religious practices, and drug use. And since the spontaneous occurrence of some events is unpredictable, trained observers cannot always be on the scene. Under these circumstances, the **survey** is a valuable tool in the researcher's arsenal. Survey data are typically gathered in one of two ways. In the first, the researcher interviews people by reading them questions from a prepared questionnaire. In the second, people receive a questionnaire in the mail, fill it out, and return it by mail.

In both interview and questionnaire surveys, researchers have to pay close attention to their sampling procedures. Should they wish information about a large population, they do not need to contact every member of that population. Instead, they can draw on a small sample to derive broad generalizations. Public opinion pollsters like the Gallup, Harris, and CBS News organizations employ a small sample of approximately 1,500 individuals to tap the opinion of 230 million Americans.

The rationale underlying sampling procedures is easy to grasp. By way of illustration, consider a jar filled with 80,000 blue, green, red, purple, and white marbles. You would not have to count all the marbles to determine their proportions. All you would need do is randomly select 1,000 marbles, sort them into appropriate piles by color, and count them. You could then estimate the proportions of the various marbles with great confidence and with only a small margin of error, so long of course as each marble in the jar had an equal chance of being represented in the count. Physicians proceed on a similar assumption when they test your blood by taking only a few drops of it.

When it comes to social behavior, however, the matter is more complicated than it is with marbles and blood. Sociologists typically employ either a random sample or a stratified random sample in their research.

In the **random sample** researchers select subjects on the basis of chance so that every individual in the population has the same opportunity to be chosen. Should sociologists prefer greater precision, they can use a **stratified random sample**. They then divide the population into relevant categories, such as age, sex, socioeconomic level, and race, and draw a random sample from each of the categories. Thus if blacks constitute 12 percent of the population and Hispanics 7 percent, blacks will comprise 12 percent of the sample and Hispanics 7 percent.

Designing good questionnaires is not easy. The wording of the questions, their number, and the format in which they appear are all critical matters. For instance, the wording of a question may systematically bias the answers. A New York Times/CBS News survey found that only 29 percent of respondents said they favored a constitutional amendment "prohibiting abortions." But in response to a later question in the same survey, 50 percent said they favored an amendment "protecting the life of an unborn child"—which amounts to the same thing (Dionne, 1980). At times politicians seek to use this tactic to their advantage (Deaux and Wrightsman, 1984). For example, a question that begins "I agree that Candidate X" is more likely to produce a positive response than a question that begins "Does Candidate X." A good deal of pretesting is required to ensure that questions are understandable, unbiased, and specific enough to elicit the desired information.

Probably the major difficulty with self-report information has to do with the issue of its accuracy. Because individuals are involved in the data they are reporting, they may intentionally or unwittingly supply biased reports. For example, they may withhold or distort information because, if they were to tell the truth, they would feel threatened or face a loss in self-esteem. Further, many people lack the self-insight required to provide certain kinds of information. At least 10 percent of the population lacks the literacy necessary to comprehend even the simplest question. Then too, from 20 to 70 percent of the people who receive a questionnaire in the mail fail to complete or return it, distorting the sample's representativeness.

Observation. Observation is one of the most pervasive activities in which we engage as we go about our everyday lives. It is also a primary tool of sociological inquiry. Observation becomes a scientific technique when it (1) serves a clear research objective, (2) is undertaken in a systematic rather than haphazard manner, (3) is carefully recorded, (4) is related to a broader body of sociological knowledge and theory, and (5) is subjected to the same checks and controls applied to all types of scientific evidence (Selltiz, Wrightsman, and Cook, 1976).

Anthropologists have long employed observation as a primary tool for studying non-Western peoples. And as early as the 1920s, sociologists trained at the University of Chicago employed the technique as the cornerstone of their studies of hobo life (Anderson, 1923), prostitution (Thomas, 1923), and gang behavior (Thrasher, 1927). Sociologists typically observe people in one of two ways. They may observe the activities of people without intruding or participating in the activities, a procedure termed **unobtrusive observation**. Or sociologists may engage in activities with the people that they are studying, a technique called **participant observation**.

Elliot Liebow's (1967) study of the black streetcorner men that we discussed earlier in the chapter involved participant observation. Liebow, a white, began his study by hanging out on the corner in front of the New Deal Carry-out Shop. Here he initiated a conversation with a 31-year-old black man, Tally Jackson. Over the course of the

next four hours the two men struck up a friendship as they drank coffee, watched people pass by, and chatted. Over the next several weeks, Liebow often ate breakfast and lunch at the Carry-out and began occasionally putting a dime in the jukebox. The streetcorner men were at first suspicious of Liebow, but Tally allayed their distrust by sponsoring Liebow as his friend.

Within a number of months, Liebow was well enough known and accepted by the streetcorner men that he was free to go to their rooms or apartments, needing neither an excuse nor an explanation for doing so. Yet even so, the fact that he was white, college-educated, and "doing research" made him an "outsider." Liebow (1967:253) observes:

[B]ut I also was a participant in a full sense of the word. The people I was observing knew that I was observing them, yet they allowed me to participate in their activities and take part in their lives to a degree that continues to surprise me. Some "exploited" me, not as an outsider but rather as one who, as a rule, had more resources than they did. When one of them came up with the resources—money or a car, for example—he too was "exploited" in the same way. I usually tried to limit money or other favors to what I thought each would have gotten from another friend had he the same resources as I. I tried to meet requests as best I could without becoming conspicuous. I was not always on the giving end and learned somewhat too slowly to accept food or let myself be treated to drinks even though I knew this would work a hardship on the giver.

In many situations observation is the only way to gather data. At times people are unable or unwilling to tell about their behavior: They may lack sufficient self-insight to report on it, or because their behavior is illicit, taboo, or deviant, they may be reluctant to do so. But observation also has many of the same limitations as the field experiment. Additionally, there is the practical problem of applying observational procedures to phenomena that occur over a long period, such as a certain historic era. For these types of investigation, archival data is particularly useful.

Archival Research. Archival research refers to the use of existing records that have been produced or maintained by persons or organizations other than the researcher. Sources include census data, government statistics, newspaper reports, books, magazines, personal letters, speeches, folklore, court records, works of art, and the research data of other social scientists. A new utilization of data already collected for some other purpose may have considerable value and merit.

Theda Skocpol's *States and Social Revolution* (1979) is a good illustration of a sociological work based on the use of historical materials. She had a number of concerns, including testing Marx's theory of revolution. In her study, Skocpol looked for similarities in the societal conditions that existed at the time of the French (1787–1800), Russian (1917–1921), and Chinese (1911–1949) revolutions. She then studied data from nations where revolutions failed or did not take place: Germany in 1848 and Russia in 1905 (revolutions that failed), England in the seventeenth century (a political revolution), and Prussia in the early 1800s and Japan in the late 1860s (where basic structural change was initiated by a ruling elite). Although Skocpol found much of value in Marx's theory of revolution, she was also critical of it. Whereas Marx saw the state as the coercive instrument of the ruling class, Skocpol (1979:27) depicts it as "a structure with a logic and interests of its own not necessarily equivalent to, or fused with, the interests of the dominant class in society" (see Chapter 8).

Skocpol also traces the roots of the French, Russian, and Chinese revolutions to the political crises that developed in the nation's "old-regime states." The crises developed when the countries became enmeshed in long-term international conflicts that resulted in military defeat. Simultaneously, domestic class tensions, particularly those between the landed aristocracy and the peasantry, made the agrarian masses receptive to revolutionary activity. Based upon her comparative-historical analysis, Skocpol concludes that successful social revolutions pass through three stages: an old regime's state apparatus collapses; the peasantry mobilizes in class-based uprisings; and a new elite consolidates political power.

Archival research has the advantage of allowing researchers to test hypotheses over a wider range of time and societies than would otherwise be possible. We gain greater confidence in the validity of a hypothesis when we can test it in a number of cultures and historical periods rather than restrict ourselves to a single group in the present time and place. However, the technique also has its disadvantages. The major problem is that missing or inaccurate records often prevent an adequate test. And when material is available, it is frequently difficult to categorize in a way that gives an answer to a research question (Deaux and Wrightsman, 1984).

RESEARCH ETHICS

Because sociological knowledge can have positive and negative consequences for individuals and institutions, ethical considerations must govern sociological research. Yet in conducting research, sociologists confront a dilemma. On the one hand, they must not distort or manipulate their findings to serve untruthful, personal, or institutional ends. On the other hand, they are obligated to consider people as ends and not means. Because of the possible conflicts between these various responsibilities, the American Sociological Association (1980) has provided a code of ethics to govern the behavior of its members. Among these principles are the following:

Sociologists must not knowingly use their research roles as covers to obtain information for other than sociological research purposes.

Research subjects are entitled to privacy and dignity of treatment.

Research must not expose subjects to substantial risk or personal harm in the research process. Where risk or harm is anticipated, full and informed consent must be obtained.

Confidential information provided by research participants must be treated as such by sociologists, even when this information enjoys no legal protection or privilege.

In sum, because sociological knowledge can be a form of economic and political power, sociologists must exercise care to protect their discipline, the people they study and teach, and society from abuses that may stem from their professional work.

SUMMARY

1. The sociological perspective encourages us to look beyond the often neglected and taken-for-granted aspects of our social environment and examine them in fresh and creative ways. As we look behind the outside of our social world and scrutinize the hidden fabric, we encounter new levels of reality.

2. The ability to see our private experiences and personal difficulties as entwined with the structural arrangements of our society and the historical times in which we live is the essence of the sociological imagination. The sociological imagination allows us to break out from the narrow vision that usually characterizes our daily activities.

3. The sociologist Auguste Comte is commonly credited with being the founder of sociology. He emphasized that the study of society must be scientific, and he urged sociologists to employ systematic observation, experimentation, and comparative historical analysis as their methods. Additionally, he divided the study of society into social statics and social dynamics.

4. Herbert Spencer depicted society as a system, a whole made up of interrelated parts, an image he based upon the organic analogy. He also set forth an evolutionary theory of historical development, one that depicted the world as growing progressively better.

5. Karl Marx has influenced sociological thinking both by his penetrating insights and by the fact that some sociologists have fashioned their work specifically against his theory. He focused his search for the basic principles of history on the economic environments in which societies develop. At each stage of history, the current state of a society's technology and its method of organizing production dictate the group that will dominate the society and the groups that will be dominated. Thus he believed that society is divided into those who own the means of producing wealth and those who do not, giving rise to class conflict.

6. Emile Durkheim was especially concerned with social solidarity, distinguishing between mechanical and or-

ganic solidarity. He contended that the distinctive subject matter of sociology should be the study of social facts—those aspects of social life that cannot be explained in terms of the biological or mental characteristics of the individual. People experience the social fact as external to themselves in the sense that it has an independent reality and forms a part of their objective environment.

7. Max Weber left a legacy of rich insights for a variety of disciplines, including sociology. He said that a critical aspect of the sociological enterprise is the study of the intentions, values, beliefs, and attitudes that underlie people's behavior. Weber employed the German word *Verstehen* in describing his approach for learning about the subjective meanings people attach to their actions. Other ideas that Weber contributed to sociology were his notions of the ideal type and a value-free science.

8. Science assumes that every event or action results from an antecedent cause—that is, cause-and-effect relationships prevail in the universe. Scientists spend a good deal of their time attempting to figure out how one thing relates to another. In so doing, they find the steps associated with the scientific method a helpful procedure. These steps entail selecting a researchable problem, reviewing the literature, formulating a hypothesis, choosing a research design,

collecting the data, analyzing the results, and stating conclusions.

9. Four major techniques of data collection are available to sociologists: experiments, surveys, observation, and archival research. In the experiment, researchers work with two groups that are identical in all relevant respects. They introduce a change in one group—the experimental group—but not in the other group—the control group. The procedure allows sociologists to test the effects of an independent variable on a dependent variable. Surveys allow sociologists to investigate people's values, beliefs, attitudes, perceptions, motivations, and feelings. Interviewing and questionnaires constitute the primary techniques for gathering survey data. Observation is a valuable tool when people lack sufficient self-insight to report on their behavior or when they are reluctant to do so. Archival research allows sociologists to test hypotheses over a wider range of time and societies than would otherwise be possible.

10. It is important that sociologists observe the ethics of their discipline in carrying out research. They have an obligation not to expose their subjects to substantial risk or personal harm in the research process and to protect the rights and dignity of their subjects.

GLOSSARY

archival research The use of existing records that have been produced or maintained by persons or organizations other than the researcher.

class conflict The view of Karl Marx that society is divided into those who own the means of

producing wealth and those who do not, giving rise to struggles between classes.

control group The group that affords a neutral standard against which the changes in an experimental group can be measured.

correlation A change in one variable associated with a change in another variable.

dependent variable The variable that is affected in an experimental setting.

dialectic The notion in Hegelian philosophy that an idea, termed a *thesis*, takes on meaning only when it is related to its opposite or contradictory idea, called an *antithesis*. The interaction between the two ideas forms a new idea, termed a *synthesis*.

dialectical materialism The application by Karl Marx of the notion of the dialectic to the material world, particularly to the study of class conflict.

experiment Researchers work with two groups that are identical in all relevant respects. They introduce a change in one group, but not in the other group. The procedure permits researchers to test the effects of an independent variable on a dependent variable.

experimental group The group in which researchers introduce a change in an experimental setting.

hypothesis A proposition that can be tested to determine its validity.

ideal type A concept constructed by a sociologist to portray the principal characteristics of a phenomenon.

independent variable The variable that causes an effect in an experimental setting.

mechanical solidarity A form of social integration that characterized early societies in which a sense of oneness was derived from the fact that all the members of the society engaged in essentially similar tasks.

operational definition Taking abstract concepts and putting them in a form that permits their measurement.

organic solidarity A form of social integration that characterizes modern societies. A society is held together by the interdependence fostered by the differences among people.

participant observation A technique in which researchers engage in activities with the people that they are observing.

random sample Researchers select subjects on the basis of chance so that every individual in the population has the same opportunity to be chosen.

social dynamics Those aspects of social life that have to do with social change and that pattern institutional development.

social facts Those aspects of social life that cannot be explained in terms of the biological or mental characteristics of the individual. People experience the social fact as external to themselves in the sense that it has an independent reality and forms a part of their objective environment.

social statics Those aspects of social life that have to do with order and stability and that allow societies to hold together and endure.

sociological imagination The ability to see our private experiences and personal difficulties as entwined with the structural arrangements of our society and the historical times in which we live.

sociology The scientific study of social interaction and group life.

stratified random sample Researchers divide a population into relevant categories and draw a random sample from each of the categories.

superstructure The notion of Karl Marx that political ideologies, religion, family organization, education, and government constitute a level of social life that is primarily shaped by the economic institution.

survey A method for gathering data on people's beliefs, values, attitudes, perceptions, motivations, and feelings. The data can be derived from interviews or questionnaires.

unobtrusive observation A technique in which researchers observe the activities of people without intruding or participating in the activities.

value-free sociology The view of Max Weber that sociologists must not allow their personal biases to affect the conduct of their scientific research.

variable The term scientists apply to something they think influences (or is influenced by) something else.

verstehen An approach to the study of social life developed by Max Weber in which sociologists mentally attempt to place themselves in the shoes of other people and identify what they think and how they feel.

2

Culture
and
Social Structure

COMPONENTS OF CULTURE

Norms
Values
Symbols and Language

CULTURAL UNITY AND DIVERSITY

Cultural Universals
Cultural Integration
Ethnocentrism
Cultural Relativism
Subcultures and Countercultures

SOCIAL STRUCTURE

Statuses
Roles
Groups
Institutions
Societies

PERSPECTIVES IN SOCIOLOGY

The Functionalist Perspective
The Conflict Perspective
The Interactionist Perspective
Using the Three Perspectives

The story of the mutiny on the *Bounty* and of the subsequent settlement on Pitcairn Island is a perennial favorite. Many of us harbor a secret dream that we might escape to a modern-day Garden of Eden, especially when it is situated on a lovely Pacific islet. And the chords of the imagination vibrate readily to the romance and drama of the mutiny and to the tale of crime and murder that accompanied the first days on Pitcairn. But our interest in Pitcairn derives primarily from another fact—it offers a unique social experiment in the founding of a society and the fashioning of a new culture.

As most of us know, in 1789 mutineers led by Fletcher Christian seized the *Bounty* shortly after the ship had departed from Tahiti. They put Lieutenant William Bligh, the ship's captain, and eighteen of his men adrift in a small cutter. The mutineers then returned to Tahiti. Sixteen of the men decided to remain on the island, while another nine, including Christian, elected to seek another island where they might escape British retribution. They induced six Tahitian men and twelve Tahitian women to sail with them to Pitcairn Island.

Imagine the problems that confronted the English and Tahitian colonists when they arrived on Pitcairn, an uninhabited South Pacific island that is less than two square miles in area. How would they find food? How would they protect themselves from the elements? How would they maintain order? How would they manage their sexual relationships, a matter of no small concern since there were fifteen men and twelve women? How would they provide for the children born of these unions?

In finding solutions to their problems, the English and Tahitian colonists could not fall back on genetically programmed answers such as those that permit ants, bees, termites, and other social insects to live a group existence. They lacked built-in responses and highly specialized appendages that would prepare them for a particular environmental niche. Instead, *Homo sapiens* are organisms for which the environment had become primarily a thing to shape and not a thing to be shaped by. The Pitcairn Islanders were not prisoners of their genes. For similar reasons, human beings find it possible to live in Arctic regions the way the

The English and Tahitian colonists on Pitcairn had to evolve a social heritage or culture that would give them viable institutional arrangements for social living. Although the early years were marked by strife, the settlers managed to establish workable patterns for organizing a peaceful, prospering community. (Culver Pictures)

COLONISTS OF PITCAIRN'S ISLAND.

Eskimoes do, in deserts as the Arab nomads of the Sahara do, and in outer space in special craft as astronauts do. The foundations of this adaptation are to be found in culture and society, the topics of this chapter.

Culture refers to the social heritage of a people—those learned patterns for thinking, feeling, and acting that are transmitted from one generation to the next, including the embodiment of these patterns in material items. It includes both **nonmaterial culture**—abstract creations like values, beliefs, symbols, norms, customs, and institutional arrangements—and **material culture**—physical artifacts or objects like stone axes, computers, loincloths, tuxedos, automobiles, paintings, hammocks, and domed stadiums. **Society** refers to a group of people who live within the same territory and share a common culture. Very simply, culture has to do with the customs of a people, and society with the people who are practicing the customs. Culture provides the fabric that enables human beings to interpret their experience and guide their action, whereas society represents the networks of social relations that arise among a people.

In fashioning a new society, the Pitcairn Islanders had the combined heritage of two cultures to draw on. Their ancestors in England and Tahiti had been confronted with similar problems of social living. Not surprisingly, the cultural patterns they evolved were a blend of their different backgrounds. Take subsistence. Since Pitcairn ecologically resembles Tahiti more than England, their food patterns consisted principally of Tahitian items, including yams, taros, sweet potatoes, pumpkins, peas, bananas, breadfruit, and coconuts. However, their tools—metal hoes, spades, and mattocks—were of English origin. Since the women took responsibility for the preparation and cooking of food, the nonmaterial aspects of Tahitian culture came to dominate in household arrangements (for instance, as in Tahiti, the

Pitcairn Islanders ate their meals in the late morning and in the early evening).

Eighteen years passed before the colonists were visited by outsiders, but even then guests came only rarely and stayed but a short time. In 1833 a Captain Freemantle found the residents to be "a well-disposed, well-behaved, kind, hospitable people." They had evolved deep attachments to their island and strong bonds of social unity. Yet the early years on Pitcairn were difficult. Things went rather peaceably and prosperously for about two years, at which time the English and Tahitian men had a falling out over the women. Two of the Tahitian men were murdered, leading to eight years of intermittent strife and bloodshed. Even so, an underlying cooperation and division of labor sustained life on the island as the colonists built homes, cultivated gardens, fished, caught birds, and constructed pits for trapping wild hogs. Had the hand of every human being been turned against that of every other person, Pitcairn society would have disintegrated.

Components of Culture

As our account of the Pitcairn Islanders testifies, culture provides individuals with a set of common understandings that they employ in fashioning their actions. In doing so, it binds the separated lives of individuals into a larger whole, making society possible by providing a common framework of meaning. Only by sharing similar perspectives with one another can we weave integrated webs of ongoing interaction. Culture allows us to "know" in rather broad terms what we can expect of others and what they can expect of us. Simultaneously, culture affords a kind of map or a set of guideposts for finding our way about life. It provides a configuration of do's and don'ts, a complex of patterned mental stop-and-go signs that tell us about the social landscape: "Notice this," "Ignore that," "Avoid this action," and "Do that" (Kluckhohn, 1960:21). If we know a people's culture—their design for living—we can understand and predict a good deal of their behavior. Let us examine more carefully a number of key components of culture.

NORMS

If we are going to live our lives in group settings, we must have understandings that tell us which actions are permissible and which are not. Only in this way do our daily lives take on an ordered and patterned existence. And only in this way can we determine which behaviors we can legitimately insist others perform and which they can legitimately insist we perform. For instance, when we enter a clothing store, begin a college course, get married, or start a new job, we already have some idea regarding the expectations that will hold for us and others in these settings. Such expectations are norms. **Norms** are social rules that specify appropriate and inappropriate behavior in given situations. They tell us what we "should," "ought," and "must" do, as well as what we "should not," "ought not," and "must not" do. In all cultures, the great body of rules deal with such matters as sex, property, and safety.

Norms afford a *means* by which we orient ourselves to other people. They provide social definitions that allow us to shape our actions so that we can align them with those of other people. But norms are also *ends*. We and others attribute to them an independent quality, making them "things" in their own right (Stokes and Hewitt, 1976). They become standards by which individuals appraise one another's actions and reward and punish various behaviors. People attach a good deal of importance to some

norms, called **mores** (singular **mos**), and they mete out harsh punishment to violators. Other norms, called **folkways**, they deem to be of less importance and they exact less stringent conformity to them (Sumner, 1906).

Folkways. Folkways have to do with the customary ways and ordinary conventions by which we carry out our daily activities. We bathe, brush our teeth, groom our hair, wear shoes or sandals, wave greetings to friends, mow our lawns, and sleep in beds. We view people who violate folkways, especially those who violate a good number of them, as somehow "different" and even "strange." However, ordinarily we do not attach moral significance to the folkways. For example, we may regard people who wear soiled clothing as crude but not as sinful, and people who are late for appointments as thoughtless but not evil. Gossip and ridicule are important mechanisms for enforcing folkways.

Mores. People take a less benign approach to violators of mores. Murder, theft, rape, treason, and child molestation bring strong disapproval and severe punishment within the United States. Mores are seen as vital to a society's well-being and survival. People usually attach moral significance to mores, and they define people who violate them as sinful, evil, and wicked. Consequently, the punishment for violators of a society's mores is severe; they may be put to death, imprisoned, outcast, mutilated, or tortured.

Folkways and mores are distinguished by the fact that they are usually enforced by people acting in a spontaneous and collective manner. For example, anthropologist Robert H. Lowie (1935) reports that the Crow Indians, acting as a community, would punish individuals who committed a serious breach of morality. In the evening someone might call out to the whole group: "Did you hear about so-and-so?" Then, amid great laughter, they would comment upon the person's transgression in the most scathing fashion and continue in this manner throughout the entire evening. Wrongdoers would be so shamed by the ridicule of their fellows that they might leave the community and not return until they had redeemed themselves.

Law. A society's mores are an important source of laws. **Laws** are rules that are enforced by a special political organization composed of individuals who enjoy the right to use force. As anthropologist E.A. Hoebel (1958:470–471) observes: "The essentials of legal coercion are general acceptance of the application of physical power, in threat or in fact, by a privileged party, for a legitimate cause, in a legitimate way, and at a legitimate time." The people who administer laws may make use of physical force with a low probability of retaliation by a third party (Collins, 1975). Laws tend to be the result of conscious thought, deliberate planning, and formal declaration. They can be changed more readily than can folkways and mores.

VALUES

Whereas norms are rules for behavior, **values** are broad ideas regarding what is desirable, correct, and good that most members of a society share. Values are so general and abstract that they do not explicitly specify which behaviors are acceptable and which are not. Instead, values provide us with criteria and conceptions by which we evaluate people, objects, and events as to their relative worth, merit, beauty, or morality. The major value configurations within the dominant American culture include the assignment of high importance to achievement and success, work and activity, efficiency and practicality, material comfort, individuality, progress, rationality, patriotism, and democracy (Williams, 1970). People tend to appeal to values as the ultimate rationales for the choices they make in life.

At times different norms are based on the same values. The value of freedom is embodied in quite different norms in the United States than it is in the Soviet Union. Americans express the value in terms of legal rights associated with free speech, freedom of religion, and other Bill of Rights guarantees. The Soviets define freedom in terms of such guarantees as the right to a job, education, and medical care. Likewise, two Americans may both place a premium on social equality; however, one may express it by supporting affirmative action programs and the other by opposing such legislation as "reverse discrimination," favoring instead "color-blind" civil rights laws.

Values are not etched in granite for all time. The advice columns of Ann Landers mirror many of the changes that have taken place in American attitudes over the past thirty years (Hays, 1984). In 1955, Landers was a bit Victorian. Although many of the letters came from wretchedly unhappy wives, Landers emphasized that the bond of marriage was virtually indissoluble. And in contrast to the "child-free" couple of the later "Me Decade," she portrayed the "childless" couple of 1955 as "a tragedy." Even in the early 1960s, we gain from the columns an image of a society guided by traditional values. But by 1970 many barriers had come down, and the columns dealt casually with homosexuality, runaway children, and marijuana. A decade later, Landers was even less likely to reply in a conservative tone. One letter of the 1980s thanked Ann for her "nonjudgmental" advice on what to do should a married lover suffer a heart attack in a hotel room. And in one of her spicier columns, Landers printed a piece by a physician who advocated masturbation as a means for dealing with sexual frustrations. The somewhat Victorian Ann had grown to accept new ideas regarding what constitutes proper behavior, as had Americans in general.

SYMBOLS AND LANGUAGE

Norms and values are nontangible aspects of social life, what sociologists term nonmaterial culture. But if they lack a physical existence, how can we get a handle on them? How in the course of our daily lives can we talk to one another about rules and standards, mull them about in our minds, and appraise people's behavior in terms of them? The answer has to do with symbols. **Symbols** are acts or objects that have come to be socially accepted as standing for something else. They come to represent other things through the shared understandings people have. Consider the word "computer," a symbol that when spoken or written stands for a physical object. It becomes a vehicle of communication because a community of users (Americans) agree that the symbol and the object are linked. Hence symbols are a powerful code or shorthand for representing and dealing with aspects of the world about us (Hewitt, 1979).

Symbols assume many different forms. Take gestures—body postures or movements with social significance (Hiller, 1933). Whereas Americans shake their heads to show a negative reaction, the inhabitants of the Admiralty Islands make a quick stroke of the nose with a finger of the right hand. Turks display negation by throwing their heads back and then making a clucking noise with the tongue. By virtue of their culture, Americans will misinterpret the meaning of these gestures. Objects such as flags, paintings, religious icons, badges, and uniforms also function as social symbols. But probably the most important symbols of all are found in **language**—a socially structured system of sound patterns (words and sentences) with specific and arbitrary meanings. Language is the cornerstone of every culture. It is the chief vehicle by which people communicate ideas, information, attitudes, and emotions to one another. And it is the principal means by which human beings create culture and transmit it from generation to generation.

The Significance of Symbols. We can gain an appreciation for the part that symbols, particularly words, play in our daily lives by recalling the experiences of Helen Keller. As most of us know, Helen Keller was stricken with a severe illness at the age of 21 months that left her deaf and blind. In her autobiography, *The Story of My Life* (1904), she recounts that in her early years she remained imprisoned in her body, having only nebulous and uncertain links to the outside world. Later, through the skilled and patient teaching given her by Anne Mansfield Sullivan, she learned the American Sign Language for the deaf.

In the following passage from her autobiography, Helen Keller (1904:21–24) tells of her early experiences:

Have you ever been at sea in a dense fog, when it seemed as if a tangible white darkness shut you in, and the great ship, tense and anxious, groped her way toward the shore with plummet and sounding-line, and you waited with beating heart for something to happen? I was like that ship before my education began, only I was without compass or sounding-line, and had no way of knowing how near the harbour was.

. . . . The morning after my teacher came she led me into her room and gave me a doll. When I had played with it a little while, Miss Sullivan slowly spelled into my hand the word "d-o-l-l." I was at once interested in this finger

play and tried to imitate it. When I finally succeeded in making the letters correctly I was flushed with childish pleasure. Running downstairs to my mother I held up my hand and made the letters for doll. I did not know that I was spelling a word or even that words existed; I was simply making my fingers go in monkey-like imitation. In the days that followed I learned to spell in this uncomprehensible way a great many words, among them pin, hat, cup and a few verbs like sit, stand and walk. But my teacher had been with me several weeks before I understood that everything has a name.

One day, while I was playing with my new doll, Miss Sullivan put my big rag doll into my lap also, spelled "d-o-l-l" and tried to make me understand that "d-o-l-l" applied to both. Earlier in the day we had had a tussle over the words "m-u-g" and "w-a-t-e-r." Miss Sullivan had tried to impress it upon me that "m-u-g" is mug and that "w-a-t-e-r" is water but I persisted in confounding the two. In despair she had dropped the subject for the time, only to renew it at the first opportunity. . . .

We walked down the path to the well-house, attracted by the fragrance of the honeysuckle with which it was covered. Some one was drawing water and my teacher placed my hand under the spout. As the cool stream gushed over one hand she spelled into the other the word water, first slowly, then rapidly. I stood still, my whole attention fixed upon the motions of her fingers. Suddenly I felt a misty consciousness as of something forgotten—a thrill of returning thought; and somehow the mystery of language was revealed to me. I knew then that "w-a-t-e-r" meant the wonderful cool something that was flowing over my hand. That living word awakened my soul, gave it light, hope, joy, set it free! . . . I left the well-house eager to learn. Everything had a name, and each name gave birth to a new thought. (Copyright 1902, 1903, 1905 by Helen Keller. Reprinted by permission of Doubleday & Co., Inc.)

Only as Helen Keller grasped the significance of symbols, particularly words, did she acquire an intelligent understanding of her environment. Indeed, the change it brought revolutionized her personality. The association between a word and an experience allowed her to use the symbol in the absence of the experience. She could now conceive of "water" apart from its actual presence. By virtue of symbolic expression, "reality" becomes internally coded in a condensed and more easily manipulated mental form. Thus Helen Keller was reluctant to apply the term "idea" or "thought" to her mental processes before she learned how to employ words. Of equal significance, she could share her experiences with other people and they could share their experiences with her. The ability to use symbols, especially language, was the ticket that admitted Helen Keller to social life and hence to full humanness.

Human beings live their lives primarily within symbolic environments. Other organisms may communicate by means of gestures, sounds, touch, and chemical odors, but the meanings of these signals are genetically programmed within them (Colgan, 1983). Psychologists have trained chimpanzees and gorillas to use American Sign Language, but human intervention was first necessary. Presumably some of the apes have understood that meanings are attached to the symbols. For instance, upon seeing a watermelon for the first time, the chimp Washoe invented the phrase drink fruit to refer to it and likewise labeled a swan a water bird. Similarly, the gorilla Koko has learned to devise novel names for new objects, such as finger bracelet for a ring, white tiger for a zebra, and eye hat for a mask. But even though various apes have displayed notable achievements, nobody is likely to mistake their capacities for those of a normal 3-year-old child (Limber, 1977). The skills exhibited by the chimps are related to human skills, but they are clearly not equivalent to human skills (Terrace, 1979; de Luce and Wilder, 1983).

The Linguistic Relativity Hypothesis. The languages found among the world's people are quite diverse. Arabs have some 6,000 words that are connected in some way with the camel, including colors, breeds (different lineages), classes (such as milk camels, riding camels, marriage camels, and slaughter camels), states of pregnancy (some 50 words), and their current activities (such as grazing, conveying a caravan, and participating in a war expedition). Inuits (Eskimos) make minute distinctions among kinds of snow and snowfall. And Americans have a vast number of words pertaining to automobiles, including make, year, model, body type, and accessories.

Do these linguistic differences mean that if people speak a certain language, they experience a different social reality than do people who speak another language? In other words, does our language shape the way we perceive and interpret the world? Edward Sapir (1949) and his student Benjamin L. Whorf (1956) answer these questions affirmatively. In what has been termed the **linguistic relativity hypothesis**, Sapir and Whorf contend that languages ''slice up'' and conceptualize the world of experience differently, creating different realities for us. Hence no two languages shape the thought of people in quite the same fashion. Conceived in these terms, we selectively screen sensory input in the way we are programmed by our language, admitting some things while filtering out others. Consequently, experience as it is perceived through one set of linguistically patterned sensory screens is quite different from experience perceived through another set (Hall, 1966).

Few sociologists challenge the basic premise of the linguistic relativity hypothesis that the words people use reflect their chief cultural concerns—camels, snow, automobiles, or whatever. But most contend that regardless of their culture people can make the same distinctions made by Arabs with regard to camels, Inuits (Eskimos) with regard to snow, and Americans with regard to automobiles. They may lack a word to name each distinction, but they are still capable of recognizing it. Rather than determining thought, language is viewed as simply helping or hindering certain kinds of thinking. Viewed in this manner, language reflects the distinctions that are of practical importance in the life of a community. In like fashion, the idioms and vernacular of sociologists, lawyers, prostitutes, baseball players, college students, drug dealers, and stamp collectors all reflect their special interests and concerns.

Cultural Unity and Diversity

The great merit of culture is that it permits human beings to circumvent the slowness of genetic evolution. Behavior patterns that are wired into organisms by their genes do not allow rapid adaptation to changing conditions. In contrast, cultural change can be rapid. Indeed, some social scientists contend that cultural evolution has swamped biological evolution as the chief source of behavior change for human beings. The functioning of the human brain is no longer rigidly prescribed by genetic programs. Instead, genes have allowed the construction of a liberated brain, one that permits a flexible repertoire of responses. The more culture human beings have acquired, the more biological capacity for culture has then evolved, leading to more culture, and so on (Barkow, 1978; Lewontin, Rose, and Kamin, 1984). The fact that culture has increasingly usurped nature as the primary moving force in human development has implications for cultural unity and diversity, a matter to which we now turn our attention.

CULTURAL UNIVERSALS

Although culture provides guideposts for daily living—a blueprint or map for life's activities—these guideposts often differ from one society to another. The "oughts" and "musts" of some societies are the "ought nots" and "must nots" of other societies; the "good" and "desirable" among this people are the "bad" and "undesirable" among that people. And so it goes. Should this fact of cultural variation lead to the conclusion that cultures are different in all respects and hence not comparable? Or to put the question another way, can we realistically speak of **cultural universals**—patterned and recurrent aspects of life that appear in all known societies?

There are indeed such common denominators or cultural constants. The reason is not hard to come by. All people confront many of the same problems. They must secure a livelihood, socialize children, handle grief, deal with deviants, provide for sex, and so on. Culture represents an accumulation of solutions to the problems posed by human biology and the generalities of the human situation.

George Peter Murdock and his associates at Yale University (1950b) have developed a classification of cultural components that has universal application. They list some eighty-eight general categories of behavior that are found among all cultures, including "food quest," "clothing," "settlements," "property," "travel and transport," "fine arts," "social stratification," "kinship," "political behavior," "death," "religious practices," and "infancy and childhood." The eighty-eight categories are subdivided into additional topics. For example, "funeral rites" always include expressions of grief, means for disposing of the corpse, and rituals to define the relations of the dead with the living. It should be emphasized, however, that universal components at no point include the specific details of actual behav-

ior. The universals relate to broad, overall categories and not to the *content of culture*. Consider marriage. Although marriage is found in all cultures, some societies favor monogamy (one spouse), others polyandry (plural husbands), and still others polygyny (plural wives) (see Chapter 9).

CULTURAL INTEGRATION

The items that form a culture tend to constitute a consistent and integrated whole. In the words of William Graham Sumner (1906:5–6), the parts are "subject to a strain of consistency with each other." However, perfect integration is never achieved for the obvious reason that historical events constantly exert a disturbing influence. Nor is it sufficient merely to know the traits of a people. Two cultures could have identical inventories of items and yet be substantially different (Kluckhohn, 1960). We need to know how the various ingredients are interrelated. An analogy may prove helpful. Take a musical sequence of three notes, C, E, and G. Knowing this information does not allow us to predict the type of sensation that the playing of these notes is likely to produce. We need to know the relationship between the notes. In what order will they be played? What will be the duration each will receive? How will the emphasis be distributed? And will the instrument on which they are played be a horn, a piano, or a violin?

Many early anthropologists made the error of viewing culture as so loosely knit together that the main task of cultural analysis consisted of disentangling the various elements and showing from which people they came. They portrayed culture as just so many patches and shreds that somehow coexisted. But increasingly social scientists have come to recognize that the parts of a culture comprise a closely interwoven fabric, so that a change in one part has consequences for other parts and for the whole. For this reason, an element undergoes modification in the process of being diffused from one society to another. Occasionally the modification of a cultural trait may take the form of *syncretism*—the blending or fusing of the trait with a like element in another culture. Our contemporary Christmas and Easter holidays are examples. In pre-Christian times, many European peoples carried out midwinter and spring ceremonies. The midwinter festival often included games, dancing, and exchange of gifts, and general merrymaking. These elements have entered into the celebration of Christmas and are summed up in the traditional greeting, "Merry Christmas!" Early Christians simply found it advantageous to locate Christmas and Easter at times of already existing festivals.

ETHNOCENTRISM

Once we acquire the cultural ways peculiar to our own society, they become so deeply engrained that they seem second nature to us. Additionally, we have difficulty conceiving of alternative ways of life. Anthropologist Ralph Linton (1945:125) notes:

It has been said that the last thing which a dweller in the deep sea would be likely to discover would be water. He would become conscious of its existence only if some accident brought him to the surface and introduced him to air. Man, throughout most of his history, has been only vaguely conscious of the existence of culture and has owed even this consciousness to contrasts between the customs of his own society and those of some other with which he happened to be brought into contact.

Given these tendencies, it is hardly surprising that we should judge the behavior of other groups by the standards of our own culture, a phenomenon sociologists call **eth-**

nocentrism. Sumner (1906:13) described this point of view as one "in which one's own group is the center of everything, and all others are scaled and rated with reference to it."

It was ethnocentrism that led China's Emperor Chien Lung to dispatch the following message to Great Britain's George III in reply to the latter's request that the two nations establish trade ties:

Our Celestial Empire possesses all things in prolific abundance and lacks no produce within its own borders. There is, therefore, no need to import the manufactures of outside barbarians in exchange for our own produce. But as the tea, silk, and porcelain, which the Celestial Empire produces, are absolute necessities to European nations and to yourselves, we have permitted, as a signal mark of favor, that foreign business houses [at Canton] be supplied, and your country thus participate in our beneficence. . . . As your Ambassador can see for himself, we possess all things. I set no value on objects strange or ingenious, and I have no use for your country's manufacturers. . . . I do not forget the lonely remoteness of your island, cut off from the world by intervening wastes of sea, and I overlook your excusable ignorance of the usages of our Celestial Empire. I have consequently commanded my Minister to enlighten your Ambassador on the subject. (Quoted in Vander Zanden, 1979:295)

Ethnocentrism is found among families, tribes, nations, cliques, colleges, fraternities, businesses, churches, and political parties. The notion that one belongs to the "best people" provides a kind of social glue cementing people together. Feelings of group pride, belonging, and collective self-awareness promote solidarity and stability. But at the same time these feelings generate intergroup conflict. Ethnocentrism, then, is a double-edged feeling. It fosters a sense of oneness, overriding divisions within a group and binding together people who otherwise are divided by economic conflicts and social gradations. And it sets people apart by promoting a longing not to belong to any other group.

CULTURAL RELATIVISM

Ethnocentrism gets in the way of the scientific study of culture. We cannot grasp the behavior of other peoples if we interpret it in the context of *our* values, beliefs, and motives. Rather, we must examine their behavior in the light of *their* values, beliefs, and motives. This approach, termed **cultural relativism**, views the behavior of a people from the perspective of their own culture. In sharp contrast to ethnocentrism, cultural relativism employs the kind of value-free or neutral approach advocated by Max Weber (see Chapter 1).

Anthropologist Elman Service (1973:10) came to appreciate the importance of cultural relativism in the course of his fieldwork among the Havasupai Indians of the Southwest. In interviewing an old man about the tribe's culture, the anthropologist periodically asked why the people behave as they do. The man would answer, "That's the way we do." Service observes: "I was looking for a key to Havasupai culture, afraid of not finding it, and right there I patently overlooked the truth: There is no key to understanding culture except on its own terms."

A perspective characterized by cultural relativism does not ask whether or not a particular trait is moral or immoral, but what part it plays in the life of a people. For instance, among some Inuit peoples, the elderly infirm are left behind to perish in the cold. Rather than condemning the practice, social scientists examine the behavior in the context of Inuit culture, where it is defined as a humane measure (Murdock, 1943). The

Inuits believe that individuals experience in the next world a standard of health similar to that which they enjoy in the period preceding death. Consequently, the Inuits see the practice as minimizing the disabilities and infirmities their loved ones will encounter in the hereafter. By the same token, social scientists point out that the practice is adaptive for a people whose subsistence is precarious and who must strictly limit their dependent population. For Americans who are appalled at the Inuit custom, it is worth noting that many Japanese find quite abhorrent our practice of placing our elderly infirm in nursing homes rather than caring for them at home.

SUBCULTURES AND COUNTERCULTURES

Cultural diversity may also be found within a society. In many modern nations, the members of some groups participate in the main culture of the society while simultaneously sharing with one another a number of unique values, norms, traditions, and life styles. These distinctive cultural patterns are termed a **subculture**. Subcultures abound in American life, and find expression in various religious, racial, ethnic, occupational, and age groups.

The Old Order Amish are a case in point. The Amish are a religious sect that originated in Germany and Switzerland during the Reformation conflicts of the sixteenth century. Because of religious persecution, many Amish migrated to Pennsylvania in the early 1700s. Most Amish families live on farms, although a minority work in skilled crafts like carpentry, furniture making, and blacksmithing. They believe in a literal interpretation of the Bible and turn their backs on modern standards of dress, "progressive" morality, "worldly" amusement, automobiles, and higher education. Above all, the Amish value hard physical work and

The United States has evolved as a pluralistic society, with a variety of subcultures. Although the larger American society expects conformity in those areas believed vital to the national well-being, some latitude exists for groups to evolve and maintain their own cultural traits and traditions in other areas of life. Here a traditional African marriage rite is performed in New York City. (Katrina Thomas/Photo Researchers)

believe that those who do not find joy in work are somehow abnormal. Far from being ashamed of their nonconformity to "worldly standards," the Amish pride themselves on being a "peculiar people" who separate themselves from the world (Hostetler, 1980; Foster, 1980).

Youth culture is another example of a subculture. Western nations have postponed the entrance of their adolescents into adulthood for economic and educational reasons and have segregated them in schools and colleges. In doing so, they have spawned conditions favorable to the devel-

opment of unique cultural patterns among their youth. These cultural patterns find expression in fads having to do with recordings, entertainment idols, and dance steps, personal adornment and hair styles, and distinctive jargons. Standards revolving about masculinity and femininity also have high priority. For boys, the critical signs of manhood are physical mastery, athletic skill, sexual prowess, risk taking, courage in the face of aggression, and a willingness to defend one's honor at all costs. For girls, the most admired qualities are physical attractiveness, personal vivaciousness, the ability delicately to manipulate various sorts of interpersonal relationships, and skill in exercising control over sexual encounters.

Large corporations like American Telephone & Telegraph also have distinctive subcultures (Langley, 1984). For over a hundred years, AT&T cultivated an incredibly strong service ethic, captured by a picture of a nineteenth-century Bell System lineman fighting to keep telephone lines open during a blizzard. This mission shaped the company's organizational structure, the kind of people it hired, and their shared value system. The breaking up of the Bell System in 1984 had a profound impact on its corporate culture. With AT&T free to enter competitive high-technology markets, the company had to abandon many of its earlier values and standards. And because it no longer operates in a regulated environment, the company has had to face fierce challenges from competitors. These changes have had profound implications for its personnel. In the new environment, AT&T's managers must shun caretaking and promote risk taking.

At times the norms, values, and life styles of a subculture are substantially at odds with those of the larger society and constitute a **counterculture**. A counterculture rejects many of the behavioral standards and guideposts that hold in the dominant culture. The "hang-loose" orientation

This famous illustration, showing an intrepid AT&T lineman working to keep the telephone lines open during a blizzard, demonstrates the commitment to service that has long been a component of AT&T's corporate subculture. (Courtesy of AT&T)

found among some youth in the early 1970s had a good many countercultural overtones. The young people questioned the legitimacy of the Establishment, rejected the hard-work ethic of their elders, turned to drugs in a search for new experience, and "dropped out" of middle-class life. Delinquent gangs and Satanic cults are other illustrations of counterculture groups.

Social Structure

Earlier in the chapter we noted that culture has to do with the customs of a people, and society with the people who are practicing the customs. Culture supplies the framework that allows people to interpret events and guide their actions; society consists of the actual web of relationships that people enter into as they go about their daily activities. For the most part, people do not interact in a haphazard or random manner.

Rather, their relationships are characterized by social ordering. Sociologists apply the term **social structure** to this social ordering—the interweaving of people's interactions and relationships in recurrent and stable patterns. It finds expression in a matrix of social positions and the distribution of people in them.

Social structure provides an organized and focused quality to our group experiences. By virtue of social structure, we link certain of our experiences, terming them, for example, "the family," "the church," "the neighborhood," and "General Motors." In somewhat similar fashion, we perceive physical aspects of our experience as structures—parts organized into wholes—and not as isolated elements. For example, when we look at a building, we do not simply see lumber, shingles, bricks, glass, and other components, but a house; when we look at a tailless amphibian, we do not merely see bulging eyes, smooth spotted skin, and long hind legs, but a frog. In so doing we relate an experience to other experiences in terms of some larger, more inclusive context.

Social structure gives us the feeling that life is characterized by organization and stability. For example, consider the social structure of your college. Each semester you enter new classes, yet you have little difficulty attuning yourself to unfamiliar classmates and professors. Courses in sociology, calculus, American history, English composition, and physical education are offered year after year. A new class enters college each fall, and another class graduates each spring. Football games are scheduled for Saturday afternoons in the autumn and basketball games for evenings during the winter months. Deans prepare budgets, allocate funds, and manage their academic domains. All the while new students, professors, coaches, players, and deans pass through the system and in due course make their exits. Yet even though the actual people that comprise a college change over time, the college endures. Likewise, a clique, a family, a rock band, an army, a business organization, a religious group, and a nation are social structures. Social structure, then, consists of the recurrent and orderly relationships that prevail among the members of a group or society.

Sociologists view social structure as a *social fact* of the sort described by Emile Durkheim (see Chapter 1). We experience a social fact as external to ourselves—as an independent reality that forms a part of our objective environment. Consequently, social structures constrain our behavior and channel our actions in certain directions. When you entered college for the first time, you felt somewhat awkward because as yet you did not fit into your college's way of doing things. The college's way is social structure, the shape or form that a particular organization has taken through the years as stu-

dents, professors, and administrators have interacted on a regular basis.

Although we use motionless structural terms as a convenient means for describing and analyzing social life, we should not allow this practice to blind us to the dynamic and changing qualities of social structure. A college is not a fixed entity that, once created, continues to operate perpetually in the same manner. All social ordering must be continually created and re-created through the interweaving and stabilizing of social relationships. For this reason, organized social life is always undergoing modification and change (Olsen, 1978) (see Chapter 12). Let us take a closer look at social structure by examining its major components.

STATUSES

In our daily conversations, we use the word "status" to refer to a person's ranking as determined by wealth, influence, and prestige. However, sociologists employ **status** somewhat differently to mean a position within a group or society. It is by means of statuses that we locate one another in various social structures. Mother, mayor, priest, friend, supervisor, male, captain, child, Cuban-American, customer, professor, and convict are all statuses.

A status has been likened to a ready-made suit of clothes (Newcomb, 1950). Within certain limits, the prospective buyer can choose regarding matters of style and fabric. But an American is not free to choose the costume of a Chinese peasant or that of a Hindu prince. We must choose from among the suits presented by our society. Furthermore, our choice is limited to a size that will fit, as well as by our pocketbooks. Having made our choice within these limits, we can have certain alterations made. But apart from minor modifications, we tend to be limited to what retailers already have on their racks. Statuses too come ready-made, and the range of choice among them is limited. Societies commonly limit competition for statuses with reference to sex, age, and social affiliations. For instance, realistically, not every American can be elected president. Women, blacks, and members of the lower class suffer severe handicaps from the outset. This observation brings us to a consideration of ascribed and achieved statuses.

Ascribed and Achieved Statuses. We have greater control over some of our statuses than others. Some statuses are assigned to us by our group or society and termed **ascribed statuses**. Age and sex are common reference points for the ascription of statuses. For instance, one cannot legally drive a car (age 16 or 17), vote (age 18), become president (age 35), or receive social security retirement benefits (age 62) without being the requisite age. Race, religion, family background, and socioeconomic status are also common bases for assigning statuses to individuals.

Other statuses we secure on the basis of individual choice and competition. We call these **achieved statuses**. No society ignores the fact that individuals differ from one another, and all societies recognize individual accomplishment and failure. This fact is reflected in the allocation of some statuses on the basis of individual achievement. Quarterback, choir director, physician, actor, college student, church deacon, county sheriff, pickpocket, president of Exxon, coach, and scuba diver are illustrations of achieved statuses.

Master Statuses. Some of our statuses overshadow other of our statuses both in our own minds and in those of other people as well. A **master status** is a key or core status that carries primary weight in a person's interactions and relationships with others. For children, age is a master status; similarly, sex is a master status in most societies. Additionally, race and occupation are particularly critical statuses in American life. Master statuses tend to lay the framework within which our goals are formulated and our training is carried out.

ROLES

A status carries with it a set of culturally defined rights and duties, what sociologists term a **role**. These expectations define the behavior people view as appropriate and inappropriate for the occupant of a status. Quite simply, the difference between a status and a role is that we *occupy* a status and *play* a role (Linton, 1936).

Sociologists have taken the notion of role from the theater, an analogy suggested by William Shakespeare in *As You Like It* (Act II, Scene 7):

All the world's a stage,
And all the men and women merely players.
They have their exits and their entrances;
And one man in his time plays many parts.

Actors perform their roles in accordance with a script (analogous to culture), what the other actors say and do, and the reactions of the audience. But the theater analogy also has its weaknesses. Whereas the theater is a world of make-believe, in life our parts are real. And as we go about our daily activities, we are seldom conscious of "acting" according to a script. Moreover, in life we must do a good deal of improvising, continually testing and changing our actions in accordance with the behavior of other people.

Roles allow us to formulate our behavior mentally so we can shape our actions in appropriate ways. In doing so, we collect the particulars of an unfolding situation and identify *who does what, when, and where*. Roles permit us to assume that in some respects we can ignore personal differences and say that for practical matters people are interchangeable. For example, every American "knows" that a physician is "a person who treats sick people" and a carpenter is "a person who uses lumber to build houses." In sum, roles enable us to collapse or telescope a range of behaviors into manageable bundles.

Role Performance. A role is the *expected* behavior we associate with a status. **Role performance** is the *actual* behavior of the person who occupies a status. In real life a gap often exists between what people should do and what they actually do. And people vary in how they implement the rights and duties associated with their roles. You frequently take such differences into account when you select one professor over another for a given course. One professor may have the reputation for coming late to class, lecturing in a relaxed, informal manner, and assigning difficult term papers. Another professor may be a distinguished authority in the field, monitor class attendance, and assign take-home examinations. Regardless of which professor you select, you will still occupy the status of student and play its associated role. However, you will have to modify your behavior somewhat depending upon your selection.

Role Set. A single status may have multiple roles attached to it, constituting a **role set**. Consider your status as a student. The status of student involves one role as a pupil, one role as a peer of other students, one role as a loyal supporter of your school's teams, one role as a user of the library, and one role as a "good citizen" of the college community. In fact, a role does not exist in isolation. Instead, it is a bundle of activities that are meshed with the activities of other people. For this reason, there can be no professors without students, no wives without husbands, no blacks without whites, and no patients without physicians.

Roles impinge on us as sets of norms that define our **duties**—the actions others can legitimately insist that we perform—and our **rights**—the actions we can legitimately insist that others perform (Goffman, 1961). Every role has at least one reciprocal role attached to it. Hence, the rights of one role are the duties of the other role. For instance, your rights as a student—to receive authoritative material in lectures, to be administered fair exams, and to be graded objectively—are the duties of your professor. And your duties—to read assigned materials, take exams, and attend classes—are your professor's rights.

One way individuals are linked together in groups is through networks of reciprocal roles. Role relationships tie us to one another because the rights of one end of the relationship are the expectations of the other. Groups consist of intricate complexes of interlocking roles, which their members sustain in the course of interacting with one another. People experience these stable relationships as social structure—a school, a hospital, a family, a gang, an army, and so on.

Role Conflict. **Role conflict** results when individuals are confronted with conflicting expectations stemming from their simultaneous occupancy of two or more statuses. A football coach whose son is a member of the team may experience role conflict when deciding whether to make his own son or another more talented player the starting quarterback. Black police officers at times are placed in a somewhat similar dilemma when their supervisors expect them to be loyal to the police department and blacks expect them to be loyal to the black community. Some college students report that they experience role conflict when their parents pay them a campus visit. They feel they are "on stage" before two audiences holding somewhat contradictory expectations of them. One way to handle role conflict is to subdivide or compartmentalize one's life and assume only one of the incompatible roles at a time. For instance, college students may attempt to segregate their school and home experiences so they do not have to appear before their parents and peers simultaneously.

Role Strain. Role strain occurs when individuals find the expectations of a single role incompatible, so that they have difficulty performing the role. Consider the relationship physicians have with their patients. Doctors are expected to be gentle healers, humanitarians, self-sacrificing saviors of the sick. Simultaneously, they are expected to be small-business retailers of knowledge that they have obtained at considerable cost and sacrifice. While aggressive bill collecting is consistent with the small-business-retailer aspects of the role, it is inconsistent with that of the gentle healer. Supervisors often confront similar difficulties. They wonder: "Should I be a good Joe and mix with my staff, or should I maintain my distance from them?" They are asked to be both commanding parent figures and reassuring, comforting big brothers or sisters. For the most part there are few well-defined or accepted answers to the dilemmas posed by these contradictory expectations.

GROUPS

Statuses and roles are building blocks for more comprehensive social structures, including groups. Sociologists view a **group** as two or more people who share a feeling of unity and who are bound together in relatively stable patterns of social interaction. As pointed out above, roles link us within social relationships. When these relationships are sustained across time, we frequently assign group properties to them. Four things usually happen as a result of these attributions. First, we come to think of the relationships as encompassed by boundaries, so that people are either "inside" or "outside" a group. Second, we attribute an "objective" existence to groups and treat them as if they are real and exact things. Third, we view a group as having a distinct subculture or counterculture—a set of unique norms and values. And fourth, we develop a sense of allegiance to a group that leads us to feel we are a unit with a distinct identity. We will examine these features at some length in Chapter 4.

A group is more than a collection of people. Sociologists distinguish it from an **aggregate**, which is simply a collection of anonymous individuals who are in one place at the same time. Shoppers in a mall, individuals waiting in line for football tickets, an audience at a concert, and a crowd watching a hockey game are examples of aggregates. Individuals shift in and out of an aggregate rather easily and frequently. Since the people interact with one another only transiently and temporarily, patterns of social ordering are short-lived. However, this quality should not lead us to dismiss aggregates as inconsequential. As we will see in Chapter 12, they provide the foundation for many forms of collective behavior.

A group also differs from a **category**, a collection of people who share a characteristic that is deemed to be of social significance. Common categories include age, race, sex, occupation, and educational attainment. Often categories are little more than statistical groupings. However, information regarding such categories can have important uses. For instance, if we know the age distribution of a population, we can make projections that anticipate the demand for various social services, including social security and Medicare benefits (see

Chapter 11). Further, people who are aware that they share certain traits may be motivated to interact. They may even establish organizations to advance their common interests. For example, some women have banded together in the League of Women Voters and NOW (National Organization for Women) by virtue of an awareness that they are a social category that shares certain problems.

INSTITUTIONS

Groups assume a particularly important part in institutional life. Sociologists view **institutions** as the principal instruments whereby the essential tasks of living are organized, directed, and executed. Each institution is built about a standardized solution to a set of problems. The family institution has as its chief focus the reproduction, socialization, and maintenance of children; the economic institution, the production and distribution of goods and services; the political institution, the protection of citizens from one another and from foreign enemies; the religious institution, the enhancement of social solidarity and consensus; and the educational institution, the transmission of the cultural heritage from one generation to the next. Admittedly this classification oversimplifies matters. An institution may perform more than one function, and several institutions may contribute to the performance of the same function.

As sociologists typically define an institution, it encompasses both the notion of cultural patterns and social structure. Thus institutions constitute (1) the more or less standardized solutions (cultural patterns) that serve to direct people in meeting the problems of social living, and (2) the relatively stable relationships that characterize people in actually implementing these solutions. Conceived in this way, a cluster of cultural patterns (a set of norms, values, and symbols) establishes the behavior that is expected of us as a certain kind of person (for instance, a student) in relation to certain other kinds of people (for example, a professor, dean, teaching assistant, departmental secretary, registrar, or bursar). This set of cultural patterns locates us within a network of relationships. The concept of institution, then, implies that we are bound within networks of relationships (groups) in which we interact with one another (play our roles) in terms of certain shared understandings (cultural patterns) that define the behavior expected of us as given kinds of people (statuses). In the chapters that follow we will have considerably more to say on these matters. In particular, Chapters 8, 9, and 10 examine specific institutions.

SOCIETIES

Societies represent the most comprehensive and complex type of social structure in today's world. As we noted earlier in the chapter, *society* refers to a group of people who live within the same territory and share a common culture. By virtue of this common culture, the members of a society typically possess similar values and norms and a common language. Its members perpetuate themselves primarily through reproduction and comprise a more or less self-sufficient social unit. A society can be as small as a tribal community of several dozen people and as large as modern nations with hundreds of millions of people.

Although we often use the term nation-state interchangeably with society, the two are not necessarily the same. As we will see in Chapter 8, a state is a political entity centering on a government. Among many peoples of the world, the state binds together nationality and tribal groups that in their own right constitute societies. Consider Europe. A large number of European nation-states contain multiple nationality groups, including Great Britain (Scottish, Welsh, and English), Belgium (Flemish and Walloons), Czechoslovakia (Czechs and Slovaks), and Switzerland (Germans, Italians, and French). Similarly, many African nation-states contain multiple tribal groups: 250 in Nigeria, 200 in Zaire, and 130 in Tanzania. Political self-determination for one nationality is often incompatible with political self-determination for another.

Sociologists have classified societies in a good many ways. One popular approach is based on the principal way in which the members of a society derive their livelihood (Lenski and Lenski, 1982). Clearly, survival confronts all peoples with the problem of how they will provide for such vital needs as food, clothing, and shelter. And the manner in which they solve the problem has vast consequences for other aspects of their lives.

Hunting and gathering societies represent the earliest form of organized social life. Individuals survive by hunting animals and gathering edible foods. Because their food-gathering techniques rather quickly reduce the supply of animals and plants in a locality, the people are constantly on the move. Mcreover, their society is typically small, consisting of about 50 or so members. Large and complex forms of social organization are virtually impossible at this level of development. Kinship—ties by blood and marriage—is the foundation for most relationships. Specialized and enduring work groups, governments, and standing armies are unknown.

Some ten thousand or so years ago, human beings learned how to cultivate a number of the plants on which they depended for food. They became less dependent on the whims of nature than their hunting and gathering ancestors had been. The digging stick, and later the hoe, provided the basis for *horticultural societies*. Horticulturalists clear the land by means of "slash and burn" technology, raise crops for two to three years, and then move on to new plots as the soil becomes exhausted. Their more efficient economies allow for the production of a social surplus—goods and services over and above those necessary for human survival. This surplus became the foundation for social stratification; the specialization of some economic, political, and religious roles; a growth in the importance of warfare; and more complex forms of culture and social structure. Even so, the upper limit for most horticultural communities is about 3,000 persons.

Five to six thousand years ago, in fertile river valleys such as those of the Middle East, the plow heralded an agricultural revolution and the emergence of *agrarian societies* (Childe, 1941). Plowing stirs up the fertile elements in the soil that in semi-arid regions sink beneath the reach of plant roots. Additionally, the harnessing of animal power (such as oxen) and the discovery of the basic principles of metallurgy greatly enhanced the value of the plow. These innovations meant larger crops, more food, expanding populations, and even more complex forms of social organization. In time sophisticated political institutions emerged, with power concentrated in the hands of hereditary monarchs. Continuing advances in both productive and military technologies contributed to a substantial growth in the power of the state, the size of the territory it controlled, and the emergence of large capital cities. The massive pyramids of Egypt, the great cathedrals of medieval Europe, the roads and aqueducts of Rome, and the far-flung irrigation systems of the Middle East and China are products of agrarian societies.

About 250 years ago, the Industrial Revolution gave birth to *industrial societies* whose productive and economic systems are based on machine technologies. The energy needed for work activities came increasingly from hydroelectric plants, petroleum, and natural gas rather than from people and animals. Economic self-sufficiency and local market systems were displaced by complex divisions of labor, exchange relationships, and national and international market systems. The ability to read and write, limited to a small minority in agrarian societies, became essential skills in advanced industrial societies and led to the growth of educational institutions. Many activities that were once the responsibility of families were relinquished to other institutions. Populations grew and people increasingly congregated in cities. Large-scale bureaucracies and formal organizations came to predominate in both the private and public spheres, finding expression in big business, big unions, big universities, big hospitals, and big government.

Some social analysts contend that the United States is currently moving in the direction of a *postindustrial society* (Bell, 1973). Other metaphors have been applied to the new and revolutionary patterns, including Alvin Toffler's (1980) *third wave* and John Naisbitt's (1982) *megatrends.* In the postindustrial society, increasing numbers of workers find employment in tertiary industry centering on the provision of services rather than the extraction of raw materials and the manufacture of goods. Simultaneously, new techniques permit the automation of many processes in the workplace with the introduction of computers and complex feedback regulation devices. All these changes are being accompanied by a knowledge explosion based on the creating, processing, and distributing of information. We will have considerably more to say on these matters in Chapter 12.

Perspectives in Sociology

Thus far in the chapter we have considered the units that comprise culture and social structure. More particularly, we have looked at a number of the crucial building blocks—norms, values, symbols, and language—that provide the foundations of culture. In a similar manner, we have examined the components of social structure—statuses, roles, groups, institutions, and society. The discussion has been largely descriptive. But how are we to bind together such a multitude of material—facts and concepts—so that we can grasp and comprehend them all at once? How are we to see relationships among the concepts and uncover implications that are not evident in isolated pieces of data? How are we to organize our search for knowledge regarding the many different, and often puzzling, aspects of human behavior? Clearly we need some sort of tool. A theoretical perspective provides such a tool. A **theoretical perspective** is a general approach to phenomena that affords a set of assumptions and interrelated concepts for depicting the world.

Through the years, sociology has come to be characterized by a number of theoretical perspectives. The adherents of each perspective ask somewhat different questions about society and provide different views of social life. We do not need to accept only one model and reject all the others; rather, theoretical perspectives are tools—mental constructs—that allow us to visualize something. Any model necessarily limits our experience and presents a tunnel image. But a good model also increases the horizon of what we can see, serving like a pair of binoculars. It provides rules of inference through which new relationships can be discovered and suggestions about how the scope of a theory can be expanded. Within contemporary sociology there are three major perspectives: the functionalist, the conflict, and the symbolic interactionist. We will be returning to them throughout the book. For now, let us briefly examine each in turn.

THE FUNCTIONALIST PERSPECTIVE

The structural-functional—or, more simply, functionalist—perspective draws substantially upon the ideas of Auguste Comte, Herbert Spencer, and Emile Durkheim (Ritzer, 1983) (see Chapter 1). Its theorists take a broad view of society and focus on the macro aspects of social life. In the 1950s and early 1960s, the functionalist theories of Talcott Parsons (1949, 1951) and his students occupied center stage in American sociology. Indeed, some proponents like Kingsley Davis (1959) argued that the approach was, for all intents and purposes, synonymous with sociology.

The Social System. Functionalists take as their starting point the notion that society is a system. A **system** is a set of elements or components that are related to each other in a more or less stable fashion through a period of time. Hence functionalists focus on the parts of society, particularly its major institutions, such as the family, religion, the economy, the state, and education. They identify the structural characteristics of the institutions much as biologists describe the principal features of the body's organs. They then appraise the functions of the institutions. For instance, as we noted earlier in the chapter, the family is said to have as its chief focus the reproduction, socialization, and maintenance of children.

One of the features of a system stressed by functionalists is its tendency toward *equilibrium,* or balance among its parts and among the forces operating on it. Hence change in one institution has implications for other institutions and for the community or society as a whole. For instance, as

women have been drawn into the wage economy, they have tended to postpone marriage and have fewer children. In turn, the schools have seen enrollments fall and authorities have often had to close school buildings. Some institutions may also change more rapidly than others, contributing to social dislocations. As increasing numbers of mothers with preschool children enter the paid labor force, new arrangements are required to take care of the children during the day. Yet licensed day care facilities are currently available for fewer than one out of six of the children with working mothers. So many children, especially those from low-income homes, are currently receiving inadequate care (Vander Zanden, 1985).

Functions and Dysfunctions. Within system analysis, functionalists pay particular attention to the functions performed by a system's parts, especially its institutions, roles, cultural patterns, social norms, and groups. **Functions** are the observed consequences that permit the adaptation or adjustment of a system (Merton, 1968). Functionalists say that if a system is to survive, certain essential tasks must be performed; should these tasks go unperformed, the system fails to maintain itself—it perishes. If society is to exist, let alone flourish, its members must make provision for certain functional requirements. Institutions are the principal structures whereby these critical tasks for social living are organized, directed, and executed. Each institution is built around a standardized solution to a set of problems.

Robert K. Merton (1968) points out that just as institutions and the other parts of society can contribute to the maintenance of the social system, they can also have negative consequences. Those observed consequences that lessen the adaptation or adjustment of a system he terms **dysfunc-**

tions. Take poverty. As shown by sociologist Herbert J. Gans (1972), poverty has both functional and dysfunctional properties. In conducting his analysis, Gans was serving neither as an apologist nor as a critic of poverty. Rather, he sought to identify the part poverty plays within American life. In terms of its functions, the existence of poverty ensures that the nation's "dirty work" is done—those jobs that are physically dirty, dangerous, temporary, dead-end, poorly paid, and menial. Poverty also creates jobs for those who serve the poor or who "shield" the rest of the population from them—police, social workers, numbers runners, Pentecostal ministers, loan sharks, and heroin pushers. Of course, large numbers of poor people may be simultaneously dysfunctional for society. Poverty intensifies a variety of social problems, including those associated with health, education, crime, and drug addiction. And the victims of poverty often experience a sense of alienation from society and as a consequence withhold their loyalty from the system.

Manifest and Latent Functions. Merton (1968) also distinguishes between manifest functions and latent functions. **Manifest functions** are those consequences that are intended and recognized by the participants in a system; **latent functions** are those consequences that are neither intended nor recognized. This distinction draws our attention to the fact that people's *conscious* motivations for engaging in a behavior are not necessarily identical with the behavior's *objective* consequences. For example, the Hopi Indians of the Southwest have a number of ceremonials designed to produce rain. Science informs us that the manifest function of the rituals is not achieved; the ceremonials do not control meteorological events. But the concept of latent functions allows us to examine the consequences of the rituals not for the rain gods, but for the

Hopi themselves. The rituals provide occasions on which the scattered members of the society assemble to engage in a common activity. The ceremonials afford a means of collective expression by which the Hopi people achieve a sense of social solidarity. Thus the rituals serve functions that are neither intended nor recognized by the Hopi.

Social Consensus. Functionalists also assume that most members of a society agree on what is desirable, worthwhile, and moral, and what is undesirable, worthless, and evil. In other words, they share a *consensus* regarding their core values and beliefs. Most Americans accept the values and beliefs that inhere in the democratic creed, the doctrine of equal opportunity, and the notion of personal achievement; most Russians agree on the desirability of a society fashioned in accordance with the communist creed. Functionalists say that a high degree of consensus provides the foundation for social integration and stability. By virtue of a long socialization process, people come to accept the rules of their society, so for the most part they live by them.

Evaluation of the Functionalist Perspective. The functionalist perspective is a useful tool for describing society and identifying its structural parts and the functions of these parts. It provides a "big picture" of the whole of social life, particularly as it finds expression in patterned, recurrent behavior and institutions. For some purposes, it is clearly helpful to "shut down" social processes and describe behavior at a given point in time. An anatomist does much the same thing when examining a cell under a microscope or a cadaver in a laboratory. Thus from the functionalist perspective we derive primarily a static picture—a sort of snapshot—of social life at a particular time in history.

However, such an approach does not

provide us with the entire story of social life. The functionalist approach has difficulty dealing with history and processes of social change. It fails to grasp the never-ending flow of action that occurs among people. Yet the real world consists of transition and flux (Olsen, 1978). Moreover, the functionalist perspective tends to exaggerate consensus, integration, and stability while disregarding conflict, dissensus, and instability. The problems that structural-functional theory has in dealing with change, history, and conflict have led critics to charge that it has a conservative bias and that it tends to support existing social arrangements (Mills, 1959; Gouldner, 1970; Abrahamson, 1978). Such is not the case with the conflict perspective: It paints quite a different picture of social life.

THE CONFLICT PERSPECTIVE

Conflict theorists, like functionalists, focus their attention on society as a whole, studying its institutions and structural arrangements. Yet the two perspectives are at odds on a good many matters (Dahrendorf, 1959; Lenski, 1966). Where functionalists depict society in relatively static terms, conflict theorists emphasize the processes of change that continually transform social life. Where functionalists stress the order and stability to be found in society, conflict theorists emphasize disorder and instability. Where functionalists see the common interests shared by the members of a society, conflict theorists focus upon the interests that divide. Where functionalists view consensus as the basis of social unity, conflict theorists insist that social unity is an illusion resting on coercion. And where functionalists often view existing social arrangements as necessary and justified by the requirements of group life, conflict theorists see many of the arrangements as neither necessary nor justified.

Diversity of Approaches. Although conflict theory derives much of its inspiration from the work of Karl Marx, the conflict framework is not necessarily Marxian (see Chapter 1). Indeed, it draws on many diverse currents, including the work of such sociologists as Georg Simmel (1908/1955, 1950), Lewis Coser (1956), and Randall Collins (1975). Moreover, because Marx's theory is so encyclopedic, a great many theorists have claimed to be working within the guidelines set down by his work, even though irreconcilable differences set them apart in warring camps (Ritzer, 1983). Further, although class conflict is the core of Marxian theory, many contemporary sociologists view conflict as occurring among many groups and interests—religion versus religion, race versus race, consumers versus producers, taxpayers versus welfare recipients, sunbelt versus snowbelt states, central city residents versus suburbanites, the young versus the elderly, and so on.

Sources of Conflict. While the conflict perspective encompasses a variety of approaches, most of them assume that human societies operate under conditions of perpetual scarcity for many of the resources people require. Wealth, prestige, and power are always in limited supply, so gains for one individual or group are often associated with losses for others. The question then becomes: Which party will win and which party will lose? **Power**—the ability to control the behavior of others, even against their will—provides the answer. As we will see in Chapter 8, power determines the outcome of the *distributive question* of who will get what, when, and how (Lasswell, 1936). And power also answers the question of which group will be able to translate its preferences for behavior (its values) into the operating rules for others—for instance, who will define whom as deviant and make their definitions of deviance stick (see Chapter 5). Conflict theorists ask how some groups acquire power, dominate other groups, and effect their will in human affairs. In so doing, they look at who benefits and who loses from the way society is organized.

How Society Is Possible. If social life is fractured and fragmented by confrontations between individuals or groups, how is a society possible? We pointed out how functionalists say that society is held together primarily by a consensus among its members regarding core values and norms. Conflict theorists reject this view, they maintain that society is often held together in the face of conflicting interests in one of two ways. Under one arrangement, one group enjoys sufficient power to make and enforce rules and shape institutional life so that its interests are served. Many conflict theorists regard the state—government and the rules it promulgates—as an instrument of oppression employed by ruling elites for their own benefit (functionalists tend to view the state as an organ of the total society, functioning to promote social control and stability). Under another arrangement, there are so many overlapping and divided interest groups that people can win or lose jointly, depending on their willingness to cooperate and compromise. Thus rewards can often be maximized and losses minimized by entering into alliances against outsiders (Sprey, 1979).

Evaluation of the Conflict Perspective. The conflict perspective provides a welcome balance to functionalist theory. Indeed, since the strengths of the one perspective tend to be the weaknesses of the other, the two approaches complement one another in many ways. Where the functionalist approach has difficulty dealing with history and social change, the conflict approach makes these matters its strength. And

where the conflict approach has difficulty dealing with some aspects of consensus, integration, and stability, the functionalist approach affords penetrating insights. Additionally, both approaches have traditionally taken a holistic view of social life, portraying societies as systems of interrelated parts (van den Berghe, 1963).

Admittedly, some proponents of the functionalist and conflict schools find their differences so great that they see no basis for reconciliation. Even so, any number of sociologists have taken on the task. For instance, sociologists like Ralf Dahrendorf (1959) and Gerhard E. Lenski (1966) view society as basically "Janus-headed," and contend that the functionalists and conflict theorists are simply studying two aspects of the same reality. They note that both consensus and conflict are central features of social life.

Other sociologists like Lewis Coser (1956) and Joseph Himes (1973), drawing upon the seminal work done by Georg Simmel (1908/1955), suggest that under some circumstances conflict is *functional* for society. It quickens group allegiances and loyalties and thus is a social glue that binds people together. For example, the Black Power movement of the 1960s and early 1970s provided blacks with a sense of dignity, belonging, self-worth, and pride. And conflict may also prevent social systems from ossifying by exerting pressure for change and innovation. The civil rights movement, although challenging established interests and racist patterns, may have contributed to the long-term stability of American institutions by bringing blacks into the "system." However, it is clear that conflict can be dysfunctional for a system, a fact highlighted by contemporary Lebanon, where the number of people who think of themselves as "Lebanese"—as opposed to being Maronite Christians, Shiite Muslims, Sunni Muslims, or Druse—is becoming smaller and smaller (Friedman, 1984).

The social fabric in modern-day Lebanon has been torn apart as Christian, Druse, Palestinian, and Moslem factions battle for ascendancy. Conflict has accentuated each group's self-consciousness and in-group loyalties. In the process, allegiance to the Lebanese nation-state has eroded and the nation's institutional life has disintegrated. (Chauvel/Sygma)

THE INTERACTIONIST PERSPECTIVE

The functionalist and conflict perspectives take a "big picture" approach to sociology, focusing on the "macro" or large-scale structures of society. In contrast, the interactionist perspective has traditionally been more concerned with the "micro" or small-scale aspects of social life. Sociologists like Charles Horton Cooley (1902/1964), George Herbert Mead (1934/1962), Manford Kuhn (1964), and Herbert Blumer (1969) have turned their attention to the individuals who make up society and have asked how they go about fitting their actions together. As with the functionalist and conflict per-

spectives, a number of themes recur in the various formulations of interactionist thought.

Symbols. Interactionists emphasize that we are social beings who live a group existence. However, in contrast with ants, bees, termites, and other social insects, we possess few, if any, innate behaviors for relating ourselves to one another. If we are largely lacking in such inborn mechanisms, how is society possible? Interactionists find the answer in the ability of human beings to communicate by means of symbols. Because they stress the importance of social interaction and the symbols people use to attune themselves to one another, these sociologists are called *symbolic interactionists*.

Meaning: Constructing Reality. Following in the tradition of George Herbert Mead (1863–1931), symbolic interactionists contend that we act toward people, objects, and events on the basis of the *meanings* we impart to them. Meaning is not something that inheres in things, it is a property that derives from, or arises out of, the interaction that takes place among people in the course of their daily lives (Blumer, 1969). Put another way, reality does not exist "out there" in the world but is *manufactured* by people as they intervene in the world and interpret what is occurring there. As social philosopher Alfred Schutz (1971) points out, there are strictly speaking no such things as facts, pure and simple. We select facts from a universal context through the activities of our mind, and for this reason all "facts" are human creations. Accordingly, symbolic interactionists say that we experience the world as **constructed reality**.

An illustration may help in grasping this point (Vander Zanden, 1984). Some cloudless night, look up into the northern heavens and find the seven stars that form the Big Dipper. Then attempt to discern in this combination of stars the image first of a bear, then a wagon, and finally a bushel basket. Most Americans have great difficulty identifying the latter objects. They conclude: "It just looks like a dipper and that's all there is to it." Other people have known this same set of stars by different names. The ancient Syrians saw the configuration as the Wild Boar; the Hindus, as the Seven Sages; the Greeks, as the Great Bear; the Poles, as the Heavenly Wagon; and the Chinese, as the Northern Bushel.

The interesting thing about all this is the influence the assignment of such names—symbolic word handles—have had on how people view this celestial configuration. From their writings, it is clear that the ancient Greeks did not just call these stars the Great Bear; when they looked into the northern sky, they *saw* the figure of a bear. Nor does it matter to most of us that some 203 other stars are visible in the same constellation—Ursa Major—and that these stars offer an infinite number of combinations and configurations. In the case of the dipper, we single out seven specific stars, label them a "dipper," and in turn we see a "dipper." For their part, the ancient Greeks saw a bear; the Syrians, a wild boar; and so on. All this leads symbolic interactionists to say that if sociologists are to understand social life, they must understand what people actually say and do from the viewpoint of the people themselves. This orientation is strongly influenced by Max Weber's concept of *Verstehen*.

Fashioning Behavior. Symbolic interactionists portray us as creatively constructing our actions in accordance with the meanings we attribute to a situation. In fashioning our behavior, we use symbols to define our perceptual inputs, mentally outline possible responses, imagine the consequences of alternative courses of action, eliminate unlikely possibilities, and finally select the optimal mode of action (Stryker, 1980). We mentally rehearse our actions before we actually act and, upon acting, serve as audiences to our own actions (see Chapter 3). This implies that a certain amount of indeterminacy or unpredictability inheres in human behavior because we must continually fashion meanings and devise ways to fit our actions together. Consequently, much of our behavior has a tentative and developing quality to it: We map, test, devise, suspend, and revise our overt actions in response to the actions of others.

Evaluation of the Interactionist Perspective. The interactionist perspective has the advantage of bringing "people" into the panorama of sociological investigation. It directs our attention to the activities of individuals as they go about their everyday lives. We see people not as robots mechanically enacting behavior prescribed by social rules and institutional arrangements, but as social beings endowed with the capacity for thought. Through interaction they acquire the symbols and the meanings that allow them to interpret situations, assess the advantages and disadvantages of given actions, and then select one of them. Thus from interactionists we gain an image of human beings as individuals who actively fashion their behavior, as opposed to an image of individuals who simply respond in a passive manner to the external dictates of structural constraints.

However, the interactionist perspective has its limitations. In their everyday lives people do not enjoy total flexibility in shaping their actions. Although interactionists acknowledge that much of our action is guided by systems of preestablished meanings, including culture and social order, some like Herbert Blumer (1969) downgrade the part social structure plays in our lives. Critics contend that symbolic interactionism can lead to a marked overemphasis on the immediate situation and an "obsessive con-

Doing Sociology: Applying the Sociological Perspectives

Fraternities and sororities have long been a fixture on many American college and university campuses. As part of a class project to apply the major sociological perspectives to an aspect of college life, introductory students at Ohio State University examined fraternities and sororities. Viewed from the functionalist perspective, the Greeks were seen as parts of a larger whole or system that constitutes the educational enterprise. More particularly, the Greek houses seem to function as social arrangements that assist college youth in weakening their emotional bonds with their parents and moving into the larger world, including the academic community. They allow youth to establish meaningful ties with peers, to exercise independence from adult controls, and to realize identities and acquire statuses in which their own activities and concerns are paramount. And the group living that characterizes Greek life enables young people to cultivate relationships and skills characterized by sociability, self-assertion, competition, cooperation, and mutual understanding among equals. By the same token, Greek involvement in campus charity drives and their support for intercollegiate athletic programs foster the esprit de corps so essential for college and university allegiances. However, fra-

ternities and sororities may also have dysfunctional properties because social and status distinctions may provide the focus for campus dissension and obligations to the Greek community may take precedence over educational concerns.

Viewed from the conflict perspective, fraternities and sororities were seen within the context of a larger social and economic order characterized by class, racial, and gender conflicts and inequalities. The Greeks appear to mirror and reproduce these social arrangements. Within their fraternity and sorority houses, privileged youth are prepared for their future lives in corporate and other large-scale organizational structures. Young people must subordinate and relegate their individual needs and aspirations to the dictates and requirements of the Greek organization in much the manner they later will be required to in large law and accounting firms, business establishments, government bureaus, hospitals, and universities. Additionally, the hierarchical structure of authority and the division of labor in the Greek houses equip youth for similar types of relationships in the bureaucratic structures of the larger world. And the social life provided by the Greeks reflects the "country-club" type of etiquette and interpersonal social skills that will be re-

quired of corporate officials and professionals. Thus, from the conflict perspective the Greek system seems to be an aspect of elitist arrangements by which the established order is perpetuated from one generation to the next.

The sociology students saw symbolic interactionists as taking a somewhat different view of fraternities and sororities. Here the emphasis falls on the ways that members of the Greek community fashion shared meanings that provide the foundations for social relationships. Greek emblems and rituals facilitate a consciousness of oneness, symbolizing the reality of the group and the relation of members to it. Simultaneously, these same mechanisms identify and highlight the boundaries of the group. An important characteristic of such boundaries is that they face in two directions. Not only do the boundaries limit Greek members from moving out to other interaction possibilities, but they prevent non-Greek members from entering the Greek sphere. Members become aware of the contours of the group; they know what kinds of experiences "belong" within its precincts and what kinds do not. In the course of their social interaction, the youth construct the reality we know as the fraternity and sorority system.

cern with the transient, episodic and fleet-ing" (Meltzer, Petras, and Reynolds, 1975:85). The perspective tends to overlook the connectedness that outcomes have to one another, particularly the links that exist among episodes of interaction (Weinstein and Tanur, 1976).

In contrast with traditional formulations of the interactionist perspective, function-alists remind us that society has a pat-terned, recurrent quality to it that limits the latitude people have in forging their actions. And conflict theorists alert us to the fact that social arrangements are not neutral, but al-locate the burdens and benefits of society unequally among different groups. To rec-tify some of these difficulties, a number of symbolic interactionists like Sheldon Stry-ker (1980) have recently undertaken to in-troduce structural and large-scale compo-nents into interactionist thought. Stryker attempts to bridge social structure and the individual with such concepts as "position" and "role." We took a somewhat similar ap-proach earlier in the chapter when we un-dertook to link the small-scale or micro as-pects of social life with its large-scale or macro aspects. We saw that the intertwined patterns of action and interaction form the foundation for groups and societies.

USING THE THREE PERSPECTIVES

The details of the three sociological per-spectives will become clearer as we encoun-ter them in the chapters to come. As we noted, each theoretical approach has its ad-vantages and its disadvantages. Each por-trays a different aspect of reality and directs our attention to some dimension of social life that the other neglects or overlooks. Functionalism highlights the functions and dysfunctions of poverty in terms of the op-eration of the larger society. Conflict theo-rists portray the inequalities that flow from the way society is organized, and they show who gains and who loses from these ar-rangements. Interactionists suggest that people define certain circumstances as de-viating from what they perceive to be an ideal standard of living, assign an unfavor-able meaning to these conditions, and apply the label "poverty" to them. Hence, each approach offers a somewhat different in-sight.

Further, each perspective affords a more effective approach, a better "fit," to some kinds of data—some aspects of social life—than other perspectives do. Each approach may have some merit and need not neces-sarily preclude the accuracy of another per-spective in explaining given data or pre-dicting particular outcomes. Indeed, each approach is useful precisely because it pro-vides us with one piece of information re-garding the exceedingly complex puzzle of social life. Just as carpenters find that a chisel, a plane, and a saw are useful tools that complement one another as they go about building a house, so we will find that all three perspectives are useful sociological tools for describing and analyzing human behavior.

SUMMARY

1. Culture provides individuals with a set of common understandings that they employ in fashioning their actions. In so doing, it binds the separated lives of individuals into a larger whole, making society possible by providing a common framework of meaning. Only by shar-ing similar perspectives with one an-

other can we weave integrated webs of ongoing interaction.

2. Norms are social rules that specify appropriate and inappropriate behavior in given situations. They afford a means by which we orient ourselves to other people. And they are also ends; we and others attribute to them an independent quality, making them "things" in their own right. Folkways, mores, and laws are types of norms. Whereas norms are rules for behavior, values are broad ideas regarding what is desirable, correct, and good that most members of a society share. Values are so general and abstract that they do not explicitly specify which behaviors are acceptable and which are not.

3. Symbols are acts or objects that have come to be socially accepted as standing for something else. Symbols assume many different forms, but language is the most important of these. Language is the cornerstone of every culture. It is the chief vehicle by which people communicate ideas, information, attitudes, and emotions. And it is the principal means by which human beings create culture and transmit it from generation to generation.

4. Cultural universals are patterned and recurrent aspects of life that appear in all known societies. The reason for such common denominators or cultural constants is not hard to come by. All people confront many of the same problems. Culture represents an accumulation of solutions to the problems posed by human biology and the human situation. The items that form a culture tend to constitute a consistent and integrated whole.

5. Once we acquire the cultural ways peculiar to our own society, they become so deeply ingrained that they seem second nature to us. Additionally, we have difficulty conceiving of alternative ways of life. Given these facts, it is hardly surprising that we should judge the behavior of other groups by the standards of our own culture, a phenomenon sociologists term ethnocentrism. Ethnocentrism gets in the way of the scientific study of culture. We must examine their behavior in the light of their values, beliefs, and motives, an approach termed cultural relativism.

6. Cultural diversity does not occur only between societies. It may also be found within a society in the form of subcultures. Subcultures abound in American life, finding expression in various religious, racial, ethnic, occupational, and age groups. At times the norms, values, and life styles of a subculture are at odds with those of the larger society, making it a counterculture.

7. For the most part people do not interact with one another in a haphazard or random manner. Instead, their relationships are characterized by social ordering. Sociologists apply the term social structure to this social ordering—the interweaving of people's interactions and relationships in recurrent and stable patterns. Social structure is a social fact of the sort described by Emile Durkheim.

8. Status represents a position within a group or society. It is by means of statuses that we locate one another in various social structures. We have greater control over some of our statuses than others. Some are assigned to us—ascribed statuses; others we secure on the basis of individual choice and competition—achieved statuses. A status carries with it a set of culturally defined

rights and duties, what sociologists term a role. A role is the expected behavior we associate with a status. Role performance is the actual behavior of the person who occupies a status. A single status may have multiple roles attached to it, constituting a role set.

9. Statuses and roles are building blocks for more comprehensive social structures, including groups. Roles link us within social relationships. When these relationships are sustained across time, we frequently attribute group properties to them. Sociologists distinguish groups from aggregates and categories.

10. Institutions are the principal instruments whereby the essential tasks of social living are organized, directed, and executed. Each institution is built around a standardized solution to a set of problems. As sociologists typically define an institution, it encompasses the notions of both cultural patterns and social structure.

11. Societies represent the most comprehensive and complex type of social structure in today's world. By virtue of their common culture, the members of a society typically possess similar values and norms and a common language. One popular approach for classifying societies is based on the way people derive their livelihood: hunting and gathering societies, horticultural societies, agrarian societies, industrial societies, and postindustrial societies. Another approach rests on the distinction between traditional and modern types.

12. The structural-functional—or, more simply, functionalist—perspective draws substantially upon the ideas of Comte, Spencer, and Durkheim. Its proponents take as their starting point the notion that society is a system. They identify the structural characteristics and functions of institutions. Functionalists also typically assume that most members of a society share a consensus regarding their core beliefs and values.

13. Although the conflict approach draws much of its inspiration from the work of Karl Marx, its framework is not necessarily Marxian. While class conflict constitutes the central core of Marxian theory, many contemporary sociologists view conflict as occurring among many groups and interests. The conflict perspective provides a welcome balance to functionalist theory.

14. Symbolic interactionists contend that society is possible because human beings have the ability to communicate with one another by means of symbols. They say that we act toward people, objects, and events on the basis of the meanings we impart to them. Consequently, we experience the world as constructed reality.

GLOSSARY

achieved status Statuses that individuals secure on the basis of choice and competition.
ascribed status Statuses assigned to an individual by a group or society.
aggregate A collection of anonymous individuals who are in one place at the same time.

category A collection of people who share a characteristic that is deemed to be of social significance.
constructed reality Our experience of the world. Meaning is not something that inheres in things, it is a property that derives from, or arises out

of, the interaction that takes place among people in the course of their daily lives.

counterculture A subculture—norms, values, and life style—that is at odds with the ways of the larger society.

cultural relativism A value-free or neutral approach that views the behavior of a people from the perspective of their own culture.

cultural universals Patterned and recurrent aspects of life that appear in all known societies.

culture The social heritage of a people; those learned patterns for thinking, feeling, and acting that are transmitted from one generation to the next, including the embodiment of these patterns in material items.

duties Actions that others can legitimately insist we perform.

dysfunctions The observed consequences that lessen the adaptation or adjustment of a system.

ethnocentrism The tendency to judge the behavior of other groups by the standards of one's own culture.

folkways Norms people do not deem to be of great importance and to which they exact less stringent conformity.

functions The observed consequences that permit the adaptation or adjustment of a system.

group Two or more people who share a feeling of unity and who are bound together in relatively stable patterns of social interaction.

institutions The principal instruments whereby the essential tasks of living are organized, directed, and executed.

language A socially structured system of sound patterns (words and sentences) with specific and arbitrary meanings.

latent functions Consequences that are neither intended nor recognized by the participants in a system.

laws Rules that are enforced by a special political organization composed of individuals who enjoy the right to use force.

linguistic relativity hypothesis The view that

different languages slice up and conceptualize the world of experience differently.

manifest functions Consequences that are intended and recognized by the participants in a system.

master status A key or core status that carries primary weight in a person's interactions and relationships with others.

material culture Physical artifacts or objects created by the members of a society.

mores Norms to which people attach a good deal of importance and exact strict conformity.

nonmaterial culture Abstract creations like values, beliefs, symbols, norms, customs, and institutional arrangements created by the members of a society.

norm A social rule that specifies appropriate and inappropriate behavior in given situations.

power The ability to control the behavior of others, even against their will.

rights The actions that we can legitimately insist that others perform.

role Expectations (rights and duties) that define the behavior people view as appropriate and inappropriate for the occupant of a status.

role conflict Situation in which individuals are confronted with conflicting expectations stemming from their simultaneous occupancy of two or more statuses.

role performance The actual behavior of the person who occupies a status.

role set The multiple roles associated with a single status.

role strain Finding the expectations of a single role incompatible, so that one has difficulty performing the role.

social structure The interweaving of people's interactions and relationships in recurrent and stable patterns.

society A group of people who live within the same territory and share a common culture.

status A position within a group or society; a location in a social structure.

subculture A group whose members participate in the main culture of a society while simultaneously sharing a number of unique values, norms, traditions, and life styles.

symbol An act or object that has come to be socially accepted as standing for something else.

system A set of elements or components related to each other in a more or less stable fashion through a period of time.

theoretical perspective A general approach to phenomena that affords a set of assumptions and interrelated concepts for depicting the world.

values Broad ideas regarding what is desirable, correct, and good that most members of a society share.

3

Socialization

FOUNDATIONS FOR
SOCIALIZATION

Nature and Nurture
Social Communication
Definition of the Situation

THE SELF

Charles Horton Cooley: The Looking-
  Glass Self
George Herbert Mead: The
  Generalized Other
Erving Goffman: Impression
  Management

SOCIALIZATION ACROSS THE LIFE
SPAN

Childhood
Adolescence
Young Adulthood
Middle Adulthood
Later Adulthood
Death

In comparison with other species, we enter the world as amazingly "unfinished" beings. We are not born human, but become human only in the course of interaction with other people. Our humanness is a social product that arises in the course of **socialization**—a process of social interaction by which people acquire the knowledge, attitudes, values, and behaviors essential for effective participation in society. By virtue of socialization, a mere biological organism becomes transformed into a person—a genuine social being.

Were it not for socialization, the renewal of culture could not occur from one generation to the next. Human beings are uniquely dependent upon a social heritage—the rich store of adaptations and innovations that countless generations of ancestors have developed over thousands of years. Through culture, each new generation can move on from the achievements of the preceding one. Without socialization, society could not perpetuate itself beyond a single generation. Individuals would lack those common understandings necessary to align their actions and to bind their separated lives into a larger whole. Both the individual and society are mutually dependent on socialization. It blends the sentiments and ideas of culture to the capacities and needs of the organism (Davis, 1948: 195).

We gain an appreciation of the importance of socialization when we examine the cases of children reared under conditions of extreme isolation. Sociologist Kingsley Davis (1949) reports on two cases from the 1940s. Anna and Isabelle were illegitimate children whose mothers had kept them hidden in secluded rooms over a period of years. They received enough care to be kept alive. When local authorities discovered them, they were about 6 years of age. They were extremely retarded and displayed few human capabilities or responses.

Anna was placed in a county home and later in a school for retarded children. She was able to learn to talk in phrases, walk, wash her hands, brush her teeth, follow simple instructions, play with a doll, and engage in other human activities. Just how fully she might have developed is not known, since she died of hemorrhagic jaundice at age 10. In contrast, Isabelle received special training from the members of the faculty of Ohio State University. Within a week after training was begun, she attempted her first vocalization. Isabelle progressed rapidly through the stages of learning and development typical of American children. She finished the sixth grade at age 14 and was judged by her teachers to be a competent, cheerful, and well-adjusted student. Isabelle is reported to have completed high school, married, and had her own normal family. The cases of Anna and Isabelle testify that much of the behavior we regard as somehow given in the human species does not occur unless it is put there through communicative and social contact with others.

More recently, Susan Curtiss (1977) has reported on the case of Genie, who was discovered at the age of 13 after having experienced a childhood of severe and unusual deprivation. From the age of 20 months she had been locked in a small room and harnessed to an infant's potty seat. Her father beat her frequently, especially when she made sounds. Under these circumstances, she never developed language. At age 13 Genie came to the attention of authorities and was admitted to a hospital. She was malformed, incontinent, and malnourished. On attainment and maturity tests she scored in the range of a 1-year-old. Specialists at nearby UCLA designed a program to rehabilitate and educate her.

Although Genie made some progress in the comprehension and production of language, her speech remained slow and resembled a somewhat garbled telegram. Additionally, her behavior was not "normal." When encountering a stranger who caught her fancy, she would ignore social norms, physically grasp the person, and refuse to let go. She would approach strangers, stand directly in front of them, and without observing an acceptable distance, peer directly into their faces. Additionally, she masturbated as often as possible, anywhere and everywhere. Genie's mother regained custody of her in 1978 and terminated the therapy and research program. One hypothesis psychologists have advanced to explain Genie's language deficiencies is that there are critical periods in the development of language capabilities and that gaps occurring in these periods cannot be successfully bridged once children enter puberty.

Foundations for Socialization

Human socialization presupposes that an adequate genetic endowment and an adequate environment are available. As we noted in Chapter 2, psychologists have taught chimpanzees and gorillas a great many things, including the use of symbols. Yet the methods by which the animals must be trained are quite different from the relatively spontaneous way in which children acquire language and many other skills. Nothing happened in the evolution of chimps and gorillas that allows them to produce their own symbols, although they evidently have the mental capabilities to make use of those fashioned by people. Thus chimps and gorillas lack the unique capacity for language and thought that characterizes normal human beings. Clearly, if human socialization is to occur, an appropriate genetic endowment is necessary. By the same token, the cases of Anna, Isabelle, and Genie testify to the inadequacy of our biological equipment for producing a normal hu-

man personality in the absence of social interaction. Humanness, then, is a product of both hereditary and environmental factors.

NATURE AND NURTURE

Every February, as spring arrives, many children on the Mediterranean island of Sardinia suddenly become listless. Over the following three months their schoolwork suffers; they fall asleep at their desks; and they complain of feeling dizzy and nauseous. In the United States, the behavior would be ascribed to spring fever, boredom, or a collective effort to disrupt the schooling process. But Sardinian teachers know that children and adults can die of the affliction, particularly after urinating quantities of blood. An estimated 35 percent of Sardinians suffer from the disorder (Harsanyi and Hutton, 1979).

In 1959 scientists investigated the disease and found that it is a hereditary condition associated with the lack of a single enzyme, called glucose-6-phosphate dehydrogenase (or, G-6-PD). However, the Sardinians display the symptoms only during the spring, suggesting that a victim's lack of G-6-PD is not the only factor activating the disease. Researchers reasoned that something in the environment had to be taking advantage of the enzyme deficiency. In other words, although the genetic defect may have been the gun, an environmental factor had to be pulling the trigger. They found that the Italian fava bean is the culprit and that susceptible Sardinians can remain free of attacks by not eating the plant and its products.

In recent years, research of the sort undertaken among the Sardinians has shown the complex relationships that exist between heredity and environment. And the old nature-nurture controversy, debated for centuries, had been found to be a nonissue. Even the classical Greek philosophers argued over whether ideas are innate to the human mind or are acquired through experience. At first scientists asked *which* factor, heredity or environment, is more important in fashioning a particular trait, such as a mental disorder or an individual's intelligence. Later they attempted to determine *how much* of the differences they found among people could be attributed to differences in heredity and *how much* to differences in environment. More recently, many of them have phrased the question in terms of *how* specific hereditary and environmental factors *interact* to produce particular characteristics and behaviors.

The early phrasing of the question caused untold difficulties. Carried to its logical conclusion, the either-or dichotomy defines biologically inborn behavior as that which appears in the absence of environment, and learned behavior as that which does not require an organism. The "how much" question also poses difficulties. It assumes that nature and nurture are related in such a way that the contribution of one is *added* to the contribution of the other. Yet in real life, the two factors *work together* to produce a given outcome, as in the case of the Sardinian disorder. Genes determine the range of potential possibilities, but the environment selects among them.

Organisms are not passive objects programmed by internal genetic forces, nor are they passive objects shaped by the external environment (Rossi, 1984). Hereditary and environmental factors interpenetrate and mutually determine each other. By way of analogy, consider the baking of a cake: The taste of the completed product is the result of a complex interaction among the components—the butter, sugar, flour, salt, and so on—exposed for a certain period to oven temperature. The outcome is not dissociable into this-or-that percent of flour, butter, and the like, although each component makes its contribution (Lewontin, Rose, and Kamin, 1984).

The human situation is even more complex than that found among other organisms. As children develop, their behavior becomes less and less dependent on *maturation*—changes in an organism that unfold more or less automatically in a set, irreversible sequence due to physical and chemical processes. Instead, learning comes increasingly to the forefront. Significantly, in learning, the human organism modifies itself by responding: the mind is not *revealed* as children mature; it is *constructed*. For this reason, human beings are not locked into an unchangeable physical body or social system.

So in a world in which complex developmental interactions are always occurring, process and history assume paramount importance. Individuals become active agents shaping both themselves and their environments. They act on and modify the world in which they live, and in turn they are shaped and transformed by the consequences of their own actions. This dynamic interplay between an individual and the environment is the foundation of human intelligence, knowledge, and culture (Vander Zanden, 1985).

SOCIAL COMMUNICATION

If they are to adapt to their environment, human beings must be able to communicate with one another. Indeed, all social interaction involves communication (Grimshaw, 1980). **Communication** refers to the process by which people transmit information, ideas, attitudes, and mental states to one another. It includes all those verbal and nonverbal processes by which we send and receive messages. Without the ability to communicate, each human being would be locked within a private world such as that experienced by Helen Keller before she acquired language. Communication allows us to establish "commonness" with one another so that senders and receivers can come together through a given message. Communication is an indispensable mechanism by which human beings attain social goals. It permits them to coordinate complex group activities, and as such it is the foundation for institutional life.

Verbal Communication. Language has enabled human beings alone of all animals to transcend biological evolution. Whereas biological evolution works only through genes, cultural evolution takes place through the linguistic transmission of information. For example, evolutionary processes took millions of years to fashion amphibians—creatures that can live on land or in water. In contrast, second amphibians—astronauts who can live in the earth's atmosphere or in the space outside it—have "evolved" in a comparatively short period of time. Human anatomy did not alter so that people could live in space. Rather, human beings increased their knowledge to the point where they could employ it to complement and supplement their anatomy. They were able to make themselves spaceworthy.

What is the source of this amazing human facility? For years many social scientists asserted that infants come into the world essentially unprogrammed for language use. But then linguists began noticing similarities in languages throughout the world. All languages have nouns and verbs and allow individuals to ask questions, give commands, and deny statements (Dale, 1976). Moreover, children acquire language with little difficulty, despite the fact that they must master an incredibly complex and abstract set of rules for transforming strings of sounds into meanings. Even deaf children have a strong bias to communicate in languagelike ways (Goldin-Meadow, 1983). And speakers can understand and produce an infinite set of sentences, even sentences they have never before heard or uttered.

In 1957, the eminent linguist Noam Chomsky put these observations together to suggest that human beings possess an inborn language-generating mechanism, what he terms the **language acquisition device**. As viewed by Chomsky (1957, 1965, 1968, 1975), the basic structure of language is biologically channeled, forming a sort of prefabricated filing system to order the words and phrases that make up human languages. All a child needs to do is learn the peculiarities of his or her society's language.

Chomsky's hypothesis has attracted interest as well as controversy. Social scientists have pointed out that simply because a biological predisposition for the development of language may be anchored in the human brain does not mean that environmental factors play no part in the acquisition of language. For instance, children do not seem to learn language simply by hearing it spoken. Two cases highlight the point. A boy with normal hearing but with deaf parents who communicated by the American Sign Language was exposed daily to television, with the expectation that he would learn English. Because he suffered from asthma, he was confined to his home, where his interactions were limited to people who communicated in sign language. By the time he was 3, he was fluent in sign language, but he neither understood nor spoke English (Moskowitz, 1978).

Similarly, a child born with a nonfunctioning immune system was kept in a germ-free bubble environment for the first four years of his life, when a bone marrow transplant provided him with a normal immune response and allowed him to return home. During his years of isolation, he communicated with the outside world by means of gestures. When released from the hospital environment, he had considerable difficulty using language and rarely initiated a conversation. Although the child had been encouraged to speak while hospitalized, his life in isolation had not provided a context in which to use language (Holland, 1983). These cases suggest that to learn a language, children must be able to *interact* with people in that language.

In sum, the acquiring of language cannot be understood by examining genetic factors and learning processes in isolation from one another. Instead, complex and dynamic interactions occur among biochemical processes, maturational factors, learning strategies, and the social environment. No aspect by itself can produce a language-using human being. Although infants possess a genetically guided ground plan that leads them toward language, that ability can be acquired only in a social context (Lenneberg, 1969; Nelson, 1977; Grimshaw, 1981).

Nonverbal Communication. Verbal symbols are only the tip of the communication iceberg (Ridgeway, Berger, and Smith, 1985). Nonverbal messages abound, and we "read" a good deal into them without necessarily being aware of doing so. Based on his experiments, psychologist Albert Mehrabian (1968) concludes that the total impact of a message is 7 percent verbal, 38 percent vocal, and 55 percent facial. Another specialist, Raymond L. Birdwhistell (1970:197), suggests that "no more than 30 to 35 percent of the social meaning of a conversation or an interaction is carried by its words."

One situation in which you are very likely aware of nonverbal communication is the pickup scene of a singles bar or a party. A rather standardized form of eye contact precedes the verbal contact. If, while gazing about a room, a man and woman spot each other and become interested, they signal with eye contact. For example, the man will hold the woman's gaze, look away, and then look back quickly once or twice. If the woman responds in kind, they may maneuver within speaking distance and strike up a conversation. A woman may also send a "flirt" sign—a sudden smile and a quick turning of the head downward or to the side. On the other hand, if you establish and hold eye contact with a stranger on an elevator, it is perceived to be a threatening communication. Similarly, in American culture you generally do not stare at another person unless you are talking (Mazur et al., 1980). You may establish eye contact with others when they are at a distance beyond that for normal conversation, but as you get closer you shift your eyes away.

There are a good many nonverbal communication systems, including the following:

Body Language: Physical motions and gestures provide signals. The "preening behavior" that accompanies courtship is a good illustration. Women frequently stroke their hair, check their makeup, rearrange their clothes, or push the hair away from the face. Men may straighten their hair, tug at their tie, readjust their clothes, or pull up their socks. These are signals that say, "I'm interested in you. Notice me. I'm an attractive person."

Paralanguage: Nonverbal vocal cues surrounding speech—voice pitch, volume, pacing of speech, silent pauses, and sighs—provide a rich source of information. Paralanguage has to do with *how* something is said rather than with *what* is said. One of the least obvious types of paralanguage is silence. Silence can communicate scorn, hostility, defiance, and sternness, as well as respect, kindness, and acceptance.

Proxemics: The way we employ social and personal space also contains messages. For instance, students who sit in the front rows of a classroom tend to be the most interested, those in the rear are more prone to mischievous activities, and students at the aisles are primarily concerned with quick departures (Sommer, 1969).

Touch: Through physical contact such as touching, stroking, hitting, holding, and greeting (handshakes), we convey our feelings to one another. However, touch can also constitute an invasion of privacy, and it can become a symbol of power when people want to make power differences visible. For example, a high-status person might take the liberty of patting a low-status person on the back or shoulder, something that is deemed inappropriate for the subordinate.

Artifacts: We commonly employ objects, including certain types of clothing, lipstick, hairpieces, eyeglasses, beauty aids, perfume, and jewelry, that tell other people our gender, rank, status, and attitude. For instance, at a singles bar, clothing and hairstyle tell potential mates

what we are and are not and say "see me" or "skip me."

Some aspects of nonverbal communication such as many gestures are especially susceptible to cultural influence (Ekman, Friesen, and Bear, 1984). The American "A-Okay" gesture made by joining the thumb and forefinger in a circle has quite different meanings, depending on the culture. An American tourist will find that what is taken to be a friendly sign in the United States has an insulting connotation in France and Belgium: "You're worth zero!" In Southern Italy it means "you're a jerk," and in Greece and Turkey it conveys an insulting or vulgar sexual invitation.

However, some facial expressions seem to have universal meanings. For example, in situations of threat and intimidation, people often use glares that very closely resemble the stare-down behavior observed in

There is substantial agreement among the members of different races and cultures about the meaning of various facial expressions, such as smiles. The muscular movements that produce these expressions are probably innate human responses. (Ira Berger/Woodfin Camp & Associates)

monkeys and apes. To investigate these matters, Paul Ekman and his associates (1972, 1980) selected a group of photographs they thought depicted surprise, disgust, fear, anger, sadness, and happiness. They showed the photos to people from five different cultures and asked them to say what the person in each photo was feeling. The overwhelming majority of the subjects identified the emotions in the same way. Even the Fore, a people in a remote part of New Guinea who have had little contact with outsiders and virtually no exposure to mass media, labeled the pictures in the same basic way. It appears, then, that the ways of displaying and interpreting certain feelings may be universal, which suggests a strong biological component. Even so, each culture provides its own "display rules," which regulate how and when given emotions may be exhibited and with what consequences.

DEFINITION OF THE SITUATION

From our discussion it is clear that human beings live in both a symbolic and a physical environment (Rose, 1962). People do not respond directly to stimuli from their sense organs, but assign *meanings* to the stimuli and formulate their actions on the basis of these meanings. For example, a "pen" is not merely a collection of visual, aural, and tactile stimuli. We give meaning to it as an object with which we can write. We may also infer from the quality of the pen something about the social rank of the user. And we may attribute magical powers to the pen as a "good luck" piece for taking unusually difficult examinations.

What we have been saying adds up to this: As we go about our everyday lives, we interpret the world about us. Our symbolic environment mediates the physical environment so that we do not simply experience stimuli, but rather a definition of the situation. A **definition of the situation** is the interpretation or meaning we give to our immediate circumstances. It is "reality" as perceived by people, the intersection of time and space within which they carry out their actions. Consequently, facts do not have an inherent or uniform existence apart from the persons who observe and assign meaning to them. "Real" facts are the ways in which people define various situations.

Because of differing definitions, people vary in their perceptions of and reactions to different situations. Take a gun. To a soldier it means one thing, to an armed robber another, to a holdup victim still another, to a hunter another, and to a gun control advocate quite another. A man mowing the lawn may be seen as beautifying his yard, avoiding his wife, getting exercise, supporting neighborhood property values, annoying a neighbor who is attempting to sleep, or earning a living by mowing lawns.

Although our definitions of the situation may differ, it is only as we arrive at common understandings that we are able to fit our action to the actions of other people. Whatever we do—play football, chat with a friend on the telephone, rob a store, make love, give a lecture, cross a busy intersection, or purchase a book—we must attribute a similar meaning to the situation if we are to achieve joint action with others. Moreover, a definition of the situation arrived at on one occasion may hold for future occasions. Viewed in this manner, we may think of culture as the agreed-upon meanings—the shared definitions of situations—that individuals acquire as members of a society. Socialization is the process by which these shared definitions are transmitted from one generation to the next.

Sociologists point out that our definitions influence our construction of reality. William I. Thomas and Dorothy S. Thomas (1928:572) captured this insight in what has become known as the **Thomas theorem**: "If men [people] define situations as real, they are real in their consequences." The Thomas theorem draws our attention to the fact that people respond not only to the objective features of a situation, but also to the meaning the situation has for them. Once the meaning has been assigned, it serves to shape not only what people do or fail to do, but also some of the consequences of their behavior. For example, for a good many generations whites defined blacks as racially inferior. Since whites controlled the centers of institutional power, they allocated to blacks a lesser share of the privileges and opportunities of society. By acting upon their racial definitions, whites fashioned social structures—institutional arrangements—in which blacks have enjoyed fewer advantages than whites. Blacks are less well educated, hold more menial jobs, live in poorer housing, and enjoy poorer health than whites. So whites have created a social order characterized by institutional discrimination (Vander Zanden, 1983).

The Self

We not only arrive at definitions of the situation; we also arrive at self-definitions as we supply answers to the question "Who am I?" These answers constitute what sociologists call the **self**—the set of concepts we use in defining who we are. The formation of the self is a central part of the socialization process. It is not a biological given, but emerges in the course of interaction with other people. Sociologist J. Milton Yinger (1965:149) observes:

[T]he self is formed out of the actions of others, which become part of the individual as a result of his having identified with these others and responded to himself in their terms. Retrospectively, one can ask "Who am I?" But in practice, the answer has come before the question. The answer has come from all the definitions of one's roles, values, and goals that others begin to furnish at the moment of birth. "You are a boy; you are my son; you are French"; "You are a good boy and fully a part of this group" (with rewards confirming the words); or "You are a bad boy" (with significant others driving the point home by the sanctions they administer).

The self represents the ideas we have regarding our attributes, capacities, and behavior. In everyday speech, we note the existence of the self in such phrases as "proud of oneself," "talking to oneself," "losing control of oneself," "ashamed of oneself," "testing oneself," "hating oneself," and "loving oneself." These conceptions represent the heart of our humanness, our awareness that each of us is a unique being apart from other beings and the same person across time. The image that each of us has that we are a distinct, bounded, coherent being gives us a feeling of psychic wholeness. Individuals who are the victims of some forms of severe mental illness, particularly schizophrenia, lack a stable self-conception and clear self-boundaries—a distinct indication of where they begin and end. Many of them therefore feel at sea in a flood of stimuli (Elliott, Rosenberg, and Wagner, 1984).

The self contributes to an **egocentric bias**, in which we typically place ourselves at the center of events (Greenwald, 1980; Zuckerman et al., 1983). By virtue of the egocentric bias, we overperceive ourselves as the victim or target of an action or event that, in reality, is not directed at us. For instance, when a professor singles out a particularly good or poor exam for a few preliminary remarks before returning the papers to the class, we commonly overestimate the likelihood that one of the papers belongs to us (Fenigstein, 1984). In similar fashion, we tend to overestimate the likelihood that we, rather than another member of a group, will be chosen to participate in an experimental demonstration. And if we are lottery players, we sense that our ticket has a far greater probability of being selected a winner than it in fact has (Goleman, 1984; Greenwald and Pratkanis, 1984). Thus the egocentric bias results in each of us experiencing life through a self-centered filter. This skewed view of reality shapes our perception of events, and later our recall of the events from memory.

We typically think of the self in static terms as an "entity" or "thing." But as the concept is employed by symbolic interactionists, it also has dynamic properties. Symbolic interactionists point out that we can be objects of our own action. We mentally take a place on the outside and, from this vantage point, become an audience to our own actions. Viewed in this manner, the self is a process by which we devise our actions in order to fit them to the ongoing actions of other people. Sociologists like Charles Horton Cooley, George Herbert Mead, and Erving Goffman have contributed a good deal to our understanding of these matters. Let us turn, then, to a consideration of their insights.

CHARLES HORTON COOLEY: THE LOOKING-GLASS SELF

At the turn of this century, the notion was prevalent in both scientific and lay circles that human nature is biologically determined. Charles Horton Cooley (1864–1929) vigorously challenged this assertion. He maintained that people transform themselves and their worlds as they engage in social interaction. In particular, Cooley (1902) contended that our consciousness arises in a social context. This notion is best exemplified by his concept of the **looking-glass self**—a process by which we imaginatively assume the stance of other people and view ourselves as we believe they see us. Our ability to take the perspective of

another person is a basic requirement of all social behavior.

Self-Awareness. Cooley suggests that the looking-glass self is an ongoing mental process characterized by three phases. First, we imagine how we appear to others. For example, we may think of ourselves as putting on weight and becoming "fat." Second, we imagine how others judge our appearance. We are aware, for instance, that people typically think of obese people as unattractive. Third, we develop some sort of self-feeling such as pride or mortification on the basis of what we perceive others' judgments to be. In this case, we are likely to experience anxiety or embarrassment regarding our "obese" state. The looking-glass self entails a subjective process and need not accord with objective reality. For example, victims of *anorexia nervosa* willfully starve themselves, denying that they are actually thin or ill, in the belief that they are too fat.

The notion of the looking-glass self does not imply that our self-conception changes radically every time we encounter a new person or a new situation. Accordingly, it is useful to distinguish between self-images and self-conceptions (Turner, 1968; Swann and Hill, 1982). A **self-image** is a mental conception or picture that we have of ourselves, which is relatively temporary; it changes as we move from one context to another. Our **self-conception** is a more overriding view of ourself, a sense of self through time—"the real me," or "I myself as I really am." Layers of self-images typically build up over time and contribute to a relatively stable self-conception. For the most part, this succession of self-images *edits* rather than supplants our more crystallized self-conception or identity.

Shyness. Since human beings are capable of self-awareness, they often experience shyness. *Shyness* is a general tendency to be tense, inhibited, and awkward in social situations. Surveys show that as many as 40 percent of adult Americans consider themselves shy. Even such celebrities as Barbara Walters, England's Prince Charles, Terry Bradshaw, Fred Lynn, Catherine Deneuve, Carol Burnett, and Warren Beatty define themselves as shy (Zimbardo, 1978). The Japanese tend to have a very high prevalence of shyness—about 60 percent. One reason seems to be that the Japanese have what is described as a "shame culture," in which individuals experience considerable pressure not to let their families down (Cheek, 1983).

Shyness takes a heavy human toll because it creates a barrier for people in achieving happiness and fulfilling their potential. Shy people are commonly big losers—in school, in business, in love, in any arena of life where people meet their needs in the course of social interaction with others. They seem too self-aware, too preoccupied with their own adequacy and the adequacy of their behavior. Consequently, their spontaneity is impaired—they are unable to "let themselves go"—and they hold back from immersing themselves in ongoing social interaction.

Choking. *Choking* is behavior in which we fail to perform up to our level of skills and abilities by virtue of experiencing social pressure (Baumeister, 1984). Like shyness, it arises when the selfhood process goes awry. For example, we often become self-conscious when we are expected to provide an excellent performance. Thus in athletic competition we may attempt to ensure the correctness of our execution—the coordination and precision of our muscle movements—by monitoring our performance. But such self-monitoring disrupts the automatic or overlearned nature of execution. Consequently, we become susceptible to mistakes. In the final and decisive game of

a championship series, such as baseball's World Series, the home team tends to choke and accordingly is at a decided disadvantage. A home crowd usually claps, shouts, and moans in response to the breaks and exploits of the home team, whereas the visitor's exploits are met either with silence or expressions of frustration. During the regular season and in early games of the World Series, such behavior may be a source of inspiration to the home team. But when a championship is imminent, failing to win it before a support audience compounds the pressures and intensifies the players' self-consciousness. As a result, they become "uptight" and error-prone (Baumeister and Steinhilber, 1984).

GEORGE HERBERT MEAD: THE GENERALIZED OTHER

George Herbert Mead (1863–1931) elaborated on Cooley's ideas and contributed many insights of his own. Mead (1934) contended that we gain a sense of selfhood by acting toward ourselves in much the same fashion that we act toward others. In so doing, we "take the role of the other toward ourselves." We mentally assume a dual perspective: we are simultaneously the *subject* doing the viewing and the *object* being viewed. In our imagination, we take the position of another person and look back on ourself from this standpoint.

Mead designates the subject aspect of the self-process the *I* and the object aspect the *Me*. Consider what sometimes happens when you contemplate whether or not to ask your professor a question. You think, "If I ask a question, he'll consider me stupid. I'd better keep quiet." In this example, you imagine the attitude of the professor toward students. In so doing, you mentally take the role of the professor and view yourself as an object or "me." It is you as the subject or "I" who decides that it would be unwise to ask the question. The use of the personal pronouns in the statement illustrates the object-subject dimensions.

According to Mead, the key to children's development of the self resides in their acquisition of language. By virtue of language, we arouse the same tendencies in ourselves as we do in others. We mentally say to ourselves, "If I want to get this person to respond this way, what will it take to do so? What would it take to get me to act in this fashion?" Mead uses the example of an instructor who asks a student to bring a chair to the classroom. The student probably would fulfill the request, but if not, the instructor would most likely get the chair herself. To ask the student to secure the chair, the instructor first must conjure up the act within her own mind. Language allows us to carry on an internal conversation. We talk and reply to ourselves in much the same manner that we carry on a conversation with others. In this fashion, we judge how other people will respond to us.

Sociologist Ralph Turner (1968) has clarified and extended Mead's ideas on the self. Turner points out that when speaking and acting, we typically adopt a state of *preparedness* for certain types of responses from the other person. If we wave to a professor, ask a police officer a question, or embrace a friend, we expect that the other person will respond with some action that will appropriately fit our own. As the other person responds, we enter a phase of *testing* and *revision*. We mentally appraise the other's behavior, determining whether or not it accords with our expectations. In doing so we assign meaning to that behavior. We then plan our next course of action. For instance, if the person responded in an unanticipated manner, we might terminate the interaction, attempt to "go back" and reassert our original intention, disregard the other's response, or abandon our initial course of action and follow the other person's lead.

Consequently, symbolic interactionists say that the process of self-communication is essential to social interaction.

According to Mead, children typically pass through three stages in developing a full sense of selfhood: the "play" stage, the "game" stage, and the "generalized other" stage. In play, children take the role of only one other person at a time and "try on" the person's behavior. The model, usually an important person in the life of the child, such as a parent, is called a **significant other**. For example, a 2-year-old child may examine a doll's pants, pretend to find them wet, reprimand the doll, and take it to the bathroom. Presumably the child views the situation from the viewpoint of the parent and acts as the parent would act.

Whereas in the play stage children take the role of only one other person at a time, in the game stage they assume many roles. As in the case of an organized game such as baseball, individuals must take into account the roles of a good many people. For example, if the batter bunts the ball down the third-base line, the person playing first base must know what the pitcher, third baseman, shortstop, and catcher will do. Each player must see his or her role as meshed with those of the other players. Likewise in life. Children must become familiar with the expectations that hold for a variety of roles if they are to play their own roles successfully.

In Mead's third stage, children recognize that they are immersed within a larger community of people and that this community has very definite attitudes regarding what constitutes appropriate and inappropriate behavior. The social unit that gives individuals their unity of self is called the **generalized other**. The attitude of the generalized other is the attitude of the larger community. Although we gain our conceptions of given rules from particular people (our mother, a teacher, or a peer), these notions

Doing Sociology: The Selfhood Process

According to symbolic interactionists, we mesh our actions with those of other individuals through the selfhood process. In our imagination, we step out of ourselves into the role of another person and attempt to view ourselves from his or her perspective. We use symbols, particularly language, to arouse the same tendencies and dispositions in ourselves as we do in others. Thus we talk and reply to ourselves in much the same manner that we carry on a conversation with other people. We become objects to ourselves, mentally monitoring and assigning meaning to our behavior and to other people's responses. For instance, when we provide a vocal utterance, a flirtatious glance, a wave of the hand, a shrug of the shoulder, or a clenched fist, we hope to signal something to another person. As the other person responds to us, we enter a phase of testing and revision. We interpret the other's behavior, noting whether or not it falls within the range of behaviors we anticipated. As we appraise the other's behavior and assign meaning to it, we plan our subsequent course of action. Thus, social interaction involves us in a process of self-communication. In the two episodes presented below, students in an introductory sociology course analyze their behavior in terms of the selfhood process:

Early in the quarter I went to the dining hall with my new neighbor, Hank. All I knew about Hank was his name. I did not know what he was like or what his interests were. Accordingly, I was uncertain how I should act toward him. After we had gotten our food and were sitting down at the dining table, I put a napkin on my lap and said, "Would you please pass me the salt?" As Hank did so, I said to myself, "Gee, what am I going to talk to this guy about?" I responded, "Perhaps I had better ask him what his major is?" I did. Hank answered in a dull monotone, "Electrical engineering." I thought to myself, "This guy is a cement block to talk to. Maybe I am too serious with him. My voice sounds serious and I seem uptight. I had better open things up somewhat." I said to myself, "If he were 'me,' what would 'I' want to hear that wasn't so serious?" In so doing I took a dual perspective, the "me" being the object aspect and the "I" the subject aspect. I responded to myself, "I like partying." So I asked, "Do you party?" Bingo! His eyes came alive and he pulled himself into an upright posture. I found a topic of mutual interest and we then hit it off quite well.

I drove home late Friday evening. I take a back highway that has little traffic on it. I had my headlights on high when a car approached also with glaring beams. I said to myself, "I want that motorist to turn down his headlights. What would it take to signal me to cut my lights?" I responded, "I would lower my beams if someone flicked his lights." So I flicked my lights from high to low a number of times, but the motorist did not respond. I thought to myself, "That motorist either doesn't think we are close enough to reduce his beams, or he has forgotten that he set them on high." As we got nearer, I said to myself, "I'll just let my beams on high. I don't envy the guy a bit. I've replaced my headlamps with more powerful ones that throw more light than standard beams. Heck, if this joker wants to play 'Blind the other driver,' I'll go along with it. He'll get it a lot worse than I will." When we were about an eighth of a mile apart, he turned his beams down to regular strength. I mentally said to myself, "Okay, fair play. I'll cut mine as well." And I proceeded to do so.

are generalized or extended to embrace all people within similar situations. To think about our behavior, then, is to interact mentally with ourselves from the perspective of an abstract community of people. According to Mead, the generalized other is the vehicle by which we are linked to society. By means of the generalized other, we incorporate, or internalize, the organized attitudes of our community within our own personalities so that social control becomes self-control.

ERVING GOFFMAN: IMPRESSION MANAGEMENT

Erving Goffman (1922–1982) has provided an additional dimension to our understanding of the self. Cooley and Mead had examined how our self-conceptions arise in the course of social interaction and how we fashion our actions based on the feedback we derive about ourselves and our behavior from other people. Goffman (1959) directs our attention to another matter. He points out that only by influencing other people's ideas of us can we hope to predict or control what happens to us. We have a stake in presenting ourselves to others in ways that will lead them to view us in a favorable light, a process Goffman calls **impression management**. In doing so, we use both concealment and strategic revelation. For example, a taxi driver may attempt to disguise from a passenger the fact that they were mistakenly traveling in the wrong direction, and a young professor fresh out of graduate school may spend several hours preparing and rehearsing a lecture in hopes of appearing "knowledgeable" to her students. You are probably aware of engaging in impression management when deciding what to wear for particular occasions, such as a party, a physician's appointment, a job interview, or a "date."

Goffman sees the performances staged in

a theater as an analytical analogy and tool for depicting and understanding social life, a perspective he called the **dramaturgical approach**. He depicts social life as a stage on which people interact; all human beings are both actors and members of the audience, and the parts are the roles people play in the course of their daily activities. Goffman illustrates his approach by describing the changes that occur in waiters' behavior as they move from the kitchen to the dining room. As the nature of the audience changes, so does their behavior. "Frontstage" in the dining room, the waiters display a servile demeanor to the guests. "Backstage" in the kitchen, they openly flaunt and otherwise ridicule the servility they must perform "frontstage." Further, they seal off the dirty work of food preparation—the gristle, grease, and foul smells of spoiled food—from the appetizing and enticing "frontstage" atmosphere. Hence, as people move from situation to situation, they drastically alter their self-expression. They undertake to define the situation for others by generating cues that will lead others to act in ways they wish.

Although Goffman is commonly classed by sociologists with interactionists, his work departs in significant ways from classical symbolic interactionist formulations (Gonos, 1977). Symbolic interactionists see each situation as somewhat unique, as freshly built up piece by piece out of the peculiar combinations of activities and meanings that operate in a particular setting. Goffman (1974) depicts social life as "frames"—structures—that have an invisible but real existence behind the visible social transactions of everyday life. These basic frameworks of understandings provide stable rules that people use in fashioning their behavior. Thus Goffman sees action as guided more by a mechanical adherence to rules than by an active, ongoing process of interpersonal negotiation.

Socialization Across the Life Span

Socialization is a continuing, lifelong process. The world about us changes and requires that we also change. The self is not carved in granite, somehow finalized for all time during childhood. Life is adaptation—a process of constant renewing and remaking. Three-year-olds are socialized within the patterns of a nursery school, engineering students within their chosen profession, new employees within an office or plant, a husband and wife within a new family, religious converts within a cult, and elderly patients within a nursing home.

In one way or another, all societies have to deal with the life cycle that begins with conception and continues through old age and ultimately death. Upon the rich tapestry supplied by the organic age grid, societies weave varying social arrangements. A 14-year-old girl may be expected to be a middle-school student in one culture and a mother of two in another; a 45-year-old man may be at the peak of a business career, still moving up in a political career, retired from a career as a professional football player—or dead and worshipped as an ancestor in some other society (Datan, 1977). All cultures divide biological time into socially relevant units. While birth, puberty, maturity, aging, and death are biological facts of life, it is society that gives each its distinctive meaning.

Some people extend their stages of life to include the unborn and the deceased. The Australian aborigines think of the unborn as the spirits of departed ancestors. These spirits are believed to enter the womb of a passing woman and gain rebirth as a child (Murdock, 1934). Likewise, the Hindus regard the unborn as the spirits of persons or animals who lived in former incarnations (Davis, 1949). The dead may also be seen as continuing members of the community. Anthropologist Ralph Linton (1936: 121–122) found that when a Tanala of Madagascar died, the individual was defined as merely surrendering one set of rights and duties for another:

Thus a Tanala clan has two sections which are equally real to its members, the living and the dead. In spite of rather half-hearted attempts by the living to explain to the dead that they are dead and to discourage their return, they remain an integral part of the clan. They must be informed of all important events, invited to all clan ceremonies, and remembered at every meal. In return they allow themselves to be consulted, take an active and helpful interest in the affairs of the community, and act as highly efficient guardians of the group's mores.

Hence each society shapes the processes of development in its own image, defining the stages it recognizes as significant.

Modern societies are ordered in ways that formally structure people's preparation for new roles. Schools and colleges are designed to transmit various skills, mental hospitals to teach healthier patterns of adjustment, prisons to "resocialize" convicts through rehabilitation programs, and conferences and seminars to familiarize a firm's staff with its operating procedures. Role socialization commonly involves three phases (Mortimer and Simmons, 1978). First, people think about, experiment with, and try on the behaviors associated with a new role, what sociologists term **anticipatory socialization**. Children informally acquaint themselves with such adult roles as spouse and parent by "playing house." Apprenticeship, intern, probationary, and rehabilitation programs are more institutionalized arrangements for acquiring new roles. Second, once individuals assume a new status, they find that they must continually alter, adapt, and remake their roles to fit changing circumstances. For instance, as a couple enter marriage, they must evolve new interpersonal skills because much of the marital role is hidden from children. Third, as individuals move through the life span, they not only enter roles, but must disengage or exit from many of them. Such rituals as graduation exercises, marriage, retirement banquets, funerals, and other rites of passage are socially established mechanisms for easing some role transitions. Let us take a closer look at some of the transitions that center on life span roles.

CHILDHOOD

In the Middle Ages, the concept of childhood as we know it was unheard of. Children were regarded as small adults (Ariès, 1962). The arts and documents of the medieval world portray adults and children mingling together, wearing the same clothes, and engaging in many of the same activities. The world we think proper for children—fairytales, games, toys, and books—is of comparatively recent origin. Until the seventeenth century, Western words for young males—"boy," garçon (French), and Knabe (German)—were used to denote a man of 30 or so years of age who enjoyed an independent position. No special word existed for a young male between the ages of 7 and 16. The world "child" expressed kinship, not an age period (Plumb, 1972). Only around the year 1600 did a new concept of childhood begin to emerge.

The notion that children should be attending school rather than working in factories, mines, and fields is of relatively recent origin. Significantly, the first industrial workers in the United States were nine children hired in 1791 as employees of a Rhode Island textile mill. In the 1820s half of the cotton mill workers in New England were children who worked twelve- to fifteen-

Nowadays we often hear that childhood has changed for the worse. Some authorities assert that today's children lack the innocence that once was associated with childhood. They say that school-age youngsters are more aware, not just of sex and violence, but also of injustice, cruelty, corruption, war, and human frailty. But what is often overlooked is that in years gone by, childhood was anything but a golden age. Indeed, prior to modern times, most children's lives were bleak. Until the eighteenth century, a very large proportion of all children were what we would today call "abused children." Even sixty years ago child labor in factory settings was common. (Culver Pictures)

hour days. Even as late as 1924, the National Child Labor Committee estimated that 2 million American children under 15 were at work, the majority as farm laborers.

Whatever definitions they hold of children, societies begin socializing them as soon as possible. Most infants are fairly malleable in the sense that within broad limits, they are capable of becoming adults of quite different sorts. The magnitude of their accomplishments over a relatively short period of time is truly astonishing. For example, by their fourth birthday most American children have mastered the complicated and abstract structure of the English language. And they can carry on complex social interactions in accordance with American cultural patterns.

Children display people-oriented responses at very early ages. Even before their first birthdays, children are already contributors to social life (Rheingold, Hay, and West, 1976). For instance, they will point at objects—a window display, an airplane, an automobile, or a picture of a cereal box—to call other people's attention to them. In doing so, children demonstrate not only that they know other people can see what they see, but also that others will look at what interests them. Often the pointing gesture is accompanied by attempts at vocalization (Leung and Rheingold, 1981). Thus, by the time children are about a year of age, they seem to have the ability to take the visual perspective of others and to begin sharing their own perspective of the world.

Some categories for classing people appear quite early. For instance, 6-month-old infants are able to distinguish between an adult and a baby, suggesting that infants employ age as one dimension to categorize the social world (Lewis and Brooks-Gunn, 1979). By 18 months, most middle-class children can pretend that they are carrying out some action, such as drinking out of a cup. This capacity suggests that they are capable of viewing themselves as agents who produce behavior. By 2 years of age, they can make a doll do something as if it were acting on its own. In so doing, they reveal an elementary ability for representing other people as independent agents. Most 3-year-olds can make a doll carry out several role-related activities, revealing knowledge of a social role (for instance, pretend to be a doctor and examine a doll). Four-year-olds can typically act out a role, meshing the behav-

ior with that of a reciprocal role (for example, pretend that a patient doll is sick and a doctor doll examines it, in the course of which both dolls make appropriate responses). During the late preschool years, children become capable of combining roles in more complicated ways (for instance, being a doctor and a father simultaneously). Most 6-year-olds can pretend to carry out several roles at the same time.

During the preschool years, children view the self and the mind as simply parts of the body (Damon and Hart, 1982). However, between 6 and 8 years of age, they begin to distinguish between mind and body. They grasp that people are unique not only because they look different, but because they have different feelings and thoughts. They come to define the self in internal rather than external terms and recognize the difference between psychological and physical attributes (Selman, 1980). The number of dimensions along which children conceptualize other people increases throughout childhood. The greatest development occurs between 7 and 8 years of age, then the rate of change in conceptualization slows. Indeed, the differences between children who are 7 years old and those who are 8 are frequently greater than the differences between 8-year-olds and 15-year-olds (Livesley and Bromley, 1973).

ADOLESCENCE

In much of the world, adolescence is not a socially distinct period in the human life span. Although young people everywhere undergo the physiological changes associated with puberty, children frequently assume adult responsibilities by age 13 and even younger. In the United States, adolescence appears to be an "invention" of the past hundred years (Demos and Demos, 1969; Kett, 1977; Thornburg, 1983). As the nation changed from a rural to an urban society, the role of children altered. They no longer had a significant economic function in the family once the workplace became separated from the home. In time, mandatory school attendance, child labor laws, and special legal procedures for "juveniles" established adolescence as a well-defined social reality.

During adolescence, individuals undergo changes in growth and development that are revolutionary. After a lifetime of inferiority, they suddenly catch up with adults in physical size and strength. Accompanying these changes is the rapid development of the reproductive organs that signals sexual maturity.

In the view of neo-Freudians like Erik Erikson (1963, 1968), the main task of adolescence is to build and confirm a reasonably stable identity. As they go about their everyday lives, people interact with one another on the basis not so much of what they actually are, as of what conceptions they have of themselves and others. Erikson (1968:165) suggests that an optimal feeling of identity is experienced as a sense of well-being. "Its most obvious concomitants are a feeling of being at home in one's body, a sense of 'knowing where one is going,' and an inner assuredness of anticipated recognition from those who count." For adolescents, Erikson says, the search for identity becomes particularly acute. Like trapeze artists, adolescents must release their hold on childhood and reach in midair for a firm grasp on adulthood. In the process, many young people confront role confusion and a blurred self-image. Their uncertain identities lead them to search for a stable anchorage by overcommiting themselves to cliques, allegiances, loves, and social causes.

Erikson's view of adolescence is in keeping with a long psychological tradition that has portrayed adolescence as a period of "storm and stress." Social scientists have suggested that Western nations make the transition from childhood to adulthood a particularly difficult one (Dragastin and Elder, 1975; Sebald, 1977; Elkind, 1979). At adolescence, boys and girls are expected to stop being children, yet they are not expected to be men and women. The definitions given them by society are inconsistent. Many non-Western societies make the shift in status more definitive by providing **puberty rites**—initiation ceremonies that symbolize the transition from childhood to adulthood. Adolescents may be subjected to thoroughly distasteful, painful, and humiliating experiences during such rituals, but they are then pronounced grownup. Boys are often terrorized, ceremonially painted, and circumcised; girls are frequently secluded at menarche. But the tasks and tests are clear-cut, and young people know that if they accomplish the goals set for them, they will acquire adult status (Herdt, 1982). Mild versions of puberty rites in Western societies include the Jewish Bar Mitzvah and Bat Mitzvah, the Catholic confirmation, securing a driver's license, and graduation from high school and college.

In recent years, however, a growing body of research has led social scientists to challenge the view that adolescence among American youth is inherently a turbulent period (Adelson, 1979; Blyth and Traeger, 1983). Although the self-images and self-conceptions of young people change, the changes are not invariably "stormy." Rather than experiencing dramatic change and disruption, adolescents gradually fashion their identities based on their sexual circumstances and their evolving competencies and skills (Offer and Offer, 1975; Dusek and Flaherty, 1981). Indeed, for most youth, their overall self-esteem increases with age across the adolescent years (McCarthy and Hoge, 1982; O'Malley and Bachman, 1983). But there are exceptions. Changes in the social environment, like the transition to middle or junior high school, can in some cases have a disturbing effect, especially for girls (Simmons and Rosenberg, 1973, Simmons et al., 1979).

Although the media make a good deal out of generational differences between adolescents and their parents, the notion of a "generation gap" vastly oversimplifies matters. Research suggests that both the family and the peer group are important anchors in the lives of most teenagers. However, the relative influence of the two groups varies with the issue involved. The peer group has the greater influence when the issues have to do with musical tastes, personal adornment, and entertainment idols, and in some cases with marijuana use and drinking. But the family has the greater influence when the issues have to do with future life goals, fundamental behavior codes, and core values (Davies and Kandel, 1981; Krosnick and Judd, 1982). In many cases, a substantial proportion of young people see no reason to distinguish between the value system of their parents and that of their friends. In part this is due to the fact that teenagers select as friends individuals who share attitudes that are compatible with those of their families (Cohen, 1983). A 1983 youth poll found that 80 percent of the students agreed with their parents on the topics of drugs, education, and work, and 60 percent agreed on the topic of sex. Said Janis Cromer (1984), an educational analyst who wrote the report: "If there was a generation gap in the 60's, it narrowed to a crack in the 1970's and it's a hairline fracture in the 1980's" (quoted by Ordovensky and Johnson, 1984:2).

YOUNG ADULTHOOD

Recent developments in the Western world—the growth of service industries, the prolongation of education, and the enormously high educational demands of post-industrial society—have lengthened the transition to adulthood. In some respects our society appears to be evolving a new status between adolescence and adulthood: youth—men and women of college and graduate school age (Keniston, 1970). In leaving home, youth in their late teens or early twenties may choose a transitional institution, such as the military or college, to start them on their way. Or young people may work (provided they can find a job) while continuing to live at home. During this time, a roughly equal balance persists between being in the family and moving out. Individuals become less financially dependent, enter new roles and living arrangements, and achieve greater autonomy and responsibility. With the passage of time, the center of gravity in young people's lives gradually shifts away from the family of origin (Levinson, 1978; Gould, 1978).

The developmental tasks confronting individuals from 18 to 30 years of age typically center on the two core tasks Sigmund Freud (1938) called *love* and *work*. Through adult friendships, sexual relationships, and work experiences, they arrive at initial definitions of themselves as adults. Ideally, they develop the capacity to experience a trusting, supportive, and tender relationship with another person (Erikson, 1963). They may cohabit with a sexual partner or marry and begin a family. And they may lay the groundwork for a career or develop one career and then discard it. They may also drift aimlessly, which often precipitates a crisis at about age 30.

In making their way through the early years of adulthood, and for that matter the middle and later years as well, individuals are strongly influenced by **age norms**—rules that define what is appropriate for people to be and to do at various ages. A cultural timetable—a sort of societal "Big Ben"—defines the "best age" for a man or woman to finish school, settle on a career, marry, be-

The primary tasks confronting young adults revolve about love and work. The center of gravity in their lives shifts steadily away from their family of origin as they move into the larger world and assume responsibility for themselves. American society holds strong expectations that young people enter a close relationship with a member of the opposite sex and equip themselves for gainful employment. (Peter Menzel)

come a parent, hold a top job, become a grandparent, and retire (Kimmel, 1980). Individuals tend to set their personal "watches" by this **social clock**, and most people readily report whether they themselves are "early," "late," or "on time" with regard to major life events (Neugarten, 1968).

However, variations do occur in the setting of one's social clock, so that the higher the social class, the later tends to be the pacing of age-linked events. Early adulthood typically lasts longer for a person in the middle class than for a member of the working class. Further, the life cycle in our society appears to be becoming more fluid; many traditional norms and expectations are changing and age is losing many of its customary meanings. As a result, we may

be witnessing what sociologist Bernice L. Neugarten (1979) has called an "age-irrelevant society" in which there is no single appropriate age for taking on given roles. She notes that it is no longer unusual to encounter the 28-year-old mayor, the 30-year-old college president, the 35-year-old grandmother, the 50-year-old retiree, the 65-year-old new father, and the 70-year-old student.

Some psychologists, like Erik Erikson (1963), have undertaken the search for what they view as the regular, sequential periods and transitions in the life cycle. They depict life as a succession of stages that resemble a stairway made up of a series of steplike levels. Erikson's chief concern is with psychological development, which he divides into the eight major stages of development described in Table 3.1. Each stage poses a unique task that revolves about a crisis—a turning point of increased vulnerability and heightened potential. According to Erikson, the crisis posed by each stage must be successfully resolved if healthy development is to take place. Consequently, the interaction that occurs between an individual and so- ciety at each stage can change the course of personality in a positive or a negative direction. Gail Sheehy took a somewhat similar approach in her best-selling book, *Passages* (1976). She too contends that each stage in life poses a unique set of problems that must be resolved before a person can successfully advance to the next stage. By pass-

TABLE 3.1

Erikson's Eight Stages of Development

Developmental Stage	Psychosocial Crisis	Predominant Social Setting	Favorable Outcome
1. Infancy	Basic trust vs. mistrust	Family	The child develops trust in itself, its parents, and the world.
2. Early childhood	Autonomy vs. shame, doubt	Family	The child develops a sense of self-control without loss of self-esteem.
3. Fourth to fifth year	Initiative vs. guilt	Family	The child learns to acquire direction and purpose in activities.
4. Sixth year to onset of puberty	Industry vs. inferiority	Neighborhood; school	The child acquires a sense of mastery and competence.
5. Adolescence	Identity vs. role confusion	Peer groups and outgroups	The individual develops an *ego identity*—a coherent sense of self.
6. Young adulthood	Intimacy vs. isolation	Partners in friendship and sex	The individual develops the capacity to work toward a specific career and to involve himself or herself in an extended intimate relationship.
7. Adulthood	Generativity vs. stagnation	New family; work	The individual becomes concerned with others beyond the immediate family, with future generations, and with society.
8. Old age	Integrity vs. despair	Retirement and impending death	The individual acquires a sense of satisfaction in looking back upon his or her life.

Source: Erik Erikson. 1953. *Childhood and society.* New York: Norton.

ing from one stage to the next—*passages*—each individual acquires new strengths and evolves an *authentic identity*.

Daniel J. Levinson (1978) has also approached adulthood from a stage perspective. He and his associates at Yale University have studied forty men in their mid-thirties to mid-forties. They designate six periods ranging from the late teens or early twenties to the late forties (see Figure 3.1). In Levinson's view, the overriding task confronting individuals throughout adulthood is the creation of a structure for life. But the structure does not become established once and for all time; it must be continually modified and reappraised. Transition periods tend to loom within two or three years of, and on either side of, the symbolically significant birthdays—20, 30, 40, 50, and 60. By interacting with the environment, each person formulates goals, works out means to achieve them, and modifies assumptions.

Some social scientists believe that unexpected events in our lives shape our development far more than the predictable transitions, such as marriage, parenthood, and

FIGURE 3.1   LEVINSON'S PERIODS OF MALE DEVELOPMENT
Daniel J. Levinson conceives of male development as characterized by a succession of stages. Each stage requires the restructuring of critical aspects of a man's assumptions regarding himself and the world. (Source: Daniel J. Levinson et al. 1978. **The Season's of a Man's Life.** *New York: Knopf, p. 57. Copyright © 1978 by Daniel J. Levinson. Reprinted by permission of Alfred A. Knopf, Inc.)*

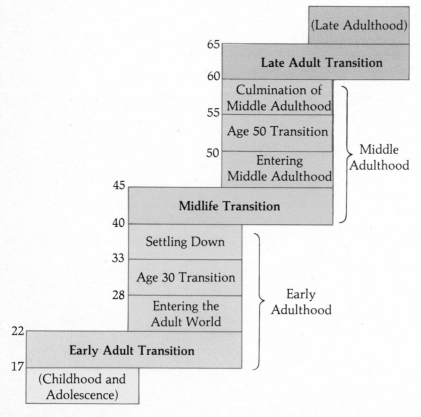

retirement (Peterson, 1984). They contend that stage theories overlook the vast differences that characterize the human experience. Adult life is not the same thing for men and women and for rich and poor. Even the era in which a person is born makes a difference—the Great Depression of the 1930s, World War II, or the Vietnam war. Moreover, these social scientists contend that people are prepared for the major transitions of life by age norms and social clocks. Consequently, people tend to take the transitions in their stride and do not perceive them as crises or unusually stressful events.

People locate themselves across the life span not only in terms of social timetables, but also in terms of **life events**—turning points at which people change some direction in the course of their lives (Hultsch and Plemmons, 1979; Brim, 1980). Some of these events are related to social clocks. But many are not, such as suffering severe injury in an accident, being raped, winning a lottery, undergoing a Born Again conversion, or living at the time of the antiwar protests of the late 1960s. Some life events are associated with internal growth or aging factors like puberty or old age. Others are the consequences of group life, including wars, national economic crises, and revolutions. Still others derive from happenings in the physical world, including fires, hurricanes, floods, earthquakes, or avalanches. And some have a strong inner or psychological component, such as a profound religious experience, the decision to leave one's spouse, or the death of a parent.

MIDDLE ADULTHOOD

Middle adulthood lacks the concreteness of infancy, childhood, and adolescence. It is a catchall category that is rather nebulous. Sometimes middle adulthood is used to refer to "people over 30," a time in life when men and women presumably have "settled down" with families and careers. But it is also employed to denote "middle-aged" individuals—those roughly between 45 and 64 years of age. Whichever meaning is attached to middle adulthood, the core tasks remain much the same as they did for men and women in young adulthood and revolve about love and work. We will defer our discussion of the "love" dimension, since much of what we will have to say in Chapter 9 deals with intimacy issues and life style options.

The central portion of the adult life span of both men and women is spent in work. As we will see in Chapter 8, people work for a great many reasons. Although economic considerations predominate, work also structures time, provides a context in which to relate to others, affords an escape from boredom, and sustains a sense of self-worth. The fact that someone will pay us for our work is an indication that what we do is needed by others and that we are a necessary part of the social fabric. Increasingly, for women as well as men, a paid job is defined as a badge of membership in the larger society. Overall, job satisfaction tends to be associated with the opportunity to exercise discretion, accept challenges, and make decisions (Kohn and Schooler, 1982; Gruenberg, 1980).

Levinson (1978) finds that in their early thirties men tend to establish their niche in the world, dig in, build a nest, and make and pursue long-range plans and goals. They usually have some dream or vision of the future that lies ahead of them. In their mid to late thirties, men seek to break out from under the authority of others and assert their independence. They often believe that their superiors control too much, delegate too little, and are insufficiently imaginative and aggressive. In their early forties men begin assessing where they stand in relation to the goals they earlier set for themselves. They may sense a gap between "what I've got now" and "what it is I really want," leading to an interval of soul-searching. Around 45, some men experience a "mid-life crisis." Stereotypes depict men of this age as "flipping out"—leaving their wives for women young enough to be their daughters, quitting their jobs to become beachcombers, or drinking to excess. Yet most individuals are able to resolve the mid-life transition through a continuous process of self-evalution that may entail a modification of some aspirations and a reassessment of priorities. Most men gradually bring their aspirations in line with their attainments without severe upset and turmoil (Mortimer and Simmons, 1978).

Levinson is currently engaged in research dealing with periods in adult female development. There is reason to believe that the phases Levinson identifies in adult male development do not necessarily apply to women. For one thing, until relatively recently, work and family were not separate spheres of life for most women. For another, women may leave the paid labor force to have and care for children, complicating their career opportunities. We will have more to say on these matters in Chapter 7 when we examine gender roles in American life.

Around 48 years of age, most women experience *menopause*—the end of menstrual activity. Many "old wives' tales" have contributed to the fear some women have of menopause. However, the research of Neugarten (1963) suggests that often the most upsetting thing about menopause is the anticipation of it. A recent survey of 8,114 Massachusetts women from 45 to 55 found that only about one-fourth of the women visit a physician because of hot flashes and other menopausal symptoms (episodes of profuse sweating, fatigue, dizziness, headaches, insomnia, and nervousness). Although a relatively high number of the women experienced hot flashes at one time or another, the severity of the episodes was considerably less than that depicted in popular folklore (Hale, 1984). Women are more

likely to feel upset if they view menopause as signaling the end of their attractiveness, usefulness, and sexuality. Such self-evaluations may be heightened by our youth-oriented culture, which tends to devalue older people.

LATER ADULTHOOD

Like other periods of the life span, the time at which later adulthood begins is a matter of social definition. In preindustrial societies, life expectancy is typically short and the onset of old age is early. For instance, one observer reported that among the Arawak of Guyana (South America), individuals seldom live more than 50 years and between the thirtieth and fortieth years in the case of men, and even earlier in the case of women, "the body, except the stomach, shrinks, and fat disappears [and] the skin hangs in hideous folds" (Im Thurn, 1883). Literary evidence also reveals that during the European Renaissance, men were considered "old" in their forties (Gilbert, 1967). Currently, as Neugarten (1977) suggests, a new division is emerging in many Western nations between the "young-old" and the "old-old." The young-old are early retirees who enjoy physical vigor, new leisure time, and new opportunities for community service and self-fulfillment. The old-old include those who are of advanced age and suffer various infirmities.

Societies differ in the prestige and dignity they accord the aged. In many rural societies, including imperial China, elders enjoyed a prominent, esteemed, and honored position (Lang, 1946). Among the agricultural Palaung of North Burma, long life was deemed a privilege reserved for those who had lived virtuously in a previous incarnation. People showed their respect to older people by being careful not to step on their shadows. Young women cultivated an older appearance because women acquired honor and privilege in proportion to their years

(Milne, 1924). In contrast to these cultural patterns, youth is the favored age in the United States. We have restricted the roles open to the elderly and accord them little prestige. Indeed, the older the elderly become, especially as they reach advanced age, the more likely Americans are to stereotype them unfavorably. They are depicted as troublesome, cranky, touchy, and sickly beings. In some respects, the very old have become the nation's lepers.

Despite the unfavorable stereotypes that persist regarding the elderly, the actual picture is substantially different. Only 12 persons out of 1,000 in the 65 to 74 age group live in nursing homes. The figure rises to 59 for those 75 to 84, and to 237 for those over 85. Overall, only one American in five who is over 65 will ever be relegated to a nursing home (Shanas, 1982). Additionally, about 3 percent of the elderly who live at home are bedridden, 5 percent are seriously incapacitated, and another 11 to 16 percent are restricted in mobility. On the other hand, from one-half to three-fifths of the elderly function without any limitation (and 37 percent of those 85 and over report no incapacitating limitation on their activity).

Old age entails exiting from some social roles. One of the most important of these is retirement from a job. On the whole, Americans are now retiring at earlier ages than in previous generations. The proportion of men aged 65 and over who were gainfully employed dropped from 68 percent in 1890, to 48 percent in 1947, to only 17 percent today. About 8 percent of women over 65 hold jobs or are seeking work, down from 9.5 percent in 1971. Of equal social significance, 85 percent of men aged 60 to 64 held jobs in 1959, whereas only 66 percent hold jobs today; during the same period, the percentage of men 55 to 59 holding jobs dropped from 93 to 86 percent (Brophy, 1984). In government, nearly two out of three civil servants retire before age 62.

Some sociologists have depicted retirement as having negative consequences for the elderly because occupational status is a master status—an anchoring point for adult identity (Blau, 1973). Much of postretirement life is seen as aimless, and giving structure to the long, shapeless day is believed to be the retired person's most urgent challenge. Further, sociologist Irving Rosow (1974) contends that in the United States people are not effectively socialized to old age. The social norms that define the expectations for old age are few, weak, and nebulous. Complicating matters, the elderly have little motivation to conform to a "roleless role"—a socially devalued status. Even if there were definitive norms for guiding people's behavior in old age, Rosow says that few people would want to conform to role expectations that exclude them from equal opportunities for social participation and rewards.

In recent years the negative view of retirement has been challenged (Glamser, 1976; George and Maddox, 1977). For one thing, attitudes toward work and retirement seem to be changing. Moreover, research reveals that it is money which is most missed in retirement, and that when people are assured an adequate income, they will retire early (Shanas, 1972; Beck, 1982). One longitudinal survey of 5,000 men found that most men who retire for reasons other than health are "very happy" in retirement and would, if they had to do it over again, retire at the same age. Only about 13 percent of whites and 17 percent of blacks said they would choose to retire later if they could choose again (Parnes, 1981). Overall, when people are healthy and their incomes are adequate, they express satisfaction with retirement.

Many elderly individuals also experience another role loss, that of being married. Although three out of four American men 65 and over are married and living with their wives, the same holds true for only one out of three women. This results from the fact that women typically outlive men by seven to eight years and from the tradition that women marry men older than themselves. Research by Helena Znaniecki Lopata (1973) reveals that the higher a woman's education and socioeconomic class, the more disorganized her self-identity and life become after her husband's death. However, once her "grief work" is accomplished, these women have more resources to form a new life style. Overall, negative long-term consequences of widowhood appear to derive more from socioeconomic deprivation than from widowhood itself (Balkwell, 1981). Of interest, Lopata found that about half of the widows in her study lived alone, and most of these said they much preferred to do so. Only 10 percent moved in with their married children. Those who lived alone cited their desire to remain independent as their chief reason.

DEATH

A diagnosis of impending death requires that an individual adjust to a new definition of self. To be defined as dying implies more than the presence of a series of biochemical processes (De Vries, 1981). It entails the assumption of a social status, one in which social structuring not only attends but shapes the dying experience. Consider, for instance, the different social definitions we typically attribute to a 20-year-old who has been given a five-year life expectancy and those we attribute to a healthy 80-year-old. Likewise, hospital personnel give different care to patients based on their perceived social worth. In a study of a hospital emergency room, sociologist David Sudnow (1967) found that different social evaluations led the staff to work frantically to revive a young child, but to acquiesce in the death of an elderly woman. Finally, although death is a biological event, it is made a social reality through such culturally fashioned events as wakes and funerals.

Changes in medical technology and social conditions have made death a different experience than in earlier times. Dying in the modern world is often drawn out and enmeshed in formal bureaucratic processes (Lofland, 1978). Only a few generations ago, most people died at home and the family assumed responsibility for laying out the deceased and preparing for the funeral. In recent times, death has been surrounded by taboos that in large measure have kept the subject out of sight and out of mind. Today the nursing home or hospital cares for the terminally ill and manages the dying experience. A mortuary—euphemistically called a "home"—prepares the body and makes the funeral arrangements or arranges for the cremation of the remains. As a result, the average American's exposure to death is minimized. The dying and the dead are segregated from others and placed with specialists for whom contact with death has become a routine and impersonal matter (Strauss and Glaser, 1970; Arias, 1981).

Institutional control of dying has reduced individual autonomy. Personal needs and desires are often subordinated to organization needs. Indeed, much criticism has been leveled at the way modern organizations and technology structure the care of the terminally ill. Public opinion surveys reveal that 73 percent of Americans believe that patients with terminal illnesses should be allowed to halt treatment even if it means certain death; 65 percent believe that physicians should be allowed to stop treating an unconscious, terminally ill patient if asked by the patient's family (Kenny, 1984). Americans tend to favor a quick transition between life and death. But the belief that "the less dying, the better" has come up against an altered biomedical technology, in which individuals are increasingly approaching death through a "lingering trajectory." Many people have a profound fear of being held captive in a state between life and death—as "vegetables" sustained entirely by life-support equipment. Consequently, growing numbers of Americans are coming to the view that too much is done for too long a period at too high a cost, all at the expense of basic human considerations and sensitivities.

Over the past decade, the hospice movement has arisen to provide a more humane approach for the care of the terminally ill. A **hospice** is a program or mode of care that attempts to make the dying experience less painful and emotionally traumatic for patients and their families. Advocates of the hospice approach say that it is difficult for physicians and nurses in hospital settings to accept the inevitability of death. Hospitals are geared to curing illness and prolonging life, and consequently incurable illness and death are sources of embarrassment to them. Thus proponents of hospice care insist that other institutional arrangements are required.

Whenever possible, hospice treatment is administered in the patient's home. Visiting physicians, nurses, social workers, and volunteers provide emotional and spiritual help in addition to medical care. A number of hospitals and nursing homes have also established hospice units. The emphasis of hospice approaches falls on comfort and care, rather than on attempts to prolong life. Patients receive painkilling medication on an as-needed basis, and they are also provided with antidepressive and antianxiety drugs should they be required. Most hospice programs also offer follow-up bereavement care for family members.

In recent years, Elisabeth Kübler-Ross (1969, 1981) has contributed a good deal to the movement to restore dignity and humanity to death. She contends that when medical personnel and the family know that a patient is dying and attempt to hide the fact, they construct a barrier that prevents all the parties from preparing for death. Moreover, the dying person typically sees through the make-believe. Kübler-Ross has found that it is better if everyone is allowed to express his or her genuine emotions and if these feelings are respected. Surveys show that four out of five persons would want to be told if they had an incurable illness.

Although there are different styles for dying—just as there are different styles for living—Kübler-Ross (1969) finds that dying people typically pass through five stages in accommodating themselves to impending death: *denial* that they will die, *anger* that life will shortly end, *bargaining* with God or fate to arrange a temporary truce, *depression* or "preparatory grief," and *acceptance*. Not everyone passes through all the stages, and individuals slip back and forth between stages. And a great many other factors also influence the dying experience, including differences in gender, ethnic membership, personality, the death environment, and the nature of the disease itself. Death cannot be understood except in the total context of a person's previous life and current circumstances. In sum, over the past decade or so, public and professional awareness of the dying person's experience has increased dramatically and has given impetus to a more humane approach to death.

SUMMARY

1. Socialization is the process of social interaction by which people acquire those behaviors essential for effective participation in society. Were it not for socialization, the renewal of culture could not occur from one generation to the next. And in the absence of socialization, society could not perpetuate itself beyond

a single generation. Both the individual and society are mutually dependent on socialization.

2. Human socialization presupposes that an adequate genetic endowment and an adequate environment are available. Organisms are not passive objects programmed by internal genetic forces, nor are they passive objects shaped by the external environment. Hereditary and environmental factors interpenetrate and mutually determine each other. The dynamic interplay between an individual and the environment is the foundation of human intelligence, knowledge, and culture.

3. If they are to adapt to their environment, human beings must be able to communicate. Communication refers to the process by which people transmit information, ideas, attitudes, and mental states to one another. It includes all those verbal and nonverbal processes by which we send and receive messages.

4. People do not respond directly to stimuli from their sense organs, but assign meanings to the stimuli and formulate their actions on the basis of these meanings. Our symbolic environment mediates the physical environment so that we do not simply experience stimuli, but rather a definition of the situation. A definition of the situation is the interpretation or meaning we give to our immediate circumstances. Our definitions influence our construction of reality, an insight captured by the Thomas theorem: "If men [people] define situations as real, they are real in their consequences."

5. We not only arrive at definitions of the situation; we also arrive at self-definitions as we supply answers to the question "Who am I?" Charles Horton Cooley contended that our consciousness arises in a social context. This notion is exemplified by his concept of the looking-glass self—a process by which we imaginatively assume the stance of other people and view ourselves as we believe they see us. It consists of three phases. First, we imagine how we appear to others. Second, we imagine how others judge our appearance. And third, we develop some sort of self-feeling such as pride or mortification on the basis of what we perceive others' judgments of us to be.

6. George Herbert Mead elaborated upon Cooley's ideas and contributed many insights of his own. He contended that we gain a sense of selfhood by acting toward ourselves in much the same fashion that we act toward others. In so doing, we "take the role of the other toward ourselves." We mentally assume a dual perspective: Simultaneously we are the subject doing the viewing and the object being viewed. According to Mead, children typically pass through three stages in developing a full sense of selfhood: the play stage, the game stage, and the generalized other stage.

7. Erving Goffman has provided an additional dimension to our understanding of the self. He points out that only by influencing other people's ideas of us can we hope to predict or control what happens to us. Consequently, we have a stake in presenting ourselves to others in ways that will lead them to view us in a favorable light, a process Goffman calls impression management. In so doing, we use both the arts of concealment and strategic revelation.

8. Socialization is a continuing, lifelong process. All societies have to deal with the life cycle that begins with concep-

tion and continues through old age and ultimately death. Upon this organic age grid, societies weave varying social arrangements. Some of these arrangements have to do with childhood. Though societies differ in their definitions of childhood, they all begin the socialization process as soon as possible. The magnitude of children's accomplishments over a relatively short period of time is truly astonishing. For instance, they display people-oriented responses at very early ages.

9. In much of the world, adolescence is not a socially distinct period in the human life span. Although people everywhere undergo the physiological changes associated with puberty, they frequently assume adult responsibilities by age 13 and even younger. In the view of Erik Erikson, the main task of adolescence is to build and confirm a stable identity. But adolescence is not necessarily a turbulent period. Nor does a sharp generation gap separate American adolescents from their parents.

10. The developmental tasks confronting young adults revolve about the core tasks of work and love. Ideally they develop the capacity to experience a trusting, supportive, and tender relationship with another person. And they lay the groundwork for a career. In making their way through the early years of adulthood, individuals are strongly influenced by age norms and tend to set their personal "watches" by a cultural Big Ben, the social clock. Some social scientists have looked for stages through which young adults typically pass. Others believe that unexpected events play a more important role in development.

11. Middle adulthood is a somewhat nebulous period. The core tasks remain much the same as they did in young adulthood. Increasingly, work is coming to be defined for both men and women as a badge of membership in the larger society. Although economic considerations predominate, people also work as a means to structure their time, interact with other people, escape from boredom, and sustain a positive self-image. As they pass through the middle years, adults confront a variety of changing circumstance and challenges to which they must fashion adaptations.

12. Like other periods of the life span, the time at which later adulthood begins is a matter of social definition. Further, societies differ in the prestige and dignity they accord the aged. Old age often entails exiting from some social roles. One of the most important of these is retirement from a job. Some sociologists have portrayed retirement in negative terms, but this view has recently been challenged. Overall, when people are healthy and their incomes are adequate, they typically express satisfaction with retirement. Many elderly adults also experience another role loss, that of being married. Women are more likely to be widowed than are men.

13. A diagnosis of impending death requires that an individual adjust to a new definition of self. It entails the assumption of a social status, one in which social structuring not only attends but shapes the course of the dying experience. Changes in medical technology and social conditions have made death a different experience from that of earlier times. Dying in the modern world is often drawn out and enmeshed in formal bureaucratic processes. The hospice movement has arisen to provide a more humane approach to the dying experience.

GLOSSARY

age norms Rules that define what is appropriate for people to be and to do at various ages.

anticipatory socialization People think about, experiment with, and try on the behaviors associated with a new role.

body language Physical motions and gestures that provide social signals.

communication The process by which people transmit information, ideas, attitudes, and mental states to one another.

definition of the situation The interpretation or meaning we give to our immediate circumstances.

dramaturgical approach The sociological perspective associated with Erving Goffman that views the performances staged in a theater as an analytical analogy and tool for depicting social life.

egocentric bias The tendency to place ourselves at the center of events, so that we overperceive ourselves as the victim or target of an action or event that, in reality, is not directed at us.

generalized other The term George Herbert Mead applied to the social unit that gives individuals their unity of self. The attitude of the generalized other is the attitude of the larger community.

hospice A program or mode of care that attempts to make the dying experiences less painful and emotionally traumatic for patients and their families.

impression management The term Erving Goffman applied to the process whereby we present ourselves to others in ways that will lead them to view us in a favorable light.

language acquisition device The view associated with Noam Chomsky that human beings possess an inborn language-generating mechanism. The basic structure of language is seen as biologically channeled, forming a sort of prefabricated filing system to order the words and phrases that make up human languages.

life events Turning points at which people change some direction in the course of their lives.

looking-glass self The term that Charles Horton Cooley applied to the process by which we imaginatively assume the stance of other people and view ourselves as we believe they see us.

paralanguage Nonverbal cues surrounding speech—voice, pitch, volume, pacing of speech, silent pauses, and sighs—that provide a rich source of communicative information.

proxemics The way we employ social and personal space to transmit messages.

puberty rites Initiation ceremonies that symbolize the transition from childhood to adulthood.

self The set of concepts we use in defining who we are.

self-conception An overriding view of ourselves; a sense of self through time.

self-image A mental conception or picture we have of ourselves that is relatively temporary; it changes as we move from one context to another.

significant other The term George Herbert Mead applied to a social model, usually an important person in an individual's life.

social clock The personal "watch" individuals use to pace the major events of their lives and which is based on cultural age norms.

socialization A process of social interaction by which people acquire the knowledge, attitudes, values, and behaviors essential for effective participation in society.

Thomas theorem The notion that our definitions influence our construction of reality. It was stated by William I. Thomas and Dorothy S. Thomas: "If men [people] define situations as real, they are real in their consequences."

4

Social Groups and Formal Organizations

GROUP RELATIONSHIPS

Primary Groups and Secondary
Groups
In-Groups and Out-Groups
Reference Groups

GROUP DYNAMICS

Group Size
Leadership
Social Loafing
Social Dilemmas
Groupthink
Conformity

FORMAL ORGANIZATIONS

Types of Formal Organization
Bureaucracy
Weber's Analysis of Bureaucracies
Disadvantages of Bureaucracy
Informal Organization
Alternative Perspectives
Humanizing Bureaucracies

We often do not appreciate the part groups play in our lives until we are separated from them. When we leave home to attend college, get married, or take a job, many of us experience "homesickness"—nostalgia for a group from which our immediate ties suddenly have been severed. Indeed, life and its satisfactions take on meaning and value primarily in the context of other people. When we confront difficulties, the social support and feedback of others help us to put the problems into perspective and often to deal more effectively with them. Additionally, groups provide the structure by which we involve ourselves in the daily affairs of life. It is hardly surprising, therefore, that people who live alone experience a substantially higher incidence of alcoholism, suicide, and other pathologies than do people who live with others (Gove and Hughes, 1980).

Prisoners who are maintained in solitary confinement reveal some of the appalling consequences of social isolation. Their orientation to the world about them is often profoundly altered (Gassian, 1983:1452–1453). One prisoner held in solitary confinement at the Massachusetts Correctional Institution at Walpole observes: "Everything gets exaggerated. After a while, you can't stand it. Meals—I used to eat everything they served. Now I can't stand the smells—the meat—the only thing I can stand to eat is the bread." Another says, "What really freaks me out is when a bee gets into the cell—such a small thing." Many inmates report difficulties with thinking, concentration, and memory. One prisoner reports: "I can't read. . . . Your mind's narcotized . . . sometimes I can't grasp words in my mind that I know." In some cases, inmates in solitary confinement impulsively mutilate themselves. "I cut my wrists—cut myself many times when in isolation. Now, it seems crazy. But every time I did it, I wasn't thinking—lost control—cut myself without knowing what I was doing."

As we pointed out in Chapter 2, a **group** consists of two or more people who share a feeling of unity and who are bound together in relatively stable patterns of social interaction. Groups are not tangible things; rather, they are products of social definitions—sets of shared ideas. As such they constitute constructed realities. In other words, we make groups real by treating them *as if* they are real, a clear application of the Thomas theorem (see Chapter 3). We fabricate groups in the course of our social interaction as we cluster people together in social units: families, teams, cliques, nationalities, races, labor unions, fraternities, clubs, corporations, and the like. In turn we *act* on the basis of these shared mental fabrications, creating an existence *beyond* the individuals who are involved. As we pointed out in Chapter 2, groups are social structures that have an existence apart from the particular relationships individual people have with one another. For this reason, many groups like colleges, sports teams, religious orders, ethnic groups, political parties, and business organizations have an existence that extends beyond the life spans of specific people (Vander Zanden, 1984).

What we have been saying adds up to this: The whole is greater than the sum of its parts. Groups have distinctive properties in their own right apart from the particular individuals who belong to them. In this sense, they are *social facts* (see Chapter 1). Groups resemble chemical compounds more than they do mixtures. For example, although hydrogen and oxygen are both gases at room temperature, they form a chemical compound—water—whose properties are different in kind from either hydrogen or oxygen. It is the joining of molecules—and the bonding of people—that produces qualitatively new entities. Accordingly, we can speak of families, cliques, clubs, and organizations without having to break them down into the separate interactions that compose them.

Group Relationships

Life places us in a complex web of relationships with other people. As we noted in Chapter 3, our humanness arises out of these relationships in the course of social interaction. Moreover, our humanness must be sustained through social interaction, and fairly constantly so. When an association continues long enough for two people to become linked together by a relatively stable set of expectations, it is called a **relationship**.

People are bound within relationships by two types of bonds: expressive ties and instrumental ties. **Expressive ties** are social links formed when we emotionally invest ourselves in and commit ourselves to other people. Through association with people who are meaningful to us, we achieve a sense of security, love, acceptance, companionship, and personal worth. **Instrumental ties** are social links formed when we cooperate with other people to achieve some goal. Occasionally this may mean working with our enemies, as in the old political saying, "Politics makes strange bedfellows." More often, we simply cooperate with others to reach some end without endowing the relationship with any larger significance.

PRIMARY GROUPS AND SECONDARY GROUPS

Sociologists have built on the distinction between expressive and instrumental ties to distinguish between two types of groups: primary and secondary. A **primary group** involves two or more people who enjoy a direct, intimate, cohesive relationship with one another (Cooley, 1909). Expressive ties predominate in primary groups; we view the people—friends, family members, and lovers—as ends in themselves and valuable in their own right. A **secondary group** entails two or more people who are involved in an impersonal relationship and have come together for a specific, practical purpose. Instrumental ties predominate in secondary groups; we perceive people as means to ends rather than as ends in their own right. Illustrations include our relationships with a clerk in a clothing store and a cashier at a service station. Sometimes primary group relationships evolve out of secondary group relationships. This happens in many work settings. People on the job often develop close relationships with co-workers as they come to share gripes, jokes, gossip, and satisfactions.

A number of conditions enhance the likelihood that primary groups will arise. First, group size is important. We find it difficult to get to know people personally when they are milling about and dispersed in large groups. In small groups we have a better chance to initiate contact and establish rapport with them. Second, face-to-face contact allows us to size up others. Seeing and talking with one another in close physical proximity makes possible a subtle exchange of ideas and feelings. And third, the probability that we will develop primary group bonds increases as we have frequent and continuous contact. Our ties with people often deepen as we interact with them across time and gradually evolve interlocking habits and interests.

We use the word "primary" in our daily conversations to refer to things that are essential and important. Clearly the term is appropriate for primary groups, since they are fundamental to us and to society. First, primary groups are critical to the socialization process. Within them, infants and children are introduced to the ways of their society. Such groups are the breeding grounds in which we acquire the norms and values that equip us for social life. Sociologists view primary groups as bridges between individuals and the larger society because they transmit, mediate, and interpret a society's cultural patterns and provide the sense of oneness so critical for social solidarity.

Second, primary groups are fundamental because they provide the settings in which we meet most of our personal needs. Within them, we experience companionship, love, security, and an overall sense of well-being. Not surprisingly, sociologists find that the strength of a group's primary ties has implications for its functioning. For example, the stronger the primary group ties of troops fighting together, the better is their combat record. During World War II the success of German military units derived not from Nazi ideology, but from the ability of the German army to reproduce in the infantry company the intimacy and bonds found in civilian primary groups (Shils and Janowitz, 1948). What made the *Wehrmacht* so

formidable was that, unlike the American army, German soldiers who trained together went into battle together. Additionally, American fighting units were kept up to strength through individual replacement, whereas German units were "fought down," then pulled back to be reconstituted as a new group (Van Creveld, 1982). And the Israelis have found that combat units hastily thrown together without time to form close bonds perform more poorly in battle and experience higher rates of psychiatric casualties than do units with close bonds (Cordes, 1984).

Third, primary groups are fundamental because they serve as powerful instruments for social control. Their members command and dispense many of the rewards that are so vital to us and that make our lives seem

Sociological research suggests that the fighting effectiveness of the Wehrmacht *in World War II derived from the strength of primary-group ties within combat units. German soldiers were likely to continue fighting so long as they had the necessary weapons, the group possessed leadership with which its members could identify, and individuals found acceptance, security, and rapport in their squads and platoons. When men felt themselves to be members in good standing in a primary group, they were more likely to be effective soldiers.*
(AP/Wide World Photos)

worthwhile. Should the use of rewards fail, members can frequently win compliance by rejecting, or threatening to ostracize, those who deviate from its norms. For instance, some religious cults employ "shunning" (a person can remain in the community, but others are forbidden to interact with them) as a device to bring into line individuals whose behavior goes beyond that allowed by the group's teachings. Even more important, primary groups define social reality for us by "structuring" our experiences. By providing us with definitions of situations, they elicit from us behavior that conforms to group-devised meanings. Primary groups, then, serve both as carriers of social norms and as enforcers of them.

IN-GROUPS AND OUT-GROUPS

It is not only the groups to which we immediately belong that have a powerful influence upon us. Often the same holds true for groups to which we do not belong. Accordingly, sociologists find it useful to distinguish between in-groups and out-groups. An **in-group** is a group with which we identify and to which we belong. An **out-group** is a group with which we do not identify and to which we do not belong. In daily conversation we recognize the distinction between in-groups and out-groups in our use of the personal pronouns "we" and "they." We can think of in-groups as "we-groups" and out-groups as "they-groups."

The concept of in-group and out-group highlight the importance of *boundaries*—social demarcation lines that tell us where interaction begins and ends. Group boundaries are not physical barriers, but rather discontinuities in the flow of social interaction. To one degree or another, a group's boundaries "encapsulate" people in a social membrane so that the focus and flow of their actions are internally contained. Some boundaries are based on territorial location, such as neighborhoods, communities, and nation-states. Others rest on social distinctions such as ethnic group, or religious, political, occupational, language, kin, and socioeconomic class memberships. Whatever their source, social boundaries face in two directions. They prevent outsiders from entering a group's sphere, and they keep insiders within that sphere so they do not entertain rival possibilities for social interaction.

At times we experience feelings of indifference, disgust, competition, and even outright conflict when we think about or have dealings with out-group members. An experiment undertaken by Muzafer Sherif and his associates (1961) has shown how our awareness of in-group boundaries is heightened and antagonism toward out-groups is generated by competitive situations. The subjects were 11- and 12-year-old boys, all of whom were healthy, socially well-adjusted youngsters from stable, middle-class homes, The setting was a summer camp where the boys were divided into two groups.

During the first week at the camp the boys in each group got to know one another, evolved group norms, and arrived at an internal division of labor and leadership roles. During the second week, the experimenters brought the two groups into competitive contact through a tournament of baseball, touch football, tug-of-war, and treasure hunt games. Although the contest opened in a spirit of good sportsmanship, positive feelings quickly evaporated. During the third week, the "integration phase," Sherif brought the two groups of boys together for various events, including eating in the same mess hall, viewing movies, and shooting off firecrackers. But far from reducing conflict, these settings merely provided new opportunities for the two groups to challenge, berate, and harass one another. The experimenters then created a series of urgent and natural situations in which the two groups would have to work together to achieve their ends, such as the emergency repair of the conduit that delivered the camp's water supply. Whereas competition had heightened awareness of group boundaries, the pursuit of common goals led to a lessening of out-group hostilities, and the lowering of intergroup barriers to cooperation.

REFERENCE GROUPS

More than a century ago, American writer Henry Thoreau observed: "If a man does not keep pace with his companions, perhaps it is because he hears a different drummer." Thoreau's observation contains an important sociological insight. We evaluate ourselves and guide our behavior by standards embedded in a group context. But since Americans are dispersed among a good many different groups—each with a somewhat unique subculture or counterculture—the frames of reference we use in assessing and fashioning our behavior differ. In brief, we have different **reference groups**—social units we use for appraising and shaping attitudes, feelings, and actions.

A reference group may or may not be our membership group. We may think of a reference group as a base we use for viewing the world, a source of psychological identification. It helps to account for seemingly contradictory behavior: the upper-class revolutionary, the renegade Catholic, the reactionary union member, the shabby gentleman, the quisling who collaborates with the enemy, the assimilated immigrant, and the social-climbing chambermaid. These individuals have simply taken as their reference group people other than those from their membership group (Hyman and Singer, 1968). The concept thus helps to illuminate such central sociological concerns as socialization and social conformity (Singer, 1981).

Reference groups provide both *normative* and *comparative* functions. Since we would like to view ourselves as being members in good standing within a certain group—or we aspire to such membership—we take on the group's norms and values. We cultivate its life styles, political attitudes, musical tastes, food preferences, and sexual practices, and drug-using behaviors. Our behavior is group-anchored. We also use the standards of our reference group to appraise ourselves—a comparison point against which we judge and evaluate our physical attractiveness, intelligence, health, ranking, and standard of living. When our membership group does not match our reference group, we may experience feelings of **relative deprivation**—discontent associated with the gap between what we have (the circumstances of our membership group) and what we believe we should have (the circumstances of our reference group). Feelings of relative deprivation often contribute to social alienation and provide fertile conditions for collective behavior and revolutionary social movements (see Chapter 12). The reference group concept, then, contains clues to processes of social change.

However, not all reference groups are positive. We also make use of negative reference groups, social units with which we compare ourselves to emphasize the differences between ourselves and others. For Cuban-Americans in Miami, Florida, the Castro regime functions as a negative reference group (Carver and Humphries, 1981). A good many of them fled their homeland after Castro came to power in the 1959 revolution. Militant opposition to the Castro regime helps the Cuban-Americans determine what they really believe in and decide who they really are. Of even greater significance, the negative reference group is a mechanism of social solidarity, an instrument by which the exile community binds itself together. It provides a common denominator for acceptance and ensures for members of the cause the benefits that accrue to true believers.

Group Dynamics

To understand groups is to understand much about human behavior. The reason is not difficult to come by, since groups are the wellsprings of our humanness. Although we think of groups as things—distinct and bounded entities—it is not their static but their dynamic qualities that make them such a significant force. We need to examine what happens within groups.

GROUP SIZE

The size of a group is important because, even though it is a structural component, it influences the nature of interaction. The smaller the group, the more opportunities we have to get to know other people well and to establish close ties with them. The popular adage "Two's company, three's a crowd" captures an important difference between two-person and three-person groups. Two-person groups—**dyads**—are the setting for many of our most intense and influential relationships, including that between parent and child and between husband and wife. Indeed, most of our social interactions take place on a one-to-one basis.

Sociologist John James (1951) and his students observed 7,405 informal interactions of pedestrians, playground users, swimmers, and shoppers, and 1,458 people in a variety of work situations. They found that 71 percent of both the informal and work interactions consisted of two people; 21 percent involved three people; 6 percent included four people; and only 2 percent entailed five or more people. Emotions and feelings tend to play a greater part in dyads

than they do in larger groups (Hare, 1976). But this factor also contributes to their relatively fragile nature: A delicate balance exists between the parties, so if one of them becomes disenchanted, the relationship collapses. And contrary to what you might expect, two-person relationships tend to be more emotionally strained and less overtly aggressive than are other relationships (Bales and Borgatta, 1955; O'Dell, 1968).

The addition of a third member to a group—forming a **triad**—fundamentally alters a social situation. Coalitions become possible, with two members joining forces against a third member (Hare, 1976). With this arrangement, one person may be placed in the role of an "intruder" or "outsider." However, under some circumstances, the third person may assume the role of a "mediator," and function as a peacemaker.

One recurring question that has attracted the interest of sociologists is this: What is the optimum group size for problem solving? For instance, if you want to appoint a committee to make a recommendation, what would be the ideal size for the group? Small group research suggests that five is usually the best size (Hare, 1976). With five members, a strict deadlock is not possible, because there is an odd number of members. Further, since groups tend to split into a majority of three and a minority of two, being a minority does not result in the isolation of one person, as it does in the triad. The group is sufficiently large for the members to shift roles easily and for a person to withdraw from an awkward position without necessarily having to resolve the issue formally. Finally, five-person groups are large enough so that people feel they can express their emotions freely and even risk antagonizing one another, yet they are small enough so that the members show regard for one another's feelings and needs. As groups become larger, they become less manageable. People no longer carry on a "conversation" with the other members, but "address" them with formal vocabulary and grammar.

LEADERSHIP

Imagine a football team without a quarterback; an army without officers; corporations without executives; universities without deans; orchestras without conductors; and youth gangs without chiefs. Without overall direction, people typically have difficulty coordinating their activities. Consequently, in group settings some members usually exert more influence than others. We call these individuals *leaders*. Small groups may be able to get along without a leader, but in larger groups a lack of leadership leads to chaos.

Two types of leadership roles tend to evolve in small groups (Bales, 1970). One, a **task specialist**, is devoted to appraising the problem at hand and organizing people's activity to deal with it. The other, a **social-emotional specialist**, focuses on overcoming interpersonal problems in the group, defusing tensions, and promoting solidarity. The former type of leadership is *instrumental*, directed toward the achievement of group goals; the latter is *expressive*, oriented toward the creation of harmony and unity. In some cases, one person assumes both roles, but usually each role is played by a different person. Neither role is necessarily more important than the other, and the situation does much to dictate the relative importance of each.

Leaders differ in their styles for exercising influence. Through the years, the classic experiments in leadership by Kurt Lewin and his associates (Lewin, Lippitt, and White, 1939; White and Lippitt, 1960) have generated considerable interest. In these pioneering investigations, adult leaders working with groups of 11-year-old boys followed one of three leadership styles. In the *authoritarian* style, the leader determined the group's policies, gave step-by-step directions so that the boys were certain about their future tasks, assigned work partners, provided subjective praise and criticism, and remained aloof from group participation. In contrast, in the *democratic* style, the leader allowed the boys to participate in decision-making processes, outlined only general goals, suggested alternative procedures, permitted the members to work with whomever they wished, evaluated the boys objectively, and participated in group activities. Finally, in the *laissez-faire* style the leader adopted a passive, uninvolved stance; provided materials, suggestions, and help only when requested; and refrained from commenting on the boys' work.

The researchers found that authoritarian leadership produces high levels of frustration and hostile feelings toward the leader. Productivity remains high so long as the leader is present, but it slackens appreciably in the leader's absence. Under democratic leadership members are happier, feel more group-minded and friendlier, display independence (especially in the leader's absence), and exhibit low levels of interpersonal aggression. Laissez-faire leadership resulted in low group productivity and high levels of interpersonal aggression. However, it should be emphasized that the study was carried out with American youngsters accustomed to democratic procedures. Under other circumstances and in different cultural settings, an authoritarian leader may be preferred. The frequency of authoritarian leaders in developing nations has suggested to some sociologists that people may prefer a directed leadership styles under highly stressful conditions (Bass, 1960). However, an equally plausible explanation is that it is easier for authoritarian leaders to seize and maintain leadership under these circumstances.

SOCIAL LOAFING

An old saying has it that "Many hands make light the work." Yet the proverb falls short of the truth. For example, we might expect that three individuals can pull three times as much as can one person and that eight can pull eight times as much. But research reveals that whereas persons individually average 130 pounds of pressure when tugging on a rope, in groups of three they average 117 pounds each, and in groups of eight only 60 pounds each. One explanation is that faulty coordination produces group inefficiency. However, when subjects are blindfolded and *believe* they are pulling with others, they also slacken their effort (Ingham, 1974). Apparently when individuals work in groups, they work less hard than they do when working individually—a process called **social loafing** (Williams, Harkins, and Latané, 1981).

When undergraduate men are asked to make as much noise as possible by shouting or clapping along with others, they produce only twice as much noise in groups of four and 2.4 times as much in groups of six as when alone (Latané, Williams, and Harkins, 1979). Presumably people slack off in groups because they feel they are not receiving their fair share of credit or because they think that in a crowd they can get away with less work. In comparable circumstances, Soviet peasants produce less when they work on collective farms than when they cultivate a small plot of land for their own use. (Although the private plots occupy less than 1 percent of Soviet agricultural lands, some 27 percent of the total value of the nation's farm output is produced on them.) We should not conclude from these findings that we can do away with work groups. Groups are essential to social life and they can accomplish many things that individuals cannot. For instance, Alcoholics Anonymous, Parents Without Partners, Weight Watchers, and other self-help groups testify to the desirable influences and outcomes that can be associated with groups.

SOCIAL DILEMMAS

The social loafing effect suggests that there is an inverse relationship between group size and individual motivation. A closely related phenomenon is termed a **social dilemma**—a situation in which members of a group are faced with a conflict between maximizing their personal interests and maximizing the collective welfare (Komorita and Barth, 1985). Garrett J. Hardin's (1968) "tragedy of the commons" is one type of social dilemma in which the long-run consequence of self-interested individual choice results in social disaster. Hardin explored the situation in which a number of herders share a common pasture. Each person may reason that by putting another cow to graze, he or she will realize a benefit from it. But if each person follows this course, the commons will be destroyed and each will ultimately lose. Hardin was addressing the problem of population growth. The notion can be applied equally well to pollution, which is the reverse of the grazing problem; where grazing takes matter out of the commons, pollution puts matter in. Social dilemmas are encountered in many other spheres of life as well. Consider the choice confronting a soldier in a foxhole at the outset of a battle. The rational choice for each soldier would be to remain in the foxhole to avoid being killed, but if every soldier makes this choice, the battle will most certainly be lost and everyone in the unit will be killed (Kerr, 1983). In many social dilemmas there is a possibility that some other member of the group can and will provide the public good, making one's own contribution unnecessary—that is termed the "free-rider mechanism."

What social mechanisms are available to influence individuals to act cooperatively rather than selfishly? Hardin sought an answer in social controls that restrict individual actions detrimental to the common good. Government often serves this function by regulating access to various resources (see Chapter 8). Group norms frequently achieve the same end through informal sanctions (Messick et all, 1983). But there are also measures that induce people to act cooperatively and that elicit prosocial behaviors. Among these mechanisms are those that highlight group boundaries and foster a superordinate group identity (Kramer and Brewer, 1984). The findings of Muzafer Sherif and his associates (1961), discussed earlier in the chapter, provide a good illustration of circumstances in which the pursuit of common goals lowers barriers to cooperation. Moreover, where individuals are made to feel that they are being rewarded for their cooperative behavior (for instance, sharing in the profits or benefits equally), they are less likely to switch to self-centered, individualistic behavior (Komorita and Barth, 1985). Groupthink is another strategy, although it is one that can have disastrous outcomes, a matter that we now consider.

GROUPTHINK

In 1961 the Kennedy administration undertook the ill-fated Bay of Pigs invasion of Cuba. Nothing went right for the 1,400 CIA-trained Cuban invaders, most of whom were killed or captured by Castro's forces. Not only did the invasion solidify Castro's leadership, it consolidated the Cuban-Soviet alliance and led the Russian leadership to attempt to place atomic missiles in Cuba. Later President John Kennedy was to ask: "How could we have been so stupid?" Not only had the president and his advisers overlooked the size and strength of the Castro army, but in many instances they even had failed to seek relevant information.

"Groupthink" among top officials in the Kennedy administration led to the uncritical acceptance of dubious assumptions and a disastrous invasion of Cuba by CIA-trained Cuban dissidents. Here President Kennedy is shown discussing Cuban policy with Secretary of State Dean Rusk and a CIA official. (Jacques Lowe/Woodfin Camp & Associates)

Social psychologist Irving Janis (1972) suggests that the president and his advisers were victims of **groupthink**—a decision-making process found in highly cohesive groups in which the members become so preoccupied with maintaining consensus that their critical faculties become impaired. In groupthink, members share an illusion of invulnerability that leads to overconfidence and a greater willingness to take risks. Its victims believe unquestioningly in the rightness of their cause—in this case, the need to overthrow the communist Castro regime, which the American leaders perceived to be the essence of evil. Members of the group demand conformity and apply pressure to those who express doubts about a proposed course of action; they withhold dissent and exercise self-censorship. In fact, later evidence showed that the Secretary of State Dean Rusk and Secretary of Defense Robert McNamara held widely differing assumptions about the invasion plan even though they had participated in the same meetings.

CONFORMITY

Groupthink research testifies to the powerful social pressures that operate in group settings and produce conformity. Although such pressures influence our behavior, we often are unaware of them. In a pioneering study, Muzafer Sherif (1936) demonstrated this point with an optical illusion. If people view a small, fixed spot of light in a darkened room, they perceive it as moving erratically in all directions. However, individuals differ in how far they think the light "moves." Sherif tested subjects alone and found their reference point. He then brought together in group settings people with quite different perceptions and asked them again to view the light and report aloud on their observations. Under these circumstances, their perceptions *converged* toward a group standard. Later, in solitary sessions, they did not return to the standard they had at first evolved, but adhered to the standard of the group. Significantly, most subjects reported that they arrived at their assessment independently and that the group had *no* influence on them.

Sherif presented subjects with an ambiguous situation; Solomon Asch (1952) asked subjects to match lines of the same length from two sets of cards displayed at the front of the room. He instructed the members of nine-person groups to give their answers aloud. However, all but one of the individuals were confederates of Asch, and they unanimously provided incorrect answers on certain trials. Despite the fact that the correct answer was obvious, nearly one-third of all the subjects' judgments contained errors identical with or in the direction of the rigged errors of the majority. Some three-fourths of the subjects conformed on at least one of the trials. Thus Asch demonstrated that some individuals conform to the false consensus of a group even though the consensus is contraindicated by the evidence of their own eyes.

The case of Patricia Hearst provides a good illustration of group conformity. As a 19-year-old student, she was kidnapped in Berkeley, California, in 1974 by members of the Symbionese Liberation Army. Although she loathed her captors, was forced to have sex with all three of the men, and was abused by the women, she did not escape even when they left her alone. She participated in bank robberies, even sometimes driving the getaway van. In her autobiography (1981), Patricia Hearst says she never believed in what the group was doing and that she was not indoctrinated by the Maoist lectures. Rather, she felt that she had been made a member of the team and wanted to perform as a team player. She asserts: "I felt I owed them something, something like loyalty." When individuals become totally dependent upon a group, they may surrender their autonomy and relinquish control over their bodies and destinies. The case of Patricia Hearst highlights the critical part groups play in our lives, particularly those groups from which we derive our identities and in which we embed ourselves in the course of our daily existence. As we will see shortly, such groups may function as total institutions.

Formal Organizations

As modern societies have become increasingly complex, so have the requirements of group life. As we noted in Chapter 2, the social organization of traditional societies revolves primarily around kin relations. The division of labor is simple; the people are culturally homogeneous; and there is no formal law. But contemporary societies composed of millions of people can no longer rely entirely on primary group arrangements to accomplish the tasks of social life. Food has to be produced, preserved, and transported over considerable distances to support large urban populations. The residents of large, anonymous communities can no longer count on family members and neighbors to enforce group norms and standards. Children can no longer be educated by the same "natural processes" by which parents teach them to walk and talk. And medical science in alliance with sophisticated technologies provides more effective treatments for illness than do folk remedies. For these and many other tasks, people require groups they can deliberately create for the achievement of specific objectives. Such groups are **formal organizations**.

In recent decades the United States has increasingly become a society of large, semiautonomous, and tightly knit formal organizations. Not only is there big government—extending from local municipal organizations to those of the federal government—but there are also big multinational corporations, big universities, big hospitals, big unions, and big farm organizations. Modern society is emerging as a web of formal organizations that appear, disappear, change, merge, and enter into countless relationships with one another. Although formal organizations have existed for thousands of years, dating back to ancient Mesopotamia, Egypt, and China, only in recent times have their scope and centrality become so pronounced. Not surprisingly, sociologist Robert Presthus (1978) calls modern society "the organizational society."

TYPES OF FORMAL ORGANIZATION

People enter formal organizations for a variety of reasons. Sociologist Amitai Etzioni (1964, 1975) classifies organizations on the basis of these reasons, identifying three major types: voluntary, coercive, and utilitarian. **Voluntary organizations** are associations that members enter and leave freely. Examples include the PTA, a coin collectors club, the League of Women Voters, the Girl Scouts, the local chapter of the National Association for the Advancement of Colored People, the auxiliary of a neighborhood church, and a bowlers league. Members are not paid for participation. Individuals join voluntary organizations to fill their leisure time, to enjoy the company of like-minded people, to perform some social service, or to advance some cause.

The fact that Americans join and support so many clubs and lodges has impressed foreign observers as one of the striking qualities of the nation's culture. Even in the 1830s, the French writer Count Alexis de Tocqueville noted: "Americans of all ages, all stations in life, and all types of disposition are forever forming associations." When voluntary organizations complete their goals, Americans often refashion them, finding new purposes to validate an enterprise. For example, once vaccines eliminated infantile paralysis, the March of Dimes organization reformulated its goals to embrace new health missions (Sills, 1957). In some cases program failure is essential, because the effective solution of the problems the organizations address would eliminate the need for their existence. Skid row rescue missions provide a good illustration of this principle (Rooney, 1980).

People also become members of some organizations—**coercive organizations**—against their will. They may be committed to a mental hospital, sentenced to prison, or drafted into the armed forces. Sociologist Erving Goffman (1961) has studied life in what he calls *total institutions*—places of residence where individuals are isolated from the rest of society for an appreciable period of time and where behavior is tightly regimented. In these environments the "inmates" or "recruits" are exposed to resocialization experiences that systematically seek to strip away their old roles and identities and fashion new ones. The induction process often includes **mortification**. Individuals are separated from families and friends who provide networks of support for old ways. They are made vulnerable to institutional control and discipline by being deprived of personal items, clothing, and accessories, and provided haircuts, uniforms, and standardized articles that establish an institutional identity. Often the new members are humiliated by being forced to assume demeaning postures, to engage in self-effacing tasks, and to endure insulting epithets (what sociologists term a *degradation ceremony*). These procedures leave individuals psychologically and emotionally receptive to the roles and identities demanded of them by the total institution.

Individuals also enter formal organizations formed for practical reasons—**utilitarian organizations**. Universities, corporations, farm organizations, unions, and government bureaus and agencies are among the organizations people form to accomplish vital everyday tasks. Utilitarian organizations fall between voluntary and coercive organizations: Membership in them is not entirely voluntary nor entirely compulsory. For example, we may not be compelled to secure employment with a corporation, but if we wish to support ourselves, doing so is an essential element of life.

BUREAUCRACY

So long as organizations are relatively small, they can often function reasonably well on the basis of face-to-face interaction. But if larger organizations are to attain their goals, they must establish formal operating and administrative procedures. Only as they standardize and routinize many of their operations can they function effectively. This requirement is met by a **bureaucracy**, a social structure made up of a hierarchy of statuses and roles that is prescribed by explicit rules and procedures and based on a division of function and authority. Sociologists use the concept in a way that differs sharply from the negative connotations bureaucracy has in popular usage. For instance, in everyday life we often employ the term to refer to organizational inefficiency. The bureaucrat is stereotyped as an officious, rule-conscious, responsibility-dodging clerk entangled in red tape and preoccupied with busywork.

Bureaucracy has developed over many centuries in the Western world (Bendix, 1977). It grew slowly and erratically during the Middle Ages and after. Only in the twentieth century has it fully flowered in response to the dictates of industrial society. As contemporary organizations have increased in size and complexity, more structural units and divisions have been required. In turn, some mechanism is needed for synchronizing and integrating the various activities. By providing for the performance of tasks on a regular and orderly basis, bureaucracies permit the planning and coordination of these activities in an efficient manner. Additionally, they aim to eliminate all unrelated influences on the behavior of their members so that people act primarily in the organization's interests. At the present time, most large, complex organizations in the United States are organized as bureaucracies.

WEBER'S ANALYSIS OF BUREAUCRACIES

German sociologist Max Weber (1946, 1947) was impressed by the ability of bureaucracies to rationalize and control the process by which people collectively pursue their

Max Weber believed that bureaucratic-type organizations provided the most rational form of social structure for carrying out tasks requiring the large-scale mobilization of people for a collective goal. Each position has a clearly defined set of duties, activities are governed by a system of rules, positions are filled on the basis of technical competence, and there are clear divisions of function and lines of authority. (David M. Campione/Taurus Photos)

goals. Although he was concerned about some of the negative consequences of bureaucracy, Weber contended that the needs of mass administration made bureaucracy an essential feature of modern organizational life. Weber dealt with bureaucracy as an *ideal type*. As pointed out in Chapter 1, an ideal type is a concept constructed by sociologists to portray the principal characteristics of a phenomenon. For example, sociologists can abstract common elements from a government agency, the Roman Catholic Church, the teamsters' union, IBM, and Yale University and arrive at a model for describing and analyzing organizational arrangements. (Figure 4.1 depicts the structure of the government of the United States.) But the model should not be mistaken for a realistic depiction of how real bureaucracies actually operate in the contemporary world.

The following are the major components of Weber's ideal bureaucracy—a sketch of a completely *rationalized* organization centered on the selection of the most appropriate means available for the achievement of a given goal:

1. Each office or position has clearly defined duties and responsibilities. In this manner, the regular activities of the organization are arranged within a clear-cut division of labor.

2. All offices are organized in a hierarchy of authority that takes the shape of a pyramid. Officials are held accountable to their superior for subordinates' actions and decisions in addition to their own.

3. All activities are governed by a consistent system of abstract rules and regu-

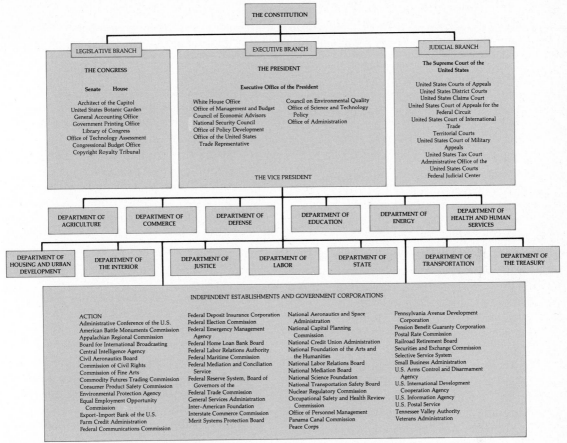

FIGURE 4.1   THE STRUCTURE OF THE GOVERNMENT OF THE UNITED STATES
(Source: U.S. Bureau of the Census.)

lations. These rules and regulations define the responsibilities of the various offices and the relationships among them. They ensure the coordination of essential tasks and uniformity in performance regardless of changes in personnel.

4. All offices carry with them qualifications and are filled on the basis of technical competence, not personal considerations. Presumably trained individuals do better jobs than those who gain an office based on family ties, personal friend-

ship, or political favor. Competence is established by certification (for instance, college degrees) or examination (for example, civil service tests).

5. Incumbents do not "own" their offices. Positions remain the property of the organization, and officeholders are supplied with the items they require to perform their work.

6. Employment by the organization is defined as a career. Promotion is based on seniority or merit, or both. After a probationary period, individuals gain the se-

curity of tenure and are protected against arbitrary dismissal. In principle, this feature makes officials less susceptible to outside pressures.

7. Administrative decisions, rules, procedures, and activities are recorded on written documents preserved in permanent files.

Weber believed that bureaucracy is an inherent feature of modern capitalism. Yet he was equally insistent that a socialist society could not dispense with the arrangement. Indeed, Weber thought that socialism would see an increase, not a decrease, in bureaucratic structures. While recognizing the limitations of capitalism, he nonetheless felt it presented the best chances for the preservation of individual freedom and creative leadership in a world dominated by formal organizations (Ritzer, 1983). Some sociologists are not this optimistic. They have expressed concern that bureaucracies may pose an inherent challenge to human liberty by turning free people into "cogs" in organizational machines (Blau and Scott, 1962). Let us take a closer look at some of these matters.

DISADVANTAGES OF BUREAUCRACY

Weber's ideal form of bureaucracy is not realized in practice for a number of reasons (Perrow, 1979). First, human beings do not exist just for organizations. People track all sorts of mud from the rest of their lives with them into bureaucratic arrangements, and they have a great many interests that are independent of the organization. Second, bureaucracies are not immune to social change. When such changes are frequent and rapid, the pat answers supplied by bureaucratic regulations and rules interfere with rational operation. And third, bureaucracies are designed for the "average" person. However, in real life people differ in intelligence, energy, zeal, and dedication, so that they are not in fact interchangeable in the day-to-day functioning of organizations.

It may have occurred to you that Weber's approach to bureaucracy has a functionalist emphasis. He views the various components of his ideal type as a functional response to the requirements of large-scale organization. These properties permit a formal organization to achieve its goals in the fastest, most efficient, and most rational manner. Other sociologists have also pointed out that bureaucracies have disadvantages, or *dysfunctions* (see Chapter 1). Let us consider a number of these problems.

Trained Incapacity. Social critic Thorstein Veblen (1921) pointed out that bureaucracies encourage their members to rely on established rules and regulations and to apply them in an unimaginative and mechanical fashion—a pattern he called **trained incapacity**. As a result of the socialization provided by organizations, individuals often develop a tunnel vision that limits their ability to respond in new ways when situations change. Because of trained incapacity, bureaucracies are often inflexible and inefficient in times of rapid change. For example, for more than a decade the American automobile industry was unresponsive and uncreative in meeting the changing tastes of the American public and in confronting the inroads of foreign competitors in the American market. Its managers continued to build the same large and fuel-inefficient cars by the same manufacturing techniques, despite the superior quality and appeal of the Japanese products.

Parkinson's Law. Weber viewed bureaucracy as a mechanism for achieving organizational efficiency. We gain a quite different picture from C. Northcote Parkinson (1962), who has gained renown as the author of **Parkinson's law**: "Work expands so as to fill the time available for its completion." Despite the tongue-in-cheek tone of his writing, Parkinson undertakes to show that "the number of the officials and the quantity of the work are not related to each other." He contends that bureaucracy expands not because of an increasing workload, but because officials seek to have additional subordinates hired in order to multiply the number of people under them in the hierarchy. These subordinates in turn create work for one another, while the coordination of their work requires still more officials.

The relentless growth of bureaucracy is reflected in American government. When George Washington was inaugurated as president in 1790, there were 9 executive units and some 1,000 employees. A century later, over 150,000 civilians worked in the Harrison administration, a rate of growth ten times as fast as that of the population. And by 1980 nearly 3 million civil servants were employed by the executive branch. Whereas only 1 of 4,000 Americans was employed by the executive branch in 1790, the figure stood at 1 in 463 in 1891 and 1 in 75 by 1980 (Porter, 1980). Of course factors other than those associated with Parkinson's Law contributed to the growth in American government, including the expansion of government services.

The Peter Principle. Weber thought that promotion on the basis of merit and competence would ensure that qualified individuals would be placed in responsible positions. But Lawrence J. Peter and Raymond Hull (1969) suggest that this may not in fact be the case. In what has become known as the **Peter principle**, they observe: "In a hierarchy every employee tends to rise to his level of incompetence" (p. 25). In other words, people get promoted so long as they are competent, but eventually many individuals reach positions that exceed their talents and abilities. Once this happens, they are unlikely to receive further promotions, although they remain in the office in which they are incompetent. Given sufficient time and an elaborate hierarchy with many ranks, Peter's corollary follows: "In time, every post tends to be occupied by an employee who is incompetent to carry out its duties" (p. 27). Even so, the work of the bureaucracy gets done: "Work is accomplished by those employees who have not yet reached their level of incompetence" (p. 27). Admittedly the Peter principle overstates the matter, but it does highlight one problem frequently encountered in bureaucratic arrangements.

Oligarchy. Organizations, like all other groups, enjoy a formidable capacity for eliciting conformity. As we noted earlier, groups do not just control and dispense rewards and punishments. They also define social reality by structuring our experiences. Given the predominant role organizations have in contemporary life, some observers have expressed concern for the future of democratic institutions. They point out that all too often the needs of organizations take priority over those of individuals. Complicating matters, Robert Michels (1911/1966), a sociologist and friend of Weber, argues that bureaucracies contain a fundamental flaw that makes them undemocratic social arrangements: They invariably lead to oligarchy—the concentration of power in the hands of a few individuals, who use their offices to advance their own fortunes and self-interests. He called this tendency the **iron law of oligarchy**—"Whoever says organization, says oligarchy" (p. 365).

Michels cites a variety of reasons for the oligarchical tendencies found in formal organizations. First, they have hierarchical structures with authority exercised downward from the top. Even when final authority is vested in the membership, the requirements of leadership and the dictates of overall administration make popular voting and related procedures inconsequential rituals. Second, officials have a great many advantages over their members. They have access to information that is unavailable to others, and they usually possess superior political skills and experience. Additionally, they control a variety of administrative resources, including communication networks, offices, and a treasury that can be used to carry out their official tasks or to ward off challengers. Moreover, they can use the rewards they control to coopt dissidents and rivals. And third, ordinary members tend to be uninterested in assuming leadership responsibilities and are apathetic toward the problems of the organization.

Michels points to the developmental course of European socialist parties and labor unions as evidence in support of his thesis that leaders seldom reflect the democratic aspirations of their organizations. Even so, not all organizations are oligarchic (Breines, 1980; Schwartz, Rosenthal, and Schwartz, 1981). For instance, the International Typographical Union (ITU), composed of typesetters, has maintained a democratic tradition by institutionalizing a "two-party system" (Lipset, Trow, and Coleman, 1956). Union elections are held on a regular basis, with the two parties putting up a complete slate of candidates. Where competing groups are active and legitimate, the rank-and-file have the potential for replacing leaders and introducing new policies. For instance, in 1964 rank-and-file Republicans nominated Barry Goldwater for president over the opposition of the established leadership, and in 1976 a political unknown and outsider, Jimmy Carter, got the Democratic party nomination.

So although the complexity of modern life requires large-scale formal organization, bureaucratic structures have their disadvantages and problems. There are limits to what larger hierarchical organizations can accomplish. Yet, as political scientist James Q. Wilson (1967:6) observes, we often lose sight of this fact:

If enough people don't like something, it becomes a problem; if the intellectuals agree with them it becomes a crisis; any crisis must be solved; if it must be solved, then it can be solved—and creating a new organization is the way to do it. If the organization fails to solve the problem (and when the problem is a fundamental one, it will almost surely fail), then the reason is "politics," or "mismanagement," or "incompetent people," or "meddling," or "socialization," or "inertia."

Hence, as Wilson points out, some problems cannot be solved, and some organizational and governmental functions cannot be performed well.

INFORMAL ORGANIZATION

The rules, regulations, procedures, and impersonal relationships prescribed by a bureaucracy only rarely correspond with the realities of organizational life for another reason. Formal organization breeds **informal organization**—interpersonal networks and ties that arise in a formal organization but are not defined or prescribed by it. Based on their common interests and relationships, individuals form primary groups. These informal structures provide means by which people bend and break rules, share "common knowledge," engage in secret behaviors, handle problems, and "cut corners." So work relationships are much more than the lifeless abstractions contained on an organizational chart that outlines the official lines of communication and authority.

The roots of informal organization are

Doing Sociology: Informal Organization

What happens in formal organizations is not necessarily what appears on the surface, or at least what is prescribed by official blueprints. In the course of working within organizations, people relate to and influence one another in ways that do not necessarily follow the formal chain of command or the formal rules and regulations. In examining organizational life, we must pay attention not only to what people are supposed to do, but also to what they actually do. Although most activity is directed toward meeting the goals and dictates of the organization—the corporation, college, church, or governmental bureau—people simultaneously pursue their own goals through informal networks and groups. This informal structure gives a human touch to bureaucratic arrangements. In the two episodes that follow, two students tell about their work experiences and the part that informal organization plays in them.

I have a job in the warehouse of a large lumber company. The guys have developed a lot of neat little gimmicks to goof off at work. Let me describe one of them. We have one supervisor but access to two restrooms. This means that the supervisor cannot cover both restrooms simultaneously. If the "super" cannot find someone, we tell him that the guy has gone to the restroom. In reality, however, the guy is hiding out, relaxing somewhere behind a pile of lumber. The "super" usually hollers, "What's taking him so G——— d——— long?" Mad as hell, he goes to get the guy, looking first in one restroom and then in the other. When the "super" heads for the first restroom, we give a little whistle. The guy hears the whistle and hustles back to work. When the "super" returns complaining that he can't find the guy, one of us says, "Oh, he's already back. He's over there loading lumber. He was in the other restroom."

Tonight at work I noticed something that often happens but that I just took for granted and never really thought about. I am a waitress at a local restaurant. The hostess seats customers within various "stations"—a group of tables served by one waiter or waitress. On their own, however, waiters and waitresses "trade" tables in their station for tables in another station. It works this way. If the hostess seats a bunch of girls at a table in my station, I will give the table to a waiter. If guys are seated at one of his tables, the waiter will give them to me. We do this because guys give girls better tips than they do men and vice versa.

embedded within formal organization and are nurtured by the formality of its arrangements. Official rules and regulations must be sufficiently general to cover a great many situations. In applying general rules to a particular situation, people must use their judgment, and so they evolve informal guidelines that provide them with workable solutions. Additionally, in order to avoid bureaucratic "red tape," employees often arrive at informal understandings with one another. Indeed, if formal organization is to operate smoothly, it requires informal organization for interpreting, translating, and supporting its goals and practices. Thus people are tied to the larger group by their membership in primary groups that mediate them and the formal organization. Further, the impersonality of bureaucratic arrangements distresses many people, and they search for warmth, rapport, and companionship in the work setting through informal relationships.

Factory workers typically evolve their

own norms regarding what constitutes a "reasonable" amount of work, and these norms often do not conform with those of management. Sociologist Michael Burawoy (1979) studied informal organization among shop workers while working for a year as a machine operator at a large Chicago-area plant. He found that relations on the shop floor were dominated by "making out"—a competitive game the machine operators played by manipulating the rules and regulations governing their work. The workers did not passively conform to the dictates of management or to the technological aspects of their work, but actively connived to put in place their own "shop-floor culture." A central theme of the culture revolved about maximizing their payoff from the firm's piecework bonus system, while simultaneously holding up high rates through restriction of output.

Research has also shown the strong influence of the work group in regulating deviance and theft among individual workers. For instance, Donald Horning (1970) studied blue-collar theft in a manufacturing plant and concluded that informal norms regulate both the type and the amount of property taken. Employee pilferage was a group-supported activity, even though the actual taking of property took place alone or in secret. And Gerald Mars (1974) reported in his study of dockworkers that materials in shipment were stolen according to the group-defined "value of the boat." In order for theft to go undetected by dock authorities, all members of a work group had to approve of and cooperate with the activity. Studies of "time theft"—on-the-job visiting, daydreaming, reading novels and magazines, and "goofing off"—reveal that the average worker in the United States "steals" three hours and forty-five minutes from his or her employer each week (*New York Times*, 1977).

ALTERNATIVE PERSPECTIVES

Until the past decade or so, Weber's approach to bureaucracy dominated American sociology. In large measure sociologists focused their attention on organizations as abstract social structures, while often neglecting the behavior of the individuals who comprise them. Indeed, sociologists Peter M. Blau and Richard A. Schoenherr (1971: viii and 357) championed such an approach, observing:

Formal organizations, as well as other social structures, exhibit regularities that can be analyzed in their own right, independent of any knowledge about the individual behavior of their members . . . it is time that we "push men [and women] out" to place proper emphasis on the study of social structure in sociology.

Many sociologists studied formal organizations without noticing the processes by which social structures are produced and reproduced in the course of people's daily interactions. But much has changed in recent years as sociologists from differing perspectives have looked at the ways in which organizational reality is generated through the actions of people and groups of people (Benson, 1977; Zey-Ferrell, 1981). We will consider three of these approaches: the conflict, the symbolic interactionist, and the ethnomethodological.

The Conflict Perspective. Conflict theorists contend that organizational goals reflect the priorities of those who occupy the top positions. Viewed in this manner, organizations are not neutral social structures, but arenas for conflicting interests in which the social issues and power relations of society are played out (Collins, 1975). Marxist social scientists have followed in the tradition of

Karl Marx (1970), who saw bureaucracy as a manifestation of the centralizing tendencies of capitalism and an instrument of class domination. They analyze organizations within the context of the broader inequalities that operate within society and find that the distribution of power and the allocation of rewards within them mirror the larger society's class structure (Edwards, 1979; Burawoy, 1983).

In *Capital* (1867/1967) Marx claimed that the modern factory is a despotic regime made necessary by the competitive pressures of the market. These pressures compel technological innovation and work intensification, all of which rest on the availability of workers, who in order to survive must sell their labor power to capitalist employers. But as we will see in Chapters 5 and 7, Marx also viewed the factory as the crucible of revolution. The domination of the working class by capital would turn into its opposite, "the revolt of the working class."

More recent studies by Marxist social scientists suggest that bureaucratic mechanisms arose as much from the need of capitalists to impose labor discipline as from abstract notions of efficiency and rationality (Friedman, 1977; Edwards, 1978). Stephen Marglin (1974) shows that nineteenth-century British entrepreneurs established the hierarchical arrangement to guarantee themselves a central role in the production process. Katherine Stone (1974) also finds that turn-of-the-century steel magnates established top-to-bottom chains of command and job ladders to isolate individual workers, break the power of skilled craftsmen, and combat growing labor militancy.

Marx thought that the bureaucratic structures inherited from capitalism would have to be altered and even eliminated by a revolutionary working class. He wrote (1966:64): "The working class cannot simply lay hold of the ready-made state machinery and wield it for its own purposes." Instead, the workers would have to create a transitional bureaucracy that was representative of and responsive to their needs and goals. Marx chose as his model the short-lived Paris Commune of 1871. By establishing the conditions for the direct participation of workers in decision-making processes, the commune democratized the bureaucracy. However, as Marx's writings were interpreted and reformulated by Lenin and implemented by Stalin, the primary elements of Bolshevik policy in the Soviet Union centered on the expansion of bureaucratic offices and the dominance of the state apparatus by a "new class" of Communist Party officials (Djilas, 1957).

The Symbolic-Interactionist Perspective. Critics of the structural or Weberian approach to organizations point out that people, not organizations, have motivations and goals. An organization's officers and managers can only offer incentives they believe will motivate employees to conform to goals that they define as paramount (Zey-Ferrell, 1981). Thus critics, particularly symbolic interactionists, contend that human beings are not spongelike, malleable organisms who passively absorb and adapt to their environments. Instead, they portray people as active agents who shape and mold their destinies and continually fashion new joint actions based on their definitions of the situation (Blumer, 1969). Organizational constraints only provide the framework within which people forge their actions as they appraise, choose, and decide on alternatives. In sum, symbolic interactionists portray organizational behavior as generated out of individual meanings that people translate into social realities (see Chapter 1).

And rather than depicting organizations

in static terms, symbolic interactionists emphasize their dynamic and changing nature. This approach was taken by Anselm Strauss and his colleagues (1963) in their study of organizational behavior in two Chicago-area psychiatric hospitals. They treated a formal organization as a **negotiated order**—the fluid, ongoing understandings and agreements people reach as they go about their daily activities. To outsiders, the hospitals appeared to be tightly structured organizations that functioned in accordance with strict bureaucratic rules and regulations. However, the researchers found that in practice the hospitals operated quite differently. The organizations were simply too complex for a single set of rules to hold or for any one person to know all the rules, much less in exactly what situations they applied, to whom, in what degree, and for how long. Matters were complicated by constant turnover in staff and patients. Not only did people differ in their goals, they also differed in their conceptions of the nature, causes, and treatment of mental illness. Given these circumstances, most house rules served more as general understandings than as commands, and they were stretched, argued, reinterpreted, ignored, or applied as situations dictated. Individuals reached agreements with one another that provided a consensus for a time, but the understandings were subject to periodic modification and revision.

Chaos did not reign in the hospitals, because the negotiations followed patterns that permitted some degree of predictability. Even so, Strauss and his colleagues concluded:

A skeptic, thinking in terms of relatively permanent or slowly changing structure, might remark that the hospital remains the same from week to week, that only the working arrangements change. . . . Practically, we maintain, no one knows what the hospital "is"
on any given day unless he has a comprehensive grasp of the combinations of rules, policies, agreements, understandings, pacts, contracts, and other working arrangements that currently obtain. In a pragmatic sense, that combination "is" the hospital at the moment, its social order. Any changes that impinge upon this order—whether ordinary changes, like introduction of a new staff member or a betrayed contract or unusual changes, like the introduction of new technology or new theory—will necessitate renegotiation or reappraisal, with consequent changes in the organizational order. There will be a new order, not merely the re-establishment of an old order or reinstitution of a previous equilibrium. It is necessary continually to reconstitute the bases of concerted action, of social order. (1963:312)

Whether or not the negotiated order model of organizations is applicable to other kinds of settings is a matter for future research. But negotiations apparently do occur in many kinds of organizations, including factories, symphony orchestras, and political organizations (Lauer and Handel, 1983).

The Ethnomethodological Perspective. Since the 1940s, sociologist Harold Garfinkel and a number of his colleagues and students have undertaken to illuminate the commonplace, taken-for-granted activities that constitute our daily experience by an approach they call **ethnomethodology**. *Ethno,* borrowed from the Greek, means "people" or "folk," while *methodology* refers to procedures by which something is done or analyzed. Thus in its most literal sense ethnomethodology refers to the procedures—the rules and activities—that people employ in making social life and society intelligible to themselves and others (Garfinkel, 1974). Ethnomethodologists study the background understandings that constitute the "stuff" out of which stable social interaction emerges. And they investigate how people go about creating and sustaining for one another the *presumption* that there is an external social reality and order.

Sociologist Don H. Zimmerman (1971) applied the ethnomethodological perspective in examining the day-by-day operations of a large-scale organization, a public welfare agency. He studied how the receptionists went about processing applicants for public assistance and apportioning them among caseworkers. A cursory inspection suggested that the receptionists were governed by the "first come, first served" rule. But a deeper inspection revealed that they were also concerned with giving the *appearance* that applicants moved through the system in a sequential and orderly manner.

In order to do this, the receptionists had to deviate from the "first come, first served" rule. They did so on the basis of tacit understandings regarding the requirements of their work—certain assumptions regarding "what everyone who works here knows." For instance, receptionists would suspend the rule and switch the order of applicants when clients said they had a doctor's appointment or had to attend to some other urgent matter. Likewise, they would allow some applicants to request a particular social worker. And they routinely assigned "difficult" and "troublesome" applicants to a caseworker known to be good at handling "special problems."

Zimmerman concludes that as we go about our activities, we continually develop and interpret what a rule means. We do not mechanically follow rules like programmed robots. Instead, we invoke rationalizations that satisfy us and others that what we are doing constitutes "reasonable" compliance with a rule. In this sense, bureaucratic rules and regulations serve as a commonsense method by which we account for our behavior. We see and report patterning and stability in our lives because we go about

"structuring" structure, collaboratively creating meanings and understandings of one another's activities. In grasping bureaucratic behavior, then, the relevant question is not "What is the rule?" but "What has to be done?" In practice, a rule may be employed or ignored depending on the context. But more importantly, it affords the members of an organization a convenient means to portray, explain, and justify their actions.

A Synthesis of Alternative Perspectives?
Sociologist Charles Perrow (1982) joins threads from the conflict, symbolic-interactionist, and ethnomethodological perspectives to argue that the notion of bureaucratic rationality masks the true nature of organizational life. He claims that our world is more "loosely coupled"—characterized by a substantial measure of redundancy, slack, and waste—than structural theories allow. Perrow says that organizations do not have goals, only constraints. Take the Sanitation Department of New York City:

To say its goal is to pick up the garbage—even to pick it up frequently, pick it all up, and do it cheaply—does not tell us much. These are not goals of that department but merely loose constraints under which those who use the organization must operate, and these are not really any more important than the following constraints: The cushy top jobs in the department can be used to pay off political debts; some groups can use the Sanitation Department as an assured source of employment and keep others out; upper management can use its positions as political jumping-off places or training spots; equipment manufacturers use it as an easy mark for shoddy goods; and, finally, the workers are entitled to use it as a source of job security and pensions and an easy way of making a living. (p. 687)

Perrow contends that private profit-making organizations are not much different. Lockheed has been described as a pension plan that makes missiles and planes on the side so that its pension plan can be funded. Steel plants are closed even though they make a respectable profit because they are worth more as tax writeoffs. The goal of making steel or even a profit does not pose a significant obstacle. Countless other organizations continue to exist even though they fail to provide decent mail service, prepare students for careers, or offer acceptable medical care. But should the organizations fail to satisfy some special interest group that lives off them, then the consequences are defined as a major social problem.

Perrow concludes:

Do organizations have goals, then, in the rational sense of organizational theory? I do not think so. In fact, when an executive says, "This is our goal," chances are that he is looking at what the organization happens to be doing at the time and saying, "Since we are all very rational here, and we are doing this, this must be our goal." Organizations, in this sense, run backward: The deed is father to the thought, not the other way around. (p. 687)

Perrow next links the conflict perspective to his analysis by arguing that social efforts at giving accounts and attributing rationality to organizations serve elites much more than they serve other people. These efforts create a world in which organizational hierarchy, technological requirements, and profit-making motives become legitimated.

HUMANIZING BUREAUCRACIES

Since large organizations play such a critical part in our daily lives, it may be well to conclude the chapter by asking, "Can we make bureaucracies more humane instruments for modern living?" If we value freedom and independence—if we are disturbed by the conformity of attitudes, values, and behavior that bureaucracies often induce—then we may wish to set up conditions that foster uniqueness, self-direction, and human dignity. Although affording no panaceas, a number of programs have been proposed that allow individuals greater range for developing their full capacities and potential in the context of organizational life. Let us briefly consider a number of these.

Employee Participation. About the same time that Japanese manufacturers vigorously entered American markets, American academicians became intrigued by Japanese management methods (Serrin, 1984a). They particularly touted "quality circles," an arrangement where a group of up to a dozen workers and one or two managers from the same department meet together on a regular basis to figure out ways of getting along better with each other, making work easier, raising output, and improving the quality of their products. Some 2,000 American companies, including General Motors, International Business Machines Corporation, and American Telephone and Telegraph, have instituted work reform programs. In some cases workers are participating in high-level decisions dealing with how work should be organized, work hours, quality standards, and the hiring of subcontractors.

Although a good many companies have adopted employee participation programs, not all firms like them. A University of Michigan survey found that 60 percent of the companies who had adopted quality circles were lukewarm or unhappy with what they were accomplishing and 7 percent had dropped them entirely (Main, 1984). Many of the programs were established for their publicity value or because managers wanted their employees to believe they were being consulted even though no real sharing of decision-making power actually occurred. Moreover, few workers participate in their companies' most important decisions, such as product choice, plant location, and investment. Conflict theorists contend that workers win gains only through aggressiveness and that the relationship between management and labor is inherently adversarial. They claim that worker participation programs are simply cosmetic efforts that mask corporate attempts to scrap collective bargaining obligations. And union officials have been distrustful of quality circles because they fear that the circles will assume some of their functions as workers' representatives.

Proponents of the programs say that where management and workers are committed to them, absenteeism, tardiness, grievances, strikes, and labor costs are reduced. Moreover, product quality improves and pilferage lessens. For instance, General Motors plants that have the most intensive programs have better performance than do automotive plants that lack the programs.

Overall, new management strategies in the 1980s have been emphasizing a lessening of hierarchy and authoritarianism. They mark a departure from the theories of Frederick Winslow Taylor, which had dominated management philosophies since the 1920s. Taylor's system of ''scientific management'' held that production could be improved by rational, technology-centered organization and that workers could be pacified by providing them with adequate training and pay. But the changes should not be overestimated. When managers must make a tough decision, they typically revert to the direct, authoritarian mode (Serrin, 1984a).

Small Work Groups. Some corporate officials say that small working groups are more productive for Americans than attempting to adopt Japanese management styles that depend on the Japanese worker's intense company loyalty (Larson and Dolan, 1983). The approach appears highly adaptable within the computer industry where small groups, given great freedom, can react quickly to abrupt technological change. Unlike other industries, where change is gradual, computer firms must regularly come up with new products or enhancements of the old, and at constantly lower prices.

Apple Computer turned to small groups to develop its Lisa and Macintosh computers. And even giant IBM has recognized the need for small groups; it formed fourteen ''independent'' business units to capture the entrepreneurial spirit for a number of projects, including the development of factory robotic systems. IBM found that centralized organization interfered with innovation. One virtue of the small group approach is that responsibility is lodged with the employees doing the actual work. And small groups can focus their energies on a single goal, foster creativity, and reward employees commensurate with their contributions.

Employee-Ownership Plans. By 1983 there were more than 5,000 employee-owned companies in the United States, up from 300 in 1976 (English, 1983). Until recently, most employee ownership plans were management vehicles for sharing a piece of the pie and increasing worker productivity without fundamentally altering a company's structure. But newer arrangements entail employees actually taking over a firm. Many of the companies, such as Hyatt Clark Industries, Weirton Steel, and Rath Packing Company, were unprofitable, and the buyouts were a last resort to save a business and jobs for workers.

In many cases employee ownership has changed the way companies operate, including their labor-management relationships. Greater employee initiative in the workplace has been found to cut costs. But much depends on a firm's profitability. When a company becomes profitable, differences tend to get smoothed over quickly. But when a firm continues to lose money, dissatisfaction mounts. Further, some workers complain that the consultation that takes place between workers and managers counts for little. So employee ownership does not guarantee labor peace.

SUMMARY

1. Groups are not tangible things that have actual substance in the real world. Rather, they are products of social definitions—sets of shared ideas. As such they constitute constructed realities. We make groups real by treating them as if they are real, a clear application of the Thomas theorem.

2. Primary groups involve two or more people who enjoy direct, intimate, cohesive relationships. Expressive ties predominate in primary groups. Secondary groups entail two or more people who are involved in impersonal, touch-and-go relationships. Instrumental ties predominate in secondary groups. Primary groups are fundamental both to us and society: They are critical to the socialization process; they provide settings in which we meet most of our personal needs; and they are powerful instruments for social control.

3. The concepts of in-group and out-group highlight the importance of boundaries—social demarcation lines that tell us where interaction begins and ends. To one degree or another, a group's boundaries "encapsulate" people in a social membrane so that the focus and flow of their actions are internally contained. Whatever their source, social boundaries face in two directions. They prevent outsiders from entering a group's sphere, and they keep insiders within the group's sphere so that they do not entertain rival possibilities for social interaction.

4. Reference groups provide the models we use for appraising and shaping our attitudes, feelings, and actions. A reference group may or may not be our membership group. We may think of a reference group as a base that we use for viewing the world, a source of psychological identification. It provides both normative and comparative functions.

5. The size of a group is of considerable importance because it influences the nature of our interaction. The smaller the group, the more opportunities we have to get to know other people well and to establish close ties with them. Emotions and feelings tend to assume a larger part in dyads than in larger groups. The addition of a third member to a group—forming a triad—fundamentally alters a social situation. In this arrangement, one person may be placed in the role of an outsider.

6. In group settings some members usually exert more influence than others. We call these individuals leaders. Two types of leadership roles tend to evolve in small groups: a task specialist and a social-emotional specialist. Leaders differ in their styles for exercising influence. Some follow an authoritarian style, others a democratic style, and still others a laissez-faire style.

7. When individuals work in groups, they work less hard than they do when working individually, a process termed social loafing. Presumably people slack off in groups because they feel they are not achieving their fair share of credit or because they think that in a crowd they can get away with less work.

8. In group settings, individuals may become victims of groupthink. Group members may share an illusion of invulnerability that leads to overconfidence and a greater willingness to take risks. Members of the group demand conformity and apply pressure to those who express doubts about a proposed course of action.

9. Groups bring powerful pressures to bear that produce conformity among their members. Although such pressures influence our behavior, we often are unaware of them. Solomon Asch shows that some individuals will conform to the false consensus of a group even though the consensus is contradicted by the evidence of their own eyes.

10. For a good many tasks within modern societies, people require groups they can deliberately create for the achievement of specific goals. These groups are formal organizations. People enter formal organizations for a good many reasons. Amitai Etzioni classifies organizations on this basis by identifying three types: voluntary, coercive, and utilitarian.

11. So long as organizations are relatively small, they can often function reasonably well on the basis of face-to-face interaction. If larger organizations are to attain their goals, they must establish formal operating and administrative procedures. This requirement is met by a bureaucracy, a social structure made up of a hierarchy of statuses and roles that is prescribed by explicit rules and procedures and based on a division of function and authority.

12. Max Weber approached bureaucracy as an ideal type. He sketched the following characteristics of a completely rationalized organization centered on the selection of the most appropriate means available for the achievement of a given goal: Each office has clearly defined duties; all offices are organized in a hierarchy of authority; all activities are governed by a system of rules; all offices carry with them qualifications; incumbents do not own their positions; employment by the organization is defined as a career; and administrative decisions are recorded on written documents.

13. Bureaucracies also have disadvantages and limitations. These include the principle of trained incapacity, Parkinson's law, the Peter principle, and the iron law of oligarchy. There are limits to what large hierarchical organizations can accomplish. The rules, regulations, procedures, and impersonal relationships prescribed by a bureaucracy only rarely correspond with the realities of organizational life.

14. Formal organization breeds informal organization. The roots of informal organization are embedded within formal organization and are nurtured by the formality of its arrangements. If formal organization is to operate smoothly, it requires informal organization for interpreting, translating, and supporting its goals and practices. People are tied to the larger group by their membership in primary groups that mediate between them and the formal organization.

15. Until the past decade or so, Weber's approach to bureaucracy dominated American sociology. Sociologists focused on organizations as abstract social structures while neglecting the behavior of the individuals who comprise them. But much has changed in recent years as sociologists from differing perspectives—particularly the conflict, symbolic interactionist, and ethnomethodological approaches—looked at the ways by which organizational reality is generated through the actions of people and groups of people.

16. Since large organizations play such an important role in our lives, we might ask how they can be made more humane. Among such programs are those that allow employee participation, small work groups, and employee ownership.

GLOSSARY

bureaucracy A social structure made up of a hierarchy of statuses and roles that is prescribed by explicit rules and procedures and based on a division of function and authority.

coercive organization A formal organization that people become members of against their will.

dyad A two-member group.

ethnomethodology Procedures—the rules and activities—that people employ in making social life and society intelligible to themselves and others.

expressive ties Social links formed when we emotionally invest ourselves in and commit ourselves to other people.

formal organization A group people deliberately form for the achievement of specific objectives.

group Two or more people who share a feeling of unity and who are bound together in relatively stable patterns of social interaction.

groupthink A decision-making process found in highly cohesive groups in which the members become so preoccupied with maintaining group consensus that their critical faculties become impaired.

informal organization Interpersonal networks and ties that arise in a formal organization but are not defined or prescribed by it.

in-group A group with which we identify and to which we belong.

instrumental ties Social links formed when we cooperate with other people to achieve some goal.

iron law of oligarchy The principle which says that bureaucracies invariably lead to the concentration of power in the hands of a few individuals who use their offices to advance their own fortunes and self-interests.

mortification Rituals employed by coercive organizations that render individuals vulnerable to institutional control, discipline, and resocialization.

negotiated order The fluid, ongoing understandings and agreements people reach as they go about their daily activities.

out-groups Groups with which we do not identify and to which we do not belong.

Parkinson's law Work expands so as to fill the time available for its completion.

Peter principle In a hierarchy, every employee tends to rise to his level of incompetence.

primary group Two or more people who enjoy a direct, intimate, cohesive relationship with one another.

reference group A social unit we use for appraising and shaping our attitudes, feelings, and actions.

relationship An association that lasts long enough for two people to become linked together by a relatively stable set of expectations.

relative deprivation Discontent associated with the gap between what we have and what we believe we should have.

secondary group Two or more people who are involved in an impersonal relationship and have come together for a specific, practical purpose.

social-emotional specialist A leadership role that focuses on overcoming interpersonal problems in a group, defusing tension, and promoting solidarity.

social dilemma A situation in which members of a group are faced with a conflict between maximizing their personal interests and maximizing the collective welfare.

social loafing When individuals work in groups, they work less hard than they do when working individually.

task specialist A leadership role that focuses on appraising the problem at hand and organizing people's activity to deal with it.

trained incapacity The term Thorstein Veblen applied to the tendency within bureaucracies for members to rely on established rules and regulations and to apply them in an unimaginative and mechanical fashion.

triad A three-member group.

utilitarian organization A formal organization set up to achieve practical ends.

voluntary organization A formal organization that people enter and leave freely.

5

Deviance

THE NATURE OF DEVIANCE
> *Social Properties of Deviance*
> *Social Control and Deviance*
> *The Social Effects of Deviance*

SOCIOLOGICAL PERSPECTIVES ON
DEVIANCE
> *The Anomie Perspective*
> *The Cultural Transmission*
> *   Perspective*
> *The Conflict Perspective*
> *The Labeling Perspective*

CRIME AND THE CRIMINAL
JUSTICE SYSTEM
> *The Criminal Justice System*
> *Forms of Crime*
> *Measuring Crime*
> *Differing Conceptions of the*
> *   Purposes of Imprisonment*

Most of us experience everyday life as having a good deal of order and regularity to it. Our interaction seems relatively patterned, producing flowing currents of activity that bind us within the larger social enterprise. Indeed, if we are to live with one another in a group environment, it is essential that we integrate and coordinate our actions. Whatever we want—food, clothing, sex, fame, football, a job, an education, or companionship—we must get it by working with and through other people. We must take up our positions in complex and organized groups and institutions—families, political parties, corporations, schools, churches, and ball teams (Cohen, 1966).

Clearly the work of the world gets done only as the actions of a great many people are fitted together. But if people are to fit their actions together, they must have common understandings about who is supposed to do what and when they are to do it. Some understandings may seem "better" than others in that they get the job done more effectively and efficiently. But the first requirement for organized social life is that there be some understandings, however arbitrary they may seem (Cohen, 1966). As we pointed out in Chapter 2, such understandings take the form of social expectations that are embedded in norms. Without norms for governing behavior, even interaction in a clique or family would be impossible. We would lack guideposts telling us what is permissible and what constitute the outer limits of allowable behavior. If we lacked norms, interaction would be a real problem because we would never know what others might do (Sagarin, 1975).

Yet there is more to the story of norms. Norms have teeth, and teeth that can bite. Rewards and penalties are associated with them. In modern societies, the *state* is the mechanism by which a good many norms—*laws*—are enforced. Laws are not neutral: They tend to favor some group's interests,

and they embody some group's preferred values. All this brings us to a consideration of deviance.

The Nature of Deviance

In all societies the behavior of some people at times goes beyond that permitted by the norms. Norms only tell us what we are supposed to do or what we are not supposed to do; they do not tell us what people *actually* do. And what some of us actually do very often runs counter to what other people judge to be acceptable behavior. In brief, social life is characterized not only by conformity, but by deviance. **Deviance** is behavior that a considerable number of people in a society view as reprehensible and beyond the limits of tolerance. We typically view behavior as deviant to the extent to which it is negatively valued and provokes hostile reactions.

SOCIAL PROPERTIES OF DEVIANCE

As viewed by sociologists, deviance is not a property *inherent* in certain forms of behavior (Erikson, 1962; Becker, 1963; Lemert, 1972); it is a property *conferred* upon particular behaviors by social definitions. In the course of their daily lives, people make judgments regarding the desirability or undesirability of this or that behavior. They then translate their judgments into favorable or unfavorable consequences for those who engage in the behavior. In this sense, then, deviance is what people say it is. Perhaps this idea can be clarified by considering a number of points.

The Relativity of Deviance. Which acts are defined as deviant vary greatly from time to time, place to place, and group to group. For example, when ordinary people break into tombs, they are labeled looters. When archeologists break into tombs, they are hailed as scientists advancing the frontiers of knowledge. Yet in both cases burial sites are disturbed and items are carted away. Likewise, in Western nations members of the Baha'i religion are accorded religious freedom. However, the Iranian regime of Ayatollah Khomeini has jailed and executed without trial thousands of members of this religion. The group advocates equality of the sexes, universal education, elimination of intergroup prejudice, and one-world government—beliefs and practices considered heretical by the ruling mullahs of Iran's predominant Muslim sect.

These illustrations highlight the point that acts are not inherently deviant. A social audience decides whether or not some behavior is deviant. This is not to say that the acts we label homicide, stealing, sexual perversion, mental disturbance, alcoholism, gambling, and child abuse would not occur without social definitions. Rather, the critical issue is how people define behavior and the specific ways in which they react to it.

The Power to Make Definitions Stick. When people differ regarding their definitions of what is and is not deviant behavior, the question becomes one of which individuals and groups will make their definitions prevail. Consider the following illustrations.

In 1776 George Washington was labeled a traitor by the British. Twenty years later, he was the first president of the United States and beloved as "the father of his country." In the 1940s Menachem Begin was portrayed by British authorities in Palestine as a Zionist terrorist (he was the leader of the Irgun Zvai Leumi, the underground military organization so instrumental in forcing the British to give up their Palestinian mandate). Thirty years later, he was the popular head of the state of Israel. Had the Americans and Jews lost their wars for independence, very likely both Washington and Begin would have been executed—or, at the very least, given long prison terms.

An apartment in Houston, Texas, is being converted to an all-nude complex, much to the displeasure of current clothes-wearing tenants. They were told by the apartment owners that they could either stay and disrobe or move out. Said Anna Marie Abar, "I'm totally outraged. They are forcing a nudist lifestyle down my throat and saying if I don't like it I'm a pervert" (Morris, 1984).

The United States government incarcerated Ezra Pound for eleven years in a Washington-area mental hospital because it wished to avoid having to accuse one of its greatest poets of treason for his pro-Nazi activities during World War II. Later, General Edwin A. Walker, who led white Southern activists in a fight against the desegregation of the University of Mississippi, was sent to a mental hospital by the government because it did not want anything on the record to show that a high-ranking military officer had incited mob action (Sagarin, 1975). In the Soviet Union, a number of prominent political dissidents, including mathematician Leonid Plyushch, biologist Zhores Medvedev, and war hero General Pyotr Griegorenko, have been diagnosed and hospitalized as "mentally ill" (Reich, 1983). Increasingly Soviet authorities are referring dissidents to psychiatrists for such diagnoses in order to avoid embarrassing public trials and to discredit dissent as the product of sick minds.

These illustrations point to the fact that who is defined as deviant and what is defined as deviance depend on who is doing

Doing Sociology: The Social Nature of Deviance

In the course of our daily lives, we continually size up people and their behavior. Not uncommonly, we assume it is "human nature" to think and act in certain ways. Consequently, behavior that deviates from our standards seems reprehensible and somehow abnormal. Yet sociologists emphasize that deviance derives from social definitions, and more particularly from the shared understandings people evolve in the course of their social interaction and from the meanings they give to one another's behavior. They point out that deviance is relative and subject to quite different appraisals depending on the situation. In the episodes that follow, students note the part social definitions play in our assessment of what people say and do:

I am still getting over my New Year's Eve hangover. It is interesting how our society taboos intoxication and yet makes it mandatory to get smashed on New Year's Eve. Actually I don't care that much for drinking, but if I don't get smashed on New Year's Eve I'd be deviant—"uptight," "straight." The same thing happens at Mardi Gras. You are supposed to live it up and do all sorts of crazy things that

you can't do on other occasions. April Fool's Day is another case. You can do all kinds of tomfoolery that would make you a kook on other days. It is weird the way society falls all over you if you violate some norms—even sends you to the Workhouse if you're drunk. Then it turns around and makes you a deviant if you don't do these very same things. On given days society institutionalizes behavior that on other days it would label deviant.

I went to a dance tonight. The theme of the dance was the 1950s. I was going to slick my hair back and try to get dressed to fit the period. But then I saw some guys on my floor who had gone all out with the grease in their hair, sunglasses, T-shirts, muscle shirts, motorcycle boots, and the whole bit. They looked so ridiculous that I could not bring myself to dress like them. When I got to the dance I saw that everyone else had dressed up like these guys. I felt extremely out of place in clothes that are currently "normal" in everyday life and that make me feel unnoticed and relaxed outside the dance. In the dance, I

felt as if I were the one that was dressed for the wrong decade, not the others.

It was a lovely fall day today so I decided to study outside on a blanket near the dorm. Other students were lying about sunbathing. As I was halfheartedly studying, an attractive girl came by, spread her blanket near me, and then proceeded to take off her clothes like she would to take a shower or make love. Underneath her jeans and T-shirt she had on a bikini. As I was taking this all in, it occurred to me that her bikini was much more revealing than if she had taken her clothes off and exhibited a bra and panties. Yet had she done the latter, she would have been deemed a deviant and been subject to arrest by campus police for indecent exposure. . . . Here a woman exposed more of her body in a bikini than would have been the case with a bra and panties. Nonetheless, her behavior was in keeping with that of the other sunbathers and was defined as acceptable. Clearly, norms are evolved by humans and exhibit all the vagaries of the human experience, at times reaching ridiculous levels.

the defining and who has the power to make the definitions stick. Within recent years, many behaviors in the United States traditionally judged to be deviant are undergoing redefinition. Not too long ago compulsive gambling, alcoholism, drug addiction, and even many forms of mental illness were defined as evil and sinful. While such notions still persist, the view has increasingly gained currency that these behaviors are medical problems. The "disorders" are considered "illnesses" analogous to physical ailments like ulcers, diabetes, and high blood pressure. Their sufferers are placed in "hospitals" where they are called "patients" and given "treatment" by "physicians."

Simultaneously, some groups such as homosexuals, lesbians, the handicapped, and welfare mothers have entered the political arena and successfully challenged official definitions that portray them as "social problems." Indeed, individuals stigmatized and victimized by prevailing social definitions see their circumstances quite differently from those who enjoy power and enforce norms that embody their moral codes. We need only remind ourselves that not too long ago in colonial times the political and religious "establishment" of Salem, Massachusetts, was preoccupied with witches and actively hunted them down. Some 200,000 to 500,000 people (85 percent of them women) were executed as witches in Eu-

Labeling theorists contend that individuals tagged as "criminals" by society take on societal definitions of themselves. Those who are imprisoned find themselves in "total institutions" where their behavior is closely regimented. The inmates are exposed to jarring resocialization experiences that strip away their old roles and identities and impose new ones. They are rendered vulnerable to prison control by being deprived of their personal clothing and accessories and given haircuts, uniforms, and standardized articles that establish their identity as "convicts." Here, new convicts change into their prison uniforms at Sing Sing in the nineteenth century. (The Bettmann Archive)

rope between the fourteenth and seventeenth centuries (Ben-Yehuda, 1980).

A Zone of Permissible Variation. In our daily lives we typically find that norms are not so much a point or a line as a zone (Williams, 1970). Even rather specific and strongly supported norms allow a zone of permissible variation. In actual practice, norms provide for bands of permissible behavior that may nonetheless depart from the strict letter of the law. For instance, professors are expected to conduct their classes with dignity and decorum. Yet one professor at a large midwestern university is known to stand on his desk or sit on a desk lectern in the course of the class period. Clearly, American culture does not define desks as appropriate for standing on or lecterns for sitting on. It is not surprising, therefore, that most students snicker and giggle when the professor steps up on the desk for his first lecture. And more than one student has wondered aloud what kind of "weirdo" is teaching the course. However, since the professor communicates well and is a recognized authority in his field, the vast majority of students are quickly won over to his antics. In their course evaluations, the students usually comment that they were initially dismayed by the professor's informality, but soon discovered that this style was an effective teaching technique. Hence a norm usually allows for *variant* behavior, new or at least different behavior that falls within the borders of the acceptable (Merton, 1959).

In sum, no behavior is deviant in itself; deviance is a matter of social definition. The same behavior may be viewed as deviant by one group but not by another. Further, much depends on the social context in which the behavior occurs. For instance, public drunkenness is frowned on in American life, yet it may be expected behavior at a New Year's Eve party. And the same behavior may be a source of social stigmatizing in one historical period but not in another. Premarital sexual relations and divorce—sources of considerable disapproval a generation or so ago—are now for the most part accepted behaviors.

SOCIAL CONTROL AND DEVIANCE

Our discussion so far has shown that if the work of the world is to get done, people must follow rules. Social order dictates that people have to be kept in line, at least most people, and the line must be adhered to within allowable limits (Sagarin, 1975). Without social order, interaction would be a real problem and expectations would be meaningless. Societies seek to ensure that their members conform with basic norms by means of **social control**, the methods and strategies that regulate behavior within society.

Functionalist and conflict theorists differ in how they view social control. As we will see in Chapter 8, functionalists see social control, particularly as it finds expression in the activities of the state, as an indispensable requirement for survival. If large numbers of people were to defy their society's standards for behavior, massive institutional breakdown and malfunctioning would result. Functionalists therefore see chaos as the alternative to effective social control. In contrast, as we will discuss at greater length in the chapter, conflict theorists contend that social control operates to favor powerful groups and to disadvantage others. They stress that no social arrangements are neutral, and these theorists see their task as disentangling and identifying the ways in which institutional structures distribute the benefits and burdens of social life unevenly, while maintaining these structures through the techniques and instruments of social control.

There are three main types of social control processes operating in social life: (1) those that lead us to internalize our society's normative expectations; (2) those that structure our world of social experience; and (3) those that employ various formal and informal social sanctions. Let us briefly consider each of these processes.

As we saw in Chapter 3, the members of a society undergo continuous socialization, a process by which individuals acquire those ways of thinking, feeling, and acting characteristic of their society's culture. For infants and young children, conformity to the expectations of others is primarily a product of external controls. As they grow older, an increasing proportion of their behavior becomes governed by *internal* monitors. These internal monitors carry on many of the functions earlier performed by external controls. In brief, **internalization** occurs: Individuals incorporate within their personalities the standards of behavior prevalent within the larger society. Such standards are often accepted without thought or questioning—indeed, we commonly experience them as "second nature." As we immerse ourselves in the life of a group, we develop self-conceptions that regulate our conduct in accordance with the norms of the group. By doing what group members do, we acquire our identities and a sense of well-being. The group is *our* group, and its norms are *our* norms. Social control thus becomes *self-control*.

Our society's institutions also shape our experiences. In large part, we unconsciously build up our sense of reality by the way our society orders its social agendas and structures social alternatives. To the extent that we are locked within the social environment provided by our culture, we inhabit a somewhat restricted world. By virtue of the biases in such arrangements, it usually does not occur to us that alternative standards exist. In this sense, we are *culture bound*. Nonconformist patterns do not come

to our minds because the alternatives are not known to our society.

Finally, we conform to the norms of our society because we realize that to do otherwise is to incur punishment. Those who break rules are met with dislike, hostility, gossip, and ostracism—even imprisonment and death—while the conformist wins praise, popularity, prestige, and other socially defined good things. It does not take us long to appreciate that there are disadvantages to nonconformity and advantages to conformity. Many of the events surrounding the Watergate scandal that compelled Richard Nixon to resign the presidency can be understood in terms of such conformity pressures. Herbert Porter of the Committee to Re-Elect the President (the 1972 Nixon campaign organization) observed during the Senate Watergate hearings in 1973 that he had not spoken up against his bosses' wrongdoings "because of the fear of [the] group pressure that would ensue, of not being [judged] a team player." He said that loyalty to the president and his team had taken precedence over loyalty to principles and to country.

THE SOCIAL EFFECTS OF DEVIANCE

Not all behavior has a purpose or a use. And the same is doubtless true for many instances of deviance. Indeed, most of us think of deviance as "bad"—as behavior that poses a "social problem." Such a view is not surprising given the negative or disruptive consequences of much deviance, or what sociologists call *dysfunctions* (see Chapter 2). But deviance also has positive or integrative consequences for social life, what sociologists call *functions*. Sociologists like Lewis A. Coser (1962), Albert K. Cohen (1966), and Edward Sagarin (1975) have contributed much to our understanding in this area.

Dysfunctions of Deviance. Apparently most societies can absorb a good deal of deviance without serious consequences, but persistent and widespread deviance can impair and even undermine organized social life. Social organization derives from the coordinated actions of numerous people. Should some individuals fail to perform their actions at the proper time in accordance with accepted expectations, institutional life may be jeopardized. For instance, when a parent deserts a family, it commonly complicates the task of child care and rearing. And when in the midst of battle a squad of soldiers fails to obey orders and runs away, an entire army may be overwhelmed and defeated.

Deviance also undermines our willingness to play our roles and contribute to the larger social enterprise. If some individuals get rewards, even disproportionate rewards, without playing by the rules—for instance, "idlers," "fakers," "chiselers," "sneaks," and "deadbeats"—we develop resentment and bitterness. Morale, self-discipline, and loyalty suffer. Consider what your reaction would be if you knew that a good number of students in a particularly difficult course were getting the top grades by cheating on examinations. Your motivation to struggle with the material and to study long hours would undoubtedly be undermined.

Moreover, social life dictates that by and large we *trust* one another. We must have confidence that others will play by the rules. In committing ourselves to the collective enterprise, we allocate some resources, forego some alternatives, and make some investment in the future. We do so because we assume that other people will do the same. But should others not reciprocate our trust—should they betray it—we feel that our own efforts are pointless, wasted, and foolish. We too often become less willing to play by the rules.

The Functions of Deviance. Although deviance may undermine social organization, it may also facilitate social functioning in a number of ways. First, it may promote conformity. Sociologist Edward Sagarin (1975:14) observes:

One of the most effective methods of keeping most people in line is to throw some people out of line. This leaves the remainder not only in better alignment but at the same time in fear of exclusion. . . . By reacting in a hostile manner to those who are not the good and the proper, a majority of the people or a powerful group may reinforce the idea of goodness and propriety and thus perpetuate a society of individuals who are conforming, more obedient, and more loyal to their ideology and rules of behavior.

Second, many norms are not expressed as firm rules or in official codes (see Chapter 2). Accordingly, as spelled out by Emile Durkheim (1893/1964), each time the members of a group censure some act as deviance, they highlight and sharpen the contours of a norm. Their negative reactions clarify precisely what behavior is disallowed by the "collective conscience." Sociologist Kai T. Erikson (1962) notes that one of the interesting features of agencies of control is the amount of publicity they usually attract. In earlier times, the punishment of offenders took place in the public market in full view of a crowd. Today we achieve much the same result through heavy media coverage of criminal trials and executions:

Why are these reports considered "newsworthy" and why do they rate the extraordinary attention they receive? Perhaps they satisfy a number of psychological perversities among the mass audience, as many commentators have suggested, but at the same time they constitute our main source of information about the normative outlines of society. They are lessons through which we teach one another what the norms mean and how far they extend. In a figurative sense, at least, morality and immorality meet at the public scaffold and it is during this meeting that the community declares where the line between them should be drawn. . . . [The trespasser] informs us, as it were, what evil looks like, what shapes the devil can assume. In doing so, he shows us the difference between kinds of experience which belong within the group and kinds of experience which belong outside it. (Erikson, 1962:310)

Third, by directing attention to the deviant, a group may strengthen itself. A shared enemy arouses common sentiments and cements feelings of solidarity. The emotions surrounding "ain't it awful" deeds quicken passions and solidify "our kind of people" ties. As we saw in Chapter 4, frictions and antagonisms between in-groups and out-groups highlight group boundaries and memberships. In the same way, campaigns against witches, traitors, perverts, and criminals reinforce social cohesion among "the good people." For instance, Erikson (1966) has shown that when the Puritan colonists thought their way of life was threatened, they created "crime waves" and "witchcraft hysterias" to define and redefine the boundaries of their community.

Fourth, deviance is a catalyst for change. Every time a rule is violated, it is being contested. Such challenges serve as a warning that the social system is not functioning properly. For instance, high robbery rates are not likely to suggest to a political elite that robbery should be legalized and the wealth of the society redistributed. But they do loudly proclaim that there are large numbers of disaffected people, that institutions for socializing youth are faltering, that power relations are being questioned, and that the moral structures of the society require reexamination. Thus deviance is often

a vehicle for placing on a society's agenda the need for social repair and remedies. By the same token, the deviant way offers an alternative to existing ways. It is simultaneously a call for an examination of old norms and a new model (Sagarin, 1975). For instance, the Rev. Martin Luther King, Jr., and his supporters called the nation's attention to the undemocratic nature of southern segregation laws by disobeying them en masse. In due course, the civil rights movements led to these laws being changed.

Sociological Perspectives on Deviance

Deviance may have both positive and negative consequences for the functioning and survival of groups and societies. But why, we may ask, do people violate social rules? Why are some acts defined as deviance? Why are some individuals labeled deviants when they engage in essentially the same behaviors as other individuals who escape retribution and who may even enjoy acclaim? And why does the incidence of deviance vary from group to group and society to society? It is these types of questions that interest sociologists.

Other disciplines are also concerned with deviance, particularly biology and psychology. But they typically ask somewhat different questions, and they make somewhat different contributions to our knowledge. Whereas sociologists focus on social factors that generate deviance, biologists and psychologists typically look at the deviant actors and ask what is "wrong"—or at least different—about them. They seek to explain rule breaking in terms of the individuals themselves and their unique characteristics.

Here we will focus primarily on the questions posed by sociologists. Our doing so is not meant to ignore or disparage the insights of other disciplines. Take *schizophrenia*. Both biology and psychology have contributed a good deal to our understanding of the disorder—a severe form of mental illness characterized by such symptoms as hallucinations, disordered and illogical thinking, inappropriate emotional responses, personality deterioration, bizarre behavior, and gradual withdrawal from reality (American Psychiatric Association, 1980). The National Institute of Mental Health (1980) estimates that about 2 million Americans—about 1 percent of the population—can be classified as schizophrenics. Individuals diagnosed as schizophrenics account for an estimated 50 percent of the resident patients in mental hospitals.

Biologists and psychologists have shown that hereditary factors predispose individuals to some forms of schizophrenia. The hereditary component seems to derive from genes that code for proteins regulating brain activity, particularly neurotransmitters (chemicals released by nerve cells that determine the rate at which other nerve cells fire). Family, adoption, and twin studies reveal that relatives of schizophrenics are more likely to be at risk for the disorder than are other people. For example, studies of identical twins show if one twin suffers from schizophrenia, the chances are 60 percent that the other twin will also be affected. The likelihood of this happening in nontwin siblings is less than 15 percent (Kendler, 1983). Additionally, children who are removed from schizophrenic mothers at birth and adopted by normal parents are more likely to develop schizophrenia than children taken from normal mothers. But even though chemical factors may underlie schizophrenia, environmental factors are also at work. In about 40 percent of the cases in which an identical twin has been diagnosed as schizophrenic, the other twin is not schizophrenic.

Psychologists point out that mental disturbance and breakdown in behavior result from both a vulnerability of the person and environmental stresses. Some people are genetically so vulnerable that it is very difficult to provide them with an environment sufficiently low in stress to prevent schizophrenic episodes. There are also people so resistant to stress that few environments would produce breakdown. For example, some political prisoners, despite being placed in solitary confinement for years and enduring periodic torture, manage to retain their sanity. Psychologists say that most people fall somewhere between these extremes in vulnerability. Thus people differ in their risk for developing psychological disorders (Zubin and Spring, 1977).

Yet an understanding of the biological and psychological factors involved in schizophrenia does not provide us with the full story. We need to take into account sociological factors as well. Consider the following example. A man living in the Ozark Mountains has a vision in which God speaks to him. He begins preaching to his relatives and neighbors, and soon he has his entire community in a state of religious fervor. People say he has a "calling." His reputation as a prophet and healer spreads, and he attracts large audiences in the rural communities of Arkansas and Missouri. However, when he ventures into St. Louis and attempts to hold a prayer meeting—blocking traffic at a downtown thoroughfare during rush hour—he is arrested. The man tells the police officers about his conversations with God, and they take him to a mental hospital. Attending psychiatrists say he is "schizophrenic" and hospitalize him for mental illness (Slotkin, 1955). Thus we return full circle to sociological concerns. Again we are reminded that deviance is not a property inherent in behavior, but a property conferred upon it by social definitions. Let us turn, then, to a consideration of four sociological approaches to deviance: the anomie, cultural transmission, conflict, and labeling perspectives.

THE ANOMIE PERSPECTIVE

As we noted earlier in the chapter, Emile Durkheim (1893/1964, 1897/1951) contended that deviance is functional for a society. He said that deviance and the punishment of the deviant reinforce the boundaries of acceptable behavior and serve as occasions on which people reaffirm their commitment to the society's moral order. Durkheim also made another contribution to our understanding of deviance with his idea of **anomie**—a social condition in which people find it difficult to guide their behavior by norms that they experience as weak, unclear, or conflicting. He pointed out that during times of rapid social change, people become unsure of what is expected of them, and find it difficult to fashion their actions in terms of conventional norms. "Old norms" do not seem relevant, and emerging norms are still too ambiguous and poorly formulated to provide effective and meaningful guidelines for behavior. Under these circumstances, Durkheim believed that an upsurge in deviant behavior could be expected.

Robert K. Merton and Anomie Theory. Sociologists Robert K. Merton (1968) has built on Durkheim's notions of anomie and social cohesion and linked them to American life. He says that for large numbers of Americans, worldly success—especially as it finds expression in material wealth—has become a cultural *goal*. However, only certain cultural *means*—most commonly securing a good education and acquiring high-paying jobs—are approved for achieving success. There might not be a problem if all Americans had equal access to the approved means for realizing monetary success. But this is not the case. The poor and minorities often find themselves handicapped by little formal education and few economic resources.

For those Americans who internalize the goal of material success—and not all individuals do—strong strains push people toward nonconformity and the use of unorthodox practices. They cannot achieve the culturally approved goals by using the culturally approved means for attaining them. One answer to this dilemma is to obtain the prestige-laden ends by any means whatsoever, including vice and crime. Contemporary professional criminals, members of organized crime, and drug dealers find much in common with Al Capone, the notorious bootlegger and mobster of the 1920s and early 1930s, who contended:

I make my money by supplying a public demand. If I break the law, my customers . . . are as guilty as I am. The only difference between us is that I sell and they buy. Everybody calls me a racketeer. I call myself a businessman. (Quoted in Klein, 1980b:1)

But Merton emphasizes that a "lack of opportunity" and an exaggerated material emphasis are not enough to produce strains toward deviance. A society with a comparatively rigid class or caste structure may lack opportunity and simultaneously extol wealth—the medieval feudal system being a case in point. It is only when a society extols *common* symbols of success for the *entire* population while structurally restricting the access of large numbers of people to the approved means for acquiring these symbols that antisocial behavior is generated.

Merton identifies five responses to the ends–means dilemma, four of them deviant adaptations to conditions of anomie (see Figure 5.1):

Conformity. Conformity exists when people accept both the cultural goal of material success and the culturally approved means to achieve the goal. Such behavior is the bedrock of a stable society.

Innovation. In innovation, individuals hold fast to the culturally emphasized goals of success while abandoning the culturally approved ways of seeking them. Such people may engage in prostitution, peddle drugs, forge checks, swindle, embezzle, steal, burglarize, rob, or extort to secure money and purchase the symbols of success.

Ritualism. Ritualism involves the abandoning or scaling down of lofty success goals while abiding compulsively by the approved means. For instance, the ends of the organization become irrelevant for many zealous bureaucrats. Instead, they cultivate the means for their own sake, making a fetish of regulations and red tape (see Chapter 4).

Retreatism. In retreatism individuals reject *both* the cultural goals and the approved means without substituting new norms. For example, skid row alcoholics, drug addicts, vagabonds, and derelicts have dropped out of society; they ''are in society but not of it.''

Rebellion. Rebels reject both the cultural goals and the approved means and substitute *new* norms for them. Such individuals withdraw their allegiance from existing social arrangements and transfer their loyalties to new groups with new ideologies. Radical social movements are a good illustration of this type of adaptation.

Merton's modes of individual adaptation deal with role behavior—not personality types. People may shift from one mode to another.

Applying Anomie Theory. A number of sociologists have applied anomie theory to the study of juvenile delinquency. Albert Cohen (1955) suggests that lower-class boys are attracted to gangs because they are constantly being judged by a middle-class measuring

FIGURE 5.1

Merton's typology of modes of individual adaptation to anomie. (Source: Reprinted with permission of The Free Press, from Social Theory and Social Structure, *rev. ed., by Robert K. Merton. Copyright 1949, 1957 by the Free Press.)*

Modes of adaptation	Cultural goals	Institutionalized means
I Conformity	+	+
II Innovation	+	−
III Ritualism	−	+
IV Retreatism	−	−
V Rebellion	±	±

+ = Acceptance

− = Rejection

± = Rejection of prevailing values and substitution of new values rod. They find themselves failing in middle-class school environments that reward verbal skills, neatness, and an ability to defer gratification. The boys respond by banding together in juvenile gangs where they evolve "macho" standards rewarding "toughness," "street smarts," and "trouble-making"—standards that allow them to succeed. Indeed, Delbert S. Elliott (1966) finds that delinquent boys who drop out of school have a lower rate of juvenile court referrals after dropping out of school than when in school. Leaving school presumably provides a temporary solution to the frustrations they experience in meeting middle-class educational expectations.

Evaluating Anomie Theory. Merton's theory of anomie draws our attention to those processes by which society generates deviance through the way it structures its culturally approved goals and means. In particular it tells us a good deal about monetary crime. His work sheds light on why there are crimes of profit and greed, white-collar and corporate crime, crimes of warmakers, and crimes of people in power and those searching for power (Sagarin, 1975).

However, critics point out that Merton overlooks the processes of social interaction by which people shape their definitions of the world about them and fashion their actions (Cohen, 1965). Merton portrays deviants as atomistic and individualistic beings—people more or less in a box by themselves, working out solutions to stressful circumstances without regard to what other people are doing. Moreover, not all deviance stems from gaps between goals and means. Merton provides an image of American society in which there is a consensus on values and goals. But critics say that American society is pluralistic, with a good many subcultures (see Chapter 2). Numerous examples exist in American life of "deviant" behavior that can be explained as

a failure to accept the same norms as are prevalent in most of the population: violations of fish and game laws among Indians; common law marriage among some ethnic minorities; cockfighting among some groups with southern rural backgrounds; the producing of "moonshine" liquor among some Appalachian groups; and marijuana use among teenagers.

THE CULTURAL TRANSMISSION PERSPECTIVE

Anomie theory provides us with insight on how society may unwittingly contribute to deviance by the way it structures its goals and opportunities. A number of other sociologists have emphasized the similarities between the way deviant behavior is acquired and the way in which other behavior is acquired. One of the first was French sociologist Gabriel Tarde (1843–1904), who in the late nineteenth century formulated a theory of imitation to explain deviance. Having spent a great part of his life as a provincial magistrate and later as director of criminal statistics for the French Ministry of Justice, Tarde was impressed by the significant part that repetition plays in human behavior. He contended that criminals, like "good" people, imitate the ways of individuals they have met, known or heard about. But in contrast to law-abiding people, they imitate other criminals.

A number of decades later, during the 1920s and 1930s, sociologists at the University of Chicago were struck by the concentration of high delinquency rates in some areas of Chicago (Thrasher, 1927; Shaw, 1930; Shaw and McKay, 1942). They undertook a series of investigations and found that in certain neighborhoods delinquency rates were stable from one period to another despite changes in ethnic composition. They concluded that delinquent and criminal behavior are culturally transmitted from

Sociologist Robert K. Merton contends that youth gangs—like the Young Lords of New York City, members of which are shown here—are a response to social conditions of anomie. American society socializes its members to pursue financial gain, yet many Americans do not have access to the socially approved means for doing so. Lower-class and minority-group members often find themselves handicapped by little formal education and few economic resources. Merton says that these circumstances invite individuals to use forbidden but nevertheless effective means for accumulating wealth. (Charles Gatewood/The Image Works)

one generation to the next. From this viewpoint, it is "natural" that youths living in high-crime areas should acquire delinquent life styles. Moreover, as new ethnic groups enter a neighborhood, their children learn the delinquent patterns from the youth already there. Hence, the Chicago sociologists contended that youths become delinquent because they associate and make friends with other juveniles who are already delinquent.

Edwin H. Sutherland and Differential Association. Edwin H. Sutherland (1939), a sociologist who was associated with the Chicago tradition of sociology, elaborated on these conclusions in developing his theory of **differential association.** This theory builds on the interactionist perspective and emphasizes the part social interaction plays in molding people's attitudes and behavior. Sutherland said that individuals become deviant to the extent to which they participate in settings where deviant ideas, motivations, and techniques are viewed favorably. For example, they may learn how to use and obtain illegal drugs, how to enjoy and go about making homosexual contacts, or how to steal and then sell stolen items. The earlier, the more frequently, the more intensely, and the longer the duration of the contacts people have in such settings, the greater the probability that they too will become deviant. But more is involved than simply imitation. Deviant behavior is not only learned; it is taught. The theory thus focuses on *what* is learned and *who* it is learned from.

The differential association theory provides a sophisticated version of the old adage that "good companions make good boys; bad companions make bad boys." When parents move to a new neighborhood to "get Mike away from his hoodlum friends," they are applying the principle of differential association. So are parole officers who try to restrict the associations of the paroled prisoners they supervise. By the same token, the theory suggests that imprisonment may be counterproductive when juveniles are incarcerated with experienced criminals.

Applying Cultural Transmission Theory. In pluralistic societies with multiple subcultures, groups differ in some of their values and expectations for behavior. Sociologist Walter B. Miller (1958, 1975) builds on this notion in his study of unlawful activity among lower-class juveniles. He sees their behavior as conformity to cultural patterns acquired through socialization in ghetto and inner-city settings. Lower-class culture, he says, attaches high value to a number of "focal concerns": *Trouble*—welcoming "encounters" with police officers, school officials, welfare investigators, and other agents of the larger society; *toughness*—showing skills in physical combat and an ability to "take it"; *smartness*—being able to outwit, dupe, and outsmart others; *excitement*—seeking thrills, taking risks, and flirting with danger; *fate*—assuming that most of life's crucial events are beyond one's control and governed by chance and destiny; and *autonomy*—desiring to be free of external controls and coercive authority. Although these concerns are not inherently or

necessarily delinquent, their pursuit creates situations in which unlawful activity is likely to emerge. For instance, an emphasis on toughness leads to verbal insult and physical attack, and the craving for excitement promotes auto theft.

Evaluating Cultural Transmission Theory. Cultural transmission theory shows that socially disapproved behaviors can arise through the same processes of socialization as socially approved ones. It is a particularly useful tool for understanding why deviance varies from group to group and from society to society. However, the theory is not applicable to some forms of deviance, particularly those in which neither the techniques nor the appropriate definitions and attitudes are acquired from other deviants. Illustrations include criminal violators of financial trust; naive check forgers; occasional, incidental, and situational offenders; nonprofessional shoplifters; non-career-type criminals; and people who commit "crimes of passion." Further, deviants and nondeviants are often reared in the same environments—criminal behavior patterns are presented to two persons, but only one becomes a criminal. The individuals may be confronted with the same patterns but perceive them quite differently, producing different outcomes.

THE CONFLICT PERSPECTIVE

Cultural transmission theorists emphasize that individuals who are immersed in different subcultures will exhibit somewhat different behaviors because they are socialized in different traditions. To this formulation conflict theorists respond, "True, groups have differing values and norms. But the question is 'Which group will be able to translate its values into the rules of a society and make these rules stick?' Moreover, the institutional order generates clashing interests among major groups—classes, sexes, racial and ethnic groups, business organizations, labor unions, and farm associations. Accordingly, we need also ask, 'Who reaps the lion's share of benefits from particular social arrangements?' Or, put another way, 'How is society structured so that some groups are advantaged while other groups are disadvantaged and even stigmatized as deviant?' "

Although in recent decades the conflict approach has taken many new directions, its early roots can be traced to the Marxist tradition (see Chapter 1). According to orthodox Marxism, a capitalist ruling class exploits and robs the masses, yet avoids punishment for its crimes. Individuals victimized by capitalist oppression are driven to commit acts in their struggle to survive that the ruling class brands as criminal (Bonger, 1936). Other types of deviance—alcoholism, drug abuse, family violence, sexual immorality, and prostitution—are products of the moral degeneration fostered by a social milieu founded on the unprincipled pursuit of profit and the subjugation of the poor, women, blacks, and other minorities. Mental and emotional problems also abound because people become estranged from one another and from themselves. Such estrangement resides in the separation of people from the means whereby they derive their livelihood—from the basis of their existence (see Chapter 8).

Richard Quinney: Class, State, and Crime.
The contemporary Marxist approach to deviance is articulated by sociologist Richard Quinney (1974, 1980). Quinney says that the American legal system reflects the interests and ideologies of the ruling capitalist class. Law makes illegal behavior that is offensive to the morality of the powerful and that threatens their privileges and property:

Law is the tool of the ruling class. Criminal

law, in particular, is a device made and used by the ruling class to preserve the existing order. In the United States, the state—and its legal system—exist to secure and perpetuate the capitalist interests of the ruling class. (1974:8)

Quinney (1980:39) contends that if we are "to understand crime we have to understand the development of the political economy of capitalist society." Since the state serves the interests of the capitalist class, crime is ultimately a class-based political act embedded in capitalist social arrangements.

In striving to maintain itself against the internal contradictions eating away at its foundations, Quinney (1980:57) says that capitalism commits *crimes of domination.* Indeed, "one of the contradictions of capitalism is that some of its laws must be violated in order to secure the existing system." These crimes include those committed by corporations and range from price fixing to pollution of the environment. But there are also *crimes of government* committed by the officials of the capitalist state, Watergate being the most recent publicized instance. In contrast, much of the criminal behavior of ordinary people, or *predatory crime*—burglary, robbery, drug dealing, and hustling of various sorts—is "pursued out of the need to survive" in a capitalist social order. *Personal crime*—murder, assault, and rape—is "pursued by those who are already brutalized by the conditions of capitalism." And then there are *crimes of resistance,* in which workers engage in sloppy work and clandestine acts of sabotage against employers.

In sum, crime is endemic to capitalism: "When a society generates social problems it cannot solve within its own existence, policies for controlling the population are devised and implemented. Crime and criminal justice are thus integral to the larger issues of the historical development of capitalism. . . ." (Quinney, 1980:viii).

Applying Conflict Theory. Conflict theory has led social scientists to investigate the ways in which the making and administration of law is biased by powerful interests. Numerous sociologists have noted that crime is defined primarily in terms of offenses against property (burglary, robbery, auto theft, and vandalism), whereas corporate crime is deemphasized (Sutherland, 1949; Michalowski and Bohlander, 1976). Moreover, the penalty for crimes against property is imprisonment, whereas the most common form of penalty for business-related offenses is a monetary fine. Sociologists Marshall B. Clinard and Peter C. Yeager (1980) found that more than 60 percent of the nation's largest firms had been involved in one or more offenses in 1975 or 1976. Yet unlike robbers and muggers, corporations and their executives got off easy. For example, after an explosive liquid that was released into the sewers of Louisville by the Ralston Purina Company blew up in 1981, causing more than $10 million in damages, the company was fined only $62,500 for violating federal clean water laws (Kelly, 1982). And while the Federal Bureau of Investigation keeps track of every murder, rape, assault, and auto theft reported in the United States, no agency keeps a record of crimes committed by corporations themselves.

Evaluating Conflict Theory. There is a good deal of truth in conflict theory. Indeed, it is obvious to most people that powerful individuals and groups make and administer the laws. In this sense, then, laws are not neutral, but favor some group's interests and embody some group's values. Yet critics charge that such intuitive insights hardly satisfy the requirements of scientific inquiry (Hagan and Leon, 1977). For example, sociologist Stanton Wheeler (1976:527) says that while the emergence of conflict theory and the rediscovery of Marx has given new

direction to our understanding of deviance, "it is my strong impression that the achievements have been more rhetorical than anything else."

Many conflict formulations need to be refined. For example, it is not always clear which specific individuals or groups are covered by such terms as "ruling elites," "governing classes," and "powerful interests." And conflict hypotheses need to be tested. For instance, William J. Chambliss and Robert Seidman (1971:475) assert: "When sanctions are imposed, the most severe sanctions will be imposed on persons in the lowest social class." Yet research results are inconsistent. Some studies find few (Bernstein, Kelly, and Doyle, 1977) or no (Chiricos and Waldo 1975) links between the status characteristics of criminal offenders and the sentences received; other studies find the relationship to be substantial (Lizotte, 1978); and still others find that the relationship depends on specific circumstances (Hagan, Bernstein, and Albonetti, 1980). And although corporations often seek to influence legislation and public policy, they do not necessarily predominate over other interest groups (Hagan, 1980). Clearly, additional research is called for. Conflict propositions can not be accepted as articles of faith, but require rigorous scientific investigation.

THE LABELING PERSPECTIVE

Conflict theorists contend that people often find themselves at odds with one another because their interests diverge and their values clash. Some people gain the power and ascendancy to translate their value and normative preferences into the rules governing institutional life. They then successfully place negative labels on violators of these rules. A number of sociologists have taken this notion and expanded on it. They are interested in the process by which some individuals come to be tagged as "deviants," begin to think of themselves as deviants, and enter on deviant careers.

Edwin Lemert, Howard S. Becker, and Kai T. Erikson: The Societal Reaction to Deviance Approach.

Proponents of the labeling perspective—sociologists like Edwin M. Lemert (1951, 1972), Howard S. Becker (1963), and Kai T. Erikson (1962, 1966)—make a number of points. First, they contend that no act by itself is inherently criminal or noncriminal. The "badness" of an act does not stem from its intrinsic content, but from the way other people define and react to it. Deviance is always a matter of social definition.

Second, labeling theorists point out that we all engage in deviant behavior by violating some norms. They reject the popular idea that human beings can be divided into those who are normal and those who are pathological. For instance, some of us exceed the speed limit, experiment with cocaine, shoplift, cheat on a homework assignment, sample homosexual publications, underreport our income to income tax authorities, swim in the nude, become intoxicated, commit vandalism in celebration of a football victory, trespass on private property, or "joy ride" in a friend's car without permission. Labeling theorists call these actions **primary deviance**—behavior that violates social norms but usually goes unnoticed by the agents of social control.

Third, labeling theorists say that whether people's acts will be seen as deviant depends both on what they do *and* on what other people do about it. In short, deviance depends on which rules society chooses to enforce, in which situations, and with respect to which people. Not all individuals are arrested for speeding, shoplifting, underreporting income on their tax returns, trespassing, or the like. Blacks may be censured for doing what whites are "allowed" to do; women censured for doing what men are "allowed" to do; certain individuals censured for doing what their friends are also doing; and some may be labeled as deviants even though they have not violated a norm, but simply because they are so accused (for instance, they appear "effeminate" and are tagged as "gay"). Of critical importance is the social audience and whether or not it *labels* the person a deviant.

Fourth, labeling people as deviants has consequences for them. It tends to set up conditions conducive to **secondary deviance**—deviance individuals adopt in response to the reactions of other individuals. In brief, labeling theorists contend that new deviance is *manufactured* by the hostile reactions of rule makers and rule abiders. An individual is publicly identified, stereotyped, and denounced as a "delinquent," "mental fruitcake," "forger," "rapist," "drug addict," "bum " "pervert," or "criminal." The label serves to lock the individual into an outsider status. Such a master status overrides other statuses in shaping a person's social experiences and results in a self-fulfilling prophecy. Rule breakers come to accept their status as a particular kind of deviant and organize their lives around this master status.

Fifth, people labeled deviant typically find themselves rejected and isolated by "law-abiding" people. Friends and relatives may withdraw from them. In some cases, they may even be institutionalized in prisons or mental hospitals. Rejection and isolation push stigmatized individuals toward a deviant group with other individuals who share a common fate. Participation in a deviant subculture becomes a way of coping with frustrating situations and for finding emotional support and personal acceptance. In turn, joining a deviant group solidifies a deviant self-image, fosters a deviant life style, and weakens ties to the law-abiding community.

In sum, labeling theorists say that it is

the societal response to an act and not the behavior itself that determines deviance. When the behavior of people is seen as departing from prevailing norms, it "sets off a chain of social reactions." Other individuals define, evaluate, and label the behavior. Norm violators then take these labels into account as they shape their actions. In many cases, they evolve an identity consistent with a label and enter on a career of deviance.

Applying Labeling Theory. Sociologist William J. Chambliss (1973) employed labeling theory to explain the differing perceptions and definitions that community members had of the behavior of two teenage gangs. At Hanibal High School, Chambliss observed the activities of the Saints, a gang of eight white upper-class boys, and the Roughnecks, a gang of six lower-class white boys. Although the Saints engaged in as many delinquent acts as the Roughnecks, it was the Roughnecks who were in "constant trouble" and universally considered to be "delinquent."

The Saints enjoyed an image as "good students" headed for college. Yet they were often truant from school and spent their weekends drinking, driving recklessly at high speeds, deliberately running red lights, shouting obscenities at women, vandalizing empty houses, removing warning signs from road repair sites, and erecting stolen barricades on highways where unsuspecting motorists would crash into them. But the Hanibal townspeople overlooked the Saints' high level of delinquency. They saw the Saints as law-abiding youths who simply went in for an occasional prank—"good boys sowing wild oats." After all, they were well-dressed, displayed middle-class manners, and drove nice cars.

But it was otherwise for the Roughnecks. Everyone agreed that "the not-so-well-dressed, not-so-well mannered, not-so-rich boys were heading for trouble." Their brawling and petty stealing were known throughout the community. Moreover, a high level of mutual distrust and hostility existed between the Roughnecks and the police. Several of the Roughnecks were arrested a number of times, and two of the boys were sentenced to six months in reform school. In sum, the community, the school, and the police related to the Saints as though they were good, upstanding youths with bright futures, but they treated the Roughnecks as young punks headed for trouble.

A number of factors contributed to the differential treatment given the two groups. For one thing, the Saints had access to automobiles and engaged in out-of-town escapades that were less visible to Hanibal citizens than those undertaken by the Roughnecks in the center of town. For another, if the Saints were confronted with an accusing police officer, they were apologetic and penitent, whereas the Roughnecks were hostile and belligerent. And finally, police officers knew that irate and influential upper-middle-class parents would come to the aid of their youngsters, whereas powerless lower-class parents would have to acquiesce in the law's definition of their sons' behavior.

Chambliss (1973:30–31) concludes:

The community responded to the Roughnecks as boys in trouble, and the boys agreed with that perception. Their pattern of deviancy was reinforced, and breaking away from it became increasingly unlikely. Once the boys acquired an image of themselves as deviants, they selected new friends who affirmed that self-image. As that self-conception became more firmly entrenched, they also became willing to try new and more extreme deviances. With their growing alienation came freer expression of disrespect and hostility for representatives of the legitimate society. This disrespect increased the community's negativism, perpetuating the entire process of commitment to deviance.

Evaluating the Labeling Perspective. Unlike anomie and cultural transmission theory, the labeling perspective does not focus on why some individuals engage in deviant behavior. Rather, labeling theory helps us to understand why the same act may or may not be considered deviant, depending on the situation and the characteristics of the individuals who are involved. In recent years, a number of labeling theorists have incorporated insights from conflict theory into their formulations. They have looked to societal inequalities to see how institutions are structured and how rules are made and enforced.

But labeling theory also has its critics. For one thing, while labeling may help us understand how individuals become career deviants, it tells us little about what initially contributed to their deviant behavior. Indeed, in many forms of deviance it is the behavior or condition of the people themselves that is primarily responsible for their being labeled in the first place. Take mental illness. It seems that a vast majority of people who are hospitalized suffer acute disturbance associated with *internal* psychological or neurological malfunctioning (Gove, 1970). Their inner turmoil and suffering cannot be explained solely in terms of the reactions of other people.

Likewise, deviance cannot be understood without reference to norms. If behavior is not deviant unless it is labeled, how are we to classify secret and undetected deviance, such as the embezzlement of funds, the failure to pay income taxes, and the clandestine sexual molestation of children? Moreover, many criminals pursue their deviant careers because they believe that crime *pays*. One study finds that about one-third of crimes against property are at least partly attribut-able to the criminal's perception that one can earn more through crime than through a legitimate job, and another third to the fact that the person is unemployed (Viccusi, 1983).

None of the sociological perspectives we have examined provides a complete explanation of deviant behavior. Each one highlights for us an important source of deviance. And deviant behavior takes a good many forms, so we must approach each form in its own right to determine the specific factors involved. We turn next to a consideration of crime, a form of deviance that is particularly prevalent in modern societies.

Crime and the Criminal Justice System

Within modern societies, law is a crucial element in social control. Unlike informal norms such as folkways and mores, laws are rules enforced by the state. **Crime** is merely an act that is prohibited by law, so not all deviant acts are crimes. For an act to be considered criminal, the state must undertake a political process of illegalizing— or *criminalizing*—it. What crimes have in common is not they are necessarily acts we regard as immoral or wicked. For instance, a good many Americans consider it no more "evil" to cheat on their income taxes than did their parents or grandparents to purchase and consume illegal alcoholic beverages during Prohibition. Rather, the distinguishing property of crime is that people who violate the law are liable to be arrested, tried, pronounced guilty, and deprived of their lives, liberty, or property. In brief, they are likely to become caught up in the elaborate social machinery of the **criminal jus-**

tice system—the reactive agencies of the state that include the police, the courts, and prisons. Let us briefly consider each of these components of the criminal justice system.

THE CRIMINAL JUSTICE SYSTEM

Judging by what they see on television, the American public is enamored with crime. The scenario of most television crime series invariably runs along these lines: A serious crime is committed; the police or detective hero sifts through the clues and tracks down the culprits; the prosecutor throws the book at them; judge and jury do their duty; and the criminals are sent to prison. In real life, however, the picture is quite different. According to statistics from the Justice Department, of every 100 felonies committed in the United States, only 33 are reported to the police. Of these 33, only 6 are cleared by arrest. Of these 6 persons arrested, only 3 are prosecuted and convicted. Of these, only 1 is sent to prison; the other two cases are rejected or dismissed due to problems with the evidence or witnesses, or the perpetrators are diverted into treatment programs. Of those sent to prison, more than half receive a sentence of at least five years. However, the average inmate is released in about two years (Moran, 1984).

The Police. Within the United States there are 490,000 police officers, plus 210,000 support employees. Of this number, 525,000 work for local governments, 100,000 for states, and 75,000 for the U.S. government. The police are a citizen's first link with the criminal justice system, and in many ways the most important one. When a crime occurs, the police are usually the first agents of the state to become involved.

Police officers are expected not only to collar lawbreakers, but also to perform a variety of community roles, from being providers of emergency first aid to being dog-catchers, leading some police officers to call themselves "do-everything guys" (despite affirmative-action programs, 95 percent of police officers are male). In towns of 50,000 population or more, on average only 45 officers are actually on patrol in the streets out of every 100 who are on duty at any given time. Indeed, police officers spend only about 15 percent of their time dealing with crime. Competing demands on their time vary from filling out reports and directing traffic to handling complaints about uncollected trash and responding to medical emergency calls.

The Courts. In the United States, the criminal justice system is an *adversary* system. The accused person—the *defendant*—is presumed to be innocent until proved guilty in a court of law by the representative of the state—the *prosecutor.* In many nations the questioning of witnesses is handled by judges, and guilt and innocence decided by a judge or panel of judges. But the American system assumes that justice is best served by pitting opposing lawyers against each other before a neutral judge and jury.

In practice, the fate of most of those accused of crime is determined by prosecutors. Prosecutors typically reject or reduce the severity of 50 to 80 percent of the charges filed by police. The reasons prosecutors cite range from the case overload to police inefficiency in producing evidence. Of the some 2 million serious criminal cases filed each year in the United States, less than one in five goes to trial. The others end in dismissals or guilty pleas.

When prosecutors decide to take a case to trial, a number of matters confront judges. They must decide whether a defendant should be released on bail, how fast a case will come to trial, the legality of police and prosecution tactics, and when the defendant is found guilty, the penalty. Should a defendant be sent to prison, the sentence can vary substantially depending on the judge. And once early releases granted by parole boards are factored in, disparities in time served can vary enormously. The average period spent in prison by convicted felons ranges from 13 months in South Dakota to 53 months in Massachusetts.

Prisons. American prisons vary from dingy, fortresslike state penitentiaries built in the 1800s to ultramodern lockups. Yet the convict population is increasing more rapidly than the capacity of prisons to hold them. In 1984 the nation's prison population reached a record of 454,000, almost double the total of ten years earlier (Pear, 1984). Another 210,000 are in local jails awaiting trial or doing time for minor infractions. In all, 1 of every 350 Americans is behind bars. The cost runs to $10 billion a year—$16,000 or more per inmate (Gest, 1984). On average, state prisons are estimated to be one-third over capacity, while federal facilities are 28 percent overfilled, leading to doubling and even tripling up in cells designed for one person.

Given bulging prison populations, some states have devised housing arrangements that are cheaper than high-security prisons. For instance, Arkansas now transfers some young convicts with nonviolent records to halfway houses in the community, where they can hold jobs, attend school, and participate in group therapy. And at least six states have set a cap on their prison populations. When the total reaches a specified level, nonviolent inmates near the end of their terms are freed immediately. Simultaneously, states throughout the nation are frenetically building new prisons and jails ($6 billion worth of construction is under way or on the drawing boards). We will have more to say later in the chapter about

the impact of prisons on inmates. But first, let us take a closer look at crime.

FORMS OF CRIME

Since crime is an act prohibited by law, it is the state that defines crime by the laws it promulgates, administers, and enforces. Thus an infinite variety of acts can be crimes. In Eastern Europe and the Soviet Union, it is a crime to organize political parties in opposition to the Communist regimes. In some nations like Iran, it is a crime to belong to religious groups barred by the dominant religious authorities. In the United States, interracial marriages were barred by many states prior to a 1967 Supreme Court decision prohibiting such statutes. And in many communities in the United States, "blue laws" make it a crime to sell various items on Sundays, particularly alcoholic beverages. Since the list of possible acts falling under the heading of crime is inexhaustible, we cannot think of crime as something clearly defined as a unit. Instead, let us consider a number of forms of crime within the United States.

White-Collar Crime. One type of crime that has been of particular interest to sociologists is **white-collar crime**—crimes committed by affluent persons, often in the course of business activities (Sutherland, 1949). Included in white-collar crime are corporate crime, fraud, embezzlement, corruption, bribery, tax fraud or evasion, stock manipulation, misrepresentation of advertising, restraint of trade, and infringements of patents. It is estimated that more than $40 billion is stolen every year in the United States by white-collar criminals (Bequai, 1984). Fraud and theft in the retail industry increase the cost of many items by at least 15 percent. The cost of public construction is increased between 10 and 50 percent because of bribery, kickbacks, and payoffs resulting in overcharges to taxpayers of more than $2 billion annually. Insurance frauds are commonplace. In fact, the biggest theft in American history was not the robbery of a bank or an armored car, but the $1 billion Equity Funding fraud masterminded by executives of a Los Angeles–based insurance conglomerate in the late 1970s. Computer-assisted crimes are mounting rapidly, and already account for more than $200 million in annual losses. And cheating taxpayers who do not tell the Internal Revenue Service exactly how much they earn cost the government an estimated $50 billion to $100 billion a year.

The American criminal justice system is ill-equipped to deal with white-collar crime. Unlike a robbery, a stock or insurance fraud is typically complex and difficult to unravel. Local law enforcement officials commonly lack the skills and resources necessary to tackle crimes outside the sphere of street crime. Federal agencies will handle only the more serious white-collar crimes. In most cities, they will not investigate a bank embezzlement unless it exceeds $8,000 to $10,000 (in New York City, the cutoff is about $50,000) (Taylor, 1984). And the handful of white-collar criminals who are prosecuted and convicted are given a slap on the wrist. Street criminals who steal $100 may find their way to prison, while the dishonest executive who embezzles $1 million may receive a suspended sentence and a relatively small fine. Figures for the late 1970s show that embezzlers at banks stole an average of $23,000 each, but only 17 percent of them went to jail. Bank robbers, by comparison, stole only one-eighth as much, yet 91 percent ended up in jail (*U.S. News & World Report*, July 23, 1979:60).

Organized Crime. Organized crime refers to large-scale bureaucratic organizations that provide illegal goods and services in public demand. Such crime is likely to arise where the state criminalizes certain activities—prostitution, drugs, pornography, gambling, and loan-sharking—that large numbers of citizens desire and are willing to pay for. Since Prohibition, syndicated crime has largely been conducted by a Sicilian-Italian syndicate, variously termed Mafia or the Cosa Nostra. So much has been written about this group that it is difficult to separate myth from fact. However, it seems to be a loose network or confederation of regional syndicates coordinated by a "commission" composed of the heads of the most powerful crime "families" (Cressey, 1969; Roberts, 1984). The Mafia operates a vast system of political corruption and employs violence and intimidation against victims, rivals, and "renegades." Having piled up enormous profits from drug dealing and gambling, the Mafia has diversified into entertainment, labor unions, construction, trucking, vending machines, garbage carting, toxic waste disposal, banking, stock fraud, insurance, and extortion.

However, organized crime is hardly an Italian monopoly. Irish and Jewish crime figures have long cooperated with the Mafia. In New York and Philadelphia, black groups and the Mafia run gambling and narcotics operations in concert. In San Francisco, Chinese gangs shake down merchants and are involved in gambling, robberies, and prostitution; the self-proclaimed Israeli Mafia extorts money in Los Angeles; and Colombian and Cuban drug rings have flooded Florida with their products (Press, 1981; Raab, 1984).

Violent Crime. The Federal Bureau of Investigation (FBI) annually reports on eight types of crime in its *Uniform Crime Reports*. These offenses are called **index crimes** and consist of four categories of violent crime against people—murder, rape, robbery, and assault—and four categories of crimes against property—burglary, theft, motor vehicle theft, and arson. It is these crimes that are covered widely by the news media, most feared by the public, and most denounced by political officials. In 1983 there were 30.9 violent crimes for every 1,000 people in the United States. Table 5.1 shows

TABLE 5.1

Odds of Becoming a Victim of Robbery or Assault (Rates per 100,000 persons in 1981)

	Robbery	Assault
Sex		
Male	10	36
Female	5	18
Age		
12–15	12	46
16–19	12	53
20–24	12	54
25–34	8	35
35–49	5	17
50–64	5	8
65 or older	4	4
Race		
White	6	26
Black	17	31
Hispanic	12	25
Income		
$3,000 or less	16	47
$3,000–$7,499	12	31
$7,500–$9,999	9	32
$10,000–$14,999	8	31
$15,000–$24,999	6	25
$25,000 or more	5	23
Job Status		
Retired	6	4
Keeping house	4	11
Unable to work	6	18
Employed	7	29
In school	11	44
Unemployed	13	60
Residence		
Central city	15	35
Suburb	6	26
Rural	3	21

Source: U.S. Department of Justice.

the odds of a person becoming a victim of robbery or assault, based on Justice Department data.

In recent years, all index crimes except rape have been on the decline. There has been a doubling of reported rapes since 1970, a rise that may partially reflect a climate in which women are more willing and able to report assaults (in 1983 there was about 1 reported rape for every 1,000 Americans). Rape is a serious offense in which an offender undertakes sexual acts to which a victim does not consent. Although rape has had a long and disturbing history, only in the past decade or so has it received societal attention. Very often a crime receives attention only when the victims have sufficient power to demand attention. Thus the focus on rape has paralleled the rise of the women's rights movement (Cann et al., 1981).

Victimless Crime. A **victimless crime** is an offense in which no one involved is considered a victim (Schur, 1965). These crimes include gambling, the sale and use of illicit drugs, and prohibited sexual relationships between consenting adults (such as prostitution and homosexuality). Usually a crime has an identifiable victim who suffers as a result of the criminal behavior. But in victimless crime, only the offenders themselves are likely to suffer. The behavior is criminalized because society, or powerful groups within a society, define the behavior as immoral.

In recent years there has been a movement to decriminalize many victimless crimes. Proponents of decriminalization argue that these crimes consume an inordinate amount of the time and money of the criminal justice system and clogs already congested courts and jails. Additionally, when goods and services that many people desire and are willing to purchase are made illegal, a black market supplied by organized crime almost invariably develops. Complicating matters, victimless crimes are often related to the corruption of police officers and others in the criminal justice system who receive bribes and payoffs from illegal suppliers and practitioners. Finally, there are those who argue that victimless crime involves acts that are private matters and thus are not rightfully the concern of government or other people. Critics of decriminalization suggest that some acts are "inherently evil" and justify public action in the same manner that those opposed to forcible rape, theft, murder, and incest undertake to impose their moral standards on society. So once again we find that deviance and crime are not matters on which all people can agree and arrive at a universal standard. Instead, competing groups seek to gain the support of the state for their morality and values.

MEASURING CRIME

Statistics on crime are among the most unsatisfactory of all social data. Official crime records—such as the FBI's annual *Uniform Crime Reports* based on incidents filed with more than 15,000 law enforcement agencies—suffer from numerous limitations (see Figure 5.2). For one thing, a large proportion of the crimes that are committed go undetected; others are detected but not reported; and still others are reported but not officially recorded when police officers and politicians manipulate their reports to show low crime rates for political purposes. For another, perceptions of crime vary from

FIGURE 5.2   CRIME CLOCK, 1983

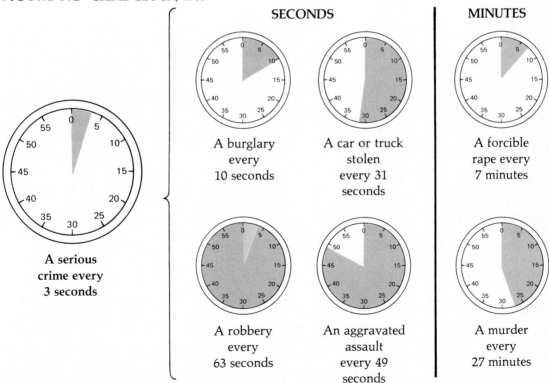

SECONDS

A burglary every 10 seconds

A car or truck stolen every 31 seconds

A robbery every 63 seconds

An aggravated assault every 49 seconds

MINUTES

A forcible rape every 7 minutes

A murder every 27 minutes

A serious crime every 3 seconds

(Source: U.S. Department of Justice, September 9, 1984.)

community to community; what is viewed as a serious crime by a citizen of a small town may be shrugged off by a big-city resident as an unpleasant bit of everyday life.

When the *Uniform Crime Reports* are compared with victim-based measures of crime (based on survey samples of American households in which individuals are asked if they or any member of their household had been victims of crime during the previous year), the rates of various crimes in the United States are substantially higher. A National Crime Survey conducted in 1979 showed that only about 30 percent of all personal crimes and 36 percent of all crimes against households were made known to the police (Department of Justice, 1981). Among offenses against the person, reported crimes of violence ranged from a 33 percent rate for assault without a weapon to a high of 66 percent for robbery with injury from serious assault. Reporting rates for offenses against property ranged from 25 percent of the household larcenies to 86 percent of car thefts. What accounts for the public's apparent reluctance to report crime? The crime survey found that the single most common reason for not reporting was that people felt the offense was not important enough to warrant police attention. The second most cited explanation was that the matter was too private or personal to share with a stranger. And many people have little faith in authorities, believing that "nothing can be done." Add to these feelings of helplessness a fear of reprisal, police insensitivity, and an unwillingness to get caught up in the slow-moving machinery of the criminal justice bureaucracy, and the reluctance of individuals to report crime becomes more understandable (Kidd and Dhayet, 1984).

Self-report-based measures of crime, involving anonymous questionnaires that ask people which offenses they have committed, also reveal much higher rates of crime than those found in official crime statistics. For instance, studies of juvenile crimes show that a good many youngsters of all social classes break some criminal laws, the amount of unreported crime is enormous, and convicted offenders are highly unrepresentative of persons violating the criminal law (Erickson and Empey, 1963; Hindelang, Hirschi, and Weis, 1981; Thornberry and Farnworth, 1982). Youths who are arrested and placed in juvenile facilities typically have limited resources or repeatedly commit serious offenses, or both.

The *Uniform Crime Reports* focus on crimes that are most likely to be committed by young people and individuals from lower socioeconomic backgrounds. Statistics on many categories of crime, such as white-collar crime and organized crime, are not routinely compiled. Many crimes committed by persons of upper socioeconomic status in the course of business are handled by quasi-judicial bodies, such as the Federal Trade Commission and the National Labor Relations Board, or by civil courts. As a result, many businesspeople are able to avoid being stigmatized as criminals. Additionally, in cases of some criminal offenses, such as income tax evasion and fraud, the crimes are also unlikely to be reported in victimization studies.

DIFFERING CONCEPTIONS OF THE PURPOSES OF IMPRISONMENT

Many Americans take a rather gloomy view of crime-fighting programs. They question whether anything works. Complicating matters, a debate ranges between "hardliners" who want tougher judges and unshackled police and "softliners" who see crime as the product of societal conditions, and urge the police to work harder on "community relations" while emphasizing rehabilitation over punishment. Criminology and penology also have been in flux,

Americans are divided on the purpose to be served by imprisonment. Some see prisons as vehicles for punishing deviants, others as centers of rehabilitation, still others as agencies of deterrence, and yet others as means for reducing crime rates. (Peter Menzel)

with the experts themselves unsure of the most effective methods for dealing with the prison population. Let us explore these matters by considering four traditional purposes of imprisonment: punishment, rehabilitation, deterrence, and selective incapacitation.

Punishment. Prior to 1800 it was widely assumed that the punishment of deviants is required if the injured community is to feel morally satisfied. But toward the latter part of the eighteenth and the early part of the nineteenth centuries, the focus changed. The idea that prisons might rehabilitate criminals came to the forefront. The word "penitentiary" was coined to describe a place where a criminal might repent and resolve to follow a law-abiding life.

In recent years there has been a renewed interest in punishment not to satisfy a de-

sire for vengeance, but to restore a sense of moral order. The argument runs like this: Certain acts are basically antisocial and heinous—for instance, murder, rape, genocide, and the sexual abuse of children—and ought to be punished. The community experiences a sense of moral outrage when behavior that is grossly immoral goes unpunished. This outrage can impair the social system, because society operates with the tacit understanding that there is some measure of fairness and normal order to life. Punishment is essential to maintain people's commitment to social order and to basic values and norms. As the discerning reader probably has gathered, this approach draws on the functionalist perspective for support.

Rehabilitation. During the last century and a half, the concept of rehabilitation has dominated penal philosophy. It has drawn on a humanistic tradition that has pressed for the individualization of justice and has demanded the fair treatment of criminals. Viewed in this manner, crime resembles "disease," something foreign and abnormal to people. Inherent in the definition of a sick person is a presumption that individuals are not to blame for the disease, and that we should direct our attention to curing them. To say, "It is not primarily the person's fault. He or she is sick," is to define the law violator as victim and not as victimizer.

Beginning in the 1960s, a number of criminologists began questioning the assumptions underlying rehabilitation strategies. And in recent years the chorus of critics has rapidly expanded. Critics of rehabilitation contend that education and psychotherapy cannot overcome or reduce the powerful tendency for some individuals to continue their criminal ways. They cite statistics on the high rate of *recidivism* (relapse into criminal behavior) to back up their argument (Martinson, 1974; Lipton, Martinson, and Wilks, 1975). And they seek to show that rehabilitative efforts result in only limited reductions in criminality, and then only for some kinds of offenders and only under certain circumstances.

One of the most prominent critics of rehabilitative procedures has been James Q. Wilson (1975, 1983), a Harvard University political scientist. He blames academic criminologists for assuming that the search for the causes of crime will lead to effective policies for controlling crime. For instance, it may be true, he says, that children growing up in a household where parents exercise ineffective control are more prone to becoming delinquent than other children. But no one knows how to give every child competent and loving parents. Wilson contends that the appeal of rehabilitative strategies rests on the notion that such strategies

get down to "basics." But he points out that it is impossible to provide delinquents with new childhoods. And prison programs that teach convicts how to read, understand their inner impulses, or repair automobiles simply increase their life alternatives. The programs do not guarantee that the inmates will prefer careers as auto mechanics to careers as professional criminals.

Deterrence. Although many social scientists, like Wilson, believe that prisons fail to rehabilitate inmates, they nonetheless favor the swift and certain punishment of law violators for deterrence purposes. For example, Wilson views human beings as rational, self-interested individuals who pursue what is best for them. He says that a good many people have discovered they can get away with crime. Crime pays for many Americans, particularly ghetto youth who find the juvenile justice system overloaded, underfunded, and ineffective, and jobs unavailable. Wilson contends that a good way to reduce crime is to make its consequences to would-be offenders more costly (by making penalties swifter, more certain, and more severe), or to make alternatives to crime more attractive (by increasing the availability and pay of legitimate jobs), or both.

The notion of deterrence rests on assumptions about human nature that are difficult to prove. Even so, sociological studies seem to suggest that the *certainty* of apprehension and punishment does tend to lower crime rates (Wolfgang, Figlio, and Sellin, 1972; Waldo and Chiricos, 1972). Few studies, however, find an association between the *severity* of punishment and crime (Tittle and Logan, 1973; Gibbs, 1975; Grasmick and Bryjak, 1980). While sociologists recognize that the prospect of punishment has some deterrent effect under some circumstances, they have been more concerned with specifying the *conditions* under which punishment influences behavior (Brown, 1978;

Erickson and Gibbs, 1978). For instance, allegiance to a group and its norms typically operates as an even stronger force than the threat of societal punishment in bringing about conformity (Anderson, Chiricos, and Waldo, 1977; Meier and Johnson, 1977). By the same token, informal standards and pressures within delinquent subcultures may counteract the deterrent effects of legal penalties (Tittle and Rowe, 1974).

Selective Confinement. There are those who argue, like Peter W. Greenwood (1982) of the Rand Corporation, that neither rehabilitation nor deterrence really works, and so it is useless to send people to prison with these goals in mind. However, imprisonment can be used to reduce crime rates. By keeping "hardcore" criminals in prison and off the streets, they are not in a position to commit crimes. For example, Marvin E. Wolfgang and his colleagues (1972) tracked the criminal records of about 10,000 young men born in 1945 who lived in Philadelphia. They found that about 6 percent, or 60, of the men were responsible for more than half the crime committed by the entire group, including most of the serious offenses.

Greenwood (1982) developed a profile of the characteristics of individuals who are most likely to engage repeatedly in crime based on surveys of 2,200 inmates serving prison terms for robbery or burglary in California, Texas, and Michigan: imprisonment for more than half of the two-year period preceding the most recent arrest, prior convictions for the same crime, a record that includes juvenile convictions before age 16, incarceration for a juvenile offense in a state or federal facility, heroin or barbiturate use as a juvenile, drug use during the two years prior to arrest, and unemployment during most of the period. Depending on the number of characteristics attributed to an individual, a subject is characterized as a low-, medium- or high-rate offender. Greenwood

asserts that incarcerating one robber who is among the top 10 percent in offense rates prevents more robberies than incarcerating 18 offenders who are at or below the median.

Yet selective incarceration also poses difficulties. For instance, individuals who engage in robbery and burglary typically retire from these careers fairly early in life; hence the "out years" in a long sentence might represent a waste of prison capacity. There is also the legal and constitutional difficulty in a democratic nation in sentencing individuals based on forecasts of their future behavior rather than on a verdict arising out of an actual crime. Further, comparable attempts by psychologists and psychiatrists to predict behavior on the basis of profile characteristics have been notoriously inaccurate (for instance, they seem to be wrong when they predict violence at least twice as often as they are right). Indeed, even according to Greenwood's own figures, only a little more than half the felons he places in the high-rate category belong there (Chaiken and Chaiken, 1982).

In recent years an estimated 75 to 100 cities, counties, and states have adopted career-criminal programs (Joseph, 1983). Although the programs vary from city to city, they typically involve special career-criminal units. Police and prosecutors dig into the criminal history of suspects to determine whether they are dealing with a "career criminal." Once law enforcers determine a suspect to be a career criminal, they prosecute faster than in other cases and demand longer sentences. Some law enforcement officers have claimed that their programs have contributed to the lowering of the crime rate in recent years. But just how much, if any, credit should be given to career-criminal programs for the decline is a matter of debate. Criminologists point out that other factors also have to be figured in the drop, including the decline in the proportion of adolescents in the general population as the last of the "baby boom" generation reaches adulthood. Young people aged 14 to 21 commit about half the index crimes. Further, any number of sociologists argue that some degree of crime is normal within modern societies. And they say that a large proportion of offenders is likewise normal, given the realities of contemporary social life (Martinson, 1974).

SUMMARY

1. In all societies the behavior of some people at times goes beyond that permitted by the norms. Norms only tell us what we are supposed to do or what we are not supposed to do. They do not tell us what people actually do. And what some of us actually do very often runs counter to what other people judge to be acceptable behavior. In brief, social life is characterized not only by conformity, but by deviance. Deviance is behavior that a considerable number of people view as reprehensible and beyond the limits of tolerance.

2. Implicit in a sociological definition of deviance is the notion that deviance is not a property inherent in certain forms of behavior; instead it is a property conferred upon particular behaviors by social definitions. In this sense, deviance is what people say it is. Definitions as to which acts are deviant vary greatly from time to time, place to place, and group to group. When people differ regarding their definitions of what is and is not deviant behavior, the question becomes one of which individuals and groups will make their definitions prevail. Even so, in our daily lives we typically find that norms are not so much a point or a line but a zone.

3. Social order dictates that people have to be kept in line, at least most people, and the line must be adhered to within allowable limits. Without social order, interaction would be a real problem and normative expectations would be meaningless. Accordingly, societies seek to ensure that their members conform with basic norms by means of social control. Social control refers to the methods and strategies that regulate behavior within society. There are three main types of social control processes operating within social life: (1) Those that lead us to internalize our society's normative expectations; (2) those that structure our world of social experience; and (3) those that employ various formal and informal social sanctions.

4. It seems that most societies can absorb a good deal of deviance without serious consequences. But persistent and widespread deviance can be dysfunctional, impairing and even severely undermining organized life. It weakens people's willingness to play their roles and to obey the rules of society. But deviance may also be functional. It may promote social solidarity, clarify norms, strengthen group allegiances, and provide a catalyst for change.

5. According to the anomie perspective, deviance derives from societal stresses. Robert K. Merton contends that American society sets forth goals of worldly success for the population at large, but withholds the means for realizing these goals from significant segments of its population. He identifies five responses to the ends–means dilemma: conformity, innovation, ritualism, retreatism,

and rebellion. Critics point out that the anomie perspective overlooks those processes of social interaction by which people shape their definitions of the world about them and fashion their actions.

6. A number of sociologists have emphasized the similarities between the way deviant behavior is acquired and the way in which other behavior is acquired—the cultural transmission perspective. Edwin H. Sutherland elaborated on this notion in his theory of differential association. He said that individuals become deviant to the extent to which they participate in settings where deviant ideas, motivations, and techniques are viewed favorably. The earlier, the more frequently, the more intensely, and the longer the duration of the contacts people have in deviant settings, the greater the probability that they too will become deviant. However, the theory is not applicable to some forms of deviance, particularly those in which neither the techniques nor the appropriate definitions and attitudes are acquired from other deviants.

7. Conflict theorists examine a variety of questions with respect to deviance. They ask "Which group will be able to translate its values into the rules of a society and make these rules stick?" and "Who reaps the lion's share of benefits from particular social arrangements?" Marxist sociologists see crime as arising from capitalist laws that make behavior illegal that is offensive to the morality of the powerful and threatens their privileges and property. Critics charge that conflict formulations have given new directions to our understanding of deviance, but that the insights have been primarily rhetorical and require scientific inquiry.

8. Labeling theorists study the processes whereby some individuals come to be tagged as deviants, begin to think of themselves as deviants, and enter on deviant careers. They say it is the societal response to an act and not the behavior itself that determines deviance. These sociologists point out that labeling people as deviants tends to set up conditions conducive to secondary deviance—deviance individuals adopt in response to the reactions of other individuals. Critics point out that labeling theory may help us understand how individuals become career deviants, but it tells us little about what contributed to their deviant behavior in the first place.

9. Crime is an act that is prohibited by law. The distinguishing property of crime is that people who violate the law are liable to be arrested, tried, pronounced guilty, and deprived of their lives, liberty, or property. They become caught up in the elaborate social machinery of the criminal justice system—the reactive agencies of the state that include the police, the courts, and prisons. Within the United States, of every 100 felonies committed, only 33 are reported to the police. Of the 33 that are reported, only 6 are cleared by arrest. Of the 6 who are arrested, only 3 are prosecuted and convicted. And only 1 is sent to prison.

10. Since crime is an act prohibited by law, it is the state that defines crime by the laws it promulgates, administers, and enforces. An infinite variety of acts can be crimes. One type of crime that has been of particular interest to sociologists is white-collar crime—crimes committed by affluent persons, often in the course of business activities. Another form of crime—organized crime—is car-

ried out by large-scale bureaucratic organizations that provide illegal goods and services in public demand. Federal agencies keep records on index crimes—violent crimes against people and crimes against property. Still another type of crime is victimless crime—offenses in which no one involved is considered a victim.

11. Statistics on crime are among the most unsatisfactory of all social data. Official crime records suffer from numerous limitations. A large proportion of the crimes that are committed go undetected; others are detected but not reported; and still others are reported but not officially recorded. Official crime records are often supplemented by victim-based measures and self-report measures.

12. There have been four traditional purposes of imprisonment: punishment, rehabilitation, deterrence, and selective incapacitation. The rationale behind punishment is that it serves to restore a sense of moral order. Rehabilitation is premised on the notion that crime resembles disease and needs to be cured. Deterrence is based on the notion that if the price of crime is too high, people will not engage in it. And selective confinement suggests that crime rates can be reduced by keeping hardcore criminals in jail and off the streets.

GLOSSARY

anomie A social condition in which people find it difficult to guide their behavior by norms they experience as weak, unclear, or conflicting.

crime An act prohibited by law.
criminal justice system The reactive agencies of the state that include the police, the courts, and prisons.

deviance Behavior that a considerable number of people in a society view as reprehensible and beyond the limits of tolerance.
differential association The notion that the earlier, the more frequently, the more intensely, and the longer the duration of the contacts people have in deviant settings, the greater the probability that they too will become deviant.

index crimes Crimes reported by the Federal Bureau of Investigation in its *Uniform Crime Reports*. These offenses consist of four categories of violent crime against people—murder, rape, robbery, and assault—and four categories of crime against property—burglary, theft, motor vehicle theft, and arson.

internalization Incorporation by individuals within their personalities of the standards of behavior prevalent within the larger society.

organized crime Large-scale bureaucratic organizations that provide illegal goods and services in public demand.

primary deviance Behavior that violates social norms but usually goes unnoticed by the agents of social control.

secondary deviance Deviance that individuals adopt in response to the reactions of other individuals.
social control Methods and strategies that regulate behavior within society.

victimless crime An offense in which no one involved is considered a victim.

white-collar crime Crimes committed by affluent persons, often in the course of business activities.

6

Social Stratification

PATTERNS OF SOCIAL
STRATIFICATION

    Open and Closed Systems
    Dimensions of Stratification
    Israeli Kibbutzim: Classless
      Communities?
    Identifying Social Classes

EXPLANATIONS OF SOCIAL
STRATIFICATION

    The Functionalist Theory of
    Stratification
    The Conflict Theory of Stratification
    A Synthesiis

THE AMERICAN CLASS SYSTEM

    The Significance of Social Classes
    What Is Happening to the Middle
      Class?
    Poverty in the United States

SOCIAL MOBILITY

    Forms of Social Mobility
    Social Mobility in the United States
    Social Mobility in Industrialized
      Societies
    Status Attainment Processes

Group living confers various collective benefits on the members of a society. Together they can accomplish a great many things that they could not otherwise achieve. But the advantages and disadvantages of the collective enterprise are not shared evenly. Most societies are organized so that their institutions systematically distribute benefits and burdens unequally among different categories of people. Sociologists call the structured ranking of individuals and groups—their grading into horizontal layers or strata—**social stratification.** Viewed in this manner, social arrangements are not neutral, but serve and promote the goals and interests of some people more than they do those of other people.

The question of "Who gets what and why?" has intrigued humankind across the centuries (Lenski, 1966). The early Hebrew prophets who lived some 800 years before Christ—particularly Amos, Micah, and Isaiah—repeatedly denounced the rich and powerful members of their society. For example, Micah accused the leading citizens of his day of coveting and seizing their neighbors' fields and homes, being "full of violence," asking for bribes, and using dishonest and "deceitful" practices. Likewise, the classical Greek philosophers, including Plato and Aristotle, discussed at length the institution of private property and slavery. Writing in *The Republic* in 370 B.C., Plato observed: "Any city, however small, is in fact divided into two, one the city of the poor, the other of the rich; these are at war with one another." And in *The Laws of Manu*, compiled by Hindu priests about 200 B.C., we find an account of the creation of the world that portrays social inequalities as divinely ordained for the good of all. Indeed, as we will see later in the chapter, viewpoints regarding social stratification have tended to polarize. Some like Micah and Plato have criticized the existing distributive system, while others like the Hindu priests have supported it.

Patterns of Social Stratification

Social stratification depends upon but is not the same thing as **social differentiation**—the process by which a society becomes increasingly specialized over time. Very early in their history, human beings discovered that a division of functions and labor contributed to greater social efficiency. Consequently, in all societies we find a separation of statuses and roles. This arrangement requires that people be distributed within the social structure so that the various statuses are filled and their accompanying roles performed. Nature helps to accomplish this task by dictating that only women should bear children, but nature does not go very much beyond this. The rest human beings have to figure out for themselves.

Although the statuses that make up a social structure may be differentiated, they need not be *ranked* with respect to one another. For instance, within our society the statuses of infant and child are differentiated, but the one is not thought to be superior in rank to the other. They are merely different. Social differentiation sets the stage for—provides the social material that may or may not become the basis for—social ranking. In other words, whenever we encounter social stratification we find social differentiation, but not the other way around. Let us begin our consideration of social stratification by examining a number of different arrangements.

OPEN AND CLOSED SYSTEMS

Stratification systems differ in the ease with which they permit people to move in or out of particular strata. As we will see later in the chapter when we discuss social mobility, people often move vertically up or down in rank or horizontally to another status of roughly similar rank. Where people can

Society has often been thought of as a rigid, unchanging structure in which each person's position was ordained by fate. This view was predominant during the Middle Ages, when serfs, at the bottom of the social hierarchy, had no freedom of geographical or social mobility. Instead, they were destined to work all their lives on the estate where they had been born. (Victoria and Albert Museum)

change their status with relative ease, we refer to the arrangement as an **open system.** In contrast, where people have great difficulty in changing their status, we call the arrangement a **closed system.** A somewhat similar distinction is conveyed by the concepts *achieved status* and *ascribed status* that we considered in Chapter 2. Achieved statuses are open to people on the basis of individual choice and competition, whereas ascribed statuses are assigned to people by their group or society.

Although there are no societies that are entirely open or entirely closed, the United States provides a good example of a relatively open system. The American dream portrays a society in which all people can alter and improve their lot. The American folk hero is Abe Lincoln, the "poor boy who made good," the "rail-splitter" who through hard work managed to move "from log cabin to the White House." The United States is founded not on the idea that all people should enjoy equal status, nor on the notion of a classless society. Rather, the democratic creed holds that all people should have an equal opportunity to ascend to the heights of the class system. In theory, the rewards of social life flow to people in accordance with their merit and competence and in proportion to their contribution to the larger social enterprise. However, in

Doing Sociology: Stratification in Campus Life

Social stratification pervades all aspects of social life. It represents structured inequality in the allocation of rewards, privileges, and resources. Some individuals—by virtue of their roles or group memberships—are advantaged, while others are disadvantaged. College life is not exempt from these patterns, despite the fact that college communities are often portrayed as rather benign settings in which administration, faculty, and students are preoccupied with the pursuit of knowledge and human betterment. Wherever one turns, social inequality confronts the members of the college community, a matter that two students discuss in the following observations:

Our math classroom is on the third floor of a building that overlooks the top floor of a parking ramp. At most three or four cars are parked up there, although it contains enough space for at least fifty cars. The lower levels of the ramp are also fairly empty. The ramp is only for the use of faculty. We students have to park some distance from campus and even then we have to get to school by 7:30 in the morning if we are to find a parking place. . . . The faculty enjoy many privileges.

They have special offices; departmental chairpersons have more spacious offices; and deans and the university president have even more magnificent offices. The faculty have "faculty restrooms" which are distinct from those simply labeled "restroom." Each dean has his own private restroom. The faculty address us by our first names, whereas we have to call them "Doctor" and "Professor."

I have been a college student now for three years. Time and again I hear it said that universities exist for students and that their primary purpose is to educate and enrich people's lives. I came to college quite idealistic, believing in its visionary commitment. But in the course of my campus experiences I have come to a quite different conclusion. Universities exist chiefly for university officials and the faculty. Student needs have minimal priority. As freshmen we are herded in mass lectures and recitation sections with little concern for our individual experiences, capabilities, or interests. We have little or no voice in what we are taught or who teaches us. These decisions

are made in an authoritarian manner by others. It seems to matter little to the powers-that-be whether teaching is good, bad, or indifferent. Professors are ultimately judged on other attributes, most particularly their ability to bring research funds to the university and "knock out" publications. In fact, students are locked in an arrangement of structured inequality. Notice how the classroom is set up. We are placed in rows of undifferentiated seats that are usually bolted to the floor. The message is clear. Students are interchangeable with one another and count for little. In contrast, professors have about a fourth to a third of the classroom, a vast territory that they can freely roam about. Commonly a solid table or lectern sets the professor apart from the class, a physical barrier that symbolically underlines the social distance and status differential that separate us. The manner in which classroom seating is laid out bars egalitarian exchanges even were the professor disposed toward them. Thus students are continually reminded of their subordinate and disprivileged position.

practice the ideal is not realized, since the American system places some measure of reliance on ascription, particularly in assigning statuses on the basis of sex, age, and race. We will examine these matters at greater length later in the chapter and in the chapter that follows.

When we think of a closed system, the Hindu caste arrangement often comes to mind, particularly as it operated in India prior to 1900. Under the traditional Hindu system, life was ordered in terms of castes in which people inherited their social status at birth from their parents and could not change it in the course of their lives. Historically there have been thousands of castes in India, although all of them have fallen into four major castes: the Brahmins, or priestly caste, who represent about 3 percent of the population; the Kshatriyas, allegedly descendants of warriors, and the Vaisyas, the traders, who together account for about 7 percent of Indians; and the Sudras, peasants and artisans, who constitute about 70 percent of the population. The remaining 20 percent are the Harijans, or Untouchables, who have traditionally served as sweepers, scavengers, leatherworkers, and swineherds.

Members of the lower castes were considered inferior, scorned, snubbed, and oppressed by higher caste members regardless of personal merit and behavior. Rigid rules of avoidance operated within the system because contact with lower caste members was believed to spiritually pollute and defile upper caste members. Even today, caste still shapes behavior in some localities, especially in rural areas, setting the rules of courtship, diet, housing, and employment. The concept of *dharma* legitimates the system, establishing the idea that enduring one's lot in life with grace is the only morally acceptable way to live. But even at its zenith, the Hindu caste system never operated to foreclose mobility up and down the social ladder. Different birth and death rates among the castes, discontent among the disadvantaged and exploited, competition between members of different castes, the introduction of modern farming technologies, conversions to Buddhism and Islam, and other factors have operated against a completely closed system (Davis, 1949; Berreman, 1960; Critchfield, 1984).

DIMENSIONS OF STRATIFICATION

We are indebted to Karl Marx and Max Weber for their contributions in unraveling the nature of social stratification. Marx believed that the key to social stratification in capitalist societies is the division between those who own and control the crucial means of production—the oppressing capitalist class or bourgeoisie—and those who have only their labor to sell—the oppressed working class or proletariat. In Marx's view, these two groups and their conflicting interests provide the foundation for stratification in capitalist nations. For Marx, social stratification consists of a single dimension.

Weber (1946) felt that Marx provided an overly simplistic image of stratification. He contended that other divisions exist within society that are at times independent of the class or economic aspect. Consequently, he took a multidimensional view of stratification, and identified three components: *class* (economic standing), *status* (prestige), and *party* (power). Each of these dimensions constitutes a distinct aspect of social ranking. Some statuses rank high in wealth, prestige, and power, such as that of most physicians. Yet the rankings of some statuses may be dissimilar. Some prostitutes and professional criminals enjoy economic privilege, although they possess little prestige or power. Members of university faculties and the clergy, while enjoying a good deal of prestige, typically rank comparatively low in wealth and power. And some public officials may wield considerable power, but receive low salaries and little prestige. For the most part, however, these three dimensions hang together, feeding into and supporting one another (Wright, 1979). Let us examine each of them in turn.

Economic Standing. The economic dimension of stratification consists of wealth and income. **Wealth** has to do with what people own. **Income** refers to the amount of money people receive. Thus wealth is based on what people *have*, whereas income consists of what people *get*. For example, one individual may have a good deal of property but receive little income from it, such as people who collect rare coins, precious gems, or works of art. Another individual may receive a high salary but squander it on high living and have little wealth.

The Federal Reserve Board estimates that in 1984 the top 2 percent of American families—those earning $100,000 or more a year—controlled 30 percent of the nation's financial assets (Columbus, Ohio, *Dispatch*, October 9, 1984a:A2). They owned 50 percent of all stocks in private hands, 71 percent of all tax-free bonds, and 20 percent of all real estate. On the basis of its study of tax returns, the Internal Revenue Service (IRS) estimates that in 1982 some 407,700 Americans had a net worth exceeding $1 million, double the number in 1976 (inflation is the principal cause of the increase—$1 million in 1982 dollars was the equivalent of $639,700 in 1976 dollars). About 31 percent of the typical millionaire's wealth is in corporate stocks, 24 percent in real estate, and 12 percent in bonds and mortgages (Wiener and Morse, 1985). (See Figure 6.1.) The average millionaire is 57 years old; only 8 percent are under age 40. Over 95 percent have

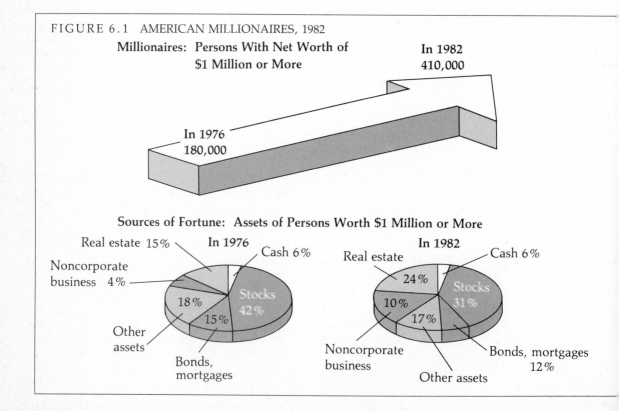

FIGURE 6.1   AMERICAN MILLIONAIRES, 1982

Millionaires: Persons With Net Worth of $1 Million or More

In 1982
410,000

In 1976
180,000

Sources of Fortune: Assets of Persons Worth $1 Million or More

In 1976
Real estate 15%
Noncorporate business 4%
Cash 6%
Stocks 42%
18%
15%
Other assets
Bonds, mortgages

In 1982
Real estate 24%
Cash 6%
Stocks 31%
10%
17%
Noncorporate business
Other assets
Bonds, mortgages 12%

attended college, and four of ten have advanced degrees (Stanley and Moschis, 1984).

Each year *Forbes* magazine compiles a list of the 400 wealthiest Americans. As economist Lester C. Thurow (1984a:27) points out, the Forbes 400 list shows that the United States is still a land of economic opportunity: there are 159 entirely self-made

millionaires on the list, and one is only 29 years old. But it also shows the considerable accumulation of economic power in the hands of the few:

Great wealth is accumulated to acquire economic power. Wealth makes you an economic mover and shaker. Projects will happen, or not happen, depending upon your decisions. It

Where the Well-to-Do Reside, by State

States with the most people with gross assets* greater than $500,000		States where people worth $500,000 make up the biggest shares of the population	
California	301,500	North Dakota	24 per 1,000
Texas	204,800	Nebraska	19 per 1,000
Florida	151,800	Iowa	18 per 1,000
New York	110,100	Wyoming	17 per 1,000
Illinois	108,000	Montana	16 per 1,000
Pennsylvania	86,800	Connecticut	16 per 1,000
Ohio	52,500	Florida	15 per 1,000
New Jersey	51,300	Texas	13 per 1,000
Iowa	50,800	Arizona	13 per 1,000
Michigan	48,100	California	12 per 1,000

* Excludes mortgages and other debts.

Taxpayers' Income Rankings

Most of America's 96.3 million personal tax returns reported adjusted gross income under $25,000. Only 1 in 1,000 showed income over $1 million.

Adjusted Gross Income	Number of Returns	Percentage of Returns
Under $15,000	34,529,701	35.8%
$15,000–$25,000	33,567,741	34.8
$25,000–$30,000	7,348,043	7.6
$30,000–$40,000	10,446,443	10.9
$40,000–$50,000	5,144,573	5.3
$50,000–$75,000	3,607,761	3.8
$75,000–$100,000	818,051	0.9
$100,000–$200,000	628,471	0.7
$200,000–$500,000	165,226	0.2
$500,000–$1,000,000	26,098	.03
Over $1,000,000	11,526	0.1

(Source: Internal Revenue Service data, 1985.)

allows you to influence the political process—elect yourself or others—and remold society in accordance with your views. It makes you an important person, courted by people inside and outside your family.

As Figure 6.1 shows, the incomes of Americans vary greatly. Whereas over 34 million Americans had adjusted gross incomes under $10,000 in 1982, 11,526 had incomes of $1 million or more. The vast majority of Americans derive their income from wages or salaries. In contrast, the wealthy secure most of their income from investments (see Table 6.1). The exception is corporate executives, 55 of whom earned $1 million or more in salaries and bonuses in 1984 (Work and Morse, 1985). Additionally, many executives receive a variety of perquisites, including a company car, club memberships, and extra life insurance. At the other extreme, as we will see later in the chapter, 15 percent of Americans live in poverty (Pear, 1984).

Prestige. Prestige involves the social respect, admiration, and recognition associated with a particular social status. It entails a feeling that we are admired and thought well of by others. Prestige is intangible, something that we carry about in our heads. However, in our daily lives we commonly seek to give prestige a tangible existence through titles, special seats of honor, deference rituals, honorary degrees, emblems, and conspicuous displays of leisure and consumption. These activities and objects serve as symbols of prestige to which we attribute social significance and meaning. Much of our interaction with others consists of subtle negotiation over just how much deference, honor, respect, and awe we are to extend and receive. Even a simple conversation frequently involves a bargain that we will be attentive to what others say to us if they in turn will be attentive to what

TABLE 6.1

Proportion of Total Income Derived from Wages or Salaries, 1980

Americans with this amount of taxable income . . .	*derived this proportion of their income from wages or salaries*
Over $1 million	17.9%
$500,000 to $1 million	34.7
$200,000 to $500,000	49.5
$100,000 to $200,000	59.7
$75,000 to $100,000	64.9
$50,000 to $75,000	73.6
$25,000 to $50,000	87.2
$20,000 to $25,000	88.6

(*Source:* Andrew Hacker, ed. *US: A Statistical Portrait of the American People.* New York: Viking, 1983, p. 171. Copyright © 1983 by Andrew Hacker. Reprinted by permission of Viking Penguin, Inc.)

we say—a mutual exchange of "ego massages."

We show deference—behavior dramatizing and confirming a person's superior ranking—in a good many ways. In *presentation rituals* we engage in symbolic acts, such as revealing regard and awe by bowing, scraping, and displaying a humble demeanor. In *avoidance rituals* we achieve the same end by maintaining a "proper distance" from prestigious figures. Consider Theodore H. White's (1961:171) account of an incident that occurred in 1960, when John F. Kennedy's presidential nomination became a certainty. As Kennedy entered his "hideaway cottage," where a number of Democratic party leaders had assembled, he walked over to his brother Bobby and his brother-in-law Sargent Shriver:

The others in the room surged forward on impulse to join him. Then they halted. A distance of perhaps 30 feet separated them from him, but it was impassable. [After a few minutes, Shriver crossed the separating space and invited the leaders over.] First Averell Harriman; then Dick Daley; then Mike DiSalle; then, one by one, Kennedy let them all congratulate him. Yet no one could pass the little open distance between him and them uninvited, because there was this thin separation about him, and the knowledge they were there not as patrons but as his clients. They could come by invitation only, for this might be a President of the United States.

Nearly ninety years ago, Thorstein Veblen (1899) highlighted the part that *conspicuous leisure* and *conspicuous consumption* play in revealing social ranking. He noted that in order to gain and hold prestige, it is not enough merely to possess wealth and power. The wealth and power must be put on public view, for prestige is awarded only on evidence. Lavish expenditure on clothing has an advantage over most other methods because our apparel gives an indication of our social ranking at a glance. The requirement that people dress in the latest fashion, coupled with the fact that the accredited fashion changes from season to season, greatly augments the amount that must be spent on a wardrobe and hence increases its symbolic significance. Automobiles serve a similar purpose. Thus Trent Tucker, in his rookie year with the New York Knickerbockers basketball team, took lessons in driving a Mercedes from his teammates. He said he learned that "professional persons, whether they're doctors, lawyers, or ballplayers, get Mercedes. They can afford it, and they think they should have one" (Stevens, 1983:21).

Veblen documents how relative success, tested by comparing one's own economic situation with that of others, becomes an established end. Such comparisons find symbolic expression, since displaying one's bankbook or stock certificates would be impractical and considered in "poor taste." A

Thorstein Veblen pointed out that the possession of wealth and power is insufficient to generate prestige. Prestige is a matter of social definitions. Accordingly, individuals ofen seek to shape the perceptions that others have of them by placing their wealth and power on display. (Steven Baratz/The Picture Cube)

good example is afforded by debutante balls—the custom whereby young women are presented to the privileged circle termed "society." In recent years the custom has enjoyed a revival (Barron, 1984). However, the estimated $250,000 that Henry Ford II spent in 1959 for the debut of his 18-year-old daughter Charlotte probably still remains the record. Ford had 2 million magnolia leaves flown in from Mississippi for the decorations, which included eighteenth-century tapestries and medieval arms and armor. Lavish charity events serve as a similar function in allowing the wealthy occasions for ritualistic displays of their wealth.

The prestige of most Americans rests primarily on their income, occupation, and life style (Coleman and Rainwater, 1978). Family background and wealth count for less than they did a generation or so ago. Simultaneously, an individual's "personality" and "gregariousness" have taken on greater importance. Although people still think that money is the most important thing, the life style individuals project and the values they reflect now assume a critical part in determining their prestige.

Power. As we will see in Chapter 8, power determines which individuals and groups will be able to translate their preferences into the reality of social life. **Power** refers to the ability of individuals and groups to realize their will in human affairs even if it involves the resistance of others. It provides answers to the question of whose interests will be served and whose values will reign. Wherever we look, from families to juvenile gangs to nation-states, we find that some parties disproportionately achieve their way. Even in such a simple matter as eye contact, we find the operation of power. Low-power people typically look less at an individual when they are speaking to a high-power person than when they are lis-

tening. In contrast, high-power people display nearly equivalent rates of looking while speaking and while listening (Ellyson et al., 1980). Not surprisingly, sociologist Amos Hawley (1963:422) observes: "Every social act is an exercise of power, every social relationship is a power equation, and every social group or system is an organization of power."

The bases of power fall into three categories. First, there are **constraints**—those resources that allow one party to add *new disadvantages* to a situation. People typically view constraints as punishments because they entail harming the body, psyche, or possessions of others. Second, there are **inducements**—those resources that allow one party to add *new advantages* to a situation. Individuals usually consider inducements to be rewards because they involve transferring socially defined good things—such as material objects, services, or social positions—in exchange for compliance with the wishes of the power wielder. Third, there is **persuasion**—those resources that enable one party to change the minds of other people *without* adding either advantages or disadvantages to a situation. By virtue of persuasion—based on one's party's reputation, wisdom, personal attractiveness, or control of the media—individuals or groups are led to prefer the same outcomes the power wielder prefers.

Power affects the ability of people to make the world work on their behalf. To gain mastery of critical resources is to gain mastery of people. To control key resources is to interpose oneself (or one's group) between people and the means whereby people meet their biological, psychological, and social needs. To the extent to which some groups command rewards, punishments, and persuasive communications, they are able to dictate the terms by which the game of life is played. At times to play the game "by the rules" means that it is no game at all—the deck is stacked, so that the outcome is a foregone conclusion.

ISRAELI KIBBUTZIM: CLASSLESS COMMUNITIES?

We have seen that social stratification entails the unequal distribution of crucial rewards, particularly wealth, income, prestige, and power. Yet as we noted earlier in the chapter, since the earliest times social inequality has troubled a good many people. In modern Western nations most egalitarian reformers have concerned themselves with narrowing the range of inequality and increasing equality of *opportunity*, rather than abolishing a system of unequal rewards altogether. However, some, including Karl Marx, have envisioned a society in which no inequality would prevail in the allocation of rewards. For Marx, the ideal society would be one based on the slogan "From each according to his ability, to each according to his need." But Marx's slogan refers only to *material* rewards. Even should complete equality be achieved in monetary income, inequalities could conceivably exist in "psychological income," particularly in prestige and power.

The experiences of the Israeli *kibbutzim*— or collective farms—provide a good many insights regarding modern efforts to establish a new type of communal existence based on the values of social equality, collective production and education, and direct participatory democracy. The first of Israel's 250 kibbutzim was founded in 1909. Today, the kibbutzim are home to 125,000 people, 3.5 percent of Israel's population. They produce 11 percent of the nation's total output and supply more than 40 percent of its agricultural products.

All major decisions in a kibbutz are taken at a general assembly of the members, which meets 35 to 40 times a year. A smaller secretariat meets weekly, and includes managers who are in charge of labor, education, and finances. Five major principles dominate kibbutz life:

1. All kibbutz property is held in common.

2. No outside hired labor should be employed.

3. The allocation of a member's time among work, study, and leisure is determined by the community.

4. All income is distributed on the basis of the norm, "From everyone according to ability—to everyone according to need."

5. Children are cared for and educated in communal children's homes.

The Israeli kibbutzim have provided a unique answer to the historical crisis of the Jewish people, who have experienced anti-Semitism, dependence, and alienation, culminating in the absolute challenge to their survival in the Holocaust. The members of the kibbutzim played a major role in the establishment of the Jewish homeland. But the movement's early idealistic pioneers had also hoped that the kibbutzim would become the model for all Israeli society. They had dreamed of creating a new society in which there would be no oppression or exploitation and in which people would devote themselves to the common good.

Despite equality in material rewards, stratification has not been eliminated from kibbutz life, since differences in prestige and power remain (Rosenfeld, 1951; Gerson, 1978). For instance, managerial positions have become associated with high prestige and power. Since collective farms typically have suffered from a lack of specially talented men and women, scarcity puts such people at a premium and gives them recognition. These individuals have opportunities to travel throughout Israel on kibbutz business and enjoy pleasures that the rank-and-file lack. And they experience the ego-expanding gratifications of being the representatives of their whole community in dealings with bankers, merchants, and government officials. Additionally, the oldtimers or kibbutz pioneers—*vatikim*—possess considerable prestige based on seniority alone.

Change has also altered kibbutz arrangements. The communities have gradually moved toward a compromise between their original communal ideals and the values of the family and the individual (Ichilov and Bar, 1980; Shipler, 1984). Increasingly, the family has become the centerpiece in the kibbutzinik's personal relationship, a situation in sharp contrast with the negation of the family in the early communes. Moreover, in increasing numbers, kibbutzim have moved children out of dormitories and into their parents' apartments. In some cases, members of certain families now enjoy advantages that are not enjoyed by other families. The standard of living has also risen sharply, and in many kibbutzim it compares with that of middle-class urban families. With economic prosperity, the kibbutzim have deferred increasingly to private desires and needs. Young people often travel abroad and acquire university educations that have no direct relevance to kibbutz-related professions.

Over 90 percent of kibbutzim now boast some form of light or heavy industry (Maital, 1982). They make pianos, plastics, cryogenic instruments, color TVs, microprocessors, and oscilloscopes. Many of the products compete favorably in world markets. But industrialization has severely taxed the kibbutzim norm against hiring outside labor. Even so, most kibbutzim have responded to industrial development by se-verely limiting managerial perquisites and periodically rotating managers back to production work. In some instances, older, established kibbutzim have funneled work to newer kibbutzim eager to take the plunge into industry. Clearly, the kibbutz experience testifies to the difficulty of establishing egalitarian societies.

IDENTIFYING SOCIAL CLASSES

In the course of our everyday conversations we talk about the "upper class," "middle class," and "lower class," referring to these social classes as distinct groups. Two views are found among sociologists concerning the accuracy of this popular conception. The first view holds that classes are real and bounded strata. Although this position has been a central element in Marxist formulations (Marx and Engels, 1848/1955; Anderson, 1971; Wright, 1979), it also emerges in the work of other sociologists who have identified a blue-collar–white-collar division in American life (Blau and Duncan, 1972; Vanneman and Pampel, 1977). The second view portrays American society as essentially classless, one in which class divisions are blurred by virtue of their continuous and uninterrupted nature. Seen in this manner, "social classes" are culturally quite alike and simply reflect gradations in rank, rather than hard-and-fast social groups (Rodman, 1968; Nisbet, 1970).

The differing conceptions derive in large measure from different approaches to identifying social classes: (1) the objective method, (2) the self-placement method, and (3) the reputational method. Although all the approaches produce some overlap in classes, there are appreciable differences in the results afforded by each (Kerbo, 1983). Moreover, each approach has certain advantages and disadvantages (see Table 6.2). Let us consider each method more carefully.

TABLE 6.2

Identifying Social Classes

Method	Advantages	Disadvantages
Objective	A clear-cut method for studying the correlates of social class. It is commonly the simplest and cheapest approach, since data can usually be obtained from government sources.	The method often does not yield divisions that people themselves employ in their daily lives.
Self-Placement	The method can be applied to a large population, since survey techniques can be employed for securing the data. A useful method for predicting political behavior, since who people think they are influences how they vote.	The class with which people identify may represent their aspirations rather than their current associations or the appraisals of other people.
Reputational	The method provides a valuable tool for investigating social distinctions in small groups and communities. It is especially useful for predicting associational patterns among people.	The method is difficult to use in large samples where people have little or no knowledge of one another.

The Objective Method. The **objective method** views social class as a statistical category. The categories are formed not by the members themselves, but by sociologists or statisticians. Most commonly people are assigned to social classes on the basis of income, occupation, or education (or some combination of these characteristics). The label "objective" can be misleading, for it is not meant to imply that the approach is more "scientific" or "unbiased" than either of the others. Rather, it is objective in that numerically measurable criteria are employed for the placement of individuals. Table 6.3 shows one way of depicting the dis-

tribution of Americans by median family income.

The objective method provides a rather clear-cut statistical measure for investigating various correlates of class, such as life expectancy, mental illness, divorce, political attitudes, crime rates, and leisure activities. It is usually the simplest and cheapest approach, since statistical data can be obtained from government agencies and the Census Bureau. But there is more to class than simply raw statistical data. In the course of their daily lives, people size one another up on a good many standards of excellence. Moreover, it is not only actual income, occupa-

TABLE 6.3

Median Family Income of Americans, 1983

If Your Family Income Is	You Fall in This Bracket
More than $75,000	Top 3%
More than $50,000	Top 13%
More than $40,000	Top 23%
More than $30,000	Top 39%
More than $25,000	Top 49%
Less than $20,000	Bottom 39%
Less than $15,000	Bottom 28%
Less than $10,000	Bottom 16%
Less than $5,000	Bottom 6%

Source: U.S. Department of Commerce.

tion, or education that matters, but the meanings and definitions others assign to these qualities. For instance, a banker, while not falling below the middle class, is not necessarily accorded the highest social position in American communities (Warner and Lunt, 1941:82).

The Self-Placement Method. The **self-placement method** (also known as the subjective method) has people identify the social class to which they think they belong. Class is viewed as a social category, one in which people group themselves with other individuals they perceive as sharing certain attributes in common with them. The class lines may or may not conform to what social scientists think are logical lines of cleavage in the objective sense. Researchers typically ask respondents to identify their social class, an approach reflected in Figure 6.2.

The major advantage of the self-placement approach is that it can be applied to a large population, whereas, as we will shortly see, the reputational approach is limited to small communities. Table 6.4 shows how Americans rank the prestige of various occupations when asked to do so.

The self-placement method is also an especially useful tool for predicting political behavior, since who people *think* they are influences how they vote. However, the approach has its limitations. The class with which people identify may represent their aspirations rather than their current associations or the appraisals of other people. Further, when placing themselves in a national class structure, people commonly use fewer categories than they do when interacting with actual people and sizing them up in terms of subtle distinctions.

The Reputational Method. In the self-placement method people are asked to rank themselves. In the **reputational method** they are asked how they classify *other* individuals. This approach views class as a social group, one in which people share a feeling of oneness and are bound together in relatively stable patterns of interaction. Thus class rests on knowledge of who associates with whom. The approach gained prominence in the 1930s when W. Lloyd Warner and his associates studied the class structure of three communities: "Yankee City" (Newburyport, Massachusetts), a New England town of some 17,000 people (Warner and Lunt, 1941, 1942); "Old City" (Natchez, Mississippi), a southern community of about 10,000 (Davis, Gardner, and Gardner, 1941); and "Jonesville" (Morris, Illinois), a Midwestern town of about 6,000 (Warner, 1949). In Yankee City and Old City, Warner identified six classes: upper-upper, lower-upper, upper-middle, lower-middle, upper-lower, and lower-lower. In the more recently settled and smaller midwestern community of Jonesville he found five classes, since individuals made no distinction between the upper-upper and lower-upper classes (the former being an "old-family" class representing "an aristocracy of birth and wealth" and the latter a class composed of the "new rich") (see Figure 6.3).

Question: If you were asked to use one of four names for your social class, which would you say you belong in: the lower class, the working class, the middle class, or the upper class?

Answer: I belong in...

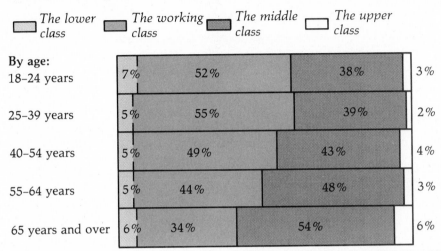

FIGURE 6.2   THE SELF-PLACEMENT METHOD FOR IDENTIFYING CLASS MEMBERSHIP
(Source: Surveys by the National Opinion Research Center, General Social Surveys, 1982, 1983, and 1984 combined. Public Opinion, *8 [February/March, 1985], p. 32.)*

The reputational method is a valuable tool for investigating social distinctions in small groups and small communities. And it is particularly useful in predicting associational patterns among people. But it is difficult to use in large samples where people have little or no knowledge of one another.

Combining Approaches. Warner undertook most of his research prior to World War II. Recently sociologists Richard D. Coleman and Lee Rainwater (1978) have updated our understanding of the class structure of urban America by combining the self-placement and reputational methods. They interviewed residents of Kansas and Boston, querying them about their perception of the levels of contemporary living. The urbanites ranked each other and themselves in the following manner:

1. *People who have really made it.* At the very top of the American class structure is an elite class of wealthy individuals. Some of these are old rich (the Rockefellers); others the celebrity rich (Paul Newman); still others the anonymous rich (a millionaire shopping center developer); and yet another group made up of the run-of-the-mill rich (a well-healed physician).

2. *People who are doing very well.* Corporate executives and professional people make up this class. These individuals reside in large, comfortable homes, belong to relatively exclusive country clubs, occasionally vacation in Europe and places known for their elite clientele, and send their children to private colleges or large, reputable state universities.

3. *People who have achieved the middle-class*

TABLE 6.4

Prestige Rankings of Occupations, 1972–1982

Occupation	Score
Physician	82
College teacher	78
Lawyer	76
Dentist	74
Bank officer	72
Airline pilot	70
Clergy	69
Sociologist	66
Secondary school teacher	63
Registered nurse	62
Pharmacist	61
Elementary school teacher	60
Accountant	56
Librarian	55
Actor	55
Funeral director	52
Athlete	51
Reporter	51
Bank teller	50
Electrician	49
Police officer	48
Insurance agent	47
Secretary	46
Mail carrier	42
Owner of a farm	41
Restaurant manager	39
Automobile mechanic	37
Baker	34
Salesclerk	29
Gas station attendant	22
Waiter and waitress	20
Garbage collector	17
Janitor	16
Shoeshiner	12

Note: Americans ranked a number of occupations in terms of prestige in national surveys conducted between 1972 and 1982. The highest possible score an occupation could receive was 90 and the lowest 10. The table shows the ranking of a number of the occupations.
(*Source:* National Opinion Research Center, 1982:299–314.)

dream. These individuals enjoy the "good life" as defined in material terms, but they lack the luxuries of those in the higher classes. More often than not they are subordinates who reside in a three-bedroom home with a family-TV room.

4. *People who have a comfortable life.* While enjoying a "comfortable" life, the members of this class have less money at their disposal than the people above them and they live in less fashionable suburbs.

5. *People who are just getting by.* Some Americans enjoy "respectable" jobs, but "the pay is not the greatest." The husband may be employed as a blue-collar worker and the wife as a waitress or store clerk. The couple may own or rent a small home, but they find that "getting by" puts a strain on their joint income.

6. *People who are having a difficult time.* Members of this group find "the going tough." Both the husband and the wife work (although periodically they may experience unemployment), but their income is low. Much of their leisure time is spent viewing television. They do, however, have one consolation: "They are not on welfare."

7. *People who are poor.* At the "bottom of the heap" are "people who are down and out." Many of them receive government assistance and benefits.

The Coleman-Rainwater divisions are somewhat unwieldy. For the most part, sociologists as well as laypeople find it easier to employ the labels "upper class," "middle class," "working class," and "lower class" (poor people) when considering class distinctions. Research suggests that these terms correspond reasonably well with objective class indicators such as income, education, occupational skill level, and manual versus nonmanual jobs (Kerbo, 1983).

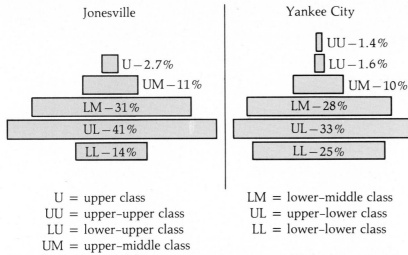

Jonesville

U – 2.7%
UM – 11%
LM – 31%
UL – 41%
LL – 14%

Yankee City

UU – 1.4%
LU – 1.6%
UM – 10%
LM – 28%
UL – 33%
LL – 25%

U = upper class
UU = upper–upper class
LU = lower–upper class
UM = upper–middle class

LM = lower–middle class
UL = upper–lower class
LL = lower–lower class

FIGURE 6.3 STRATIFICATION IN JONESVILLE AND YANKEE CITY

In Jonesville, a midwestern community, W. Lloyd Warner and his associates found five classes: one upper class, two middle classes, and two lower classes. In Yankee City, a considerably older eastern seaboard community, they identified six classes, the upper class being divided by an "old family"–"new family" chasm. Birth was crucial for membership in the "old-family" (upper-upper) class. Its members could trace their lineage and wealth through many generations. In terms of wealth, the "new-family" (lower-upper) class could meet the means test, but its members failed to meet the lineage test so essential for upper-upper class membership. (Source: Adapted from W. Lloyd Warner. 1949. Democracy in Jonesville. New York: Harper & Row.)

However, the terms mask important divisions and interests among groups in our society. Moreover, they do not necessarily correspond with self-placement identifications. Even so, these class terms remain useful both because they have the most meaning for the most people and because they are significantly related to major occupational and property divisions.

Explanations of Social Stratification

Throughout human history, the question of why social inequality and division should characterize the human condition has been a matter of lively concern (Lenski, 1966).

And as with earlier philosophers, the issue has provided a central focus of the new science called sociology (Dahrendorf, 1968). Through the years, two strikingly divergent answers have emerged. The first—the conservative thesis—has supported existing social arrangements, contending that an unequal distribution of social rewards is a necessary instrument for getting the essential tasks of society performed. In sharp contrast, the second view—the radical thesis—has been highly critical of existing social arrangements, viewing social inequality as a dog-eat-dog and exploitative mechanism arising out of a struggle for valued goods and services in short supply. Contemporary theories of inequality fall broadly into one or the other tradition. Those with roots in the conservative tradition are labeled *func-*

tionalist theories; those stemming from the radical tradition are called *conflict* theories. Hence, as sociologists Seymour Lipset and Reinhard Bendix (1951:150) remark, "Discussions of different theories of class are often academic substitutes for a real conflict over political orientations."

THE FUNCTIONALIST THEORY OF STRATIFICATION

The functionalist theory of social inequality holds that stratification exists because it is beneficial for society. This theory was most clearly set forth in 1945 by Kingsley Davis and Wilbert Moore, although it has been subsequently modified and refined by other sociologists. Davis and Moore argue that social stratification is both universal and necessary, and hence no society is ever totally unstratified or classless. In their view all societies require a system of stratification if they are to fill all the statuses comprising the social structure and to motivate individuals to perform the duties associated with these positions. Consequently, society must motivate people at two different levels: (1) It must instill in certain individuals the desire to fill various positions, and (2) once in these positions it must instill in the occupants the desire to carry out the appropriate roles.

Society must concern itself with human motivation because the duties associated with the various statuses are not all equally pleasant to the human organism, are not all equally important to social survival, and are not all equally in need of the same abilities and talents. If social life were otherwise, it would make little difference who got into which positions, and the problem of social placement would be greatly reduced. Moreover, the duties associated with a good many positions are viewed by their occupants as onerous. Hence, in the absence of motivation, many individuals would fail to act out their roles.

On the basis of these social realities, Davis and Moore contend that a society must have, first, some kind of rewards that it can use as inducements for its members, and second, some way of distributing these rewards among the various statuses. Inequality is the motivational incentive that society has evolved to meet the twin problems of filling all the statuses and getting the occupants to enact the associated roles to the best of their abilities. Since these rewards are built into the social system, social stratification is a structural feature of all societies.

Employing the economists' model of supply and demand, Davis and Moore say that the positions most highly rewarded are those (1) that are occupied by the most talented or qualified incumbents (supply) and (2) that are functionally most important (demand). For instance, to ensure sufficient physicians, a society needs to offer them high salaries and great prestige. If it did not offer these rewards, Davis and Moore suggest that we could not expect people to undertake the "burdensome" and "expensive" process of medical education. So, people at the top must receive the rewards they do. If they did not, the positions would remain unfilled and society would disintegrate.

This structure-function approach to stratification has been the subject of much criticism (Tumin, 1953; Collins, 1975). For one thing, critics charge that people are *born* into family positions of privilege and disprivilege (Anderson, 1971). As we will see later in our discussion of social mobility, where people end up in the stratification system depends in good measure on birth. Even in open class systems like the United States, the starting blocks in the competitive race are so widely staggered that the runners in the rear have only a remote chance of catching up with those ahead, while those starting ahead must virtually quit to lose ground. Indeed, conflict theorists contend that society is structured so that individuals *maintain* a ranking that is determined by birth and that is *irrespective* of their abilities (Bottomore, 1966).

Randall Collins (1975:420) directs another argument against the implied labor market model behind the Davis-Moore theory:

Following through the pure market model leads us to a startling conclusion: The system must tend toward perfect equality in the distribution of wealth. In a situation where labor is totally free to move wherever it wishes, jobs that pay high wages tend to attract a surplus of workers, which in turn will lead to a decline in their income. Jobs paying low wages tend to produce the opposite effect. Wherever jobs pay above or below the average, processes are set in motion through labor mobility which eventually bring wages back into line with all the others.

Conflict theorists point out that the labor market does not operate freely, as functionalists imply, because power is distributed unequally and educational requirements exist for employment.

Critics also point out that many of the positions of highest responsibility in the United States—government, science, technology, and education—are not financially well-rewarded. The officers of large corporations earn considerably more than do the president of the United States, cabinet members, and Supreme Court justices. In 1984 the median pay for chairpersons of large corporations was $780,769. Table 6.5 shows the 1984 earnings received by a number of prominent people in noncorporate jobs. Moreover, one may ask whether garbage collectors, despite their lower pay and prestige, are more important to the survival of the United States than top athletes who receive incomes in seven figures. In sum, the notion that many low-paying positions are functionally less important to society than are high-paying positions is difficult to support.

THE CONFLICT THEORY OF STRATIFICATION

The conflict theory of social equality holds that stratification exists because it benefits individuals and groups who have the power to dominate and exploit others. Whereas functionalists stress the common interests the members of society share, conflict theorists focus on the interests that divide people. Viewed from the conflict perspective, society is an arena in which people struggle for privilege, prestige, and power, and advantaged groups enforce their advantage through coercion.

The conflict theory draws heavily on the ideas of Karl Marx. As discussed in Chapter 1, Marx believed that a historical perspective is essential for understanding any society. To grasp how a particular economic system works, he said that we must keep in mind the predecessor from which it evolved and the process by which it grows. According to Marx, the current state of technology and the method of organizing production are the primary determinants of the evolutionary direction of society. At each stage of history, these factors determine the group that will dominate the society and the groups that will be subjugated. For instance, under the feudal arrangement, the medieval lords were in control of the economy and dominated the serfs. Under the capitalist system, the manor lord has been replaced by the modern capitalist and the serf by the "free" laborer—in reality a propertyless worker who "has nothing to sell but his hands."

Marx contended that the capitalist drive to realize surplus value is the foundation of modern class struggle—an irreconcilable clash of interests between workers and capitalists. *Surplus value* is the difference between the value that workers create (as determined by the labor-time embodied in a commodity that they produce) and the value that they receive (as determined by

TABLE 6.5

Pay for Important Jobs

Chairpersons of large corporations (median)	$ 780,769	Thomas O'Neil, Speaker, U.S. House of Representatives	$94,600
Martina Navratilova, tennis player	$4,174,000	Constance Clayton, superintendent of schools, city of Philadelphia	$85,000
Mike Schmidt, third baseman, Philadelphia Phillies baseball team	$2,000,000	Benjamin Ward, police commissioner, New York City	$82,000
Marshall Manley, senior partner, Finley, Kumble law firm, New York	$850,000	Tom Bradley, mayor, city of Los Angeles	$76,865
Jackie Presser, president, Teamsters Union	$491,056	Charles Robb, governor, state of Virginia	$75,000
Ronald Reagan, President United States	$200,000	Paul Volcker, chairman, Federal Reserve Board	$72,600
David Gardner, president, University of California	$165,000	Gen. John W. Vessey, chairman, Joint Chiefs of Staff	$65,998
A. W. Clausen, president World Bank	$150,000	Judy Goldsmith, president, National Organization for Women	$51,402
Lane Kirkland, president, AFL-CIO	$110,000	Ralph Rickett, sanitation commissioner, city of Cleveland	$34,650
Richard Schubert, president, American Red Cross	$110,000	Joseph Cardinal Bernardin, archbishop, Catholic Archdiocese of Chicago	$12,000
Warren Burger, Chief Justice, U.S. Supreme Court	$104,700		

(Source: *U.S. News & World Report*, April 29, 1985, p. 62. Copyright, 1985, U.S. News and World Report, Inc.)

the subsistence level of their wages). Capitalists do not create surplus value; they appropriate it through their exploitation of workers. Consequently, as portrayed by Marx, capitalists are thieves who steal the fruits of the laborer's toil. The capitalist accumulation of capital (wealth) derives from surplus value and is the key to—indeed, the incentive for—the development of contemporary capitalism. Marx believed that the class struggle will eventually be resolved when the working class overthrows the capitalist class and establishes a new and equitable social order.

Marx held that classes do not exist in isolation, independent of other classes to which they are opposed: "Individuals form a class only in so far as they are engaged in a common struggle with another class" (quoted by Dahrendorf, 1959:14). Under capitalism, workers at first are blinded by a *false consciousness*—an incorrect assessment of how the system works and of their subjugation and exploitation by capitalists. But through a struggle with capitalists, the workers' "objective" class interests become translated into a subjective recognition of their "true" circumstances and they formulate goals for organized action—in brief, they acquire *class consciousness*. Hence, according to Marxists, if the working class is to take on its historic role of overturning capitalism, "it must become a class not only 'as against capital' but also 'for itself'; that is to say, the class struggle must be raised from the level of economic necessity to the level of conscious aim and effective class consciousness" (Lukacs, 1968:76). It is not enough for the working class to be a "class in itself"; it must become a "class for itself."

Much of the appeal of Marx's work lies in its seemingly straightforward simplicity. He seems to strip away the superficial verbiage and qualifications of which college professors seem so fond. But it is this very simplicity that is deceiving. Conflict is a pervasive feature of human life and is not restricted to economic relations. As Ralf Dahrendorf (1959:208) observes: "It appears that not only in social life, but wherever there is life, there is conflict." Dahrendorf holds that group conflict is an inevitable aspect of society, and he rejects Marx's view that the proletarian revolution will eliminate class conflict.

Even in the realm of property, the Marxist dichotomy between the capitalist class and the working class hides or distorts other dynamic processes. Debtor and creditor have also stood against each other throughout history. For example, a dominant feature of nineteenth-century politics was the cheap-money cry of agrarians (the Greenback and Free Silver movements). Consumers and sellers have also confronted one another, a factor feeding the ghetto outbreaks of the 1960s (Dynes and Quarantelli, 1968). And divisions among racial and ethnic groups, skilled workers and unskilled laborers, and union organizations have been recurrent features of the American landscape.

Ownership of property in the form of the means of production constitutes only one source of power. The possession of the *means of administration* provides another.

The Soviet Union and Eastern European nations provide a good illustration of this. Milovan Djilas (1957), a Yugoslavian Marxist and one-time lieutenant of President Tito, has vigorously condemned the rise of what he calls "the new class" in these nations. The communist new class is "made up of those who have special privileges and economic preference because of the administrative monopoly they hold" (p. 39). The party bureaucracy comprises the new elite: "It is the bureaucracy which formally uses, administers, and controls both nationalized and socialized property as well as the entire life of society. The role of the bureaucracy in society, i.e., monopolistic administration and control of national income and national goods, consigns it to a special privileged position" (p. 44). Djilas charges: "Power is an end in itself and the essence of contemporary Communism" (p. 169).

Even within the United States, one can go a long way nowadays without property. As we will see in Chapter 8, a good deal of power derives from office rather than ownership in large multinational corporations. Not only do executives hold comparatively little in the way of property, but their influence lasts only as long as they hold their particular positions. Their hold on power is often tenuous, and they are easily replaceable. Much the same picture emerges from government. Neither Harry S Truman, Dwight D. Eisenhower, Lyndon B. Johnson, Richard M. Nixon, Gerald Ford, nor Ronald Reagan launched their careers from a base of financial, industrial, or landed property, yet each reached the pinnacle of power in the United States.

Recently Erik Olin Wright (1978a, 1978b, 1979) has investigated class relations in the United States using Marx's idea that class must be defined in terms of people's relation to the means of production. He identifies four classes: capitalists, managers, workers, and the petty bourgeoisie (small entrepreneurs). Using samples of people in the labor force, Wright finds that these categories are about as good in explaining differences in income among people as are occupation and education. Even allowing for the effects on income of occupation, education, age, and job tenure, capitalists have higher incomes than do the other classes. Thus Wright concludes that being a capitalist makes a difference.

A SYNTHESIS

Any number of sociologists have noted that both the functionalist and conflict theories have merit, but that each is better than the other in answering different questions (Sorokin, 1959; van den Berghe, 1963). For instance, Harold R. Kerbo (1983) observes that a supply and demand relation such as that proposed by structure-function theorists explains some of the distribution of rewards within the occupational structure. But he also notes that supply and demand is not free and unrestricted, the position taken by conflict theorists. Kerbo agrees with Marxian theorists that economic conflicts are among the most important sources of division in capitalist societies, but not the only sources. He views stratification systems as socially evolved mechanisms—institutional arrangements—for reducing conflict over the distribution of valued goods and services in society.

Some sociologists like Ralf Dahrendorf (1959) contend that society is basically "Janus-headed," and that functionalists and conflict theorists are simply studying two aspects of the same reality. Sociologist Gerhard E. Lenski (1966) builds on this observation and looks for ways of integrating the two perspectives to arrive at a workable synthesis. He tends to agree with functionalists that the chief resources of society are allocated as rewards to people who occupy vital positions and that stratification fosters

a rough match between scarce talents and rewards. But as a society advances in technology, it becomes capable of producing a considerable surplus of goods and services. This surplus gives rise to conflicts over who should control it. Power provides the answer to the question of control and determines the distribution of the surplus. Consequently, with technological advance, an increasing proportion of the goods and services available to a society are distributed on the basis of power. In short, Lenski holds that both the functionalist and conflict positions are true, but that neither contains the whole truth.

The American Class System

Sociologists may disagree regarding the sources of social stratification. However, they agree that social inequality is a *structured* aspect of contemporary life. When sociologists say that social inequality is structured, they mean more than that individuals and groups differ in the privileges they enjoy, the prestige they receive, and the power they wield. Structuring means that inequality is hardened or institutionalized, so that there is a system for determining who gets what. Inequality does not occur in a random fashion, but follows recurrent, relatively consistent and stable patterns. Further, these inequalities are typically passed on from one generation to the next. Individuals and groups that are advantaged commonly find ways to ensure that their offspring will also be advantaged.

Sociologists have borrowed the term "stratification" from geology. However, it is important to realize that it is somewhat more difficult to classify individuals within strata than it is to categorize rocks. Geologists usually find it rather easy to determine where one stratum or rocks ends and another begins. But as we pointed out earlier

The United States is a stratified society, like most others, with great contrasts in its members' standards of living. Social stratification finds expression in the unequal distribution of various scarce, divisible "good things." (Billy Barnes/ Southern Light)

in the chapter, social strata often shade off into one another so that their boundaries are dim and indistinct. Even so, sociologists and laypeople typically use the labels "upper class," "middle class," "working class," and "lower class" in discussing the American class system, and we will follow this usage here.

THE SIGNIFICANCE OF SOCIAL CLASSES

Few aspects of social life affect so strongly the way people behave and think as does social class. For one thing, it largely determines their **life chances**—the likelihood that individuals and groups will enjoy desired goods and services, fulfilling experiences, and opportunities for living healthy and long lives. Broadly considered, life chances has to do with people's level of living and their options for choice. For instance, the members of the higher social classes need to devote a smaller part of their resources to survival needs than do members of the lower social classes. Sociologist Paul Blumberg (1980) finds that Americans in the highest tenth of the class hierarchy spend about 11 percent of their income for food, as compared to over 40 percent for those in the lowest tenth. And the members of the higher classes also benefit in nonmaterial ways. Their children are more likely to go further in school and perform better than the children of parents who occupy lower socioeconomic positions (DiMaggio, 1982).

Likewise, the infants of parents of the higher classes are more likely to survive than are infants of parents of the lower classes (Wicks and Stockwell, 1984). And among the elderly, the active life expectancy is greater for the nonpoor than for the poor (Katz, 1983). Moreover, a survey conducted for the California Department of Mental

Health found that income is associated with health. Fifty-three percent of those paid $30,000 or more a year felt well physically; only 29 percent of those whose family income was $10,000 or less felt tip-top (*Columbus Dispatch*, 1980). And research consistently shows that those in the lower social classes have higher rates of mental illness (Myers and Bean, 1968; Goodman et al., 1983).

Social class also affects people's **style of life**—the magnitude and manner of their consumption of goods and services. Convenience foods—TV dinners, potato chips, frozen pizza, and Hamburger Helper—are more frequently on the menus of lower-income than higher-income households. Lower-class families drink less vodka, scotch, bourbon, and imported wine, but consume more beer and blended whiskey. Families in the middle and upper classes tend to buy living-room furniture one piece at a time from specialty stores; lower-class families are more likely to buy matched living-room sets from discount department stores or regular furniture stores. And lower-income families spend more of their leisure time watching television than do higher-income families (Bridgwater, 1982).

Social class is similarly associated with various patterns of behavior. For instance, differences exist in religious affiliation. Among Americans, income averages $16,300 for Lutherans, $17,000 for Methodists, $20,500 for Presbyterians, $21,700 for Episcopalians, $17,400 for Catholics, $23,000 for Jews, and $17,600 for people with no religious affiliation (Smith, 1984). Class also influences political participation. Voting increases with socioeconomic status in most Western nations (Verba, Nie, and Kim, 1978; Zipp, Landerman, and Luebke, 1980). And class is an important determinant of sexual behavior (Weinberg and Williams, 1980). For example, the lower classes are more likely to experience sexual inter-course and other sexual behaviors at earlier ages than are the higher classes. In sum, one's social class leaves few areas of life untouched.

WHAT IS HAPPENING TO THE MIDDLE CLASS?

According to an increasing number of observers of the economic and social scene, the American middle class is an endangered species (Steinberg, 1983; Thurow, 1984b; Zonana, 1984; Blackburn and Bloom, 1985). The view is based largely on U.S. Census Bureau reports of household income. These statistics show that families with annual earnings of between $15,000 and $35,000 (using the purchasing power of 1982 dollars as a basis) made up 44 percent of all families in 1982, down from 53 percent in 1970. Moreover, the richest one-fifth of American families received nearly 43 percent of the country's total money income in 1982—nine times as much as the poorest fifth, up from seven-and-a-half times as much a decade earlier. These trends suggest to some social scientists that the United States has moved in the direction of becoming a nation of "haves" and "have-nots," with fewer people in between.

Those who consider the middle class to be declining link the trend to industrial change in the United States that is eliminating high-paying jobs and replacing them with low-paying ones. Smokestack industries, like machine tools, autos, and steel, with their high-wage, skilled blue-collar workers, provide many middle-income jobs. Over the last decade, their share of total employment has fallen sharply. And when these industries shrink, the middle class shrinks with them.

At the same time that jobs in manufacturing were declining over the past decade, nearly nine out of ten new jobs were created in the service and trade sectors of the economy (more than half of them in health, business services, finance, and eating and drinking places). According to economists Barry Bluestone and Bennett Harrison (1982), it takes two department store jobs or three restaurant jobs to equal the earnings of one manufacturing job. Overall, service industries display a two-hump distribution in income—high and low. In 1980, production workers in manufacturing earned an average of $15,000 per year, and managers and professionals $23,000. However, in the service sector nonsupervisory employees made an average of $9,900 per year, while their supervisors averaged nearly $30,000.

Projections by the Bureau of Labor Statistics suggest that the jobs most likely to grow over the next decade are at opposite ends of the earnings spectrum (Steinberg, 1983). Strong growth is expected in the number of professional and technical workers. But even stronger growth is expected at the lower end, among such service workers as janitors, fast-food workers, and hospital orderlies. Overall, the eating and drinking industry is projected to *add* nearly three times as many jobs as will *exist* in the computer industry by 1990.

Political liberals have tended to accept the notion of a shrinking middle class. Conservative analysts have taken a more optimistic view. For instance, Fabian Linden (1984) blames the statistics showing a shrinking middle class primarily on the postwar baby boom. As young baby boomers entered the work force in recent years, they have swelled the ranks of low-income households. But as the baby boomers grow older, Linden says their incomes will rise. He also points out that the second-fastest-growing age group in the United States has been people 65 and over. Thus, all told, some three-fifths of all homes with incomes under $15,000 consist of individuals under 35 over 65. Simultaneously, with the increase in separations and divorces, families

headed by women grew from 12 percent of all households in 1970 to 16 percent today. Linden concludes that the demise of the middle class is a "fiction" based on a misreading of the effects of large changes in the age and living arrangements of adult Americans.

Those who see the emergence of a bipolar income distribution and the eclipse of the middle class express concern for American democracy. According to conventional American sociological wisdom, a healthy middle class is essential for a healthy democracy. A society composed of rich and poor lacks a political and economic mediating group. This observation underlay Marx's prediction that revolution would ensue as the economy generated a bipolar income distribution consisting of rich and poor. In part Marx was proved wrong because he did not foresee the rise of a middle class that had an interest in preserving capitalism and whose presence gave the poor hope that they too could escape poverty. But a shrinking middle class may now contribute to such a polarization. Downward social mobility for large numbers of a population can chill the soul and contribute to social meanness. Thus Richard M. Cyert (1984:3), president of Carnegie-Mellon University, says: "I expect that the twenty-first century will be a period of intense social struggle that will test the cohesiveness of our society." All this brings us to the matter of poverty in the United States.

POVERTY IN THE UNITED STATES

Historians may well look back on the 1980s as a time of rising affluence in the United States side by side with rising poverty. The growth in affluence is attributable to an increase in professional and technical jobs, along with more two-career couples whose combined incomes provide a "comfortable living." Simultaneously, Census Bureau statistics reveal a rapid increase in poverty since 1979, even if the value of food stamps, public housing, Medicare and Medicaid benefits is counted as income (Pear, 1984a, 1984b) (see Figure 6.4).

Defining Poverty. The definition of poverty is a matter of debate. In 1795, a group of

English magistrates decided that a minimum income should be "the cost of a gallon loaf of bread, multiplied by three, plus an allowance for each dependent" (Schorr, 1984). Today the Census Bureau defines the threshold of poverty in the United States as the minimum amount of money families need to purchase a nutritionally adequate

FIGURE 6.4   POVERTY RATES IN THE UNITED STATES, 1973–1983
A family of four was classified as poor if it had cash income of less than $10,178 in 1983. Income figures are expressed in percents. (Source: Bureau of the Census, news release, August 2, 1984.)

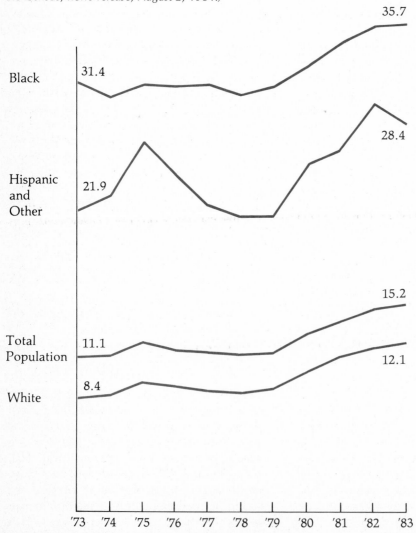

diet, assuming they use one-third of their income for food. Liberals contend the line is too low because it fails to take into account changes in the standard of living (Blumberg, 1980). Conservatives say it is too high because the poor receive in-kind income in the form of public assistance, including food stamps, public housing subsidies, and health care (Pear, 1983).

Who Are the Poor? Some twenty years after President Lyndon Johnson made his famous war on poverty speech on March 16, 1964, urbanites—not the Appalachians who were the focus of media attention in the 1960s—dominate the ranks of the poor. About 62 percent of the nation's poor lives in large cities, and their numbers are growing. Poverty also has become increasingly the lot of single and divorced mothers. Although fatherless families represent 15 percent of the nation's families, they constitute 46 percent of the households living in poverty. Children in particular are its victims. In 1983 one out of every four American children under 6 years of age was poor (Pear, 1984b). Nearly 50 percent of all black children, 40 percent of all Hispanic youngsters, and slightly more than 15 percent of all white children live in poverty.

Children under 16 years of age and elderly individuals over age 65 account, respectively, for 36 percent and 11 percent of the American poor. Farmers are also more likely to be poor than their city cousins. About 22 percent of white farmers and 49 percent of black farmers have incomes below the poverty line (Schreiner, 1983). Additionally, there are thousands of American farm workers who are poor, many of whom lack access to toilets and clean water at their work sites and suffer levels of parasitic illness rarely encountered in developed nations (Keller, 1984). And if individuals are handicapped, they are more than twice as likely as other workers to be poor (Census Bureau, 1984). About 23 percent of working-age people who receive food stamps and 37 percent of Medicaid recipients are disabled.

Theories of Poverty. Various theories have been advanced through the years to explain poverty. One approach looks to the characteristics of the poor to explain their difficulties. According to the **culture of poverty** thesis, the poor in class-stratified capitalist societies lack effective participation and integration within the larger society (Lewis, 1959, 1961, 1966). Clustered in large ghettos in cities like New York, Mexico City, and San Juan, the poor develop feelings of marginality, helplessness, dependence, and inferiority. These circumstances allegedly breed weak ego structures, lack of impulse control, a present-time orientation characterized by little ability to defer gratification, and a sense of resignation and fatalism. The resulting lifeways are both an adaptation and a reaction of the poor to their disadvantaged positions. They become self-perpetuating patterns as the ethos associated with the culture of poverty is transmitted to successive generations.

Many sociologists argue that the culture of poverty thesis has serious shortcomings (Valentine, 1968; Critchfield, 1978). For instance, as we pointed out in Chapter 1, Elliot Liebow depicts the economically poor streetcorner men of Washington, D.C., as very much immersed in American life and not as carriers of an independent culture of poverty. They too want what other American men want, but they are blocked from achieving their goals by a racist social order.

Another view sees poverty as largely *situational*. A study undertaken by the University of Michigan's Institute for Social Research (Duncan, 1984) portrays the poverty population as a kind of pool, with people flowing in and out. The findings are based on a survey of 5,000 American families chosen in 1968 and followed for a decade thereafter. The study cast doubt on the culture of poverty thesis that being poor at one time means being poor always. In the ten-year period, only 2.6 percent of the sample could be classed as persistently poor, as failing to meet the government's income standard for poverty in eight or more of the ten years. The 25 percent of the families in the sample who had received welfare at some time over the decade often received it for very short periods. Many people who slip into poverty do so for a limited time after major adverse events, such as divorce or illness. For many families, welfare serves as a type of insurance protection, something they use for a brief period but dispose of as quickly as they can.

Although women who were unmarried heads of households with children were somewhat more likely to be receiving welfare if they had come from welfare families, most women from welfare families did not receive welfare. The Michigan researchers found "little evidence that individual attitudes and behavior patterns affect individual economic progress." To a far greater extent, individuals "are the victims of their past, their environment, luck, and chance." The study supports the view that the overwhelming majority of Americans, given any reasonable choice, would prefer to work to support themselves than live on welfare.

Still another view portrays poverty as a *structural* feature of capitalist societies. The cyclical movements between economic expansion and contraction—boom and bust—contribute to sharp fluctuations in employment. Marx contended that an *industrial reserve army* is essential for capitalist economies. The industrial reserve army consists of individuals at the bottom of the class structure who are laid off in the interests of corporate profits during times of economic stagnation, then rehired when needed for producing profits during times of economic prosperity. It is disproportionately composed of minorities, who traditionally have been the last hired and the first fired. And proponents of the structural view charge that it is workers who bear the brunt of changes in industry, as seen in the persistent unemployment currently being experienced by many former workers in the auto and steel industries (Kerbo, 1983).

Poverty Programs. "The poor you always have with you," says St. John's Gospel. But the poor have not always been treated in the same way. For much of Western history, assistance to the poor has taken the form of private almsgiving, sporadically augmented with public relief. Because of the holy merit in giving, charity served the dual purpose of improving the spiritual state of the almsgiver while relieving want. But government has also intervened, although not necessarily in a charitable manner. For instance, in eighteenth-century England, poor laws provided workhouses for the able-bodied indigent to discourage people from adding themselves to the ranks of paupers. Of interest, much of the eighteenth- and nineteenth-century debate surrounding definitions of poverty and its remedies is startlingly similar to that of today (Himmelfarb, 1984).

Within the United States, President Lyndon Johnson's Great Society produced a flurry of social programs rivaling those of Franklin Roosevelt's New Deal. Some are gone, while others were severely cut or revamped by the Reagan administration in the early 1980s. Among the major antipoverty programs still available are the following:

Food Stamps. Fewer than 1 million recipients were enrolled in this nutrition program in its first year, 1964. In 1984 it spent $11.2 billion to help feed 21 million people.

Job Corps. The Labor Department spends $610 million a year to train about 80,000 disadvantaged young people annually in 107 residential centers.

Legal Services. The poor receive free legal assistance through state and local agencies that receive $281 million a year in federal aid.

Head Start. Close to $1 billion is spent each year on a comprehensive education program for about 430,000 underprivileged children.

VISTA. About $12 million is provided to fund more than 1,900 Volunteers in Service to America, who work in health, education, and social welfare projects in poor communities.

Medicaid. The health plan was begun in 1966 with expenses of $770 million. It is a federal-state program that provides health care to more than 20 million people who are poor or just above the poverty level at an annual cost of $20 billion. Another program, Medicare, finances health care for 29.5 million elderly and disabled people.

Aid to Families with Dependent Children (AFDC). AFDC is the oldest welfare program for poor children and their custodial parents. In 1935, when AFDC was created by the Social Security Act, the program paid benefits only to children. However, in 1950 the program was amended to include benefits for the custodial parent. And in 1961, states were permitted to provide aid to dependent children whose fathers were unemployed. In 1979 an average of 72 children received aid under the program for every 100 poor youngsters. But cutbacks in government funding resulted in only 53 of every 100 poor children receiving such aid in 1982. About 3.6 million households receive AFDC payments.

Two explanations have been advanced for the growth of welfare expenditures in contemporary Western nations. One view holds that relief institutions are a response to societal problems. As people's "needs" increase and the "capacity" of the economy grows, both consequences of industrialization and economic development, so do the responses of governmental relief-giving agencies. Seen in this fashion, the state is a "neutral arbiter" serving the common good. The other view portrays the state as an agency of ruling elites. The state is said to dole out welfare as a means of placating the rebellious poor and lessening popular opposition to existing social arrangements. Sociologists Larry Isaac and William R. Kelly (1981) looked into these matters, employing data from the black protest movement of the 1960s and early 1970s. While they found some support for both explanations, they found more support for the latter. As one observer (Kerbo, 1983:326) notes: "Hungry people in need don't bring more welfare; an angry poor who take their anger to the streets do."

Social Mobility

America has long been viewed as the "land of opportunity." Early in this century, the stories of Horatio Alger enjoyed wide appeal. The stories told of poor boys who "made good" in American life by reason of personal virtue, pluck, diligence, and hard work. More recently, best-selling books have described how individuals can achieve success by investing in real estate, bonds, collectibles, or the stock market, by dressing right, by intimidating others, by getting right with God, or by psyching themselves up. Underlying these notions is the assumption that individuals or groups can move from one level (stratum) to another in the stratification system, a process called

social mobility. Whereas social inequality has to do with differences in the distribution of benefits and burdens and social stratification with a structured system of inequality, social mobility refers to the shift of individuals or groups from one social status to another.

There are at least two basic reasons why social mobility takes place within society. First, societies change, and whether change is rapid or slow, it leads to new circumstances. Social change alters the division of labor, introducing new positions, undermining old ones, and shifting the allocation of scarce, divisible resources. Additionally, the exclusion from high rank of capable members of the lower strata often contributes to social strains that lead them to challenge the established arrangement and overthrow it, modify it, or extract concessions from privileged groups. Second, shifts occur in the availability of different types of talent. Although elites may monopolize the opportunities for training and education, they do not control the natural distribution of talent and ability. Thus, very often people must be recruited from the lower ranks.

FORMS OF SOCIAL MOBILITY

Social mobility can take a number of forms. Mobility may be vertical or horizontal. **Vertical mobility** involves movement from one social status to another of higher or lower rank. As we saw in Table 6.4, Americans differ in the prestige ratings of various occupations. If an auto mechanic (prestige score 37) became a bank officer (score 72), this shift would constitute upward mobility. On the other hand, if the auto mechanic became a garbage collector (score 17), this change would involve downward mobility. If the auto mechanic took a job as a restaurant manager (score 39), this shift would represent horizontal mobility. **Horizontal**

mobility entails movement from one social status to another that is approximately equivalent in rank.

Sociologists also distinguish between intergenerational and intragenerational mobility. **Intergenerational mobility** involves a comparison of the social status of parents and their children at some point in their respective careers (for example, as assessed by the rankings of their occupations at roughly the same age). Research shows that a large minority, perhaps even a majority of the American population, moves up or down at least a little in the class hierarchy in every generation. **Intragenerational mobility** entails a comparison of the social status of a person over an extended time period. Studies show that a large proportion of Americans have worked in different jobs and occupations in their lifetime (Sorensen, 1975; Duncan, 1984). But there are limits to the variety of most people's mobility experience. Short-distance movements tend to be the rule and long-distance movements the exception. Let us examine these matters more closely.

SOCIAL MOBILITY IN THE UNITED STATES

When sociologists talk about social mobility, they usually have intergenerational occupational mobility in mind. And given the traditional operation of sexism in the labor market, which until recent decades relegated women to the home or to low-paying jobs, much more is known about the mobility of men than of women. Perhaps the most impressive studies of social mobility in the United States have been undertaken by Peter M. Blau and Otis Dudley Duncan (1972), and more recently by David Featherman and Robert Hauser (1978b). The Blau and Duncan study employed data collected by the Census Bureau in 1962 from a sample of over 20,000 men, while that of Featherman and Hauser consisted of a sample of over 30,000 men in 1973.

Summarizing the data from these and related studies, it seems that about 50 percent of American men are immobile, remaining in their father's stratum (Davis, 1982). About 25 percent are upwardly mobile, moving from farm or blue-collar jobs to white-collar jobs. Another 10 percent are downwardly mobile, moving from white-collar to blue-collar jobs. And 15 percent move from farm to blue-collar positions.

There are two primary explanations for the higher rate of upward than downward intergenerational mobility in the United States. First, the *occupational structure* has been changing. More jobs were created toward the top of the occupational structure than toward the bottom with technological advances. Consequently, more people were needed in top positions. Second, *fertility* plays a role, with white-collar fathers generating fewer sons than blue-collar fathers. Hence, with higher-occupation fathers producing fewer sons and the top of the occupational structure expanding, there is more room toward the top of the class hierarchy. Overall, more than twice as many men have moved into white-collar jobs as have moved out of them (Davis, 1982).

In Chapter 7 we will consider the special circumstances of blacks and women in the United States and how racism and sexism have affected their mobility opportunities. However, it is important to point out here that the class system has proved to be much more rigid for blacks than for the general population (Blau and Duncan, 1972; Featherman and Hauser, 1978b; Wright, 1978b). Moreover, black fathers who have attained white-collar jobs have historically had greater difficulty than white fathers in passing their advantage to their sons. But this pattern may now be changing for those blacks able to break into higher occupational positions (Clark, 1983). Research also shows that working women are less likely to be in an occupational status close to their father's than are men (Hauser and Featherman, 1977). Traditionally women have been concentrated in lower nonmanual and white-collar clerical jobs. Thus, regardless of whether their fathers are higher or lower in occupational rank, women are commonly pushed up to, or down to, the lower white-collar positions.

SOCIAL MOBILITY IN INDUSTRIALIZED SOCIETIES

Concern with social mobility has reflected interest in the extent to which various societies have realized the ideal of equality of opportunity. Sociological evidence reveals that no contemporary society comes close to allowing all its members the same chance to acquire desired statuses. In all industrial societies, a family's class position plays a large part in determining the status placement of offspring. But by the same token, no modern society denies its male members the opportunity to be upwardly mobile. In each nation for which data are available, a large proportion of men have moved up or down between generations (Lipset, 1982).

Overall there is little difference among various industrialized countries in the rates of occupational mobility between the blue-collar and white-collar classes. The basic processes affecting rates of social mobility, once people of rural origin are set aside, appear to be structural—linked to the pace of economic development, rather than to political or economic systems. Thus rates of mobility are comparable in socialist and capitalist nations. A comparison of social mobility in six Communist countries (Bulgaria, Czechoslovakia, Hungary, Poland, Romania, and Yugoslavia) and seven non-

Communist ones (Australia, France, Italy, Norway, Sweden, the United States, and West Germany) reveals that blue-collar nonfarm sons (workers) are mobile into nonmanual jobs in 29.2 of the cases in the Communist average, and in 28.2 in the non-Communist sample (Connor, 1979). Although upward mobility may be somewhat higher in the United States than in most other countries, the United States does not appear to be significantly more open to mobility than other industrialized nations (Tyree, Semyonov, and Hodge, 1979; McRoberts and Selbee, 1981; Grusky and Hauser, 1984).

STATUS ATTAINMENT PROCESSES

In recent years, considerable sociological research has dealt with the factors underlying status transmission and attainment. Blau and Duncan (1972) have developed a technique for studying the course of an individual's occupational status over the life cycle. Called the **socioeconomic life cycle,** it involves a sequence of stages that begins with birth into a family with a specific social status and proceeds through childhood, socialization, schooling, job seeking, occupational achievement, marriage, and the formation and functioning of a new family unit. The outcomes of each stage are seen as affecting subsequent stages in the cycle. In order to capture the specific contributions of each stage, Blau and Duncan (1972:163) analyze their data by means of a statistical procedure called *path analysis:*

We think of the individual's life cycle as a sequence in time that can be described, however partially and crudely, by a set of classificatory or quantitative measurements taken at successive stages. . . . Given this scheme, the questions we are continually raising in one form or another are: how and to what degree do the circumstances of birth condition [determine]

subsequent status? And how does status attained . . . at one stage of the life cycle affect the prospects for a subsequent stage?

Blau and Duncan conclude that the social status of a man's parents typically has little *direct* impact on his occupational attainment. Instead, the primary influence of parental status is *indirect,* through its effect on level of schooling. (One of the virtues of path analysis is its ability to sort out direct from indirect effects). Overall, education (years of schooling completed) is the fact that has the greatest influence on a man's occupational attainment, both early and late.

Another factor that has a sizable effect is the level in the occupational status ladder at which a man starts his career. The lower he begins, the higher he has to rise, and the less likely he is to reach the top positions. Entry into some positions is conditional on performance in temporally prior ones. All societies have ways of "remembering" socially relevant aspects of an individual's biography, and that information is employed to shape his current opportunities (Maddox and Wiley, 1976).

William Sewell and his associates have also investigated the status attainment process. They based their work on a survey of Wisconsin high school seniors conducted in 1957 and a follow-up study of one-third of them from 1964 through 1967. They conclude that educational and occupational attainment are the outcome of two related processes: those by which status aspirations are formed, and those by which the aspirations become translated into an actual position in the status hierarchy. The Wisconsin data reveal that practically the entire effect of a family's socioeconomic status on a child's educational and occupational attainments is the result of the personal influences it exerts upon the child's status aspirations during adolescence. Other early factors that play a part are parental and teacher encouragement to attend college and the college plans of the adolescent's best friend.

But once these factors are controlled (statistically taken into account and allowed for), the effects of parental social status become insignificant and have no other direct influence upon status attainment. Rather, as Blau and Duncan also conclude, it is level of schooling that has the primary influence on subsequent occupational attainment. Overall, these sociological studies suggest that the contribution of schooling to father–son occupational inheritance consists of two separate steps: a relation between father's occupation and education, and a second relation between son's occupation and education.

Critics of status attainment research contend that it has a functionalist bias (Coser, 1975; Horan, 1978). Social positions are viewed as levels of performance, which are differentially evaluated and rewarded within a competitive market system. An underlying assumption is that the job market is fully open to individuals who acquire positions on the basis of competence. In contrast, conflict theorists argue that class categories are critical in determining the rewards Americans receive. Based on their ownership or nonownership of the means of production, people are channeled into class positions. In sum, the attainment process is seen as differing substantially for the members of a capitalist society (Wright, 1978a, 1978b; Smith, 1981).

Critics also contend that there are two sectors of the economy, or a **dual labor market.** The primary or *core* sector offers "good jobs" that provide high pay, security, and ample promotion possibilities. The other—the secondary or *periphery* sector—consists of "bad jobs" that provide low pay, poor working conditions, and little room for promotion. Recruitment to these two sectors varies, with blacks and women found more often in the secondary or periphery sector (Beck, Horan, and Tolbert, 1978, 1980). We will examine these matters at greater length in the next chapter.

SUMMARY

1. Most societies are organized so that their institutions systematically distribute benefits and burdens unequally among different categories of people. Sociologists call the structured ranking of individuals and groups—their grading into horizontal layers or strata—social stratification. Social stratification depends upon but is not the same thing as social differentiation—the process by which a society becomes increasingly specialized over time.

2. Stratification systems differ in the ease with which they permit people to move in or out of particular strata. Where people can change their status with relative ease, sociologists refer to the arrangement as an open system. In contrast, where people have great difficulty in changing their status, sociologists term the arrangement a closed system.

3. Sociologists typically take a multidimensional view of stratification, identifying three components: economic (wealth and income), prestige, and power. The rankings of some statuses may be dissimilar. For the most part, however, these three dimensions hang together, feeding into and supporting one another.

4. Three primary methods are employed by sociologists for identifying social classes. The objective method views social class as a statistical category. People are assigned to social classes on the basis of income, occupation, or education (or some combination of these characteristics). The self-placement method has people identify the social class to which they think they belong. Class is viewed as a social category, one in which people group themselves with other individuals they perceive as sharing certain attributes in common with them. The reputational method asks people how they classify other individuals. This approach views class as a social group.

5. The functionalist theory of social inequality holds that stratification exists because it is beneficial for society. According to sociologists Kingsley Davis and Wilbert Moore, society must concern itself with human motivation because the duties associated with the various statuses are not all equally pleasant to the human organism, are not all equally important to social survival, and are not all equally in need of the same abilities and talents. Consequently, society must have, first, some that it can use as inducements for its members, and second, some way of distributing these rewards differentially among the various statuses. Social stratification is the mechanism by which societies solve these twin problems.

6. The conflict theory of social inequality holds that stratification exists because it benefits individuals and groups who have the power to dominate and exploit others. The conflict perspective draws heavily on the ideas of Karl Marx. Marx contended that the capitalist drive to realize surplus value is the foundation of modern class struggle—an irreconcilable clash of interests between workers and capitalists. Initially workers are blinded by false consciousness, but through struggle with capitalists they evolve class consciousness.

7. Any number of sociologists have noted that both functionalist and conflict theories have merit, but that each is better than the other in answering different questions. They have sought a synthesis of the two positions. Thus Gerhard E. Lenski has looked for ways of integrating the two perspectives.

8. Few aspects of social life affect so strongly the way people behave and think as does social class. For one thing, it largely determines their life chances— the likelihood that individuals and groups will enjoy desired goods and services, fulfilling experiences, and opportunities for living healthy and long lives. Social class also affects people's style of life—the magnitude and manner of their consumption of goods and services.

9. Controversy surrounds the issue of whether or not the American middle class is an endangered species. Those who consider the middle class to be declining link the trend to industrial change in the United States that is eliminating high-paying jobs and replacing them with low-paying ones. Others see the demise of the middle class as a "fiction" based on a misreading of the effects of large changes in the age and living arrangements of adult Americans.

10. The Census Bureau defines the threshold of poverty in the United States as the minimum amount of money families need to purchase a nutritionally adequate diet, assuming they use one-

third of their income for food. Children and the elderly account for nearly half of Americans living in poverty. Three theories predominate regarding poverty. One explains the difficulties of the poor as stemming from a culture of poverty. Another view sees poverty as largely situational. Still another view portrays poverty as a structural feature of capitalist societies.

11. Social mobility takes a number of forms. It may be vertical or horizontal. And it may be intergenerational or intragenerational. When sociologists talk about social mobility, they usually have intergenerational occupational mobility in mind. Although upward mobility may be somewhat higher in the United States than in most other countries, the United States does not appear to be significantly more open to mobility than other industrialized nations.

12. Sociologists see education as a critical factor in the social mobility of individuals in the United States. It seems that education has the greatest influence on occupational attainment. William Sewell and his associates contend that educational and occupational attainment are the outcome of two related processes: those by which status aspirations are formed, and those by which the aspirations become translated into an actual position in the status hierarchy. Critics of status attainment research contend that it has a functionalist bias.

GLOSSARY

closed system A stratification system in which people have great difficulty changing their status.

constraints Those resources that allow one party to add new disadvantages to a situation.

culture of poverty The view that the poor possess self-perpetuating lifeways characterized by weak ego structures, lack of impulse control, a present-time orientation, and a sense of resignation and fatalism.

dual labor market An economy characterized by two sectors. The primary or core sector offers "good jobs," and the secondary or periphery sector offers "bad jobs."

horizontal mobility Movement from one social status to another that is approximately equivalent in rank.

income The amount of money people receive.

inducements Those resources that allow one party to add new advantages to a situation.

intergenerational mobility A comparison of the social status of parents and their children at some point in their respective careers.

intragenerational mobility A comparison of the social status of a person over an extended period of time.

life chances The likelihood that individuals and groups will enjoy desired goods and services, fulfilling experiences, and opportunities for living healthy and long lives.

objective method An approach to the identification of social classes that employs such yardsticks as income, occupation, and education.

open system A stratification system in which people can change their status with relative ease.

persuasion Those resources that enable one party to change the minds of other people without adding either advantages or disadvantages to the situation.

prestige The social respect, admiration, and recognition associated with a particular social status.

power The ability of individuals and groups to realize their will in human affairs even if it involves the resistance of others.

reputational method An approach to identifying social classes that involves asking people how they classify others.

self-placement method An approach to identifying social classes that involves self-classification.

social differentiation The process by which a society becomes increasingly specialized over time.

social mobility Individuals or groups moving from one level (stratum) to another in the stratification system.

social stratification The structured ranking of individuals and groups; their grading into horizontal layers or strata.

socioeconomic life cycle A sequence of stages that begins with birth into a family with a specific social status and proceeds through childhood, socialization, schooling, job seeking, occupational achievement, marriage, and the formation and functioning of a new family unit.

style of life The magnitude and manner of people's consumption of goods and services.

vertical mobility Movement of individuals from one social status to another of higher or lower rank.

wealth What people own.

7

Inequalities of Race, Ethnicity, and Gender

RACIAL AND ETHNIC
  STRATIFICATION

Minorities
Prejudice and Discrimination
Dominant Group Policies
The Functionalist and Conflict
  Perspectives
Racial and Ethnic Groups in the
  United States

GENDER STRATIFICATION

Gender Roles and Culture
Gender Roles and Biology
Acquiring Gender Identities
The Functionalist and Conflict
  Perspectives on Gender
  Stratification
Gender Roles in the United States

Stratification contains the answer to the question of *who gets what, when, and how.* As a consequence, a society's "good things"—particularly income, wealth, prestige, and power—are distributed unevenly. So are the burdens and unpleasant chores. In sum, stratification represents institutionalized inequality in the distribution of social rewards and burdens. People are locked into an arena of social relationships in which they differ sharply in their life chances and styles of living. In Chapter 6 we examined the class system of stratification. In this chapter we turn our attention to two additional systems of stratification, race and/or ethnicity and gender.

Within the United States, blacks, Hispanics, Native Americans (Indians), Asian-Americans, and Jews have been the victims of prejudice and discrimination. They have historically been confined to subordinate statuses that are not justified by their individual abilities and talents. The same has held true for women. Traditionally it is men who have gotten the best jobs, who have been exempt from menial household chores, who have enjoyed the top political offices, and who have had the prerogative of initiating sexual activity.

Social scientists have noted many similarities between the status of blacks and that of women within the United States (Myrdal, 1944; Hacker, 1951, 1974; Smith and Steward, 1983). Take racist and sexist stereotypes. Both blacks and women have been portrayed as intellectually inferior, emotional, irresponsible, dependent, and childlike. The rationalization for their subordination has been similar—the myth of "contented blacks who know their place" and the notion that "women's place is in the home." Recent generations of both blacks and women have challenged those stereotypes by participating in social movements for equal rights.

Traditionally, the American family system operated to bind women to domestic and child-rearing roles. To the extent that women are confined to the home by the linkage of social and reproductive functions (and thus blocked from direct access to material and social resources in the larger community), women become dependent on those who do participate in the public sphere: men. (Culver Pictures)

Racial and Ethnic Stratification

Although racial and ethnic stratification is similar to other systems of stratification in its essential features, there tends to be one major difference. Racial and ethnic groups often have the *potential* for carving their own independent nation from the existing state. Political separatism may offer racial and ethnic groups a solution that is not available to disadvantaged class and gender groups. Class and gender groups typically lack the potential for becoming self-sufficient political states because they do not function as self-sufficient social or economic groups.

Although separatist tendencies and their chances for success vary enormously among nations, the underlying potential for such movements exists in most nations with diverse racial and ethnic groups. Unlike class stratification, the issue is not replacement of one elite by another or even a revolutionary change in the political system. Instead, the question is one of whether the racial or ethnic segments of the society will be willing to participate within the existing nation-state arrangement (Lieberson, 1970). Class conflicts threaten governments, but they rarely pose alternative definitions of the territorial boundaries of the nation (Geertz, 1963). Examples abound in the contemporary world of separatist movements, including the Palestinians in the Middle East, the Irish Catholics of Northern Ireland, the Ibo of Nigeria, various tribal groups in Katanga province of Zaire, the various Muslim and Christian factions in Lebanon, and the French Canadians of Quebec Province.

MINORITIES

Societies throughout the world contain peoples with different skin colors, languages, religions, and customs. These physical and cultural traits provide high social visibility that serve as identifying symbols of group membership. In turn, individuals are ascribed statuses in the social structure based on the group to which they belong (see Chapter 2).

Races. People in various parts of the world differ in certain hereditary features, including the color of their skin, the texture of their hair, their facial features, their stature,

and the shape of their heads. But by the same token, the features that humans everywhere share are substantially larger and of considerably greater importance than their differences. Even so, we readily recognize that *groups* of Norwegians, Chinese, and Ugandans differ in their physical characteristics. The concept of **race** is used to refer to this fact. Races are populations that differ in the incidence of various hereditary traits.

Although we readily recognize that populations differ in physical appearance, scientists have considerable difficulty identifying races and categorizing people in terms of them. For the most part, races are not characterized by fixed, clear-cut differences, but by fluid, continuous differences. It is often next to impossible to tell where one population ends and another begins. For instance, where and among what people in Africa or Europe can one say with certainty that here and among these people Caucasoids (whites) cease, and there and among those people Negroids (blacks) start? With respect to skin color, hair form, stature, and head shape, populations grade into one another. Additionally, peoples differ in a great many ways, and these variations occur independently of one another. Hence, classifications based on skin color do not necessarily yield the same results as those based on some other characteristic. For example, extremely kinky hair is found among the moderately pigmented San of the Kalahari Desert (South Africa), and straight or wavy hair among some dark-pigmented peoples of southern India (Vander Zanden, 1983).

Because human beings do not lend themselves readily to cut-and-dried "racial" classifications, scientists are far from agreement in dividing human populations into "races." But what interests us here is the social significance people attach to various traits. By virtue of individuals' social definitions, skin color or some other trait becomes a "sign" or "mark" of a social status.

Ethnic Groups. Groups that we identify chiefly on cultural grounds—language, folk practices, dress, gestures, mannerisms, or religion—are called **ethnic groups.** Within the United States, Jewish-Americans, Italian-Americans, and Hispanics are examples of ethnic groups. Ethnic groups often have a sense of peoplehood, and to one degree or another many of them deem themselves to be a nation.

We often confuse nationalism (a feeling of loyalty to a nation or an ethnic group) with a feeling of loyalty to the state (a political unit). Yet a nation and a state are distinctive social entities. Consider Europe. Virtually every territory of Europe has combined at some time or other with almost every one of its neighbors. In fact, the territories covered by European political states have never been, and could not possibly be, exactly the same as the territories inhabited by various ethnic groups. Very often ethnic groups occupy small pieces of territory or are dispersed by residence and place of occupation throughout a territory. Thus political self-determination for one ethnic nationality is often incompatible with political self-determination for another. Many European political states contain multiple nationality groups: Great Britain (English, Scottish, Welsh, Northern Irish), Belgium (Flemish and Walloons), Czechoslovakia (Czecks and Slovaks), and Switzerland (Germans, French, and Italians). The consequence is that many political states periodically experience ethnic strife and even violence that derives from the minority status of some groups.

Properties of a Minority Group. Sociologists commonly distinguish five properties as characteristic of minority groups (Wagley and Harris, 1964; Vander Zanden, 1983):

1. A minority is a social group whose members experience discrimination, segregation, oppression, or persecution at the hands of another social group, the *dominant group.* As a result of power differential between the two groups, the members of a minority are disadvantaged. Equally important, they are the source of the dominant group's advantages, since the oppression of one people confers privilege and status on another.

2. A minority is characterized by physical or cultural traits that distinguish it from the dominant group. By virtue of these traits, its members are lumped together and "placed" in less desirable positions in the social structure.

3. A minority is a self-conscious social group characterized by a consciousness of oneness. Its members possess a social and psychological affinity with others like themselves, providing a sense of *peoplehood.* This consciousness of oneness is accentuated by the members' common suffering and burdens.

4. Membership in a minority group is generally not voluntary. It is an ascribed position, since an individual is commonly born into the status. Thus a person does not usually choose to be black or white.

5. The members of a minority, by choice or necessity, typically marry within their own group (endogamy). The dominant group strongly discourages its members from marrying members of the minority group, and usually scorns those who do. The minority may encourage its members to marry among themselves to preserve their unique cultural heritage.

We may define a **minority group** as a racially or culturally self-conscious population, with hereditary membership and a high degree of in-group marriage, which suffers oppression at the hands of a dominant segment of a nation-state (Williams, 1964).

PREJUDICE AND DISCRIMINATION

Prejudice and discrimination are so prevalent in contemporary life that we often assume they are merely "part of human nature." Yet this view ignores the fact that individuals and societies vary enormously in levels of prejudice and discrimination. Even in Hitler's Germany, some "Aryans" opposed anti-Semitism and helped Jews flee the Nazi Holocaust. And whereas Asians have found acceptance in Hawaii and have prospered there, on the West Coast and in British Columbia they have had a long history of persecution (Glick, 1980). Similarly, whites held a positive image of blacks in the ancient world, a situation in sharp contrast with recent history (Snowden, 1983).

Prejudice. Prejudice refers to attitudes of aversion and hostility toward the members of a group simply because they belong to it and hence are presumed to have the objectionable qualities ascribed to it (Allport, 1954). As such prejudice is a state of mind—a feeling, opinion, or disposition. Sociologist Herbert Blumer (1961) notes that four feelings typically characterize dominant group members: (1) A sense that they are superior to members of the minority group; (2) a feeling that minority members are by their nature different and alien; (3) a sense that dominant group members have a proprietary claim to privilege, power, and prestige; and (4) a fear and suspicion that members of the minority have designs on dominant group benefits. In this respect, prejudice frequently reflects a "sense of group position."

Sociologists John B. McConahay and Joseph C. Hough, Jr. (1976) detect the emergence in recent years of a new form of prejudice against blacks among affluent, suburban whites. They label it **symbolic racism.** Symbolic racism is not the racism of the Old South, with its doctrines of racial inferiority and legal segregation. Instead, it is a new form of racism in which three components converge. First, there is the feeling among many whites that blacks have become too demanding, too pushy, and too angry, and that they are getting more than they rightly deserve. Second, there is the belief that blacks do not play by "the rules of the game," typified by the traditional American values of hard work, individualism, and delay of gratification. And third, many whites stereotype blacks in the imagery of black welfare, urban riots, black mayors, crime in the streets, and quota systems. Other sociologists have also noted the prevalence of these notions (Kluegel and Smith, 1982). Such attitudes lead whites to vote against political candidates who support antipoverty programs and to consider "racism" as "somebody else's" problem (Kinder and Sears, 1981).

Discrimination. Whereas prejudice is an attitude or a state of mind, discrimination is action. **Discrimination** involves the arbitrary denial of privilege, prestige, and power to members of a minority group whose qualifications are equal to those of members of the dominant group. Prejudice does not necessarily coincide with discrimination—a one-to-one relationship does not inevitably hold between attitudes and overt actions. Sociologist Robert K. Merton (1968) identifies four relationships between prejudice and discrimination and adds folk labels to the types of individuals so described:

1. *The all-weather liberal*—the unprejudiced person who does not discriminate.

2. *The reluctant liberal*—the unprejudiced person who discriminates in response to social pressures.

3. *The timid bigot*—the prejudiced person who does not discriminate in response to social pressures.

4. *The all-weather bigot*—the prejudiced person who unhesitatingly acts on the beliefs he or she holds.

Merton points out that equal opportunity legislation has the greatest impact on the reluctant liberal and the timid bigot.

In the years since World War II, whites have shifted from more blatant forms of discrimination to more subtle forms (Crosby, Bromley, and Saxe, 1980). Similarly, public opinion surveys over the past forty years show a steady but gradual shift toward greater liberalism on race issues among whites. The greatest change took place between 1970 and 1972. Much of the long-term change derives from individuals born after 1940 who are typically less prejudiced than those born earlier in the century (Taylor, Sheatsley, and Greeley, 1978; Opinion Roundup, 1982).

Institutional Discrimination. Discrimination is not practiced just by individuals. In their daily operation, the institutions of society also systematically discriminate against the members of some groups in what is called **institutional discrimination.** The civil rights activist Stokely Carmichael and the political scientist Charles Hamilton (1967) have shown that businesses, schools, hospitals, and other key institutions need not be staffed by prejudiced individuals in order for discrimination to occur. Take employment. Employers often specify the qualifications candidates must have in order to be considered for particular jobs. Usually the qualifications have to do with prior job-related experience and some measure of formal education. The standards appear non-discriminatory because they apply to all individuals regardless of race, creed, or color.

But when members of some racial and ethnic groups lack equal opportunities to gain job experience and to receive college and professional degrees, they enter the job market at disadvantage.

Blacks have been particularly victimized by institutional discrimination. For centuries they have been the victims of inequality and low status. As we will see later in the chapter, the handicaps associated with poverty, an absence of skills, inadequate education, and low job seniority have been left largely untouched by civil rights legislation. Indeed, low status has self-perpetuating qualities. Twenty years ago, President Lyndon B. Johnson made this point in his June 1965 commencement address at Howard University. He asserted:

You do not take a person who for years has been hobbled by chains and liberate him, bring him up to the starting line of a race and . . . say, you're free to compete with all the others, and still justly believe that you have been completely fair.

In brief, equality of opportunity, even if realized in American life, does not necessarily produce equality of outcome: On the contrary, to the extent that winners imply losers, equality of opportunity almost ensures inequality. Consequently, blacks and many other minorities have concerned themselves not merely with removing the barriers to full opportunity, but with achieving the fact of *equality of income*—parity in family income, in housing, and in the other necessities for keeping families strong and healthy. It has been this sentiment that has propelled proponents of affirmative action programs.

One mechanism by which institutional discrimination is maintained is **gatekeeping**—the decision-making process whereby people are admitted to offices and positions of privilege, prestige, and power within a society. Generally gatekeepers are profes-

Doing Sociology: Institutional Discrimination

The institutions of modern societies are often structured in ways that deny equal opportunities to the members of some ethnic and racial groups. Students in introductory sociology classes at Ohio State University have examined a number of ways in which institutional discrimination has operated to restrict the entrance of blacks to major state universities. For instance, although blacks comprise about 10 percent of the population of Ohio, they represent less than 5 percent of the students enrolled on the Columbus campus of Ohio State University (4.8 percent of undergraduates, 4.9 percent of graduate students, and 3.8 percent of students in the professional colleges). Despite the fact that the university has inaugurated a variety of programs and scholarships to attract black students, the proportion of black students has fallen in recent years. Blacks are also vastly underrepresented in premed, engineering, and accounting programs, majors that afford career lines to the most prestigious and remunerative professions and occupations.

Examining their own backgrounds, students point out that a selective process already at work in the elementary and middle-school years shaped their later academic opportunities. Suburban school systems, overwhelmingly white in composition, provide solid preparation in mathematics. Students from these schools are given the training essential for attacking premed, engineering, and accounting courses. In many cases, the students were tested in the seventh grade, and those who showed superior aptitude in mathematics were placed in advanced courses. These students had a head start—they could master introductory algebra in eighth grade and take calculus in twelfth grade. In contrast, students in inner-city schools with large black enrollments typically have had access to less rigorous programs in mathematics. Consequently, many black youth are less adequately prepared for college curriculums, and disproportionate numbers of black students find themselves in remedial math programs at the university. Thus the differences in education provided to white and black youngsters affect later performance in college.

Although black students are underrepresented at Ohio State University and in programs leading to the most prestigious and remunerative professions and occupations, the same cannot be said for the football and basketball programs. At a major state university like Ohio State, the athletic program is a "big business," with an annual budget in excess of $12 million. Sports programs are major vehicles for winning financial support for the institution from state legislators, alumni, and corporate contributors. As a result, universities feel it necessary to field winning football and basketball teams. Significantly, the football and basketball programs—the two principal and most financially remunerative sports—are carried disproportionately by black youth (in contrast, swimming, golf, and tennis—"country-club" type sports—are dominated by whites). However, participation in "big-time" sports is exceedingly time-consuming, and students have difficulty combining participation with more rigorous academic programs like premed, engineering, and accounting. Thus football and basketball players are more apt to pursue majors in education and communications, occupations that usually do not provide a "fast track" to economic success. Plus, there are jobs for fewer than 5,000 professional athletes.

Although basketball and football may provide opportunities for black youth, sports is hardly colorblind. For the most part, coaches are white. Further, blacks are more likely to play peripheral positions in football that are away from the decisions of play, including wide receiver, running back, and defensive back. Few blacks play quarterback, center, or middle linebacker. Similarly, in basketball white players are more apt to fill the play-making guard position, the leadership position on the court. And in baseball, blacks are more likely to be fielders than they are to be catchers or pitchers. Thus although sports allows select black youth entrance to a university, it limits their chances to enter more remunerative professions. And if they are fortunate enough to join professional teams, their positions will probably be limited. Institutional arrangements thus structure the opportunities available to youth and contribute to the perpetuation of social inequalities.

sionals with experience and credentials in the fields they monitor—for example, individuals in personnel, school admission, and counseling offices. Although in theory they assess candidates on the basis of merit, skills, and talents—and not in terms of race, ethnicity, class, family, or religion—their decisions have been biased (Erickson, 1975). Merit, skills, and talent are relative matters. The issue of which group's *values* will be used for judging who is "capable," "bright," "conscientious," and "resourceful" comes to the forefront. Will the standards of excellence be those of the white middle class? the black? the Puerto Rican? or Chinese-American community? And which group's members will be the *judges* who determine the people who meet the qualifications? Historically, gatekeepers have been white and male, and they have selected candidates who have resembled themselves in family patterns, dress, hair style, personal behavior, and the ownership and use of property.

DOMINANT GROUP POLICIES

Dominant groups have pursued a variety of policies toward minorities. At times these policies may parallel those of the minority; at other times they run counter to minority group aims. Sociologists George E. Simpson and J. Milton Yinger (1972) identify six major types of policies: assimilation, pluralism, legal protection of minorities, population transfer, continued subjugation, and extermination. Let us examine each of these more closely:

Assimilation. One way that dominant groups seek to "solve" a minority group "problem" is to eliminate the minority by absorbing it through assimilation. **Assimilation** refers to those processes whereby groups with distinctive identities become culturally and socially fused. Minorities may also prefer this method, as have many immigrant groups in the United States. However, dominant groups and minority groups often approach assimilation differently. Within the United States, two views toward assimilation have dominated. One—the "melting pot" tradition—has seen assimilation as a process whereby peoples and cultures would fuse within the nation to produce a new people and a new civilization. The other—the "Americanization" tradition—has viewed American culture as an essentially finished product on the Anglo-Saxon pattern, and has insisted that immigrants promptly give up their cultural traits for those of the dominant American group.

Pluralism. Some minorities do not wish to be assimilated. They value their separate identities and customs, and they prefer a policy of **pluralism**—a situation in which diverse groups coexist side by side and mutually accommodate themselves to their differences. The groups cooperate when this is essential to their well-being, particularly in political and economic matters. Switzerland provides a good illustration of pluralism. Historically, the Swiss nation arose from the desire of heterogeneous communities to preserve their local independence through a system of mutual defense alliances. There is no Swiss language. Instead, the Swiss speak German, French, or Italian, with all federal documents translated into the three "official languages." The various cantons, in addition to their language differences, also have somewhat different cultural patterns. And while the majority of Swiss are Protestant, there is a sizable Catholic population. Although religious and ethnic prejudices are by no means absent, the Swiss have learned to live harmoniously with their differences.

Legal Protection of Minorities. Closely related to pluralism is the legal protection of minorities through constitutional and diplomatic means. In some nations, significant segments of the population reject coexistence with minorities on equal terms. Under these circumstances, the government may make legal provision for the protection of the interests and rights of all individuals. The Thirteenth, Fourteenth, and Fifteenth Amendments to the United States Constitution, although not pluralistic in intent, have attempted to protect the rights of minorities, especially those of blacks. Recent civil rights legislation has had a similar objective.

Population Transfer. At times dominant groups have resorted to population transfer to reduce the presence of the minority. This approach matches the secessionist aim of some minorities—both hope to reduce intergroup difficulties through physical separation. At times the migration is forced. For instance, the separation of Pakistan from India after World War II was accompanied by the migration of more than 12 million Muslims and Hindus, in part induced by terrorism and in part arranged under government auspices. People may also flee before invaders. Recently Afghans have fled to Pakistan and Cambodians to Thailand in the face of the respective Russian and Vietnamese invasions of their homelands.

Continued Subjugation. The policies just discussed attempt to incorporate minorities into a society or to drive them out. Often, however, the dominant group prefers to retain its minorities, although it seeks to keep them "in their place"—subservient and exploitable. This approach often finds expression in "internal colonialism." For example, South African whites have sought *apartheid* arrangements that allow for the political and economic subjugation of blacks and other non-Europeans. Likewise, it has been difficult to enforce laws restricting the migration of Mexicans into the United States because powerful business groups in the southwest and elsewhere want an exploitable minority.

Extermination. Intergroup conflict may become so intense that the physical destruction of one group by the other becomes the overriding goal. History abounds with examples of **genocide**—the deliberate and systematic extermination of a racial or ethnic group. North American whites destroyed more than two-thirds of the Indian population. Even as late as 1890, U.S. army forces armed with machine guns mowed down nearly 300 Sioux at Wounded Knee, South Dakota. The Boers of South Africa looked upon the Hottentots as scarcely more than animals and hunted them ruthlessly. And between 1933 and 1945, the Germans murdered 6 million Jews. It should be emphasized that these policies are not mutually exclusive, and several may be practiced simultaneously.

THE FUNCTIONALIST AND CONFLICT PERSPECTIVES

Functionalist and conflict theorists take differing views of racial and ethnic stratification. Yet as we noted in Chapters 1 and 6, the perspectives complement each other. Each draws our attention to aspects of social life that the other tends to overlook.

The Functionalist Perspective. Functionalists conceive of society as resembling a living organism in which the various parts of a system contribute to its survival. Accordingly, they look to the functions and dysfunctions associated with given social patterns. Although at first sight racial and ethnic conflict would seem to impair social solidarity and stability, functionalists point out that conflict may nonetheless be functional for a society (Coser, 1956). First, conflict promotes group formation, and groups are the building blocks of a society. It facilitates a consciousness of kind—an awareness of shared or similar values. The distinction between "we," or the in-group, and "they," or the out-group, is established in and through conflict (see Chapter 4). Groups in turn bind people together within a set of social relationships. And they define the statuses people occupy in the social structure, particularly positions that are ascribed.

Second, not only is a group defined and its boundaries established through conflict, but conflict promotes group cohesion. It makes group members more conscious of their group bonds and may increase their social participation. Some social scientists have pointed out that anti-Semitism and anti-black sentiment may be functional in that they provide dominant group members who lack a sense of cohesion within the society with an anchor—with a sense of group membership (Ackerman and Jahoda, 1950; Bettelheim and Janowitz, 1950; Adorno, 1950). It highlights their racial and ethnic membership, providing them with a means of identification in an uncertain, alienated world.

Third, ethnic and racial conflict may function as a safety valve for the society as a whole. Prejudice provides for the safe release of hostile and aggressive impulses that are culturally tabooed within other social contexts. By channeling hostilities from within family, occupational, and other crucial settings onto permissible targets, the stability of existing social structures may be promoted. This is the well-known *scapegoating* mechanism.

And fourth, functionalists point out that a multiplicity of conflicts between large numbers of differing groups within a society may be conducive to a democratic as opposed to a totalitarian order. The multiple group affiliations of individuals contribute to a variety of conflicts crisscrossing society. The groups thus operate as a check against one another. A person's segmental participation in numerous groups, rather than total absorption by one group, results in a kind of balancing mechanism and prevents deep cleavages along one axis (for instance, it prevents cleavage along rigid class lines that results in class struggle). In contrast, in totalitarian societies, there is a maximum concentration of power in one institution—the monolithic state.

The dysfunctions of racial and ethnic conflict are often more readily apparent than its functions. Conflict may reach a frequency and intensity that imperils the whole social system, as is the case in Lebanon today. Further, energy and resources are drained and dissipated by friction that might otherwise be directed within more productive channels and cooperative activities. Fears and expectations of conflict may lead to an inefficient and ineffective employment of human resources and individual talents.

The Conflict Perspective. Whereas functionalists emphasize social stability and the mechanisms that promote or interfere with it, conflict theorists see the world as in continual struggle. Conflict theorists contend that prejudice and discrimination can best be understood in terms of tension or conflict among competing groups. They point out that three ingredients commonly come into play in the emergence and initial stabilization of racism (Noel, 1972; Vander Zanden, 1983): ethnocentrism, competition, and unequal power.

As we noted in Chapter 2, *ethnocentrism* involves the tendency to judge the behavior of other groups by the standards of one's own. Individuals assume that it is the nature of things that all people should be organized according to the same assumptions that characterize their own group. When individuals are strongly ethnocentric, they find it easy to perceive the out-group as an object of loathing—as a symbol of strangeness, evil, and even danger. Ethnocentrism provides a fertile soil for prejudicial attitudes and stereotypes.

Competition intensifies ethnocentric sentiments and may lead to intergroup strife. In human affairs, conflict theorists point out that people typically seek to improve their outcomes with regard to those things—particularly privilege, prestige, and power—that they define as good, worthwhile, and desirable. When they perceive their group outcomes as mutually exclusive and legitimate, so that each can realize its goals only at the expense of the other, intergroup tensions are likely to mount. For the most part, the attitudes people evolve toward outgroups tend to reflect their perceptions of the relationships they have with the groups. Where the relations between two groups are viewed as competitive, negative attitudes—prejudice—will be generated toward the out-group. The boys' camp experiment undertaken by Muzafer Sherif and his associates (1961) and described in Chapter 4 documents this process.

Competition provides the motivation for systems of social inequality, and ethnocentrism channels competition along racial and ethnic lines, but power determines which group will subordinate the other (Noel, 1972). Without power, prejudices cannot be translated into discrimination, and groups cannot turn their claims on scarce resources into institutional discrimination. In brief, power is the mechanism by which domination and subjugation are achieved.

Marxists take the conflict thesis even further. They say that racial prejudice and exploitation arose in the Western world with the rise of capitalism (Cox, 1948; Szymaski, 1976, 1978; Geschwender, 1978). Marxist theorists contend that racist notions serve the economic interests of the capitalist class in four ways. First ideologies of racial superiority make colonialism and racist practices palatable and acceptable to the white masses. Second, racism is profitable, since capitalists can pay minority workers less and thus generate greater profits for themselves. Third, racist ideologies divide the working class by pitting white workers and minority workers against one another—a tactic of "divide and conquer." And fourth, capitalists require minority workers as an industrial reserve army that can be fired during times of economic stagnation and rehired when needed for producing profits during times of prosperity (see Chapter 6).

Marxists blame capitalists for generating racism, but sociologist Edna Bonacich (1972, 1975) says that economic competition within a **split labor market** underlies the development of tensions among ethnic groups. A split labor market is an economic arena in which large differences exist in the price of labor at the same occupational level. Bonacich notes that when a group sells its labor at rates substantially lower than the prevailing ones, higher-paid labor faces severe competition to maintain its advantage. When the cheaper labor is of a differing racial or ethnic group, the resulting class antagonism takes the form of racism. The antagonism focuses on racial or ethnic issues, although the source of the conflict is one of class.

Bonacich contends that the more expensive labor resists displacement through exclusion or a caste system. The anti-Chinese movement, which flourished in California in the 1870s, illustrates an exclusion strategy. White workers sought to drive the Chinese from their communities through harassment and violence and to shut off the entry of new immigrants. The racial caste system was the strategy employed in the post–Civil War period. White labor erected social and legal barriers—Jim Crow segregation arrangements—to avoid competition with black workers.

Regardless of the precise form that conflict theories take, and they do differ substantially from one another, they nonetheless contrast sharply with functionalist theories that look to the forces which contribute to stability rather than those which divide.

RACIAL AND ETHNIC GROUPS IN THE UNITED STATES

We have considered the nature of minority groups, prejudice, discrimination, and institutional discrimination and discussed the functionalist and conflict perspectives. Let us now turn to an examination of the circumstances of a number of groups within the United States: blacks, Hispanics, Native Americans (Indians), and Asian-Americans.

Blacks. It is very likely that the first black came to the New World with Columbus. However, black settlement in the New World did not begin until 1619, when English colonists at Jamestown, Virginia, purchased twenty blacks from a Dutch man-of-war. It seems that the blacks were accorded the status of indentured servants, much in the fashion of whites. But in the 1660s legal recognition was given to the enslavement of blacks for life, and the first law was passed banning interracial sexual relations.

The growth of slavery closely paralleled the development of the plantation system of agriculture in the South. At the time of the first federal census, taken in 1790, there were 757,208 blacks in the new nation, 20 percent of its total population. But, it was not until Eli Whitney invented the cotton gin in 1793 that cotton became the major crop of the South (slaves had previously

been used primarily in commercial agriculture based on tobacco, rice, indigo, and naval stores). Through the early 1800s, the production of cotton increased at a phenomenal rate and was accompanied by a substantial growth in the slave population, which reached 1.8 million people in 1820.

The subjugation of blacks was well rooted in the British colonies, and the tradition was carried on by the new American nation. Southerners succeeded at the Constitutional Convention of 1787 in winning additional representation in Congress on the basis of slavery, in securing federal support for the capture and return of fugitive slaves, and in preventing the closing of the African slave trade before 1808. In point of fact, the American nation arose as a Greek-style democracy, one in which democracy was extended only to the male, white population. The doctrine of black inferiority or "differences" placed blacks beyond the pale of the American democratic creed. Although American mythology says that the Civil War was fought to free the slaves, historians agree that the political struggle which unfolded between the North and the South was primarily a contest between a southern plantation elite and northern industrial, mercantile, and agrarian interests.

During Reconstruction, the Radical Republicans were in part motivated by the abolitionist argument that a legalized caste system was not compatible with American institutions. But they were also concerned lest the southern states reenter the Union with the old planter elite still in control. Indeed, the North's lack of commitment to black rights doomed Reconstruction. However, the institution of Jim Crow—legalized segregation—did not follow automatically on the overthrow of the Reconstruction regimes (Woodward, 1966). The principle of hard-and-fast segregation did not become the rule until the 1890s. Before this time, blacks still voted in substantial numbers and received equal treatment on common carriers, trains, and streetcars. Even so, blacks and whites attended separate schools, and whites did not accept blacks as social equals. It was during the 1890s and early 1900s that lynching attained its most staggering proportions and that Jim Crow laws mandating segregation were passed throughout the South.

With World War II came a new era of change in the South. Major assaults were directed against segregation from a good many quarters. The stage was set for even more drastic change when the Supreme Court ruled on May 17, 1954, that mandatory school segregation was unconstitutional. In the years that followed, the Supreme Court moved toward outlawing legalized segregation in all areas of American life. Simultaneously, the civil rights movement of the 1960s galvanized popular support for the enactment of new civil rights legislation, particularly the Civil Rights Act of 1964, 1965, and 1968. However, as the United States entered the 1970s, resistance mounted among segments of the white community to additional programs and to affirmative action measures. By the 1980s, under the Reagan administration, the nation began moving down a road that has involved the dismantling of the War on Poverty and various federal programs for minorities and the poor. Budget cutting and budget balancing have taken a severe toll in social programs.

By 1984 there were 27 million blacks in the United States, comprising about 12 percent of the population (Robey, 1984). Although a predominantly rural people at the turn of the century, less than one-fifth of blacks currently remain on farms and in small towns. While blacks have made progress in recent years, the economic gap between whites and blacks nonetheless remains enormous. The median income of black *married* couples rose almost 7 percent

(after allowing for inflation) between 1971 and 1981. However, married couples declined from 64 percent of all black families to 55 percent. Consequently, median income for all types of black families—single-parent combined with married-couple—fell over 8 percent during the decade, and blacks fell further behind whites. In 1971, the median income of black families was 60 percent of the median income of white families, but in 1981 it was only 56 percent. And although blacks are about 12 percent of the population, they control only 1 percent of the nation's financial assets.

In recent decades the black unemployment rate has remained more than twice that of whites, while the black poverty rate is almost three times that of whites. Less than 55 percent of black men over the age of 16 are employed, and almost 50 percent of black children are growing up in poverty. Given these statistics, it is hardly surprising that black infants die at a rate twice that of white infants. And in 1982, black life expectancy was 69.3 years versus 75.1 years for whites (Schwartz, 1984). In the case of cancer, 47 percent of white patients survive the disease at least five years (an indicator of a cure), but only 35 percent of black patients do so.

Hispanics. America's Spanish-speaking ethnic groups—Hispanics—have been growing rapidly. As of 1983, there were 16 million Hispanics in the United States, up from the 9 million recorded in the 1970 census and the 14.8 million in the 1980 head count. California and Texas account for more than half the nation's Hispanics, primarily Mexican-Americans. Puerto Ricans are the predominant Hispanics in New York City, where about half of mainland Puerto Ricans reside; Cubans are the largest Hispanic group in Florida, where about 60 percent of Cuban-origin Hispanics live. Some 88 percent of all Hispanics live in metropolitan areas, as compared with 75 percent of the general population. They are also younger than the total U.S. population, on average, with a median age of 23, as contrasted to the national median of 30.

Mexican-Americans have a long history in the United States that stretches back to the period before New England was colonized. Many of them trace their ancestry to the merging of the native Indian population with Spanish settlers. In 1821 Mexico secured its independence from Spain, and shortly thereafter a substantial portion of the new Mexican nation became part of the United States (resulting from the annexation of Texas, the conquest of northern Mexico, and the Gadsden Purchase). Like blacks and American Indians, people of Mexican ancestry did not originally become a part of American society through voluntary immigration. With the exception of the American Indians, they are the only American minority to enter the society through the conquest of their homeland.

In recent decades the Spanish-speaking population of the United States has grown substantially through immigration. Persons of Hispanic origin now account for about half the legal immigration into the United States. Additionally, vast numbers enter the United States illegally. An increasing number are Salvadorans and other Central Americans fleeing guerrilla war, political oppression, and economic deprivation. But the largest group continues to be Mexicans who see little chance of earning a satisfactory living in their crowded nation. To enter the United States illegally, many pay $250 to $350 each to smuggler-guides, called *coyotes*, who sometimes beat and rob them. If they elude the U.S. Immigration and Naturalization Service (INS), the illegal aliens can usually find jobs paying less than the minimum wage as farm laborers, janitors, hospital orderlies, unskilled construction workers, chambermaids, or dishwashers

(Crewdson, 1983). Estimates of the resident illegal population range from a low of about 2 million to a high of 15 million. The INS, which counts itself lucky to nab half the incoming illegal aliens, tabulated 1,251,357 arrests during 1983, up 22 percent from the previous year and about double the figure a decade earlier. The overwhelming majority are from Central and Latin America. At least 50 percent of those deported find their way back to the United States.

The 1980 census found that only 46 percent of Hispanic males—compared with 53 percent of black males and 72 percent of white males aged 25 and over—had completed four years of high school or more. In the same year, 36 percent of Hispanic 18- and 19-year-olds were high school dropouts, more than double the figure for all whites that age (16 percent) and almost double that of blacks (19 percent). In some cities, such as Chicago, about 70 percent of Hispanic children never graduate from high school. Only 12 percent of Mexican-American men in the labor force and 15 percent of Puerto Ricans, compared to 31 percent of all working men over 20, held jobs in the highest-paid professional and administrative occupations (Population Reference Bureau, 1983). The median Hispanic family income in 1982 stood at $16,200, about 70 percent of the figure of $23,900 for white families (Census Bureau, 1984b). McAllen, Laredo, and Brownsville, Texas, communities along the Rio Grande Valley, rank as the poorest metropolitan areas in the United States.

Although Hispanics are commonly lumped together in the public mind as a single group, they embrace cultures as rich and varied as the United States itself. This fact is evident in the names used to describe them: Hispanic, Latino, Chicano, and Spanish-speaking. Some people of Spanish descent dislike the term ''Hispanic,'' preferring to identify themselves by their own

Historically, the hardest, lowest-paying jobs in the United States have been taken by recent immigrants who, unlike established, earlier groups of immigrants, are willing to work long hours at unskilled labor. Today, large numbers of Mexican nationals enter the United States as seasonal, migrant farm workers; some return to Mexico with their earnings, but others remain illegally. Such minority groups serve an important economic function as a source of labor that can be hired cheaply and fired easily. (Peter Menzel)

ethnic group: Cuban, Nicaraguan, Guatemalan, Dominican, Puerto Rican. Some Mexican-Americans like the name Chicano. Others of Spanish origin prefer using Latino. Although public opinion surveys reveal that 70 percent of Hispanics agree that the Spanish language creates a strong common bond among them, 30 percent perceive significant differences among the various Hispanic ethnic groups (Russell, 1983). However, in recent years there has been a blurring of differences among Mexican, Puerto Rican, and Cuban ethnic groups, making Hispanic Americans more conscious of themselves as a homogeneous group (Rangel, 1984).

Native Americans (Indians). The 1980 census counted 1.4 million Native Americans (Indians, Eskimos, and Aleuts) within the United States. They compose the 173 tribes officially recognized by the U.S. government and the more than 300 tribes recognized by Native Americans themselves. The tribes or nations vary in size from those with less than 100 members (the Chumash of California and the Modocs of Oklahoma) to those with more than 160,000 members (the Navajo of the Southwest). An additional fifty or more tribes have vanished through massacres by whites, disease, destruction of their economic base, or absorption by other groups. Overall, native American peoples vary substantially in their history, life styles, kin systems, language, political arrangements, religion, economy, current circumstances, and identities.

Estimates vary widely as to how many Native Americans were found in the area north of the Rio Grande in 1492. Some anthropologists place the figure as low as 700,000, and others as high as 15 million. Contrary to popular mythology, most nations were not nomadic hunting peoples, but farming and fishing peoples with relatively stable communities. Initially the European powers treated the Native American groups as alien nations that could be enemies or allies against their European adversaries. But as time passed, the tribal territories of the Native Americans were appropriated and their inhabitants either annihilated or driven inland.

After the revolutionary war, the American government followed a policy of negotiating treaties of land cession with the Native Americans. When the Native Americans failed to agree, they were confronted with military force. The 1830 Removal Act provided for the relocation of all Eastern tribes to lands west of the Mississippi River. This forced migration is widely regarded as one of the most dishonorable chapters in American history, and is known as "the Trail of Tears." At least 70,000 people were removed, of whom more than 20,000 died en route. West of the Mississippi, the tragedies of defeat and expropriation were repeated. The federal government merely extended to the western Indians the system of treaties and reservations it had used to dispossess the Indians of the East. When the Native Americans resisted, they were systematically slaughtered.

Until 1871, the United States treated the native American tribes as sovereign yet dependent domestic nations with whom it entered into "treaties." But in the 1870s it shifted its policies to one making Native Americans "wards" of the federal government. The new policy had as its aim forced assimilation. These policies had a devastating impact on the native Americans and their cultures. And they created massive poverty and appalling health problems. In 1929 the government reversed its policy and

encouraged Native Americans to retain their tribal identifications and cultures. But during the Eisenhower administration the federal government returned to assimilationism, encouraging Native Americans to leave the reservations and settle in urban areas. Then, during the 1970s, the goal of national policy was again reversed, as the government sought to strengthen Native Americans' control over their own affairs without cutting them off from federal concern and support. The course of governmental policy toward Native Americans shifted repeatedly, oscillating between separatist and assimilationist extremes.

Native Americans have paid dearly for these inconsistencies and vacillations. The Bureau of Indian Affairs estimates that slightly more than 50 percent of Native Americans live on reservations, which cover 52.4 million acres in 27 states. The largest reservation, the Navajo in Arizona, New Mexico, and Utah, is 15 million acres. On the reservations, 48 percent live below the poverty line; 55 percent of reservation housing is substandard; 58 percent of reservation children drop out of school before finishing eighth grade; and unemployment in some cases runs as high as 80 percent. In 1979, the last year for which full statistics are available, the death rate among Native Americans was 770.2 per 100,000, against 588.8 for the entire country. Deaths caused by pneumonia, diabetes, tuberculosis, alcoholism, suicide, and homicide were two to eight times that of the population as a whole. Alcohol is solace to many Native Americans. Indeed, many Native American leaders look upon alcohol as an especially devastating problem, one that over time confronts their people with "genocide without firing a single bullet" (Huntley, 1983).

Asian-Americans. Asian-Americans totaled 3.5 million in 1980, about 1.5 percent of the American population. Of these, 806,000 were of Chinese ancestry, 775,000 of Filipino ancestry, 701,000 of Japanese ancestry, and 362,000 of Asian-Indian ancestry. It was during the gold rush period in California that the first large-scale immigration of Chinese to the United States took place. At first the Chinese were welcomed as a source of cheap labor. But when the speculative gold bubble burst, whites faced competition with Chinese workers. The cry became, "The Chinese must go." In the post–Civil War period, the Chinese were the victims of mob violence, bloodshed, pillage, and incendiarism. California led the nation in the passage of anti-Chinese laws, many of which remained in effect until the 1950s (for instance, the California state constitution provided that corporations could neither directly nor indirectly employ Chinese and empowered cities and towns to remove Chinese from within city limits). Although some Chinese responded to this persecution by returning to China, most dispersed eastward. They took up residence in Chinatowns, ghettos made up of Chinese.

By the end of World War II, except for a few large cities, Chinatowns had largely disappeared from the American scene. But in recent years the Chinatowns of New York City, San Francisco, and a few other large cities have obtained a new lease on life and have expanded as a result of sharp increases in immigration from Hong Kong and Taiwan (made possible by the passage of new immigration legislation in 1965 that did away with the old quota system, under which only 105 Chinese were allowed entry each year). Above the gaudy storefronts of the nation's Chinatowns, Chinese families are jammed into tiny flats. In some cities, including San Francisco, more than a quarter of the residents of Chinatown live below the poverty level. In recent years, New York City's Chinatown has become the center of the city's apparel industry, which is second only to the restaurant business as the chief

source of employment for Chinese immigrants.

The Japanese have also been victims of prejudice and discrimination. On two occasions the government launched an effort to exclude them from American life. In 1907 President Theodore Roosevelt reached an agreement with Japan to limit the immigration of Japanese to the United States. Later, during World War II, the government placed some 120,000 Japanese (two-thirds of whom were American citizens) in ten concentration camps. The action had more to do with racism than with national security, since none of the nation's other so-called enemies-in-residence (Germans and Italians) were subjected to internment—and not one Japanese-American was ever convicted of spying.

In recent years the nation's media have heralded Asian-Americans as "the model minority" (Kasindorf, 1982; McBee, 1984). They now enjoy the highest median family income of the nation's ethnic groups ($22,075 in 1982). Through thrift, strong family ties, and hard work, many Asian-Americans have managed to achieve upward mobility. Recent immigrants have included a high proportion of doctors and engineers, and fully 33 percent of Asian adults have completed college (compared with 17.5 percent of whites). The National Center for Education Statistics finds that Asian-American students are more likely than other students to enroll in college preparatory programs (47 percent take the academic program, compared with 37 percent of whites, 29 percent of blacks, and 23 percent of Hispanics). They also take more math and science courses and spend more time on homework than do other students (Zigli, 1984). But Asian-American leaders also point out that the "model minority" myth obscures such problems as crime, high suicide rates, mental disorders, and disintegrating families among poor refugees and immigrants who have difficulty coping with a strange, new society.

Gender Stratification

Men and women differ in their access to privilege, prestige, and power. The distribution problem of who gets what, when, and how has traditionally been answered in favor of males. Although women do enjoy some positions of power, these tend to be the exception, as evidenced by newspaper accounts that note "she is the only female" or "she is the first woman."

Until relatively recently, Americans did not conceive of women as a subordinate group. It is true, of course, that women do not reside in ghettos, although this is increasingly the fate of single-parent black women. Even though prestigious Ivy League institutions and medical, engineering, law, and business schools traditionally catered to male students, women have not been segregated in inferior schools. Moreover, they freely interact with—even live with—men, the presumed dominant group. How then can they be viewed as a minority? Let us return to the five properties of a minority group we considered earlier in the chapter.

1. Historically, women have encountered *prejudice and discrimination.* We will examine this matter at greater length later in the chapter.

2. Women possess *physical and cultural traits* that distinguish them from men, the dominant group.

3. Through the efforts of the women's liberation movement and consciousness-raising groups, women have increasingly become a *self-conscious social group* characterized by an awareness of oneness.

4. *Membership is involuntary,* since gender is an ascribed status that is assigned to a person at birth.

5. Only the fifth characteristic does not apply to women, since *endogamy* (in-group marriage) is not the rule.

It is clear that women and other minority groups share many characteristics in common. Noting that sexism pervades the social fabric, sociologist Jessie Bernard observes:

[*Sexism is*] *the unconscious, taken-for-granted, assumed, unquestioned, unexamined, unchallenged acceptance of the belief that the world as it looks to men is the only world, that the way of dealing with it which men have created is the only way, that the values which men have evolved are the only ones, that the way sex looks to men is the only way it can look to anyone, that what men think about what women are like is the only way to think about what women are like. (Quoted in Gornick and Moran, 1971:xxv)*

Before examining these matters in greater detail, let us turn to a consideration of gender roles and identities.

GENDER ROLES AND CULTURE

It seems that all societies have seized on the anatomical differences between men and women to assign **gender roles**—sets of cultural expectations that define the ways in which the members of each sex should behave. Anthropological evidence suggests that gender roles probably represent the earliest division of labor among human beings. Consequently, we are all born into societies with well-established cultural guidelines for the behavior of men and women.

Anthropologist George P. Murdock (1935) finds in his cross-cultural survey of 224 societies that vast differences exist in the social definitions of what constitutes appropriate masculine and feminine behavior. Indeed, as shown in Table 7.1, the allocation of duties often differs sharply from that of our own society. For instance, for generations American communities have had laws restricting the weights that a working woman is permitted to lift. Moreover, women have been excluded from many jobs because the men who control these jobs define women as "stupid," delicate," and "emotional." Yet among the Arapesh of New Guinea, it was the women who were assigned the task of carrying heavy loads because their heads were believed to be harder and stronger than those of men. Among the Tasmanians of the South Pacific, the most dangerous type of hunting—

swimming out to remote rocks in the sea to stalk and club sea otters—was assigned to women. Moreover, women formed the bodyguard of Dahomeyan kings because they were deemed to be particularly fierce fighters. And although most peoples believe that it is the men who should take the initiative in sexual matters, among the Maori and the Trobriand Islanders this prerogative falls to women (Ford and Beach, 1951).

The great variation in the gender roles of men and women from one society to another points to a social foundation for most of these differences. So do the changes observed from one time to another in sex-linked behavior patterns within the same society. Not too long ago in Western history,

TABLE 7.1

The Division of Labor by Sex in 224 Societies

Activity	Number of Societies and Sex of Person by Whom the Activity Is Performed				
	Men Always	Men Usually	Either Sex	Women Usually	Women Always
Hunting	166	13	0	0	0
Trapping small animals	128	13	4	1	2
Herding	38	8	4	0	5
Fishing	98	34	19	3	4
Clearing agricultural land	73	22	17	5	13
Dairy operations	17	4	3	1	13
Preparing and planting soil	31	23	33	20	37
Erecting and dismantling shelter	14	2	5	6	22
Tending and harvesting crops	10	15	35	39	44
Bearing burdens	12	6	35	20	57
Cooking	5	1	9	28	158
Metalworking	78	0	0	0	0
Boat building	91	4	4	0	1
Working in stone	68	3	2	0	2
Basket making	25	3	10	6	82
Weaving	19	2	2	6	67
Manufacturing and repairing of clothing	12	3	8	9	95

(Source: Adapted from George P. Murdock, "Comparative Data on the Division of Labor by Sex," Social Forces [1935], 15:551–553.)

the dashing cavalier wore long curls and perfume; he had a rapier and a stallion; and he also employed powder and lace and soft leather boots that revealed a well-turned calf. In the 1950s men who wore long hair were labeled "sissies" and "queers." But in the 1960s long hair came into style, and today more intermediate hair styles are in vogue. All this suggests that gender roles are largely a matter of social definition and socially constructed meanings.

GENDER ROLES AND BIOLOGY

When a baby is born, the first thing people want to know is whether it is a boy or a girl. The biological aspects of gender consist of the physical differences between men and women: Women have the capacity to menstruate, carry a fetus until delivery, and provide it with milk after birth; men have the ability to produce and transmit sperm. But beyond these matters, the role biology plays in producing behavioral differences between men and women is shrouded in controversy. Until relatively recently, it was generally believed that two quite separate gender roads exist, one leading from XX chromosomes at conception to womanhood and the other from XY chromosomes to manhood. But medical researchers at Johns Hopkins Medical Center are finding that there are not two roads, but one road with a number of forks where each of us turns in either a male or female direction. In other words, it appears that we become male or female by stages (Money and Ehrhardt, 1972; Money and Tucker, 1975; Ehrhardt and Meyer-Bahlberg, 1981).

In the early weeks following conception, XX and XY embryos proceed along a sexually neutral course. Around the sixth week, the Y chromosome sends a message to the two gonads to become testes. Apparently at this point the neutral and female roads converge. Likewise, at later forks in the road, without a push in the male direction, the fetus takes a female turn. Other important points in shaping gender occur with the secretion of sex hormones and the fashioning of sex organs. When the developmental process goes awry at one or more critical junctions, individuals develop reproductive organs of both sexes. Individuals whose reproductive structures are sufficiently ambiguous that it is difficult to define them exclusively as male or female are called **hermaphrodites.**

The Johns Hopkins Medical Center researchers find that social definitions play a crucial role in influencing the gender identities of hermaphrodites. At birth the child is classed as a boy or a girl, and a whole series of environmental forces then come into play (Money and Tucker, 1975: 86–89):

The label "boy" or "girl" . . . has tremendous force as a self-fulfilling prophecy, for it throws the full weight of society to one side or other as the newborn heads for the gender fork [in the road], and the most decisive sex turning point of all. . . . [At birth you were limited to] something that was ready to become your gender identity. You were wired but not programmed for gender in the same sense that you were wired but not programmed for language.

Some researchers suggest that the human embryo has a bisexual potential. It seems that biological factors do not themselves produce differences in male or female behavior, but affect the threshold for the elicitation of such behavior. Hormonal differences may "flavor" a person for one kind of gender behavior or another. But even so, hormones do not dictate that the behavior be learned. Rather, hormones make it easier for a person to learn certain gender-related behaviors. And these behaviors are constantly being shaped and modified by the environment (Money and Tucker, 1975; Scarf, 1976; Imperato-McGinley et al., 1981).

Psychologists Eleanor E. Maccoby and Carol N. Jacklin (1974), based on survey of over 2,000 books and articles on sex differences, conclude that there are four fairly "well-established" differences between boys and girls:

1. Beginning about age 11, girls show greater verbal ability than boys.

2. Boys are superior to girls on visual-spatial tasks in adolescence and adulthood, although not during childhood.

3. At about 12 or 13 years of age, boys move ahead of girls in mathematical ability.

4. Males are more aggressive than females.

However, other psychologists have launched new surveys of the literature regarding gender differences and have come to quite different conclusions. For instance, Julia Sherman (1978) and Janet Shibley Hyde (1981) looked at the evidence for the alleged cognitive differences (verbal ability, visual-spatial ability, and mathematical ability). They concluded that the magnitude of the differences is at best quite small. The matter of gender differences in aggression is also controversial. Psychologist Todd Tieger (1980), based on his survey of the literature, says that such differences become observable in children's spontaneous behavior only at about 5 years of age. During these early years, social factors foster the differential learning and expression of aggression by boys and girls. Whereas adults encourage boys to display aggression, girls are pressured to inhibit it. Commenting on Tieger's review, Maccoby and Jacklin (1980) see little reason to alter their earlier conclusions. Nevertheless, they do emphasize that aggressiveness is less a trait of individuals than it is behavior which characterizes people in some kinds of situations. Women, like men, can be expected to exhibit aggression where the norms support such displays, and inhibit it in other domains. In sum, it seems that there is little that is psychologically either male or female, although our cultural definitions often make it appear so.

ACQUIRING GENDER IDENTITIES

Gender identities are the conceptions we have of ourselves as being male or female. As such they are invisible, something that can not be established by appearance. For most people, there is a good fit between their anatomy and their gender identity. Boys generally come to behave in ways their culture labels "masculine," and girls learn to be "feminine." But there are some individuals for whom this is not the case. The most striking examples are *transsexuals*—individuals who have normal sexual organs, but who psychologically feel like members of the opposite sex. In some cases, as with Jan Morris, Christine Jorgensen, Renee Richards, and Roberta Cowell, medical science has found a way, through surgery and hormones, to reduce the incompatibility by modifying the person's anatomy to conform with the gender identity.

As we have noted in our discussion of culture and biology, learning plays a key part in the acquisition of gender identities. However, the exact nature of this learning has been the subject of considerable debate. According to Sigmund Freud and his followers, gender identity and the adoption of sex-typed behaviors are the result of an *Oedipus conflict* that emerges between the ages of 3 and 6. During this period, children discover the genital differences between the sexes. According to Freudians, this discovery prompts children to see themselves as rivals of their same-sex parent for the affection of the parent of the opposite sex. Such desires and feelings give rise to considerable anxiety. Freud said the anxiety is resolved through complicated psychological maneuvers in which children come to identify with the parent of the same sex. By virtue of this identification, boys acquire masculine self-conceptions and girls learn feminine self-conceptions. However, research that has tried to test Freud's theory has been either inconclusive or at odds with it. Additionally, cross-cultural research suggests that the Oedipus conflict does not occur among all peoples, including the Trobriand Islanders of the South Pacific (Malinowski, 1929).

Unlike Freud and his followers, *cultural transmission* theorists contend that the acquisition of gender identities and behaviors is not the product of an Oedipus conflict, but rather is a gradual process of learning that begins in infancy (Bandura, 1971; 1973). They suggest that parents, teachers, and other adults shape a child's behavior by reinforcing responses that are deemed appropriate to the child's gender role and discouraging inappropriate ones. Moreover, children are motivated to attend to, learn from, and imitate same-sex models because they think of same-sex models as more like themselves (Mischel, 1970). Children are given cues to their gender roles in a great variety of ways. Parents often furnish boys' and girls' rooms differently, decorating those of boys with animal motifs and those of girls with floral motifs, lace, fringe, and ruffles (Rheingold and Cook, 1975). The toys found in the rooms also differ. Boys are provided with more vehicles, military toys, sports equipment, toy animals, and mechanical toys; girls, more dolls, doll houses, and domestic toys.

Cultural transmission theory draws our attention to the part socialization plays in shaping the sex-typed behavior of children.

However, the image we gain from the theory is one of essentially passive individuals who are programmed for behavior by adult bearers of culture. *Labeling theory* (also called cognitive-developmental theory) provides a corrective to this perspective by calling our attention to the fact that children actively seek to acquire gender identities and roles. According to developmental psychologist Lawrence Kohlberg (1966, 1969; Kohlberg and Ullian, 1973), children come to label themselves as "boys" or "girls" when they are between 18 months and 3 years of age. Once they have identified themselves as males or females, they want to adopt behaviors consistent with their newly discovered status. This process is called *self-socialization*. According to Kohlberg, children form a stereotyped conception of maleness and femaleness—an oversimplified, exaggerated, cartoonlike image. Then they use this stereotyped image in organizing behavior and cultivating the attitudes and actions associated with being a boy or a girl.

Both the cultural-transmission and labeling theories of gender-role learning have received research support (Maccoby and Jacklin, 1974). Increasingly, social and behavioral scientists are coming to the view that any full explanation of gender-role acquisition must incorporate elements from both theoretical approaches.

THE FUNCTIONALIST AND CONFLICT PERSPECTIVES ON GENDER STRATIFICATION

The functionalist and conflict perspectives offer interpretations of gender stratification that resemble and parallel their positions on class and racial/ethnic stratification. Functionalists suggest that a division of labor originally arose between men and women because of the woman's role in reproduction. By virtue of the fact that women were often pregnant or nursing, preindustrial societies assigned domestic and childrearing tasks to them. In contrast, by virtue of their larger size and greater muscular strength, men were assigned hunting and defense tasks. Functionalists contend that a gender division of labor promoted the survival of the species and therefore was retained.

Sociologists Talcott Parsons and Robert Bales (1955) have built upon principles derived from the study of the dynamics of small groups in refining the functionalist position. They argue that two types of leaders are essential if a small group is to function effectively (see Chapter 4). *Instrumental leaders* (task specialists) devote their attention to appraising the problem at hand and organizing people's activity to deal with it. *Expressive leaders* (social-emotional specialists) focus on overcoming interpersonal problems in the group, defusing tensions, and promoting solidarity. Parsons and Bales suggest that families are also organized along instrumental-expressive lines. Men specialize in instrumental tasks (particularly roles associated with deriving a livelihood), and women in expressive tasks (nurturing roles that are allegedly an extension of their reproductive and nursing functions).

Conflict theorists reject functionalist arguments as simply offering a rationale for male dominance. They contend that a sexual division of labor is a social vehicle devised by men to assure themselves of privilege, prestige, and power in their relationships with women. By relegating women to the home, men have been able to deny women those resources they need to succeed in the larger world. More particularly, conflict theorists have advanced a number of explanations for gender stratification (Collins, 1975; Vogel, 1983). Some argue that the motivation for gender stratification derives from the economic exploitation of women's labor. Others say that the fundamental motive is men's desire to have women readily available for sexual gratifi-

cation. And still others emphasize that the appropriation of women is not for copulation but for procreation, especially to produce male heirs and daughters who can be used as exchanges in cementing political and economic alliances with other families. In order to appraise the matters raised by functionalist and conflict theorists, let us turn to an examination of gender roles in the United States.

GENDER ROLES IN THE UNITED STATES

The gender roles defined by a society have profound consequences for the lives of its men and women. They constitute master statuses that carry primary weight in people's interactions and relationships with others (see Chapter 2). In doing so, they place men and women in the social structure, establishing where and what they are in social terms. Thus gender roles establish the framework within which men and women gain their identities, formulate their goals, and carry out their training. Additionally, gender roles are a major source of social inequality. Just as our society structures inequalities based on race and ethnic membership, so it institutionalizes inequalities based on gender.

The Family. In large measure, sexual inequality has historically been sustained by assigning the economic-provider role to men and the childrearing role to women. The division between the public and domestic spheres has been a compelling one. Labor in the public sphere has been rewarded by money, prestige, and power, whereas labor in the domestic sphere has been typically isolated and undervalued. Surveys of occupational ratings show considerable complexities in people's evaluation of the domestic role (Nilson, 1978). It ranks higher in prestige than all but highly skilled blue-collar jobs for a woman and roughly the same as the skilled clerical jobs. Only "higher" white-collar jobs in the professions, the arts, and management accord women higher prestige.

The gender division of labor has operated to bind women to their reproductive function. Until the past decade or so, motherhood has been central to American definitions of the female role. Each woman has been expected to raise one man's children in an individual household viewed as private property and private space. Male dominance implied the notion that men "owned" a woman's sexuality. Women were viewed as providing a man with sexual and domestic services in exchange for his financial support. Within this arrangement, a sexual double standard prevailed that permitted men, but not women, considerable sexual freedom and adventure. Until the twentieth century, English and American common law viewed women as undergoing "civil death" upon marriage. Women lost their legal identity when they married and, in the eyes of the law, became "incorporated and consolidated" with their husbands. A wife could not own property in her own right or sign a contract. And a husband could require his wife to live wherever he chose and to submit to sexual intercourse against her will.

Although American men, particularly younger men, are shifting their views on doing housework, the burden still falls primarily upon women (Dowd, 1983b; Lee, 1984). There is a striking gap between men's intentions and their actions when it comes to housework and caring for children. In their study of American couples, sociologists Philip Blumstein and Pepper Schwartz (1983) found that even when the wives had full-time jobs, they did most of the household chores. Only 22 percent of the men as opposed to 59 percent of the women contributed 11 or more hours a week to household duties. Other research suggests that the higher a wife's earnings, the more likely her husband is to do a share of the housework. But men whose pay far exceeds that of their wives generally do less around the house (Mirowsky and Ross, 1984).

The Workplace. Over the past several decades, the growing participation of women in the American labor force has produced the greatest change in the nation's employment picture. In the United States some 54 percent of adult women are now in the paid labor force (the percentage of men is 76 percent). Since 1950, the number of mothers employed outside the home has nearly tripled. In many cases, the woman is the family's main breadwinner, with 15.5 percent of families now headed by women and nearly 6 million women earning more than their husbands. Women currently make up one-quarter of students in medical schools, almost one-third in law schools, and one-third in business schools (Trafford et al., 1984).

Despite these changes, many of the current figures on the employment of women bear a striking resemblance to those of previous decades. There has been little substantial change in the gender segregation of occupations since 1900 (Scott, 1982). The increase in female employment has come largely through the displacement of men by women in some low-paying categories and through the rapid expansion of the "pink-collar" occupations. As shown in Table 7.2, women fill more than 90 percent of all secretarial, bookkeeping, and receptionist positions. And positions at the top still elude American women. Only 5 percent of top executives are women. Moreover, although women constitute 71 percent of the nation's classroom teachers, they account for less than 2 percent of school district superintendents.

Women also earn less than men do. In 1983 a woman working full time earned 62 cents for each dollar earned by her male

TABLE 7.2

Sexism in the Labor Force, 1982

Occupation	Percent Women	Median Income	Occupation	Percent Men	Median Income
Secretaries	99.2%	$12,636	RR switch operators	100%	$22,828
Receptionists	97.5	$10,764	Firefighters	99.5	$20,438
Typists	96.6	$11,804	Plumbers, pipefitters	99.2	$21,944
Registered nurses	95.6	$18,980	Auto mechanics	99.1	$15,964
Sewers, stichers	95.5	$8,632	Carpet installers	98.8	$15,392
Keypunch operators	94.5	$12,480	Surveyors	98.5	$17,472
Bank tellers	92.0	$10,348	Truckdrivers	97.9	$17,160
Telephone operators	91.9	$13,988	Garbage collectors	97.3	$12,116

(*Source:* Bureau of Labor Statistics, 1984.)

counterpart. Earnings in traditionally "female" jobs and professions are substantially lower than those in comparable male-dominated occupations. Sociologists David L. Featherman and Robert M. Hauser (1978a) calculate that discrimination accounts for 84 percent of the earnings gap between men and women. Significantly, the lifetime earnings of a woman with five or more years of college will reach only 63.5 percent of that of a man with equal education (see Figure 7.1). In colleges and universities, women in the top three professorial ranks combined earn 19 percent less, on average, than their male counterparts (Evangelauf, 1984). The earnings of contemporary women still seem to be determined by the Old Testament rule, as stated in Leviticus 27:3–4: "A male

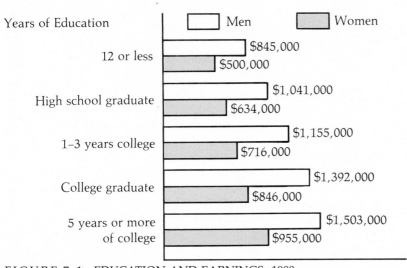

FIGURE 7.1 EDUCATION AND EARNINGS, 1980
The average college graduate who was 18 in 1980 and is currently employed full time will earn $1.1 million over the life span. But the figures differ substantially for men and women. (Source: U.S. Bureau of the Census.)

between 20 and 60 years old shall be valued at 50 silver shekels. . . . If it is a female, she shall be valued at 30 shekels" (see Table 7.3).

Overall, the career patterns of women are quite different from those of men. Given our contemporary family and work arrangements, the economic advancement of women is complicated by the social organization of child care (Van Velsor and O'Rand, 1984). Economist Lester C. Thurow (1981) points out that women who have children encounter a substantial career disadvantage. The years between 25 and 35 are critical in the development of a career. During this phase of the life span, lawyers and accountants become partners in the top firms, business managers make it to the fast track, college professors secure tenure at good universities, and blue-collar workers find positions that generate high earnings and seniority. Yet it is this time when women are most likely to leave the labor force to have children. When they do, they suffer in their ability to acquire critical skills and to achieve promotions. Even when new mothers return to work within a few months, male managers typically conclude that the women are no longer free to take on time-consuming tasks and pass them over for promotion (Fraker, 1984).

Politics and Government. In 1984, for the first time in American history, a woman was named to the presidential ticket of a major political party. Geraldine Ferraro became the Democratic party's vice-presidential candidate. Her nomination reflected other gains, especially at the state and local levels. Between 1969 and 1984, the number of women elected to state legislatures had more than tripled—from 301 to 995 (comprising 13 percent of the total). One woman was also a governor, three were lieutenant governors, and 11 were secretaries of state, as were 7 percent of the nation's mayors.

And Justice Sandra Day O'Connor of the United States Supreme Court headed a list of 72 women on federal benches (of 27,845 judges presiding in the United States, 4,762 were women).

Although women have shown increasing strength in the political arena, their numbers as officeholders still do not reflect the fact that 53 percent of the voting-age population are women and that more women vote than men. And even though in 1972 both houses of Congress approved the Equal Rights Amendment, the proposal died in June 1982, still three states short of the 38 state legislatures needed for ratification. Women have also had to run for office differently than men. Colorado Congresswoman Patricia Schroeder says that a woman runs for office "to discuss the issues, and is scrutinized for her hairstyle or her clothing. You'd never hear someone ask 'Why is that man wearing the same shirt three days in a row?' or 'What statement is he making with a blue blazer?'" (Belkin, 1984:2E).

The Women's Movement. Over the past twenty years, no social movement has had a more substantial impact on the way Americans think and act than the women's movement (Klemesrud, 1983). Such movements have arisen throughout human history, particularly within the context of social revolutions and movements for national independence. Initially women get caught up in the same broad currents that engulf a nation. But then they begin to extend the ideology of social justice and equality to their circumstances. The suffragist movement of the 1830s developed out of the abolitionist movement when women discovered strong parallels between their conditions and those of blacks. In the 1960s, the women's movement gained impetus from the involvement of women in the civil rights movement (Freeman, 1973).

TABLE 7.3

Men and Women: Same Job, Different Pay

Occupation	Weekly Earnings, Men	Weekly Earnings, Women	Earnings Ratio: % Women to Men
Lawyer	$653	$492	75.3
Engineer	592	479	80.9
Health administrator	587	394	67.1
Social scientist	580	420	72.4
Bank financial officer and manager	574	336	58.5
Computer systems analyst	568	428	75.3
Elementary–secondary school administrator	566	338	59.7
Physician	564	412	73.0
Life and physical scientist	553	378	68.3
Public relations specialist	550	341	62.0
Operations and systems analyst	547	417	76.2
Personnel and labor relations worker	530	354	66.7
College and university teacher	528	415	78.5
Designer	526	302	57.4
Public administrator	501	392	78.2
Computer programmer	478	382	79.9
Accountant	468	325	69.4
Vocational and educational counselor	459	348	75.8
Editor and reporter	451	325	72.0
Advertising agent, sales worker	449	286	63.6
Real estate agent	435	292	66.8
Insurance agent, underwriter	419	284	67.7
Wholesale, retail buyer	412	271	65.7
Elementary school teacher	411	339	82.4
Secondary school teacher	411	357	86.8

(*Source:* Bureau of Labor Statistics, *Current Population Survey,* 1982.)

The revival of feminist activity in the 1960s was spearheaded by a variety of groups. Some, like the National Organization for Women (NOW), were organized at the national level by well-known women. Others were grassroots groups that engaged in campaigns for abortion reform or welfare rights, consciousness-raising rap sessions, or the promotion of the interests of professional or gay women. After fifteen years of feminist activism, a 1983 *New York Times* poll found that a quarter of the American public believed the women's movement had made their own lives better (Kle-

mesrud, 1983). Those women who spoke favorably about the movement often did so in terms of the jobs they believe it helped them secure.

Persistence and Change. As we will discuss at greater length in Chapter 9, traditional family roles are in a state of flux. The image of the nuclear family with a breadwinning male and a full-time female homemaker represents only 12 percent of American households. In more than 60 percent of families, both husband and wife work. Some 66 percent of women who are single parents are

The past two decades have brought considerable economic and social change in the status of women. One of the most significant trends has been the movement of women into fields that traditionally have been closed to them. Yet it is easy to overestimate the magnitude of the gains that women have made. For instance, even though women constitute 53 percent of the voting-age population, less than 18 percent of the nation's judges are women. (Michal Heron/Woodfin Camp & Associates)

in the work force. And 33 million children have mothers who work full-time. Increasingly the dilemma posed for women is how to balance a job with marriage and motherhood.

Recent polls show that the majority of American men and women have adopted a number of "liberated" beliefs about women.

However, they are reluctant to abandon traditional notions of "women's work" when it comes to housekeeping and rearing children (Dowd, 1983a; *Los Angeles Times*, 1984). More than half still agree with the statement, "It is much better for everyone involved if the man is the achiever outside the home, and the woman takes care of the home and the family." Whereas men are more able to pursue their careers single-mindedly, women feel that they must try to balance their responsibilities on the job with their duties at home. Although 1970 polls showed 53 percent of American women cited motherhood as one of the best parts of being a woman, in 1983 just 26 percent did. In 1970 working outside the home was more peripheral, with only 9 percent of the women listing it as an enjoyable part of their lives; in 1983, 26 percent did. In 1983 some 58 percent of working women said they would rather work than stay home; so did 31 percent of nonworking women. Fifty-nine percent of all women, and 44 percent of men, think employed women are as good, or better, mothers as women who do not work outside the home. Yet old ways also persist. Forty-four percent of American working women say they have been discriminated against in the workplace; 80 percent agree that to get ahead a woman must be better at what she does than a man. Both persistence and change characterize the status of women in American life.

Summary

1. Stratification represents institutionalized inequality in the distribution of social rewards and burdens. People are locked within an arena of social relationships in which they differ sharply in their life chances and styles of living. In Chapter 5 we examined the class system of stratification; in this chapter we turned to two additional systems of stratification, race and/or ethnicity and gender.

2. Although racial and ethnic stratification is similar to other systems of stratification in its essential features, there is one overriding difference. Racial and ethnic

groups have the potential to carve their own independent nation from the existing state. Unlike class stratification, the issue is not replacement of one elite by another or even a revolutionary change in the political system. Instead, the question is one of whether the racial or ethnic segments of the society will be willing to participate within the existing nation-state arrangement.

3. Racial groups are populations that differ in the incidence of various hereditary traits. Ethnic groups are identified on the basis of distinctive cultural backgrounds. Racial and ethnic groups are often minority groups. Five properties characterize minorities: (l) Its members experience discrimination, segregation, oppression, or persecution at the hands of a dominant group; (2) it is characterized by physical or cultural traits that distinguish it from the dominant group; (3) it is a self-conscious social group; (4) membership in a minority is generally involuntary; and (5) the members of a minority, by choice or necessity, typically marry within their own group.

4. Prejudice is a state of mind—a feeling, opinion, or disposition. In contrast, discrimination is action, what people actually do in their daily activities. Discrimination is not practiced just by individuals. In their day-to-day operation, the institutions of society also systematically discriminate against the members of some group—a process called institutional discrimination. Gatekeeping is one mechanism by which institutional discrimination occurs.

5. Dominant groups have pursued a variety of policies toward minorities. At times these policies may parallel those of the minority; at other times they run counter to minority group aims. The chapter examined six types of dominant group policies: assimilation, pluralism, legal protection of minorities, population transfer, continued subjugation, and extermination.

6. Functionalist and conflict theorists take differing views of racial and ethnic stratification. Functionalists look to the functions and dysfunctions it has for the survival of the social system and its parts. They note that conflict promotes group formation and solidarity. Simultaneously, conflict may imperil the larger social system. Conflict theorists contend that prejudice and discrimination can best be understood in terms of tension or conflict among competing groups. Often three ingredients come into play in the emergence and stabilization of racism: ethnocentrism, competition, and unequal power.

7. Within the United States blacks, Hispanics, Native Americans (Indians), and Asian-Americans have been the victims of prejudice and discrimination. The subjugation of blacks extends to the period of exploration and colonialization. Like blacks, people of Mexican heritage and Native Americans did not originally become a part of American society through voluntary immigration. Both Native Americans and Mexicans entered the society through conquest of their homeland. Asian-Americans have also encountered considerable difficulty in the United States, but in recent decades the circumstances of many of them have greatly improved.

8. Men and women differ in their access to privilege, prestige, and power. The distribution problem of who gets what, when, and how has traditionally been answered in favor of males. Women exhibit four of the five properties commonly associated with a minority

group. Apparently all societies have seized on the anatomical differences between men and women to assign gender roles—sets of cultural expectations that define the ways in which the members of each sex should behave.

9. The biological aspects of gender consist of the physical differences between men and women: Women have the capacity to menstruate, carry a fetus until delivery, and provide it with milk after birth; men have the ability to produce and transmit sperm. But beyond these matters, the role biology plays in producing behavioral differences between men and women is shrouded in controversy. Some researchers suggest that the human embryo has a bisexual potential. It seems that biological factors do not themselves produce differences in male or female behavior, but affect the threshold for the elicitation of such behavior.

10. Gender identities are the concepts we have of ourselves as being male or female. Three theories seek to account for the process by which children acquire their gender identities. According to Freudians, the adoption of sex-typed behaviors is the result of an Oedipus conflict that emerges between the ages of 3 and 6. Cultural transmission theorists draw our attention to the part socialization plays in the process. Labeling theories examine the process whereby children come to label themselves as "boys" or "girls" and cultivate the appropriate gender-related behaviors.

11. The functionalist and conflict perspectives offer interpretations of gender stratification that resemble and parallel their positions on class and racial/ethnic stratification. Functionalists suggest that families are organized along instrumental-expressive lines, with men specializing in instrumental tasks and women in expressive tasks. Conflict theorists contend that a sexual division of labor is a social vehicle devised by men to assure themselves of privilege, prestige, and power in their relationships with women.

12. The gender roles defined by a society have profound consequences for the lives of its men and women. They constitute master statuses that carry primary weight in people's interactions and relationships with others. In so doing, they place men and women in the social structure, establishing where and what they are in social terms. Thus gender roles set the framework within which men and women gain their identities, formulate their goals, and carry out their training. Additionally, gender roles are a major source of social inequality.

Glossary

assimilation Those processes whereby groups with distinctive identities become culturally and socially fused.

discrimination The arbitrary denial of privilege, prestige, and power to members of a minority group whose qualifications are equal to those of members of the dominant group.

ethnic group A group identified chiefly on cultural grounds—language, religion, folk practices, dress, gestures, mannerisms.

gatekeeping The decision-making process whereby people are admitted to offices and positions of privilege, prestige, and power within a society.

gender identities The conceptions we have of ourselves as being male or female.

gender roles Sets of cultural expectations that define the ways in which the members of each sex should behave.

genocide The deliberate and systematic extermination of a racial or ethnic group.

hermaphrodites Individuals whose reproductive structures are sufficiently ambiguous that it is difficult to define them exclusively as male or female.

institutional discrimination Systematic discrimination against the members of some groups by the institutions of society in their daily operation.

minority group A racially or culturally self-conscious population, with hereditary membership and a high degree of in-group marriage, which suffers oppression at the hands of a dominant segment of a nation-state.

pluralism A situation where diverse groups co-exist side by side and mutually accommodate themselves to their differences.

prejudice Attitudes of aversion and hostility toward the members of a group simply because they belong to it and hence are presumed to have the objectionable qualities ascribed to it.

race Populations that differ in the incidence of various hereditary traits.

split labor market An economic arena in which large differences exist in the price of labor at the same occupational level.

symbolic racism A form of racism in which whites feel that blacks are too aggressive, do not play by the rules, and have negative characteristics.

8

Political and Economic Power

POWER, AUTHORITY, AND
   THE STATE

The State
*The Functionalist Perspective on the
   State*
The Conflict Perspective on the State
Legitimacy and Authority

ECONOMIC POWER

Comparative Economic Systems
Corporate Capitalism
Work and the Workplace

POLITICAL POWER

Types of Government
Political Power in the United States
Models of Power in the United States

Power pervades all aspects of social life. It furnishes the resources to get things done—to provide the direction essential for coordinating and integrating individual activity so that collective goals can be achieved. And it determines which individuals and groups will be able to translate their preferences into the reality of day-to-day social organization. *Power,* as we noted in Chapter 6, refers to the ability of individuals and groups to realize their will in human affairs even if it involves the resistance of others. By virtue of power, change is brought about in one party—in attitude, behavior, motivation, or direction—that would not have occurred in its absence.

Power is institutionalized in a patterned, recurrent manner and hence is embedded in social arrangements. It gives direction to human affairs, channeling people's actions along one course rather than another. Yet power entails not only the ability to get things done, but to get them done in the way that one party prefers they be done. Alexander Hamilton alluded to this attribute of power when he wrote in *The Federalist* in 1788: "In the general course of human nature, a power over a man's subsistence amounts to a power over his will." Thus the power that makes a real difference in the way social life works is the power that flows from the dominant organizations and institutions. This chapter examines "power that makes a real difference." It focuses on the economic and political institutions.

Power, Authority, and the State

Because the collective enterprise—group life—makes us mutually dependent on one another, we can achieve many of our goals only by influencing other people's behavior. As we pointed out in discussing social stratification in Chapter 6, power affects the abil-

ity of people to make the world work on their behalf. Those individuals and groups who control critical resources—rewards, punishments, and persuasive communications—are able to dictate the way social life is ordered. To command key organizations and institutions is to command people. Indeed, power is the bedrock of social organization (Bierstedt, 1950). It contributes to the creation and perpetuation of social groups and institutions. The state is such an organization and institution.

THE STATE

The **state**—the political institution—is an arrangement that consists of people who exercise an effective monopoly in the use of physical coercion within a given territory. In the final analysis the state rests on **force**—power whose basis is the threat or application of punishment. Clearly the ability to take life and inflict suffering affords a critical advantage in human affairs. In effect, force constitutes a final court of appeals; there is usually no appeal from force except the exercise of superior force. For this reason, sovereign nations restrict, and even prohibit, the independent exercise of force by their subjects. If it were otherwise, governments could not suppress forceful challenges to their authority (Lenski, 1966). But even though force is ultimately the basis of the state, it is only in unusual situations that societal power actually takes this form.

Two views have prevailed regarding the state. Conservatives see government as employing force as an instrument of right to restrain and rebuke those who would place their self-interest above the common good. In contrast, radicals maintain that the state employs force to suppress right and defend selfish interests. The conservative view sees the state as a social contract; the radical view, as an organization of violence that serves the interests of elites.

The social contract perspective was articulated by seventeenth- and eighteenth-century philosophers like Thomas Hobbes (1588–1679) who contended that human beings were "naturally" a perverse and destructive lot. In order to rid themselves of rampant brutality, violence, and chaos, people voluntarily entered into a social agreement that provided for central authority and collective defense. Hobbes took a particularly dismal view of humankind: "During the time men live without a common power [government] to keep them in awe, they are in that condition which is called war; and such a war . . . of every man against every man." Hobbes said that human beings at first had no law, since law was created by government. Indeed, there was no justice or right or wrong. But since human beings had reason they could improve themselves, and they did so by establishing government. Together, they entered into a covenant, agreeing "to confer all their power and strength upon one man . . ." thereby creating a sovereign.

But other philosophers disagreed with Hobbes. The eighteenth-century philosopher Jean Jacques Rousseau (1712–1778) argued that "man is born free, and everywhere he is in chains." According to Rousseau, the first institution humankind established was private property. Once the institution of property was established, the state necessarily followed, to define and defend property rights. In their original "state of nature," Rousseau said, human beings were "noble savages"—spontaneous, outgoing, loving, kind, and peaceful. They lived in harmony with their environment. However, the advent of private property brought corruption and oppression, and obedience to a privileged class replaced obedience to the "common will."

These contrasting views of the state have been modified and refined by generations of social scientists. The conservative and

According to the eighteenth-century philosopher Jean Jacques Rousseau, humankind in its original state was free and unfettered. Peoples like the American Indians were thought of as "noble savages" who lived in harmony with their environment and with one another until they were corrupted by "civilization." (Culver Pictures)

radical perspectives have found expression in the functionalist and conflict formulations. Let us examine these formulations more carefully.

THE FUNCTIONALIST PERSPECTIVE ON THE STATE

Functionalists contend that there is a good reason why the state arose, and why it has assumed a dominant position in contemporary life. They say that society must maintain order and provide for the common good. More particularly, they point to four primary functions performed by the state.

Enforcement of Norms. It is easy to take the state for granted. Yet the eminent anthropologist George Peter Murdock (1950a:716) tells us:

[F]or 99 percent of the approximately one million years that man has inhabited this earth, he lived, thrived, and developed without any true government whatsoever, and . . . as late as 100 years ago half the peoples of the world— not half the population but half the tribes or nations—still ordered their lives exclusively through informal controls without benefit of political institutions.

As we pointed out in Chapter 2, where people lack a formal political institution, they enforce their folkways and mores through the spontaneous and collective action of community members. Thus the Crow Indians subjected violators of their mores to scathing ridicule. But in modern, complex societies characterized by a preponderance of secondary relationships, these arrangements are no longer adequate. A special body or organization is required to ensure law and order—the state.

Planning and Direction. Rapid social change dictates that people can no longer rely on the gradual, more or less spontaneous evolution of folkways and mores to provide guidelines for daily life. New norms become indispensable. Such norms—*laws*— result from conscious thought, deliberate planning, and formal declaration. And laws have an added advantage: They can be changed more easily than folkways and mores. By way of illustration, the folkways of fairness that regulated traffic in horse and buggy days are no longer adequate for the congested conditions of the nation's highways. Nor are the laws governing automobiles suitable for handling congested air traffic over airports.

In addition, the complexity and scope of many activities requires overall coordination and integration. Under contemporary urban conditions, people find that personal and informal arrangements no longer suffice to provide highways, fire and police protection, public sanitation, safeguards to public health, and assistance to the poor and infirm. These and many other activities dictate central direction. Similarly, in times of war, financial panic, or natural disaster, people often cannot cope with the magnitude of the crisis through independent and individual actions. The efficient and effective coordination and channeling of the human endeavor requires planning and direction. This task can be performed by only one or at most a few individuals. And these individuals must have the power and authority to implement their plans (Davis, 1949).

Arbitration of Conflicting Interests. Because many resources are scarce and divisible—particularly privilege, prestige, and power—people find themselves in conflict as they pursue their goals. If no bonds other than the pursuit of immediate self-interest were to unite people, society would quickly degenerate into a Hobbesian nightmare in which "war against all" comes to prevail. If conflicts among different social strata, races, religions, and special interest groups were to become deep and intense, the entire social fabric would be imperiled. Some agency is required that is sufficiently strong to contain conflict within tolerable limits—and that agency is the state (Goode, 1972).

Protection against Other Societies. Throughout human history, societies have felt it necessary to protect their members and interests against outside groups and to advance their fortunes through acts of aggression against other groups. Two primary means for achieving these ends have been war and diplomacy. However, both war and diplomacy call for centralized control and mobilization if a people are to maximize their position relative to their adversaries. The state meets this requirement.

In sum, functionalists view the state much in the fashion of social contract philosophers. They deem it to be a social mechanism—a necessary institution—that evolved as societies moved from more traditional to modern ways of life (see Chapter 2).

THE CONFLICT PERSPECTIVE ON THE STATE

Functionalists see the state as a rather benign institution. Not so conflict theorists! They contend that the state is a vehicle by which one or more groups impose their values and stratification system upon other groups. As they view the matter, the state has its origin in the desire of ruling elites to give permanence to social arrangements that benefit themselves. More fundamentally, they depict the state as an instrument of violence and oppression. Conflict sociologist Randall Collins (1975:351–352) asserts:

What we mean by the state is the way in which violence is organized. The state consists of those people who have the guns or the other weapons and are prepared to use them; in the version of political organization found in the modern world, they claim monopoly on their use. The state is, above all, the army and the police, and if these groups did not have weapons we would not have a state in the classical sense. This is a type of definition much disputed by those who like to believe that the state is a kind of grade-school assembly in which people get together to operate for their common good. . . . [However, the basic question is] who will fight or threaten whom and who will win what?

Conflict theorists see the state arising in history with the production of a social surplus—goods and services over and above what is necessary for human survival. In hunting and gathering societies, land is communally owned, and the members of the community share the food derived from it. Agricultural societies are less egalitarian than hunting and gathering groups (see Chapter 2). Intensive agriculture produces food surpluses, so it is no longer essential that every human hand be employed in subsistence activities. Some individuals can apply their talents and abilities to new occupations, such as pottery, masonry, and weaving. Of equal significance, some members of society can live off the surplus produced by others—elites who become the beneficiaries of privilege (Lenski, 1966). Political scientists Kenneth Prewitt and Alan Stone (1973:12–13) observe:

If craftsmen produce artifacts and ornaments, these status symbols become the possessions of the ruling class. If warriors venture forth to conquer and return with slaves and women, the slaves will serve in the fields and kitchens of the ruler and the women will be placed in their harems. If the productive labor of society is used to build palaces, temples, and monuments, these edifices will be inhabited by or dedicated to the members of the ruling class. It has been a constant fact of history that much more than an equal share of the social surplus is retained by the rulers for private pleasures.

Anthropologists Charles Wagley and Marvin Harris (1964:242) also point out that the rise of the state had other social consequences. It gave rise to subject peoples (dominant–minority group relationships):

Only with the development of the state did human societies become equipped with a form of social organization which could bind masses of culturally and physically heterogeneous "strangers" in a single social entity. Whereas primitive peoples derive their cohesion largely from a common culture and from kinship and other kinds of personal ties, state societies are held together largely by the existence of a central political authority which claims a monopoly of coercive power over all persons within a given territory. Theoretically, with a sufficiently strong development of the apparatus of government, a state society can extend law and order over limitless subgroups of strangers who neither speak the same language, worship the same gods, nor strive for the same values.

There is a difference of opinion among conflict theorists regarding the nature of the state. Some Marxists (*instrumental Marxists*) have taken literally the *Communist Manifesto's* dictum that "the executive of the modern state is but a committee for managing the common affairs of the whole bourgeosie." Seen in this manner, the state is an instrument that is manipulated, virtually at will, by the capitalist class (Beirne, 1979). As we will see later in the chapter, several studies seek to show that economic power inheres in the ownership or control of the means of production (factories, banks, and large farms) and is typically transformed into political influence (Kolko, 1962; Miliband, 1969; Domhoff, 1970). Capitalists, it is alleged, accomplish this transformation through lobbying, campaign financing, intermarriage within the capitalist class, and the corruption by business of the judiciary and federal and state legislatures.

Other Marxists (*structural Marxists*) contend that the state apparatus exercises "relative autonomy" in its relationship with the capitalist class. State structures are said to have independent histories that are not simply the products of dominant class interests or class struggles (Skocpol, 1980; Quadagno, 1984). According to this view, relentless class war between capitalists and workers, boom and bust economic cycles, and intercorporate conflict place constraints on the ability of the capitalist class to manipu-

late political institutions at will. Although the state may promote a climate favorable to capitalist enterprise, it must also legitimate the sanctity of the social order and maintain internal peace (O'Connor, 1973). By virtue of this latter requirement, the state routinely pursues policies that are at variance with the interests of *some* capitalists. For instance, it enacts welfare legislation that supports unemployed and nonproductive workers; places restrictions on rent that inhibit the ability of landlords to receive open market rentals; passes and enforces antitrust legislation; and imposes taxes on corporations (Beirne, 1979). Accordingly, the state apparatus is seen as standing above the individual elements of the economy, even though in its basic orientation it promotes a social environment conducive to capitalist arrangements. In this fashion the unity of the capitalist class is maintained (Poulantzas, 1973; Mollenkopf, 1975; Block, 1977). Thus, while Marxists may differ in their views on some matters, they nonetheless tend to agree that the state manages the collective interests of the capitalist class in preventing economic crises and handling crisis periods to prevent revolutionary changes.

LEGITIMACY AND AUTHORITY

Both functionalist and conflict theorists see force as the foundation of sovereignty. But as we pointed out earlier in the chapter, they disagree on the ends served by the state's use of force. Functionalists see force as restraining those who would put their self-interests above the public good, whereas conflict theorists see force as an instrument of subjugation and exploitation. In Chapter 1 we noted that a number of sociologists have sought to reconcile the two positions by emphasizing that consensus and coercion give a Janus-headed character to society: Both consensus and conflict are seen as central elements of social life.

Although force may be an effective means for seizing power, and though it remains the ultimate foundation of the state, it is not the most effective means for political rule (Lenski, 1966). As the officials of the Soviet-imposed regime in modern-day Poland are discovering, force is both inefficient and costly. Moreover, honor, normally a prized possession, is denied to those who rule by force alone. And finally, if an elite is inspired by revolutionary visions for building a new social order, the ideals remain unfulfilled unless the masses come to embrace the new order as their own. The English leader and orator Edmund Burke (1729–1797) captured the essence of these matters when he noted that the use of force alone is but temporary: "It may subdue for a moment; but it does not remove the necessity of subduing again; and a nation is not governed, which is perpetually to be conquered."

All this highlights the importance of the distinction that sociologists make between power that is legitimate and power that is illegitimate. Legitimate power is **authority.** When individuals possess authority, they have a recognized and established *right* to determine policies, pronounce judgments, settle controversies, and, more broadly, act as leaders. Legitimacy—the social justification of power—takes a number of forms. Sociologist Max Weber (1921/1968) has suggested a threefold classification of authority based on the manner in which the power is socially legitimated: legal-rational, traditional, and charismatic.

Weber's interest in authority derived from his broader political interests. Indeed, Weber has often been called the "bourgeois Marx" because of the similarities in the two men's intellectual interests and the differences in their political orientations. Al-though critical of modern capitalism, Weber did not advocate revolution, preferring instead gradual change (Ritzer, 1983). Let us consider Weber's three bases of authority.

Traditional Authority. In **traditional authority,** power is legitimated by the sanctity of age-old customs. People obey their rulers because "this is the way things have always been done." Additionally, they may perceive a ruler's power as eternal, inviolable, and sacred. Many Roman Catholics invest the Pope with infallibility deriving from divine guidance when he acts in matters pertaining to the Church. Similarly, medieval kings and queens ruled in the name of "a divine right" ordained by God. It was this type of authority that Emperor Hirohito enjoyed until the American occupation authorities imposed a legal-rational system on Japan following World War II. A good deal of moral force stands behind traditional authority. Often the claim to such authority rests on birthright; it is generally inherited, since royal blood is thought to be somehow different from and superior to the blood of commoners.

Legal-Rational Authority. In **legal-rational authority,** power is legitimated by explicit rules and rational procedures that define the rights and duties of the occupants of given positions. It is this type of authority that Weber depicted as prevailing in his ideal-type bureaucracy, discussed in Chapter 4. Under this arrangement, officials claim obedience on the grounds that their commands fall within the impersonal, formally defined scope of their office. Obedience is owed not to the person, but to a set of impersonal principles that have been devised in a rational manner.

In the United States, the authority of government leaders is accepted because Americans accept the premise that the law is supreme. Americans accept the exercise of power because they have come to believe that policies and orders are formulated in accordance with rules to which they subscribe. They accept the authority of a newly elected president even when the election campaign was waged in bitterness and anger. The system would crumble were large numbers of Americans to reject these "rules of the game." In fact, this occurred in 1861, when southern states rejected the election of Abraham Lincoln and federal authority, seceding from the Union and initiating the Civil War. And it was the perception by Americans that President Richard M. Nixon had failed to abide by the rules in the Watergate case that led to his downfall. Ideally, then, legal-rational authority is "a government of laws, not of people."

Charismatic Authority. In **charismatic authority,** power is legitimated by the extraordinary superhuman or supernatural attributes people attribute to a leader. Founders of world religions, prophets, military victors, and political heroes commonly derive their authority from charisma (meaning literally "gift of grace"). Miracles, revelations, exceptional feats, and baffling successes are their trademarks. They are the Christs, Napoleons, Caesars, Hitlers, Castros, Joan of Arcs, and Ayatollah Khomeinis that dot the pages of history. At times such leaders have a sense of being "called" to spread the new word. They communicate a sense that the past is decadent but that a new day awaits people who follow them, as symbolized in Christ's injunction, "It is written . . . , but I say unto you. . . ."

Weber viewed each of these three bases of authority as ideal types. As we noted in Chapter 1, ideal types are concepts sociologists construct to portray the principal characteristics of a phenomenon. Hence, in practice, any specific form of authority may involve various combinations of all three.

For example, Franklin Delano Roosevelt gained the presidency through legal-rational principles. By the time he was elected president for the fourth time, his leadership had a good many traditional elements to it. And many Americans viewed him as a charismatic leader.

Economic Power

All societies confront three basic economic problems. *What* goods and services should they produce and in what quantities? *How* should they employ their limited resources—land, water, minerals, fuel, and labor—to produce the desired goods and services? And *for whom* should they produce the goods and services? The manner in which they answer these questions has profound consequences for the nature and the structure of their societies. For instance, if they decide to produce guns and weaponry in large quantities, their citizens' standard of living will be lower than if they emphasize the satisfaction of consumer needs. How they go about producing the desired goods and services shapes the world of work, how it is organized, the satisfactions it provides, and the status it accords. And decisions regarding the "for whom" question influence the distribution of wealth, income, and prestige. Clearly the answers to these questions derive from the structuring of power within societies.

As we pointed out in Chapter 2, people have responded somewhat differently over the course of human history to the dictates posed by economic survival. Hunting and gathering economies were the earliest form of organized social life. Horticultural, agrarian, and industrial modes of production followed. And some social analysts say that advanced nations are currently moving in the direction of postindustrial social organization. Changes in the way people produce, distribute, and consume goods and services result in strong pressures for change in other institutional arrangements as well.

In the contemporary world, two differing types of economic systems are competing for people's allegiance. One is characterized by a capitalist market economy and the other by a socialist command economy. Each takes a quite different approach to economic power. And each has substantially different social and political implications. Let us examine these matters more carefully.

COMPARATIVE ECONOMIC SYSTEMS

Modern economic systems differ from one another in two important respects. First, they provide different answers to the question, How is economic activity organized—by the market or by the plan? Second, they provide different answers to the question, Who owns the means of production—individuals or the state? However, these questions do not demand an "either/or" answer. Each question allows for a range of choice, with a great many gradations in between. And no contemporary nation falls totally at one or the other pole, although the United States and the Soviet Union typically supply opposite answers to both questions.

In practice, we commonly merge the two features and talk about contrasting economic systems. We think of **capitalist economies** as relying heavily on free markets and privately held property; **socialist economies** as relying primarily on state planning and publicly held property. Yet the two characteristics are not necessarily equivalent. For instance, in Nazi Germany the government controlled and planned the economy, although ownership remained mainly in private hands. And in contemporary Yugoslavia the means of production are socially owned, although the economy is largely organized by markets.

In a market economy, consumers determine which goods and services should be provided and in what quantities by registering their dollar votes. Those things that they do not want, or that are overproduced, fall in price. Items that are in short supply rise in price. Price movements act as signals to profit-making individuals and firms. They cut back on goods with falling prices and increase the production of goods with rising prices. Economists call this mechanism *consumer sovereignty.* Underlying this approach is the ideological notion that if each economic unit is allowed to make free choices in pursuit of its own best interests, the interests of all will be best served. However, many social reformers fault consumer sovereignty for promoting such ills as violence in television programming and high-sugar, low-nutrient breakfast cereals. In command economies, the state or central planning authority determines the items that will be produced and their quantities. The problem with this arrangement is highlighted by the Soviet Union, where there are fewer automobiles and more copies of Lenin's books than consumers desire.

Free-market and command economies also differ in how they go about allocating their available resources to various productive activities. Ideally, societies allocate their resources to productive activities and use known productive techniques in such a way that no reallocation of resources or change of technique would yield more of any good without yielding less of another. For instance, if we try to grow oranges in South Dakota and wheat in Florida, we are unlikely to have as much success as if we reverse these land utilization patterns. In free-market economies, competition among suppliers of goods and labor services is thought to ensure the most efficient and productive use of resources. Command economies, in contrast, are based on the assumption that rational decision making affords better results than the haphazard operation of market forces.

Finally, market and command economies differ in how they handle the "for whom" issue—how income is distributed. Market economies rely on the same price system that determines wages, interest rates, and profits for determining the distribution of income among people in the society. Historically, one of the major criticisms of the market system has been that it does not distribute income in an equitable manner. Income payments go in substantial amounts to private owners of physical capital—capitalists. And critics allege that the economic and political power held by capitalists limits the government in working toward a more just and equal social system. Accordingly, their solution is to have the state own the primary instruments of production and direct their use in "the public good."

In the contemporary world we would be hard pressed to find a pure form of either a capitalist market economy or a socialist command economy. To one degree or another, most nations are characterized by mixed economies. For instance, in the United States the nation's tax laws influence investment decisions by providing tax incentives and shelters for investors in real estate and mineral exploration. Regulatory agencies impose pollution controls, standards for work conditions, rates for electric utility companies, and licensing of prescription drugs. Additionally, some enterprises, such as the Tennessee Valley Authority (TVA), the Postal Service, Amtrak, and Conrail, operate as publicly owned agencies. Likewise, in the Soviet Union there is a small "capitalist" sector in which peasants are permitted to sell what they grow on their small private plots of land.

Even more mixed economies are found in many Western European nations. In Great Britain, for instance, most industries are privately owned, except for those deemed "basic" to the economy (coal, steel, and railroads). Scandinavian capitalism—sometimes mistakenly taken for socialism—is a form of "welfare statism." For example, in Sweden some 90 percent of the nation's enterprises are privately owned, although income taxes on profits run as high as 80 percent. The revenues secured in this fashion are used to promote an extensive system of social benefits providing cradle-to-grave care for everyone. Japan has also evolved a unique system whereby industry and government work closely together. Some large firms, particularly those engaged in exporting, receive substantial government preferences. In sum, societies approach their economic problems in a variety of ways.

CORPORATE CAPITALISM

The government is an important participant in the American economy, but the primary productive role is played by private business. In 1984 there were some 17 million businesses in the United States. Most were small, owned by an individual or family, and concentrated in services, construction, and retail and wholesale trade. Although most businesses are small, large corporations have the greatest impact on the economy. In 1982, the 275 largest industrial corporations owned two-thirds of the assets of manufacturing firms and realized nearly three fourths of the profits (*Statistical Abstracts of the United States,* 1984). The largest American corporation, Exxon, netted a profit of over $5.5 billion in 1984 (see Table 8.1). IBM's $6.5 billion profit was tops.

The Power of National Corporations. When you drive a car, work on a computer terminal, replace a light bulb, purchase gasoline, or eat a breakfast cereal, you are using products manufactured by an oligopoly. An **oligopoly** is a market dominated by a few firms. When we look at such giants of

TABLE 8.1
The 25 Largest U.S. Industrial Corporations, Ranked by Sales, 1984

Rank	Company	Sales $ Thousands	Assets $ Thousands	Rank	Net Income (Profit) $ Thousands	Rank	Employees Number	Rank
1	Exxon	$90,854,000	$63,278,000	1	$5,528,000	2	150,000	10
2	General Motors	83,889,900	52,114,900	2	4,516,500	3	748,000	1
3	Mobil	56,047,000	41,851,000	4	1,268,000	13	178,900	8
4	Ford Motor	52,366,400	27,485,600	8	2,906,800	4	383,700	3
5	Texaco	47,334,000	37,744,000	6	306,000	62	68,088	46
6	International Business Machines	45,937,000	42,808,000	3	6,582,000	1	394,930	2
7	E.I. du Pont de Nemours	35,915,000	24,098,000	11	1,431,000	11	157,783	9
8	American Tel. & Tel.	33,187,500	39,826,600	5	1,369,900	12	365,000	4
9	General Electric	27,947,000	24,730,000	10	2,280,000	6	330,000	5
10	Standard Oil (Indiana)	26,949,000	25,734,000	9	2,183,000	7	53,581	62
11	Chevron	26,798,000	36,358,000	7	1,534,000	9	37,761	101
12	Atlantic Richfield	24,686,000	22,130,000	12	567,000	30	39,400	94
13	Shell Oil	20,701,000	23,729,000	13	1,772,000	8	34,699	112
14	Chrysler	19,572,700	9,062,700	31	2,380,000	5	100,435	18
15	U.S. Steel	18,274,000	18,989,000	14	493,000	37	88,753	27
16	United Technologies	16,331,757	9,904,536	25	645,015	24	205,500	7
17	Phillips Petroleum	15,537,000	16,965,000	17	810,000	18	29,300	132
18	Occidental Petroleum	15,373,000	12,273,100	20	568,700	29	40,630	91
19	Tenneco	14,779,000	18,205,000	15	631,000	25	98,000	22
20	Sun	14,466,000	12,789,000	19	538,000	31	37,000	104
21	ITT	14,000,988	13,277,188	18	448,046	43	252,000	6
22	Procter & Gamble	12,946,000	8,898,000	32	890,000	16	61,700	51
23	R.J. Reynolds Industries	11,902,000	9,272,000	29	1,210,000	14	97,551	23
24	Standard Oil (Ohio)	11,692,000	17,487,000	16	1,488,000	10	44,200	79
25	Dow Chemical	11,418,000	11,419,000	21	585,000	27	49,800	69

(Source: Fortune, April 29, 1985:266–267.)

American business as General Motors, IBM, and General Electric, we find oligopolies. General Motors must compete with Ford, Chrysler, Toyota, and Honda; IBM with Apple, Control Data, and Hewett-Packard; and General Electric with Westinghouse (in the electrical generator market) and with Pratt and Whitney (in the jet engine market).

Such gigantic firms exercise enormous power in American life. The decisions made by their officials have implications and ramifications that reach throughout the nation. Take the automobile industry. Until recently, the car business pumped $40 billion a year into 30,000 suppliers, made products equivalent in value to 8 percent of the nation's gross national product (GPN) and 26 percent of total retail sales, and employed a large fraction of the work force (Abernathy, Clark, and Kantrow, 1983). But as the big auto firms matured, their management failed to adapt in ways that would sustain both efficiency and innovation. As a result, the American auto companies lost a substantial market share to foreign manufacturers, experienced massive layoffs of workers, and found themselves with dated plants and equipment. They became trapped in a commitment to big, comfortable cars that returned handsome profits (the profit margins on such big cars as Cadillacs, Lincolns, and Oldsmobile Cutlass Supremes range from $2,000 to $6,000 per car) (Fisher, 1984). Says Michael Driggs, a deputy assistant secretary of commerce in the Reagan administration: "They [the auto makers] have chosen to skim the cream off the market, producing fewer cars than they could profitably sell in order to profit more from the ones they do sell" (quoted by Anderson, 1984:72).

Meanwhile, Japanese car makers learned to make subcompacts for $1,600 to $2,500 less than their American counterparts (Fisher, 1984). The Big Three American automakers have responded to this situation by all but abandoning new efforts in small cars. Instead they have sought joint ventures with Japanese and South Korean automakers. Simultaneously, voluntary agreements between the United States and Japan have limited Japanese auto imports. A study by Wharton Econometrics calculates that it costs American consumers an extra $5 billion a year for cars by virtue of the higher price tags that result from the import limits (Wayne, 1984). Whereas in 1972 it took the average consumer 30 weeks to earn enough to afford the average automobile, in 1984 it took 40 weeks (Anderson, 1984).

The American steel industry affords another illustration of the impact large corporations have on American life. Steel was once the backbone of the nation's economy. It was hardly an accident that President Truman temporarily seized the steel mills, or that President Kennedy lashed out at price increases by United States Steel. But miscalculations by the steel corporations have devastated the industry. In the five years between 1979 and 1984, industry employment fell by 200,000 workers, or more than two-fifths of the total (Samuelson, 1984). Believing that demand for steel was growing, American firms retained inefficient plants and failed to introduce new technologies. Thus in 1982, less than a third of American crude steel was produced via the more efficient continuous-casting process, contrasted with four-fifths in Japan. According to a report by the Congressional Budget Office, between 1980 and 1984 steel companies spent an average of $2.2 billion annually on capital projects, $3.3 billion less than was required if they were to remain competitive (Williams, 1984). What money they did invest frequently went into nonsteel areas. United States Steel purchased Marathon Oil, National Intergroup moved into financial institutions, and Armco diversified into insurance.

Although in theory large corporations

operate in the private sector, their impact on national life and the nation's welfare is so enormous that the federal government often intervenes to bail them out when they are threatened with bankruptcy. In recent years it rescued Chrysler and Lockheed, and in 1984 the federal government saved the Continental Illinois National Bank & Trust Co. of Chicago. The Comptroller of the Currency, Todd Conover, told Congress that the federal government could not allow any of the nation's eleven largest banks to fail. Recounting a discussion with the heads of the Federal Reserve Board, the Federal Deposit Insurance Corporation, and the Treasury Department, Conover said: "We recognized that we could very well have seen a national, if not an international, financial crisis" if the government did not rescue Continental. He estimated that more than 100 banks with deposits in the troubled Chicago bank would have failed and that dozens of the bank's corporate customers could also have collapsed had the government not intervened with its $4.5 billion rescue (Carrington, 1984).

The Power of Multinational Corporations. The rise of multinational corporations and the growing internationalization of the world economy has given a new dimension to economic power (Bornschier, Chase-Dunn, and Rubinson, 1978; Szymanski, 1981; Fennema, 1982). **Multinational corporations** are firms that have their central office in one country and subsidiaries in other countries. The economic integration of less developed nations into the structures of a world economy can be traced to European exploration and colonization beginning in the fifteenth century. The arrangement has been characterized by the differentiation of core and periphery regions (Wallerstein, 1974; 1980). **Core regions** consist of geographical areas that dominate the world economy and exploit the rest of

The economic influence and power of multinational corporations extend beyond the confines of a single nation-state. For instance, it is not unusual for large banks like the First National Bank of Boston to have subsidiaries in other nations, such as Brazil. (Allan Tannenbaum/Sygma)

TABLE 8.2

The World's 25 Largest Industrial Corporations, Ranked by Sales, 1984

Rank	Company	Headquarters	Sales ($000)	Net Income ($000)
1	Exxon	New York	90,854,000	5,528,000
2	Royal Dutch/Shell Group	The Hague/London	84,864,598	4,872,148
3	General Motors	Detroit	83,889,900	4,516,500
4	Mobil	New York	56,047,000	1,268,000
5	Ford Motor	Dearborn, Mich.	52,366,400	2,906,800
6	British Petroleum	London	50,662,063	1,474,466
7	Texaco	Harrison, N.Y.	47,334,000	306,000
8	International Business Machines	Armonk, N.Y.	45,937,000	6,582,000
9	E.I. du Pont de Nemours	Wilmington, Del.	35,915,000	1,431,000
10	American Tel. & Tel.	New York	33,187,500	1,369,900
11	General Electric	Fairfield, Conn.	27,947,000	2,280,000
12	Standard Oil (Ind.)	Chicago	26,949,000	2,183,000
13	Chevron	San Francisco	26,798,000	1,534,000
14	ENI	Rome	25,798,221	(50,119)
15	Atlantic Richfield	Los Angeles	24,686,000	567,000
16	Toyota Motor	Toyota City	24,110,656	1,255,936
17	IRI	Rome	23,353,993	N.A.
18	Unilever	London/Rotterdam	21,598,790	637,065
19	Shell Oil	Houston	20,701,000	1,772,000
20	Elf-Aquitaine	Paris	20,662,330	742,576
21	Matsushita Electric Industrial	Osaka	19,993,170	1,009,532
22	Chrysler	Highland Park, Mich.	19,572,700	2,380,000
23	Pemex (Petróleos Mexicanos)	Mexico City	19,404,780	7,283
24	Hitachi	Tokyo	18,485,905	707,385
25	U.S. Steel	Pittsburgh	18,274,000	493,000
	Totals		$1,296,328,945	$59,942,260

(*Source: Fortune,* August 19, 1985, p. 179. N. A. = Not Available.)

the system; **periphery regions** consist of those areas that provide raw materials to the core and are exploited by it. At first the peripheral areas exported spices, coffee, tea, and tobacco to Europe. Later, they become suppliers of agricultural and mineral raw materials, while their advantaged classes provided markets for industrial goods from Europe (Bornschier and Hoby, 1981).

Through the years, multinational corporations have played an increasing role in the structuring of the division of labor within the world economy. Table 8.2 lists the twenty-five largest multinational corporations. Only two non-American corporations are among the top ten firms (Royal Dutch/Shell and British Petroleum, both large oil concerns). The annual income from sales of the largest corporations exceed the gross national products of most countries in which they do business. In fact, about half of the largest economic units in the world are not nations but multinational corporations.

But multinational firms do not only rival nations in wealth. They also frequently operate as "private governments," pursuing their worldwide interests by well-developed "foreign policies." In some instances, multinational corporations have posed a threat to the sovereignty of the nations in which they operate. For instance, International Telephone and Telegraph (ITT) flagrantly intervened in Chile's domestic political life in the early 1970s when it assisted the opponents of Salvador Allende. When Allende, a Marxist, was elected president of Chile, ITT worked with the Central Intelligence Agency to overthrow his legally constituted government by a coup that installed a military dictatorship. Nor have developed nations been exempted. In an attempt to secure foreign military contracts, Lockheed made payments to politically influential people in a number of countries. Among those touched by the scandal were a former Japanese prime minister and a member of the Dutch royal family. Since their operations extend across a great many national boundaries, a government has difficulty holding multinational firms accountable to its laws. And the governments of host countries find it more difficult to deal with a multinational corporation than with a domestic firm, because the multinational corporation can exercise the option of leaving a nation to carry out business elsewhere.

Companies become multinational for a variety of reasons. The traditional answer has been that they go abroad to develop a source of cheap raw materials. But in recent years they have also gone abroad in search of lower wages. For instance, textile, shoe, and electronic firms have opened factories in Hong Kong, Taiwan, and South Korea to produce labor-intensive products. Likewise, American automakers have stepped up their imports of parts made more cheaply by foreign suppliers. These developments have led American labor to complain that multinational corporations are "exporting American jobs."

There is considerable controversy regarding the impact multinational corporations have on less developed or peripheral nations in the Third World. One view, associated with mainstream Marxism, asserts that international capitalism has transformed the economies of precapitalist countries, made them capitalist, and established the foundation for worker-led socialist revolutions. Sociologist Albert Szymanski (1981) contends that prior to the 1960s, Western colonialism posed obstacles to Third World industrialization. But he says that in recent decades imperialist obstacles have been removed, and capital has flowed to low-wage areas. The contrasting view argues that Third World nations have been capitalist for centuries, have de-developed in the face of the onslaught from advanced capitalist nations, and continue to be exploited (Baran and Sweezy, 1966; Wallerstein, 1974, 1980). Sociologist Volker Bornschier and his associates (1978, 1981) claim that foreign investment in a country creates dependencies that have a long-term negative effect on the nation's rate of economic growth. Moreover, they find that the penetration of multinational corporations weakens the power of labor and middle-class groups and strengthens the hand of traditional power holders (Rubinson, 1976).

It is difficult to arrive at overall generalizations regarding the economic impact of multinational corporations on Third World nations because the impact often differs from one time to another and from country to country (Newman, 1979, 1983; Evans, 1981). Nations like South Korea, Taiwan, Hong Kong, and Singapore have used multinational firms as organizational vehicles to begin raising their populations out of poverty. But in many other cases, trade and investment by multinational firms have made jobs disappear. For example, the introduction of machinery has often led to a loss of agricultural jobs. Moreover, the economies of Third World nations frequently become tied to a single industry, increasing dependence on foreign investors, distorting patterns of national economic development, and rendering the nations especially vulnerable to bust and boom economic cycles.

The Control of Corporations. We have seen that the decisions made by corporations have vast consequences not only for the citizens of one country, but for the global community. They have a substantial impact upon employment opportunities, economic conditions (depression and inflation), consumer choices, and political authority. All this raises the question of who controls corporations—who are their decision makers? In 1932 Adoph Berle, Jr., and Gardiner C. Means published *The Modern Corporation and Private Property* , a book that has had a profound impact on scholarly thought on the matter. They said that corporate power resides with chief executives, who themselves have little financial stake in the firms they manage. The logic of their argument rested on the assertion that the stock of most large corporations is widely dispersed. Consequently, no shareholders possess a sufficient block of stock to impose corporate policy on the managers who make the day-to-day decisions for their firms. Economist John Kenneth Galbraith (1971:xvii) contends that the separation of ownership and effective control means that "The decisive power in modern society is exercised not by capital but by organization, not by the capitalist but by the industrial bureaucrat." This state of affairs has been labeled "the managerial revolution" (Burnham, 1941).

Some social scientists see the managerial revolution as the source of many of America's current economic problems. Harvard Business School professors Robert H. Hayes and William J. Abernathy say that corporations pile rewards on executives who display impressive short-term results (Wayne,

1982). Consequently, managers show an excessive concern for short-run profits. Fearing a dip in today's profits, American executives keep research and technology on short rations and skimp on the investment needed to ensure competitiveness in the future. They manage their businesses like an investment portfolio, with the various units or divisions viewed as investment opportunities competing for scarce funds. All units are held strictly accountable by a common yardstick—the return they immediately yield from the resources they consume. Since research and technology and long-term capital expenditures do not produce short-term profits, these areas receive minimal resources. The auto and steel industries provide good examples of these patterns.

Critics also charge that managers have turned from making goods to making money by means other than production (Melman, 1983). They contend that American industries are managed by persons increasingly oriented toward realizing profits by financial strategems, commodity speculation, and fast-return investments. One example of this trend has been corporate mergers that have given rise to **conglomerates**—companies that operate in a variety of completely different markets and produce unrelated products. For example, Beatrice Foods has pursued an aggressive acquisitions strategy that steadily transformed the Chicago concern into a $10 billion-a-year conglomerate with 50 companies that sell everything from luggage to orange juice (Madrick, 1983). Managers often run conglomerates like stock portfolios, with companies bought and sold because they provide a good return on investment at the moment.

Critics also say that top executives are slow to innovate while shunning risk. And they adopt strategies that allow substantial expense accounts and high salaries for themselves. For instance, in 1983 Ford Motor Chairman Philip Caldwell earned $7.3 million (largely because of stock options) (Holusha, 1985). And in announcing his company's $3.7 billion profit for 1983, General Motors Chairman Roger B. Smith boasted that GM had contributed $180 million to the company's executive bonus plan. But others contend that the objective of any pay program is for rewards to correlate with results. Assessed by the standard of profit performance, the system seems to work (James and Soref, 1981; Byrne, 1984). A group of economists at the University of Rochester's Graduate School of Management tracked over 300 top-paid chief executives and compared their salaries and bonuses to their companies' stock performances from 1977 through 1980. When share and dividend gains were among the top 10 percent, the chief executive received a 9 percent pay increase. When the company trailed among the bottom 10 percent, the top official averaged a 4 percent annual pay cut. Additionally, when highly paid executives do not deliver, the odds are that they will be replaced.

The managerial perspective, with its emphasis on leadership discretion, has largely dominated the thinking of American sociologists and economists since the 1930s. However, over the past decade a growing chorus of social scientists have advanced the view that important constraints operate on managers in discharging their responsibilities (Mintz and Schwartz, 1981a; Glasberg and Schwartz, 1983). For one thing, suppliers of raw materials and customers for finished products place limits on the maneuverability of corporate executives. Even greater constraints are imposed by large banks (eight major New York City commercial banks are responsible for making over 50 percent of all industrial bank loans).

Through their control of capital resources, major corporate lenders can decide which projects will be pursued and which will remain unfunded.

Other constraints also operate. Large institutional investors—mutual, trust, and pension funds—now control over 40 percent of all corporate stock in the United States (Kerbo and Fave, 1984). At least 70 percent of all the stock traded is controlled by such investors (Herman, 1981). Such institutions buy and sell large blocks of stock, with enormous consequences for corporate affairs. For instance, when they sell in tandem, they can squelch financing and expansion plans and undermine a firm's morale. Similarly, corporate policies can be established through intercorporate ownership. And corporate interlocks—networks of individuals who serve on the boards of directors of multiple corporations—also place constraints on what the managers of one firm can undertake without reference to the needs and requirements of other firms (Mintz and Schwartz, 1981b).

In sum, it is clear that professional managers exercise considerable authority in corporate decision making. But even though they may own little or none of a corporation's stock, executive officers continue to be governed by the requirement that they optimize profits. The ascendance of corporate managers has not freed corporations to pursue goals and policies that consistently run counter to profit maximization. The vision of a "soulful corporation" has not been realized. Rather, an arrangement characterized by a "constrained management" has evolved. While in many cases the separation of ownership from control has given managers greater range for autonomy, it has also rendered managers subservient to the constraints of an institutionalized system of rational profit seeking (Herman, 1981). The dictates of the drive for profits limit and circumscribe managerial discretion by tying managerial compensation and promotion to investors' rate of return. Hence, corporations remain fundamentally capitalist in goal and in practice.

WORK AND THE WORKPLACE

Power extends into the workplace. Among other things, it determines whether or not work will be available, how work will be organized, and the manner in which work will be remunerated. In a capitalist market economy, such as that found in the United States, the problem of organizing economic activity begins with a system of property rights involving the uses of resources and a structure of authority for mobilizing these resources (Stinchcombe, 1983; Burawoy, 1983). Property rights consist of the claims an individual or group have on objects; conversely, they define the conditions under which some individuals or groups are excluded from the use or enjoyment of these objects. As we noted earlier in the chapter, under a capitalist market economy the means by which people secure their livelihoods (the factories, mines, offices, and farms) are privately owned and oriented to the production of profits.

The work experience of Americans has undergone significant change over the past 150 years. Although more than 70 percent of the labor force worked on the farm in 1820, by 1910 only 31 percent of Americans were engaged in agriculture. Today employment in the service industries is approaching the same 70 percent that were involved in farming a century and a half ago (Ginzberg, 1982) (see Table 8.3). These changes have been accompanied by a shift from a nonindustrial to an industrial society. In nonindustrial societies, the family overshadows and dominates other institutional spheres. Work (earning a living) is not readily distinguishable from other social activities. The situation is quite different in industrial societies (Dubin, 1976). First, the workplace is physically segregated from the home. Second, working time is temporally separated in the daily cycle from leisure time. Third, specialized organizational structures—complex authority hierarchies —take over the management of work activities (Stinchcombe, 1983). And finally, the economic institution increasingly becomes the focus of other institutions, with the family, government, religion, and education accommodating to its requirements.

TABLE 8.3

Percentage of the Labor Force in Various Sectors of the U.S. Economy, 1910–1980

Year	Agriculture	Blue Collar/ Manufacturing	White Collar/ Service Workers
1910	31%	38%	31%
1920	27	40	33
1930	21	40	39
1940	17	40	43
1950	12	41	47
1960	6	41	54
1970	3	37	60
1980	3	30	67

(*Source:* Data from Bureau of the Census and Bureau of Labor Statistics.)

The Significance of Work. People work for a good many reasons. "Self-interest" in its broadest sense, including the interests of family and friends, is a basic motivation for working in all societies. But self-interest need not involve just providing for subsistence or accumulating wealth. For instance, among the Maori, a Polynesian people of the South Pacific, a desire for approval, a sense of duty, a wish to conform to custom and tradition, a feeling of emulation, and a pleasure in craftsmanship are additional reasons for working (Hsu, 1943). Even within the United States, we cannot understand work as simply a response to economic necessity. Studies show that the vast majority of Americans would continue to work even if they inherited enough money to live comfortably (Morse and Weiss, 1955; Kaplan and Tausky, 1972; Opinion Roundup, 1980).

Work has a good many social meanings (Levinson, 1964). When individuals work, they gain a contributing place in society. The fact that they receive pay for their work indicates that what they do is needed by other people, and that they are a necessary part of the social fabric. Work is also a major social mechanism for placing people in the larger social structure and affording them identities. Much of who individuals are, to themselves and others, is interwoven with how they earn their livelihood. In the United States it is a blunt and ruthlessly public fact that to do nothing is to be nothing and to do little is to be little. Work is commonly seen as the measure of an individual's worth.

Satisfaction and Alienation in Work. Sociologists find that individuals in occupations that combine high economic, occupational, and educational prestige typically show the greatest satisfaction with their work and the strongest job attachment (Blauner, 1969; Kohn and Schooler, 1973, 1982). However,

the prestige factor partly subsumes a number of other elements, including the amount of control and responsibility that goes with an occupation. The opportunity to exercise discretion, accept challenges, and make decisions has an important bearing on how people feel about their work (Kalleberg, 1977; Gruenberg, 1980). The most potent factors in job satisfaction are those that relate to workers' self-respect, their chance to perform well, their opportunities for achievement and growth, and the chance to contribute something personal and quite unique. Public opinion polls show that on the whole the vast majority of Americans (at least 85 percent) are satisfied with the work they are doing (Opinion Roundup, 1980). Even so, only about 40 percent would keep their present job if they had the opportunity to choose some other job.

When individuals fail to find their work fulfilling and satisfying, they may experience **alienation**—a pervasive sense of powerlessness, meaninglessness, normlessness, isolation, and self-estrangement (Seeman, 1959). One expression of alienation is *job burnout*—individuals no longer find their work fulfilling and satisfying, leading to a sense of boredom, apathy, reduced efficiency, fatigue, frustration, and despondency (Brody, 1982). In burnout, individuals complain that they feel drained and used up, and that they have nothing more to give to their work. They become cynical, callous, and insensitive toward the people they encounter in the work setting. Frequently, victims of burnout are highly efficient, competent, and energetic individuals with high ideals and expectations. Nurses, teachers, and police officers seem to be particularly prone to burnout (Farber, 1983).

Two somewhat different perspectives on alienation are provided by Karl Marx and Emile Durkheim (Lukes, 1977). Marx saw alienation as rooted in capitalist social arrangements. For Marx, work is our most important activity as human beings. Through work we create our world and ourselves. The products of our labor reflect our nature, and form the basis for our self-evaluations. Further, through work we experience ourselves as active beings who shape the world about us. But, according to Marx (1844/1960:500), individuals in capitalist societies lose control of their labor and become commodities, objects used by others:

Labor . . . is external to the worker, i.e., it does not belong to his essential being; . . . in his work, therefore, he does not affirm himself but denies himself. . . . His labor is . . . merely a means to satisfy needs external to it. . . . It belongs to another; it is the loss of self.

Thus Marx portrayed workers under capitalism as alienated from productive activity, the products of their labor, their coworkers, and their own human potential. Rather than being a process that is inherently satisfying, work becomes an unfulfilling activity that simply produces a subsistence wage. Workers sell their labor to capitalists who use the workers in any manner they see fit. As a result, human beings are reduced to little more than beasts of burden or inanimate machines. Under capitalism, then, work violates people and deadens the human spirit.

Marx saw alienation as the outcome of social forces that inhere in capitalist arrangements and separate human beings from meaningful, creative, and self-realizing work. In contrast, Durkheim depicted alienation as arising from the breakdown of the cohesive ties that bind individuals to society. For Durkheim, the central question was whether or not people are immersed in a structure of group experiences and memberships that provide a meaningful and valued context for their behavior. A group either coheres and makes life comprehensible and viable for individuals or it fails to do

so, engendering pathology (akin to what we called *anomie* in Chapter 5). Whereas Marx emphasized freedom from social constraint as the source of human happiness, Durkheim stressed that human happiness depends on a society that provides people with rules. Rules, said Durkheim, integrate individuals into cohesive social groups and give direction and meaning to their activity.

Both Marx and Durkheim identify forces that can result in alienation. Since much of life is spent at work, people's work experiences profoundly affect how they come to think about themselves and the satisfactions they realize. Yet, by the same token, group bonds are also associated with human happiness. However, individuals show considerable differences in their reactions to their work and group experiences. What one person finds a challenge, another may view as an unendurable pressure. Even assessments of monotony vary widely. In fact, almost any job will seem boring to some people (Stagner, 1975). And we need hardly be reminded that people differ enormously in what they view as adequate or inadequate contact with other people and in their requirements for formal rules and direction (Lowenthal, 1964).

Political Power

Controlling the means of economic production is one resource for exercising power. But it is not the only one. Modern societies contain a rather wide array of fairly distinct dimensions of power, including those found in religion, science, the arts, medicine, education, and the media. Sociologist Suzanne Keller (1963) suggests that each of these spheres can have its own set of powerful individuals and groups—what she terms **strategic elites**. These elites—people with significant power—operate primarily in their own rather specialized domains.

But, as we pointed out earlier in the chapter, the state assumes a particularly critical role in contemporary life. It seems that some form of centralized government is indispensable to modern society. The possession of the means of administration is, as Max Weber contended, an alternative to the possession of the means of production as a basis of social power. This distinction is most obvious in the case of present-day Communist nations in which there is no ownership of the means of production and the state controls the economy. Of course, power in one sphere can also be employed to achieve power in other spheres. Within the United States, economic power is often converted into political power (the Kennedy family provides a classic illustration of the process). By the same token, political power can be used to advance one's economic status (the "poor boy–successful politician" syndrome reflected in the career of Lyndon B. Johnson is a good example). Let us explore the matter of political power at greater length.

TYPES OF GOVERNMENT

Government entails those political processes which have to do with the authoritative formulating of rules and policies that are binding and pervasive throughout a society. In contemporary nations, the decisions made by government profoundly affect the everyday lives of their citizens, and very often the citizens of other nations as well. Policies relating to the state of the economy, the direction of economic development, military expenditures, issues of war and peace, drug trafficking, education, health care, social welfare, and environmental issues leave no individual untouched by their consequences and ramifications. In dealing with these matters, two quite different types of government have competed in recent generations for people's allegiance: totalitarianism and democracy. Each can be considered an ideal type, for in practice many nations have regimes with mixtures of totalitarian and democratic elements.

Totalitarianism. It is exceedingly difficult for most of us to maintain value neutrality in considering totalitarianism, since this type of government runs counter to many of our fundamental values. **Totalitarianism** is a "total state," one in which the government undertakes to control all parts of the society and all aspects of social life (Olsen, 1978). Those individuals and groups (elites) who dominate the state apparatus seek to control all subordinate governmental units, all institutions (including the economy, education, religion, medicine, the arts, science, and communication), all associations (labor unions, churches, occupational and professional organizations, special-interest associations, and youth groups), and even individual families and cliques. All organizations become an extension of the state and act as its agent. The hallmark of totalitarianism is its power structure, not its economic order. The two major prototypes of totalitarianism—Nazi Germany under Hitler and Communist Russia under Stalin—remind us that this form of government can incorporate either a capitalistic or a socialistic economy.

Totalitarian regimes typically seek to justify their control of society on the grounds that they are in the process of building a new and utopian type of society that will eventually benefit everyone (Olsen, 1978). The elite claims that it seeks to promote the common welfare. As a prelude to the massive restructuring of society, it undertakes to weaken and destroy existing social arrangements. Coercion and violence are often employed, although war and economic chaos frequently contribute to similar outcomes. Sociologist Robert Nisbet (1962:202

and 205) points out: "The political enslavement of man requires the emancipation of
man from all the authorities and memberships . . . that serve, in one degree or another, to insulate an individual from external political power. . . . The monolithic case
of the totalitarian State arises from the sterilization or destruction of all groups and
statuses that, in any way, rival or detract
from the allegiance of the masses to [the]
State."

A totalitarian society typically has three
characteristics: a monolithic political party,
a compelling ideology, and pervasive social
control. One political party is permitted,
and it brooks no opposition. Only a small
proportion of the population are party
members, although party membership is a
requisite for all important social positions.
A totalitarian ideology proclaims the official
values of the entire society, is utopian in
nature, pertains to all areas and aspects of
life, and establishes universal goals. It stip-
ulates grandiose schemes for social reconstruction and societal betterment that provide the moral basis for the extension of
state power. To enforce its power and prop-
agate its ideologies, a totalitarian regime
employs every available means of social
control. It uses the educational and communications networks, while simultaneously exercising terror by a secret police.

From a purely functional perspective, totalitarianism provides a workable model for
organizing and structuring social life. For
instance, the Soviet style of government has
operated for over 65 years. Accordingly,
criticism of totalitarian systems must be essentially a value judgment (Olsen, 1978).

Democracy. **Democracy** is a political system
in which the powers of government derive
from the consent of the governed, and in
which regular constitutional avenues exist
for changing government officials. It is an
arrangement that permits the population a
significant voice in decision making through
people's right to choose among contenders
for political office. Quite clearly, democratic
governments are not distinguished from totalitarian regimes by the absence of powerful officials (indeed, it is questionable
whether on the critical issues that affect the
survival of humankind the president of
the United States has less power than does
the premier of the Soviet Union). And for
the most part democracy is not characterized by the rule of the people themselves.
Only in relatively rare instances, such as the
New England town meeting of colonial
times, do we encounter *direct democracy*—
face-to-face participation and decision making by the citizens. Rather, most democratic
nations are characterized by *representative
democracy*—officials are held accountable to
the public through periodic elections that
confirm them in power or else replace them
with new officials.

A number of sociologists have undertaken a search for those factors that promote
a social climate favorable to a stable democracy (Kornhauser, 1959; Gusfield, 1962; Nisbet, 1962; Lipset, 1963). One factor they
identify is the existence of conflict and
cleavage associated with a competitive
struggle over positions of power, challenges
to incumbents, and shifts in the parties
holding office. Many well-organized but
countervailing interest groups serve as a
check against one another. Each group is
limited in influence because, in the process
of governing, officials must also take into
account the interests of other groups as
well. Simultaneously, interest groups provide independent power bases from which
citizens can interact with government. Consequently, the citizenry enjoys the protection of many groups and institutions against
the encroachment of any one of them. No
group or institution can attain a monopoly

of power. This state of affairs is in sharp contrast to totalitarian societies, where isolated and vulnerable individuals confront an omnipotent state.

Multiple loyalties likewise serve to prevent the polarization of society into rigidly hostile camps. Each person is a member of multiple groups, with membership in one group cutting across membership in others. For instance, American Catholics are found in both the working and upper classes, and the same holds for Protestants. Consequently, in terms of their religious affiliations, Catholics and Protestants are counterposed to one another. Simultaneously, however, working-class Catholics and Protestants are united on many economic issues by their class membership and set apart from upper-class Catholics and Protestants. In sum, people's loyalties cleave along plural axes, a crisscrossing of ties that does not allow clear-cut political cleavage. In contrast, deep-seated religious divisions in Lebanon and racial divisions in South Africa divide people into militant camps that make compromise difficult.

Relatively stable economic and social conditions also seem to favor a democratic order. Significant institutional failure confronts people with stressful circumstances that can make them vulnerable to extremist social movements (see Chapter 12). For example, Germany underwent ruinous inflation and economic dislocation in the 1920s that made the middle classes susceptible to Nazism. In this economic and social environment, the middle classes felt their status eroding and their financial fortunes collapsing before the onslaught of large-scale capitalist enterprise and a powerful labor movement. Finding themselves precariously situated in a world that seemed increasingly incomprehensible and that was swallowing them up in a torrent of social change, they turned to Nazism as the road to salvation.

The result was the death knell of Germany's fragile democratic institutions. In somewhat like fashion, the chaos and social breakdown accompanying their defeat in war made the Russian people susceptible to the revolutionary slogans of communism in 1917.

Finally, a stable democracy benefits from an underlying consensus among the populace that a democratic government is desirable and valid. The various groups accord legitimacy to the political institution. They believe they can realize their goals within the existing organizational framework because they enjoy "fair play" access to the seats of power. As we will see, voting is a key mechanism for achieving consensus. For instance, although Americans wage their election campaigns with great fury and fervor, once the election returns are in, the candidates and parties accede to the results. The losers recognize the legitimacy of the process and do not resort to extralegal and violent remedies. Rather, they criticize the incumbent officials and prepare to "throw the rascals out" at the *next* election.

These formulations, however, are not accepted by all sociologists. As we will note later in the chapter, many conflict theorists reject the pluralistic model of American society these formulations imply. Instead, they contend that the United States is governed by a "power elite." For instance, although acknowledging that political parties, labor unions, and other voluntary and occupational associations have an impact on the "middle levels" of power, sociologist C. Wright Mills (1956) contends that a "power elite" uses these organizations as administrative vehicles for carrying out predetermined policies and as mechanisms for controlling the rest of society. But before turning to these matters, let us look more generally at political power in the United States.

Political parties undertake to get their candidates elected to public office. Since they aim to control government, political parties are relatively pragmatic in shaping their programs to achieve the greatest appeal to voters. Interest groups may attempt to "capture" a mass-based political party in order to advance their policies. But success may be counterproductive, beccause single-issue campaigns often narrow the popular base and appeal of a political party. (John Crispin/Woodfin Camp & Associates)

POLITICAL POWER IN THE UNITED STATES

Both totalitarian and democratic governments are marked by competition for political positions. But what distinguishes democracies and the American system is that the contest for positions of power is legitimized—norms define political competition and opposition as expected and appropriate. Free and competitive elections, the right to form opposition parties, freedom to criticize those in power, freedom to seek public office, and popular participation are among the commonly accepted hallmarks of democratic procedures. Central to the process are political parties, popular electoral participation, interest group lobbying, and the mass media.

Political Parties. A **political party** is an organization designed to gain control of the government by putting its people in public office. It is not the same thing as an interest group, an organization that undertakes to affect policy without assuming the responsibilities of running the government. Members of an interest group seek control over government decisions as a means to an end. But a political party pursues the control of government as an end. Thus mass-based political parties tend to abandon or modify policy views that interfere with their gaining or maintaining political office.

Within American life, the major political parties function as brokers or intermediaries between the people and the government. The relatively pragmatic nature of the parties reflects this fact, as well as the structural peculiarities of a two-party system. In order to win control of the government, each party must shape itself to afford the widest possible appeal to the electorate. This requirement tends to pull each party to a centrist position, leaving the more extreme elements at the fringes. In close elections, both the Republican and Democratic parties strive for the support of the same uncommitted, often middle-of-the-road, voters. In many respects, then, they end up resembling one another. Occasionally one of their more extreme factions gains control of the presidential nominating machinery. But then they commonly suffer electoral disaster, the fate of the Goldwater Republican right in 1964 and the McGovern Democratic left in 1972. Critics of the American system say that centrist forces and pressures result in the voters not getting a real choice. But proponents point out that what is really happening is that the parties are performing one of their chief functions: compromising different and conflicting points of view prior to the election (Olson and Meyer, 1975).

Electoral Participation and Voting Patterns. The American political system is rooted in the participation of its citizenry in the governmental process through periodic elections. The principle that each person has one vote is seen as a basic mechanism for offsetting the inequalities that otherwise abound in the society by virtue of class, gender, and racial inequalities. Yet many Americans do not vote. Over the past fifty years, between 52 and 64 percent of the electorate has voted in presidential elections. Nonvoters are apt to be younger, less educated, and poorer than those who do vote (in 1980, 70 percent of those aged 45 to 64 voted, compared with 40 percent of those aged 18 to 24; 80 percent of college graduates went to the polls, compared with only 43 percent of those whose schooling stopped after the elementary grades; and 70

percent of those with family incomes of $25,000 or more voted, compared with 39 percent of those with family incomes under $5,000).

The turnout rate in presidential elections is typically 25 to 30 percent lower in the United States than in most Western European nations. Political scientists estimate that at least 9 percentage points of the difference is attributable to American personal registration statutes (Glass, Squire, and Wolfinger, 1984). In Western Europe, Canada, Australia, and New Zealand, it is the responsibility of the state to compile and maintain electoral registers. The United States is the only nation where the entire burden of registration falls on the individual rather than the government. Additionally, many nonvoters view their success or lack of success in life as a matter of "luck" and hence not as something that can be influenced by political participation (Hadley, 1978). Generally speaking, higher-status people see a relationship between politics and their own lives. But many lower-status people do not see the political system as offering them anything, or anything they can relate to effectively.

As reflected in Table 8.4, there are also important differences in how various segments of the population vote. As a general rule, older voters are more likely to vote for Republican candidates than are younger voters. Likewise, voters who are better off tend to support Republican candidates and those who are less well off tend to support Democratic candidates. Even so, Democrats still receive a significant proportion of their votes from higher-status people and the Republican Ronald Reagan did well among blue-collar workers. Prior to the 1930s black voters tended to support the party of Abraham Lincoln and black emancipation, but since Franklin D. Roosevelt and the New Deal they have overwhelmingly voted Democratic. Although the voting patterns of

TABLE 8.4

Voting by Groups in Recent Presidential Elections

Percent of 1984 total		The Vote in 1980			The Vote in 1984	
		Reagan	*Carter*	*Anderson*	*Reagan*	*Mondale*
	Total	*51%*	*41%*	*7%*	*59%*	*41%*
47%	Men	55	36	7	61	37
53	Women	47	45	7	57	42
86	White	55	36	7	66	34
10	Blacks	11	85	3	9	90
3	Hispanics	33	59	6	33	65
24	18–29 years old	43	44	11	58	41
34	30–44 years old	54	36	8	58	42
23	45–59 years old	55	39	5	60	39
19	60 and older	54	41	4	63	36
8	Less than high school education	46	51	2	50	49
30	High school graduate	51	43	4	60	39
30	Some college	55	35	7	60	38
29	College graduate	52	35	11	59	40
51	White Protestant	63	31	6	73	26
26	Catholic	49	42	7	55	44
3	Jewish	39	45	15	32	66
15	White born-again Christian	63	33	3	80	20
26	Union household	43	48	6	45	53
15	Under $12,500 in Income	42	51	6	46	53
27	$12,500–24,999	44	46	8	57	42
21	$25,000–34,999	52	39	7	59	40
18	$35,000–50,000	59	32	8	67	32
13	Over $50,000	63	26	9	68	31
24	From the East	47	42	9	52	47
28	From the Midwest	51	40	7	61	38
29	From the South	52	44	3	63	36
18	From the West	53	34	10	59	40
41	White men	59	32	7	68	31
45	White women	52	39	8	64	36
4	Black men	14	82	3	12	85
5	Black women	9	88	3	6	93
11	Men, 18–29 years old	47	39	11	61	37
13	Women, 18–29 years old	39	49	10	55	45
17	Men, 30–44 years old	59	31	4	62	37
18	Women, 30–44 years old	50	41	8	54	46
11	Men, 45–59 years old	60	34	5	63	36
12	Women, 45–59 years old	50	44	5	58	41
9	Men, 60 and older	56	40	3	62	37
10	Women, 60 and older	52	43	4	64	35

(*Source:* New York Times/CBS News Poll, *New York Times* [November 8, 1984]:11. Copyright © 1984 by The New York Times Company. Reprinted by permission.)

men and women have not traditionally differed, in recent years women have been more apt to support the Democratic party than have men. Overall, there is a persistence of voter identifications with particular parties. Nonetheless, changes do occur, although not as precipitously as is commonly imagined.

Interest-Group Lobbying. People who share common concerns or points of view are called **interests,** and the groups that organize them are called **interest groups.** One distinction that is often made is between special-interest groups and public-interest groups. **Special-interest groups** are interest groups that primarily seek benefits from which their members would derive more gains than the society as a whole. Examples include chambers of commerce, trade associations, labor unions, and farm organizations. **Public-interest groups** are interest groups which pursue policies that presumably would be of no greater benefit to their members than to the larger society. Consumer protection organizations are good illustrations of public-interest groups.

One type of special-interest group that has attracted considerable controversy are **political-action committees (PACs),** an interest group that is set up to elect or defeat candidates, but not through the organization of a political party. PACs were specifically authorized by the 1971 Federal Election Campaign Act, but they had existed before then as well. In 1984, political action committees set up by unions, corporations, and special interests numbered more than 3,800 (Green and Guth, 1984). Money is important in an era of multimillion-dollar campaigns. In the 1984 elections, winning a seat in the House of Representatives cost on average about $500,000. A Senate seat ran ten times this amount (Walsh, 1984). Herbert Alexander, director of the Citizens Research Foundation (located at the University of Southern California), estimates that outlays for all 1984 elections, from courthouse to White House, approached $2 billion. Even before elections are in full swing, PACs are in action. For instance, Common Cause, a public-interest lobby, says that PACs gave nearly $14.6 million to 73 Senate candidates in the 18 months before July 1, 1984—more than two-thirds of it going to incumbents. Moreover, many political action committees hedge their bets by contributing to both candidates in a campaign, assuring that they later will have access to the winner.

The Mass Media. The **mass media** consists of those organizations—newspapers, magazines, television, radio, and motion pictures—that undertake to convey information to a large segment of the public. Whereas earlier generations of Americans depended primarily on newspapers for their political information, recent generations have depended chiefly on television. Studies show that two-thirds of Americans get most of their news from television, and over half get *all* their news in this manner (Shea, 1984). The public secures information about candidates from television through news broadcasts and paid advertising. Although there is little credible evidence that the television networks knowingly favor particular presidential candidates, they do influence public attitudes by their selection of news events. They slant their programs toward the exciting, the provocative, the timely, and the unusual, which encourages candidates to make "news" and provide good "visuals."

For example, Jimmy Carter and his advisers correctly judged that the winner of the Iowa caucuses, the first real event of the 1976 campaign season, would emerge as the "front runner." Accordingly, beginning in 1974, and for two years thereafter, the Carter campaign concentrated its efforts on Iowa. Even though Carter did not really win Iowa (he finished second to "uncommitted"), the media portrayed him as the state's winner and he quickly became the center of media attention. One month earlier only 3 percent of the American public had known who Jimmy Carter was (a former governor of Georgia). The rest is history.

More and more campaigns are being turned over to high-powered professionals who advise candidates on every detail, ranging from which issues they should tackle to the images they should project in their media appearances. Increasingly physical appearance and "good looks" are surfacing as paramount matters in an era when packaging candidates for the media is so critical. Moreover, TV advertising, for which candidates spend nearly half their campaign funds, gives greater emphasis to style and personality over substance. Professionals cite evidence showing that a colorful event in which a candidate utters a few catch one-liners wins more votes than an earnest discussion of the issues. Computer technology is also being employed to target specific voter groups, and then bombard them with TV advertising and direct-mail appeals specifically tailored to their interests. And campaign managers are employing public opinion polls not only to find out how voters perceive their candidates, but to determine what voters want to hear their candidates say (Mashek, 1984; Walsh, 1984). These matters raise the question, "How does the political system actually operate, and who makes it run?" Different answers have been proposed.

MODELS OF POWER IN THE UNITED STATES

One of the longest-running debates in the social sciences has to do with the nature of power in the United States. Is power concentrated in the hands of the few, or distributed widely among various groups within American life? What is the basis of

power? Is the exercise of power in the United States unrestricted, or is it limited by the competing interests of numerous groups? Social scientists have supplied quite different answers to these questions, represented by three theoretical perspectives: the Marxist (or ruling class), the elitist, and the pluralist.

The Marxist Perspective. Marxist theory has had a profound impact on sociological thinking about power and social organization. Not only has it influenced the work of conflict sociologists, but it has provided a backdrop—even a target—in terms of which non-Marxist sociologists have formulated their rival interpretations (see Chapter 1). Sociologists following in the Marxist tradition, like J. Allen Whitt (1979, 1982), hold that political processes must be understood in terms of the institutional structure of society as it is shaped by underlying class interests and conflict.

Whitt contends that the ways in which the major social institutions (especially the economic institution) are organized have critical implications for how power is exercised. Rather than focusing primarily upon the individuals who control the seats of power (as do power elite theorists), Whitt looks to the *biases* inherent in social institutions as shaping political outcomes. He portrays society as structured in ways that place constraints on decision makers and render their formulation of policy largely a foregone conclusion. Given the capitalist logic of institutions in Western nations, the ruling class usually need not take direct action to fashion outcomes favorable to its interests. The political outcomes are built within the capitalist ordering of affairs by the way agendas are set and alternatives are defined.

The Elitist Perspective. The elitist perspective found early expression in the ideas of such late nineteenth- and early twentieth-century European sociologists as Vilfredo Pareto, Gaetano Mosca, and Robert Michels. They undertook to show that the concentration of power in a small group of elites is inevitable within modern societies (Olsen, 1970). These theorists rejected Marx's idealistic vision of social change that would bring about a classless and stateless society. Instead, they depicted all societies past the bare subsistence level—be they totalitarian, monarchical, or democratic—as dominated by the few over the many. The masses, they held, cannot and do not govern themselves. Even so, change occurs across time through the gradual circulation of elites—one elite comes to replace another.

Within the United States, elitist theory has taken a somewhat different course, particularly as it is formulated in the work of sociologist C. Wright Mills (1956). Mills contends that the major decisions affecting Americans and others—especially those having to do with issues of war and peace—are made by a very small number of individuals and groups whom he terms the Power Elite. The real rulers of the United States, says Mills, come from three groups: corporation executives, the military, and high-ranking politicians. They are the ones who made such fateful decisions as those surrounding the Bay of Pigs invasion of Cuba, the bombing of North Vietnam, the supplying of military assistance to pro-American elements in Central America, and the procurement of major weapon systems.

The elitist model depicts elites as unified in purpose and outlook because of their similar social backgrounds, their dominant and overlapping positions in key social institutions, and the convergence of their economic interests (Domhoff, 1970). For instance, sociologist Michael Useem (1983) contends that an "inner circle" of interconnected corporate officers and directors assume the stewardship of American political

and social affairs. He finds that inner-group members are more likely to belong to an exclusive social club, have upper-class parents, participate in major business associations, serve on government advisory boards, belong to the upper levels of nonprofit and charitable organizations, gain media coverage for themselves, maintain informal contacts with government leaders, and prefer one another's company. According to elitist theorists, elites invariably get their way whenever important public decisions are at stake. They manage conflicts in the larger society in such a way as to produce outcomes favorable to themselves. Their power is pervasive; it leaves few areas of social life untouched and results in a relatively stable distribution of power.

The Pluralist Perspective. The pluralist perspective sharply contrasts with both the power elite and Marxist models. Pluralist theorists start with interest groups as the basic feature of organized political life. They say that no one group really runs the government, although many groups have the power to veto policies that run counter to their interests (Riesman, 1953; Dahl, 1961). Important decisions are made by different groups depending on the institutional arena— business organizations, labor unions, farm blocs, racial and ethnic associations, and religious groups. When their interests diverge, the various interest groups compete for allies among the more or less unorganized public. But the same group or coalition of groups does not set broad policies. Instead, their power varies with the issue.

Most groups remain inactive on most issues and mobilize their resources only when their interests are immediately at stake. Viewed in this fashion, the resulting distribution of power tends to be unstable because interests and alliances are typically short-lived, and new groups and coalitions are always being organized as old ones dis-integrate. Moreover, government achieves substantial autonomy by operating as a broker or balancing agent among competing interest groups.

Some pluralists say that so many interest groups have sprung up in the United States in recent years, each demanding special attention to its own concerns, that government has become paralyzed. All too often it is unable to respond effectively and efficiently in dealing with major problems (Shea, 1984). Stalemate results when powerful and nearly equal opposing interests confront one another on an issue. Policymakers also become preoccupied with certain highly focused and emotional issues, and ignore the less dramatic but vital ones. Whether it is abortion, gun control, pollution, nuclear power, or tax deductions for business lunches, increasing numbers of groups are singlemindedly pursuing their narrow interests. Such outcomes tend to go with single-issue politics.

Conclusions. What conclusions can we draw from the contending models of power? At the outset, it should be stressed that elitist theorists like Mills and even Marxian-oriented theorists do not argue that a power elite or governing class domi-nates American society. Given the many interest groups in the United States, no one group can achieve complete dominance. Even so, when important decisions are made—especially on the critical issues of war and peace and on matters fundamentally affecting the economy—some corporate and political power centers clearly have greater input than do other groups.

Yet given the divisions within the highest echelons of American government on the B-1 bomber, the MX missile, levels of defense spending, military intervention in Central America, and tax policies, it is exceedingly difficult to make a convincing case for a unified power elite. At the same time, it is hard to deny that major corporate, military, and political interests have a common stake in preserving existing institutional arrangements. And it is also true, as structural Marxists remind us, that the political and economic institutions seem to gain an existence separate from the specific individuals who have ownership or positions of authority within them. Thus the question is not only "Who runs America?" but also "What runs America?" In sum, each model contains a kernel of truth, and a synthesis of the formulations seems at present to afford the most satisfactory approach.

Summary

1. Power pervades all aspects of social life. It furnishes the resources that provide direction essential for coordinating and integrating individual activity so that collective goals can be achieved. And it determines which individuals and groups will be able to translate their preferences into the reality of day-to-day social organization. Social interaction is the essence of power because power always exists within social relationships.

2. The state—the political institution—is an arrangement that consists of people who exercise an effective monopoly in the use of physical coercion within a given territory. In the final analysis the state rests on force—power whose basis is the threat or application of punish-

ment. Two views have prevailed regarding the state. Conservatives see government as employing force as an instrument of right to restrain and rebuke those who would place their self-interest above the common good. In contrast, radicals maintain that the state employs force to suppress right and defend selfish interests. The conservative view sees the state as a social contract; the radical view, as an organization of violence that serves the interests of elites.

3. Functionalists contend that there is a good reason why the state arose, and why today it has assumed a dominant position in contemporary society. They point to four primary functions performed by the state: the enforcement of norms, overall social planning and direction, the arbitration of conflicting interests, and the protection of a society's members and interests against outside groups.

4. Conflict theorists contend that the state is a vehicle by which one or more groups impose their values and stratification system upon other groups. As they view the matter, the state has its origin in the desire of ruling elites to give permanence to social arrangements that benefit themselves. More fundamentally, they depict the state as an instrument of violence and oppression.

5. Although force may be an effective means for seizing power, and though it remains the ultimate foundation of the state, it is not the most effective means for political rule. Accordingly, sociologists distinguish between power that is legitimate and power that is illegitimate. Legitimate power is authority. Sociologist Max Weber suggests that power may be legitimated by tradisional, legal-rational, and/or charismatic means.

6. Modern economic systems tend to differ from one another in two important respects. First, they provide a different answer to the question of how economic activity is organized—by the market or by the plan. Second, they provide a different answer to the question of who owns the means of production—individuals or the state. In practice, we commonly merge the two features and talk about contrasting economic systems. We think of capitalist economies as relying heavily on free markets and privately held property; socialist economies as relying primarily on state planning and publicly held property.

7. The government is an important participant in the American economy. But the primary productive role is played by private business. Large corporations exercise enormous power in American life. The decisions made by their officials have implications and ramifications that reach throughout the nation. The rise of multinational corporations and the growing internationalization of the world economy have given economic power a new dimension. Such firms rival nations in wealth and frequently operate as private governments pursuing their worldwide interests by well-developed foreign policies. Some social scientists say that a managerial revolution has separated ownership and effective control in corporate life. But other social scientists point to the institutional constraints that operate on corporate decision makers. Hence, corporations remain fundamentally capitalist in goal and in practice.

8. Power extends into the workplace. It determines whether or not work will be available, how work will be organized, and the manner in which work will be remunerated. People work for a good many reasons in addition to "self-interest." And work has many social meanings, especially those that define a person's position in the social structure. Individuals in occupations that combine high economic, occupational, and educational prestige typically show the greatest satisfaction with their work and the strongest job attachment. When individuals fail to find their work satisfying and fulfilling, they may experience alienation. Marx saw alienation as the outcome of social forces that inhere in capitalist arrangements and separate human beings from meaningful, creative, and self-realizing work. Durkheim depicted alienation as arising from the breakdown of the cohesive ties that bind individuals to society.

9. Government entails those political processes that have to do with the authoritative formulating of rules and policies that are binding and pervasive throughout a society. Totalitarianism is a "total state"—one in which the government undertakes to extend control over all parts of the society and all aspects of social life. A totalitarian society typically has three characteristics: a monolithic political party, a compelling ideology, and pervasive social control. Democracy is a political system in which the powers of government derive from the consent of the governed, and in which regular constitutional avenues exist for changing government officials. A number of factors promote a social climate favorable to a stable democracy: countervailing interest groups, multiple loyalties, stable economic and social conditions, and an underlying political consensus.

10. A constitutional system of government defines and prescribes the boundaries within which political power is pursued in the United States. Central to American political processes are political parties, popular electoral participation, interest-group lobbying, and the mass media. Political parties are organizations designed to gain control of the government by putting their people in public office. They operate in a political environment in which the citizenry participates in the governmental process through periodic elections. Additionally, people who share common concerns or points of view form interest groups to advance their concerns. Since the mass media are the chief source of people's political information, political parties and interest groups are increasingly tailoring candidates and issues in ways that capture media attention.

11. One of the longest-running debates in the social sciences has to do with the nature of power in the United States. Marxist theory holds that political processes must be understood in terms of the institutional structure of society as it is shaped by underlying class interests and conflict. The elitist model depicts major decisions as being made by a power elite who constitute the real rulers of the United States. The pluralist perspective contends that no one group really runs the government because interest groups constitute countervailing and balancing political forces. Each model contains a kernel of truth, and a synthesis of the formulations seems at present to afford the most satisfactory approach.

Glossary

alienation A pervasive sense of powerlessness, meaninglessness, normlessness, isolation, and self-estrangement.

authority Legitimate power.

capitalist economy An economic system relying primarily on free markets and privately held property.

charismatic authority Power that is legitimated by the extraordinary superhuman or supernatural attributes people attribute to a leader.

conglomerates Companies that operate in completely different markets and produce largely unrelated products.

core regions Geographical areas that dominate the world economy and exploit the rest of the system.

democracy A political system in which the powers of government derive from the consent of the governed, and in which regular constitutional avenues exist for changing government officials.

force Power whose basis is the threat or application of punishment.

government Those political processes which have to do with the authoritative formulating of rules and policies that are binding and pervasive throughout a society.

interest groups Organizations of people who share common concerns or points of view.

interests People who share common concerns or points of view.

legal-rational authority Power that is legitimated by explicit rules and rational procedures which define the rights and duties of the occupants of given positions.

mass media Those organizations—newspapers, magazines, television, radio, and motion pictures—that undertake to convey information to a large segment of the public.

multinational corporations Firms that have their central office in one country and subsidiaries in other countries.

oligopoly A market dominated by a few firms.

periphery regions Geographical areas that provide raw materials to the core and are exploited by it.

political action committees An interest group set up to elect or defeat candidates, but not through the organization of a political party.

political party An organization designed to gain control of the government by putting its people in public office.

public-interest groups Interest groups which pursue policies that presumably would be of no greater benefit to their members than to the larger society.

socialist economy An economic system relying primarily on state planning and publicly held property.

special-interest groups Interest groups that primarily seek benefits from which their members would derive more gains than the society as a whole.

state An arrangement that consists of people who exercise an effective monopoly in the use of physical coercion within a given territory.

strategic elites Powerful individuals and groups who exercise significant power in their own rather specialized domains.

totalitarianism A "total state"—one in which the government undertakes to control all parts of the society and all aspects of social life.

traditional authority Power that is legitimated by the sanctity of age-old customs.

9

The Family

STRUCTURE OF THE FAMILY

Forms of the Family
Forms of Marriage
The Functionalist Perspective on the Family
The Conflict Perspective on the Family
The Interactionist Perspective on the Family

MARRIAGE AND THE FAMILY IN THE UNITED STATES

Choosing a Marriage Partner
Married Couples
Parenthood
Employed Mothers
Two-Income Families
Family Violence, Child Abuse, and Incest
Divorce
Stepfamilies
Care for the Elderly

ALTERNATIVE LIFE STYLES

Singlehood
Unmarried Cohabitation
Childless Marriages
Single Parenthood
Gay Couples
Communes

Many of us believe, as does social scientist Urie Bronfenbrenner (1977:47), that "the relationships in families are the juice of life, the longings and frustrations and intense loyalties. We get our strength from those relationships, we enjoy them, even the painful ones. Of course, we also get some of our problems from them, but the power to survive those problems comes from the family, too."

Given these sentiments, it is hardly surprising that a good many Americans have been concerned about the directions in which family life has been moving in recent decades. They tend to be of two minds regarding the matter. There are those who say that the family is a timeless entity, rooted in our social and animal nature. But since the institutional structure of society is always changing, the family must change to reflect this fact. Accordingly, although a durable feature of the human experience, the family is said to be a resilient institution (Bane, 1976). The other view holds that the family is in crisis, showing many signs of decay and disintegration. This latter view is currently the more fashionable. The evidence in support of it seems dramatic and, on the surface, incontrovertible. Divorce rates have soared; birth rates have fallen; the proportion of unwed mothers has increased; single-parent households have proliferated; mothers of young children have entered the labor force in large numbers; and the elderly are placing growing reliance on the government rather than the family for financial support (Fuchs, 1983).

Laments about the current decline of the family imply that at an earlier time in history the family was more stable and harmonious than it currently is. Yet, despite massive research, historians have not located a "golden age of the family" (Flandrin, 1979; Degler, 1980). For instance, the marriages of seventeenth-century England and New England were based on family and property needs, not on choice by affection. Families were often devastated by desertion and death. Loveless marriages, the tyranny of husbands, high death rates, and the beating and abuse of children add up to a grim image (Shorter, 1975). Indeed, concerns about the family have a long history (Greer, 1979). Educators of the European medieval and Enlightenment periods were worried about the strength and character of the family. In colonial and frontier times people expressed anxiety about the disruption of family life. And in the nineteenth and early twentieth centuries, worry about the family was cloaked in recurrent public hysteria regarding the "peril" posed to the nation's Anglo-American institutions by the arrival of immigrant groups with "alien cultures." In sum, the "family question," despite its many guises, is not new. It is a recurrent theme, one that is the subject matter of this chapter.

Structure of the Family

What is the family? Although we all use the term and doubtless have a clear idea of what we mean by it, the "family" is exceedingly difficult to define. When we set about separating families from nonfamilies, we encounter all sorts of problems (Stephens, 1963). Many of us think of the family as a social unit consisting of a married couple and their children, living together in a household. But as we will see in the course of the chapter, such a definition is too restrictive. In many societies it is the kin group, and not a married couple and their children, that is the basic family unit. And there are those who argue that psychological bonds are what families are all about. Defined in this fashion, long-term relationships, heterosexual or homosexual, should be considered as families. Clearly, defining the family is not simply an academic exer-

This nineteenth-century family portrait reflects the sentimental and idealized image of the family prevalent at the time. The elder male assumed the central position, and female members were assigned a peripheral status relative to the male members. (EKM-Nepenthe)

cise. How we define it determines the kinds of families we will consider normal and the kinds we will consider deviant, and what rights and obligations we will recognize as legally and socially binding (Skolnick, 1981).

For our purposes in the chapter, we will define a **family** as a group of people defined by the members of a community as a household unit. Typically, these individuals are related by blood, adoption, or marriage, and cooperate economically. Viewed in this manner, the family is an institution (see Chapter 2). As such, it provides (1) more or less standardized solutions that serve to direct people in meeting the problems of social living, and (2) the relatively stable relationships that characterize people in actually implementing these solutions. In sum, the family is one of the principal instruments whereby the critical tasks of social living are organized, directed, and executed. Let us consider some of the patterns found in human families.

FORMS OF THE FAMILY

As we look about the world, and even in our own society, we encounter a good many differences in the ways in which families are organized. Families vary in their composition and in their descent, residence, and authority patterns.

Composition. Social relationships between adult males and females can be organized within families by emphasizing either spouse or kin relationships. In the **nuclear family** arrangement, spouses and their offspring constitute the core relationship; blood relatives are functionally marginal and peripheral. In contrast, in the **extended family** arrangement, kin—individuals related by common ancestry—provide the core relationship; spouses are functionally marginal and peripheral. The nuclear family pattern is the preferred arrangement among most Americans. In the course of their lives,

Americans typically find themselves members of two nuclear families. First, an individual belongs to a nuclear family that consists of oneself and one's father, mother, and siblings, what sociologists call the **family of orientation.** Second, since over 90 percent of Americans marry at least once, the vast majority of the population are members of a nuclear family that consists of oneself and one's spouse and children, what sociologists call the **family of procreation.**

Extended families are found in numerous forms throughout the world. In one case, that of the Nayar—a soldiering caste group in the pre-British period of southwestern India—spouse ties were virtually absent (Gough, 1959, 1965; Dumont, 1970; Fuller, 1976). When a woman was about to enter puberty, she was ritually "married" to a man chosen for her by a neighborhood assembly. After three ceremonial days, she was ritually "separated" from him and was then free to take on a series of "visiting husbands" or "lovers." Although a woman's lovers gave her regular gifts on prescribed occasions, they did not provide support. When a woman had a child, one of the men—not necessarily the biological father—paid a fee to the midwife and thus established the child's legitimacy. However, the man assumed no economic, social, legal or ritual rights or obligations toward the child. It was the mother's kin who took responsibility for the child.

For some time, sociologists assumed that industrialization undercut extended family patterns while fostering nuclear family arrangements. For instance, William J. Goode (1963) surveyed families in many parts of the world and concluded that industrialization weakens extended family patterns in a number of ways. First, industrialism requires that people move about in search of new job and professional opportunities,

weakening kin obligations that depend on frequent and intimate interaction. Second, industrialism facilitates social mobility, creating friction among relatives of different class rankings. Third, industrialism substitutes nonkin agencies for kin groups in handling such common problems as police protection, education, military defense, and moneylending. And fourth, industrialism emphasizes achievement over ascription, reversing the traditional pattern and thereby lessening people's dependence on their families. However, in recent years sociologists have taken a new look and have found that industrialization and extended family arrangements are not necessarily incompatible (Smelser, 1959). For instance, Tamara K. Hareven (1982) examined family life in a textile community of New Hampshire in the nineteenth century and discovered that industrialism promoted kin ties. Not only did different generations often reside together in the same household, they provided a good deal of assistance to one another. And in England, by virtue of high mortality rates, the nuclear family had come to prevail before industrialization got under way (Laslett, 1974, 1976; Stearns, 1977; Quadagno, 1982).

Descent. Societies trace descent and pass on property from one generation to the next in one of three ways. Under a **patrilineal** arrangement, a people reckon descent and transmit property through the line of the father. Under a **matrilineal** arrangement, descent and inheritance take place through the mother's side of the family. The Nayar were a matrilineal people. A child owed allegiance to the mother's brother and not the father. Property and privileged positions passed from maternal uncle to nephew. Under the **bilineal** arrangement, both sides of an individual's family are equally important. Americans are typically bilineal, reckoning descent through both the father and the mother (however, the surname is transmitted in a patrilineal manner).

Residence. Societies also differ in the location where a couple take up residence after marriage. In the case of **patrilocal** residence, the bride and groom live in the household or community of the husband's family. The opposite pattern prevails in **matrilocal** residence. For example, among the Hopi, a Southwest Pueblo people, the husband moves upon marriage into the dwelling of his wife's family, and it is here that he eats and sleeps. In the United States, newlyweds tend to follow **neolocal** patterns in which they set up a new place of residence independent of either of their parents or other relatives.

Authority. Although the authority a man or woman enjoys in family decision making is influenced by their personalities, societies nonetheless dictate who is expected to be the dominant figure. Under **patriarchal** arrangements, it is usually the eldest male or the husband who fills this role. The ancient Hebrews, Greeks, and Romans and the nineteenth-century Chinese and Japanese provide a few examples. Logically, the construction of a **matriarchal** family type is very simple and would involve the vesting of power in women. Yet true matriarchies are rare, and considerable controversy exists as to whether the balance of power actually rests with the wife in any known society (Stephens, 1963). Even though matriarchies may not be the preferred arrangement in most societies, they often arise through default upon the death or desertion of the husband. In a third type of family, the **egalitarian** arrangement, power and authority are equally distributed between husband and wife. This pattern has been on the increase in recent years in the United States, where marriage is changing from a one-vote system in which men make the decisions to a system in which the couple sort out choices jointly.

FORMS OF MARRIAGE

The fact that the parties to a marriage must be members of two different kin groups has crucial implications for the structuring of the family. Indeed, the continuity, and therefore the long-term welfare, of any kin group depends on obtaining spouses for the unmarried members of the group from other groups. By the same token, a kin group has a stake in retaining some measure of control over at least a portion of its members after they marry (Lee, 1977). Accordingly, we need to take a closer look at marital arrangements, particularly marriage. **Marriage** refers to a socially approved sexual union between two or more individuals that is undertaken with some idea of permanence.

Exogamy and Endogamy. All societies regulate the pool of eligibles from which individuals are expected to select a mate. A child's kin generally have more in mind than simply getting a child married. They want the child married to the *right* spouse, especially where marriage has consequences for the larger kin group. Two types of marital regulations define the "right" spouse: *endogamy* and *exogamy.* **Endogamy** is the requirement that marriage occur within a group. Under these circumstances, people must marry within their class, race, ethnic group, or religion. **Exogamy** is the requirement that marriage occur outside a group. Under these circumstances, people must marry outside their kin group, be it their immediate nuclear family, clan, or tribe.

Regulations relating to exogamy are

based primarily on kinship and usually entail **incest taboos,** rules that prohibit sexual intercourse with close blood relatives. Such relationships are not only prohibited, but bring reactions of aversion and disgust. Incest taboos were once singled out by social scientists as the only universal norm in a world of diverse moral codes. But sociologist Russell Middleton (1962) found that brother-sister marriage was not only permitted but frequently practiced by the ancient Egyptians. He speculates that brother-sister marriage served to maintain the power and property of a family and prevented the splintering of an estate through inheritance. A similar arrangement apparently also occurred among the royal families of Hawaii, the Inca of Peru, and the Dahomey of West Africa. Additionally, the degree of kinship covered by incest varies from society to society. For example, in colonial New England it was incestuous if a man were to marry his deceased wife's sister. But among the ancient Hebrews, the custom of the levirate required that a man had to marry his deceased brother's widow under some circumstances.

There have been numerous attempts to account for both the existence and the prevalence of incest taboos. Anthropologist Claude Levi-Strauss (1956) suggests that incest taboos promote alliances between families and reinforce their social interdependence. Anthropologist George Peter Murdock (1949) says that incest taboos prevent destructive sexual jealousies and rivalries within the family. Sociologist Kingsley Davis (1960) contends that incestuous relationships would hopelessly confuse family statuses (for example, the incestuous male offspring of a father–daughter union would be the son of his own sister, a stepson of his own grandmother, and a grandson of his own father). And sociobiologists, noting that children raised together on Israel's kibbutzim seldom marry each other, argue that

this behavior is prewired by genes (Wilson, 1975; Lumsden and Wilson, 1981). Admittedly, these matters remain unresolved, and social scientists continue to find themselves perplexed about the real basis of incest taboos.

Types of Marriage. The relationship between a husband and wife may be structured in one of four ways: **monogamy,** one husband and one wife; **polygyny,** one husband and two or more wives; **polyandry,** two or more husbands and one wife; and **group marriage,** two or more husbands and two or more wives. Monogamy appears in all societies, although other forms may not only be permitted but preferred. It was the preferred or ideal type of marriage in less than 20 percent of 862 societies included in one cross-cultural sample (Murdock, 1967).

Polygyny has enjoyed a wide distribution throughout the world, with 83 percent of the 862 societies permitting husbands to take plural wives. The Old Testament, for example, records polygynous practices among the Hebrews: Gideon had many wives, who bore him seventy sons; King David had several wives; King Solomon reportedly had seven hundred wives and three hundred concubines; King Solomon's son Rehoboam had eighteen wives and sixty concubines; and Rehoboam's sons in turn had many wives.

The lot of husbands with several wives rarely if ever conforms to the Hollywood image of the Arabian sheik whose harem is ready and waiting to provide him every pleasure. Indeed, anthropologist Ralph Linton (1936:183–184) believes that the polygynous husband should be pitied, not envied, by other men:

[T]here are few polygynous societies in which the position of the male is really better than it is under monogamy. If the plural wives are not congenial, the family will be torn by feuds in

which the husband must take the thankless role of umpire, while if they are congenial he is likely to be confronted by an organized female opposition.

Although Linton overstated the case, his point is worth considering. And generally, it is only the economically advantaged males who can afford to have more than one wife (for example, in China, India, and the Islamic countries, polygyny has usually been the privilege of the wealthy few). Polygyny involves far more than sex; it is closely tied to economic production and status considerations (Heath, 1958). The arrangement tends to be favored where large families are advantageous and women make substantial contributions to subsistence.

Although polygyny has a wide distribution, polyandry is exceedingly rare. Polyandry usually does not represent freedom of sexual choice for women; often, it involves the right or the opportunity of younger brothers to have sexual access to the wife of an older brother. If a family cannot afford wives or marriages for each of its sons, it may find a wife for the eldest son only. Anthropologist W. H. R. Rivers (1906:515) studied polyandrous practices among the Todas, a non-Hindu people in India, and observed:

The Todas have a completely organized and definite system of polyandry. When a woman marries a man, it is understood that she becomes the wife of his brothers at the same time. When a boy is married to a girl, not only are his brothers usually regarded as also the husbands of the girl, but any brother born later will similarly be regarded as sharing his older brother's rights. . . . The brothers live together, and my informants seemed to regard it as a ridiculous idea that there should even be disputes or jealousies of the kind that might be expected in such a household. . . . Instead of

adultery being regarded as immoral . . . according to the Toda idea, immorality attaches rather to the man who grudges his wife to another.

Social scientists are far from agreement on whether group marriage has ever existed as a cultural norm. There is some evidence that it did occur among the Kaingang of the jungles of Brazil, the Marquesans of the southern Pacific, the Chukchee of Siberia, and the Todas of India. At times, as among the Todas, polyandry appears to slip into group marriage, where a number of brothers share more than one wife (Stephens, 1963).

THE FUNCTIONALIST PERSPECTIVE ON THE FAMILY

As we have noted in other chapters, functionalist theorists stress that if a society is to survive and operate with some measure of effectiveness, it must guarantee that certain essential tasks are performed. The performance of these tasks—or *functions*—cannot be left to chance (see Chapter 2). To do so would run the risk that some activities would not be carried out, and the society would disintegrate. Although acknowledging that families show a good deal of variation throughout the world, functionalists seek to identify a number of recurrent functions families typically perform.

Reproduction. If a society is to perpetuate itself, new members have to be created. Sexual drives do not necessarily take care of the matter, because many people are aware that they can satisfy their sexual needs in the absence of procreation. For instance, the "pill," coitus interruptus, intrauterine devices (IUDs), condoms, abortion, infanticide, the rhythm method, and countless other techniques allow couples to separate sexual enjoyment from reproduction. Consequently, societies commonly motivate people to have children. Among peasant peoples, children are often defined as an economic asset. Likewise, religious considerations may operate (in pre-Communist China, where ancestor worship provided the foundation for religious life, one's comfort in the hereafter could be assured only by having numerous sons). And in the United States, many Americans still define marriage and children as affording the "good life"; in fact, the absence of children is often viewed as a misfortune (in a recent Gallup survey, 45 percent of the respondents said that childless people are more likely to be unfulfilled, and 64 percent felt that the childless are lonely)(Pebley and Bloom, 1982).

Socialization. At birth, children are uninitiated in the ways of culture, and thus each new generation subjects society to a recurrent "barbarian invasion" (see Chapter 3). Most infants are fairly malleable in that within broad limits they are capable of becoming adults of quite different sorts. It is urgent, therefore, that they become the "right" kind of adults. Through the process of socialization, children become inducted into their society's ways, and it is the family that usually serves as the chief culture-transmitting agency. The family functions as an intermediary in the socialization process between the larger community and the individual.

Care, Protection, and Emotional Support. Whereas the offspring of lower animals can survive independently of their parents within a matter of days or weeks, this is not true of human children. Their prolonged dependency dictates that they be fed, clothed, and provided with shelter well into puberty. Throughout the world, the family has been assigned the responsibility for shielding, protecting, sustaining, and other-

wise maintaining children, the infirm, and other dependent members of the community. Moreover, since people are social beings, they have a variety of emotional and interpersonal needs that can be met only through interaction with other human beings. The family provides an important source for entering into intimate, constant, face-to-face contact with other people. Healthy family relationships afford companionship, love, security, a sense of worth, and a general feeling of well-being.

Assignment of status. Societies constantly confront a continual stream of raw material in the form of new infants who must be placed within the social structure. This function can be accomplished by assigning some statuses to an individual on the basis of family membership, what sociologists call *ascribed statuses* (see Chapter 2). The family confers statuses that (1) orient a person to a variety of interpersonal relationships, including those involving parents (parent-child), siblings (brothers and sisters), and kin (aunts, uncles, cousins, and grandparents), and that (2) orient a person to basic group memberships, including racial, ethnic, religious, class, national, and community relationships.

Regulation of Sexual Behavior. As we noted earlier in the chapter, a society's norms regulate sexual behavior by specifying who may engage in sexual behavior with whom and under what circumstances. In no known society are people given total freedom for sexual expression. Although some 70 percent of the world's societies permit some form of sexual license, even these societies typically do not approve of childbirth out of wedlock—this is the **norm of legitimacy** (like other norms, this one is occasionally violated, and those who violated it are usually punished). Legitimacy has to do with the placement of a child in a kinship network that defines the rights the newborn has to care, inheritance, and instruction (Goode, 1960; Malinowski, 1964). A great many social complications result when this norm is violated. Take the matter of the small but growing number of unmarried women who are becoming pregnant through artificial insemination by an anonymous male donor. The artificially conceived child is born into a legal limbo. Says Leonard Loeb, chair of the American Bar Association's family law section (Dullea, 1979:A18):

If a woman inseminates herself it becomes like a marriage without a clergyman or a judge. You must have someone authorized to give it sanctity. I know of no state that sanctifies artificial insemination by donor to an unmarried woman. It may be coming but I think you'd have a hell of a time getting that one past any legislature.

In sum, the functionalist perspective draws our attention to the requirements of group life and to the structural arrangements whereby these requirements are met. But critics point out that these tasks can be performed in other ways. Indeed, by virtue of social change, many of the economic, child-care, and educational functions once performed by the family have been taken over by other institutions. Even so, the family tends to be the social unit most commonly responsible for reproduction, socialization, and the other functions considered above.

THE CONFLICT PERSPECTIVE ON THE FAMILY

Functionalists spotlight the tasks carried out by the family that serve the interests of society as a whole. Many conflict theorists have seen the family as a social arrangement benefitting some people more than others.

Friedrich Engels (1884/1902), Karl Marx's close associate, viewed the family as a class society in miniature, with one class (men) oppressing another class (women). He contended that marriage was the first form of class antagonism in which the well-being of one group derived from the misery and repression of another group. The motivation for sexual domination was the economic exploitation of a woman's labor.

Sociologist Randall Collins (1975) says that historically men have been the "sexual aggressors" and women the "sexual prizes for men." He traces male dominance to the greater strength, size, and aggressiveness of men. Women have been victimized by their smaller size and their vulnerability as childbearers. Across an entire spectrum of societies women have been seen as sexual property, taken as booty in war, used by their fathers in economic bargaining, and considered as owned by their husbands. Collins (1975:232) says that "men have appropriated women primarily for their beds rather than their kitchens and fields, although they could certainly be pressed into service in the daytime too."

According to Collins, men have ordered society so that women are their sexual property. They claim exclusive sexual rights to a woman much in the manner that they determine access to economic property like buildings and land. Marriage becomes a socially enforced contract of sexual property. Hence, within Western tradition, a marriage was not legal until sexually consummated, sexual assault within marriage was not legally rape, and the principal grounds for divorce was sexual infidelity. A woman's virginity was seen as the property of her father and her sexuality as the property of her husband. Thus rape has often been seen less as a crime perpetrated by a man against a woman than as a crime perpetrated by one man against another man.

In recent years, however, economic and

political changes have improved women's bargaining position. When they were no longer under the control of their fathers, they became potentially free to negotiate their own sexual relationships. But women often found that within the free marriage market, they had to trade their sexuality for the economic and status resources of men. Collins suggests that in an economic world dominated by men, the most favorable female strategy became one in which a woman maximized her bargaining power by appearing both as sexually alluring and as inaccessible as possible. She had to hold her sexuality in reserve as a sort of grand prize that she exchanged for male wealth and status, stabilized by a marriage contract. Under such an arrangement, femininity and female virginity came to be idealized, and women were placed on a pedestal so that an element of sexual repression was built into courtship. But as women have increased their economic opportunities, freeing themselves from economic dependence on men, they have gained the resources to challenge the "double standard" of sexuality. The sexual bargains they strike can focus less on marriage and more on immediate pleasure, companionship, and sexual gratification.

Although conflict theory reverberates with the seminal ideas of Friedrich Engels and Karl Marx, other social scientists have approached the issue of conflict somewhat differently. At the turn of the century, psychoanalyst Sigmund Freud (1930/1961) and sociologist Georg Simmel (1908/1955, 1908/1959) also advanced a conflict approach to the family. They contended that intimate relationships inevitably involve antagonism as well as love. More recently, sociologists like Jetse Sprey (1979) have developed these ideas and suggest that conflict is a part of all systems and interactions, including the family and marital interactions. They see

family members as confronting two conflicting demands: to compete with one another for autonomy, authority, and privilege, and simultaneously to share one another's fate in order to survive and even flourish. Viewed in this fashion, the family is a social arrangement that structures close interpersonal relationships through ongoing processes of negotiation, problem solving, and conflict management. This view is quite compatible with the interactionist perspective.

THE INTERACTIONIST PERSPECTIVE ON THE FAMILY

As we saw in Chapters 2 and 3, symbolic interactionists emphasize that human beings create, use, and communicate with symbols. They interact through role taking, a process of reading the symbols used by others and attributing meaning to them. Interactionists portray humans as a unique species because they have a mind and self. The mind and self arise out of interaction and provide the foundation for enduring social relationships and group life. Thus when they enter interactive situations, people define the situation by identifying the expectations that will hold for themselves and others. They then organize their own behavior in terms of these understandings.

The symbolic interactionist perspective is a useful tool for examining the complexities of a relationship. Thus, should the roles of one family member change, invariably there are consequences for the other family members as well. For example, later in the chapter we will see that parenthood alters the husband-wife relationship by creating new roles and increasing the complexity of the family unit. Likewise, family life is somewhat different in homes where a mother is in the paid labor force or where an economic provider is unemployed. And the loss of critical family roles, such as occurs at the time of divorce, has vast implications for family functioning. The symbolic interactionist perspective draws our attention to the complex interconnections that bind people within relationships. We encounter individuals as active beings who evolve, negotiate, and rework the social fabric that constitutes the mosaic of family life.

In sum, functionalist theorists focus on the structural properties and functions of family systems. Conflict theorists portray the family as a system of perpetual "give and take" and conflict regulation (Dahrendorf, 1965). And symbolic interactionists see the family as a dynamic entity through which people continually fashion ongoing relationships and construct a group existence. Although each perspective yields differing insights, each offers a complementary lens through which to view institutional life.

Marriage and the Family in the United States

The issues that divide functionalist and conflict theorists are also encountered among the American public. Indeed, the family has become such a debated topic that sociologists Brigitte Berger and Peter L. Berger (1983) title their recent book *The War over the Family.* To its critics on the political left and among some feminists, the nuclear family is the source of many modern woes. To political conservatives, the family is the last bastion of morality in a world that is becoming increasingly decadent. And to the army of helping professionals, the family is a problem, an institution in grave difficulty. Let us see what we can make of all this by taking a closer look at marriage and the family in American life.

CHOOSING A MARRIAGE PARTNER

Since marriage brings a new member into the inner circle of a family, a child's relatives have a stake in the person who is to be the spouse. Random mating might jeopardize these interests. If children were permitted to "fall in love" with anybody, they might choose the *wrong* mate. Although love has many meanings, we usually think of the strong physical and emotional attraction between a man and a woman as **romantic love**. The ancient Greeks saw such love as a "diseased hysteria," an overwhelming force that irresistibly draws two people together and leads them to become passionately preoccupied with one another.

The Social Regulation of Love. Although most societies recognize that some people may be "smitten" by love, Americans have capitalized on these feelings and elevated them to an exalted position in national life. Many other peoples have viewed romantic love quite differently. Consider these words of the elders of an African tribe who, in discussing the problems of "runaway" marriages and illegitimacy, complained in the 1883 Commission on Native Law and Custom: "It is all this thing called love. We do not understand it at all. . . ." (quoted by Gluckman, 1955:76). The elders saw romantic love as a disruptive force. Given their cultural traditions, marriage did not imply a romantic attraction toward the spouse-to-be, marriage was not the free choice of partners, and considerations other than love determined the selection of a mate.

Sociologist William J. Goode (1959) finds that romantic love is given more emphasis in some societies than in others. At one extreme, societies view marriage without love as mildly shameful; at the other, they define strong romantic attachment as a laughable or tragic aberration. The American middle class falls toward the pole of positive approval; the nineteenth-century Japanese and Chinese fell toward the pole of disapproval; and the Greeks after Alexander and the Romans of the empire took a middle course.

Societies undertake to "control" love in a variety of ways. One approach is *child marriage.* This pattern was employed at one time in India. A child bride went to live with her husband in a marriage that was not physically consummated until much later. Another approach involves the *social isolation* of young people from potential mates. For instance, the Manus of the Admiralty Islands secluded their young women in a lodge built on stilts over a lagoon. Still another approach entails the *close supervision* of couples by chaperons, an arrangement found among seventeenth-century Puritans. And finally *peer and parental pressures* may be brought to bear to ensure that youngsters "go with the right people." For example, in the United States parents often threaten, cajole, wheedle, and bribe their children to limit their social contacts to youths with "suitable" ethnic, religious, and educational backgrounds. Regardless of the arrangement employed, the net result is the same—a person's range of choice is narrowed by social barriers.

Factors in Mate Selection. Given a field of eligible mates, why do we fall in love with and marry one person and not another? A variety of factors seem to be at work. One is **homogamy,** the tendency of like to marry like. People of similar ages, races, religions, nationalities, education, intelligence, health, stature, attitudes, and countless other traits tend to marry one another to a degree greater than would be found by chance. Although homogamy seems to operate with respect to social characteristics, the evidence is less clear for such psychological factors as personality and temperament.

Physical attractiveness also plays a part in mate selection. On the whole, Americans share similar standards for evaluating physical attractiveness (Urdy, 1965). Moreover, we prefer the companionship and friendship of attractive people to that of unattractive people (Reis, Nezlek, and Wheeler, 1980; Marks, Miller, and Maruyama, 1981). And we believe that attractive people are more likely to find good jobs, to marry well, and to lead happy and fulfilling lives—in brief, we think that "what is beautiful is good" (Dion, 1972; Dion, Berscheid, and Walster, 1972). When talking on the telephone to a man they believe to be physically attractive, women are more poised, more sociable, and more vivacious than when they talk to a man they believe to be physically unattractive (Brody, 1981). However,

From a field of eligible individuals, we typically select as a mate a person who resembles us in race, religion, education, health, and numerous other traits. Moreover, we tend to choose partners with about the same degree of physical attractiveness as we have ourselves. (Judy S. Gelles/Stock, Boston)

since the supply of unusually beautiful or handsome partners is limited, in real life we tend to select partners who have a degree of physical attractiveness similar to our own (Murstein, 1972, 1976; White, 1980). According to the **matching hypothesis,** we typically experience the greatest payoff and the least cost when we follow this course, since individuals of equal attractiveness are the ones most likely to reciprocate our advances.

Still another factor operates in choosing a mate. We feel most comfortable with people who have certain personality traits, while those with other traits "rub us the wrong way." Sociologist Robert F. Winch (1958) has taken this everyday observation and formulated a theory of **complementary needs.** This concept refers to two different personality traits that are the counterparts of each other and that provide a sense of completeness when they are joined. For instance, dominant people find a complementary relationship with passive people, and talkative people find themselves attracted to good listeners. Roles also complement one another (Murstein, 1976). By way of illustration, a bedroom athlete is likely to be attracted to a lusty, passionate partner, rather than a cool, cerebral one with little "animal" sensuousness. Thus interpersonal attraction also depends on how well each partner fulfills the role expectations of the other and how mutually gratifying they find their "role fit."

Exchange theory provides a unifying link among these three factors. It is based on the notion that we like those who reward us and dislike those who punish us (Blau, 1964; Nye, 1978; Burgess and Huston, 1979). Many of our acts derive from our confidence that from them will flow some benefit—perhaps a desired expression of love, gratitude, recognition, security, or material reward. In the course of interacting with one another, we reinforce the relationship by rewarding

each other. Thus people with similar social traits, attitudes, and values are mutually rewarded by validating one another's life style and supporting it at very low cost. In selecting partners of comparable physical attractiveness, we minimize the risk of rejection while maximizing the profit from such a conquest. And the parties in complementary relationships offer each other high rewards at low cost to themselves. In sum, exchange theory proposes that people involved in a mutually satisfying relationship will exchange behaviors that have low cost and high reward.

MARRIED COUPLES

Most adult Americans hope to establish an intimate relationship with another person and make the relationship work. This finding underlies a recent study of American couples undertaken by sociologists Philip Blumstein and Pepper Schwartz (1983). They investigated the experiences of four types of couples: married, cohabitating, homosexual male, and lesbian. The study centered on New York City, Seattle, and San Francisco, where the researchers secured 12,000 completed questionnaires. From these, Blumstein and Schwartz selected 300 couples for in-depth interviews. Eighteen months later, they sent half the couples a follow-up questionnaire to determine if they were still living together. As with most volunteer samples, the survey was not wholly representative, since it was weighted toward white, affluent, well-educated Americans. The researchers believe that any bias is toward the liberal side, and that the nation is probably even more conservative in its family patterns than their results show.

Blumstein and Schwartz had expected American couples to be less conventional than they were. Take work. Although 60 percent of the wives were employed outside the home, only 30 percent of the men and

In many respects, college functions as a transitional institution that assists young people in moving out of their families and entering the adult world. In the late teens and early twenties, many young people find themselves in a phase of life in which a roughly equal balance exists between "being in" the family and "moving out." Developmental psychologists say that getting across the boundary of the family is a major developmental task during these years. Individuals must become less financially dependent, enter new roles and living arrangements, and achieve greater autonomy and responsibility. Students in introductory sociology courses at Ohio State University have found a number of sociological insights helpful in understanding their experiences. A number of these insights are provided below:

It seems that in the past I have always dated girls who are very talkative, assertive and outgoing. I am a rather quiet person and I find I need someone who can carry on most of the conversation. In truth, I am a much better listener than talker. I have noticed that whenever I have gone out with a retiring or shy girl that nothing ever got said and the date bombed. I have been going with my present girlfriend for a year now. My dad is always complaining to me about her. He says she drives him nuts, that all she does is talk, talk, talk, and that she is much too pushy. Actually we work out real well together. She is able to pull me out of my shell and she makes me feel comfortable in social situations. As Robert F. Winch points out in his complementary need theory of mate selection, we look for persons who provide us with the maximum gratification of our needs. We generally feel most comfortable when one person has one personality trait and the other person has its counterpart so that when the traits are joined they produce a sense of completeness. In this way the two people supply each other's lack and supplement each other.

Tonight my mother sat me down for a mother-daughter talk. The subject was my boyfriend and marriage. Mother said that I should be more careful in selecting a boyfriend so as to go with someone like our family. She told me she regretted marrying a "goy" (non-Jew) and that I would find life a lot easier if I found a "nice Jewish boy" who understood my upbringing and the ways of my family. She told me that it was awkward and inconsiderate of me to bring my "goy" boyfriend to dinner on the Sabbath. She said it made the family uncomfortable and furthermore it was not fair to my boyfriend since he didn't understand why or what we were doing—it put him in an awkward position. She explained that things would be a lot easier all around if I would find someone of the same religious background.

Although in theory mate selection in the United States is free, in practice a good many pressures operate "to control" love. My mother was attempting to bring pressure on me to marry within the Jewish group (an endogamous marriage).

Before I moved into a coed dormitory I wondered about the relationships between the guys and girls in the same dorm. Having lived in a coed dorm for a while now, it has turned out differently from what I had expected. Very few of the guys date girls in our dorm. Rather, we date girls from "outside." With girls from our dorm we become "friends"—more a "brother-sister" relationship. I was surprised that so little sexual promiscuity occurred among the members of the opposite sexes in the same coed dormitory. A semi-incest taboo operates within a coed dormitory. I think the reason for this is that romantic and sexual involvement would complicate our relationships. Romantic ties might fragment our relationships and pose barriers in relating to other people. A guy involved with a particular girl wouldn't like her associating on a day-to-day basis with the other guys he lived with (and vice versa); you would come to resent or feel suspicious of your roommates. And if the relationship with a particular girl broke up, it would be a strain living in the same dorm together and continually coming in contact with one another.

39 percent of the women believed that both spouses should work. Even when the wives had full-time jobs, they did the greater part of the housework. Whereas 59 percent of the women contributed eleven or more hours a week to household chores, only 22 percent of the men contributed this amount of time. Indeed, husbands so objected to doing housework that the more they did of it, the more unhappy they were, the more they argued with their wives, and the greater were the chances the couple would divorce. In contrast, if a man did not contribute what a woman felt to be his fair share of the housework, the relationship was not usually jeopardized.

American men seem preoccupied with dominance and power. In fact, they could take pleasure in their partner's success only if it was not superior to their own. In contrast, women were found to be happier and relationships were more stable when the male partners were ambitious and successful. Most married couples pooled their money. However, regardless of how much the wife earned, they measured their financial success by the husband's income only.

Most of the married couples had sexual relations at least once a week. People who had sex infrequently were just as likely to have a long-lasting relationship as those who had sex often. While couples were happier when the opportunity to initiate and refuse sex was shared equally by the partners, in more than half of the cases the husbands were still the primary initiators. But whereas the women tended to link sex and love, men often did not. Less than a third of the couples engaged in extramarital activities. Husbands were more often repeatedly unfaithful than wives, but their transgressions did not necessarily represent dissatisfaction with either their partner or the relationship as a whole. Women, in contrast, often strayed just once, mostly out of curiosity; but for them, infidelity was more likely to blossom into a full-fledged love affair.

Early in the marriage men were more likely than women to feel encroached upon by the relationship and to complain that they needed more "private time." But in long-standing marriages, it was the wives who more often complained that they did not have enough time by themselves. Further, women were more likely than men to say they were the emotional caretakers of the family, although 39 percent of the men indicated that they focused more on their marriage than they did on their work. In about a quarter of the marriages, both partners claimed they were relationship-centered.

Like Blumstein and Schwartz, Theodore Caplow and his colleagues (1982) expected to find the American nuclear family in trouble when they undertook a restudy of "Middletown," a pseudonym for Muncie, Indiana. Robert S. and Helen Merrill Lynd (1929, 1937) had made Middletown into a leading sociological laboratory in their celebrated 1920s study. Sociologists generally agree that the Lynd's research represents one of the best large-scale uses of anthropological methods in the study of an American community. The Lynds portrayed Middletown as a small city whose residents were straining to enter the twentieth century, but who nevertheless clung to a nineteenth-century faith in the value of work, church, family, and country.

On the surface, much seems to have changed in Middletown in the intervening fifty years. High school students wear blue jeans and T-shirts to classes; mothers leave their children at day care centers and take jobs; there is bloodshed on television and graphic sex in the movies; and some junior high school girls visit the Planned Parenthood center to get their birth control pills. But Caplow and his associates conclude that the doomsayers are wrong, and the family has not lost its attractiveness. They observe (1982:323):

Tracing the changes from the 1920s to the 1970s, we discovered increased family solidarity, a smaller generation gap, closer marital communication, more religion, and less mobility. With respect to the major features of family life, the trend of the past two generations has run in the opposite direction from the trend nearly everyone perceives and talks about.

They say their findings were as surprising to them "as they may be to our readers."

Although divorce rates have soared, the research described above and other studies reveal that Americans have not given up on marriage. Public opinion surveys confirm that Americans depend very heavily on marriage for their psychological well-being (Glenn and Weaver, 1981). As Table 9.1 shows, marriage is the most prevalent American life style. However, increasing numbers of Americans no longer view marriage as a permanent institution, but rather as something that can be ended and reentered.

PARENTHOOD

Nuclear families that are not disrupted by divorce, desertion, or death typically pass through a series of changes and realignments across time, what sociologists call the **family life cycle** (Hill, 1964; Rapoport, Rapoport, and Strelitz, 1976; Nock, 1979). These changes and realignments are related to the altered expectations and requirements imposed on a husband and wife as children are born and grow up. The family begins with the husband-wife pair and becomes increasingly complex as members are added, creating new roles and multiplying the number of relationships. The family then stabilizes for a time, after which it begins shrinking as each of the adult children is launched. Finally, it returns once more to the husband-wife pair, and eventually terminates with the death of a spouse.

Each modification in the role content of one family member has implications for all the other members. The arrival of the first child compels the reorganization of a couple's life, since living as a trio is more complicated than living as a pair. Parents have to juggle their work roles, alter their time

TABLE 9.1

Marital Status of Americans

	1980	Percent
Males, 15 and over	83,839,270	100.0%
Single	25,074,755	29.9
Married	50,518,621	60.3
Separated	1,588,846	1.9
Widowed	2,125,493	2.5
Divorced	4,531,555	5.4
Females, 15 and over	91,414,347	100.0
Single	21,037,493	23.0
Married	50,138,720	54.8
Separated	2,404,936	2.6
Widowed	11,231,965	12.3
Divorced	6,601,233	7.2

(*Source:* U.S. Bureau of the Census.)

schedules, change their communication patterns, and relinquish some privacy. And parenthood competes with the husband/wife role. Women with a first child are more likely than childless women to report that their husbands are not paying enough attention to them (Ryder, 1973). Moreover, marital adjustment ratings fall after the birth of a first child (Belsky, Spanier, and Rovine, 1983). Overall, it seems that although their initial encounter with parenthood may be stressful, most couples do not find it sufficiently stressful to warrant calling the experience a crisis (Lamb, 1978; McLaughlin and Micklin, 1983). Contemporary parents appear to have a less romantic and more realistic view of the probable effects of children on their lives than did earlier generations of parents. And despite the changes a child brings to their lives, most couples report enormous satisfaction with parenthood.

As a couple have additional offspring, their children are also affected. An only child, an oldest child, a middle child, and a youngest child all experience a somewhat different world because of the different social webs that encompass their lives. For instance, research suggests that first-born children are fortune's favorites (Cicirelli, 1978). First-borns are overrepresented in college populations, at the higher IQ levels, among National Merit and Rhodes Scholars, in *Who's Who in America*, among American presidents (52 percent), among men and women in Congress, and in the astronaut corps. One explanation is that the first-born plays a parent surrogate role in dealing with later-born siblings. The eldest child functions as a sort of intermediary between later-borns and the parents, encouraging the development of the older child's verbal, cognitive, and leadership skills. Later children tend to be more relaxed and gregarious and less inhibited than the eldest child, because parents are typically more relaxed in

their parenting than they are with first-borns (Brooks, 1984).

Clinical psychologists and psychiatrists have stressed the problem parents face when their children leave home. Dissatisfaction is most common among couples who had used their children's presence to disguise the emptiness of their own relationship. But most couples do not experience difficulty with the "empty-nest" period; the majority view this stage as a time of "new freedoms." Indeed, national surveys show that middle-aged women whose children have left home experience greater general happiness and enjoyment of life, in addition to greater marital happiness, than middle-aged women with children still living at home (Vander Zanden, 1985).

EMPLOYED MOTHERS

As we pointed out in Chapter 7, sexual inequality has been sustained historically by assigning the economic provider role to men and the child-rearing role to women. However, over the past several decades, increasing numbers of mothers with children have found employment outside the home. In 1984 some 60.5 percent of children under age 18 had working mothers—fully 32 million children (see Figure 9.1). About half of all mothers with preschool children were employed outside the home, as were 41 percent of mothers with children under age 1 (Census Bureau, 1984a).

Serious concern is frequently voiced about the future of the nation's children as more and more mothers enter the work force. Many people fear that the working mother represents a loss to children in terms of supervision, love, and cognitive enrichment. But an accumulating body of research suggests that there is little difference in the development of children whose mothers work and children whose mothers remain at home (Farel, 1981; Schacter, 1981;

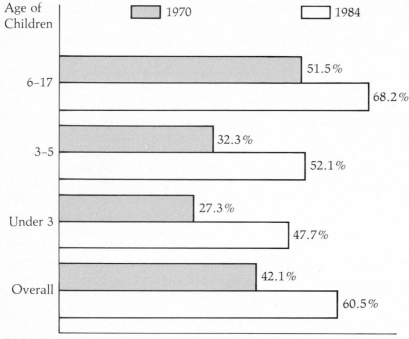

Age of Children

■ 1970   □ 1984

6–17   51.5%   68.2%

3–5   32.3%   52.1%

Under 3   27.3%   47.7%

Overall   42.1%   60.5%

FIGURE 9.1   MORE WORKING MOTHERS
More than six of 10 mothers with children under age 18 are in the labor force—up 44 percent from 1970. (Source: U.S. Department of Labor.)

Stith and Davis, 1984). In fact, many psychologists and sociologists are no longer asking whether it is good or bad that mothers work. Instead, they are finding that a more important issue is whether the mother, regardless of employment, is satisfied in her situation (Hoffman and Nye, 1974; Sweeney, 1982; Stuckey, McGhee, and Bell, 1982). The working mother who gets personal satisfaction from employment, who does not feel excessive guilt, and who has adequate household arrangements is likely to perform as well or better than the nonworking mother. Women who are not working and would like to, and working mothers whose lives are beset by harassment and strain, are the ones whose children are mostly likely to display maladjustment and behavior problems.

With the entry of women into the labor force, arrangements for child care are shifting from care in the home to care outside the home (Census Bureau, 1984a). Even so, between 1977 and 1982 the use of group care rose only from 13 to 15 percent. Of working mothers with at least one child under age 5, 26 percent had the child cared for at home, either by a husband, relative, or another person. Another 44 percent placed their preschool child in another person's home while they were at work. Only 6.2 percent cared for the child while on the job. The most likely users of group care services are well-educated women who work full-time and have high family incomes.

In 1984 some 5 million American children under the age of 10 had no one to look after them when they came home from school in the afternoon. An additional 500,000 preschoolers were in the same predicament.

For significant portions of the day or night, many working parents are unable to care personally for their children, and they lack relatives or friends to whom they turn for reliable babysitting. One answer to this problem is day care. But the quality of the day care currently available and affordable leaves many people dissatisfied. Ralph Nader, the consumer activist, describes some centers as "children's warehouses." And sex-abuse scandals at centers from California to New York have terrified a good many parents (Watson, 1984). Additionally, low-quality facilities are more likely to spread a variety of diseases, especially colds, diarrhea, and dysentery (Ricks, 1984).

The United States is one of the few industrialized nations that does not have a comprehensive day care program. European nations—particularly Sweden—have established nationally subsidized support systems. More than a thousand American companies offer help with day care, but such programs are still in their infancy (Peterson, 1984). Child care advocates warn that failure to develop a national policy toward child care will result in "a generation of neglected children" (Palmer, 1984).

There is, however, one encouraging note. Most child psychologists agree that *high-quality* day care and nursery schools provide acceptable child care arrangements (Belsky and Steinberg, 1978; Kagan, Kearsley, and Zelazo, 1978; Etaugh, 1980). Such programs are characterized by small group size, high staff-child ratios, well-trained staffs, good equipment, and attractive and nurturing environments. Most children show remarkable resilience. Throughout the world, children are raised under a great variety of conditions, and the day care arrangement is just one of them. The effects of day care depend to some extent on the amount of time a child spends at a center and on the quality of parent–child interaction during the time the family is together (Stith and Davis, 1984). Moreover, working mothers provide a somewhat different role model for their children that is associated with less traditional gender-role concepts and a higher evaluation of female competence (Gold and Andres, 1978; Shreve, 1984).

TWO-INCOME FAMILIES

Some 27.7 million American households—67 percent of all married couples—have two breadwinners. Even so, women still continue to shoulder the primary responsibility for household tasks and child care (Berk and Berk, 1979; Skinner, 1983). A 1980 national survey found overwhelming numbers of working women reporting that they did not have enough time to meet their home and work responsibilities (General Mills, 1981). When women are expected to contribute more than men to the household division of labor, they may be less effective on the job than they otherwise might be and they may not realize their true career potential. Alternatively, they may fall victim to the "superwoman" syndrome and attempt to excel both on the job and at home.

In two-income families, the man typically has a larger voice in major household decisions than the woman does. Junior–senior relationships commonly operate, with the wife usually secondary (O'Barr, 1979; Gappa, O'Barr, and St. John-Parsons, 1979). For instance, should a husband be offered a better position in another area of the country, the wife typically makes the move regardless of the effect the transfer has on her career. Moreover, some wives fear that should they take over responsibility for their own finances, their husbands will feel that their masculinity is threatened. However, if they relinquish control of their income to the husband, they often experience resentment and bitterness. Consequently, many couples maintain separate accounts or pool only a portion of their incomes.

Scheduling time together is a frequent source of tension for dual-career couples (Moore, 1984). But the conflict often masks problems of commitment, lack of intimacy, and divergent goals. Arguments over work schedules usually have more to do with "how much does he/she care" than with the amount of time the couple actually spends together. Another source of tension derives from income differences. On average, wives earn only 62 percent as much as their husbands do as full-time, year-round workers. However, of the 49 million wives in the United States, 5.9 million, or 12.1 percent, earn more than their husbands (Bianchi, 1984b). Men often feel their self-esteem threatened in this situation, and such couples run a higher risk of psychological and physical abuse, marital conflict, and sexual problems (Kessler and McRae, 1981; Rubenstein, 1982). Yet the difficulties are not insurmountable, provided couples can come to terms with old expectations and new realities and learn what works best for them. Women are growing more confident of their knowledge and abilities, while increasing numbers of men are learning to share family responsibility and power. The dynamics of family decision making are currently in transition as many dual-income couples evolve new patterns and traditions for family living (Huber and Spitze, 1983; Bird, Bird, and Scruggs, 1984).

FAMILY VIOLENCE, CHILD ABUSE, AND INCEST

Mounting evidence suggests that family violence, child abuse, and incest are much more common than most Americans had suspected. The expression "coming out of the closet" is an apt one when applied to battered women and victims of child abuse and sexual molestation. They have been as reluctant to reveal their plight as gay persons have been to reveal their sexual preferences. Traditionally they have attempted to keep the indignities they have experienced locked inside the family home.

Estimates of family violence vary widely. One nationally representative survey found that 16 percent of those sampled reported some kind of physical violence between the husband and wife during the year of the study; 28 percent said marital violence had occurred at some point in their marriage (Straus, Gelles, and Steinmetz, 1980). *Time* magazine estimates that nearly 6 million wives are abused by their husbands and some 2,000 to 4,000 women are beaten to death each year (O'Reilly, 1983). Although both men and women engage in violence, men typically do more damage than their female partners. Some men find it easier to control the weaker members of the family by force, because it does not require negotiation or interpersonal skills. Women put up with battering for a variety of reasons (Strube and Barbour, 1983). For one thing, the fewer the resources a wife has in the way of education or job skills, the more vulnerable she is in the marriage. For another, Americans place the burden of family harmony on women, with the implication that they have failed if the marriage disintegrates. Finally, the more a wife was abused by her parents and witnessed violence in her childhood home, the more likely she is to remain with an abusive husband.

Children also suffer abuse and neglect. From interviews with 2,143 married couples representing a cross section of American families, sociologist Murray A. Straus and his colleagues (1980) estimate that parents kick, punch, or bite some 1.7 million children a year, beat up 460,000 to 750,000 more, and attack 46,000 others with knives or guns. A great many factors are related to abuse and violence. Researchers find that social stress, including the loss of a job or divorce, is associated with the maltreatment of children (Conger, Burgess, and Barrett, 1979; Steinberg, Catalano, and Dooley, 1981). Moreover, families that are socially isolated and outside neighborhood support networks are more at risk for child abuse than are families with rich social ties (Garbarino and Sherman, 1980). Additionally, abusive parents are themselves likely to have been abused when they were children (Straus, Gelles, and Steinmetz, 1980; Kalmuss, 1984).

Although incest has been called the last taboo, its status as a taboo has not kept it from taking place, but merely from being talked about. Indeed, most people find it so offensive that parents may be sexually attracted to their children they prefer not to think about it. There are about 10 female victims of incest for every male victim (Hinds, 1981). The perpetrator is commonly the father, uncle, or other male authority figure in the household. In cases of father-daughter incest, the fathers are typically "family tyrants" who employ physical force and intimidation to control their families (Finkelhor, 1979; Herman and Hirschman, 1981). The mothers in incestuous families are commonly passive, have a poor self-image, and are overly dependent on their husbands, much the same traits found among battered wives. The victims of molestation are usually shamed or terrified into treating the experience as a dirty secret (Gordon and O'Keefe, 1984). Not uncommonly, childhood incest leads to serious emotional and psychological problems, low self-esteem, guilt, isolation, mistrust of men, difficulties in establishing intimate relationships, sexual precociousness, drug and alcohol abuse, and even suicide (Emslie and Rosenfeld, 1983; Husain and Chapel, 1983). Victimized women tend to show lifetime patterns of psychological shame and stigmatization (Brozan, 1984; Stark, 1984).

Over the past decade, the problems of family violence, child abuse, and incest have emerged as major issues. Even so, considerable ambivalence still exists on these subjects. Much needs to be done to assist the victims. Social service agencies need to be restructured so that battered family members can find real help. Remedial laws need to be enacted. Perhaps of even greater importance, a cultural revolution of attitudes and values is required to eradicate the abuse of women and children (Vander Zanden, 1985).

DIVORCE

Divorce is on the upswing. When today's elderly were establishing families, divorce was relatively infrequent. In 1980, only 15 percent of Americans aged 65 to 74 reported that their first marriage had ended in divorce. By contrast, roughly half of those aged 25 to 35 in 1980 had either ended their first marriage in divorce or expected to do so before they reached age 75 (Glick, 1984). Yet rising divorce rates tell us little about the level of marital satisfaction or even stability. Changes in official divorce statistics do not inform us about unofficial separation, or the proverbial poor family's divorce—desertion. Moreover, the current rate of marital breakup through divorce is approaching the level of marital breakup through death in earlier centuries. Indeed, by adding desertion to death, a greater proportion of middle-aged couples in the nineteenth century suffered marital dissolution than do their contemporary counterparts (Skolnick, 1981).

In 1982 divorces in the United States reached a high of 1.2 million, and more than half of the couples who divorced had children. Researchers find that the households of divorced mothers and fathers are substantially more disorganized than those of intact families (Hetherington, 1979; Hetherington, Cox, and Cox, 1982). The first two years after divorce are especially difficult.

Divorced parents do not communicate as well with their children, are less affectionate, and are more inconsistent discipliners than are parents in intact families (Wallerstein and Kelly, 1980; Fine, Moreland, and Schwebel, 1983). Divorced mothers with teenage sons find their situation particularly stressful. Financial problems complicate the difficulties of many women. Only half of divorced mothers receive any money at all from their children's fathers, and this is seldom much (Jencks, 1982).

A study of the long-term effects of divorce finds that children who are very young when their parents divorce have fewer psychological problems ten years later than do their older brothers and sisters (Wallerstein, 1984). Young preschool-age children often regress to stages of dependency and feel responsible for driving their fathers away. Even five years after a marriage breaks up, younger children seem more depressed and emotionally scarred than do their older siblings. But after ten years, children who were preschoolers when their parents divorced carry fewer memories of stressful events than do older brothers and sisters who are more likely to retain vivid, damaging memories. The split-up of their parents causes older siblings to be apprehensive about new relationships, and they are more likely to view marriage with caution. For these children, the divorce remains a central aspect of their lives.

Although divorce may be more commonplace today, it is hardly a routine experience. In many cases, divorce exacts a greater emotional and physical toll than almost any other type of stress, including widowhood (Brody, 1983; Masterson, 1984). Separated and divorced people are overrepresented in mental institutions, more likely to die from cardiovascular disease, cancer, pneumonia, and cirrhosis of the liver, and more prone to die from accidents, homicides, and suicides. Middle-aged and elderly women are especially devastated by divorce. These women—called *displaced homemakers*—often dedicated themselves to managing a home and raising children, and then find themselves jettisoned after years of marriage. Within the United States, some 100,000 people over the age of 55 divorce each year. Many of the women find themselves ill-equipped to deal with the financial consequences. Frequently they have not worked outside their homes since they were married some forty or more years earlier. And the women are cut off from their ex-husband's private pension and medical insurance plans.

Most divorced people remarry. About five of every six divorced men and three of every four divorced women marry again. Divorced men are more likely to remarry than women. For one thing, divorced men are more likely to marry someone not previously married. For another, because men usually marry younger women, divorced men have a larger pool of potential partners to choose from (Glick, 1984). Should the divorced remarry, they are more likely to divorce again than are individuals in first marriages. If current projections hold, about 61 percent of men and 54 percent of women in their thirties who remarry will undergo a second divorce. It seems that individuals drag into the new marriage many of the insecurities and personality problems that disrupted the previous one. And with one divorce under their belt, they are less hesitant about securing a second one should trouble appear (Cherlin, 1978; Furstenberg and Spanier, 1984).

STEPFAMILIES

Remarriage frequently results in stepfamilies. Because more than half of remarried persons are parents, for better or worse, their new partners become stepparents. One in six American families is a stepfamily;

35 million Americans live in one, including 20 percent of the nation's children under age 18. By 1990, the number of stepfamilies and single-parent households will outnumber families with two biological parents.

Most stepparents attempt to re-create a traditional family because it is the only model they have. But a stepfamily functions differently than the traditional nuclear family (Mills, 1984). For one thing, the stepparent role does not necessarily approximate that of a biological parent, particularly in authority, legitimacy, and respect. For another, the family tree of a stepfamily can be very complex and convoluted, populated not only by children of both spouses, but by six sets of grandparents, relatives of former spouses, relatives of new spouses, and the people former spouses marry. The more complex the social system of the remarriage, the greater the ambiguity about roles within the family and the greater the likelihood of difficulties (Clingempeel, 1981). Matters are further complicated because stepparents and stepchildren do not have a mutual history or a previous opportunity to bond.

Stepfamilies often start on a highly idealistic note. But as the months go by, their outlook on the family changes, and individuals gain a more realistic view. Misunderstandings in stepfamilies take many forms. Most often, they are caused by conflicting family traditions, unfulfilled expectations, financial pressures, loyalty conflicts, unresolved power struggles, and ill-defined behavior standards for the children. Discipline is a frequent problem, because children often see the stepparent as an intruder. Society also lacks a clear picture of how members should relate to one another; for instance, how should a son relate to his stepparent and vice versa, and how should the custodial stepparent relate to the former spouse?

Most stepparents are stepfathers. Although growing numbers of fathers are winning child custody cases, the vast majority of children still live primarily with their mothers. Stepfathers usually underrate their parenting skills and their contributions to the lives of their stepchildren. Indeed, their stepchildren and spouses give them higher marks than they give themselves (Bohannan and Erickson, 1978). Children living with stepfathers apparently do just as well, or just as poorly, in school and in their social life as do children living with natural fathers. And children with stepfathers on the whole do better than do children from father-absent homes (Robinson, 1984; Ganong and Coleman, 1984).

The stepfamily must adjust to many types of challenges not encountered by most natural families. In order to succeed, the stepfamily must loosen the boundaries that encapsulated the two previous biological families and structure a new social unit (Papernow, 1984). As old arrangements "unfreeze," members must evolve a oneness that allows the new family to act together for common ends. Most workable solutions leave some of the "old" ways of doing things intact while fashioning new rituals, expectations, and rules. When the restructuring is successful, the members no longer need to give constant attention to relationships and can relate to one another spontaneously and comfortably.

CARE FOR THE ELDERLY

Despite the significant changes that have occurred in family roles in recent decades, it is grown children who still bear the primary responsibility for their aged parents. The sense of obligation is strong even when the emotional ties between the parent and child are weak (Cicirelli, 1981, 1983; Neugarten, 1982; Baruch and Barnett, 1983). In 80 percent of the cases, any care an elderly person requires is provided by their families. This assistance supplements what the elderly receive from savings, pensions, social security, Medicare, and Medicaid.

Some 40 percent of Americans between the ages of 55 and 59 and 20 percent of those 60 to 64 have at least one living parent (Brody et al., 1983). Social scientists call middle-aged adults the *sandwich generation* because they find themselves with responsibilities for their own teenage and college-age children and for their elderly parents. Care for the elderly falls most often on daughters and daughters-in-law. These women have historically functioned as our society's "kin-keepers" (Lang and Brody, 1983). Despite the changing roles of women, when it comes to the elderly, the old maxim still applies: "A son's a son till he takes a wife, but a daughter's a daughter for the rest of her life." Yet 61 percent of the women also work. Although being employed substantially reduces the hours of assistance that sons provide their elderly parents, it does not have an appreciable effect on that provided by daughters (Stoller, 1983). Not surprisingly, women of the sandwich generation are subjected to role overload stresses that are often compounded by their own age-related problems, including lower energy levels, the onset of chronic ailments, and family losses (Brody et al., 1983).

The motivations, expectations, and aspirations of the middle-aged and the elderly at times differ because of their different positions in the life cycle. Intergenerational strain is usually less where financial independence allows each generation to maintain separate residences. Both the elderly and their adult offspring seem to prefer intimacy "at a distance" and opt for independent households as long as possible. Elderly parents who call upon their children for assistance are more likely to be frail, severely disabled, gravely ill, or failing mentally. When middle-aged adults fail to take responsibility for an ailing parent, it may re-flect not "hardheartedness," but a realization that the situation is more stressful than they can cope with. But to do so commonly produces strong feelings of guilt (Hess and Waring, 1978).

Alternative Life Styles

Despite popular perceptions that the American family is a dying institution, the evidence we have reviewed in the chapter suggests that the family tree is as deeply rooted as ever in the social landscape. It is, however, sprouting varied branches. Family relationships are becoming more tangled as a result of people living longer and occasionally changing mates to suit the seasons of their lives. Increasing numbers of children are growing up with several sets of parents and an assortment of half and step brothers and sisters. Simultaneously, by virtue of the rapid expansion in life style options, Americans now enjoy more alternatives in tailoring their relationships to individual choice. A **life style** is the overall pattern of living people evolve to meet their biological, social, and emotional needs. Let us examine a number of life style options.

SINGLEHOOD

Despite our couples-oriented society, single-person households are outpacing the growth of most other household types (in 1983, married couples occupied 59 percent of all households, compared with 70 percent in 1970). The number of Americans living alone has increased 77 percent since 1970, much faster than the 12 percent growth in married couples (Census Bureau, 1984d). By 1990, there will be 24 million single households, so that one of every four occupied dwelling units will have only one person in it. Yet singles are hardly a monolithic group, with the divorced (11.5 million), widowed

*From the various liberation movements of the 1960s has come a wider accept-
ance of pluralistic standards that permit a far wider range of life styles than had
been the case. The freedom to pursue a life style based on individual preference and less constrained by external standards of "normality" or "respectabili-
ty" has been enhanced by increases in material affluence and cultural
sophistication. (Melanie Wall/Southern Light)*

(12.7 million), and never-married (45.7 million) constituting distinct groups of those
aged 15 and older. The high incidence of
divorce, the ability of the elderly to maintain
their own homes alone, and the deferral of
marriage among young adults have contributed to the high rate of increase in the number of nonfamily households.

In 1982, almost 12 percent of women and
17 percent of men aged 30 to 34 had never
married. These figures were almost double
the proportion of never-married singles in
1970, when 6 percent of women and 9 percent of men had never married. A similar
trend is evident among people in their mid-
to late twenties: 23 percent of women and
more than a third of men in these age
groups were still single in 1982, compared
with 11 percent of women and 19 percent
of men in 1970 (see Figure 9.2). Although
many of these men and women may simply
have postponed marriage, the changes sug-

gest that a growing proportion of Americans may elect never to marry at all (Census
Bureau, 1984d). Overall, rates of nonmar-
riage increase as education increases, particularly for women. Even so, the population remaining single today is smaller than
it was at the turn of the century, when fully
42 percent of all American adult men and
33 percent of adult women never married
(Kain, 1984).

There are degrees of singleness. A person may be single, then choose to cohabit
or marry, and perhaps decide later to divorce and become single again. Singlehood
is a reclaimable status. As sociologist Roger
W. Libby (1977:49–50) points out, singlehood as a life style for younger Americans
is quite varied:

*Between the extreme images of the swinging
and always elated single and the desperately
lonely, suicidal single lies a continuum of*

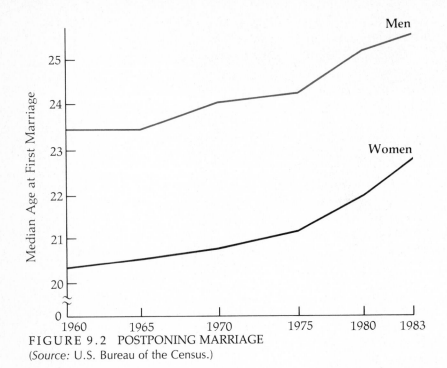

FIGURE 9.2 POSTPONING MARRIAGE
(*Source:* U.S. Bureau of the Census.)

single people with joys and sorrows similar to those of people electing other life-styles. . . . We are left, then, with the impression that singlehood (like marriage) is not a lifelong commitment for most people. Choices are usually replaced by new choices.

In recent years, the notion that people must marry if they are to achieve maximum happiness and well-being has been increasingly questioned (Cargan and Melko, 1982). A good many Americans no longer think of singlehood as a residual category for the unchosen and lonely. Singles have found that as their numbers have grown, a singles subculture is available to them in most metropolitan areas. They can move into a singles apartment, go to a singles bar, take a singles vacation, join a singles consciousness-raising group, and so on. And if they wish, they can lead an active sex life without acquiring an unwanted mate, child, or reputation. However, there has been a marked decrease in casual sex in the United States in recent years, in part a response to fears surrounding such diseases as acquired immune deficiency syndrome (AIDS) and genital herpes (Lyons, 1983).

UNMARRIED COHABITATION

The number of adults who share living quarters with an unrelated adult of the opposite sex has increased in recent decades to nearly 2 million individuals, 4 percent of all couples (Census Bureau, 1984d). About half of all individuals living together have been married previously, and three in ten unmarried couples have one or more children present in the household. Cohabitation is particularly attractive to young adults. One-fourth of the men and nearly two-fifths of the women are under 25 years of age; two-thirds of the men and three-fourths of the women are under 35 (Spanier, 1983) (see Table 9.2). The dramatic increase

TABLE 9.2
Cohabiting Couples, 1981

| | Women | | Men | |
Age	Number	Percent	Number	Percent
Under 25	687,000	38.0%	435,000	24.1%
25–34	686,000	37.9	780,000	43.1
35–44	151,000	8.4	252,000	13.9
45–64	185,000	10.2	230,000	12.7
65 and over	99,000	5.5	111,000	6.1
Prior Marital Status				
Never married	991,000	54.8	958,000	53.0
Ever married	817,000	45.2	850,000	47.0
Total	1,808,000	100.0%	1,808,000	100.0%

(*Source:* U.S. Bureau of the Census, 1982.)

in the numbers and proportion of unmarried couples is related to the growing social acceptance of the arrangement. Another factor has been the sustained increase in the average age at first marriage.

Although the media often label cohabiters "unmarried marrieds" and their relationships "trial marriages," the couples typically do not see themselves this way. College students commonly define cohabitation as part of the courtship process, rather than as a long-term alternative to marriage. One study of students in the Boston area found cohabiting couples to be no less likely to marry, and no more likely to break up, than noncohabiting students who were "going together" (Risman et al., 1981). Although about a fourth to a third of students at major universities had cohabiting experiences in the mid-1970s (Macklin, 1974, 1978), the pattern may be reversing itself in the 1980s. Many college students look on cohabitation as a restricting and demanding life style. At the same time, there has been a shift toward more conservative values and stronger religious conviction among students (Pentalla, 1983).

Couples living together but not married are far less liberated about money, sex, and housework than their nontraditional living arrangement might suggest. As with married men, cohabiting men are more likely to be the ones who initiate sexual activity, make most of the spending decisions, and do far less of the housework than do their working women partners (Blumstein and Schwartz, 1983). Cohabiting couples experience many of the same sorts of problems as married couples (Gross, 1977). However, unmarried couples see themselves as less securely anchored than married couples, and accordingly feel more tentative about their ability to endure difficult periods. Perhaps these insecurities contribute to the higher incidence of interpersonal violence among cohabiting couples (Yllo and Straus, 1981).

CHILDLESS MARRIAGES

Some married couples prefer not to have children (and some couples are involuntarily childless due to infertility). Over the past two decades, increasing numbers of couples have come to view childbearing not as an inevitable part of their lives, but as a choice to be made after a rational weighing of pros and cons (Bloom, 1984). Couples cite a variety of reasons for not wanting to have children. Some couples feel they are unsuited to parenthood. Others desire a life style that allows for greater freedom, spontaneity, privacy, and leisure than that permitted by children. And still others say that a career is the primary focus of their lives. Between 1976 and 1982, the proportion of women between the ages of 35 and 39 who had not had children rose from 11 to 14 percent. Of equal significance, there has been a substantial increase in the proportion of young women who are postponing childbirth. Whereas in 1960 24 percent of married women between the ages of 20 and 24 did not have children, by 1982 the figure had reached 43 percent (Hall, 1984). Although many of these women see themselves as simply delaying parenthood, in some cases the delay will mean that they will not have children at all (their marriages will break up, they will encounter fertility problems, or they will become more involved with their careers).

As couples enter their thirties, some of them change their minds and decide that they want children. As a result, the birth rate among women in their early thirties is beginning to increase (Pebley and Bloom, 1982). The delay in childbearing has occurred primarily among urban professional women. Many of these women wanted to complete their educations and establish their careers before beginning a family. They repeatedly deferred having children and then came to see that a deadline was approaching. Further, during the 1980s a renewed family traditionalism set in. And finally, many couples find that the thirties are a more comfortable time to have children, because they have already faced and gone through a good many of their own crises. In some cases, the desire to nurture and be a parent is strong enough to inspire deliberate unwed motherhood (Langway, 1981; Peterson, 1984).

SINGLE PARENTHOOD

If current trends continue, about half of all children born in the 1980s will live in a single-parent household for at least a portion of their childhood. Nearly 13 percent of American families were headed by single parents in 1982 (about 22 percent of all households with children) (see Figure 9.3). Of the 10.3 million single-parent households, 8.2 million were headed by women and 2.1 million by men. About 70 percent of these families originate through divorce or separation. Another 10 percent result from the death of a spouse, and still another 20 percent through the birth of a child to an unmarried woman. In about half of the households, the parent marries or remarries within five years, creating a parent-stepparent arrangement.

As we pointed out in Chapter 6, female-headed households are likely to be low-income households. A basic reason is that marital separation produces a precipitous decline in household income. The reduction of income in single-parent households is met by a proportionate reduction in expenditures for food, housing, and other items, and the drop in living standards persists indefinitely. There is a critical difference between the married poor with children and the single-parent poor: On average the married poor move out of poverty; the single-parent poor do not (Weiss, 1984). Nearly half of families headed by single-parent mothers live below the poverty level, and many are dependent on government agencies for assistance.

Women heading a single-parent family typically experience greater stress than women in two-parent families (McLanahan, 1983). For one thing, their lower incomes are sources of chronic strain. For another, the responsibilities for the family fall entirely on one adult rather than two. Female heads report much lower self-esteem, a

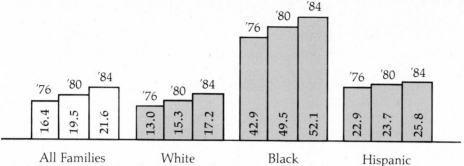

'76 16.4
'80 19.5
'84 21.6
All Families

'76 13.0
'80 15.3
'84 17.2
White

'76 42.9
'80 49.5
'84 52.1
Black

'76 22.9
'80 23.7
'84 25.8
Hispanic

FIGURE 9.3 SINGLE–PARENT FAMILIES AS A PERCENTAGE OF FAMILIES WITH CHILDREN, 1976–1984
(*Source:* U.S. Bureau of the Census.)

lower sense of effectiveness, and less optimism about the future than their counterparts in two-parent settings. Many single-parent mothers complain of a lack of free time, spiraling child care costs, loneliness, and unrelenting pressures associated with the dual demands of home and job.

Single-parent fathers also encounter many of the same problems. Juggling work and child care poses a good deal of difficulty, especially for fathers with preschool youngsters. Many fathers first attempt to have someone come into their homes and care for the children there while they are at work. But the vast majority find that this arrangement does not work out. Many fathers then gravitate toward day care centers and nursery schools where they feel that the staff has a professional commitment to children (Mendes, 1976). Once the children start elementary school, fathers usually allow them to stay alone after school. Many single fathers report that their greatest difficulty in making the transition to single parenthood is losing their wife's help and companionship; they say that it is more difficult for them to become single than to become a single parent (Smith and Smith, 1981).

Many families headed by single parents survive their hardships with few ill effects—some even blossom as a result of the spirit of cooperation brought by their difficulties. However, a disturbing number of children and their parents are saddled with problems. Some studies show that juvenile delinquency is twice as likely to occur in a single-parent home as in a two-parent home. Lack of parental supervision and persistent social and psychological strains are usually complicated by problems of poverty (Mann, 1983). Moreover, children living in single-parent families are much more likely to be enrolled below the grade that is modal for their age than children living with both parents (Bianchi, 1984). In sum, single parents are in need of a variety of services not currently available in most communities. These services include day care facilities that are affordable and convenient to home or work, various forms of counseling, child care enrichment, after school programs, and parent education (Turner and Smith, 1983).

GAY COUPLES

Few people within the history of Western society have been more scorned, feared, and stigmatized than gays. However, in recent years straight Americans have shown a greater willingness to accord homosexuals and lesbians the same rights and protections they accord other Americans. Even so, there has been little change between 1973 and 1982 in polling results that show about 70 percent of the public saying homosexual relations are "always wrong" (Schneider and Lewis, 1984). Further, by a five to one margin, the public thinks gays are less likely than straights to lead happy, well-adjusted lives. Although gays have won some important victories in their drive to prohibit discrimination on the basis of sexual orientation, discharges from the military for homosexuality have continued, doubling from 875 in 1974 to 1,796 in 1983 (Benedetto, 1984). Thus, while homosexuals and lesbians have made gains on some fronts, they as yet do not enjoy the freedom to practice a gay life style openly in all spheres of American life.

Homosexuality is a preference for an individual of the *same sex* as a sexual partner. The Alfred C. Kinsey Institute for Sex Research estimates that 5 to 6 percent of the adult population is predominantly homosexual. However, since there are so many gradations in sexual behavior and preferences, many sociologists and psychologists take the view that there are heterosexual or homosexual *practices*, but not homosexual *individuals* (Bell, Weinberg, and Hammersmith, 1981). Further, gays are a varied group (Bell and Weinberg, 1978). They are found in all occupational fields, political persuasions, religious faiths, and racial and ethnic groups. Some are married, have children, and lead lives that in most respects are indistinguishable from those of the larger population. Others enter homosexual unions that are relatively durable. Still others engage in casual sex with a good many partners.

Reseachers at the Kinsey Institute (Bell and Weinberg, 1978:216) have concluded that "homosexual adults who have come to terms with their homosexuality, who do not regret their sexual orientation, and who can function effectively sexually and socially, are no more distressed psychologically than are heterosexual men and women." Their

research shows that lesbians tend to form more lasting ties than do male homosexuals. However, whereas lesbian and heterosexual couples place considerable emphasis on fidelity, male homosexual couples tolerate outside sexual relations quite well (Blumstein and Schwartz, 1983). About 90 percent of homosexual men with established partners engage in sexual relations with other men. On the whole, the men define fidelity not in terms of sexual behavior, but in terms of each individual's commitment to the other. Homosexual men are more likely to break up over money issues and other incompatibilities than over sexual faithfulness. They tend to sort household duties out according to each person's skills and preferences and only rarely on the basis of stereotyped roles of "husband" and "wife."

COMMUNES

Communes are groups or communities that people intentionally form in order to establish familylike relationships among unrelated individuals. The idea of communal living dates back into antiquity. And such communities have had a long history in American life, including such groups as the Shakers, Fourierists, Zoarites, Spiritualists, Hutterites, the Amana Community, and the Oneida Community. Communal living underwent a revival in the late 1960s and early 1970s when some two to three thousand communes were formed in the United States. Not uncommonly, communes spring up during periods when people feel traditional institutions are disintegrating and long for a meaningful new order (Zablocki, 1980).

Communes vary greatly. There are those that assume an anarchistic form and stress warmth, intimacy, and involvement, have few or no formal rules, demand no long-term commitment, provide a vague philosophical foundation, are open to all comers, and have a weak financial base. At the opposite extreme, there are those that are rigorously structured and set stringent entrance requirements, enforce a strict normative code, demand a firm philosophical commitment, and foster economic survival through communal financial enterprises. Some communes, such as the nineteenth-century Shakers, have insisted on celibacy; others have practiced monogamy; and still others have encouraged unrestricted sexual promiscuity. Although historically most communes were founded in rural settings, many modern communes have taken the form of collective households in urban areas where the members have renovated old mansions or brick two-flats (Cornfield, 1983).

Sociologist Rosabeth Moss Kanter (1973) finds that many people are attracted to communal households in response to crises in their lives. It is not surprising, then, that communes tend to be rather fragile undertakings. This is most apparent among anarchistic communes, where relationships are often tentative and easily terminated. Most urban communes have attempted to equalize the status of men and women, but in practice a heritage of sexism has pervaded the households. Further, most communes have problems with members who fail to do their share of the work or carry out their responsibilities. Finally, personality clashes, conflicts of interest, and financial difficulties have doomed many communes (Zablocki, 1980; Cornfield, 1983).

Summary

1. When we set about separating families from nonfamilies, we encounter all sorts of problems. The way in which we define the family is not simply an academic exercise. It determines the kinds of families we will consider to be normal and the kinds we consider to be deviant, and what rights and obligations we will recognize as legally and socially binding. For our purposes in the chapter, we define the family as a group of people the members of a community define as a household unit. Typically these individuals are related by blood, adoption, or marriage, and cooperate economically. Viewed in this fashion, the family is an institution.

2. As we look about the world, and even in our own society, we encounter a good many differences in the ways families are organized. Families vary in composition and in descent, residence, and authority patterns. Social relationships between adult males and females can be organized within families by emphasizing either spouse or kin relationships. In the nuclear family arrangement, spouses and their offspring constitute the core relationship; blood relatives are functionally marginal and peripheral. In the extended family arrangement, kin provide the core relationship; spouses are functionally marginal and peripheral.

3. The fact that the parties to a marriage must be members of two different kin groups has crucial implications for the structuring of the family. The continuity, and therefore the long-term welfare, of any kin group depends on obtaining spouses for the unmarried members of the group from other groups. By the same token, a kin group has a stake in retaining some measure of control over at least a portion of its members after they marry. All societies

regulate the pool of eligibles from which individuals are expected to select a mate. They also structure the relationship between a husband and wife in one of four ways: monogamy, polygyny, polyandry, and group marriage.

4. Functionalist theorists stress that if a society is to survive and operate with some measure of effectiveness, it must guarantee that essential tasks are performed. The performance of these tasks—or functions—cannot be left to chance. Although acknowledging that families show a good deal of variation throughout the world, functionalists identify a number of functions families typically perform: reproduction; socialization; care, protection, and emotional support; assignment of status; and regulation of sexual behavior.

5. Functionalists spotlight the tasks carried out by the family that serve the interests of society as a whole. Conflict theorists have seen the family as a social arrangement benefitting some people more than others. Friedrich Engels viewed the family as a class society in miniature, with one class (men) oppressing another class (women). Randall Collins sees the family as an instrument for maintaining male claims to women as sexual property. Other conflict sociologists say that intimate relationships inevitably involve antagonism as well as love.

6. Societies undertake to regulate the process whereby young people choose a marriage partner. Romantic love is given more emphasis in some societies than in others. Societies "control" love in a variety of ways, including child marriage, social isolation of young people, close supervision of couples, and peer and parental pressures. A variety of factors operate in the selection of a mate: homogamy, physical attractiveness, and complementary needs. Exchange theory provides a unifying link among these factors. It proposes that people involved in a mutually satisfying relationship will exchange behaviors that have low cost and high reward.

7. Most adult Americans hope to establish an intimate relationship with another person and make the relationship work. Despite the considerable change in family patterns in recent decades, American couples remain rather conventional in their marital relationships. Divorce rates have soared, but Americans have not given up on marriage. However, increasing numbers of Americans no longer view marriage as a permanent institution, but rather as something that can be ended and reentered.

8. Nuclear families that are not disrupted by divorce, desertion, or death typically pass through a series of changes and realignments across time, what sociologists call the family life cycle. These changes and realignments are related to the altered expectations and requirements imposed on a husband and wife as children are born and grow up. Each modification in the role content of one family member has implications for all the other members.

9. Increasing numbers of mothers are working. Many social scientists are no longer asking whether it is good or bad that mothers work. Instead, they are finding that a more important issue is whether the mother, regardless of employment, is satisfied in her situation. Two-income couples are also on the increase. Even so, women still continue to shoulder the primary responsibility for household tasks and child care.

10. Mounting evidence suggests that family violence, child abuse, and incest are much more common than most Americans had suspected. These patterns appear to be transmitted through socialization processes from one generation to another. Divorce is also on the upswing in American life. Although it may be more commonplace, it is hardly a routine experience; it exacts a considerable emotional and physical toll from all family members. Most divorced people remarry, and remarriage frequently results in stepfamilies. Despite the significant changes that have occurred in family roles in recent decades, it is grown children who still bear the primary responsibility for their aged parents.

11. By virtue of the rapid expansion of life style options, Americans now enjoy more alternatives in tailoring their relationships to individual choice. A life style is the overall pattern of living people evolve to meet their biological, social, and emotional needs. Among the varying life style options open to Americans are singlehood, unmarried cohabitation, childless marriage, single parenthood, gay relationships, and communes.

Glossary

bilineal Reckoning descent and transmitting property through both the father and the mother.

commune A group or community that people intentionally form in order to establish familylike relationships among unrelated individuals.

complementary needs Two different personality traits that are the counterparts of each other and that provide a sense of completeness when they are joined.

endogamy The requirement that marriage occur within a group.

egalitarian An arrangement in which power and authority is equally distributed between husband and wife.

exchange theory The view which proposes that people involved in a mutually satisfying relationship will exchange behaviors that have low cost and high reward.

exogamy The requirement that marriage occur outside a group.

extended family A family arrangement in which kin—individuals related by common ancestry—provide the core relationship; spouses are functionally marginal and peripheral.

family A group of people defined by the members of a community as a household unit. Typically, these individuals are related by blood, adoption, or marriage, and cooperate economically.

family life cycle Changes and realignments related to the altered expectations and requirements imposed on a husband and wife as children are born and grow up.

family of orientation A nuclear family that consists of oneself and one's father, mother, and siblings.

family of procreation A nuclear family that consists of oneself and one's spouse and children.

group marriage The marriage of two or more husbands and two or more wives.

homogamy The tendency of like to marry like.

homosexuality A preference for an individual of the same sex as a sexual partner.

incest taboos Rules that prohibit sexual intercourse with close blood relatives.

life style The overall pattern of living that people evolve to meet their biological, social, and emotional needs.

marriage A socially approved sexual union between two or more individuals that is undertaken with some idea of permanence.

matching hypothesis The notion that we typically experience the greatest payoff and the least cost when we select partners who have a degree of physical attractiveness similar to our own.

matriarchy The vesting of power in the family in women.

matrilineal Reckoning descent and inheritance through the mother's side of the family.

matrilocal A bride and groom live in the household or community of the wife's family.

monogamy The marriage of one husband and one wife.

neolocal Newlyweds set up a new place of residence independent of either of their parents or other relatives.

norm of legitimacy The rule that children not be born out of wedlock.

nuclear family A family arrangement in which the spouses and their offspring constitute the core relationship; blood relatives are functionally marginal and peripheral.

patriarchy The vesting of power in the family in men.

patrilineal Reckoning descent and inheritance through the father's side of the family.

patrilocal A bride and groom live in the household or community of the husband's family.

polyandry The marriage of two or more husbands and one wife.

polygyny the marriage of one husband and two or more wives.

romantic love The strong physical and emotional attraction between a man and a woman.

10

Religion and Education

RELIGION

Varieties of Religious Behavior
Religious Organizations
The Functionalist Perspective on
  Religion
The Conflict Perspective on Religion
Reaffirming Tradition: The Iranian
  Islamic Revolution
Promoting Secular Change: The
  Protestant Ethic
Adapting Tradition: The
  Fundamentalist Revival
Mainline Religious Groups
State–Church Issues

EDUCATION

The Functionalist Perspective on
  Education
The Conflict Perspective on
  Education
The Bureaucratic Structure of
  Schools
The Effectiveness of the Schools
The Availability of Education

Institutions are a central component of social structure (see Chapter 2). They are strategic instruments through which human life is patterned, stabilized, and made predictable. Because of institutions, we feel there is an appreciable element of regularity, efficiency, and certainty in our daily activities. Indeed, we organize our relationships with other people and carry out the essential tasks of group life within the context of institutions. So there is a vital link between a society's institutional arrangements and the private experiences of its members.

In Chapter 8 we considered the political and economic institutions and in Chapter 9 the family institution. In this chapter we turn our attention to the religious and educational institutions. Each of these institutions is focused on the solution to a set of problems encountered in social living (see Chapter 2). The units comprising institutions, churches within the broader religious institution and schools within the educational institution, have evolved to meet basic social needs. As we will see in the pages that follow, the tasks performed by the two institutions differ. Even so, the functions performed by the religious and educational institutions converge in many contemporary societies, fostering a standardized culture that is essential for the creation and operation of large-scale organizations (see Chapter 4). Moreover, they shape the cultural fabric within which individuals fashion their ideological and political allegiances. And they often serve as the seedbeds of new ideas and organizational arrangements (Collins, 1981). In sum, the religious and educational institutions play a vital part in keeping society going.

Religion

Religion has to do with those socially shared ways of thinking, feeling, and acting that have as their focus the realm of the supernatural or "beyond." As Emile Durkheim (1912/1965) points out, religion is centered in beliefs and practices that are related to *sacred* as opposed to *profane* things. The **sacred** involves those aspects of social reality that are set apart and forbidden. The **profane** has to do with those aspects of social reality that are everyday and commonplace. The sacred, then, is extraordinary, mysterious, awe-inspiring, and even potentially dangerous—it "sticks out" from normal, routine life (Berger, 1967). The same object or behavior can be profane or sacred depending on how people define it. A wafer made of flour when seen as bread is a profane object, but it becomes sacred to Catholics as the body of Christ when it is consecrated in communion. Because the sacred is caught up with strong feelings of reverence and awe, it can usually be approached only through **rituals**—social acts prescribed by rules that dictate how human beings should comport themselves in the presence of the sacred. In their religious behavior, human beings fashion a social world of meanings and rules that govern what they think, feel, and act in much the same way that they do in other realms of life.

VARIETIES OF RELIGIOUS BEHAVIOR

Religious behavior is so varied that we have difficulty thinking about it unless we use some classificatory means for sorting it into relevant categories. Although no categories do justice to the diversity and richness of the human religious experience, sociologist Reece McGee (1975) provides us with one scheme that is both insightful and manageable: simple supernaturalism, animism, theism, and a system of abstract ideals.

Simple supernaturalism is prevalent in preindustrial societies. It entails the notion of **mana,** a diffuse, impersonal, supernatural force that exists in nature for good or evil. With mana people do not entreat spirits or gods to intervene on their behalf.

Rather, they compel a superhuman power to behave as they wish by manipulating it mechanically. For instance, the act of carrying a rabbit's foot is thought to bring the bearer good luck; the capacity to bring good luck is as much an attribute of the rabbit's foot as is its color or weight. One need not talk to the rabbit's foot or offer it gifts, but only carry it. Similarly, the act of uttering the words "Open Sesame" serves to manipulate impersonal supernatural power. Many athletes use lucky charms, elaborate routines, and superstitious rituals to ward off injury and bad luck in activities based on uncertainty (Zimmer, 1984). Mana is usually employed to reach "here-and-now" goals—control of the weather, assurance of a good crop, cure of an illness, good performance on a test, success in love, or victory in battle. It functions much like an old-fashioned book of recipes or a home medical manual.

Animism involves a belief in spirits or otherworldly beings. People have seen spirits throughout nature—in animals, plants, rocks, stars, rivers, and at times in other individuals. Since spirits are personified and are believed to act on the basis of associated motives and emotions, individuals customarily employ techniques in dealing with them similar to those they employ in their human relationships. Love, punishment, reverence, and gifts have all been used to deal with superhuman spirits. And cajolery, bribery, and false pretenses may be seen as effective as awe. Additionally, in animism, as with mana, supernatural power is often harnessed through rituals that compel a spirit to act in a desired way.

In **theism** religion is centered in a belief in gods who are thought to be powerful, to have an interest in human affairs, and to merit worship. Judaism, Christianity, and Islam are forms of **monotheism,** or belief in one god. They all have established religious organizations, religious leaders or priests, traditional rituals, and sacred writings. Ancient Greek religion and Hinduism (prac-

Religion has always influenced people's views of themselves, their relationships, and the world around them. Here, a priest of ancient Rome practices divination by examination of the entrails of a bird. (EKM-Nepenthe)

ticed primarily in India) are forms of **polytheism,** or belief in many gods with equal or relatively similar power. Hindu gods are often tribal, village, or caste deities associated with a particular place—a building, field, or mountain—or a certain object—an animal or a tree.

Some religions focus on a set of abstract ideals. Rather than centering on the worship of a god, they are dedicated to achieving moral and spiritual excellence. Many of the religions of Asia are of this type, including Taoism, Confucianism, and Buddhism. Buddhism is directed toward reaching an elevated state of consciousness, a method of purification that provides a release from suffering, ignorance, and selfishness. In the Western world, humanism is based on eth-

ical principles. Its adherents discard all theological beliefs about God, heaven, hell,
and immortality, and substitute for God the
pursuit of good in the here and now.
Heaven is seen as the ideal society on earth
and hell as a world in which war, disease,
and ignorance flourish. The soul is the human personality, and immortality is deeds
that live on after death for good or evil in
the lives of other people.

RELIGIOUS ORGANIZATIONS

Norms, beliefs, and rituals provide the cultural fabric of religion. But there is more to
the religious institution than its cultural heritage. As with other institutions, there is
also the structural mosaic of social organization whereby people are bound together
within networks of relatively stable relationships. We need to examine not only the
religious customs of a people, but the ways
in which people organize their religious life.

Sociologists distinguish among four
ideal types of religious organization:
churches, denominations, sects, and cults
(Niebuhr, 1929; Troeltsch, 1931; Pope, 1942;
Johnstone, 1975; Wallis, 1975). Whereas
churches and denominations typically exist
in accommodation with the larger society,
sects and cults often find themselves at
odds with established social arrangements
and practices. Cults differ from sects in that
cults are viewed by their members as being
pluralistically legitimate, providing one
among many alternative paths to truth or
salvation. In this respect, cults resemble denominations. In contrast, the sect, like the
church, defines itself as being uniquely legitimate and possessing exclusive access to
truth or salvation. This model is depicted in
Figure 10.1.

The Church. The **church** is a religious organization that considers itself uniquely legitimate and typically enjoys a positive re-

	Positive relationship with society	Negative relationship with society
Claims lone legitimacy	CHURCH	SECT
Accepts pluralistic legitimacy	DENOMI-NATION	CULT

FIGURE 10.1   TYPES OF RELIGIOUS OR-
GANIZATION
(*Source:* Adapted from Roy Wallis, *Sectarianism:
Analyses of Religious and Non-Religious Sects.*
New York: Wiley, 1975, p. 41. Reprinted by per-
mission of Peter Owen Ltd.)

lationship with the dominant society. It
usually operates with a bureaucratic structure and claims to include most of the members of a society. In fact, members are *born
into* the church if their parents are affiliated
with it; they do not have to *join* the church.
The aim of the church is professedly universal. Its message is *Extra ecclesiam nulla
salus*—"Outside the church there is no salvation." Its response to competing groups
is to suppress, ignore, or coopt them (see
Table 10.1).

The church typically makes its peace with
the secular aspects of social life. It tends to
be a conservative body and allies itself with
the advantaged classes. For the most part,
it does not champion new causes or social
reform but accepts the dominant goals and
values of society. It also frequently looks
back to an earlier way of life. When groups
within the church attempt to give it new
directions, church officials frequently attempt to block the changes. A good illustration of this is the opposition of Vatican leaders to the theology of liberation that has
gained strength in Latin America. The theology of liberation is a body of teachings
that draws on Marxist analysis in emphasizing the special commitment of Roman Cath-

TABLE 10.1
Church–Sect Differences

Characteristic	Church	Sect
Size	Moderate to large	Small
Church property	Extensive	Little
Religious Services	Limited degree of congregational participation	High degree of congregational participation
Emphasis	On religious education and transmission of religion to the children of members	On evangelism and adult members
Clergy	Specialized; professional; full-time	Unspecialized; little formal training; part-time
Doctrines	Literal interpretation of Scriptures; emphasis on worldly concerns	Literal intepretation of Scriptures; emphasis upon other worldly concerns
Social class of members	Mainly advantaged classes	Mainly disadvantaged classes
Relationship with other religious groups	Disdain or pity for all sects	Suspicion of rival sects
Relationship with secular world	Affirms prevailing culture and social arrangements	Renounces or opposes prevailing cultural standards and social arrangements
Hymns	Stately music coming out of more remote liturgical tradition	Resemble contemporary folk music
Sources of membership	Born into the faith; seeks universal membership	Join the group; voluntary, confessional bases of membership

(*Source:* Adapted from Liston Pope. 1942. *Millhands & Preachers: A Study of Gastonia.* New Haven, Conn.: Yale University Press.)

olics to the poor. The Vatican has condemned the theology of liberation advanced by the Brazilian Franciscan friar Leonardo Boff as endangering "the healthy doctrine of the faith" and leading to "the destruction of the authentic sense of the sacraments and the word of faith" (Dionne, 1985).

The church attaches considerable importance to the means of grace that it administers, to a system of doctrine that it has formulated, and to the administration of rituals that it controls through an official clergy. It strives to dominate all aspects of social life—to teach and guide the members of society and dispense saving grace. The church type is exemplified by the Roman Catholic Church of thirteenth-century Europe and the Theravada Buddhism of feudal Southeast Asia. Vestiges of the church arrangement are found in contemporary nations with mandated "official" religions, including the Islamic Shiites of Iran; the Catholic Church of Italy, Monaco, and Spain; the Lutherans of Denmark, Iceland, Norway, and Sweden; the Hindus of Nepal; the Jews of Israel; the Buddhists of Burma;

the Greek Orthodox Church of Greece; and the Church of England.

The Sect. The **sect** is a religious organization that considers itself uniquely legitimate, but is at odds with the dominant society. It usually consists of a small, voluntary fellowship of converts, most of whom are drawn from disadvantaged groups. The sect does not attempt to win the world over to its doctrines, but instead practices exclusiveness; it follows literally the phrase, "Come out from among them and be ye separate." It is often founded by individuals who break away from a church and claim that they represent the true, cleansed version of the faith from which they split (Stark and Bainbridge, 1979). Members who entertain heretical opinions or engage in immoral behavior are subject to expulsion. Occasionally group pressures can be so powerful—as in the case of Rev. Jim Jones and the People's Temple in Guyana—that even suicide may not be an individual option, but a group requirement. The sect thinks of itself as an elect—a religious elite. Sect members believe that other religious interpretations are in error, and they portray the larger society as decadent and evil (see Table 10.1). It is often a form of social dissent, exemplified by the Anabaptists of Reformation times, and the Mormons, Shakers, and Quakers of the eighteenth and nineteenth centuries. Some new religions such as the Children of God and the Rev. Sun Myung Moon's Unification Church are also sectlike.

The experience of the Northeast Community Church of Island Pond, Vermont, highlights the tensions that often develop between a sect and the larger community (Butterfield, 1984; Clendinen, 1984). Complaints by townspeople led the Vermont state police in 1984 to round up 112 children of sect believers and detain them for three days to check for reported signs of abuse

and neglect. The children were released after a district judge denied the state's request for temporary detention orders. Members of the sect, who number about 300, live in a group of communally run houses on the northern side of Island Pond, an isolated community near the Canadian border. Townspeople say that sect members beat their children, but the sect holds that "the infliction of pain upon a child's rear end with the use of a reedlike rod is not child abuse, but rather their salvation." The sect is reportedly run by a small group of elders. Its members say they are establishing "a Kingdom of God on earth" and depict the rest of the world as "the Kingdom of Satan." Members work in communally run businesses, including a deli, a used clothing store, and a construction and plumbing cooperative.

Most sects are small, and many of them fail to grow larger. Their high state of tension with the larger society serves to cut them off from potential recruits (Stark and Bainbridge, 1981). Should they survive and gain adherents, they tend to become more churchlike. A number of factors seems to be at work (Niebuhr, 1929). For one thing, the problem of training the children of the original members almost inevitably causes some compromise to be made in the rigid requirements for membership evolved in the sect's early years. The Presbyterians, for instance, inaugurated the Half-Way Covenant so that children whose "calling and election" was not yet sure could be held within the fold. For another, as a sect gains adherents and the promise of success, it begins to reach out toward greater influence within the society. In the process it gradually accommodates itself to the larger culture it is attempting to conquer, and attracts an increasing number of persons who enjoy social and economic privileges. Finally, the nature of the religious impulse renders it difficult to sustain. Fervor begins to be replaced with reasoned faith and bureaucratic structures.

The Denomination. The **denomination** accepts the legitimacy claims of other religions and enjoys a positive relationship with the dominant society. In many cases it is a sect in an advanced stage of development and adjustment to the secular world. The membership of the denomination comes largely from the middle class. The moral rigor and religious fervor of the sect are relaxed. It usually has an established clergy who have undergone specialized training to prepare for their positions at a theological seminary. Although conversions provide one source for new members, most individuals are born into the group. Accordingly, church officials are particularly concerned with developing a training program to prepare the children of members to become adult adherents of their faith.

Members often define church-going as one of the duties of upstanding members of the community and as an integral part of involvement in the "okay world." The denomination is content to be one organization among many, all of which are deemed acceptable in the sight of God. Examples of denominations include most of the major religious groups in the United States: Presbyterians, Baptists, Congregationalists, Methodists, Unitarians, Lutherans, Episcopalians, Roman Catholics, and Reformed and Conservative Jews.

The Cult. The **cult** accepts the legitimacy of other religious groups, but finds itself at odds with the dominant society. Like the denomination, the cult does not lay claim to *the* truth, but unlike the denomination it tends to be critical of society. The cult does not require its members to pass strict doctrinal tests, but instead invites all to join its ranks. It usually lacks the tight discipline of sects whose rank-and-file members attempt

to hold one another "up to the mark." And unlike the sect, it usually lacks prior ties with an established religion, constituting instead a new and independent religious tradition (Stark and Bainbridge, 1979). The cult frequently focuses on the problems of its members, especially those who are confronted with loneliness, fear, inferiority, tension, and similar problems. Some cults are built about a single function, such as spiritual healing or spiritualism. Others, like various New Thought cults, seek to combine elements of conventional religion with ideas and practices that are essentially nonreligious. Still others direct their attention toward the pursuit of self-awareness, self-realization, wisdom, or insight, such as Vedanta, Soto Zen, the Human Potential Movement, and Transcendental Meditation.

THE FUNCTIONALIST PERSPECTIVE ON RELIGION

Functionalist theorists look to the contributions religion makes to society's survival. They reason that if every known society seems to have something called religion, its presence cannot be dismissed as a social accident (Davis, 1951). If religion were not adaptive, societies would long since have evolved without it. Accordingly, they ask what functions are performed by religion in social life.

Durkheim: Religion as a Societal Glue. In *The Elementary Forms of Religious Life* (1912/ 1965), the last of his major works, Emile Durkheim brought his concern with group forces to an analysis of the functions of religion. He selected for his study the Arunta, an Australian aboriginal people. The Arunta practice **totemism**, a religious system in which a clan (a kin group) takes the name of, claims descent from, and attributes sacred properties to a plant or animal. Durkheim says that the totem plant or animal is not the source of totemism, but a stand-in for the real source, society itself. He contends that religion—the totem ancestor, God, or some other supernatural force—is the symbolization of society. By means of religious rituals, the group in effect worships itself. Society harnesses the awesome force inherent in people's perception of the sacred for animating a sense of oneness and moral authority. The primary functions of religion are the creation, reinforcement, and maintenance of social solidarity and social control. (See box.)

Durkheim observes that if we are left to ourselves, our individual consciousness—our inner mental states—are closed to one another. Our separate minds cannot come in contact and communicate except by "coming out of themselves." Consequently, social life dictates that the internal be made external—the intangible, tangible. Our inner consciousness is transformed into a *collective* consciousness through the symbolic device of religious rituals. By uttering the same cry, pronouncing the same word, or performing the same gesture, we inform one another that we are united in a shared state of mind. Simultaneously, we mentally fuse ourselves within a social whole. We generate a sort of electricity or collective euphoria that lifts us to an intense state of exaltation which overrides our individual beings. Religious rituals thus operate in two ways: First, they provide vehicles by which we *reveal* to one another that we share a common mental state; second, they *create* among us a shared consciousness that contributes to a social bonding.

Durkheim emphasizes the similarity in our attitudes toward society and toward God. Society inspires the sensation of divinity in the minds of its members because of its power over them. Moreover, society, like God, possesses moral authority and can inspire self-sacrifice and devotion. And finally, religion is capable of endowing in-

dividuals with exceptional powers and motivation. Accordingly, Durkheim says that the religious person is not the victim of an illusion. Behind the symbol—religion—there is a real force and reality: society. Durkheim concludes that when religion is imperiled and not replaced by a satisfying substitute, society itself is jeopardized: Individuals pursue their private interests without regard for the dictates of the larger social enterprise.

Additional Functions. Durkheim draws our attention to how religion functions as a "societal glue" that contributes to social cohesion and solidarity by integrating and unifying the members of a community. Moreover, when a society links its morality to religion, social control may be furthered. The enforcement of norms is greatly enhanced if recourse can be had to priests, the unknown, the divine, idealism, and supernatural agents.

Sociologists have shown that religion may perform other functions as well. For one thing, it helps people in dealing with life's "breaking points" (Ebaugh, Richman, and Chafetz, 1984). Much of the human experience is uncertain and insecure. Humankind is recurrently confronted with crises and haunting perplexities—floods, epidemics, droughts, famines, wars, accidents, sickness, social disorder, personal defeat, humiliation, injustice, the meaning of life, the mystery of death, and the enigma of the hereafter. Religion deals with these ultimate problems of life, provides "answers," and often offers the prospect of hope through magical control or spiritual intercession. Moreover, it assists people in the transitional stages of life. Most religions celebrate and explain the major events of the life cycle—birth, puberty, marriage, and death—through *rites of passage* (ceremonies marking the transition from one status to another).

Religion may also be an impetus to social

Doing Sociology: Intercollegiate Rivalries

Emile Durkheim contended that religious rituals function as an important source for creating reinforcing, and maintaining social solidarity. Observations by students in introductory sociology classes at Ohio State University suggest that intense intercollegiate rivalries serve a similar function, particularly traditional, season-concluding football games such as those between Ohio State and Michigan. The sociology students point out that American colleges and universities recruit students from a great many differing backgrounds and with diverse affiliations, allegiances, interests, and traditions. Given the influx of large numbers of new students each year, how are colleges and universities to instill in the new arrivals a consciousness of oneness and a sense of belonging to a common group? One particularly potent mechanism is a rivalry between the in-group and an out-group, especially an intercollegiate game. Such encounters afford a powerful device for highlighting the boundaries of a group, fostering "we-group" sentiments, and cementing bonds among group members. Thus traditional games provide occasions for the members of a college community to engage in a variety of activities that have symbolic significance in promoting their collective consciousness.

Durkheim pointed to the part that a totem ancestor played among the Arunta in symbolizing their society. The college mascot performs a somewhat similar function for the college community—the Badger, the Gopher, the Tiger, the Wolverine, the Trojan, and so on. The "totem" of Ohio State University is Brutus Buckeye. The significance of this symbol was highlighted before a recent Ohio State–Michigan football game, when the "head" of Brutus Buckeye was stolen. The thief demanded a ransom for its return, and the story quickly became the focus of local media attention. Ohio State football fans felt an emptiness and loss—a sense that the absence of Brutus Buckeye at the game would create a void and perhaps even mystically result in "bad luck" for the team. Although the thief was never apprehended, the head was found in a dumpster before game time and the finder received a reward of $2,000.

The Arunta inhabit a semidesert region in central Australia. They are a hunting-and-gathering people who range over a vast area in small bands of two or three families each. Their religious ceremonies provide occasions when the nearly 2,000 members get together and renew their societal ties. In a somewhat similar fashion, big games like that between Ohio State and Michigan afford occasions when alumni and longtime Ohio State supporters assemble to reestablish and heighten their sense of oneness and to reaffirm their allegiance to the university (including their willingness to render financial support).

The Arunta engage in elaborate ceremonials in which members dress in ritual garments, dance, and recall myths telling of the heroic deeds of their totemic ancestors. Again, sociology students note many parallels with the Ohio State–Michigan game. The football players, cheerleaders, and band members outfit themselves in distinctive uniforms, and fans wear the unique scarlet and gray colors of Ohio State. Radio and television stations carry special programs recalling previous Ohio State–Michigan games, presenting gridiron stars of earlier years, and interviewing current players and coaches. Campus-area stores display Ohio State slogans, souvenirs, and memorabilia. Students and alumni attend a gigantic pep rally the evening before the game. At game time the university band plays rousing songs such as the "Buckeye Battle Cry" and "Carmen Ohio" to fire the enthusiasm of the crowd. Cheerleaders and Brutus Buckeye orchestrate chants that build collective excitement. On the field, the football players become the symbolic embodiment—a tangible expression—of the university and its community. What is otherwise rather ill-defined and indistinct—a gigantic university with over 50,000 students, thousands of faculty and staff, and countless alumni—becomes in the course of a Saturday football afternoon a living and profoundly meaningful social reality—indeed, a distinctive social entity.

Bishop Desmond Tutu, who received the Nobel Peace Prize in 1984, has been a leading figure in the movement against apartheid in South Africa. Apartheid is the white government's offical policy of racial separation. Bishop Tutu insists that apartheid must be dismantled, not just reformed, arguing that "You can't improve something that is intrinsically evil." (Pam Hasegawa/Taurus Photos)

change. For instance, black churches have historically made a significant contribution to the mobilization of protest, as was evident in the civil rights movements of the 1950s and 1960s. The black ministers of Montgomery, Alabama, organized a bus boycott in 1955 and 1956 that was instrumental in bringing about the desegregation of the city's buses after Mrs. Rosa Parks was arrested for violating a local bus segregation ordinance. And the Southern Christian Leadership Conference (SCLC), led by the Rev. Martin Luther King, Jr., and other black ministers, was at the forefront of the black protest movement of the 1960s. In recent years Roman Catholic bishops in the United States have also been major propo-

nents of social change. In a pastoral letter in 1983 they said that nuclear war is a morally unacceptable means of resolving differences and that "the intentional killing of innocent civilians is always wrong." And in 1984 they called for a program of economic justice and urged Americans to reexamine the nation's economic priorities in light of the Church's "preferential option for the poor."

Functional Equivalents. We frequently overlook the religious overtones in behavior otherwise thought to be nonreligious and even antireligious. The search for a doctrine that reveals the meaning of existence and answers fundamental questions may lead one person to God and another to "the party," nationalism, science, or sport. It is a mistake to disregard the differences these choices indicate, but it is equally a mistake to overlook the similar functions they often perform.

Communist movements share a variety of elements with many Christian groups. Communism provides a philosophical world view; a promise of a messianic era in a Communist utopia; an explicit program for personal conduct; a priesthood of Party theologians and officials; saints and martyrs of the "cause"; annual rites of renewal such as May Day parades; Party missionaries; revered texts such as the *Communist Manifesto* and *Capital*; heresies; inquisitions; sacred shrines like Lenin's tomb in Moscow's Red Square; and iconic statues of Marx, Lenin, Mao, and other "prophets." Novelist Arthur Koestler (1949:23) describes his "conversion" to communism (which he later recanted) in terms reminiscent of converts to religious sects:

By the time I had finished with Feuerbach and State and Revolution [books by Marx and Lenin], something had clicked in my brain which shook me like a mental explosion. To say that one had "seen the light" is a poor description of the mental rapture which only the convert knows (regardless of what faith he has been converted to). The new light seems to pour from all directions across the skull; the whole universe falls into pattern like the stray pieces of a jigsaw puzzle assembled by magic at one stroke. There is now an answer to every question, doubts and conflicts are a matter of the tortured past—a past already remote, when one had lived in dismal ignorance in the tasteless, colorless world of those who don't know.

Contemporary nationalism has also taken on many religious qualities (Schuman, 1933:287–288):

The cult of nationalism has its high priests, its rituals, and its theology no less than other cults. . . . The patriot has learned reverence for the land of his ancestors—for merrie England, America the beautiful, la Patrie, *or* das Vaterland. *This involves both ancestor worship and territorial fetishism. . . . Living political leaders are judged by the degree to which they appear to come up to or fall short of the traditional standards set by the departed figures of national myths and legend. Similarly, the patriot worships the land of his nation—the hallowed soil, watered by the blood of heroes. . . . The national flag is everywhere a peculiarly sacred symbol, always to be respected and never to be defiled.*

In sum, nationalism has assumed the properties of a political religion.

For some, science has come to be the source of meaning in life, serving for them as a sort of secular religion. Similarly, sport in America, for a good many athletes and spectators, is like a religion (Vance, 1984). Some runners, wrestlers, and other athletes describe their sport experiences as a profound communion and oneness with nature that propels them out of ordinary space and time. Athletes and sportswriters often employ words in talking and writing about sport that are traditionally associated with religion, including "faith," "dedication," "sacrifice," "ritual," "commitment," "spirit," and "peace." But although communism, nationalism, science, and sport function somewhat like religions, they are not religions in the sense that Christianity or Judaism are religions.

THE CONFLICT PERSPECTIVE ON RELIGION

From the writings of functionalist theorists we gain a view of religion as a vital source for social integration and solidarity. We derive a quite different image from conflict theorists. Some of them depict religion as a weapon in the service of ruling elites who use it to hold in check the explosive tensions produced by social inequality and injustice. Others see religion as a source of social conflict and point to the religious wars of the Middle Ages and to present-day religious strife in the Middle East, India, and Ireland. Still others see religion as a source of social change.

Marx: Religion as the Opium of the People. The stimulus for many of the contributions made by conflict theorists comes from the work of Karl Marx. Marx (1844/1963:43–44) portrayed religion as a painkiller for the frustration, deprivation, and subjugation experienced by oppressed peoples. He said it soothes their distress, but any relief it may provide is illusory because religion is a social narcotic:

Religious suffering is at the same time an expression of real suffering and a protest against real suffering. Religion is the sigh of the oppressed creature, the sentiment of a heartless world, and the soul of soulless conditions. It is the opium of the people.

Marx saw religion as producing an otherworldly focus that diverts the oppressed from seeking social change in this world. It leads people to project their needs and desires into the realm of make-believe and obscures the real source of social misery and class conflict. More particularly, religion engenders a false consciousness among the working class that interferes with its attainment of true class consciousness. A Marxist reading of English history suggests that the development of Methodism in nineteenth-century England prevented revolution by redirecting workers' discontent and fevor into a religious movement (McGuire, 1981). And the Russian revolutionary Leon Trotsky was so aware of the similarity of revolutionary Marxism to religious sectarianism that in the late 1890s he successfully recruited the first working-class members of the South Russian Workers' Union among adherents of religious sects.

Marx viewed religion as an expression of human alienation. People shape social institutions with the expectation that they will serve their needs, but find instead that they themselves become the servants of the institutions they have created. Social institutions, rather than providing for the wants and enriching the lives of the entire community, are taken over by the ruling class and used to oppress and victimize people. Thus people fashion Gods, lose their knowledge that they have done so, and then find themselves having to live their lives at the behest of these same Gods. As with the economic, family, and legal institutions, people no longer see themselves as the authors of their own products, but as part of an encompassing natural order that dominates and directs them. Hence, in much the manner that they are alienated from their labor (see Chapter 8), the members of the working class are alienated from the larger social environment: "The more powerful becomes the world of objects which they create . . . , the poorer they become in their inner lives, and the less they belong to themselves. It is just the same as in religion. The more of themselves humankind attributes to God, the less they have in themselves" (Marx, 1844/1963:122).

Any number of sociologists have agreed with Marx that there is an inherently conservative aspect to religion (Yinger, 1957; Glock, Ringer, and Babbie, 1967). The sense of the sacred links a person's present experience with meanings derived from the group's traditional past. Religious beliefs and practices provide taken-for-granted truths that are powerful forces militating against new ways of thinking and behaving. Practices handed down from previous generations, including institutional inequalities and inequities, become defined as God-approved ways and highly resistant to change. For instance, American slavery was justified as part of God's "natural order." In 1863, the Presbyterian church, South, met in General Synod and passed a resolution declaring slavery to be a divine institution, ordained by God. More recently segregation was justified on similar grounds. Said Louisiana State Senator W. M. Rainach in defending segregation in 1954: "Segregation is a natural order—created by God, in His wisdom, who made black men black and white men white" (*Southern School News*, 1954:3). Likewise, the Hindu religion threatens believers who fail to obey caste rules with reincarnation (rebirth) at a lower caste level or as an animal.

Religion may also legitimate changes favoring powerful and wealthy groups. Imperialism has often been supported by religious or quasi-religious motivations and beliefs. In the 1890s President William McKinley explained his decision to wage the expansionist war against Spain and seize Cuba and the Philippines as follows (quoted by McGuire, 1981:188):

I am not ashamed to tell you, gentlemen, that I went down on my knees and prayed Almighty

*God for light and guidance more than one
night. And one night late it came to me this
way. . . . There was nothing left for us to do
but to take them all and to educate the Filipinos
and uplift and civilize and Christianize them
and by God's grace do the very best we could
by them, as our fellow men for whom Christ
also died.*

Religion, then, can be a potent force in the
service of the established order. Religious
organizations themselves are frequently
motivated to legitimate the status quo because they also have vested interests to protect, including power, land, and wealth
(Collins, 1981).

Religion and Social Change. A number of
conflict theorists have recently taken a new
look at the relationship between religion
and social change (McGuire, 1981). They see
religion not as a passive response to the
social relations of production, but as an active force shaping the contours of social life.
Thus it can play a critical part in the birth
and consolidation of new social structures
and arrangements. While acknowledging
that some aspects of religion inhibit change,
they point out that others challenge existing
social arrangements and encourage change.
Under some circumstances religion can be
a profoundly revolutionary force that holds
out a vision to people of how things might
or ought to be. So religion is not invariably
a functional or conservative factor in society,
but often one of the chief, and at times the
only, channel for bringing about a social revolution.

Throughout history, religion has provided an unusually effective vehicle for
change because of its ability to unite people
and their social lives. American history has
been no exception. The religious movements associated with the Great Awakening
in the late eighteenth and early nineteenth
centuries were an important impetus to the
abolitionist movement and later to the tem-

perance and prohibition movements. They
also had an impact on the democratization
of the American political system, promoting
popular participation in what was largely
an oligarchy of the economically privi-
ledged. The civil rights and peace movements of recent decades have likewise
drawn strength from religious motivations
and the resources of religious organizations.

Sociologist Peter L. Berger (1979) suggests that in the clash between traditional
and modern social arrangements, religious
sentiments and organizations can be used
in three contrasting ways. First, religion can
be mobilized in opposition to modernization and for the reaffirmation of traditional
authority. This is the route taken by the
Ayatollah Khomeini and his Shiite followers
in Iran. Second, religion can adapt to the
secular world and harness religious motivations for secular purposes. This is the
path taken by John Calvin and his Protestant followers. And third, religion can retain
its fundamental roots while applying them
to contemporary concerns. This is the road
taken by the fundamental revivalist movement in the United States. Let's examine
each of these alternatives in turn.

REAFFIRMING TRADITION: THE IRANIAN ISLAMIC REVOLUTION

In February 1979, Ayatollah Khomeini returned to Iran from exile in Paris and led a
revolution that toppled Shah Mohammed
Riza Pahlevi. The Iranian monarchy was replaced by a theocratic regime rooted in Islamic traditions and anti-Western fervor.
Nine months later, a militant crowd seized
control of the United States Embassy in Teh-
eran and launched 444 days of tension that
appreciably affected the 1980 American
presidential election. In the intervening
years, the new Islamic state has weathered
a power struggle and the purging of many
of the revolution's prominent figures, a
campaign of bombings and assassinations

by internal enemies, severe economic difficulties, and a war with neighboring Iraq (Kifner, 1984).

A number of forces converged to produce the Iranian revolution (Akhavi, 1980; Fischer, 1980). For one thing, the Islamic clergy, or mullahs, found their authority and wealth severely eroded as the shah sought to modernize and secularize the nation. The shah's policies tightened the cohesiveness of the clergy and transformed the mullahs into a revolutionary force. Although weakened, the clergy retained control of the religious institution and used the network provided by mosques as a power base to attack the shah's order and ultimately to bring the state apparatus under clerical domination. The rural migrants who were flooding Iranian cities—the "disinherited," as they were called by anti-shah activists—steadfastedly supported the Islamic clergy. From them, the mullahs recruited and organized the Revolutionary Guards, the paramilitary force that served as the foot soldiers of the revolution. The clergy rallied the Iranian masses against the decadence and degradation they perceived in Iranian life, against Western practices and fashions, and against rampant materialism and modernization. Religion thus became an idiom for political and nationalistic expression.

In the face of intense foreign pressures and destabilizing internal conditions and tensions, the beleaguered masses took refuge in religion. Resentment against persistent Western dominance and the imposition of Western ways fed revolutionary fervor. Young people rediscovered their grandparents' traditions as they sought a religious source for their social and cultural identities. The new power that oil conferred and the West's insatiable dependence on it made defiance seem feasible. The oil boom had also enriched a privileged class, brought accusations that the money had not been spent for the good of the people, and upset traditional economic and social patterns. Complicating matters, the brutality of the shah's secret police alienated Westernized intellectuals, students, civil servants, technical experts, and traditional merchants of the bazaar.

Since the revolution, the mullahs have secured political dominance by filling nearly all the seats in Parliament through their Islamic Republican party. The local mosques have served as the building blocks of power, functioning as an amalgam of political clubhouse, government office, police station, and educational center. A system of Islamic law and justice has superseded secular law and a formal judiciary. A systematic campaign has been undertaken to purge Western ways, alcohol, gambling, prostitution, and pornography from Iranian life. Women must wear head scarves, and those who neglect to do so may be sent to a "reeducation center." The Islamic state employs surveillance and intimidation to impose strict conformity to rules of dress, social conduct, and religious observance. Iranian authorities admit to some 2,000 to 3,000 executions of dissidents, although opposition leaders say the figure is closer to 30,000. Homosexuals, drug dealers, and unfaithful wives also have been targets for the firing squads. On the international scene, the regime deems it to be its religious duty to export revolution until an Islamic empire stretches from the Persian Gulf to the Mediterranean and beyond (Ibrahim, 1984; Iyer, 1984; Smith, 1984).

PROMOTING SECULAR CHANGE: THE PROTESTANT ETHIC

People's orientations to their gods and the supernatural can inhibit secular change and modernization. But their religious beliefs and practices can also promote socioeconomic change. Max Weber (1904, 1916, 1917) studied several world religions in order to discern how a religious **ethic**—the perspective and values engendered by a religious way of thinking—can affect people's behavior. He suggests that there are periods in historical development when circumstances push a society toward a reaffirmation of old ways or toward new ways. At such critical junctures, religion—by supplying sources of individual motivation and defining the relationship of individuals to their society—can be a source of historical breakthrough. While a religious ethic does not mechanically determine social action, it can give it impetus by shaping people's perceptions and definitions of their material and ideal interests.

In *The Protestant Ethic and the Spirit of Capitalism* (1904), Weber turned his sociological eye to one historic breakthrough—the development of capitalism. He sought a link between the rise of the Protestant view of life and the emergence of capitalist social arrangements in Western society. He maintained that the development of capitalism depended upon the creation of a pool of individuals who had the attitudes and values necessary to function as entrepreneurs. Once capitalism is established, it carries on in a self-perpetuating fashion. The critical problem, Weber said, is to uncover the origin of the motivating spirit of capitalism in precapitalist society. He believed that Protestantism, particularly Calvinism, was crucial to, but not the only factor in, the rise of this spirit. Calvinism is based on the teachings of the French theologian and reformer John Calvin (1509–1564) and found expression in a variety of religious movements, including Puritanism, Pietism, and Anabaptism.

Weber noted that Protestantism and modern capitalism appeared on the historical scene at roughly the same time. There were other links as well. First, capitalism initially attained its highest development in Protestant countries, particularly the United States and England, whereas Catholic nations like Spain and Italy lagged behind. Second, in nations with both Protestant and Catholic regions, such as Germany, it seemed to be the Protestant regions that pioneered in capitalist development. And third, Weber marshaled evidence that suggested it was by and large the Protestants, not the Catholics, who became the early capitalist entrepreneurs. Based on these observations, Weber (1904/1958:64) concluded that the **protestant ethic,** particularly as it was embodied in Calvinist doctrine, instilled an "attitude which seeks profit rationally and systematically."

The Calvinist ethos had other elements that fed capitalist motivation, particularly its *doctrine of predestination*. Calvin rejected the idea prevalent in Catholicism of the Middle Ages that a person's status in the afterlife is determined by the way he or she behaves here on earth. Instead, Calvin taught that at birth every soul is predestined for heaven or hell. This notion was especially disquieting, since people did not know whether they were among the saved or the damned. According to Weber, Calvin's followers, in their search for reassurance, came to accept certain earthly signs of **asceticism** as proof of their salvation and genuine faith: hard work, sobriety, thrift, restraint, and the avoidance of fleshly pleasures. As people are wont to do, the Calvinists, preoccupied with their fate, subtly began to cultivate these very behaviors. More important, self-discipline and a willingness to delay gratification are qualities that lead people to amass capital and achieve economic success. Capitalist entrepreneurs could ruthlessly pursue profit and feel that they were fulfilling their Christian obligation. Thus the Calivinist ethos took the spirit of capitalism out of the realm of individual ambition and translated it into an ethical duty.

A good many scholars since Weber have raised serious questions regarding his hypothesis (Tawney, 1926; Robertson, 1933; Samuelsson, 1961; Cohen, 1980). They have looked to other factors in explaining the origins of capitalism, including a surge in commerce during the fifteenth and sixteenth centuries, technological innovations, the influx of capital resources from New World colonies, unrestrained markets, and the availability of a free labor force. Further, sociologist Randall G. Stokes (1975) has shown that the beliefs comprising the Protestant ethic do not necessarily lead people to engage in entrepreneurial activities. Calvinism did not produce capitalist outcomes when it was transplanted by Dutch and French Huguenot settlers (Afrikaners) to South Africa. Although Afrikaner Calvinism was theologically identical to European Calvinism, it had a conservative rather than an innovative economic impact. It is worth noting that *The Protestant Ethic and the Spirit of Capitalism* was one of Weber's earlier works. In lectures given shortly before his death, Weber incorporated many new elements in his analysis of the origins of large-scale capitalism (Collins, 1980). Even so, his early work, although not necessarily accurate in all its particulars, remains a sociological landmark. It demonstrates the impact religion can have on human affairs in producing outcomes that are not necessarily intended or foreseen by its adherents.

ADAPTING TRADITION: THE FUNDAMENTALIST REVIVAL

We have seen that religion may be a conservative force, impeding modernization and reaffirming traditional authority, as in contemporary Iran. It may also be a powerful agent for social change, creating a perception of the world that gives an impetus to innovation and rationalized economic activity, as in the case of Calvinism. Finally, religion may draw upon people's spiritual yearnings and adapt them to modern life. The current fundamentalist revival in the United States represents an attempt to capture the roots of religious inspiration and shape them to the contemporary world.

The 1980s have witnessed a return to religiousness among Americans, what some have dubbed "a spiritual reawakening" (O'Driscoll, 1984; Schumer, 1984; Briggs, 1984c) Gallup polls show 56 percent more Americans saying they were reliant on God in 1984 than was the case five years earlier. "Christian" schools and academies are booming, with an estimated 25,000 such schools in the United States. Bible study and prayer groups are springing up in many settings, from suburban living rooms to corporate boardrooms. Retreat centers run by various religious groups have spurted in recent years. And prayer has increasingly come back in vogue, no longer shunted aside as an outmoded flight of fancy.

Even so, Gallup polls show church memberships still hovering around 70 percent of the nation's population, unchanged since the early 1970s. Attendance is also static— about 40 percent of the American public attends religious services weekly. It appears that many people feel more comfortable expressing their new fervor outside organized religion. Quiet, informal gatherings and discussion groups appear to be a particularly popular mode of religious expression. Unlike the more impassioned swing to "born-again" Christianity in the late 1970s and to Eastern religions in the late 1960s, the current revival is a more sober affair, with tradition back on the agenda as a positive force. The "born-again" movement was marked by outward revivalism and a dramatic conversion, whereas the newer movement emphasizes the inward nurture of the soul and a deepening of faith. Many Americans seem to be searching for a religious rootedness, as opposed to the extreme emphasis on individualism and self that was the focus of much religious interest in the 1970s.

The Campus Religious Revival. Religion has also enjoyed a rebirth on college campuses. The Gallup Organization finds that the number of Americans between the ages of 18 and 29 taking part in religious education more than doubled to 35 percent between 1980 and 1984. And the proportion of college students who say religion is important to them has grown from 39 to 50 percent (Mann, 1984). Students of all major religious faiths—Protestants, Catholics, and Jews—are displaying a renewed interest in spiritual matters, with enrollment in theology courses, involvement in volunteer work, and attendance at campus worship services on the increase. Religious workers report that students seem more concerned with basic values and religious essentials than were students in the 1960s and 1970s.

Students, like their elders, appear to be looking for a quiet, secure religious life that is both humane and compassionate. Many of them have lost confidence in social engineering and are searching for something worth living for. Overall, there is a revived interest in traditional religion and the questions it raises and seeks to answer (Schumer, 1984).

The Electronic Church. Television has become a major vehicle for religious expression in American life. A 1984 survey found that about 13.6 million Americans—6.2 percent of the television audience—regularly watch religious programs. About half of the audience is over 50 years of age. Nearly two-thirds of the viewers are women, and 79 percent are white. To a considerable extent, the audience uses television as a supplement, rather than as a substitute, for attendance at religious services. Although complicated theological issues are rarely de-

Contemporary American college students are displaying a renewed interest in traditional religion and the questions it raises and seeks to answer. Here, college students participate in an outdoor prayer meeting. (Paul Conklin)

bated, political issues are discussed on more than half the programs. In recent years a flurry of new religious-oriented talk shows, soap operas, documentaries, gospel music, and magazine-format programs have been added to the fare of television programming. While preachers like Pat Robertson and Jim Bakker employ a talk-show format, the highest-rated religious programs have a Sunday church style, including those of Robert Schuller, Oral Roberts, Jimmy Lee Swaggart, Rex Humbard, and Jerry Falwell (Doan, 1984).

The practitioners of televangelism have pressed hard to restore "morality" and traditional family values to American life. They see "secular humanism" as the root of contemporary ills—liberal policies that seek to deal with social life "independently of God." They say that nonfundamentalist efforts are empty or futile because there cannot be a rationale for life apart from God. Most fundamentalists see the traditional male-dominated nuclear family as sacrosanct. They equate abortion with murder, define homosexuality as an ungodly perversion, vigorously denounce pornography and smut (including sex education in the public schools), and promote prayer in the nation's classrooms. The fundamentalists are passionate about social and political matters because they believe their positions are totally biblical. Running through their messages is the notion that God has a message and a plan ("Believe in Him; trust in Him.") and that enormous benefit can be derived from taking a positive approach to life. Television allows viewers to "privatize" religious worship, to gain a feeling of immediate and personal help in coping with their troubles, and to enjoy the illusion of a face-to-face relationship with a dynamic religious leader (Hadden and Swann, 1981).

The Christian Right. In 1965, priests, nuns, rabbis, and ministers marched in Selma, Al-

abama, in an effort to secure a national voting rights act. In the decade that followed, many mainstream Protestant denominations, including the Methodists, Episcopalians, Congregationalists, and Presbyterians, made active efforts on behalf of civil rights, peace, and other social issues, usually on the side embraced by political liberals. Many of these religious groups were characterized by a "modern theology"—the attempt to make traditional religious teachings plausible and understandable in the modern world. These developments raised the ire of fundamentalists, and as the nation moved in a more politically conservative direction in the late 1970s, they began to organize around issues of interest to them. Among these groups were the Moral Majority associated with the Rev. Jerry Falwell, Christian Voice, and the Religious Roundtable (Guth, 1983).

Fundamentalists have insisted that discussing public policy and politics without reference to moral principles is wrong. They are skeptical about modern science and technology, and place their faith in the search for spiritual answers, rather than purely technical solutions to modern problems. Among the issues that galvanized fundamentalists for political action have been freedom for Christian schools, prayer and Bible reading in the public schools, a constitutional ban on abortion, tighter restrictions on pornography and homosexuality, free enterprise, anticommunism, and a stronger military (Himmelstein, 1983; Herbers, 1984b). They became deeply involved in partisan support of Ronald Reagan and other conservative candidates in the 1980 and 1984 elections. The Christian Right has relied on up-to-date methods of computerized direct mail solicitation, fundraising, mass media publicity, political organization, and targeted lobbying. Whether fundamentalist political organizations will be as ephemeral as the civil rights movement's Southern

Christian Leadership Conference and the Student Nonviolent Coordinating Committee (SNCC) or whether they will continue as an important force on the national political scene remains to be determined.

MAINLINE RELIGIOUS GROUPS

If religious denominations were basically the same, then it would matter little that Americans are divided among more than a thousand religious groups (see Table 10.2). However, surveys find substantial differences in attitudes and practices among Americans of different denominations (Smith, 1984). Nearly 90 percent of Protestant fundamentalists believe in an afterlife, but among more moderate and liberal Protestant groups the figure slips to 80 percent. About 75 percent of Catholics believe in an afterlife, compared with 46 percent of those with no religious affiliation and 25 percent of Jews. While only 20 percent of Protestant fundamentalists are willing to allow an atheist to make a speech, teach in college, or have a book in a public library, about 40 percent of all Catholics, 54 percent of Episcopalians, 61 percent of Jews, and 72 per-

cent of those with no religious affiliation support all three civil rights for atheists. Similar patterns hold in other spheres as well, with Protestant fundamentalists taking the strictest view toward sin and biblical teachings, and being the least likely to smoke, drink, go to bars, or favor the legalization of marijuana. Overall, Catholics tend to resemble the Protestant center with respect to traditional values, whereas Jews fall toward the liberal pole.

Surveys by the Gallup Organization reveal that about 71 percent of the American population believes there is a Heaven and 53 percent a Hell (Opinion Roundup, 1983). Of those believing in Heaven, 66 percent say they have an excellent to good chance of going there, whereas 34 percent believe they have only a fair to poor chance. Although virtually every home in the United States has at least one Bible, biblical illiteracy is widespread. Less than half of adult Americans can name four or more of the Ten Commandments, and only 12 percent of the public claims to read the Bible daily. Yet Americans consider themselves a religious people, with 86 percent of the population saying that religion is important or

TABLE 10.2

Largest American Christian Denominations, 1982

	Total Members	Share of U.S. Population
Roman Catholic	52,088,774	22.5%
Southern Baptist	13,991,709	6.0
United Methodist	9,457,012*	4.1
Lutheran Church in America	2,925,655	1.3
Mormon	2,864,000	1.2
Episcopal	2,794,139	1.2
Lutheran, Missouri Synod	2,630,823	1.1
American Lutheran	2,346,710	1.0
United Presbyterian	2,342,441	1.0
United Church of Christ	1,716,723	0.9

* Latest Methodist figure is for 1981.
(*Source:* National Council of Churches, 1984.)

fairly important in their lives and about 94 percent indicating that they believe in God (compared with 98 percent in India, 88 percent in Italy, 76 percent in Great Britain, 72 percent in France, and 63 percent in Scandinavia).

Protestants. Protestants comprise about 64 percent of the adult population of the United States. American Protestant groups can be ranked along a continuum in terms of their religious traditionalism (Smith, 1984). At the conservative end are the fundamentalists, including the Southern Baptists, Pentecostals, and Jehovah's Witnesses. Near the middle fall the moderate religious groups, including Lutherans and Methodists. At the liberal end come Unitarians, Congregationlists, Presbyterians, and Episcopalians. Religious attachment is the strongest among Protestant fundamentalist groups, with 51 percent reporting they attend church weekly and 58 percent rating their faith as strong. Among Lutherans and

Methodists, weekly attendance is about 23 percent, and the proportion with strong religious faith ranges between 33 and 40 percent. In contrast, about 18 percent of Episcopalians attend church weekly, and 31 percent rate their faith as strong.

Over the past two decades, the major Protestant denominations have seen their memberships shrink. During the same period, conservative and fundamentalist groups have grown (see Table 10.3). A variety of factors have contributed to the loss of members among Methodist, Lutheran, Presbyterian, and Episcopalian groups. First, their members frequently marry outside their own denomination and relinquish their church memberships in the process. Second, the trend toward greater individualism, personal freedom, and tolerance of diversity that took place during the sixties and seventies, especially among young people, turned many individuals away from the religious patterns of their parents and fostered a "pick-and-choose" type of Christi-

TABLE 10.3

Gains and Losses in Protestant Church Membership

Evangelical Churches	1973	Latest	Change
Southern Baptist Convention	12,295,400	14,185,454	Up 15%
Church of Jesus Christ of Latter-day Saints	2,569,000	3,593,000	Up 40%
Assemblies of God	1,099,606	1,879,182	Up 71%
Seventh-day Adventists	464,276	623,563	Up 34%
Church of the Nazarene	417,732	507,574	Up 22%
Mainline Churches			
United Methodist Church	10,192,265	9,405,083	Down 8%
Presbyterian Church (U.S.A.)	3,715,301	3,157,372	Down 15%
Lutheran Church in America	3,017,778	2,925,655	Down 3%
Episcopal Church	2,917,165	2,794,139	Down 4%
Christian Church (Disciples of Christ)	1,330,747	1,156,458	Down 13%

(*Source: U.S. News & World Report*, April 30, 1984, p. 82. Copyright, 1984, U.S. News & World Report, Inc.)

anity (Riche, 1982; Chittister and Marty, 1983). Third, the fertility of the members of moderate and liberal Protestant denominations has tended to be low (Smith, 1984). And finally, they have run against the swelling tide of religious conservatism. In order to meet these challenges, denominations like the Methodists have been cutting back on politics, returning to the grassroots evangelism of their founders, and building a stronger spiritual base (Briggs, 1984a, 1984b).

Catholics. Roman Catholics constitute the nation's largest religious denomination, representing nearly a quarter of the adult population. About 42 percent of Catholics attend church each week and some 41 percent say their faith is strong (Smith, 1984). Catholics have seen their church undergo an astounding array of changes since the Second Vatican Council in 1962–1965: Mass is said in English rather than Latin; the laity can receive communion wafers into their own hands or take wine from the chalice; power is less rigorously centralized; the role of the lay members has been expanded; secrecy in church affairs has been diminished; and non-Catholics are no longer defined as heretics.

Yet on the issue of birth control, divorce, abortion, women's inclusion in the priesthood, and mandatory celibacy for priests, large numbers of American Catholics seem to be turning a deaf ear to the Pope's insistence on traditional beliefs and practices. On questions of sexual morality the differences are most marked, with 95 percent of young Catholic adults approving of artificial birth control and 89 percent approving of remarriage after divorce. Nearly half of American Catholics do not consider premarital sex wrong, and 32 percent say that sexual activity between members of the same sex is not categorically wrong. Of the estimated 1.5 million American women who

have an abortion in a given year, about one-quarter are Catholic (Sciolino, 1984). These shifts in sentiment have resulted in a growing tension between the Vatican and segments of the American church. Underlying the changes have been the success, power, and prosperity Catholics have achieved in the United States. In a few generations, large numbers of Catholics have made their way from immigrant status—many of them poor and crowded into industrial cities of the Northeast and Middle West—into the mainstream of American life as well-educated, affluent suburbanites (Greeley, 1982, 1985).

The growing independence of conscience is accepted—or at least tolerated—by many parish priests and nuns, who define their chief pastoral mission as one of meeting the everyday needs of the faithful (Sciolino, 1984). But turbulence in the American church has contributed to about a fifth of the priests and a higher proportion of nuns withdrawing from the active ministry. The result has been a growing shortage of priests and nuns. Two decades ago, the American church had 48,000 seminarians; currently there are fewer than 12,000, of whom only 60 percent are likely to take their final vows. Fewer Catholic families regard the priesthood as a higher calling than marriage, and more and more young men are hesitating to make a permanent commitment to a life of celibacy and service to others. Complicating matters, 20 percent of younger priests quit within the first ten years; an additional 17 percent quit by 15 years; by their twenty-fifth anniversary, 50 percent have left the priesthood (Briggs, 1984). At the same time, the ranks of nuns are dwindling, having dropped 35 percent since reaching a peak of 181,421 in 1966 (half of all nuns in the United States are now 60 years of age or older). Increasing numbers of nuns are rebelling against their second-class ecclesiastical status. Following Vatican

Council II, many jettisoned their cumbersome habits, relaxed rigid convent rules, and made social justice central to their mission. Although 10 percent of the nuns still choose cloistered lives in a traditional setting, another 10 percent have pursued secular careers as lawyers, academics, administrators, social activists, and government officials (Woodward, 1984).

The priorities of the American church have changed in recent years with the issues of the lot of the poor and peace moving to the forefront of the concerns of The National Conference of Catholic Bishops. The bishops have called the level of poverty and unemployment in the United States a "social and moral scandal" and have supported a "freeze" on nuclear weapons production. And although Catholics who go to church every week or almost every week are evenly split over a constitutional amendment banning abortions, many bishops of the Northeast have militantly opposed abortion (Herbers, 1984a). The result has been an increasingly bitter debate within the church on the activist direction taken by the nation's bishops (Kennedy, 1984).

As noted earlier in the chapter, liberation theology, which has its roots in Latin America, has also been the source of much controversy and opposition from Vatican officials. It emphasizes that the world is the theater of God's activity and borrows some of its ideas from Marxist sociology. Instead of taking the lead from church teachings or a clerical hierarchy, liberation theology emphasizes the importance of following the example of Jesus, particularly as He identified Himself with the poor and society's outcasts. Followers of liberation theology work not only for the spiritual salvation of the poor, but for an improvement in their social and economic conditions. Thus it is a movement that encourages social and political involvement. In sum, for American Catholics, as well as Catholics in other parts of the world, the meaning of belonging to the Church and being a Catholic has been changing.

Jews. Jews constitute about 2 to 3 percent of the nation's adult population. Like their Protestant and Catholic counterparts, the nation's Jews have experienced a good deal of change over the past two decades. A particularly significant statistic has been the rapid increase in intergroup marriages, with indications that the rate of Jewish-gentile intermarriage may be approaching 50 percent. However, there is not necessarily a loss to the Jewish community, since the non-Jewish partner often converts to Judaism. Overall, Jewish leaders have been concerned with the passive erosion of religious practice among their members. While many Jews continue to identify themselves with their faith, most do not take an active part in religious activities. Only 8 percent of the nation's Jewish population reports attending religious services each week, although 42 percent rate their faith as strong (Smith, 1984). A commitment to the survival of Israel has also given psychological unity to the Jewish community and fostered a Jewish identity (Sanoff, 1983).

The American Jewish Committee places the world's Jewish population at about 14.3 million. The United States, with about 5.8 million Jews, has the largest Jewish population, outstripping Israel, which counts 3.1 million, and the Soviet Union, with 2.7 million. A tripartite structure of religious organizations in American Jewish communities resembles Protestant denominationalism in its representation of various shades of belief and practice (Harrison and Lazerwitz, 1982). Orthodox Jews display the greatest degree of traditionalism, followed by Conservative Jews, who are intermediate in rank, and Reform Jews, who are the least traditional.

In a manner paralleling the Protestant

and Catholic communities, many Jews have turned in recent years to a more personal type of religion for solace and sustenance. They are returning to some of the old ways, while remaining contemporary in outlook. Many Reform Jews are again wearing skull-caps and prayer shawls during services. Simultaneously, attendance at all-day Jewish schools has soared from 62,000 in 1962 to 110,000 in 1983, despite a decline in Jewish birth rates. Large numbers of Jews have also turned to *havurah*, a movement designed to make the Jewish religious experience more meaningful. A *havurah* usually consists of about ten families who meet together on a regular basis to pursue Jewish interests. The members may study together, worship and celebrate holidays, and render service to the Jewish community. Given developments such as these, Jewish leaders are optimistic regarding the continued vitality of Judaism in the United States in the years ahead (Sanoff, 1983).

STATE–CHURCH ISSUES

The First Amendment to the American Constitution states: "Congress shall make no law respecting an establishment of religion, or prohibiting the free exercise thereof. . . ." While this prohibition applies only to Congress, the Supreme Court has held it applicable to the states by virtue of the due process clause of the Fourteenth Amendment. It has provided the foundation for the principle of the separation of church and state, by which organized religion and government have remained substantially independent of each other. Compared with many other nations, the United States has maintained a remarkably hands-off attitude toward religion. In a number of cases, however, laws have been enacted and upheld by the Supreme Court that have impinged upon religious practices, including those against polygamy among Mormons and

against snake-handling by charismatic Christians.

The separation of church and state has not denied a religious dimension to the American political scene. Although most Americans deem an individual's religious beliefs and practices to be a strictly private matter, there are nonetheless certain common elements of religious orientation most Americans share. These religious dimensions are expressed in a set of beliefs, symbols, and rituals that sociologist Robert Bellah (1970; Bellah and Hammond, 1980) calls **civil religion.** Its basic tenet is that the American nation is not an ultimate end in itself, but a nation under God with a divine mission. Although religious pluralism prevents any one denomination from supplying all Americans with a single source of meaning, civil religion compensates by providing an overarching sacred canopy. President Reagan captured this sentiment when he observed at a Dallas prayer breakfast in August 1984: "I believe that faith and religion play a critical role in the political life of our nation, and always has, and that the church—and by that I mean all churches, all denominations—has had a strong influence on the state, and this has worked to our benefit as a nation."

Civil religion finds expression in the statements and documents of the Founding Fathers, presidential inaugural addresses, national holidays, historic shrines, mottos, and patriotic expressions in times of crisis and peril. There are four references to God in the Declaration of Independence. Every president has mentioned God in his inaugural address (except George Washington in his second inauguration). Thanksgiving is a national holiday celebrated as a day of public thanksgiving and prayer. And the government engages in many religious practices, from the phrase "In God We Trust" on its currency to the prayers said in Congress.

Throughout American history, the influence of religion on secular politics and government has remained strong. As noted earlier in the chapter, religion has historically played a major role in a good many American social movements. Today groups armed with moral agendas are also seeking to gain public support for their programs. For instance, liberal religious organizations and the nation's Catholic bishops are pushing a set of issues that includes disarmament and improved social services for the disadvantaged. The Christian right has likewise come to the fore with an appeal to recover the Christian roots, heritage, and values of an older America. The result has been a reopening of the debate over the role religion should play in public policy. At issue is not the right of religious activists to enter the political arena and lobby for laws consistent with their beliefs. Rather, the issue has been one of defining the place a religiously defined morality has in a pluralist society. The main controversies have resided in those areas in which private morality and public policy overlap. Abortion provides a good illustration. There are those who insist that abortion is a private moral choice and that the state has no right to make the practice illegal. Others, particularly anti-abortion groups, contend that abortion is no more a matter of private moral choice than slavery was and that the state has an obligation to stop it. Other equally emotional issues have related to prayer in public schools, pornography, and the rights of homosexuals.

The current debate suggests that religion remains a powerful moving force in American life. In some respects, Americans are no closer to resolving how to relate people's religious lives to their civil lives than was the case in the days of Thomas Jefferson and James Madison. Clearly the issue is not one to be decided once and for all. Each generation of Americans must tackle its own version of the church-state question. The strength of the nation's pluralistic system has historically resided in a built-in check in which a backlash or countermovement sets in when any one group pushes too hard for its religious values.

Education

Controversy also envelops the educational institution. This fact is hardly surprising, since in modern societies few individuals and groups do not have a substantial stake in the educational enterprise. The reason is not difficult to discern: Learning is a fundamental process in our lives. It allows us to adapt to our environment by building on previous experience. Through our successes and failures in coping with our life circumstances, we derive an accumulating body of information that serves as a guide to decisions and actions. Social scientists view **learning** as a relatively permanent change in behavior or capability that results from experience. Since learning is so vital to social life, societies do not usually leave it to chance. Societies may undertake to transmit particular attitudes, knowledge, and skills to their members through formal, systematic training—what sociologists call **education.** Education is one aspect of the many-sided process of socialization by which people acquire behaviors essential for effective participation in society (see Chapter 3). It entails an explicit process in which some individuals assume the status of teacher and others the status of student and carry out their associated roles.

THE FUNCTIONALIST PERSPECTIVE ON EDUCATION

Schools initially came into existence several thousand years ago to prepare a select few for a limited number of leadership and professional positions. However, in the past century or so public schools have become the primary vehicles by which the members of a society are taught the three Rs, affording them the literacy skills required by large-scale industrial and bureaucratic organizations. Viewed from the functionalist perspective, the schools make a number of vital contributions to the survival and perpetuation of modern societies.

Completing Socialization. Many preliterate and peasant societies lack schools. They socialize their youngsters in the same "natural" way that parents teach their children to walk or talk. Consider the following account of the Copper Eskimos by anthropologist Diamond Jenness (1922:170,219):

A girl . . . is encouraged to make dolls and to mend her own clothing, her mother teaching her how to cut out the skins. Both boys and girls learn to stalk game by accompanying their elders on hunting excursions; their fathers make bows and arrows for them suited to their strength. One of their favourite pastimes is to carry out, in miniature, some of the duties they will have to perform when they grow up. Thus little girls often have tiny lamps in the corners of their huts over which they will cook some meat to share with their playmates. . . . The children naturally have many pastimes that imitate the actions of their elders. . . . Both boys and girls play at building snow houses. In summer, with only pebbles to work with, they simply lay out the ground plans, but in winter they borrow their parents' snow-knives and make complete houses on a miniature scale.

The content of culture among the Copper Eskimos is quite similar for everyone, and people acquire it mostly in an unconscious manner through daily living. Unlike the Copper Eskimos, adults in modern societies cannot afford to shape their children in their own image. Too often parents find themselves with obsolete skills, trained for jobs that are no longer needed. The knowledge and skills required by contemporary living cannot be satisfied in a more or less automatic and "natural" way. Instead, a specialized educational agency is needed to transmit to young people the ways of thinking, feeling, and acting mandated by a rapidly changing urban and technologically based society.

Social Integration. Functionalists say that the education system functions to inculcate the dominant values of a society and shape a common national mind. Within the United States students learn what it means to be an American, become literate in the English language, gain a common heritage, and acquire mainstream standards and rules. In this fashion youngsters from diverse ethnic, religious, and racial backgrounds are immersed within the same Anglo-American culture and prepared for "responsible" citizenship (see Chapter 7). Historically, the nation's schools have played a prominent part in Americanizing the children of immigrants. Likewise, the schools are geared to integrating the poor and disadvantaged within the fabric of dominant, mainstream institutions. How well the educational institution performs these functions is a debatable matter. As we will note later in the chapter, conflict theorists see educational activities directed toward these ends as serving the interests of elite classes and groups.

Screening and Selecting. As we noted in Chapter 2, all societies ascribe some statuses to individuals independent of their unique qualities or abilities. Other statuses are achieved through choice and competition. No society ignores entirely individual differences or overlooks individual accomplishment and failure. Modern societies in particular must select certain of their youth for positions that require special talents. The educational institution commonly performs this function, serving as an agency for screening and selecting individuals for different types of jobs. By conferring degrees, diplomas, and credentials that are prerequisites for many technical, managerial, and professional positions, it determines which young people will have access to scarce positions and offices of power, privilege, and status (see Table 10.4). For many Americans, the schools function as "mobility escalators," allowing able, gifted individuals to ascend the social ladder. Again, as we will see later in the chapter, conflict theorists contest this point and allege instead that the schools serve to guarantee that the sons and daughters of the elite—having acquired the "proper" credentials—are able to secure the best positions.

Research and Development. For the most part, schools are designed to produce people who fit into society, not people who set out to change it. However, schools, particularly universities, may not only transmit culture; they may add to the cultural heritage. Contemporary American society places a good deal of emphasis on the development of new knowledge, especially in the physical and biological sciences, medi-

cine, and engineering. In recent decades, the nation's leading universities have increasingly become research centers. Indeed, by virtue of their research roles, 88 colleges and universities are among the top 500 contractors for the U.S. Department of Defense (see Table 10.5). This emphasis on research has led universities to judge professors not primarily in terms of their competence as teachers, but as researchers. Promotions, salary increases, and other benefits are usually contingent on research and publication, with "publish or perish" and "publish and prosper" being the governing tenets of university life. Critics contend that academic success is most likely to come to those who have learned to "neglect" their teaching duties to pursue research activities. But defenders say that even when students are not themselves involved in research projects, they benefit from the intellectual stimulation a research orientation brings to university life.

Latent Functions. Schools perform a good many latent functions, consequences that may not be recognized nor intended (see Chapter 2). Within American life, the educational institution performs of a number of these functions. First, it provides a custodial or babysitting service, keeping youngsters out from under the feet of adults and from under the wheels of automobiles (as the number of households in which both parents work increases, pressure has mounted to start public schooling at the age of 4 rather than 5 or 6). Second, schools serve as a marriage market, providing young people with opportunities to select mates of similar class and social backgrounds as themselves. Third, schools provide settings in which students develop a variety of interpersonal skills needed for entering into friendships, participating in community affairs, and relating to others in the workplace. Fourth, the age segregation of stu-

Table 10.4
How Education Raises Income

Heads of Family (age 25 or older)	Median Family Income, 1983
5 or more years of college	$43,834
Finished college	$37,467
1 to 3 years of college	$29,097
Finished high school	$24,506
1 to 3 years of high school	$17,469
Finished grade school	$15,977
Did not finish grade school	$12,233

(*Source:* U.S. Department of Commerce.)

dents in school environments encourages the formation of youth subcultures. Fifth, schools "warehouse" many unoccupied individuals who otherwise might remain idle (Walters, 1984). And finally, formal compulsory education keeps children and adolescents out of the labor market and hence out of competition with adults for jobs.

THE CONFLICT PERSPECTIVE ON EDUCATION

Conflict theorists see the schools as agencies that reproduce and legitimate the current social order through the functions they perform. By reproducing and legitimating the existing social order, the educational institution is seen as benefiting some individuals and groups at the expense of others (Collins, 1977, 1979).

Reproducing the Social Relations of Production. Some conflict theorists depict American schools as reflecting the needs of capitalist production and as social instruments for convincing the population that private ownership and profit are just and in the best interests of the entire society (Apple, 1982; Apple and Weis, 1983). In *Schooling and Capitalist America* (1976), Samuel Bowles and Herbert Gintis set forth the **correspondence principle**—that the social relations of work find expression in the social relations of the school. They say that the schools mirror the workplace and hence on a day-to-day basis prepare children for adult roles in the job market. The authoritarian structure of the school reproduces the bureaucratic hierarchy of the corporation, rewarding diligence, submissiveness, and compliance. The system of grades employed to motivate students parallels the wage system for motivating workers. In short, the schools are seen as socializing a compliant labor force for the capitalist economy.

The Hidden Curriculum. In the eyes of conflict theorists, the **hidden curriculum** of the schools plays a similar role. The hidden curriculum consists of a complex of unarticulated values, attitudes, and behaviors that subtly mold children in the image preferred by the dominant institutions. Teachers model and reinforce traits that embody middle-class standards—industry, responsibility, conscientiousness, reliability, thoroughness, self-control, and efficiency. Children learn to be quiet, to be punctual, to line up, to wait their turn, to please their teachers, and to conform to group pressures. Thus schools provide a bridge between the values of intimacy and acceptance pervading the family and the more demanding, impersonal rules of a competitive, materialistic society.

Control Devices. Conflict theorists agree with functionalist theorists that schools are agencies for drawing minorities and the disadvantaged into the dominant culture. But they do not see the function in benign terms. Sociologist Randall Collins (1976) contends that the educational system serves the interests of the dominant group by defusing the threat posed by minority ethnic groups. In large, conflict-ridden, multi-ethnic societies like the United States and the Soviet Union, the schools become instruments to Americanize or Sovietize minority people. Compulsory education erodes ethnic differences and loyalties and transmits to minorities and those at the bottom of the social hierarchy the values and life ways of the dominant group. Schools, then, are viewed as control devices employed by established elites.

Productive Capital. Conflict theorists see the research and development function of the universities quite differently than do functionalist theorists. For instance, Michael W. Apple (1982) gives a Marxist twist

Table 10.5

Universities Ranked among the Top 500 Defense Contractors, 1983*

	Amount of Contracts (add 000)	Rank in Top 500		Amount of Contracts (add 000)	Rank in Top 500
Massachusetts Inst. of Technology	$247,845	15	University of Massachusetts	3,158	250
Johns Hopkins University	226,703	17	Texas A&M U. Research Foundation	3,121	252
Illinois Institute of Technology	42,054	51	University of Michigan	3,064	254
University of California	39,956	54	University of Arizona	2,991	260
Stanford University	25,993	67			
			Rensselaer Polytechnic Institute	2,906	264
Georgia Institute of Technology Research Institute	25,160	70	Princeton University	2,848	267
			New York University	2,693	272
University of Texas	23,250	72	Boston College	2,677	276
Pennsylvania State University	20,436	77	University of Rhode Island	2,566	282
University of Rochester	20,393	78			
University of Southern California	18,762	81	George Washington University	2,524	287
			Florida State University	2,519	288
			Oklahoma State University	2,476	290
University of Washington	15,269	89	University of Pittsburgh	2,431	293
University of Dayton	14,809	93	University of Colorado	$2,377	296
New Mexico State University	14,013	96	Northeastern University	2,362	298
Carnegie-Mellon University	12,248	106	Georgia Institute of Technology	2,355	299
University of New Mexico	10,522	114	Lehigh University	2,298	300
			Purdue U. Research Foundation	2,279	301
University of Illinois	10,426	116			
Utah State University	8,745	133	University of North Carolina	2,157	309
Columbia University	7,165	149	New York State U. Research Foundation	2,144	310
University of Maryland	6,790	154	University of Florida	2,140	311
Cornell University	5,227	177	New Mexico Institute of Mining and Technology	2,138	312
California Institute of Technology	4,808	188	University of Hawaii	2,138	313
Ohio State U. Research Foundation	4,522	197	Brown University	2,109	316
Yale University	4,462	198	University of Iowa	1,941	326
University of Utah	4,304	203	Case Western Reserve University	1,878	330
University of Wisconsin	4,285	204	Georgetown University	1,869	332
			Clemson University	1,852	336
University of Pennsylvania	3,947	211			
Oregon State University	3,924	213	Colorado State University	1,815	343
Harvard University	3,920	214	University of Minnesota	1,795	346
Boston University	3,476	234	North Carolina State University	1,731	349
University of Miami	3,333	242	University of Denver	1,698	352
			Northwestern University	1,686	353
Virginia Polytechnic Inst. & State U.	3,286	246	University of Virginia	1,670	357

Table 10.5   *Continued*

	Amount of Contracts (add 000)	Rank in Top 500		Amount of Contracts (add 000)	Rank in Top 500
Michigan State University	1,531	370	Wentworth Inst. of Technology	1,171	441
University of Alabama	1,464	378	Texas Tech University	1,126	446
New York Polytechnic Institute	1,458	381	State U. of New York	1,119	448
University of Tennessee	1,328	401			
			Rutgers University	1,089	456
Louisiana State University	1,319	405	Washington State University	1,086	457
University of Missouri	1,306	407	Purdue University	1,033	469
Stevens Institute of Technology	1,266	414	Catholic University of America	1,009	475
Duke University	1,247	418	Drexel University	952	488
University of Central Florida	1,203	424			
			University of Houston	938	493
Emmanuel College (Mass.)	1,186	431	Washington University (Mo.)	933	495
Michigan Technological			Auburn University	904	498
University	1,182	433	Regents of the U. of Michigan	901	499

* Colleges and universities received about 6 percent of Department of Defense contract funds for research, development, testing, and evaluation in fiscal year 1983.
(*Source:* U.S. Department of Defense.)

to the functionalist argument by contending that the educational institution produces the technical and administrative knowledge necessary for running a capitalist order. Viewed in this manner, education is part of the system of production. It not only reproduces existing social arrangements, but develops the knowhow needed by capitalists to fuel the economy and gain competitive advantage in world markets.

Credentialism. Collins (1979) also downplays the functionalist argument that schools serve as mobility escalators. He cites evidence that students acquire little technical knowledge in school and that most technical skills are learned on the job. Although more education is needed to obtain most jobs, Collins says that this development is not explained by the technical requirements of the job. The level of skills required by typists, receptionists, salesclerks, teachers, assembly-line workers, and many others is not much different than it was a generation or so ago. Collins calls these tendencies **credentialism**—the requirement that a worker have a degree for its own sake, not because it certifies skills needed for the performance of a job. Since education functions more as a certification of class membership than of technical skills, it functions as a means of class inheritance.

Whereas at one time a college degree brought an elite occupational status with elite pay, today it brings a middle-class status with middle-class pay. There has been a progressive reduction in the occupational and income return for each year of education (Featherman and Hauser, 1978b; Jencks et al., 1979). The growth of junior and community colleges is a good illustration of these processes. Conflict theorists portray these schools as an upward extension of the public school tracking system, keeping minority and working-class youngsters at the same class level as their parents (Karabel,

1977). These youths are led to believe that a junior- or community-college education will increase their chances for upward mobility. In reality, however, such schooling does not typically open corporate or professional career lines. Much in the manner of "marks" in a con game, working-class and minority youth find themselves involved in an educational "cooling-out" process. For instance, fewer than 10 percent of the students who enroll at one of California's 106 two-year community colleges (with 1.1 million students in 1985) complete a two-year program and move on to a four-year college (Lindsey, 1985). In brief, as a population gains more education, the relative position of different groups in the stratification system remains basically the same.

THE BUREAUCRATIC STRUCTURE OF SCHOOLS

Until a few generations ago, schooling in the United States usually took place in a one-room schoolhouse. One teacher taught all eight grades, with the more advanced and older students helping the less capable and younger students with their lessons. So long as the schools remained relatively small, they could operate on the basis of face-to-face interaction. But like hospitals, factories, and businesses, schools grew larger and more complex. In order to attain their goals, they had to standardize and routinize many of their operations and establish formal operating and administrative procedures. In brief, they turned to a bureaucratic arrangement, a social structure made up of a hierarchy of statuses and roles prescribed by explicit rules and procedures and based on a division of function and authority (see Chapter 4).

Like other complex organizations, schools do not exist in a social vacuum, but are tightly interlocked with other institutions. At the very top of this organizational arrangement is the federal government, which through a variety of agencies, including the Department of Education and the federal court system, profoundly influences educational life. Consider, for instance, court rulings in desegregation cases and recent policies mandating practices relating to the education of handicapped children. State educational authorities also provide encompassing standards and regulations, like those setting the number of days in a school year, and they allocate state monies for specified programs.

The formal organization of American schools and colleges typically consists of four levels: (1) the board of education or trustees, (2) administrators, (3) teachers or professors, and (4) students. The control of most schools and colleges is vested in an elected or appointed board of laypeople. It generally appoints and assigns administrators and teachers, decides on the nature of educational programs, determines building construction, and approves operational budgets. The administrators—superintendents, principals, presidents, chancellors, and deans—are responsible for executing the policies of the board. Although in theory the board determines policy, in actual practice many policy questions are settled by administrators. Teachers are the immediate day-to-day link between the larger system and individual students, the latter occupying the lowest position in the school bureaucracy. Elementary and secondary teachers usually enjoy less authority in decision making than their counterparts in higher education. In sum, the school system is characterized by a chain of command, a network of positions functionally interrelated for the purpose of accomplishing educational objectives.

By virtue of bureaucratic arrangements, school environments are remarkably standardized in both their physical and their social characteristics. Physical objects, social relations, and major activities remain much the same from day to day, week to week, and even year to year. These patterns are most apparent at the elementary and secondary school levels. For instance, time is highly formalized. The pledge of allegiance is followed by math at 8:35, which is followed by reading at 9:10, which is followed by recess, and so on over the course of the day. The music teacher comes for fifty minutes on Tuesday afternoons and children go to gym on Wednesday and Friday mornings at 10:20. There is almost a holy aura about the "daily grind" as mandated by the schedule.

Individual behavior is rigidly governed by sets of rules—no loud talking during seat work, raise your hand to talk during discussions, keep your eyes on your paper during tests, and no running in the halls. The physical layout of the school and the omnipresent symbols of adult authority emphasize and reinforce the subordinate status of the pupils. Cloakrooms and lunchrooms have a special space reserved for the teachers and a separate space for children. The teacher has a special desk in a special part of the classroom. Although the teacher may inspect a child's desk and possessions at will, the child is denied a similar right. It is a system that encourages student passivity and makes the school a relatively uninteresting place, resembling in many ways what sociologist Erving Goffman (1961) has called a *total institution* (see Chapter 4).

THE EFFECTIVENESS OF THE SCHOOLS

In recent years a number of national reports have appeared decrying the state of the American educational system. In the words of the National Commission on Excellence in Education (1983), we are a "nation at risk" because of a "rising tide of mediocrity" in the schools. Likewise, a Carnegie Foundation (1983) report argues that "the teaching profession is in crisis in this country," the National Task Force on Education for Economic Growth (1983) says that "a real emergency is upon us," and the National Association of High School Principals (Sifzer, 1984) claims the American high school is an outdated institution providing a "warmed-over version of principles promulgated in 1918." The reports mention many of the same indicators, including poor achievement test scores, a long-term fall in college entrance test scores (see Table 10.6), declines in both enrollments and achievement in science and mathematics, the poor performance of American students on international tests (see Table 10.7), the high cost incurred by business and the military for

Table 10.6

Scores on National College Entrance Examinations

Testing Year	ACT*	SAT†
1970	19.9	948
1971	19.2	943
1972	19.1	937
1973	19.2	926
1974	18.9	924
1975	18.6	906
1976	18.3	903
1977	18.4	899
1978	18.5	897
1979	18.6	894
1980	18.5	890
1981	18.5	890
1982	18.4	893
1983	18.3	893

* The ACT (American College Testing Program Assessment) is scored on a scale of 1 to 36. The ACT test is used primarily by schools in Midwest, South, Southwest, Mountain, and Plains states.
† SAT's (Scholastic Aptitude Test) total possible score is 1,600. It is used primarily by elite colleges and universities on the East and West coasts.
(*Source:* American College Testing Program and College Board.)

Table 10.7

Twelfth-Grade Math Skills (average percentage of correctly answered questions)

	U.S.	World*
Sets and relations	59%	62%
Number systems	45	50
Algebra	48	57
Geometry	37	42
Elementary functions/ calculus	36	44
Probability and statistics	45	50
Finite mathematics	36	44†

* In addition to the United States, the countries covered in the survey were Australia, Belgium, Canada, Chile, England, Finland, France, Hong Kong, Hungary, Ireland, Israel, Ivory Coast, Japan, Luxembourg, Netherlands, New Zealand, Nigeria, Scotland, Swaziland, Sweden, and Thailand.
† Estimated average score.
(Source: Second International Mathematics Study, 1984.)

remedial and training programs, and the substantial levels of functional illiteracy found among American adults and children.

A University of Michigan study shows that American schoolchildren lag behind schoolchildren in Japan and Taiwan from the day they enter school (Fiske, 1984) (see Table 10.8). The poorer performance of the American youngsters seems to be related to the way American schools manage instruction. For one thing, the average school year is shorter in the United States—180 days versus 240 in Japan and Taiwan—and the school day is a half hour to two hours shorter. For another, American children spend less than half as much time as the Taiwanese and less than two-thirds as much as the Japanese on academic activities. Finally, cultural differences also appear to af-

fect performance. Japanese and Taiwanese parents seem to place greater emphasis than their American counterparts on the importance of children working hard at school and on homework. However, despite the lower achievement levels of American children, parents in the United States are more satisfied with their children's schools than are parents in Japan and Taiwan.

Social scientists have also examined what makes a school effective. Child psychiatrist Michael Rutter (1979) led a University of London team in a three-year study of students entering twelve London intercity secondary schools. The researchers found that schools only a scant distance apart and with students of similar social backgrounds and intellectual abilities had quite different educational results. The critical element distinguishing the schools was their "ethos" or "climate." The successful schools fostered expectations that order would prevail in the classrooms, and they did not leave matters of student discipline to be worked out by individual teachers for themselves. As a result, it was easier to be a good teacher in some schools than others. Additionally, the effective schools emphasized academic concerns—care by teachers in lesson planning, group instruction, high achievement expectations for students, a high proportion of time spent on instruction and learning activities, the assignment and checking of homework, and student use of the library. The researchers also found that schools that fostered respect for students as responsible people and held high expectations for appropriate behavior achieved better academic results. In the more successful schools, many students assumed responsibilities as group captains or as participants in school assemblies. However, there was no relationship between the size and age of the school building and student discipline or achievement.

Other research supports the conclusion

TABLE 10.8
Academic Achievement in the United States, Japan, and Taiwan

	Mean Number of Questions Answered Correctly		Percent of Class Time Spent on Reading	Percent of Class Time Spent on Math	Percent of the Time Students Paid Attention in Class
	Math	Reading Comprehension			
First Grade					
United States	17.1	21.3	50.6%	13.8%	45.3%
Japan	20.1	22.8	36.2	24.5	66.2
Taiwan	21.2	25.6	44.7	16.5	65.0
Fifth Grade					
United States	44.4	82.6	41.6	17.2	46.5
Japan	53.8	82.5	24.0	23.4	64.6
Taiwan	50.8	84.6	27.6	28.2	77.7

(*Source:* H. W. Stevenson, University of Michigan, 1984.)

that successful schools foster expectations that order will prevail and that learning is a serious matter (Clark, Lotto, and McCarthy, 1980; Winn, 1981). Much of the success enjoyed by private and Catholic schools has derived from their ability to provide students with an ordered environment and strong academic demands (Coleman et al., 1982a). Academic achievement is just as high in the public sector when the policies and resulting behavior are like those in the private sector (Coleman et al., 1982b). In sum, successful schools possess "coherence": things stick together and bear predictable relationships with one another.

THE AVAILABILITY OF EDUCATION

Since 1975 the average tuition charges for public and private four-year colleges have more than doubled (see Figure 10.2), and in recent years the costs of a college education have been surging ahead at double the rate of inflation. Over the past decade, a variety of federal financial-assistance programs has lent substantial support to both students and schools. In addition to the Job Training Partnership Act and the Vocational Education Program that primarily aid non-college youth, there are those programs that assist college students, including low-interest guaranteed loans, federally subsidized student jobs, Pell Grants, direct federal loans, and certain government grants that require no repayment by recipients. In 1985 more than 3.4 million college students received financial help from federally sponsored programs. However, many of these programs are now being curtailed. In its effort to cut federal budget deficits, the Reagan administration has sought a return to a traditional emphasis on parent and student responsibility for financing college costs and the elimination of aid to students from higher-income families (Engelgau, 1985).

There are a good many reasons why a college education is costly. For one thing, education is a labor-intensive industry, with about three-quarters of a college's budget going for faculty and staff salaries. Yet compared with other professionals, college professors hardly seem overpaid. Full professors earn an average of $37,400 a year; assistant professors make an average of

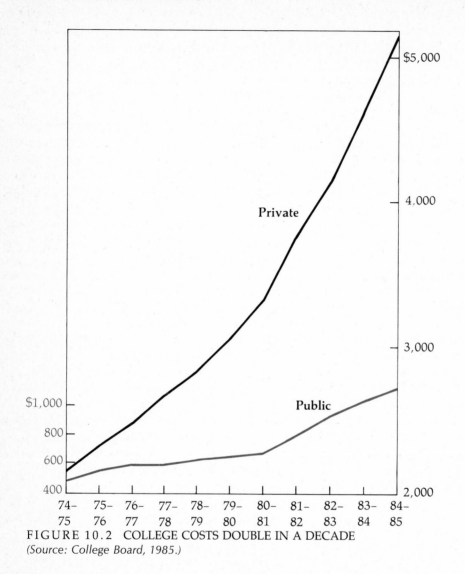

FIGURE 10.2   COLLEGE COSTS DOUBLE IN A DECADE
(Source: College Board, 1985.)

$23,210, less than executive secretaries. Indeed, college faculty members make 19 percent *less* than they did in 1971, adjusting for inflation. Other costs have also mounted. College utility bills have doubled over the past decade. And years of deferred maintenance have meant growing costs in keeping buildings functional (Williams, 1985).

Even with substantial increases, tuition does not cover the real costs of educating a student. On average, tuition at private colleges covers three-fourths of the cost (private gifts and investment income provide the rest), whereas at lower-priced public institutions it covers about 25 percent (public institutions are subsidized by state taxes). The cutback in federal subsidies is complicating the educational cost crunch. Youth from middle-income, working-class, and minority families have been particularly affected. According to the American Association of State Colleges and Universities, financial obstacles were taking a growing toll in the college enrollment of minority and disadvantaged students even prior to the cutback in federal funds (Ordovensky, 1985). Although more blacks and Hispanics have graduated from high school in recent years than in 1975, smaller percentages are attending college. Whereas 29 percent more blacks graduated from high school in 1982 than in 1975, black college enrollment fell 11 percent. During the same time period, the Hispanic high-school graduation rate was up 38 percent, but Hispanic enrollment in college was down 16 percent. In contrast, white high-school graduates were up 7 percent and white college enrollment was down less than 1 percent. As a result of these shifts, federal financial aid to white students rose 7.9 percent from 1978 to 1983, while aid to black students fell 4.7 percent.

The cutbacks in federal aid to students have also affected the nation's colleges and universities, particularly small private colleges. They have found their enrollments jeopardized by the inability of many students to afford steep tuition payments. Indeed, T. H. Bell (1985), President Reagan's first secretary of education, has assailed the cutbacks as an "unwitting assault on the nation's private colleges and universities." He claims that the changes will force thousands of students to transfer from private colleges, strain the budgets of the states by transferring higher-education expenses from the federal to state governments and effectively preclude able students from low-income families from setting their sights on "our distinguished institutions." The Reagan administration responds that the federal aid program has "run amok" and must be cut back "before the public loses all confidence in it" (Elmendorf, 1985).

Summary

1. Religion is centered in beliefs and practices that are related to sacred as opposed to profane things. The sacred is extraordinary, mysterious, awe-inspiring, and even potentially dangerous. The same object or behavior can be profane or sacred, depending on how people define it. Because the sacred is caught up with strong feelings of reverence and awe, it can usually be approached through rituals.

2. Religious behavior is so varied that we have difficulty thinking about it unless we use some classificatory means for sorting it into relevant categories. One scheme distinguishes between simple supernaturalism, animism, theism, and a system of abstract ideals. Simple supernaturalism entails the notion of mana—a diffuse, impersonal, supernatural force that exists in nature for good or evil. Animism involves a belief in spirits or otherworldly beings. Theism is a religion centered in a belief in gods who are thought to be powerful, to have an interest in human affairs, and to merit worship. And finally, some religions focus on a set of abstract ideals that are oriented to achieving moral and spiritual excellence.

3. Sociologists distinguish among four ideal types of religious organization: churches, denominations, sects, and cults. Whereas churches and denominations exist in a state of accommodation with the larger society, sects and cults find themselves at odds with established social arrangements and practices. Cults differ from sects in that cults are viewed by their members as being

pluralistically legitimate, providing one among many alternative paths to truth or salvation. In this respect, cults resemble denominations. In contrast, the sect, like the church, defines itself as being uniquely legitimate and possessing exclusive access to truth or salvation.

4. Functionalist theorists look to the contributions religion makes to societal survival. According to Emile Durkheim, religion—the totem ancestor, God, or some other supernatural force—is the symbolization of society. By means of religious rituals, the group in effect worships itself. Viewed in this manner, the primary functions of religion are the creation, reinforcement, and maintenance of social solidarity and social control. In addition, religion helps people in dealing with life's "breaking points." And it may be an impetus to social change.

5. Some conflict theorists depict religion as a weapon in the service of ruling elites who use it to hold in check the explosive tensions produced by social inequality and injustice. Karl Marx portrayed religion as a painkiller for the frustration, deprivation, and subjugation experienced by oppressed peoples. Other conflict theorists see religion not as a passive response to the social relations of production, but as an active force shaping the contours of social life. It can play a critical part in the birth and consolidation of new social structures and arrangements.

6. Sociologist Peter L. Berger suggests that religion can be employed in three contrasting ways. First, it can be mobilized in opposition to modernization and to the reaffirmation of traditional authority. This is the route taken by the Aya-

tollah Khomeini and his Islamic Shiite follwers in Iran. Second, religion can adapt to the secular world and harness religious motivations for secular purposes. According to Max Weber, this is the path taken by John Calvin and his Protestant followers. Third, religion can retain its fundamental roots while applying them to contemporary concerns. This is the road taken by the fundamental revivalist movement in the United States.

7. If religious denominations were basically the same, then it would matter little that Americans are divided among more than a thousand religious groups. However, surveys find that substantial differences in attitudes and practices among Americans of different denominations are expressed in a set of beliefs, symbols, and rituals that sociologists call civil religion.

9. Education is one aspect of the many-sided process of socialization by which people acquire behaviors essential for effective participation in society. It entails an explicit process in which some individuals assume the status of teacher and others the status of student and carry out their associated roles.

10. Viewed from the functionalist perspective, schools make a number of vital contributions to the survival and perpetuation of modern societies. A specialized educational agency is needed to transmit the ways of thinking, feeling, and acting mandated by a rapidly changing urban and technologically based society. The educational system serves to inculcate the dominant values of a society and shape a common national mind. It functions as an agency for screening and selecting individuals for different types of jobs. And schools,

particularly universities, may add to the cultural heritage through research and development.

11. Conflict theorists see the schools as agencies that reproduce and legitimate the current social order through the functions they perform. By reproducing and legitimating the existing social order, the educational institution is seen as benefiting some individuals and groups at the expense of others. Some conflict theorists depict American schools as reflecting the needs of capitalist production and as social instruments for convincing the population that private ownership and profit are just and in the best interests of the entire society.

12. So long as the schools remained relatively small, they could operate on the basis of face-to-face interaction. But like hospitals, factories, and businesses, schools grew larger and more complex. In order to attain their goals, they had to standardize and routinize many of their operations and establish formal operating and administrative procedures. Like other complex organizations, schools do not exist in a social vacuum, but are tightly interlocked with other institutions. The formal organization of American schools and colleges typically consists of four levels: (1) the board of education or trustees, (2) administrators, (3) teachers or professors, and (4) students.

13. Social scientists have examined what makes a school effective. Successful schools foster expectations that order will prevail and that learning is a serious matter. Much of the success enjoyed by private and Catholic schools has derived from their ability to provide students with an ordered environment and strong academic demands.

Glossary

animism A belief in spirits or otherworldly beings.

asceticism A way of life characterized by hard work, sobriety, thrift, restraint, and the avoidance of earthly pleasures.

church A religious organization that considers itself uniquely legitimate and enjoys a positive relationship with the dominant society.

civil religion Elements of nationalism and patriotism that take on the properties of a religion.

correspondence principle The notion set forth by Samuel Bowles and Herbert Gintis that the social relations of work find expression in the social relations of the school.

credentialism The requirement that a worker have a degree that does not provide skills needed for the performance of a job.

cult A religious organization that accepts the legitimacy of other religious groups, but finds itself at odds with the dominant society.

denomination A religious organization that accepts the legitimacy of other religious groups and enjoys a positive relationship with the dominant society.

education The transmission of particular attitudes, knowledge, and skills to the members of a society through formal, systematic training.

ethic The perspective and values engendered by a religious way of thinking.

hidden curriculum A complex of unarticulated values, attitudes, and behaviors that subtly fit children in the image of the dominant institutions.

learning A relatively permanent change in behavior or capability that results from experience.

mana The notion that there is in nature a diffuse, impersonal, supernatural force operating for good or evil.

monotheism The belief in one god.

polytheism The belief in many gods with equal or relatively similar power.

profane Those aspects of social reality that are everyday and commonplace.

Protestant ethic The Calvinist ethos that embodied the spirit of capitalism.

religion Those socially shared ways of thinking, feeling, and acting that have as their focus the realm of the supernatural or "beyond," and that are centered in beliefs and practices that are related to sacred things.

rituals Social acts prescribed by rules that dictate how human beings should comport themselves in the presence of the sacred.

sacred Those aspects of social reality that are set apart and forbidden.

sect A religious organization that considers itself uniquely legitimate, but is at odds with the dominant society.

theism A religion centered in a belief in gods who are thought to be powerful, to have an interest in human affairs, and to merit worship.

totemism A religious system in which a clan (a kin group) takes the name of, claims descent from, and attributes sacred properties to a plant or animal.

11

The Human Environment

THE ECOLOGICAL
ENVIRONMENT

*The Functionalist Perspective on the
    Environment*
*The Conflict Perspective on the
    Environment*
Environmental Concerns
The Effects of Crowding

POPULATION

Elements in Population Change
Population Composition
Malthus and Marx
Demographic Transition
Population Policies
The American Health Care System

THE URBAN ENVIRONMENT

The Origin and Evolution of Cities
Patterns of City Growth
Ecological Processes
*Urban Crisis and the Future of
    American Cities*

Sociology highlights for us the critical part the social component plays in the human experience. But since humans are also physical beings, their very nature dictates that they be located within space in some sort of habitat. Accordingly, human populations must achieve a working relationship with their environment (Hawley, 1950, 1984; Agnew, 1981; Micklin and Choldin, 1984). The **environment** consists of all the surrounding conditions and influences that affect an organism or a group of organisms. Like other forms of life, human beings confront their environment not so much as individuals, but as units in cooperative association. Among their chief adaptive mechanisms are social organization and technology. As we noted in Chapter 2, the subsistence strategy a population employs—hunting and gathering, horticulture, agriculture, or industrialism—has critical implications for its culture and social structure.

One way of viewing the environment is as an **ecosystem**—a relatively stable community of organisms that have established interlocking relationships and exchanges with one another and their natural habitat. Consider, for instance, the links that bind together fish, a marine environment, and a small hunting and gathering population. In surface waters fish excrete organic waste that is converted by marine bacteria to inorganic products; the latter serve as nutrients for algal growth; the algae are eaten by the fish; human beings consume fish; human waste products decompose and provide nutrition for plants; plants assist in oxygenating the atmosphere, which is essential for sustaining the marine bacteria, algae, fish, and human beings. In brief, all components are caught up in a complex and delicately balanced cycle of life.

The process achieves the self-purification of the environment. Wastes produced in one step in the cycle become the necessary raw materials for the next step. We gain an appreciation for the efficiency of the arrangement when things go wrong. If the marine environment is overloaded with sewage and industrial effluents, the amount of oxygen required to support waste decomposition by the bacteria of decay may be insufficient. Lacking the necessary oxygen, the marine bacteria and fish die, and the entire cycle is halted. In this fashion countless streams, rivers, and lakes have become devoid of life and human beings have lost a vital resource. In sum, each component in the ecosystem is tied to others in an astonishingly complex web involving the circular flow of energy and materials within the living and nonliving environment.

The Ecological Environment

Ecology is the study of the interrelations between the living and nonliving components of an ecosystem. Sociologists are particularly interested in the human environment. One way of viewing the human ecological complex is to examine the relationships among population (P), organization (O), environment (E), and technology (T), the so-called POET complex. Take the matter of air pollution in Los Angeles (Duncan, 1959, 1961). Residents of Los Angeles experience periodic episodes of bluish-gray haze in the atmosphere that reduces visibility and irritates the eyes and the respiratory tract (E $\rightarrow$ P). The smog also damages plants (E $\rightarrow$ E) and erodes a variety of metals (E $\rightarrow$ T). Through the years, Los Angeles residents have organized various civic movements to deal with the problem and have secured the enactment of a variety of regulatory measures (E $\rightarrow$ O). Among other things, industrial plants have been required to install pollution-abatement devices (O $\rightarrow$ T).

Meanwhile, chemists have confirmed the

"factory in the sky" theory of smog formation—combustion and related processes release unburned hydrocarbons and oxides of nitrogen into the atmosphere which, when subjected to strong sunlight, form smog (T → E). Also implicated in the problem is the frequent occurrence of temperature inversion in the Los Angeles area, which keeps polluted air from rising very far above ground level (E → E). The problem has intensified with the growth in the population, leading residents to spread out over a wide territory (P → E) and heightening dependence on the automobile as the principal means of transportation (T → O). Duncan (1961:146) notes the following paradox: "Where could one find a more poignant instance of the principle of circular causation . . . than that of the Los Angelenos speeding down their freeways in a rush to escape the smog produced by emissions from the very vehicles conveying them?"

THE FUNCTIONALIST PERSPECTIVE ON THE ENVIRONMENT

Functionalist theorists approach the ecological environment by examining the interconnections among the various parts composing the ecosystem. They see the ecosystem as exhibiting a tendency toward equilibrium, in which its components maintain a delicately balanced relationship with one another. The notion of equilibrium implies that the system, despite internal changes and the impingement of external forces, remains on a relatively even keel. The perspective is nicely captured by the notion of Spaceship Earth—the idea that our planet is a vessel in the void of the universe, a closed system with finite resources that, if destroyed or depleted, cannot be replaced. Life exists only in the biosphere, a thin skin of air, soil, and water on the surface of the planet. The earth's biosphere has served humankind well. We have multiplied to over 4.8 billion people and expanded almost to all corners of the globe. In large part our remarkable success has derived from our ability to alter the environment and take from it the resources we need. But functionalists stress that our survival depends on our ability to maintain a precarious balance among the living and nonliving components comprising the biosphere. They fear that our pollution of the environment and our depletion of the earth's natural resources are jeopardizing the very environment that is the basis for life.

A graphic example of the reciprocal ties that bind human beings and their physical environment is provided by the sub-Saharan region of Africa. The tragedy of the region has been captured in recent years by television portrayals of the massive sufferings of its people. The scenes are familiar: pale deserts haunted by starving people, infant bellies swollen by want, and dead cattle. An estimated 35 million people in Africa live on the interfaces of deserts and arable land and are threatened by hunger. The overworking of marginal lands for crops, grazing, and firewood has resulted in "desert creep." Much of this "desertification" is not attributable to basic climatic change. Rather, the introduction of Western techniques, such as irrigation, deep plowing, and the use of chemical fertilizers has served to compound the region's problems (Cowell, 1984a). For instance, irrigated land became waterlogged, accumulated too much salt, and became useless. And the wells dug in arid regions led to people and cattle congregating in the vicinity of the wells, with the herds overgrazing the pastures and trampling the ground with their hoofs. Thus a vicious circle has been at work in which people intensify their exploitation of the land in order to compensate for desert creep, only to complicate their problems as this misuse in turn feeds new desert expansion. Functionalists emphasize that human beings must become more sensitive to both the manifest and latent consequences of their actions on the environment in order to avoid this type of damage to the ecosystem.

THE CONFLICT PERSPECTIVE ON THE ENVIRONMENT

As is true on many other issues, the conflict perspective does not offer a unified point of view on environmental matters. Some conflict theorists depict environmental problems as due more to the distribution of the world's resources than to a limited amount of resources available in the world. They say that the basic issue is not how much is available, but rather one of which individuals and groups will secure a disproportionate share of what is available. Hence, the critical decisions that affect the environment are made not in the interests of present and future generations, but in the interests of those groups that can impose their will on others. Conflict theorists also point out that people tend to be separated into two camps on environmental issues. On the one side there are those who favor economic development and growth even if it results in some measure of environmental damage. On the other side there are those who see environmental preservation as their primary goal and believe that the environment must take precedence over economic goals. The two groups are at odds and contest each other in the political arena.

Conflict theorists see many of the same circumstances in Africa as do the functionalists, but come to somewhat different conclusions. They point out that according to World Bank figures, sub-Saharan Africa's foreign debt increased almost tenfold between 1970 and 1982, from $5.7 billion to $51.3 billion (Cowell, 1984a). This growing indebtedness exerted pressure on African governments to promote cash crops for export rather than food crops for their people.

Simultaneously, commodity prices have fallen on the world market. Consequently, the African nations cannot repay their debts, nor can they afford to purchase food from other nations. Complicating matters, the money provided by Western aid agencies during the 1970s was diverted to highly visible projects, such as roads, port facilities, airports, and office buildings. Thus the aid money was recycled to Western corporations, while small African farmers were neglected. Moreover, when Western nations have provided food to African governments, they have found an outlet for surplus food in need of a market and have benefited American and European farmers. Finally, assistance is often rendered to African governments that are friendly toward the donor nations, in the process stabilizing the existing regimes (Cowell, 1984b).

ENVIRONMENTAL CONCERNS

Functionalist and conflict theorists disagree about many things. However, it is not uncommon for individuals from both camps to express distress over what they see as our deteriorating environment and our depletion of critical resources. By way of illustration, consider the following matters that are a source of considerable concern to many Americans:

Within the United States, more than 71 billion gallons of waste chemicals from ammonia to zinc are generated by industry each year. According to the Environmental Protection Agency, up to 90 percent of this chemical debris is improperly disposed of in open pits and ponds or leaky barrels (Work and Taylor, 1984). A report of the Office of Technology Assessment says that there are more than 10,000 disposal sites for hazardous waste around the country that urgently require cleanup to protect the public. It estimates that the total costs of cleaning up these sites could approach $100 billion. The General Accounting Office finds 378,000 hazardous waste sites that could be addressed under cleanup programs, although it says that many of them may not require priority attention (Shabecoff, 1985). Hazardous sites contain toxic chemicals, metals, and other substances that contaminate water sources and pose health hazards. For example, some 800 families had to leave Niagara's Love Canal area in 1979 after health experts linked unusually high rates of illness and death there to chemicals leaking from an old industrial dump.

A growing body of evidence shows that forests throughout the Eastern United States and Central Europe are in decline. Many species of trees are being dwarfed and deformed—and some have stopped growing at all. Moreover, the trees are losing their vitality and resistance to insects and disease. Environmentalists claim that "forest death" is resulting from acid rain. When coal, oil, and other fossil-based fuels are burned, the emissions are converted in the upper atmosphere into particles that return to earth in the form of highly acidic rain, snow, or fog (Taylor, 1984) (see Figure 11.1).

Since the beginning of this century, the population of the United States has increased about 200 percent, while per capita water use has shot up 500 to 800 percent. By 1980, water use in the nation came to some 2,000 gallons per day for each man, woman, and child. Complicating matters, the nation's reserves of

FIGURE 11.1 AILING AMERICAN WOODLANDS

The shading indicates areas where trees are being stunted or damaged by unusual illness.
(Source: U.S. News & World Report, April 23, 1984, p. 58. Copyright, 1984, U.S. News & World Report, Inc.)

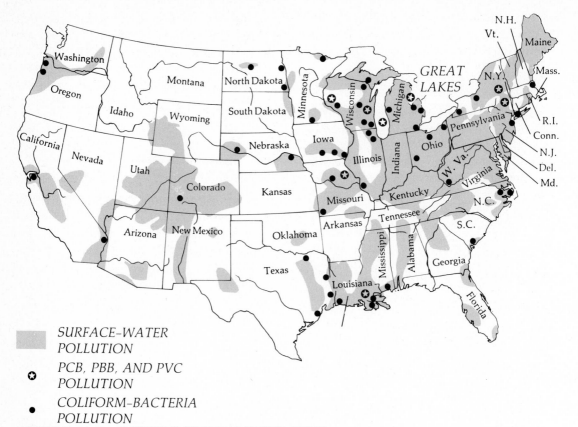

FIGURE 11.2 AMERICA'S GROWING WATER CRISIS

Increasing numbers of rivers and lakes are polluted with acid rain, chemicals like PCB's, and coliform bacteria from sewage. Below ground, water is being drawn from the network of aquifers more rapidly than it is flowing in. Complicating matters, as fresh water moves out, salt water seeps in from oceans and other sources. (Source: U.S. Water Resources Council and NOAA/USDA Joint Agricultural Weather Facility.)

water are being stretched thin as more rivers, lakes, and aquifers become polluted and undrinkable. Without more water, booming urban centers such as Los Angeles and Phoenix will stop growing and conceivably begin to shrivel. The shift of industry from the snow belt to the sun belt could be halted and huge agricultural areas could revert to desert (Sheets, 1983) (see Figure 11.2).

In 1982, Richard S. Schweiker, then secretary of Health and Human Services, admitted that the above-ground atomic

bomb tests in Nevada in the 1950s and 1960s probably caused human cancers as a result of radioactive fallout. Perhaps even more ominous are the warnings of scientists like Carl Sagan who cite evidence to support the view that the immense clouds of smoke and dust raised by even a medium-scale nuclear war could bring about a global "nuclear winter" (Turco et al., 1984). They say that land and water would freeze, causing global effects unrelated to radiation hazards. The upshot, they contend, would be the extinction of a significant propor-

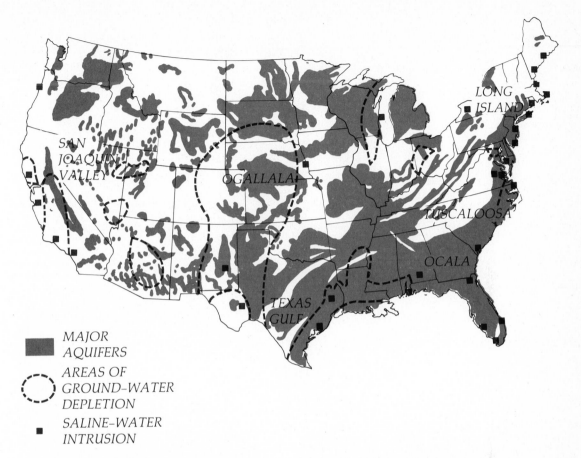

MAJOR
AQUIFERS

AREAS OF
GROUND-WATER
DEPLETION

SALINE-WATER
INTRUSION

tion of the earth's animals and plants, including very likely the human race (see Figure 11.3).

In 1984 the Environmental Protection Agency said that ethylene dibromide, the most powerful cancer-causing chemical the agency has tested, has so pervaded the nation's food supply that banning the substance would not eliminate it from America's diet for years. The chemical, known as EDB, has been used widely for more than two decades as a soil treatment and post-harvest fumigant for fruits, vegetables, and grains (Shabecoff, 1984).

Most people agree that these situations are serious. But what about the future? Are matters likely to get better or worse? Experts are in disagreement regarding the long-term effects of economic growth and development. Some take a pessimistic view, while others find considerable room for optimism.

The Pessimistic Scenario. Many authorities express grave concern about the prospects for the earth. Some, like sociologist William R. Catton (1980), say that capitalist and socialist nations alike have committed themselves to policies of economic growth that disregard the pollution of the biosphere and the rapid consumption of nonrenewable resources. Catton contends that we are not "approaching" a resource limit, but have already exceeded the earth's carrying capacity for human beings. He estimates that more than 90 percent of our species is sustained by energy resources that are not

5,000 megatons in bombs (one–third of world's nuclear arsenal) explode.

Bombs ignite huge fire–storms; 250 million tons of smoke and debris fill sky.

Winds, weather systems merge smoke, dust clouds from widespread blasts.

Clouds block 90% of sunlight. Temperatures fall below zero for months. Plants die. Animals, millions of people starve.

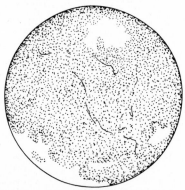

FIGURE 11.3   THE DESOLATION OF NUCLEAR WINTER
Carl Sagan and other scientists predict that nuclear winter would be a devastating after-effect of nuclear war. The figure depicts how the severe climatic changes would occur. (Source: USA Today, March 27, 1985, p. 5A. Copyright, 1985, USA Today. Reprinted by permission.)

replenishable. As these energy resources become exhausted and pollution systematically undermines the· environment, a "crash" or decrease in population is inevitable. The situation is like a population of yeast cells feeding on a vat of freshly pressed grape juice. The large supply of sugar allows exuberant growth until the resource is exhausted and the concentration of alcohol (pollution) it produces becomes too great. The yeast population then becomes extinct. The world's problems are complicated by the fact that three-quarters of the earth's population uses about 25 percent of the resources; the other 75 percent are consumed by the affluent, industrialized quarter of humanity. Catton suggests the possibility that various social antagonisms and ills, including racism, social inequalities, nazism, war, and student unrest, may result from population pressure in an environment with too few resources.

Sobering conclusions are also contained in *The Global 2000 Report to the President* issued in 1980 by the Council on Environmental Quality. It insists that because the earth is of finite weight and the population is ever-increasing, we soon will be running out of natural resources. The report's main conclusion is that "The world in 2000 will be more crowded, more polluted, less stable ecologically, and more vulnerable to disruption than the world we live in now. Serious stresses involving population, resources and environment are clearly visible ahead." The report contends that the world is likely to be confronted with subtantially higher prices for food, oil, minerals, and fertilizer. In less-developed countries, it sees increasing soil erosion, little room for the expansion of cropland, water shortages, deforestation, loss of species, more overcrowding, and more pollution. It concludes that the world's people will be "poorer in many ways" and life will be "more precarious" by the year 2000 "unless the nations of the world act decisively to alter current trends." The only way out, the report says, would be centralized government planning, controls on the allocation of scarce resources, and internationalism.

The Optimistic Scenario. Economist Julian L. Simon and the late futurist Herman Kahn (1984) explicitly contradict the wording in *Global 2000,* saying: "If present trends continue, the world in 2000 will be less crowded (though more populated), less polluted, more stable ecologically, and less vulnerable to resource-supply disruption than the world we live in now. Stresses involving population, resources, and environment will be less in the future than now." Based on historical trends, they predict declining scarcity, falling prices for raw materials, and increased wealth. Given time to adjust to shortages with known methods and new inventions, Simon and Kahn say that free people create additional resources. For instance, plastics were originally developed as substitutes for elephant ivory in billiard balls after tusks began to grow scarce. Thus an actual or perceived shortage eventually leaves us better off than if the shortage had never arisen, thanks to resulting new techniques. The free play of market forces is fundamental to the vision of Simon and Kahn, who place considerable faith in human ingenuity and the rate of technological advance. They view government intervention in the market as more often the cause of, rather than a solution to, the problems of the world.

Pessimists look at the economic resources already discovered in the world and conclude that the rest will be more difficult to find and more expensive to extract. But Simon (1981) says cost is not a function of scarcity, but of technology. He notes that once upon a time ships were dispatched to kill whales for their oil. Then resourceful individuals began to spread blankets on the surface of oily pools and wring them out by hand to extract the petroleum. Next human beings turned to drilling holes in the ground to get oil. Overall, he finds that the history of raw materials and energy is one of steadily declining prices.

Simon rejects the warnings of those who talk about "nonrenewable resources" in a "finite world," noting that our "spaceship earth" is a body of 260 billion cubic miles of material. Nor does he accept the specter of environmental ruin. He argues that pollution was far worse in nineteenth-century cities, with coal dust, horse manure, and human excrement posing serious health hazards. Simon looks for proof that the environment is improving in data showing lower age-specific death rates and increased life expectancies. He rejects claims that we are destroying our "delicately balanced" ecology, noting that ecologists once pronounced Lake Erie to be "eternally dead," yet today it is teeming with fish. And he finds fault with forecasts of global famine, citing statistics to show that throughout the world people are eating better than ever because the amount of cropland and yields per acre are increasing. According to Simon, people who are engaged in work and creating knowledge are "the ultimate resource." Wealth, rather than being a fixed quantity, is produced by people. Simon would leave the world more or less to its own devises, especially to the operation of unimpeded market forces, a point of view many ecologists dismiss as naive and foolhardy.

The ability of pessimists and optimists to use the *identical* data to arrive at diametrically opposite conclusions leads us again to the insight supplied by symbolic interactionists that social problems (as well as environmental problems) are matters of social definition. Even more crucially, the question becomes one of which individuals and groups will be able to translate their vision of reality into official public policy.

THE EFFECTS OF CROWDING

We commonly think that crowding is bad for people. Popular belief holds that it breeds family breakdown, mental illness, suicide, alcoholism, crime, and violence. The notion has found support in research which shows that population buildup has

bad effects on deer, rats, and a variety of other organisms (Christian, 1983). For instance, John Calhoun (1962) studied overcrowding among Norway rats and found that high population densities led to the disintegration of family life, high infant mortality rates, small litters, inadequate nest building, abandonment of the young, cannibalism, and sadism. Calhoun labeled the situation a "behavioral sink."

In contrast, the impact of crowding on human behavior is more complex, and it does not invariably result in pathology (Choldin, 1978). Take crime. Implausible as it may seem, over the past thirty years American urban density and household crowding have declined sharply, while crime rates have soared. Additionally, crowded cities, including Tokyo, London, Buffalo, and Providence, have low crime rates, whereas relatively uncrowded cities, including Los Angeles, Houston, and New Orleans, are characterized by high crime rates. Likewise, in New York City no relationship has been found between neighborhood crowding and the crime rate. When the economic level of neighborhoods is equated, population density is not associated with the crime rate or any other type of social, mental, or physical pathology. And although researchers have attempted to link crowding to aggression, studies typically show that there is no significant independent association between the two factors (Sundstrom, 1978). Such findings seemingly suggest that the source of social pathology must be elsewhere.

It would be amiss, however, to conclude that crowding has no impact on human behavior. It does. Social scientists distinguish between density and crowding. **Density** has to do with the physical compactness of people in space. **Crowding** is the perception people have that too many other individuals are present in the situation. Crowding, then, is not a product of absolute numbers,

Crowded conditions have long prevailed in urban environments. This 1912 photo shows row tenements on Elizabeth Street in New York City. (RH Photo Archive)

but of people's social definitions. Thus architectural designs—the arrangement of doors, windows, partitions and other dividers—that give people a greater sense of privacy lead them to feel less crowded, even though the density remains the same. Similarly, the sense of crowding that students often experience in long-corridor dormitories can be lessened by modifying the hallways so as to cluster the residents into suites with fewer than 20 members (Baum and Davis, 1980).

A good many factors influence whether or not people define a situation as being crowded (Sundstrom, 1978). Duration is one factor. For instance, people typically find it easier to tolerate a brief exposure to high-density conditions such as a ride on a crowded elevator than prolonged exposure on a cross-country bus. A second factor is predictability. People typically find crowded settings even more stressful when they are unable to predict them. A third factor has to do with frame of mind. There are times when individuals welcome solitude and other times when they prefer the presence of others. A fourth factor involves the environmental setting. People generally report that they can tolerate crowding better in impersonal settings such as a shopping center or an airline terminal than they can in more personal settings like their home or apartment. Finally, crowding seems to intensify people's definition of a situation (Freedman, 1975). If people are fearful and antagonistic—or excited and friendly—crowding tends to intensify the feelings. Crowding makes a doctor's waiting room and a subway car all the more unpleasant, whereas it makes a football game and a party all the more enjoyable. And even though a crowded New York subway car turns people off, a crowded San Francisco cable car, crammed with people hanging over the sides, is defined as a "tourist attraction."

Population

It is difficult to consider the human environment without turning rather quickly to a discussion of the world's population. **Demography** is the science dealing with the size, distribution, composition, and changes in population. Demographic data show that world population growth is at once both awesome and sobering. The earth gains 150 new human beings each minute, 9,100 each hour, 218,000 each day, and some 80 million each year. World population is growing so rapidly that every three years the new additions equal the total population of the United States. As we go back in time, population statistics become increasingly fragmentary and unreliable, so that the earliest figures represent at best informed guesses (Wilford, 1981). It is estimated that some 40,000 years ago the world population stood at about three million. At 8000 B.C., the dawn of agriculture, it was 5 million. At the time of Christ, it was 200 million, an estimate believed to have a fair degree of accuracy. By 1650, it had climbed to 500 million, and by 1830, to 1 billion. At the end of World War II and the advent of the nuclear age, it stood at 2.3 billion. In 1985 there were some 4.8 billion people on the globe. Thus it took millions of years for humankind to reach 1 billion in number, but within a century it had reached 2 billion and within an additional quarter century, 4 billion (see Figure 11.4). However, it is anticipated that world population will "stabilize" at just over 11 billion people by the year 2150 (Population Reference Bureau, 1984).

ELEMENTS IN POPULATION CHANGE

All population change within a society can be reduced to three factors: the birth rate, the death rate, and the migration rate into or out of the society.

Birth Rate. The **crude birth rate** is the number of live births per 1,000 members of a population in a given year. In 1982 the crude birth rate for Americans was 16 per 1,000, substantially lower than that of nations like Kenya in eastern Africa, with a crude birth rate of 53.8 per 1,000. The measure is called "crude" because it obscures important differences among races, ethnic groups, classes, age groups, and other categories within the population by lumping all births within a single figure (see Table 11.1). The **general fertility rate** indicates the annual number of live births per 1,000 women aged 15 to 44. In 1983, the general fertility rate for American women in their primary childbearing years was 73.2 per 1,000. Demographers also calculate **age-specific fertility,** or the number of live births per 1,000 women in a specific age group, such as from 25 to 29 or 30 to 34. Fertility rates provide us with information regarding the *actual* reproductive patterns of a society. By contrast, the potential number of children that could be born if every woman of childbearing age bore all children she possibly could is called **fecundity.**

As Figure 11.5 shows, the number of children born in recent years has risen to near the baby-boom highs of the late 1950s. The reason the number of births has risen is that the number of women of childbearing age has increased as the large generation born during the baby boom of the 1950s has reached adulthood. However, the average number of children born to women of childbearing age is only about half of what it was three decades ago. As noted in Chapter 9, childbearing is up sharply among women in their early thirties who postponed having babies until their schooling was completed and their careers begun. Between 1980 and 1983, births jumped 15 percent among women aged 30 to 34 (women in this category averaged 69.1 births per 1,000 women in 1983, up from 60.0 in 1980). Rates for

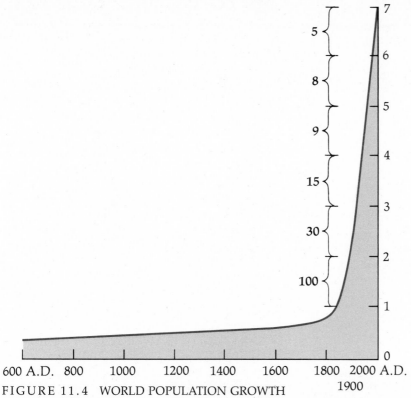

FIGURE 11.4   WORLD POPULATION GROWTH
The bold numbers inside the graph indicate the rapidly decreasing number of years required to increase the world's population by 1 billion people. (Source: Population Reference Bureau, Inc.)

other age groups have remained fairly constant during the same period.

Young American women say they want so few children that, if they actually have that number of children, their generation will not replace itself. The average number of children that a woman aged 18 to 24 expects to have in her lifetime is currently 1.8. It takes an average of 2.1 children per woman for a modern population to replace itself without immigration, the level of **zero population growth (ZPG).** Some 12 percent of all women aged 18 to 34 indicate that they do not plan to have children. These trends reflect the dramatically changing roles of women in American life and in the work force (Census Bureau, 1983).

Death Rate. The **crude death rate** is the number of deaths per 1,000 members of a population in a given year. In 1982 the crude death rate for Americans was 8.6 per 1,000, substantially lower than that of a nation like Chad in central Africa, which had a crude death rate of 44.1 per 1,000. As in the case of birth rates, demographers are interested in **age-specific death rates,** or the number of deaths per 1,000 individuals in a specific age group. For instance, in 1982 the death rate for American children ages 1 to 14 was .36 per 1,000 (36 per 100,000); for adolescents and young adults 15 to 24, 1.05 (105 per 100,000); and for those 25 to 64, 4.63 (463 per 100,000). The **infant mortality rate** is the number of deaths among infants un-

TABLE 11.1

Births in the United States in 1981 per 1,000 Women Age 18–44

By Age	
18–24	92.1
25–29	112.8
30–34	67.3
35–39	28.6
40–44	7.1
By Race	
White	68.5
Black	81.3
Hispanic (all races)	99.2
By Marital Status	
Married	96.8
Divorced, widowed	27.8
Never married	27.0
By Education	
Not high school graduates	88.2
High school graduates	70.3
College graduates	64.7
By Status as Worker	
Employed	40.6
Unemployed	78.2
Not in labor force	126.1
By Family Income	
Less than $5,000	95.5
$5,000–$14,999	80.4
$15,000–$24,999	76.9
More than $25,000	52.4

(*Source:* U.S. Departments of Commerce and Health and Human Services.)

der 1 year of age per 1,000 live births. In 1982 the infant mortality rate in the United States was 11.2 per 1,000. Fifteen nations report infant mortality rates lower than this, the lowest being reported in Sweden, Japan, and Finland, with rates of 6.7, 7.4, and 7.7, respectively. In contrast, the infant mortality rate among Ethiopians is 229.

The life expectancy of Americans reached a high of 74.7 years in 1983. White females

born in 1983 can expect to live 78.8 years, and black females 73.8 years. In contrast, white males born in 1983 have a life expectancy of 71.6 years, and black males a life expectancy of 65.2 years. As a result of the greater longevity of women, there are currently in the United States three women for every two men over the age of 65; in the over-85 bracket, the margin is better than two to one. Genetic differences may play a part in these sex differences (Epstein, 1983). Women appear to be more durable organisms because of an inherent sex-linked resistance to some types of life-threatening disease. For instance, the female hormone estrogen is a protective factor against cardiovascular disease. Life-style differences also seem to play a part. One factor has been the higher incidence of smoking among men (Holden, 1983). But with the rising incidence of smoking among teen age girls, women may lose some of their statistical advantage in the years ahead.

Migration Rate. The **net migration rate** is the increase or decrease per 1,000 members of the population in a given year that results from people entering (immigrants) or leaving (emigrants) a society. Migration is the product of two factors. There are those forces—*push* factors—that encourage people to leave a habitat they already occupy. And there are those forces—*pull* factors—that attract people to a new habitat. Before people actually migrate, they usually compare the relative opportunities offered by the present and the anticipated habitats. If the balance is on the side of the anticipated habitat, they typically migrate unless prevented from doing so by a Berlin Wall, immigration quotas, lack of financial resources, or some other compelling reason. In the 1840s the "push" of the potato famine in Ireland and the "pull" of employment opportunities in the United States made this country appear attractive to many Irish people. Likewise,

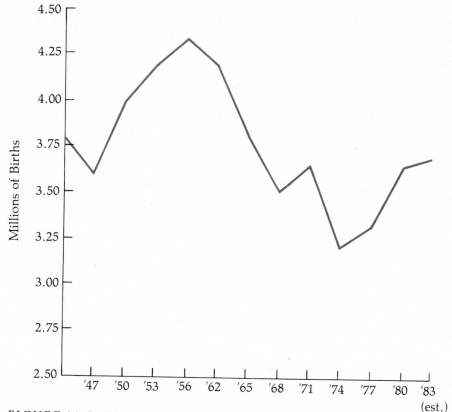

FIGURE 11.5   INCREASE IN U.S. BIRTHS, 1947 TO 1983
Figures are rounded to the nearest million, and adjustment is made for under-registration. (Source: National Center for Health Statistics.)

the "push" resulting from the failure of the 1848 revolution and the "pull" of American political freedom led many Germans to seek their fortunes in this country. At the present time, both "push" and "pull" factors are contributing to the entry into the United States of large numbers of illegal aliens from Mexico. Low agricultural productivity and commodity prices in Mexican agriculture have served as a "push" factor, and high American wages have served as a "pull" factor (see Chapter 7). Movement of people from one nation to another is called **international migration.**

People also move about within a nation—**internal migration.** Data from the census

taken in the United States every ten years reveal the impact of changing migration patterns. The 1980 census showed two historic firsts: For the first time, a majority of the American population resides in the South and West. And for the first time since the Industrial Revolution, rural and small-town communities in the nation are growing more rapidly than metropolitan areas. Once-vast empty areas of the United States are filling as modern communications, transportation, and economic growth allow more and more corporations and individuals to locate outside the major urban centers.

Somewhat similar trends are occurring in

The Sun Belt states of the South and West have been growing more rapidly than other regions of the nation. Dallas, Texas, shown here, has experienced particularly rapid growth. Changes in population distribution mean that new facilities must be provided in growing areas, while existing facilities in areas of out-migration are likely to be underused. Derivative changes range far and wide in other areas of life, including housing, schools, roads, hospitals, and shopping facilities. (Cary Wolinsky/Stock, Boston)

Canada and the heavily industrialized countries of northwestern Europe (Belgium, Denmark, France, the Netherlands, and West Germany). Since the beginning of the Industrial Revolution, the transition from an agrarian economy to an industrial one typically has been accompanied by an increasing concentration of a nation's population in high-density "core" areas. Populous metropolitan centers become distinct from the sparsely peopled "hinterland" or "periphery" areas. This growth was fostered by *economies of scale* in the organization of an industrial society. An economy of scale is the saving that results from making an investment in an area where the concentration of people and industry is already high. For instance, such services as schools, roads, hospitals, sewage, and drinking water systems, and fire and police forces are already in place in established urban centers. The fact that migration into the core of developed countries is being replaced by

a flow toward the periphery suggests that the advantages of the economies of scale have been reduced. New technology and the development of service industries allows for the dispersion of offices and plants (Vining, 1982).

Growth Rate. The **growth rate** of a society is the difference between births and deaths, plus the difference between immigrants and emigrants per 1,000 population. In 1983 the United States had a growth rate of 0.9 percent. The highest annual population growth rate is 11.3 percent in the United Arab Emirates. The growth rate of the Soviet Union is roughly comparable to that of the United States. However, a number of nations, including East Germany, West Germany, and Hungary have negative annual growth rates, which means that without immigration they will lose population. If we consider merely the difference between the birth and death rates (the rate of natural increase), it takes a population with an annual rate of increase of 1 percent 69 years to double its population; a 4 percent annual rate increase leads to a doubling of the population in 17 years.

The Census Bureau predicts that by the year 2000, six of every ten Americans will live in the South and West (see Figure 11.6). The West will continue to be the fastest-growing region, increasing by 45 percent. The South will increase by 31.2 percent over the next two decades. By contrast, the North Central region is expected to increase by only 1.5 percent, while population in the Northeast will contract by 5.5 percent. The Census Bureau cautions that a good deal can happen in fifteen years and its assump-

tions that current migration patterns will continue could prove wrong (Schellhardt, 1983).

POPULATION COMPOSITION

Births, death, and migration affect population *size*. Sociologists are also interested in the *composition* or characteristics of a population. Among these characteristics are sex, age, rural or urban residence, race, religion, national origin, marital status, income, education, and occupation. The sex composition of a population is of particular significance. It is measured by the *sex ratio*—the number of males per 100 females. At birth, there are roughly 105 males for every 100

FIGURE 11.6   PROJECTED STATE-BY-STATE PERCENTAGE CHANGES IN POPULATION, 1980 TO 2000
(Source: U.S. Bureau of the Census, 1983.)

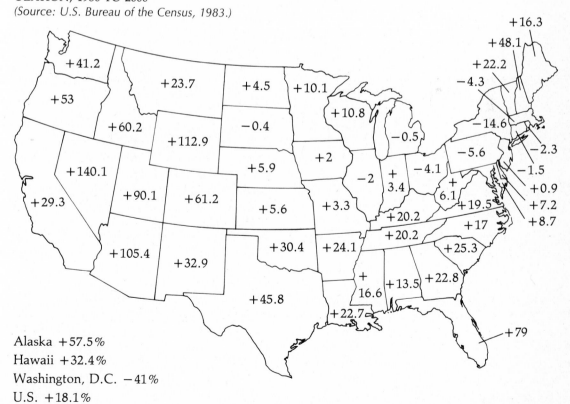

Alaska +57.5%
Hawaii +32.4%
Washington, D.C. −41%
U.S. +18.1%

females. But around age 20, women begin to outnumber men, and the rate accelerates as people grow older. Typically, frontier, mining, cattle-raising, and lumbering areas attract a disproportionate number of males. Females, in contrast, are found in greatest numbers in cities that concentrate on commercial and clerical activities (for instance, Hartford, Connecticut, and Washington, DC).

Another important population characteristic is its age composition. A population heavily concentrated in the 20 to 65 years range has a large labor force relative to its nonproductive population. Its dependency burdens tend to be light. In contrast, a population concentrated at either extreme of the age distribution—either under 20, over 65, or both—has a heavy dependency ratio (a large number of nonproductive individuals relative to its productive population). We can gain an appreciation for the social significance of these matters by examining population pyramids.

Population Pyramids. The age and sex composition of a population can be portrayed by a **population pyramid,** often called the "tree of ages" (see Figure 11.7). It is based either on absolute numbers or on proportions. Age groupings are placed in order on a vertical scale, with the youngest age group located at the bottom and the oldest age group at the top of the diagram. On the horizontal axis are plotted the numbers or proportions that each specified age group represents of the total, with the sum or portion corresponding to the male segment placed to the left of the central dividing line and that comprising the female segment placed to the right of it. The pyramid itself represents the entire population.

Social Significance of Population Changes. The population pyramid for 1900 shown in Figure 11.7 has the shape of a true pyramid,

typical of a population that is increasing by virtue of a high birth rate and a declining death rate. The 1940 and 1980 pyramids reveal a different picture. They are the product of a decline in both the birth rate and the death rate. Notice that the bases of the 1940 and 1980 pyramids are contracted, reflecting the decline in the birth rate in 1930 and 1970. Next notice the short bars in the 40 to 50 age group in the 1980 pyramid; those individuals occupying the base bars in the 1940 pyramid have now moved slightly above the middle-age range.

Pyramids based on absolute numbers, like that shown in Figure 11.7, are of particular value to public officials, educators, investors, and planners. From this type of pyramid it is possible to project the age structure of the population at various time intervals in the future. From the 1980 pyramid we can project that population changes are likely to cause a shortage of military recruits in the near future, a continued slump in businesses that serve teenagers, a substantial growth in household consumption in the 1980s, and heavy pressure on health and pension systems in the next century.

Many current population effects are due to the large "bulge" of persons born after World War II that is now making its way through the age groups. Sandwiched between two much smaller generations—the children born during the Great Depression of the 1930s and the "baby bust" group of the 1970s—the baby boom generation has swelled and strained American institutions at every stage. Demographers liken their progress through the population pyramid to that of a watermelon swallowed by a python. The bumper crop of 64 million infants born between 1946 and 1961 are now 25 to 40 years old and make up nearly a third of the American population. In the 1950s the baby boomers made the United States a child-oriented society of new schools, sub-

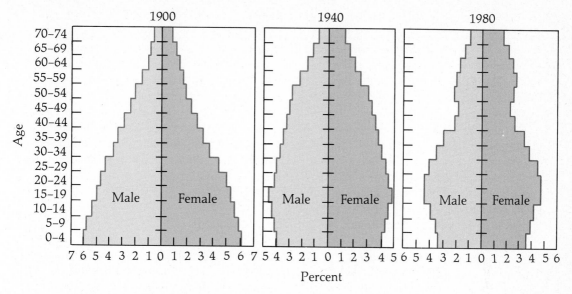

Population Pyramids, 1900, 1940, and 1980, Based on Proportions

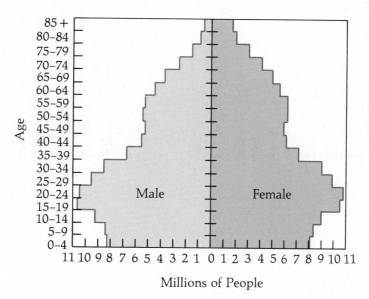

Population Pyramid, 1980, Based on Absolute Numbers

FIGURE 11.7   POPULATION PYRAMIDS, UNITED STATES
(Source: U.S. Bureau of the Census.)

urbs, and station wagons. The baby boomers born before 1955 were on their generation's cutting edge. They provided the nation with Davy Crockett and rock'n'roll, went to Woodstock and Vietnam, and fueled the student, civil rights, and peace movements of the 1960s and early 1970s. The younger boomers, in contrast, tend to be more politically conservative. They find that their older brothers and sisters have already filled the better jobs, in many cases blocking their career ladders. Moreover, the younger boomers are entering the job market at a time of economic difficulty and seeking housing at a time when high prices and interest rates have put many homes out of their financial reach. The imbalance in the size of the nation's generations is likely to cause additional problems when the baby boom children reach old age. By the year 2030, one out of every five Americans will be 65 or older and dependent on a Social Security and Medicare system that must be supported by the smaller generations behind them. The Social Security dependency ratio—the number of workers compared with the number of recipients—was five to one in 1965, but will drop to two to one by 2035.

Many of the new schools built to accommodate the large numbers of baby boomers in the 1960s are now closed or half empty. Colleges are already scrambling to keep enrollments up. The college-age population (individuals aged 18 to 24) peaked in 1981 at 30 million people. By 1995, only 24 million people will be 18 to 24 years old, a 22 percent decline from 1981. College presidents are turning to adult education in hopes of maintaining their enrollments. There are currently more than 3 million people between the ages of 25 and 34 enrolled in school, double the number ten years ago. As college graduates become more numerous, the competitive employment advantage will belong to those who have secured

graduate education. Additionally, some elementary schools may face overcrowding soon, an echo of the baby boom. As noted earlier in the chapter, the large number of baby boom women now entering their prime childbearing years is responsible for the increase. In sum, the periodic rise and fall of births in the United States creates waves of people who move through the age groups, alternately building up and eroding major institutional arrangements and changing the social landscape.

MALTHUS AND MARX

The relationship between population growth and the level of a nation's welfare has long been a central concern for those interested in population problems. The concern has been especially pronounced since 1798, when the English historian and political scientist Thomas Robert Malthus (1766–1834) first published his *Essay on the Principle of Population*. Many of the issues he raised are still being debated today. Malthus took an extremely pessimistic view, asserting that human populations tend to increase at a more rapid rate than the food supply needed to sustain them. Human beings, Malthus said, confront two unchangeable and antagonistic natural laws: (1) the "need for food," and (2) the "passion between the sexes." He contended that, whereas agricultural production tends to increase in arithmetic fashion (1-2-3-4-5-6-7-8), population has a tendency to increase in geometric fashion (1-2-4-8-16-32-64-128). Based on this formulation, Malthus took a dim view of the future, for if populations always increase to the ultimate point of subsistence, progress can have no lasting effect. Population will invariably catch up, and literally "eat" away the higher levels of living. He considered famine, war, and pestilence to be the chief deterrents to excessive population growth. But Malthus also recognized that preventive checks might reduce the birth rate—what he called "moral restraint." But since he was also an ordained minister, it either did not occur to him that people might use birth control, or he viewed birth control as a sin and beneath human dignity.

Many questions have since been raised regarding the Malthusian thesis. For one thing, Malthus failed to appreciate the full possibilities of the Industrial Revolution and its ability to expand productive capacities to an extent unknown in his time. Additionally, there is no clear evidence that food always and everywhere can increase only in arithmetic ratio. For example, within the United States the application of technology—farm machinery, irrigation, fertilizers, pesticides, and hybrid plants and animals—has resulted in subsistence growing as fast and even faster than population. Indeed, there is a growing body of evidence that demographic pressure stimulates technological evolution, leading to more productive agricultural techniques (Boserup, 1965; Cohen, 1977). And as noted above, Malthus did not foresee the possibility of new birth control methods or their application within the context of a value system favoring small families.

In some respects, Malthus may be seen as an intellectual predecessor of the political conservatives of the present (Dupaquier, Fauve-Chamoux, and Grebenik, 1983). When they attempt to do good, Malthus thought that governments end up doing evil. By fostering early marriage, he contended, the English Poor Law that subsidized the incomes of workers with families merely increased the numbers of the poor. Even so, Malthus did encourage public policies that would lead people to consider rationally the future consequences of their actions.

Karl Marx (1906) took issue with many Malthusian notions and formulations. He insisted that an excess of population, or more particularly of the working class, depends on the availability of employment opportunities, not a fixed supply of food. Marx believed that a deepening crisis of the capitalist system would inevitably force increasing numbers of workers into the ranks of the unemployed, leading some individuals to conclude that society is overpopulated. Thus he traced the problems associated with population growth to capitalist society, and sought cures in a fundamental restructuring of the social and economic order. Viewed in this fashion, population is always relative to the social structure. In sum, whereas Malthus looked primarily to the individual to restrain population growth through self-control, Marx looked to collective action to refashion institutional life.

DEMOGRAPHIC TRANSITION

A number of social scientists have employed the idea of **demographic transition** to map out the population growth characteristic of the modern era (Davis, 1945; Notestein, 1945). Viewed as history, the notion seeks to explain what has happened in European nations over the last two hundred years. Viewed as theory, it has been used to predict what will happen in developing nations in the future. Demographic transition theory holds that the process of modernization is associated with three stages in population change (see Figure 11.8):

Stage 1: High potential growth. Societies untouched by industrialization and urbanization are characterized by a high birth rate and a high death rate. As a result, the population remains relatively stable. The stage is described as having "high potential growth" because, once the societies gain control over their death rates, their growth is likely to be rapid.

Stage 2: Transitional growth. Modernization has its initial impact on mortality levels. Improved housing, better levels of nutri-

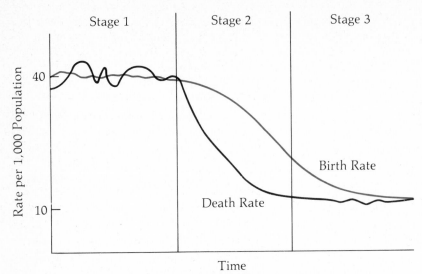

FIGURE 11.8   TRENDS IN BIRTH AND DEATH RATES ACCORDING
TO THE THEORY OF DEMOGRAPHIC TRANSITION

tion, and improvements in health and sanitary measures bring about a steady decline in death rates. Since a decisive reduction in the death rate has traditionally been associated with a marked drop in the infant mortality rate, a larger proportion of the huge yearly crop of babies survives and in time themselves become parents. Thus a drop in the death rate, while the birth rate of a population remains unchanged, results in a marked increase in the rate of population growth. But as time passes, couples begin to realize that with lower infant mortality rates, fewer births are required to produce the same number of surviving children, and they adjust their fertility accordingly. Moreover, the costs and benefits associated with children change as modernization progresses, making small families economically advantageous. The second stage ends when the birth rate sinks to meet the death rate.

Stage 3: Population stability. Modernization allows couples to gain control of their fertility through effective birth control techniques while simultaneously undermining religious proscriptions against their use.

The result, according to demographic transition theorists, is that modern societies come to be characterized by low mortality and low fertility, a situation approximating zero population growth.

Social scientists have debated whether modernization produces these stages in a reliable, regular way (Tilly, 1978b; Eberstadt, 1981). For one thing, they are not sure that the stages represent an accurate portrayal of European demographic history. For instance, demographer William Petersen (1960) finds that the Netherlands followed a quite different demographic course than that suggested by the theory. In the modern era, the Netherlands underwent a more or less continuous growth in population, although its death rate did not decline until the twentieth century. Indeed, in the period between 1750 and 1850, the death rate apparently rose. Dutch population growth was a product of a rise in fertility that followed the breakdown of traditional inhibitions against procreation. Likewise, the transition process in many other European nations did not follow the scenario outlined by proponents of the theory. Nor does demographic transition theory apply directly to the poor countries of today's world. For example, in some nations, such as Jamaica, fertility has actually gone up in recent decades as an initial response to economic advance (Tilly, 1978b). Other theories fare little better. For example, the French experience does not lend support to conflict and Marxist theories contending that specific modes of production are associated with particular demographic patterns (McQuillan, 1984). Apparently, a great many variables come to bear in quite different interrelationships to produce widely different demographic outcomes.

POPULATION POLICIES

There are three basic schools of thought relating to fertility-reduction policies (Grunstaff, 1981). The first approach involves *family planning*. Its proponents contend that if contraceptives are made readily available, and information regarding the value and need for birth planning is disseminated throughout a society, people will reduce their fertility. In turn, a reduction in fertility will allow investment in economic development. Yet it is easy to fall into the "technological fallacy"—adopting a blind faith in the gadgetry of contraception—without fully appreciating the *social* changes that may first be required. Even the best technique will not be employed unless people want to use it. The simple truth is that people in many parts of the world do *not* want to limit their number of children. For many individuals, children are their chief protection against the buffetings of life, providing care when they are unemployed, sick, or elderly. Birth rates come down when people are motivated to lower their fertility, whether or not they have modern contraceptives available to them. Throughout hu-

man history, people have been quite enterprising in separating sexual enjoyment from procreation.

A second approach entails a *developmentalist* strategy. According to this school of thought, fertility is a pattern of behavior tied closely to the institutional and organizational structure of society. Its proponents call upon Western nations to share their wealth and not exploit the resources of Third World nations. At the 1974 UN World Population Conference in Bucharest, delegates from many Communist countries recommended a policy of laissez-faire: "Take care of the people and population will take care of itself," or "Development is the best contraceptive." Although modernization has often been associated with a decline in fertility, as our discussion of the demographic transition theory reveals, the relation is not clear-cut enough to justify a simple causal link between industrialization and smaller families.

A third approach involves a *societalist* perspective. The government fashions policies designed to produce changes in demographic behavior. Demographer Kingsley Davis (1971:403) suggests a number of social reforms that would reduce fertility by rewarding low fertility and penalizing high fertility:

[T]he most effective social changes would be those that offer opportunities and goals that compete with family roles. For instance, giving advantages in housing, taxes, scholarships, and recreation to single as compared to married people, would discourage early marriage. Giving special educational and employment opportunities to women would foster career interests and therefore lessen motherhood as a woman's sole commitment. . . . Discontinuing the custom of family names, giving more complete control over children to nursery and elementary schools while holding parents responsible for the costs. . . . As for methods of *birth control, including abortion, these could be provided free of charge.*

A number of nations have used coercion to reduce fertility. For a period in the 1970s, India inaugurated a program of forced sterilization that resulted in just under 1 million vasectomies being performed each month (Kaufman, 1979). And in recent years China has instituted harsh methods to curb population growth, including punishing couples who have two or more children and fining a woman pregnant with a second child 20 percent of her pay if she refuses to have an abortion (there were 74 abortions for 100 live births in Peking in 1982, and 84 abortions for 100 live births in Shunyi County outside Peking) (Wren, 1984). Such programs have aroused considerable indignation among many citizens in Western nations. Clearly, programs for reducing fertility remain quite controversial, both in terms of their effectiveness and their morality.

THE AMERICAN HEALTH CARE SYSTEM

The health of a people forcefully affects key demographic factors. Accordingly, a society's health care system assumes critical importance. In American life the medical institution, through its control of health services, has become an important, independent source of power (Starr, 1982). By the late nineteenth century, physicians had largely absorbed or eliminated other health approaches, including homeopaths and herbal doctors, and had become sole arbiters of all health-related occupations and care systems. The authority of physicians was institutionalized through a system of medical school training, state licensing, and physician control of hospital personnel and technology. Over the past century, the private practitioner has been the primary provider of medical services, while hospitals

have been the central focus of health care delivery. But in order to take advantage of special income-sheltering provisions of the tax codes and economies of scale, physicians have increasingly incorporated their practices. The proportion of doctors in group practices is now 25 percent, compared with only 1 to 2 percent after World War II. Moreover, 1 out of 3 hospital beds belongs to a chain, and 1 out of 8 to a for-profit chain. Corporate medicine is growing in American life.

Although there has been a dramatic reduction in deaths from infectious diseases in the last century and steady gains have been made in containing major killer diseases like cancer and heart disease, health care in the United States is falling victim to runaway costs. Public and private expenditures on health care rose from 5 to 11 percent of the gross national product between 1960 and 1983. By 1983 Americans spent $1,459 for the health care of every man, woman, and child, and hospital expenditures were 35 times what they were in 1950 (see Figure 11.9). However, as economist Lester C. Thurow (1984c) points out, no set of expenditures can indefinitely rise faster than the gross national product. Already the mounting costs of the American medical care system are having consequences for the nation's economic performance and international competitiveness. Thurow calculates that in terms of cash wages, American auto workers make only slightly more ($11.80 per hour) than Japanese auto workers ($10.27 per hour). But when fringe benefits are included, the differential is substantially greater—$13.50 in Japan, versus almost $22 in the United States. At the Chrysler Corporation, health insurance premiums account for nearly $3 of these fringe benefits.

One approach to cutting medical costs has been prepayment plans, of which health maintenance organizations (HMOs)

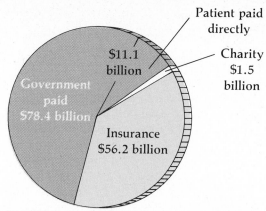

Patient paid directly

Charity $1.5 billion

$11.1 billion

Government paid $78.4 billion

Insurance $56.2 billion

FIGURE 11.9   WHO PAYS THE HOSPITAL BILL?
The figure shows how Americans paid their $147.2 billion hospital bill in 1983. (Source: U.S. Health Care Financing Administration.)

are a prominent example (Wells, 1984). For a fixed sum of money each year, the HMO provides its members with comprehensive health care (if it provides more services than its premiums permit, the HMO loses money, and hence it is motivated to stay within its limits). HMOs have proved economical. On average, they use 30 percent fewer hospital days than the traditional fee-for-service provider. Were the entire country suddenly to be converted to an HMO style of practice, there would be 11 million fewer hospital admissions each year, at an annual savings of $15 to $20 billion (Schwartz, 1984).

However, reduced hospital admissions will not be able to control the long-term costs of American health care. Each year the American population is growing both larger and older, contributing about 1 percentage point a year to the total annual increase of 7 percent in real costs. Likewise, the costs of goods and services that hospitals must purchase rise more rapidly than inflation, because the cost of labor is a very large portion of their budget. And finally, the continual upgrading in medical services as-

sociated with technological advances, including new diagnostic techniques, hip replacement, coronary-bypass surgery, and even liver, kidney, and heart transplantations, raise rather than lower medical costs.

Given the continued surge in health costs, Americans will have to find some way to expend a growing portion of the gross national product for medical care, or they will have to ration hospital services. And should they take this latter approach, Americans will then have to say to some people, "Yes, a new kidney would be good for you, but as a society we cannot afford it." Thus far, Americans have been reluctant to say "no" to those requiring expensive medical procedures. But each new advance in medical technology poses the same question: "How will this medical service be financed?" The dilemma Americans must increasingly confront is that, given limited resources, the nation cannot afford to give certain high-cost kinds of treatment to everyone. Indeed, to save money, Massachusetts has mandated that hospitals spend no more in each succeeding year than the increase in inflation minus 1.5 percent. This measure has effectively prevented the state's hospitals from performing certain transplant operations and from exploiting new technological advances to the fullest. The British have already confronted a similar problem. They spend half as much per capita on hospital care as Americans do, and accordingly their physicians have had to shape medical judgment to fit economic scarcity. For instance, up to the age of 45 or 50, the British rate of dialysis and transplantation for chronic kidney disease is nearly the same as in the United States. But few patients over 55 are referred to dialysis centers. It would seem that Americans will have to come to some social consensus concerning the tradeoff between the rising cost of medical services and life-extending benefits they provide.

The Urban Environment

We have seen that both population size and composition have a great many ramifications for all phases of social life. The distribution of a population in space also assumes critical significance. The "where" may be an area as large as a continent or as small as a city block. Between these extremes are world regions, nations, national regions, states, cities, and rural areas. Changes in the number and proportion of people living in various areas are the cumulative effect of differences in fertility, mortality, and net migration.

One of the most significant developments in human history has been the development of cities. Although many of us take cities for granted, they are one of the most striking features of our modern era. A **city** is a relatively dense and permanent concentration of people who secure their livelihood chiefly through nonagricultural activities. The influence of the urban mode of life extends far beyond the immediate confines of a city's boundaries. Many of the characteristics of modern societies, including the problems, derive from an urban existence. Perhaps we can gain a better appreciation for these matters by first considering the origin and growth of cities.

THE ORIGIN AND EVOLUTION OF CITIES

Cities constitute a relatively recent development in human history. Not until the Neolithic period did conditions become ripe for the existence of large settlements of people. The domestication of plants and the husbandry of animals were critical innovations that allowed human beings to become a partner with nature rather than a parasite on nature. In contrast with their hunting and gathering ancestors, human beings now achieved the ability to "produce" food, allowing for population expansion in settled communities (Childe, 1941, 1942).

Preindustrial Cities. Early Neolithic communities were more a matter of small villages than of cities. A number of innovations had to be added to the Neolithic complex before towns evolved. Between 6000 and 4000 B.C., the invention of the ox-drawn plow, the wheeled cart, the sailboat, metallurgy, irrigation, and the addition of new plants—when taken together—afforded a more intensive and productive use of Neolithic innovations. When this enriched technology came to be applied in locales where climate, soil, water, and topography were most favorable, the result was a sufficiently productive economy to permit the concentration in one place of people who did not grow their own food. These favoring conditions were found in broad river valleys with alluvial soil that was not exhausted by successive use, with a dry climate that minimized the leaching of soil, with ample days of sunshine, and with a nearby river that afforded a supply of water for irrigation.

Among the early centers of urban development were Mesopotamia, the Nile Valley of Egypt, the Indus Valley of India, and the Yellow River Basin of China (Davis, 1955, 1967). Yet by itself a productive economy was not sufficient to allow for the growth of cities. Rather than providing food for a surplus of city dwellers, cultivators can, at least in theory, multiply on the land until they end up producing just enough to sustain themselves. New forms of social organization were also required. Bureaucratic structures and stratification systems arose that enabled government officials, religious personnel, merchants, and artisans to appropriate for themselves part of the produce grown by cultivators (see Chapters 4 and 5).

For the most part, preindustrial cities did not exceed 10 percent of the population of an area. Cities of 100,000 or more were rare, although under favorable social and economic conditions some cities surpassed this size. Rome in the second century A.D., Constantinople as the political successor to Rome, Baghdad before A.D. 1000, the cities of Sung China between A.D. 1100 and 1300, and Tokyo, Kyoto, and Osaka in seventeenth- and eighteenth-century Japan all had populations well above 100,000, and in some cases, possibly even a million (Sjoberg, 1960). However, the size of preindustrial cities was restricted by a variety of factors. First, the roads and vehicles could not accommodate the transportation of bulky materials for long distances. And the preservation of perishable commodities, including foodstuffs, was difficult. Second, early cities had trouble securing the hinterlands. Their inhabitants were constantly threatened and often conquered by neighboring cities and nonurban peoples. Indeed, in time even mighty Rome succumbed to foreign invaders. Third, the absence of modern medicine and sanitation meant that urban living was frequently deadly. The water supply was often polluted by sewage, and as commercial centers, cities attracted transients who served as carriers of contagious diseases. Finally, serf, slave, and caste arrangements bound the peasantry to the land and prevented rural-urban migration. These and other factors made early cities primarily small affairs (Davis, 1955).

Industrial-Urban Centers. Urbanization has proceeded quite rapidly during the past 180 years. In 1800 there were fewer than 50 cities in the world with 100,000 or more population. By 1950 there were 906 cities, and by 1980 2,202 cities with over 100,000 inhabitants. By size, there are currently 26 cities with over 5 million people, 71 cities with between 2 and 5 million inhabitants, and 128 cities with between 1 and 2 million people. Most early urban communities were

city-states, and many modern nations have evolved from them. Even where the nation became large in both size and land area, the city has remained the focus for political and economic activities, and the core and magnet of much social life. To people of other nations, the city often represents the nation, and this tradition survives in the modern use of a city, such as Washington, London, and Moscow, as a synonym for a nation.

Both social factors and technological innovations contributed to the acceleration of urban growth. Organizational changes permitted greater complexity in the division of labor (see Chapter 4). Simultaneously the events labeled the Industrial Revolution allowed human beings to use steam as a source of energy, reinforcing those forces promoting the widespread use of machines.

Power-driven machines accelerated social trends that were drawing manufacturing out of the home to a centralized factory. As the factory system expanded, increasing numbers of workers were needed. People flocked to the factories, attracted not only by the novelty of urban life, but by the opportunity to realize greater economic rewards. In Europe city growth was also stimulated by the demise of feudal systems and the emergence of nation-states. Under the impetus of nationalism, large geographic areas were consolidated, enlarging internal markets, integrating transportation systems, providing for common coinage and weights, and abolishing internal duties on goods.

Metropolitan Cities. Industrial-urban centers have typically been geographically scattered, and although dominating their hinterlands, have had only tenuous economic and social relations with them. More recently, metropolitan cities have emerged. This phase in urban development does not represent a sharp break with the industrial-urban tradition, but rather a widening and deepening of urban influences in every area of social life. Increasingly cities have become woven into an integrated network. The technological base for the metropolitan phase of urbanism is found in the tremendous increase in the application of science to industry, the widespread use of electrical power (freeing industry from the limitations associated with steam and belt-and-pully modes of power), and the advent of modern forms of transportation (the automobile and rapid transit systems have released cities from the limitations associated with foot and hoof travel, which had more or less restricted growth to a radius of 3 miles from the center).

Steam and belt-and-pully power techniques had produced great congestion in urban areas by the beginning of the twentieth century. But a number of factors have increasingly come to the foreground and bucked earlier centripetal pressures, including rising city taxes, increased land values, traffic and transportation problems, and decaying and obsolescent inner zones. These and other forces have accelerated the centrifugal movement made technologically possible by electric power, rapid transit, the automobile, and the telephone. The result has been the development of satellite and suburban areas, broad, ballooning urban bands linked by beltways that constitute cities in their own right. In population, jobs, investment, construction, and shopping facilities, they rival the old inner cities. They are the sites of industrial plants, corporate offices and office towers, fine stores, independent newspapers, theaters, restaurants, superhotels, and big-league stadiums.

The conventional distinction between cities and rural areas is eroding in many Western societies as the world is becoming, in Marshall McLuhan's oft-quoted phase, a "global village." In many cases, the rural interstices between metropolitan centers have filled with urban development, mak-

ing a "strip city" or **megalopolis.** The Northeastern Seaboard is a good illustration of this process. A gigantic megalopolis lies along a 600-mile axis from southern New Hampshire to northern Virginia, encompassing 10 states, 117 counties, 32 cities larger than 500,000 people, and embracing nearly a fifth of the U.S. population. Urban projections suggest that by the year 2050, if not sooner, another urbanized strip will extend from New York State through Pennsylvania, Ohio, northern Indiana and Illinois to Green Bay, Wisconsin, and Minneapolis–St. Paul (see Figure 11.10).

PATTERNS OF CITY GROWTH

A good deal of the sociological enterprise is directed toward identifying recurrent and stable patterns in people's social interactions and relationships (see Chapter 2). In like fashion, sociologists are interested in understanding how people order their relationships and conduct their activities in space. They provide a number of models that attempt to capture the ecological patterns and structures of city growth (see Figure 11.11).

Concentric Circle Model. In the period between World Wars I and II, sociologists at the University of Chicago viewed Chicago as a social laboratory and subjected it to intensive study. The **concentric circle model** enjoyed a prominent place in much of this work (Park, Burgess, and McKenzie, 1925). The Chicago group held that the modern city assumes a pattern of concentric circles, each with distinctive characteristics. At the center of the city—*the central business district*—are retail stores, financial institutions, hotels, theaters, and businesses that cater to the needs of downtown shoppers. Surrounding the central business district is an area of residential deterioration caused by the encroachment of business and indus-

1. Metropolitan Belt
1A. Atlantic Seaboard
1B. Lower Great Lakes
2. California Region
3. Florida Peninsula
4. Gulf Coast
5. East Central Texas–
   Red River

6. Southern Piedmont
7. North Georgia–
   South East Tennessee
8. Puget Sound
9. Twin Cities Region
10. Colorado Piedmont
11. St. Louis
12. Metropolitan Arizona

13. Willamette Valley
14. Central Oklahoma–
    Arkansas Valley
15. Missouri–Kaw Valley
16. North Alabama
17. Blue Grass
18. Southern Coastal Plain
19. Salt Lake Valley

20. Central Illinois
21. Nashville Region
22. East Tennessee
23. Memphis
24. El Paso–
    Ciudad Juarez

FIGURE 11.10   MEGALOPOLISES IN THE YEAR 2000
Projections suggest that the heavily urban shaded areas on the map will characterize many sections of the United States by the year 2000. The megalopolitan areas shown here are numbered in order of population size. (Source: Adapted from Population Growth and American Future. *Washington D.C.: U.S. Government Printing Office.)*

try—*the zone in transition.* In earlier days these neighborhoods had contained the pretentious homes of wealthy and prominent citizens. In later years they became slum areas and havens for marginal business establishments (pawnshops, secondhand stores, and modest taverns and restaurants). The zone in transition shades into the *zone of workingmen's homes* that contains

two-flats, old single dwellings, and inexpensive apartments inhabited largely by blue-collar workers and lower-paid white-collar workers. Beyond the zone occupied by the working class are *residential zones* composed primarily of small business proprietors, professional people, and managerial personnel. Finally, out beyond the areas containing the more affluent neighborhoods is a ring of encircling small cities, towns, and hamlets, *the commuters' zone.*

The Chicago group viewed these zones as ideal types, since in practice no city conforms entirely to the scheme. For instance, Chicago borders on Lake Michigan, so that a concentric semicircular rather than a circular arrangement holds. Moreover, critics point out that the approach is less descriptive of today's cities than cities at the turn of the twentieth century. And apparently some cities like New Haven have never approximated the concentric circle pattern (Davie, 1937). Likewise, cities in Latin America, Asia, and Africa exhibit less specialization in land use than in the United States.

The Sector Model. Homer Hoyt (1939) has portrayed large cities as made up of a number of sectors rather than concentric circles—the **sector model** (see Figure 11.11).

Low-rent districts often assume a wedge shape and extend from the center of the city to its periphery. In contrast, as a city grows, high-rent areas move outward, although remaining in the same sector. Districts within a sector that are abandoned by upper-income groups become obsolete and deteriorate. Thus, rather than forming a concentric zone around the periphery of the city, Hoyt contends that the high-rent areas typically locate on the outer edge of a few sectors. Furthermore, industrial areas evolve along river valleys, watercourses, and railroad lines, rather than forming a concentric circle around the central business district. But like the concentric circle model, the sector model does not fit a good many urban communities, including Boston (Firey, 1947).

The Multiple Nuclei Model. Another model—the **multiple nuclei model**—depicts the city as having not one center, but

FIGURE 11.11 THEORETICAL PATTERNS OF URBAN STRUCTURE
(Source: Reprinted from "The Nature of Cities" by Chauncey D. Harris and Edward L. Ullman in Volume 242 of The Annals of The American Academy of Political and Social Science. © *1945 by The American Academy of Political and Social Science.)*

Concentric Zone Theory   Sector Theory   Multiple Nuclei Theory

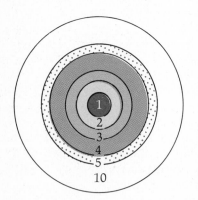
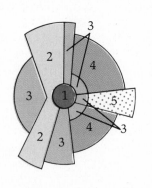
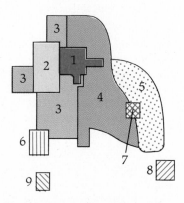

1. Central Business District
2. Wholesale Light Manufacturing
3. Low–Class Residential
4. Medium–Class Residential
5. High–Class Residential
6. Heavy Manufacturing
7. Outlying Business District
8. Residential Suburb
9. Industrial Suburb
10. Commuters' Zone

several (Harris and Ullman, 1945). Each center specializes in some activity and gives its distinctive cast to the surrounding area. For example, the downtown business district has as its focus commercial and financial activities. Other centers include the "bright lights" (theater and recreation) area, "automobile row," a government center, a wholesaling center, a heavy manufacturing district, and a medical complex. Multiple centers evolve for a number of reasons. First, certain activities require specialized facilities—for instance, the retail district needs to be accessible to all parts of the city; the port district requires a suitable waterfront; and a manufacturing district dictates that a large block of land be available near water or rail connections. Second, similar activities often benefit from being clustered together—for instance, a retail district profits by drawing customers for a variety of shops. Third, dissimilar activities are often antagonistic to one another—for example, affluent residential development tends to be incompatible with industrial development. And finally, some activities cannot afford high-rent areas and hence locate in low-rent districts—for instance, bulk wholesaling and storage. The multiple nuclei model is less helpful in discovering universal spatial patterns in all cities than in describing the unique patterns peculiar to particular communities.

Social Area Analysis. The concentric circle, sector, and multiple nuclei models attempt to identify the spatial patterns that govern the ecological structure of urban centers. Eshref Shevky and Marilyn Williams (1949) provide a different approach—**social area analysis**—that focuses on the social characteristics of an urban population. They compile indexes of the social, family, and ethnic properties of a community to discern linkages between changing dimensions of social life and the use of space. For example,

individuals who reside in inner-city neighborhoods tend to be unmarried and of lower socioeconomic rank. Those living in the suburbs are more likely to be married and of higher socioeconomic rank. By measuring these and related indexes at various points in time, sociologists can identify major trends and currents in urban living. It should be stressed that all these models of urban growth rest primarily on studies of North American cities and are not necessarily applicable to cities in other parts of the world.

ECOLOGICAL PROCESSES

The structural patterning of cities derives from a number of underlying ecological processes. As we have seen, people relate to one another and undertake their activities in ways that result in geographic areas taking the form of **natural areas** with distinctive characteristics. One process by which natural areas are formed is **segregation**—a process of clustering wherein individuals and groups are sifted and sorted out in space based on their sharing certain traits or activities in common. This clustering takes place voluntarily when people find that close spatial proximity is advantageous. For instance, the multiple nuclei model of city growth suggests that certain similar activities profit from cohesion provided by a segregated district. Likewise, some nationality and cultural groups prefer to live in close proximity to one another. This arrangement facilitates communication, understanding, and rapport, and fosters we-group identifications and loyalties. Additionally, a segregated neighborhood protects against the intrusion of strange values, norms, and beliefs, while simultaneously providing political leverage with City Hall through bloc voting. Of course segregation may also be involuntary. Residential neighborhoods frequently attempt to exclude incompatible commercial and industrial activities through zoning ordinances. And as we noted in Chapter 7, ethnic and racial groups may systematically exclude from their neighborhoods other groups, including blacks and Jews. Surveys of mortgage-lending practices reveal that, relative to whites of comparable income, black applicants are more likely to be denied mortgages (called *redlining*) and to pay higher interest rates when they do get mortgages (Vander Zanden, 1983).

Invasion and succession are also critical ecological processes. **Invasion** takes place when a new type of people, institution, or activity enroaches on an area occupied by a different type. Should the invasion continue until the encroaching type displaces the other, **succession** is said to have occurred. Although a neighborhood's ecological function may remain unchanged (for instance, residential), it typically becomes a less desirable place to live or work. Yet the reverse process also takes place. Georgetown, in Washington, DC, was an abject slum in the 1920s. More recently, private individuals have restored many of the crumbling pre-Civil War mansions, providing expensive and attractive housing in which government, business, and professional leaders reside. **Urban gentrification**—the return of the middle class, usually young, white, childless professionals (sometimes called *Yuppies*, for Young Urban Professionals), to older neighborhoods—is happening in large cities throughout the United States (Haight-Ashbury in San Francisco, Queen Village in Philadelphia, Mount Adams in Cincinnati, New Town in Chicago, German Village in Columbus, Ohio, and Brooklyn Heights in New York). The process typically culminates in the displacement of the poor and minorities from these neighborhoods by upwardly mobile whites with financial resources and clout. Many older cities are counting on urban gentrification to counteract their eroding population and tax bases.

Young, upwardly mobile professionals have been attracted to a number of older neighborhoods in the nation's larger cities. This "urban gentry" has restored the old homes and displaced low-income groups in a process known as "gentrification." Shown here is a row of well-maintained townhouses in Brooklyn Heights, which has become a chic residential neighborhood. (Christa Armstrong/Rapho-Photo Researchers)

However, even though the "back-to-city" movement has transformed some neighborhoods, it has hardly been a panacea for urban ills (indeed, it may compound the ills when poor are displaced and pushed into adjoining neighborhoods). Moreover, urban gentrification appears to have slowed in recent years (Schill and Nathan, 1983; Gale, 1984; Chall, 1984).

URBAN CRISIS AND THE FUTURE OF AMERICAN CITIES

Looking out over Chicago from the 94th-floor observatory of the John Hancock building, one sees a city that resembles an old Oriental rug: It is bright and vital in some places and worn and bare in others. The bare spots on the face of Chicago and other older American cities began to appear in the mid-1950s, and by the 1970s the exodus of residents and corporations had become a serious problem. Left behind were vast areas of abandoned houses, apartment buildings, neighborhood stores, and factories. St. Louis, Cleveland, Pittsburgh, and Detroit suffered population declines of 13 percent or more from 1970 through 1976, a rate that if continued would result in their being virtually uninhabited by the year 2000. However, in recent years the big-city population drain has slowed, and in some places, including Washington and Boston, it has reversed (Klein, 1980a).

The "donut structure" is an apt description of the course of metropolitan development in many American cities since World War II. The hole in the doughnut is the decaying central city, and the ring is a prosperous and growing suburban and exurban region. In some cases, such as New York City's Manhattan, the hole is a core area that is being revitalized, and the ring is a surrounding part of the city that is becoming progressively blighted. A number of trends have contributed to the phenomenon. For one thing, since World War II the suburbs and exurbs of most American cities have grown more rapidly than the cities themselves (Sternlieb and Hughes, 1980). For another, the rural population is now growing as rapidly as the urban population (Long and DeAre, 1983). Finally, large numbers of people from the northeastern and east-central states have moved to the southwestern and western regions of the nation. People tend to follow jobs and migrate to areas where they believe there are better employment opportunities. Additionally, cities are less likely to lose population to their suburbs if both the city and the suburbs are comparable in public services and costs (Bradbury, Downs, and Small, 1982).

Urban decline is both descriptive and functional. *Descriptive decline* has to do with the loss of population or jobs. *Functional decline* refers to a deterioration in city services and the social amenities of urban life. Descriptive decline occurs as people who have the resources to leave the city do, while those who are poor have little choice but to remain. The proportion of poor residents increases as their number is swelled by recent migrants who are also poor. Urban ills are aggravated and require an increasing share of a city's resources. Life in the city then becomes less agreeable and more costly for middle- and upper-income residents, who move out of the city. This reinforcing pattern hurts the city and complicates its ability to be responsive to people's needs. All this means that American cities are less able to fulfill one of their historical functions—namely, helping society assimilate and integrate the poor and immigrants (Bradbury, Downs, and Small, 1982). Cities require sustained infusions of resources from the outside, particularly the federal government, at the very time that deficit cutting and austerity are curtailing federal urban programs.

Functional decline is reflected in the decay in older industrial cities of the urban infrastructure—the network of roads, bridges, sewers, rails, and mass transit systems. Currently half of all American communities cannot expand because their water treatment systems are at or near capacity. Many roads and bridges are bearing far greater burdens than they were designed to accommodate. For instance, Boston's six-lane Southeast Expressway, built in 1959 for 75,000 autos a day, now carries 150,000 cars daily. Forty-five percent of the nations 248,500 bridges are structurally deficient or obsolete. In response to the fiscal crises of the 1970s, many local officials balanced budgets by canceling preventive maintenance and deferring necessary repairs of public works. One major obstacle to infrastructure maintenance is the diversity and multiplicity of responsibility, which falls upon more than 100 federal agencies, not to mention 50 states, more than 3,000 counties, and thousands of local agencies. In addition, corruption on the part of construction firms, labor unions, public officials, and organized crime have wastefully dissipated public funds. In sum, in past decades public works made the United States a nation of highways, automobiles, water systems, and cities that have been the envy of the world. Today's hard choices—or social drift and inattention—will determine the shape of urban life for decades to come (Beck, 1982).

Summary

1. Since humans are physical beings, their very nature dictates that they be located within space in some sort of habitat. Accordingly, human populations must achieve a working relationship with their environment. One way of viewing the environment is as an ecosystem—a relatively stable community of organisms that have established interlocking relationships and exchanges with one another and their natural habitat. Sociologists find it useful to study the relationships among population (P), organization (O), environment (E), and technology (T), the POET complex.

2. Functionalist theorists approach the human environment by examining the interconnections among the various parts comprising the ecosystem. They see the ecosystem as exhibiting a tendency toward equilibrium in which its components maintain a delicately balanced relationship. The perspective is nicely captured by the notion of Spaceship Earth—the idea that our planet is a vessel in the void of the universe, a closed system with finite resources that, if destroyed or depleted, cannot be replaced.

3. Some conflict theorists depict environmental problems as due more to the distribution of the world's resources than to a limited amount of resources available in the world. They say that the basic issue is not how much is available, but rather which individuals and groups will secure a disproportionate share of what is available. The critical decisions that affect the environment are made, not in the interests of present and future generations, but in the interests of those groups that can impose their will on others. Conflict theorists also point out that people tend to be separated into two camps on environmental issues. On the one side there are those who favor economic development and growth even if it results in some measure of environmental damage. On the other side there are those who see environmental preservation as their primary goal and believe the environment must take precedence over economic goals.

4. Experts are in disagreement regarding the long-term effects of economic growth and development. Many authorities express grave concern about the prospects for the planet. They say that capitalist and socialist nations alike have committed themselves to policies of economic growth which disregard the pollution of the biosphere and the rapid consumption of nonrenewable resources. Other authorities take a more optimistic view. They look to technology to save us. The free play of market forces is fundamental to their vision.

5. Pollution buildup has bad effects on deer, rats, and a variety of other organisms. In contrast, the impact of crowding on human behavior is more com-

plex, and does not invariably result in pathology. Social scientists distinguish between density and crowding. Density has to do with the physical compactness of people in space. Crowding is the perception people have that too many other individuals are present in the situation. Crowding, then, is not a product of absolute numbers, but of people's social definitions.

6. All population change within a society can be reduced to three factors: the birth rate, the death rate, and the migration rate into or out of the society. The number of children born in recent years in the United States has risen to near the baby boom highs of the late 1950s. The reason the number of births has risen is that the number of women of childbearing age has increased as the large generation born during the baby boom of the 1950s has reached adulthood. Even so, young American women say they want so few children that, if they have the children they say, their generation will not replace itself. The life expectancy of Americans has now reached a high of 74.7 years. Migration is the product of two factors. There are those forces—push factors—that encourage people to leave a habitat they already occupy. And there are those forces—pull factors—that attract people to a new habitat.

7. Birth, death, and migration affect population size. Sociologists are also interested in the composition or characteristics of a population. They are particularly interested in the sex ratio (the number of males per 100 females) and age composition. A population pyramid is a useful tool for analyzing population change and discerning population trends.

8. Thomas Robert Malthus held that, whereas agricultural production tends to increase in arithmetic fashion, population has a tendency to increase in geometric fashion. Based on this formulation, Malthus took a dim view of the future. For if populations always increase to the ultimate point of subsistence, progress can have no lasting effect. However, Malthus failed to appreciate the full possibilities of the Industrial Revolution and its ability to expand productive capacities to an extent unknown in his time. Additionally, there is no clear evidence that food always and everywhere can increase only in an arithmetic ratio. Karl Marx took issue with Malthus, insisting that an excess of population is related to the availability of employment opportunities, not to a fixed supply of food.

9. A number of social scientists have employed the idea of demographic transition to map out the population growth characteristic of the modern era. Viewed as history, the notion seeks to explain what happened in European nations over the last two hundred years. Viewed as theory, it has been used to predict what will happen in developing nations in the future. Demographic transition theory holds that the process of modernization is associated with three stages in population change: Stage 1: high potential growth; stage 2, transitional growth; and stage 3, population stability.

10. There are three basic schools of thought relating to fertility-reduction policies. The first approach involves family planning. Its proponents contend that if contraceptives are made readily available and information regarding the value and need for birth planning is disseminated throughout a society, people will reduce their fertility. A second approach entails a developmental-

ist strategy. It holds that modernization automatically decreases fertility. A third approach involves a societalist perspective. The government fashions policies designed to produce changes in people's demographic behavior.

11. Within American life the medical institution, through its control of health services, has become an important, independent source of power. Although there has been a dramatic reduction in deaths from infectious diseases in the last century and steady gains have been made in containing major killer diseases like cancer and heart disease, health care in the United States is falling victim to runaway costs. Given the continued surge in health costs, Americans will have to find some way to expend a growing portion of the gross national product for medical care, or they will have to ration hospital services.

12. Cities constitute a relatively recent development in human history. Not until the Neolithic period did conditions become ripe for the existence of large settlements of people. Preindustrial cities were primarily small affairs. Urbanization has proceeded rapidly during the past 180 years, resulting in industrial-urban centers. More recently, metropolitan cities have emerged. This phase in urban development does not represent a sharp break within the industrial-urban tradition, but rather a widening and deepening of urban influences in every area of social life. In many cases, the rural interstices between metropolitan centers have filled with urban development, making a "strip city" or megalopolis.

13. Sociologists are interested in understanding how people order their relationships and conduct their activities in space. They provide a number of models that attempt to capture the ecological patterns and structures of city growth: the concentric circle model, the sector model, the multiple nuclei model, and social area analysis.

14. The structural patterning of cities derives from a number of underlying ecological processes. People relate to one another and undertake their activities in ways that result in geographic areas taking the form of natural areas with distinctive characteristics. One process by which natural areas are formed is segregation. Invasion and succession are also critical ecological processes.

15. Urban decline in many American cities has been both descriptive and functional. Descriptive decline has to do with the loss of population or jobs. Functional decline refers to a deterioration in city services and the social amenities of urban life. Descriptive decline occurs as people who have the resources to leave the city do, while those who are poor have little choice but to remain. Functional decline is reflected in the decay in older industrial cities of the urban infrastructure—the network of roads, bridges, sewers, rails, and mass transit systems.

Glossary

age-specific death rate The number of deaths per 1,000 individuals in a specific age group.
age-specific fertility The number of live births per 1,000 women in a specific age group.

city A relatively dense and permanent concentration of people who secure their livelihood chiefly through nonagricultural activities.
concentric circle model The approach to city

growth which says that the modern city assumes a pattern of concentric circles, each with distinctive characteristics.

crowding The perception that people have that too many other individuals are present in a situation.

crude birth rate The number of live births per 1,000 members of a population in a given year.

crude death rate The number of deaths per 1,000 members of a population in a given year.

demographic transition theory A view of population change which holds that the process of modernization passes through three stages: high potential growth, transitional growth, and population stability.

demography The science dealing with the size, distribution, composition, and changes in population.

density The physical compactness of people in space.

ecology The study of the interrelations between the living and nonliving components of an ecosystem.

ecosystem A relatively stable community of organisms that have established interlocking relationships and exchanges with one another and their natural habitat.

environment All the surrounding conditions and influences that affect an organism or a group of organisms.

fecundity The potential number of children that could be born if every woman of childbearing age bore all the children she possibly could.

general fertility rate The annual number of live births per 1,000 women aged 15 to 44.

growth rate The difference between births and deaths, plus the difference between immigrants and emigrants per 1,000 population.

infant mortality rate The number of deaths among infants under 1 year of age per 1,000 live births.

internal migration Population movement within a nation.

international migration Population movement among nations.

invasion A new type of people, institution, or activity that encroaches on an area occupied by a different type.

megalopolis A strip city formed when the rural interstices between metropolitan centers fill with urban development.

multiple nuclei model The approach to city growth which assumes a city has several centers, each of which specializes in some activity and gives its distinctive cast to the surrounding area.

natural areas Geographic areas with distinctive characteristics.

net migration rate The increase or decrease per 1,000 members of the population in a given year that results from people entering (immigrants) or leaving (emigrants) a society.

population pyramid The age and sex composition of a population as portrayed in the tree of ages.

sector model The approach to city growth which assumes that large cities are made up of sectors—wedge-shaped areas—rather than concentric circles.

segregation A process of clustering wherein individuals and groups are sifted and sorted out in space based on their sharing certain traits or activities in common.

social area analysis An approach to examining urban patterns that focuses on the social characteristics of the population by areas.

succession Invasion that continues until the encroaching type of people, institution, or activity displaces the previous type.

urban gentrification The return of the middle class—usually young, white, childless professionals—to older urban neighborhoods.

zero population growth The point at which a modern population replaces itself without immigration—2.1 children per woman.

12

Social Change

A WORLD OF CHANGE

Sources of Social Change
Perspectives on Social Change
Social Change in the United States
Social Change in Third World
    Nations

COLLECTIVE BEHAVIOR

Varieties of Collective Behavior
Preconditions for Collective Behavior
Explanations of Crowd Behavior

SOCIAL MOVEMENTS

Types of Social Movements
Social Revolution
Terrorism
Causes of Social Movements

LOOKING TO THE FUTURE

Social life is not a material or substance to be molded: rather, it is an ongoing process constantly renewing, remaking, changing, and transforming itself. Indeed, life is never static but always in flux. In nature there are not any fixed entities, only transition and transformation (Whitehead, 1929; Sheldon, 1954). According to modern physics, the objects you normally see and feel consist of nothing more than patterns of energy that are forever moving and altering (Sears, Zemansky, and Young, 1982). Conceptions of "stuff," mass in the old sense of quantity or matter, have largely been displaced by more dynamic notions of process. Atoms, once supposedly fixed and solid, have broken down into protons, neutrons, and electrons, and these in turn have been broken down into energy and motion. From electrons to galaxies, from amoebas to humans, from families to societies, every phenomenon exists in a state of continual "becoming" (Olsen, 1978).

The dynamic quality of life often eludes us by virtue of our perceptual and conceptual limitations. Our thinking apparatus demands that we be furnished with discrete and identifiable "things." For instance, we "benchmark" time in seconds, minutes, hours, days, weeks, and years and, as we have done repeatedly in this text, capsulate epochs in such statements as "since World War II" and "the 1960s." Structure-function approaches help us to partition social life into discrete structures, including statuses and institutions. They allow us to place a "handle" on the fluid quality of life so that we may grasp, describe, and analyze it, making it understandable and intelligible. But as many conflict and symbolic interactionist theorists emphasize, the dichotomy between structure and process gives birth to problems that are frequently unnecessary. For one thing, the dichotomy produces difficulty in handling change. Indeed, the word "change" itself is saturated with certain nonprocess connotations, implying a shift from one static and relatively stable "state" to another. Admittedly, the English language does not help us in formulating these matters, since the nouns that provide the subjects of most of our sentences chiefly refer to static objects, not to ongoing process (Olsen, 1978). Given these problems and limitations, in this chapter we will address social change and process, the dynamic quality of social life.

A World of Change

Sociologists refer to fundamental alterations in the patterns of culture, structure, and social behavior over time as **social change.** It is a process by which society becomes something different while remaining in some respects the same. The impact of social change is strikingly apparent when we reflect on events that influenced the national mood only a few short years ago but that have since faded in importance as millions of Americans who are too young to have experienced them have entered adulthood. If we assume that age 10 is a time in life when events begin to form lasting memories for us, then of today's 237 million Americans (*U.S. News & World Report*, January 23, 1984):

98 percent do not remember a United States without a federal income tax (1913)

94 percent are too young to remember the first time women voted (1920)

89 percent cannot recollect Charles Lindbergh's solo flight to Paris (1927)

87 percent do not remember the stock market crash that marked the onset of the Great Depression (1929)

76 percent do not recall Pearl Harbor and the entry of the United States into World War II (1941)

JUST A MINUTE

CUSHION AND PNEUMATIC WIRE WHEEL VEHICLES

HERE'S A PROPOSITION. Take a good look at these two styles. They are right in season, and we honestly believe that they are two of the best selling light vehicles we have ever built. If you will let us know which one of these you want—the Runabout or the Stanhope—we will make you a special summer price. We can't deliver but a few more, so write soon if you want to take advantage of this proposition.

THE **SCHACHT MFG. CO.**

CINCINNATI OHIO

Mention THE CARRIAGE MONTHLY when writing advertisers

We begin to appreciate the impact that social change has upon our lives when we reflect upon what life was like in the not too distant past. A century ago automobiles were unknown; instead, consumers were invited to consider the styling and comfort of horse-drawn carriages. Yet in less than a century the automobile has given impetus to the steel, rubber, oil, glass, and insurance industries and has altered the residential patterns of cities. (The Bettmann Archive)

69 percent are too young to recall life without television (1948)

49 percent have no recollection of the assassination of President John F. Kennedy (1963)

30 percent cannot recall the end of the Vietnam war or the Arab oil embargo (1973)

25 percent do not remember the nation's Bicentennial (1976)

Forecasts by the World Future Society likewise highlight for us the significance of social change. Among its forecasts are (*Columbus Dispatch*, 1984b):

By the year 2000 there will be 100,000 Americans over the age of 100

Animal and plant species will disappear at the rate of 10,000 a year by 1990, with one species becoming extinct each hour

NASA may have a permanent base on the moon by 2007

Blue-collar workers will make up only 10 percent of the American work force by the end of the century

In the absence of a drastic downturn in population growth, more people will be born worldwide in the year 2050 than were born in the 1,500 years after the birth of Christ

Scientific information currently grows about 13 percent each year, but by the year 2000 the rate will jump above 30 percent

Some 35,000 robots will be installed in the United States by 1990, multiplying in the near future at about 30 percent a year

Given the impact that social change has on our lives, let us begin our discussion by examining some of its sources.

SOURCES OF SOCIAL CHANGE

Social change confronts people with new situations and compels them to fashion new forms of action. A great many factors interact to generate changes in people's behavior and in the culture and structure of their society. Sociologists identify a number of particularly critical factors, the impact of which differs with the situation and the time and place.

The Physical Environment. As we saw in Chapter 11, humans are physical beings who are located in some sort of habitat. If they are to survive, they must achieve a working relationship with their environment. Among the chief adaptive mechanisms available to a population are social organization and technology. But the social organization and technology that is adaptive to one environment is not necessarily adaptive to another. Hunting and gathering, horticultural, agricultural, and industrial societies all present different types of adaptations. Should the environment change for any reason, those who have evolved a given type of adaptation must respond by making appropriate institutional changes, fashioning new forms of social organization and new technologies. Droughts, floods, epidemics, earthquakes, and other forces of nature are among the ever-present realities that compel people to alter their lifeways. Additionally, as we noted in Chapter 11, human beings also have an impact on their physical environment. Hazardous-waste dumps, acid rain, pollution of the water and air, overtaxing water resources, erosion of topsoil, and desertification result from human damage to the ecosystem. Thus human beings are tied to their environment in a chain of complex interchanges.

Population. Changes in the size, composition, and distribution of a population also affect culture and social structure. In Chapter 11 we saw the impact that the baby-boom generation is having on American life as the large "bulge" of persons born after World War II makes its way through the age groups. Already they have left their mark on musical tastes and the political climate. And what some have called the "narcissism of the '70s" appears to be on the wane as maturing members of the baby-boom generation look for close relationships and commitments. Likewise, the graying of the American population is having vast social

ramifications. It is a principal factor in the nation's soaring Social Security, Medicaid, and health care costs (those 85 and over are the fastest-growing part of the population). The graying of the society is also posing thorny dilemmas in the workplace, as large numbers of middle-age workers jockey for advancement. Increasing numbers of people are lining up for promotion, but there are fewer slots opening up than there are people willing to fill them. This situation can lead to frustration and an increase in midlife career changes, although people may also respond by pouring more of their energies into hobbies or family and community pursuits.

Clashes over Resources and Values. As we have repeatedly noted in this text, conflict is a form of interaction in which people are involved in a struggle over resources or values. Individuals and groups find themselves at odds; they feel separated by incompatible objectives. Not surprisingly, conflict is a basic source of social change. Members of a group must marshal their resources for competition. For instance, during wartime they must alter their customary ways of ordering their daily lives, and they may invest greater authority in military leaders. Of course, conflict also often involves negotiation, compromise, or accommodation. The swirling currents produced by these dynamic processes result in new institutional arrangements. Yet history demonstrates that the outcome of such interaction is rarely the total fulfillment of the goal or goals of the parties involved. Most commonly, the end result is not a simple quantitative mixing of aspects of the opposing programs, but a completely new qualitative entity. Who could have foretold in 1870 the South that eventually emerged from the contest between the reconstructionists and their opponents? In 1918, the Europe and Russia that arose following a war "to end all wars" and "to make the world safe for democracy"? In 1933, the economic and social America that developed from the struggle between Roosevelt supporters and anti-New Dealers? In 1965, the nation that would emerge twenty years later after a decade of social turbulence? Thus old social orders continually erode and new ones arise.

Supporting Values and Norms. A society's values and norms act as "watchdogs" or "censors" permitting or inhibiting certain innovations. They may also serve as "stimulants." It is interesting to compare our readiness to accept technological innovations with our resistance to changes in economic theory, religion, or the family. Our use of the word "inventor" reflects this cultural bias. The inventor is one who innovates in material things, whereas the inventor of intangible ideas is often called a "revolutionary" or "radical," words with odious connotations. Among Samoans, considerable allowance is made for innovation in decorative arts, yet this freedom is negated by the culture's failure to give the innovator much recognition. Contrast this outlook with the Israelites of the eighth and seventh centuries B.C. who felt a strong need for spiritual interpretation and thus gave honor and followership to prophets who could find new ways of interpreting the will of God in the interests of the society (Herskovits, 1945).

Innovation. A **discovery** represents an addition to knowledge, whereas an **invention** uses existing knowledge in some novel form. Thus a discovery constitutes the perception of a relationship or fact that had not previously been recognized or understood. Einstein's theory of relatively and Mendel's theory of genes were discoveries. In contrast, an invention involves a new combination of old elements. The automobile was composed of six old elements in a new combination: a liquid gas engine, a liquid gas receptacle, a running-gear mechanism, an intermediate clutch, a driving shaft, and a carriage body.

Innovations—both discoveries and inventions—are not single acts, but a cumulative series of transmitted increments plus a series of new elements. Consequently, the greater the number of cultural elements on which innovators may draw, the greater the frequency of discovery and invention. And just as a prolific couple gives birth to descendants who may multiply geometrically, so a pregnant invention may bring forth a geometrically increasing number of progeny. For example, glass gave birth to lenses, costume jewelry, drinking goblets, windowpanes, test tubes, X-ray tubes, light bulbs, radio and television tubes, mirrors, and many other products. Lenses in turn gave birth to eyeglasses, magnifying glasses, telescopes, cameras, searchlights, and so on. Such developments reflect the *exponential principle*—as the cultural base increases, its possible uses tend to grow in geometric ratio.

Diffusion. **Diffusion** is the process by which culture traits spread from one social unit to another. Each culture contains a minimum of traits and patterns unique to or actually invented by it. It is easy, for instance, for Americans to minimize their debt to other peoples. We point with pride to what other societies have acquired from us, yet we often neglect to note what we have gained from them. As an illustration, consider the following account of the cultural content in the life of a "100 percent" American written as satire by anthropologist Ralph Linton (1937:427–429):

[D]awn finds the unsuspecting patriot garbed in pajamas, a garment of East Indian origin; and lying in a bed built on a pattern which *originated in either Persia or Asia Minor. He is muffled to the ears in un-American materials: cotton, first domesticated in India; linen, domesticated in the Near East; wool from an animal native to Asia Minor; or silk whose uses were first discovered by the Chinese. . . .*

If our patriot is old-fashioned enough to adhere to the so-called American breakfast, his coffee will be accompanied by an orange, domesticated in the Mediterranean region. He will follow this with a bowl of cereal made from grain domesticated in the Near East. . . . As a side dish he may have the egg of a bird domesticated in Southeastern Asia or strips of the flesh of an animal domesticated in the same region. . . .

In sum, a great number of social forces are at work, making for a continual process of social change.

PERSPECTIVES ON SOCIAL CHANGE

Many of sociology's roots lie in the effort to unravel the "meaning" of history and to establish laws of social change and development. The founders of sociology, particularly Auguste Comte and Herbert Spencer, looked to the grand sweep of history, searching for an understanding of how and why societies change. Many contemporary sociologists continue to be intrigued by these "big questions." The major sociological perspectives on social change fall within four broad categories: evolutionary perspectives, cyclical perspectives, functionalist perspectives, and conflict perspectives.

Evolutionary Perspectives. Much sociological thinking during the nineteenth century was dominated by the doctrine of social progress and a search for underlying evolutionary laws. According to Social Darwinists like Spencer, social evolution resembles biological evolution and results in the world growing progressively better. In his theory

of *unilinear evolution*, Spencer contended that change has persistently moved society from homogeneous and simple units toward progressively heterogeneous and interdependent units. He viewed the "struggle for existence" and "the survival of the fittest" as basic natural laws. Spencer equated this struggle with "free competition," insisting that "men ignore it to their sorrow." If unimpeded by outside intervention, particularly government, those individuals and social institutions that are "fit" will survive and proliferate while those that are "unfit" will in time die out.

As we pointed out in Chapter 1, Spencer's Social Darwinism mirrored the orientation of laissez-faire capitalism. Governmental regulation and welfare legislation were depicted as fostering social degeneration by "artificially preserving" the unfit and restricting the fit in their inheritance of the earth. Social Darwinism was a doctrine well-suited to expansionist imperialism and provided a justification for Western colonialism. The white race and its cultures were extolled as the highest forms of "humanity" and "civilization." Other peoples and cultures were "lower" in evolutionary development, and so it was only proper that Europeans, being "fitter," should triumph in the "struggle for existence." However, such blatant ethnocentrism did not stand the test of scientific research. Simultaneously, the notion of unilinear evolution came under scientific scrutiny and was found wanting. Anthropologists demonstrated that non-Western societies—and many European nations as well—did not pass through the same sequence of stages. In brief, there is not one scenario, but many scenarios of social change. The course of change is not neatly preprogrammed by natural law in some rigidly fashioned mold.

Although evolutionary theory fell into disrepute for some fifty years, it has undergone a revival in recent decades (Steward, 1955; White, 1959; Lenski, 1966; Service,

1971). Contemporary approaches take a *multilinear* view of evolution. Their proponents recognize that "change" does not necessarily imply "progress," that change occurs in quite different ways, and that change proceeds in many different directions. Indeed, interest in evolutionary theory has moved so centrally into mainstream sociology that even such a leading structure-function sociologist as the late Talcott Parsons (1966, 1977) came to fashion a theory of "evolutionary change." While disclaiming that societal evolution is either a continuous or a simple linear process, Parsons suggests that societies tend to become increasingly *differentiated* in their structures and functions. But differentiation is not sufficient, since the new structural arrangements must be more functionally adaptive than previous arrangements, leading to *adaptive upgrading*.

Sociologist Gerhard Lenski (1966; Lenski and Lenski, 1982) likewise takes an evolutionary perspective that does not regard changes in social organization as necessarily leading to greater human happiness or satisfaction. He holds that evolution depends largely on changes in a society's level of technology and its mode of economic production. These changes in turn have consequences for other aspects of social life, including stratification systems, the organization of power, and family structures. According to Lenski, there is an underlying continuum in terms of which all societies can be ranked: hunting and gathering societies, simple horticultural societies, advanced horticultural societies, agrarian societies, and industrial societies. More specialized evolutionary bypaths include herding societies and "hybrid societies" such as fishing and maritime societies.

Cyclical Perspectives. Evolutionary theories, particularly those with a unilinear focus, depict history as divided into steplike levels that constitute sequential stages and that are characterized by an underlying trend. Cyclical theorists take a different approach and look to the rise and fall of civilizations. Their objective is not to predict the long-term direction of human history, but rather to predict the course of a civilization or society. Nor do cyclical theorists seek to place societies on some sort of linear or historical scale. Instead, they compare societies in a search for generalizations regarding their stages of growth and decline. In sum, evolutionalists tend to be relatively jolly people who see humankind as ever striving to reach new heights in a challenging future, whereas cyclists tend to be relatively pessimistic individuals who forecast the demise of every civilization.

The nineteenth century was a time of faith in evolution and human progress. But the catastrophe of World War I and the periodic economic crises that have plagued industrial nations led some scholars to express doubt regarding the course of human history. One of these was the German scholar Oswald Spengler (1880–1936), whose *The Decline of the West* (1918) became a best seller. He contended that culture passes through the same stages of growth and decline as individuals: a period of development, followed by maturity, eventual decline, and death. Based on his examination of eight cultures, Spengler says that each culture possesses a life span of approximately a thousand years. Western culture, he held, emerged about A.D. 900, and therefore its end is close at hand (hence the title of his book and the interest it provoked).

English historian Arnold J. Toynbee (1934/1954) also sought to depict uniformities in the growth and decline of civilization and to identify the principles that underlie this development. Like Spengler, he believes that the course of most civilizations is uniform, although he does not ascribe a time interval to their rise and decline. Toynbee says that civilizations arise in response to some challenge. A challenge may derive from natural forces, such as severe climate, or from human factors, such as warlike neighbors. A civilization grows and flourishes when the challenge is not too severe and when a creative minority (an intelligent elite) finds an adequate response to the challenge. When the creative minority fails to find a response adequate to a challenge, the civilization breaks down and disintegrates. In the course of disintegrating, the minority transforms itself into a ruling elite and imposes its will by force. This development hastens the decline, because it intensifies internal strife. However, careful examination of Toynbee's work shows it to rely primarily upon Hellenic and Western experiences and to neglect Arabic, Egyptian, and Chinese histories that reveal somewhat different patterns. Thus his theory tends to be arbitrarily imposed on the history of other civilizations rather than being inductively derived from a study of them.

Functionalist Perspectives. As we saw in Chapter 2, the concept of system is central to the structure-function model of society. A system is a set of elements or components related in a more or less stable fashion over a period of time. One of the features of a system stressed by structure-function theorists is its tendency toward *equilibrium*. Even though contending forces are never equal, final, or permanent, there is a tendency for a system to achieve some sort of balance among them. Although time can be introduced as a factor within the model, American structure-function sociologists have stressed static over dynamic processes. Of course things are not static in the sense of being dead; things happen all the time. Children are born, people die, and institutional structures functionally contribute to the regular performance of essential tasks across time (Dahrendorf, 1968).

As we pointed out earlier in the chapter, structure-function sociologists like Parsons (1966, 1977) have introduced the notion of evolution to the perspective. In so doing, they have attempted to broaden the concept of equilibrium to include *developing* properties in addition to those that are *self-maintaining*. Following the organic analogy, the social group is portrayed as living in a state of dynamic or moving equilibrium. Upsetting forces introject themselves into the equilibriated system, functioning as innovative stimuli. The equilibriated social system responds adjustively to these disturbances, accommodating them within the functioning structure and establishing a new level of equilibrium. Hence, even though society changes, it remains stable through new forms of social integration.

Sociologist William F. Ogburn (1922) drew upon evolutionary models to fashion a functionalist approach to social change. He distinguishes between *material* and *nonmaterial culture* and locates the source of change in material invention—tools, weapons, and technical processes. Nonmaterial culture refers to social values, norms, beliefs, and social arrangements, including law, religion, and the family. Ogburn saw the impetus for social change coming from material culture. Nonmaterial culture must adapt or respond to changes in material culture. Since nonmaterial culture must constantly "catch up" with material culture, an adjustment gap develops between the two forms of culture. Ogburn called this gap **cultural lag.** Although the notion of cultural lag contains a valuable insight, it vastly oversimplifies matters. No one factor is capable of explaining social change since in real-life situations a vast array of forces converge in complex interaction with one another to give society its dynamic properties.

Social life abounds with examples where the rate of change in various segments of society is uneven and results in social dislocation. For instance, the automobile has fostered a whole host of changes. It spawned such secondary industries as oil refineries, tire and glass conglomerates, and the giant accident insurance industry. It induced massive investments in single-family homes and in extensive road systems that move traffic from the central city to outer suburban rings. But in doing so, the automobile has contributed to the despoiling of the natural environment and to an exodus of the central city's affluent population. Thus, as depicted by Ogburn, social problems ensue from the "social disorganization" that occurs when social institutions lag behind changing technology.

Conflict Perspectives. Conflict theorists hold that tensions between competing groups are the basic source of social change. Nowhere does one find a clearer exposition of the conflict perspective than that provided by Karl Marx, particularly as it finds expression in his notion of the *dialectic*. As we saw in Chapter 1, the dialectic depicts the world in dynamic terms as a world of *becoming* rather than *being*. According to Marxian dialectical materialism, every economic order grows to a state of maximum efficiency, all the while developing internal contradictions or weaknesses that contribute to its decay. Class conflict is a particularly powerful source of change, and Marx saw it as the key to understanding human history. As noted in Chapter 6, class conflict derives from the struggle between those who own the means of producing wealth and those who do not.

Marx said that all change is the product of a constant conflict between opposites. It arises from the contradiction inherent in all things and all processes. All development— social, economic, or human—proceeds through the resolution of existing contradictions and the eventual emergence of new contradictions. The outcome of the clash between opposing forces is not a compromise (an averaging out of the differences among them). It is an entirely new product, one born of struggle. In this manner, both individuals and societies change. It is a dynamic process of complex interchanges between all facets of social life. As Marx (1906) observed, "By acting on the external world and changing it, he [the individual] at the same time changes his own nature."

We have dealt with conflict theorists at some length in several chapters. We have noted that many conflict theorists regard Marx's view that "all history is the history of class conflict" as a vast oversimplification (Coser, 1956, 1957; Dahrendorf, 1958). They contend that other types of conflict are equally and in some instances, more important, including conflict between nations, ethnic groups, religions, and economic interest groups. Sociologist Ralf Dahrendorf (1958:174–175), an advocate of conflict theory, asserts:

1. *Every society is subjected at every moment to change: social change is ubiquitous.*

2. *Every society experiences at every moment social conflict: social conflict is ubiquitous.*

3. *Every element in a society contributes to its change.*

4. *Every society rests on constraint of some of its members by others.*

Dahrendorf sees these points as complementing the functionalist model, which highlights the integrated and configurational aspects of social life.

SOCIAL CHANGE IN THE UNITED STATES

To live in the United States is to gain an appreciation for Dahrendorf's assertions that social change is ubiquitous. It high-

Doing Sociology: Patterns of Social Change

Social change is ubiquitous. Yet it is easy to overlook the social change that affects our daily lives. In my classes at Ohio State University, I have students examine some aspect of their lives that has been touched by social change. Below, a student discusses the change that has occurred in student living arrangements over the past thirty years.

I have lived in the dorms for two years now. But like a good many other students, I would prefer to live in an apartment. Two other guys and I looked around the campus area and found several three-bedroom apartments. But none of them really appealed to us. It so happened that in the course of our search, we came across a four-bedroom apartment very much to our liking. We decided we wanted it, since it is an attractive place and convenient to campus. The only problem was finding a fourth roommate. I approached one of

my male friends with the idea of moving in with us but he wasn't interested. However, his girlfriend was with him, and she jokingly suggested herself as the fourth roommate. She had planned to get an apartment with one of her friends, but the girlfriend had dropped out of school. It wasn't long before the idea of her becoming the fourth person took on a serious note. The four of us reviewed the idea, thought about the problems we might encounter, and decided to go ahead with it. So the four of us signed the leases.

There was one problem that I had not given much thought to, namely how my parents would take the news of three guys and a woman sharing an apartment. I thought I had better have a chat with my dad first, because his opinion carries a good deal of weight with my mom. This past weekend I went home and told my dad about our plans. He just

laughed (I wonder if he would have laughed had it been my sister) and began telling me about his experiences at the University of Wisconsin at Madison in the 1950s. Even though it is a university with a long tradition of political liberalism and student activism, at that time women, but not men, had "hours." Freshmen and sophomore women had to be back to their dorms by 10:00 P.M. on weekdays and 12:00 P.M. on weekends; junior and senior women had 12:00 A.M. hours on both weekdays and weekends. If a woman did not return on time, she was "grounded" by a discipline committee for a number of weeks. Women could stay overnight off-campus only if they had written permission from their parents and a suitable chaperon. At that time the ground floor of most of the women's dorms had what the students called "passion pits"—"stalls" along a hallway where a

lights the maxim that "To live is to change." Let us examine one aspect of change in American life, that associated with the rapid introduction of technology within the workplace.

The Computer Revolution. Many of use are fascinated by the Industrial Revolution. But when we ask why the Industrial Revolution was a revolution, we find that it was not the machines that made it so. Certainly the steam engine, the cotton gin, the locomo-

tive and rails, and the power loom were extraordinary inventions. But the primary reason that they were revolutionary is because they were agents for great social change. They took people out of the fields and brought them into factories. They gave rise to mass production and, through mass production, to a society in which wealth was not confined to the few (Diebold, 1983). In somewhat like fashion, computers promise to revolutionize the structure of American life, particularly as they free the human young woman might entertain a guest. The "passion pits" had chairs but little else. There was no wall along the hallway so the couples could be supervised to insure they "would not go too far."

My dad said that when he became a graduate student, he secured an apartment in a rundown building in which the landlord resided. Although my dad was then 24 years old, being single he was still subject to university rules and was barred from having women visitors to his apartment. My dad said he ignored the rules. When he returned to his apartment one day, he noticed that the landlord had tacked on the door a copy of the university rules that stipulated women were not permitted in the rooms or apartments of single university men. My dad took the rules down and threw them out. When he went to pay his rent at the end of the month, the landlord told my

dad he was not allowed to have women in his apartment. My dad firmly informed the landlord that it was his apartment and he would have whomever he wished visit him. That was the last he heard from the landlord. However, had university officials learned of his behavior, my dad could have been expelled from the university.

The college campus of 30 years ago sounds like a very repressive place, one that I have a hard time imagining. And it was an extremely sexist arrangement, since "hours" applied only to the female students. The impetus for change in the 1960s with the student power, civil rights, women's, and peace movements. Old arrangements crumbled as students confronted their elders and university officials, challenging their right to dictate student life styles. These movements served to "liberate" segments of the American public who until then had

not enjoyed the full rights of American citizenship, particularly blacks and women. As a result, students at many colleges can now have members of the opposite sex to their dormitory rooms and can reside with members of the opposite sex in off-campus housing. Most universities no longer have responsibility for supervising the sexual "morality" of their students.

I have also been reflecting on the changes that I may confront 30 years from now. Are there new directions in which "human liberation" may proceed? One area that comes to mind is the right of people to choose a "healthy death." Today the terminally ill are kept alive by barbaric life-support systems that override their individual autonomy and personhood. But I suspect that in the years ahead people will gain a greater voice in determining when and under what circumstances they will be permitted to die.

mind and open new vistas in knowledge and communication (Feigenbaum and McCorduck, 1983). It is the capacity of the computer for solving problems and making decisions that represents its greatest potential and poses the greatest difficulties in predicting its impact on society. Even so, a number of issues have been repeatedly raised about the social impact of computers (Hallblade and Mathews, 1980).

First, the computer promises to automate some workplace activities that are now per-

formed by people. The Industrial Revolution centered on the supplementation and ultimate replacement of the *muscles* of humans and animals by introducing mechanical methods. The computer goes beyond this development to supplement and replace some aspects of the *mind* of human beings by electronic methods. Both changes have vast implications for the world of work.

Second, information is a source of power, and computers mean information. The centralized accumulation of data permits the concentration of considerable power in those who have access to the computer. A power gap tends to develop between those who are trained to use and understand computers and those who are not. Some authorities believe that widespread access to computers will produce a society more democratic, egalitarian, and richly diverse than any previously known (Feigenbaum and McCorduck, 1983). But the expectations of computer enthusiasts may be nothing more than wishful thinking. It may be that computer technology intelligently structured and wisely applied might help a society raise its standard of literacy, education, and general knowledgeability. But there is no automatic, positive link between knowledge and its enlightened use (Winner, 1984).

Third, computers alter the way people relate to one another. On a telephone, we hear the other person's voice. In face-to-face contact, we see people smile, frown, and nod. But there is no such feedback in computer exchanges. When people use a computer to send electronic mail, they lack access to nonverbal cues. Thus computers may have consequences for our sense of individuality. It also makes computer exchanges less predictable. For one thing, people are less likely to hold back strong feelings when communicating by computers; they show a greater tendency to swear, insult others, and communicate abruptly. For another, in face-to-face meetings, one person is likely to talk considerably more than another. But on a computer, people tend to talk about the same amount because they are less self-conscious and are protected by a feeling of anonymity. Moreover, computer technology changes people's awareness of themselves, of one another, and of their relationship with the world. A machine that appears to "think" challenges our notions not only of time and distance, but of mind (Turkle, 1984).

Finally, computers have implications for individual privacy and the confidentiality of our communications and personal data. The growing use of computers to collect data and store information provides the technical capability for integrating several information files into networks of computerized data banks. With such networks, personal data that we provide for one purpose can potentially be accessed for other purposes. Thus as people handle more and more of their activities through electronic instruments—mail, banking, shopping, entertainment, and travel plans—it becomes technically feasible to monitor these activities with unprecedented ease. Such opportunities for matching and correlating data have a menacing, Orwellian potential to them.

Technology and Jobs. Visionaries look to technology to make human lives richer and freer. They say that the new electronics allows people to have access to vast stores of information, expanded human resources, and opportunities for working and relating with one another on a more flexible, cheaper and convenient basis (Hiltz and Turoff, 1978) (see box). More specifically, they see a variety of benefits deriving from technological advances. For one thing, tasks that are boring, repetitive, and narrowly defined can be performed by machines. As automation removes low-level work, opportunities grow for greater free time in which people can be more creative and productive. For another, new technologies dictate that workers understand how the entire production process fits together, rather than seeing themselves as working with only a small piece of it. And as routine tasks are taken over by computers and robots, the ability and willingness of workers to solve unexpected problems and to reprogram production in response to shifting requirements assumes greater significance (Eckholm, 1984). Further, some experts see computer systems as offering opportunities to disadvantaged groups to acquire the skills and

Utopian Visions of Earlier Technological Periods

Not only computers have been heralded as a panacea for our ills. In earlier times much the same claims were made for steam, electrical power, and electronics.

From the Age of Steam: "Fellow Men! I promise to show the means of creating a paradise within ten years, where everything desirable for human life may be had by every man in super-abundance, without labor, and without pay; where the whole face of nature shall be changed into the most beautiful of forms, and man may live in the most magnif-icent palaces, in all imagin-able refinements of luxury, and in the most delightful gardens; where he may ac-complish, without labor, in one year, more than hitherto could be done in thousands of years."
—J.A. Etzler, *The Paradise within the Reach of all Men, with Labor, by Powers of Nature and Machinery* (1842)

From the Age of Electrical Power: "Centralization has claimed everything for a century: the results are ap-parent on every hand. But the reign of steam ap-proaches its end: a new stage in the industrial revo-lution comes on. Electric power, breaking away from its servitude to steam, is be-coming independent. Elec-tricity is a decentralizing form of power: it runs over distributing lines and subdi-vides to all the minutiae of life and need. Working with it, men may feel the thrill of control and freedom once again."
—Joseph K, Hart, *The Sur-vey Graphic No. 51*, March 1, 1924

From the Age of Electron-ics:"The electric age of ser-vomechanisms suddenly re-leases men from the mechanical and specialist servitude of the preceding machine age. As the ma-chine and the motorcar re-leased the horse and pro-jected it onto the plane of entertainment, so does auto-mation with men. We are suddenly threatened with the liberation that taxes our in-ner resources of self-employ-ment and imaginative partic-ipation in society. . . . Panic about automation as a threat of uniformity on a world scale is the projection into the future of mechanical standardization and special-ism, which are now past."—
Marshall McLuhan, *Under-standing Media* (1964)
—(From Winner, 1984)

social ties they require to become fully func-tioning members of society.

But not all experts are so optimistic. They point to a number of studies, including those of the U.S. Bureau of Labor Statistics, which suggest that most of the new jobs will be menial service positions paying rel-atively low wages (Winner, 1984). New technologies often result in a two-tier work force with a small group of creative people performing spirit-enhancing and mind-chal-lenging tasks at the top and a large work force of people with low job skills who are paid correspondingly low wages at the bot-tom. Perhaps even more critically, new tech-nologies often eliminate jobs. Critics say that as computers and robots take over many office and factory duties, the only work that will remain will be primarily for janitors, hospital orderlies, and fast-food helpers. According to this view, technology has the double impact of job creation and job displacement, eliminating semiskilled and unskilled jobs while increasing the de-mand for technically trained workers. For instance, it is estimated that in the 1980s robots will eliminate between 13,500 and 24,000 jobs in Michigan, while creating only 5,000 to 8,000 jobs (Silk, 1982).

Yet there are those who contend that the

United States is not deindustrializing or losing its manufacturing base. Economist Kenneth M. Brown of the American Enterprise Institute cites statistics showing that manufacturing output as a percentage of gross national product has remained "quite stable" (Myers, 1984). He calculates that it was 24.5 percent in 1950, 23.3 percent in 1960, 24.1 percent in 1970, 23.8 percent in 1980, and 23.8 percent in 1984. Brown concludes that the share of *employment* in manufacturing is declining steadily because productivity has increased more rapidly in manufacturing than in services. When the "troubled industries"—motor vehicles, steel, textiles, shoes, and apparel are set aside (20 percent of the nation's manufacturing and about 3 percent of the labor force—employment in manufacturing rose 6 percent and output 14 percent between 1977 and 1982.

Other matters are also in dispute. Some experts contend that the most obvious beneficiaries of the new electronics are multinational corporations (Winner, 1984). Computer technologies provide large firms with the means for organizing their work and marketing operations more efficiently, while enhancing their ability to achieve centralized control. Thus computer technology increases the power of those who already enjoy power. With the mushrooming growth of office work—about one-half of the nation's work force is now employed in processing and handling information—large corporations are coming to recognize that office productivity has lagged significantly, and that vast productivity improvements in office work must be achieved if profit levels are to be maximized (Serrin, 1984b).

Likewise, advances in telecommunications and satellite transmissions permit the shifting of office work from central cities to suburban or rural areas and even to foreign countries (Serrin, 1984b). This migration of jobs complicates the crisis of the nation's large cities (see Chapter 11). Additionally, high-technology manufacturing processes lend themselves to the kind of systematized, rote-assembly processes that make low-cost labor attractive. For this reason, the Atari, Inc., unit of Warner Communications moved many of its videogame and computer operations to Hong Kong and Taiwan, idling about 1,700 American workers.

Increasingly, critics are also questioning whether the new technology is improving the lot of office workers (Andrew, 1983). Indeed, some labor leaders contend that office automation has created the electronic equivalent of the moving assembly line, with the computer system programmed to monitor workers' performance. A study by the U.S. Public Health Service offers some support for the criticism. The study looked at three categories of workers: clerical workers who did data processing with video display terminals, professionals who occasionally use video display terminals, and clerical workers who processed data by manual methods. The clerical workers using the video display terminals reported substantially greater physical and mental stress than did workers in other categories. The terminal users had to follow rigid work procedures that did not allow them any control over their work. Instead, the machine controlled them. Contemporary "electronic factories" are mostly a creation of banks, insurance companies, credit-card concerns, and firms with large data-processing requirements. In appearance the work settings are quite similar: a large, quiet room with video display terminals grouped in clusters or rows with data processors serving as electronic-age stevedores, loading and retrieving information.

Although considerable controversy surrounds the impact technology has on the workplace, it is clear that some individuals come out the losers. Frequently, the human consequences are so massive and pervasive that a single company, industry, or state cannot cope with them. Under these circumstances, a national response is essential if programs are to be set in place for shifting workers to industries and regions with jobs and for retraining workers for new jobs. A modern society ignores at its peril a situation where a growing number of its population cannot find gainful employment.

SOCIAL CHANGE IN THIRD WORLD NATIONS

It is difficult today to read a newspaper or view a television newscast without gaining a feeling for the powerful currents of change that continually encompass the world. Iran, the Middle East, Central America, South Africa, and countless other global centers conjure images of boiling cauldrons of social transition and transformation. Sociologists have approached social change in Third World nations from two somewhat different perspectives: modernization and world systems.

Modernization. **Modernization** describes the process by which a society moves from traditional or preindustrial social and economic arrangements to those characteristic of industrial societies. Implicit in the notion of modernization is the assumption that there is basically one underlying cause of development—namely, that followed by advanced Western nations and Japan. Viewed in this manner, modernization entails a pattern of *convergence* as societies become increasingly urban, industry comes to overshadow agriculture, the size and density of the population increases, the division of labor becomes more specialized, and the knowledge base grows larger and more complex.

The momentum for change derives from *internal* forces and processes. The chances that a Third World country will evolve in the direction of liberal Western democracies is thought to be enhanced when a nation's economy provides for literacy, education, and communication, creates a pluralistic

rather than a centrally dominated social order, and prevents extreme inequalities among the various social strata (Dahl, 1971). Efficient systems of communication and a diversity of social groups and organizations are believed to distribute political resources and skills among multiple segments of the community and provide the foundation of counterbalancing and effective opposition parties.

World Systems. **World-system** (or *dependency*) approaches view development within the context of an international, geographical division of labor. For instance, sociologist Immanuel Wallerstein (1974, 1980) distinguishes between three components of the global economic and political community: the core, the periphery, and the semiperiphery (see Chapter 8). In general, the *core* geographical area dominates the world economy and exploits other social and economic units. The *periphery* consists of those regions that supply raw materials to the core and are severely exploited by it. The *semiperiphery* are those areas that fall somewhere between the exploiting and exploited segments of the world economy.

According to world-system analysis, Third World nations cannot recapitulate the developmental trajectory of Western nations and Japan. An unequal exchange takes place between core and periphery nations, with development at the former end of the chain coming at the cost of underdevelopment at the other end (Delacroix and Ragin, 1981). More particularly, specialization in the production and export of raw materials is said to be detrimental to the long-term growth prospects of developing nations. Such specialization distorts these nations' economies because they become responsive to the demands of the world market rather than to internal developmental needs. Thus the momentum and course of development is shaped primarily by *external* forces and processes (Wolf, 1982). Further, investments in the production or mining of raw materials monopolize capital to the detriment of other types of investment (Stokes and Jaffee, 1982). And class formation in the dependent nations results in a small elite whose economic interests are linked to foreign investors in the core countries (Rubinson, 1976). In sum, whereas modernization approaches look to convergences in political and economic development, world-system analysis looks to divergences.

Collective Behavior

As we experience social life, it tends to be settled, patterned, and recurrent. We go about our daily activities, carrying out our roles and guiding our behavior by norms that define what we are supposed to do in given situations. Yet as we have seen in this chapter, it is easy to overemphasize the structured nature of social life. Some forms of group behavior are not organized in terms of established norms and institutionalized lines of action. This is particularly true of **collective behavior**—ways of thinking, feeling, and acting that develop among a large number of people and that are relatively spontaneous and unstructured. Human history is replete with episodes variously labeled by contemporaries as "psychic epidemics," "collective seizures," "group outbursts," "mass delusions," "crazes," and "group pathologies." Indeed, from earliest recorded times people have thrown themselves into a great many types of mass behavior, including social unrest, riots, manias, fads, panics, mass flights, lynchings, crowd excitement, religious revivals, and rebellions. All these forms of behavior are more likely to occur during times of rapid social change. Moreover, they often provide an impetus to social change. Accordingly, no discussion of social change can neglect collective behavior.

VARIETIES OF COLLECTIVE BEHAVIOR

Collective behavior comes in a great many forms. In order to gain a better appreciation for the impact such behavior has on our lives, let us consider a number of varieties of collective behavior at greater length.

Rumors. A **rumor** is a difficult-to-verify piece of information transmitted from person to person in relatively rapid fashion. We often think of rumors as providing false information, and in many cases this is true. But they also may be accurate, or, at the very least, contain a kernel of truth. Rumors typically arise in situations in which people lack information or distrust the official sources of information. They are a substitute for hard news, a collective attempt by people to achieve information and understanding about matters that are important to them but about which they are ignorant (Shibutani, 1966; Rosnow and Fine, 1976). As such, rumors are both a form of collective behavior and an important element in most other forms of collective behavior.

Periods of anxiety, tension, and sagging economic conditions provide an environment that lead to a proliferation of rumors (Rosnow and Kimmel, 1979; Koenig, 1982). Under these circumstances, rumors give people a way to make sense out of their social world and to structure reality. One type of rumor that is particularly common involves alleged contamination. Indeed, in recent years a variety of unfounded rumors have hurt the sales of some of the nation's largest corporations. For instance, McDonald's has had to fight rumors that it puts earthworms in hamburgers (perhaps suggested by the fact that raw hamburger resembles red worms). Some people have seen a communist connection in the clenched-fist symbol of Arm and Hammer, the baking soda. And Procter & Gamble removed its 135-year-old moon-and-stars trademark (see Figure 12.1) from its prod-

FIGURE 12.1 THE PROCTER & GAMBLE TRADEMARK
The Procter & Gamble trademark was the subject of recurrent rumors in various parts of the nation contending that the design was a symbol of Satanism. Despite the company's repeated assurances that the trademark represented nothing more sinister than the man in the moon and the 13 original American colonies, the rumors persisted. Eventually, Procter & Gamble announced in 1985 that it would no longer use the symbol on its product packages.

ucts when it was unable to dispel persistent rumors that the symbol was a sign of devil worship (Solomon, 1984; Salmans, 1985).

Rumors tend to evolve and take on new details as people interact and talk. Some research suggests that highly anxious people spread rumors much more frequently than do less anxious ones. Likewise, rumor participants—people who are eager to listen or pass on a rumor—are often individuals who wish to attract attention. Typically they are people who are on the edge of the group or relatively low in status. For a brief instant—when they are circulating a sensational story—they become somebody (Koenig, 1982).

Fashion and Fads. We typically think of folkways and mores as having considerable durability—as being relatively fixed and slow to change. Yet human beings often yearn for something new, for variety and novelty. At first it may seem impossible that this desire could be satisfied through norms, since norms emphasize conformity (see Chapter 2). Yet curiously, human beings manage to be conformists even when they seek change. They achieve this strange anomaly by a set of norms that demand some measure of conformity while they endure, but that last only a short time (Davis, 1948). Such norms are termed *fashions* and *fads*.

A **fashion** is a folkway that lasts for a short time and enjoys widespread acceptance within society. Fashion finds expression in such things as styles of clothing, auto design, and home architecture. By virtue of fashion, the suit that was in vogue five years ago seems out of place today. The automobile of three years past that appeared so exquisitely beautiful and appropriate looks outdated and even somewhat odd now. And "gingerbread" and brownstone houses no longer suit the tastes of many home buyers.

A **fad** is a folkway that lasts for a short time and enjoys acceptance among only a segment of the population. Indeed, the behavior is often scorned by most people. Fads often appear in amusements, new games, popular tunes, dance steps, health practices, movie idols, and slang. Adolescents are particularly prone toward fads. It seems that the identities of adolescents are as yet rather diffuse, uncrystallized, and fluctuating, and that teenagers are frequently at sea with themselves and others. This ambiguity and absence of stable social anchorage lead many youths to overcommit themselves to fads. The fads become a vehicle whereby young people can gain a sense of identity and belonging, with aspects of dress and gesture arbitrarily serving as signs of an in-group or out-group status (E. Erikson, 1968). For the most part, fads typically play only an incidental part in the

Breakdancing is a fad, a form of collective behavior that lasts for a short time and finds acceptance among a limited segment of the population. Adolescents seem especially susceptible to fads. They provide a means whereby young people can define who they are relative to their peers and can establish in-group memberships. (John P. Cavanagh/Archive)

lives of the individuals who adopt them. Some fads, however, come to preoccupy individuals, becoming all-consuming passions. Such fads are called **crazes.** Financial speculation at times assume craze proportions. In the famous Holland tulip mania in the seventeenth century, the value of tulip bulbs came to exceed their weight in gold; the bulbs were not planted, but bought and sold among speculators. In the Florida land boom of the 1920s, lands were sold and resold at skyrocketing prices without the purchasers even seeing their purchases.

Mass Hysteria. Mass hysteria refers to the rapid dissemination of behaviors involving contagious anxiety, usually associated with some mysterious force. For instance, medieval witchhunts rested on the belief that many social ills were caused by witches. Likewise, some "epidemics" of assembly-line illness—*mass psychogenic illness*—derive from hysterical contagion. In recent years episodes of mass psychogenic illness have occurred in American plants packing frozen fish, punching computer cards, assembling electrical switches, sewing shoes, making dresses, and manufacturing lawn furniture. In most cases, the workers complain of headaches, nausea, dizziness, weakness, and breathing difficulty. However, health authorities, including physicians, industrial hygienists, and toxicologists, find no bacteria, virus, toxic material, or other pathogenic agent to explain the symptoms. The episodes are most prevalent among poorly paid, female assembly-line workers who perform the same repetitive task over and over. Mass psychogenic illness is usually a collective response to severe stress caused by job dissatisfaction, monotony, overwork, noise, crowding, or poor management. An event such as a speedup or required overtime commonly triggers the outbreak (Colligan, Pennebaker, and Murphy, 1982).

We should not conclude that illnesses associated with contagious hysteria are simply in the workers' "heads." The individuals suffer real physical symptoms. For example, something—perhaps unusual stress—causes them to breathe rapidly (hyperventilate). The more rapidly a person breathes, the more carbon dioxide is blown off, and the higher becomes the pH level (acid-alkaline content) of the blood. The human body performs poorly at high pH levels, and such symptoms as headache, nausea, numbness in the feet and hands, and weakness can ensue.

Panic. **Panic** involves irrational and uncoordinated but collective actions among people induced by the presence of an immediate, severe threat. For instance, people commonly flee from a catastrophe such as a fire or flood. The behavior is collective, since social interaction intensifies people's fright. Consider what happened on Halloween evening, 1938, when a radio drama of H. G. Wells's novel *War of the Worlds* stirred up incidents of panic behavior in the United States (Cantril, 1940). The broadcast, carried by CBS stations, purported to describe an invasion of Martians. The story, narrated by Orson Welles and a number of other actors, was related in the form of special news bulletins and on-the-spot reports, interspersed with interviews with "eyewitnesses," "scientists," "public officials," and "commentators." The program began with dance music, purportedly coming from a hotel orchestra. Suddenly the music was interrupted with a special news bulletin (Cantril, 1940:22–23):

Ladies and gentlemen, I have a grave announcement to make. Incredible as it may seem, both the observations of science and the evidence of our eyes lead to the inescapable assumption that those strange beings who landed in the Jersey farmlands tonight are the vanguard of an invading army from the planet Mars. The battle which took place tonight at Grovers Mill has ended in one of the most startling defeats ever suffered by an army in modern times; seven thousand men armed with rifles and machine guns pitted against a single fighting machine of the invaders from Mars. One hundred and twenty known survivors. The rest strewn over the battle area from Grovers Mill to Plainsboro crushed and trampled to death under the metal feet of the monster, or burned to cinders by its heat-ray.

Dramatic announcements came in quick succession. As the broadcast proceeded, people ran to tell others by word of mouth and by phone. Some ran to the streets in panic. Others took to their cars to drive as far as possible from the place of invasion. Still others fell to the floor in prayer, or sat immobilized, waiting for the inevitable end. Estimates suggest that at least a million Americans were disturbed by the story. By the following morning, when newspapers and radio broadcasts reported the affair as a hoax, the excitement ended.

Crowds. The **crowd** is one of the most familiar and at times spectacular forms of collective behavior. It is a temporary, relatively unorganized gathering of people who are in close physical proximity. Since a wide range of behavior is encompassed by the concept, sociologist Herbert Blumer (1946) distinguishes among four basic types of crowd behavior. The first, a **casual crowd,** is a collection of people who have little in common except that they may be viewing a common event, such as looking through a department store window. The second, a **conven-**

tional crowd, entails a number of people who have assembled for some specific purpose and who typically act in accordance with established norms, such as people attending a baseball game or concert. The third, an **expressive crowd,** is an aggregation of people who have gotten together for self-stimulation and personal gratification, such as occurs at a religious revival or a rock festival. And fourth, an **acting crowd** is an excited, volatile collection of people who are engaged in rioting, looting, or other forms of aggressive behavior in which established norms carry little weight.

Although crowds differ from one another in many ways, they also share a number of characteristics in common:

1. *Suggestibility.* Crowd members tend to be more suggestible than they are in established social settings. Their behavior is not guided in a straightforward manner by conventional norms. Accordingly, individuals are usually more susceptible to images, directions, and propositions emanating from others.

2. *Deindividualization.* **Deindividualization** is a psychological state of diminished identity and self-awareness (Zimbardo, 1969). Anonymity—a sense that one is among strangers and "lost in the crowd"—contributes to deindividualization. Under such circumstances people no longer feel as inhibited in committing disapproved acts as they would among close associates. Reduced self-consciousness and a lowered concern for social evaluation also contribute to the deindividualization process (Mann, Newton, and Innes, 1982). Thus feelings of individual distinctiveness and uniqueness diminish as individuals increasingly make the group their focus of attention and activity.

3. *Invulnerability.* In crowd settings individuals often acquire a sense that they are more powerful and invincible than they are in routine, everyday settings. Moreover, they feel that social control mechanisms are less likely to be applied to them as individuals. Under these conditions, there may be an increase in behavior not normally approved by society, such as aggression, risk taking, self-enhancement, stealing, vandalism, and the uttering of obscenities (Dipboye, 1977; Mann, Newton, and Innes, 1982).

We will return to a consideration of crowds shortly, considering several theories of crowd behavior. But first, let us examine a number of preconditions for collective behavior.

PRECONDITIONS FOR COLLECTIVE BEHAVIOR

Sociologist Neil J. Smelser (1963) provides a framework for examining collective behavior based on the value-added model popular among economists. **Value-added** is the idea that each step in the production process—from raw materials to the finished product—increases the economic value of manufactured goods. Consider, for instance, the stages by which iron ore is converted into finished automobiles. As raw ore, the iron can be fashioned into an auto fender, a kitchen range, a steel girder, or the muzzle of a cannon. Once it is converted into thin sheets of steel, however, its possible uses are narrowed. Although it can still be fashioned into an auto fender or a kitchen range, it can no longer be employed for making a steel girder or the muzzle of a cannon. After the steel sheet is cut and molded in the shape of a fender, its use is further limited; it is no longer suitable for making a kitchen range. Each step in the process adds a specific "value" to the iron ore while simultaneously subtracting from previous possibilities.

As viewed by Smelser, episodes of collective behavior are like automobiles in that they are produced in a sequence of steps that constitute six determinants of collective behavior. In order of occurrence, they are (1) structural conduciveness, (2) structural strain, (3) growth and spread of a generalized belief, (4) precipitating factors, (5) mobilization of participants for action, and (6) the operation of social control. Each determinant is shaped by those that precede it and in turn shapes the ones that follow. Moreover, as in the case of automobiles, as each successive determinant is introduced in the value-added sequence, the range of potential final outcomes becomes progressively narrowed. Smelser contends that each of the six factors in the scheme is a *necessary* condition for the production of collective behavior, while all six are believed to make collective behavior virtually inevitable. Let us take a closer look at each of the determinants in Smelser's model.

Structural Conduciveness. Structural conduciveness refers to social conditions that *permit* a particular variety of collective behavior to occur. For instance, before a financial panic is possible, such as the stock market crash of 1929, there must be a money market where assets can be exchanged freely and rapidly. This basis does not exist in societies where property can be transferred only to the first-born son on the father's death, because the holders of property lack sufficient maneuverability to dispose of their assets on short notice. In like manner a race riot—a battle between two racial groups—dictates that two racial populations be in close physical proximity to one another.

Structural Strain. Structural strain is said to occur when important aspects of a social system are "out of joint." Wars, economic crises, natural disasters, and technological change disrupt the traditional rhythm of life and interfere with the way people normally carry out their activities. As stress accumulates across time, individuals become increasingly susceptible to courses of action not defined by existing institutional arrangements. They experience *social malaise*—a feeling of underlying and pervasive discontent. Thus, as we noted earlier in the chapter, mass psychogenic illness typically is a response to job strain where workers are under pressure to increase production. What the workers seem to be saying when they become ill is, "This place makes me sick."

The Growth of a Generalized Belief. Structural strain and a sense of social malaise by themselves are not sufficient to produce collective behavior. People must define a situation as a problem in need of a solution. In the course of social interaction, they evolve a shared view of reality and common ideas as to how they should respond to it. A generalized belief is required that provides people with "answers" to their stressful circumstances. For instance, in panic behavior, a belief evolves that empowers an ambiguous element in the environment with a generalized capacity to threaten or destroy. It was this type of belief regarding Martian invaders that precipitated the panic associated with the 1938 Halloween broadcast.

Precipitating Factors. Still another ingredient is required. Some sort of event is needed to "touch off" or "trigger" mass action. A precipitating event creates, sharpens, or exaggerates conditions of conduciveness and strain. Additionally, it provides adherents of a belief with explicit evidence of the workings of evil forces or greater promise of success. Revolutions, for example, are often precipitated in this manner: General Gage's 1775 march from Boston to Concord and Lexington; the seizure of the royal prison fortress by an angry French crowd in 1789; and the March 11, 1917, Tsarist decrees against Petrograd strikers. Likewise, in panic behavior it is usually a specific event that sets the flight in motion. A dramatic event—a broadcast of a Martian "invasion," an explosion, a government collapse, or a bank failure—provides the structuring essential to such behavior.

The Mobilization of Participants for Action. Once the above determinants have been put in place, the only necessary condition that remains is to bring the participants into action. This point marks the outbreak of crowd hostilities, the beginning of a revolution, or the onset of panic. In the Martian panic, the broadcast itself contained mobilizing communications (Cantril, 1940:29):

> *This in Newark, New Jersey . . .*
>
> *This is Newark, New Jersey . . .*
>
> *Warning! Poisonous black smoke pouring in from Jersey marshes. Reaches South Street. Gas masks useless. Urge population to move into open spaces . . . automobiles use routes 7, 23, 24. . . . Avoid congested areas. Smoke is now spreading over Raymond Boulevard. . . .*

In turn, listeners sounded the alarm to others. Through contagion, panic creates fear that feeds on itself.

Operation of Social Control. The sixth factor in Smelser's scheme is the operation of social control. It is not like the other determinants of collective behavior. Social control is basically a counterdeterminant that prevents, interrupts, deflects, or inhibits the accumulation of the others. Social control typically takes two forms. First, there are controls designed to *prevent* the occurrence of an episode of collective behavior by lessening conductiveness and strain (for example, welfare programs that seek to pacify the underclasses). Second, there are controls that attempt to *repress* an episode of collective behavior *after* it has begun (for example, police measures and curfews). In the case of the Martian broadcast, 60 percent of the stations carrying the program periodically interrupted it to make local explanatory announcements when it became evident that a misunderstanding was abroad. Such announcements helped curb panic behavior in the localities that received them.

In some instances, however, the activities of the agents of social control precipitate collective behavior and even violence. A good illustration of this occurred in the spring of 1963, when Rev. Martin Luther King, Jr., took the civil rights fight to Birmingham, Alabama, alleged to be the most segregated large city in the South. He and his followers organized a "siege of demonstrations" against Birmingham's segregation ordinances. More than 3,000 Birmingham blacks were arrested, while newspapers, magazines, and television stations beamed to the nation pictures of blacks facing snarling police dogs and being bowled over by high-pressure fire hoses. Although the demonstrations did not immediately succeed in overturning Birmingham's racist laws, the civil rights issue quickly became the number-one topic not only in the South, but throughout the United States. The brutality against Birmingham blacks gave impetus to some 1,122 civil rights demonstrations in the following four months in cities throughout the nation. These demonstrations culminated on August 28, 1963, in the March on Washington in which some 200,000 civil rights marchers demonstrated "for jobs and freedom." The wave of demonstrations spurred the Kennedy administration to sponsor new civil rights legislation that was passed by Congress the following year.

Assessing the Value-Added Model. Smelser's value-added model provides a useful tool for grasping the complexity of collective behavior. We see that collective behavior requires more than discontent and effective leaders (Marx and Woods, 1975). But the approach does have serious limitations. In some cases of collective action, all six stages do not necessarily occur, or they do not take place in the sequence Smelser specifies (Milgram, 1977). Additionally, some forms of crowd behavior are better explained by other perspectives. Let us consider a number of these approaches.

EXPLANATIONS OF CROWD BEHAVIOR

One of the characteristics of crowd behavior is the substitution of new forms and patterns of behavior for those that normally prevail in everyday life. Although crowd members differ in a great many ways, their behavior seems to derive from a common impulse and to be dominated by a single spirit. But is this indeed the case? What happens in the course of crowd behavior? And what processes fashion people's behavior under crowd conditions? Three somewhat different answers have been supplied by sociologists to these questions.

Contagion Theory. Contagion theory emphasizes the part that rapidly communicated and uncritically accepted feelings, attitudes, and actions play in crowd settings. Its proponents assume that unanimity prevails within a crowd, since crowd members often seem to act in identical ways and to be dominated by a similar impulse. Thus a crowd is often spoken of in the singular, as

if it were a real thing—"the crowd roars" and "the angry mob surges forward." This view of the crowd embodied in the influential work of the nineteenth-century French writer Gustave Le Bon (1896:23–24), who set forth the "law of the mental unity of crowds":

Under certain given circumstances . . . an agglomeration of men [people] presents new characteristics very different from those of the individuals composing it. The sentiments and ideas of all the persons in the gathering take one and the same direction, and their conscious personality vanishes.

Hence, Le Bon believed that people undergo a radical transformation in a crowd. They can become cruel, savage, and irrational—Jekylls turned into Hydes. In the crowd people become capable of violent, destructive, and terrible actions that would horrify them if they engaged in the actions when alone.

Le Bon's contagion theory depicts the crowd as characterized by a "mob mind" that overpowers and submerges the individual. A uniform mood and imagery evolve contagiously through three mechanisms: *imitation*—the tendency for one person to do the same thing that others are doing; *suggestibility*—a state in which individuals become susceptible to images, directions, and propositions emanating from others; and *circular reaction*—a process whereby the emotions of others elicit the same emotions in oneself, in turn intensifying the emotions of others in a reciprocal manner (for instance, A sees B becoming excited and in response also becomes excited, intensifying the excitement of B, leading A to become all the more excited and so on). However, Le Bon's concept of the crowd mind as some sort of supra-individual entity—one that is endowed with thinking processes and a capacity for feeling and believing—is rejected by most social scientists (Milgram and Toch, 1969). Only as individual entities with individual brains and nervous systems are human beings capable of thought and emotion.

Convergence Theory. The spread of an infectious disease is a good analogy for the contagion theory. In contrast, the heart surgery ward of a hospital provides the best analogy for **convergence theory.** The patients on the ward share a common problem, but not because they have transmitted the infection to one another. Rather, they select themselves out from the public because they share a common complaint and assemble on the ward with a common purpose. Likewise, some social scientists say that crowds select out a special class or category of people who are "crowd-prone." Whereas contagion theorists see normal, decent people being *transformed* under crowd influence, convergence theorists propose that a crowd consists of a highly unrepresentative body of people who assemble *because* they share the same predispositions. For instance, social psychologist Hadley Cantril (1941), in his study of the Leeville, Texas, lynching, contends that the active members came chiefly from the lowest economic bracket, and several had previous police records. As a class, poor whites were most likely to compete for jobs with blacks and were most likely to find their own status threatened by the presence of successful blacks. These individuals provided a reservoir of people who were ready for a lynching with a minimum of provocation.

Emergent-Norm Theory. The **emergent-norm theory** challenges the image of the crowd contained in both contagion and convergence theory. It stresses the *lack* of unanimity in many crowd situations and the *differences* in motives, attitudes, and actions that characterize crowd members: the presence of impulsives; suggestibles; opportunistic yielders; passive supporters; cautious activists; passers-by; and so on. The approach denies that people find themselves spontaneously infected with the emotions of others to the extent that they want to behave as others do (Turner, 1964; Turner and Killian, 1972).

Emergent-norm theory draws upon the work of Muzafer Sherif (1936) and Solomon Asch (1952) that deals with social conformity in ambiguous situations (see Chapter 4). According to sociologists like Ralph H. Turner and Lewis M. Killian (1972), collective behavior entails an attempt by people to find meaning in an uncertain social setting. Individuals search for cues to appropriate and acceptable behavior. And like the subjects in Sherif's experiments, who developed group norms that were different from the standards they developed when they were alone, crowd members collectively evolve new standards for behavior. For example, they may develop a norm that one should loot, burn, or harass police. Crowd members then proceed to enforce the norm: they reward behavior consistent with it, inhibit behavior contrary to it, justify proselyting, and institute actions that restrain dissenters. Since the new behavior differs from that in noncrowd situations, the norm must be specific to the situation—hence, an *emergent* norm.

Assessing the Perspectives. The three perspectives provide differing views of crowd behavior. Even so, they are not mutually exclusive. Consider what happens at a homecoming football game. Contagion contributes to the excitement through a process of circular reaction. Convergence operates, since loyal alumni and football enthusiasts are selected out from the larger population and come together in the stadium. Finally, an emergent norm defines what constitutes an appropriate response to a particular event and suppresses incongruous behavior. In sum, each perspective affords a useful tool for understanding crowd behavior.

Social Movements

Like collective behavior, social movements often appear in times of rapid social change. Both frequently provide an impetus to social change. Indeed, both occur outside the institutional framework that forms everyday life and break through the familiar web of ordered expectations. But even though social movements and collective behavior resemble one another, they differ in an important way (Traugott, 1978). Whereas collective behavior is characterized by spontaneity and a lack of internal structure, social movements possess a considerable measure of internal order and purposeful orientation. It is this organizational potential that allows social movements to challenge established institutions. Thus sociologists view a **social movement** as a more or less persistent and organized effort on the part of a relatively large number of people to bring about or resist change.

Central to the concept of social movement is the idea that people intervene in the process of social change. Rather than responding passively to the flow of life or to its troubling aspects, people seek to alter the course of history. Of equal significance, they undertake joint activity. Individuals consciously act together with a sense of engaging in a common enterprise. In sum, social movements are vehicles whereby people collectively seek to influence the course of human events through formal organization (see Chapter 4). It is little wonder, then, that social movements are the stuff of which history books are written: accounts of great leaders, the rise and fall of political movements, and the social dis-

locations and changes brought about by revolutions. Christianity, the Crusades, the Reformation, the American Revolution, the antislavery movement, the labor movement, Zionism, and fascism—like other social movements—have profoundly affected the societies they have touched.

TYPES OF SOCIAL MOVEMENTS

Historian Crane Brinton (1938) in his classic study *The Anatomy of Revolution,* writes, "No ideas, no revolution." He might equally well have noted, "No ideas, no social movement." In brief, a set of ideas—an **ideology**—is critical to a social movement. An ideology provides individuals with conceptions of the movement's purposes, its rationale for existence, its indictment of existing conditions or arrangements, and its design for action. Thus an ideology functions as a kind of glue that joins people together in a fellowship of belief, thereby cementing solidarity. But an ideology does even more. It not only binds together otherwise isolated and separated individuals, it unites them with a *cause.* In doing so, it prepares them for self-sacrifice on behalf of the movement—at times even to lay down their lives for the "True God," "the New Nation," or "the Revolution."

Social movements can be distinguished on the basis of their ideologies, or more particularly, by the goals their ideologies set forth. Some movements pursue objectives that aim to change society through challenging fundamental values or by seeking modifications within the framework of the existing value scheme. The former, **revolutionary movements,** advocate the *replacement* of the existing value scheme; the latter, **reform movements,** pursue changes that will *implement* the existing value scheme more adequately. The civil rights movement identified with the leadership of the Rev. Martin Luther King, Jr., had a reform em-

Members of social movements seek to bring about or resist social change.
Here feminists protest night assaults with a mass march at night to the dangerous Fenway area of Boston. (Ellis Herwig/Stock, Boston)

phasis. It sought to extend values that were already acknowledged to inhere in political democracy to the black population of the United States. In contrast, a number of black nationalist groups that arose in the late 1960s had a revolutionary emphasis. They sought to institute basic changes in the American republican form of government, to rearrange the American class structure, and to inaugurate a system of greater black autonomy.

Movements arise not only for the purpose of instituting change, but also to block change or to eliminate a previously instituted change—**resistance movements.** Indeed, movement begets countermovement. Thus the southern movement for civil rights unleashed a white counterattack beginning in the 1950s that found expression in the organization of White Citizens Councils and Ku Klux Klan groups. Historian Arthur Schlesinger, Jr., has argued that from its earliest days the United States has been dominated by alternating political currents: the conservative (Tory or Hamiltonian) philos-

ophy and the liberal (Whig or Jeffersonian) philosophy. Liberal periods witness an emphasis on popular rights, programs of reform, and efforts to share power with the unrepresented. In contrast, the emphasis during conservative periods falls on property rights, safety of the propertied classes, and efforts to perpetuate the power of the status quo. Schlesinger points out that liberal gains typically remain on the statute books even after the conservatives recover power. The conservatives acquiesce in the new social arrangements. However, they attempt to sabotage the reform measures by halfhearted enforcement and reduced appropriations (Vander Zanden, 1983).

Still other types of movements—**expressive movements**—are less concerned with institutional change than with a renovating or renewing of people from *within* (frequently with the promise of some future redemption). Pentecostal and holiness religious sects illustrate this kind of movement. Although they are arise primarily among the underprivileged, the sects do not seek comprehensive social change; they do not aim to save the world, but to save individuals from a world that is becoming progressively degenerate. They commonly believe that the second coming of the Messiah is near at hand and that there is no hope for the unsaved except through conversion and regeneration.

SOCIAL REVOLUTION

A **social revolution** involves the overthrow of a society's state and class structures and the fashioning of new social arrangements. Revolutions are most likely to occur under certain conditions (Skocpol, 1979; Goldstone, 1982). First, a good deal of political power is concentrated in the state so that there is a centralized governing apparatus. Accordingly, the state can become the focus for collective anger and attack. Second, the military's allegiance to the established regime is weakened so that the army is no longer a reliable tool for suppressing domestic disorders. Where army officers are drawn from elites in conflict with the central government, or when troops sympathize with their civilian counterparts, the unreliability of the army increases the vulnerability of the state. Third, political crises—often associated with long-term international conflicts that result in military defeat—weaken the existing regime and contribute to the collapse of the state apparatus. And fourth, a substantial segment of the population must mobilize in uprisings that bring a new elite to power. Peasant revolts usually stem from landlords taking over peasant lands, substantial increases in taxation or rents, or famines. Urban uprisings commonly derive from sharp jumps in food prices and unusually high levels of unemployment.

A number of historians and sociologists have surveyed important revolutions of the West in search of common stages and patterns in their development (Edwards, 1927; Brinton, 1938; Goldstone, 1982). Among the revolutions that they have examined are the English Revolution of 1640, the American Revolution of 1776, the French Revolution of 1789, and the Russian Revolution of 1917. From this work has stemmed a number of observations regarding the sequence of events that typically unfold in the course of major social revolutions, an approach called the **natural history of revolutions.**

Prior to the revolution, intellectuals—journalists, poets, playwrights, essayists, lawyers, and others—withdraw support from the existing regime and demand major reforms. Under increasing attack, the state attempts to meet the criticisms by instituting a number of reforms (for example, the reforms of Louis XVI in France, the Stolypin reforms in Russia, and the Boxer reforms in China). The onset of the revolution is heralded by the weakening or paralysis of the state, usually brought on by the government's inability to deal with a major military, economic, or political problem. The collapse of the old regime brings to the forefront divisions among conservatives who attempt to minimize change, radicals who seek fundamental change, and moderates who try to steer a middle course. Coups or civil war often ensue. The first group to gain the reins of power are usually moderate reformers (for instance, in Iran, Bazargan, the moderate critic, first took power after the shah's government was forced out).

The moderates seek to reconstruct governmental authority on the basis of limited reform, often employing organizational structures left over from the old regime. Simultaneously, radical centers of mass mobilization spring up with new organizations (in France, the moderate Girondin assembly confronted the radical Jacobin clubs; in America, the moderate Continental Congress was outpaced by the radical Patriots Societies; and in contemporary Iran the moderates led by Bazargan, Bani-Sadr, and

Gotbzadeh were supplanted by the radical Islamic clerics). The moderates find themselves heirs to the same problems and liabilities that felled the old regime, and in turn they are replaced by the radicals. The disorder that follows the revolution and the seizure of power by the radicals results in coercive rule. This is the stage of "Terror" that characterized the guillotine days of the French Revolution, Stalin's Gulag, and Mao's Cultural Revolution. Turmoil persists and allows military leaders to move into ascendancy (for instance, Washington, Cromwell, Napoleon, Ataturk, Mao, Tito, Boumedienne, and Mugabe). Finally, radicalism gives way to a phase of pragmatism and the consolidation of a new status quo. The "excesses" of the revolution are condemned and the emphasis falls on the fashioning of stable institutions. In France, this phase was marked by the fall of Robespierre; in the Soviet Union, by Khrushchev's repudiation of Stalin; and in China, by the fall of Mao's allies (the "gang of four"). Although not all revolutions pass through the identical sequence of stages, this approach does draw our attention to recurrent patterns in the unfolding of revolutionary activity.

TERRORISM

Terrorism may be viewed as the use of force or violence against persons or property to intimidate or coerce a government, a formal organization, or a civilian population in furtherance of political, religious, or social objectives. In practice, as with a great many other behaviors, what constitutes terrorism is a matter of social definition. Thus it is often difficult to distinguish "your terrorist" from "our freedom-fighter" or to differentiate aid to "terrorists" from "covert support of friendly forces," as with the Reagan administration's controversial support of the Nicaraguan contras, or counterrevolution-

ary fighters in the mid-1980s. In like fashion, the Federal Bureau of Investigation labeled a "terrorist" the antinuclear activist who in 1982 drove up to the Washington Monument in a truck that he pretended was loaded with explosives, whereas the agency has failed to apply that label to those responsible for firebombing abortion clinics.

For many years social scientists and historians treated terrorism primarily as a nuisance. But more recently they have increasingly come to see it as a new mode of warfare with far-reaching implications. What distinguishes much contemporary terrorism is not so much its motivation or purpose but rather the extent of state involvement in carrying out well-planned and highly destructive acts against adversary nations. The 1983 attack on the U.S. Marine barracks in Beirut that resulted in the death of 241 Americans is a good illustration of this.

Another feature of contemporary terrorism has been the extent to which it has become a media event. Very often terrorism is aimed at a media audience, not the actual victims. Although the terrorists write the script and perform the drama, the "theater of terror" becomes possible only when the media afford the stage and access to a worldwide audience. Measured in terms of the worldwide attention terrorism garners, and not in terms of the number of lives lost, it can be quite effective in the amount of terror it creates at relatively low cost to the perpetrators.

The act of media coverage also often enhances the importance of the issue that allegedly led to the terrorist activities. Newspaper readers and television viewers see the issue as of substantially greater importance and as justifying resolution by national or international action (Cunningham, 1984). For instance, the 1983 bombing of the Marine barracks led many Americans, including members of Congress, to oppose American involvement in Lebanon. The media portrayed grotesque scenes of the bodies of young Marines being pulled out of the rubble, chilling a good many people and making the American public desirous of avoiding further entanglement in Lebanon's affairs.

Shiite Muslims have been implicated in a good many of the bombings that have occurred in the Middle East in recent years. Some social scientists have sought explanations in that religion's history and tradition honoring martyrdom and even encouraging suicide as a holy act. But others have seen strong similarities with the acts of political terrorists (Cunningham, 1984). Among the latter groups have been factions of the Palestine Liberation Organization, the Red Brigades (Italy), the Red Army Faction (West Germany), Fighting Communist Cells (a Belgian anti-NATO group), a FLNC (a Corsican nationalist group in France), ETA (a Basque nationalist group in Spain), and the Irish Republican Army (Northern Ireland). There also has been a trend in recent years toward issue-oriented terrorism (in France, the Committee for the Liquidation of Computers has bombed computer centers; in the United Kingdom, the Animal Rights Militia has set off bombs and incendiary devices at laboratories conducting animal experiments; in Switzerland, the Radical Ecologists firebombed two power lines leading from a nuclear plant near Basel; and in Canada, the Wimmins Fire Brigade has made arson attacks on video shops selling pornography).

Nor has the United States been exempt from terrorism. Over the past decade or so a variety of terrorist groups have surfaced, such as the Symbionese Liberation Army, the Weather Underground, the Armed Resistance Group, the United Freedom Front, the Black Liberation Army, and the World Liberation Front. A number of groups have had nationalist aims, including anti-Turkish Armenians, nationalist Puerto Ricans, Croatian separatists, and anti-Castro Cubans. Some groups have advanced programs of racial and religious hatred, including such right-wing extremist organizations as the Order, the Silent Brotherhood, the Covenant, and the Aryan Nations (in 1985 the federal government indicted 24 members of the Order, charging them with the murder of Denver talk-show host Alan Berg, the attempted murder of FBI agents in gun battles in Washington and Oregon, armed robberies that included the paramilitary assault on a Brink's truck in Ukiah, California, which netted $3.6 million, and counterfeiting). Many of the same factors that underlie social movements also feed terrorism, a matter to which we now turn our attention.

CAUSES OF SOCIAL MOVEMENTS

Clearly the concept of social movement covers a good many different kinds of behavior. But why should a social movement form? What factors lead people to undertake joint action on behalf of some cause? Sociologists have been of two minds on these matters. There are those who seek the roots of social movement in social misery, and more particularly, in social and economic deprivation. Other sociologists do not find this argument particularly convincing. They note that most societies contain a considerable reservoir of social discontent and that oppression and misery have been widespread throughout history. Yet social movements are quite rare. These sociologists look to the resources and organizations that aggrieved persons can muster as providing the key to an understanding of social movements. Let us examine each of these approaches at greater length.

Deprivation Approaches. As noted in earlier chapters, Karl Marx held that capitalist exploitation leads to the progressive impoverishment of the working class. He expected that over time conditions would become so abominable that workers would be compelled to recognize the social nature of their misery and overthrow their oppressors. Yet Marx also recognized that abject misery and exploitation do not necessarily result in revolutionary fervor. He pointed out that the suffering of the underclasses (what he labeled the *lumpenproletariat*) can be so intense and their resulting alienation so massive that all social and revolutionary consciousness is deadened. Although the "progressive misery," or *absolute deprivation*, argument is found in Marx's more political writings, he also gave recognition to a type of *relative deprivation*. He foresaw that the working class could become better off as capitalism advanced, but that the gap between owners and workers would widen and produce among the latter deepening feelings of comparative disadvantage (Giddens, 1973; Anderson, 1974; Harrington, 1976).

A number of sociologists have suggested that a major factor in the evolution of the black protest in the 1960s was the emergence among blacks of a growing sense of **relative deprivation**—a gap between what people actually have and what they have come to expect and feel to be their just due (Geschwender, 1964; Gurr, 1970; Vander Zanden, 1983). The prosperity of the 1950s and 1960s gave many blacks a taste of the affluent society. They gained enough to arouse realistic hopes for more. Hence, grievances revolving about squalid housing, limited job opportunities, persistent unemployment, low pay, and police brutality were felt as severely frustrating. The civil rights movement arose not so much as a protest fed by despair, as one fed by *rising* expectations.

Sociologist James Davies (1962, 1969, 1974) finds that relative deprivation may also be fostered under another condition—

that characterized by his "rise-and-drop," or "J curve," hypothesis (see Figure 12.2). He contends that revolutions are most likely to take place when a prolonged period of social and economic betterment is followed by a period of sharp reversal. People fear that the gains they achieved with great effort will be lost, and their mood becomes revolutionary. Davies illustrates the rise-and-drop hypothesis by events as varied as Dorr's rebellion in Rhode Island in 1842, the Pullman strike of 1894, the Russian Revolution of 1917, and the Egyptian revolution of 1953.

Resource Mobilization Approaches. Deprivation approaches seek to find out why people are attracted to social movements. Resource-mobilization approaches take a different tack. According to the resource-mobilization school, social discontent is more or less constant and thus endemic within all modern societies (Tilly, 1978a; Zald and McCarthy, 1979; Jenkins, 1983). Accordingly, its proponents deem it unnecessary to explain the forces that energize and activate a social movement. Instead, they emphasize the importance of structural factors, such as the availability of resources for pursuing particular goals and the network of interpersonal relationships that serve as the focus for membership recruitment. People are seen as participating in a social movement not as the result of deprivation, but as a response to a rational decision-making process whereby they weigh the costs and benefits of participation.

In many cases, resources and organizations outside the protest group are crucial in determining the scope and outcomes of collective action. External support is especially critical for movements of the poor. Sociologists J. Craig Jenkins and Charles Perrow (1977) illustrate the point with historical materials dealing with farm worker insurgencies within the United States. They

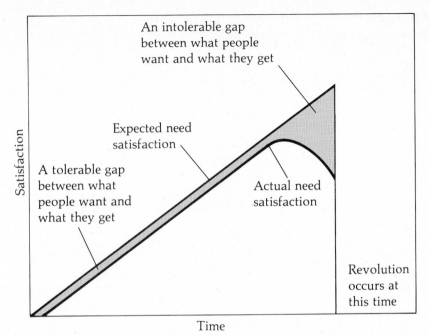

An intolerable gap
between what people
want and what they get

Expected need
satisfaction

A tolerable gap
between what
people want and
what they get

Actual need
satisfaction

Satisfaction

Revolution
occurs at
this time

Time

FIGURE 12.2   DAVIES' J-CURVE THEORY OF REVOLUTION
The figure illustrates Davies' theory that revolutions are often fostered when a
period of social and economic betterment is succeeded by sharp reversals,
fueling concern that the gains will be lost. (Adapted from James C. Davies.
"Toward a Theory of Revolution." American Sociological Review, *Vol. 27*
(February 1962), Fig. 1, p. 6.)

contrast the unsuccessful attempt to organize farm workers by the National Farm Labor Union from 1946 to 1952 with the successful organization of Mexican farm workers by the United Farm Workers from 1965 to 1972. Both groups pursued similar ends (union contracts), employed similar tactics (mass agricultural strikes and boycotts supported by organized labor), and encountered comparable obstacles. Yet the United Farm Workers prevailed where the National Farm Labor Union failed. Jenkins and Perrow contend that the United Farm Workers succeeded because internal divisions in government neutralized oppositional elites, while the support of the liberal-labor coalition during the reform years of the 1960s and early 1970s turned the tide in favor of the farm workers.

The grievances of the farm workers did not change in the post-World War II period, nor did the basic conflicts of interest that were embedded in the nation's institutional life. What changed were the resources and opportunities for collective action that were available to the farm workers—most particularly, the availability of powerful allies. Hence, the success or failure of a social movement derives from strategic factors and the political processes in which it becomes enmeshed.

Assessing the Approaches. Some resource-mobilization theorists overstate their case. It may be true that social unrest is endemic within society, but there are instances where suddenly imposed grievances do generate organized protest. The rapid emergence of organized action groups in the communities surrounding the Three Mile Island area following the 1979 nuclear accident provides a good illustration of this process (Walsh, 1981). Much the same holds for countermovements—resistance or "anti" movements—that arise in response to the social change pursued by other movements (Mottl, 1980). The antisegregation movement in the South (Vander Zanden, 1965) and the Boston antibusing movement provide examples of movements that gain support among people who believe themselves threatened by impending change (Useem, 1980). However, resource-mobilization approaches have the advantage of drawing social movement analysis within the larger arena of social and political conflict. We gain an image of social movements as formal organizations clashing over the direction of public policy and the use of political power (Tilly, 1978a). Indeed, we come to view social movements as instruments or vehicles of power.

Looking to the Future

We look to the past for the roots of the present and to both the past and the present for what the future may hold. In fact, we undertake many of our daily activities in anticipation of the future. We carry out our job responsibilities in the expectation that we will be paid at the end of the week or the month. We make arrangements for future events, including football games, parties, spring break, final examinations, and graduation exercises. We invest our money, energy, and time in an education based on the assumption that there will be a job payoff down the road. We may involve ourselves in environmental and antinuclear movements in order to have a voice in the fashioning of tomorrow's world. Because the future is so important to us, we look to

experts from a wide range of disciplines to give us some idea of what we can expect in the weeks, years, and decades ahead. Some individuals, known as **futurists,** specialize in the study of the future, seeking to understand, predict, and plan the future of society.

The complexity of society makes it exceedingly difficult to predict the distant future with accuracy, and even the not too distant future is often hard to anticipate. Even so, one thing seems certain: We shall not live all our lives in the world into which we were born, nor shall we die in the world in which we worked in our maturity. Futurists have identified two changes that seem to be central to contemporary social life. First, the United States is being restructured from an industrial to an information society. Second, modern societies are increasingly shifting from a national to a global economy. Futurists have applied a good many metaphors to these changes, including Daniel Bell's "postindustrial society," Alvin Toffler's (1980) "the third wave," and John Naisbitt's (1982) "megatrends." Common to these metaphors is the notion that American society is shifting from the production of goods to the production of services, and from a society based on the coordination of people and machines to a society organized around knowledge. These changes, it is contended, will afford a myriad of choices. The world will increasingly be one of many flavors, not just vanilla or chocolate.

Many observers of contemporary American life believe that we are witnessing a historical change and the first major impact of the shift from an energy economy to an information economy (Drucker, 1985). For three hundred years technology has been cast in a mechanical model, one based on the combustion processes that go on inside a star like the sun. The steam engine opened the mechanical age and it reached its apex with the discovery of nuclear fission and nuclear fusion, which replicated the energy-producing processes of a star. But we now seem to be moving toward a biological model based on information and involving the intensive use of materials. Although biological processes need physical energy and materials, they tend to substitute information for both. Biological processes "miniaturize" size, energy, and materials by "exploding" information. The human brain is some ten times the size and weight of the brain of a lemur (a lower primate). But it handles a billion times more information. The miniaturization is on the order of 10 to the ninth power, and it is far ahead of what the microchip has achieved with miniaturization. As a result, high-tech industries are information-intensive rather than energy- or materials-intensive. Sociologists have played and will continue to play an important role in assessing and interpreting these developments and other aspects of change.

Summary

1. Human life is never static, but always in flux. However, the dynamic quality of life often eludes us because of our perceptual and conceptual limitations. Sociologists refer to fundamental alterations in the patterns of culture, structure, and social behavior over time as social change. It is a process by which society becomes something different while remaining in some respects the same.

2. Social change confronts people with new situations and compels them to fashion new forms of action. A great many factors interact to generate changes in people's behavior and in the culture and structure of their society. Sociologists identify a number of particularly critical factors, including the physical environment, population, clashes over resources and values, supporting values and norms, innovation, and diffusion.

3. Many of sociology's roots lie in the effort to unravel the "meaning" of history and to establish laws of social change and development. The major sociological perspectives on social change fall within four broad categories: evolutionary perspectives, cyclical perspectives, functionalist perspectives, and conflict perspectives. Evolutionary theorists, particularly those with a unilinear focus, depict history as divided into steplike levels that constitute sequential stages and that are characterized by an underlying trend. Cyclical theorists look to the course of a civilization or society, searching for generalizations regarding their stages of growth and decline. Functionalist theorists see society as a system that tends toward equilibrium. And conflict theorists hold that tensions between competing groups are the basic source of social change.

4. The computer revolution is having a broad impact on people's lives. Computers promise to automate some workplace activities now performed by people. They have consequences for the use and manipulation of social power. Computers alter the manner in which people relate to one another. And they have implications for individual privacy and the confidentiality of communications and personal data. Visionaries look to technology to make human lives richer and freer. Pessimists see technol-

ogy as creating a two-tier work force with a small group of creative people performing spirit-enriching and mind-challenging tasks at the top and a large work force of people with low job skills who are paid correspondingly low wages at the bottom.

5. Sociologists have approached social change in Third World nations from two somewhat differing perspectives. The modernization approach sees development as entailing a pattern of convergence as societies become increasingly urban, industry comes to overshadow agriculture, the size and density of the population increases, the division of labor becomes more specialized, and the knowledge base grows larger and more complex. The world system or dependency approach views development within the context of an international, geographical division of labor. According to world system analysis, an unequal exchange takes place between core and periphery nations, with development at the former end of the chain coming at the cost of underdevelopment at the other end.

6. Some forms of group behavior are not organized in terms of established norms and institutionalized lines of action. This is particularly true of collective behavior. Collective behavior comes in a good many forms, including rumors, fashions and fads, mass hysteria, panic, and crowds.

7. Sociologist Neil J. Smelser provides a framework for examining collective behavior based on the value-added model popular among economists. As viewed by Smelser, episodes of collective behavior are produced in a sequence of steps that constitute six determinants of collective behavior. In order of occurrence, they are (1) structural conducive-

ness, (2) structural strain, (3) growth and spread of a generalized belief, (4) precipitating factors, (5) mobilization of participants for action, and (6) the operation of social control. Each determinant is shaped by those that precede it and in turn shapes the ones that follow.

8. Sociologists offer three somewhat different approaches to crowd behavior. According to contagion theory, rapidly communicated and uncritically accepted feelings, attitudes, and actions play a critical part in crowd settings through processes of imitation, suggestibility, and circular reaction. Convergence theory suggests that a crowd consists of a highly unrepresented body of people who assemble because they share the same predispositions. The emergent-norm theory challenges the image of the crowd contained in both contagion and convergence theory. According to this view, crowd members evolve new standards for behavior that they then enforce in normative ways.

9. Central to the concept of social movement is the idea that people intervene in the process of social change. Of equal significance, they undertake joint activity. Social movements are vehicles whereby people collectively seek to influence the course of human events through formal organizations. Common forms of social movement include revolutionary, reform, resistance, and expressive movements.

10. Social revolutions are most likely to occur under certain conditions. First, a good deal of political power is concentrated in the state, so that there is a centralized governing apparatus. Second, the military's allegiance to the established regime is weakened, so that the army is no longer a reliable tool for suppressing domestic disorders. Third,

political crises weaken the existing regime and contribute to the collapse of the state apparatus. And fourth, a substantial segment of the population must mobilize in uprisings that bring a new elite to power. A number of historians and sociologists have surveyed important revolutions of the West in search of common stages and patterns in their development, giving rise to the natural history of revolutions approach.

11. Sociologists are of two minds regarding the causes of social movements. There are those who seek the roots of social movement in social misery, and more particularly in social and economic deprivation. Other sociologists do not find this argument particularly convincing. They note that most societies contain a considerable reservoir of social discontent and that oppression and misery have been widespread throughout history. These sociologists look to the resources and organizations aggrieved persons can muster as providing the key to an understanding of social movements.

Glossary

acting crowd An excited, volatile collection of people who are engaged in rioting, looting, or other forms of aggressive behavior in which established norms carry little weight.

casual crowd A collection of people who have little in common with one another except that they may be viewing a common event, such as looking through a department store window.

collective behavior Ways of thinking, feeling, and acting that develop among a large number of people and that are relatively spontaneous and unstructured.

conventional crowd A number of people who have assembled for some specific purpose and who typically act in accordance with established norms, such as people attending a baseball game or concert.

contagion theory An approach to crowd behavior which emphasizes the part that rapidly communicated and uncritically accepted feelings, attitudes, and actions play in crowd settings.

convergence theory An approach to crowd behavior which says a crowd consists of a highly unrepresentative body of people who assemble because they share the same predispositions.

crazes Fads that become all-consuming passions.

crowd A temporary, relatively unorganized gathering of people who are in close physical proximity.

cultural lag The view that immaterial culture must constantly "catch up" with material culture, resulting in an adjustment gap between the two forms of culture.

deindividualization A psychological state of diminished identity and self-awareness.

diffusion The process by which culture traits spread from one social unit to another.

discovery An addition to knowledge.

emergent-norm theory An approach to crowd behavior which says crowd members evolve new standards for behavior in a crowd setting and then enforce the expectations in the manner of norms.

expressive crowd An aggregation of people who have gotten together for self-stimulation and personal gratification, such as occurs at a religious revival or a rock festival.

expressive movement Movements that are less concerned with institutional change than with a renovating or renewing of people from within.

fad A folkway that lasts for a short time and enjoys acceptance among only a segment of the population.

fashion A folkway that lasts for a short time and enjoys widespread acceptance within society.

futurist Individuals specializing in the study of the future; they seek to understand, predict, and plan the future of society.

ideology A set of ideas that provides individuals with conceptions of the purposes of a social movement, a rationale for the movement's existence, an indictment of existing conditions, and a design for action.

invention The use of existing knowledge in a new form.

mass hysteria The rapid dissemination of behaviors involving contagious anxiety, usually associated with some mysterious force.

modernization The process by which a society moves from traditional or preindustrial social and economic arrangements to those characteristic of industrial societies.

natural history of revolutions The view that social revolutions pass through a set of common stages and patterns in the course of their development.

panic Irrational and uncoordinated but collective action among people that is induced by the presence of an immediate, severe threat.

reform movement A social movement that pursues changes which will implement the existing value scheme of a society more adequately.

relative deprivation A gap between what people actually have and what they have come to expect and feel to be their just due.

resistance movement A social movement that arises to block change or eliminate a previously instituted change.

revolutionary movement A social movement that advocates the replacement of a society's existing value scheme.

rumor A difficult-to-verify piece of information that is transmitted from person to person in relatively rapid fashion.

social change Fundamental alterations in the patterns of culture, structure, and social behavior over time.

social movement A more or less persistent and organized effort on the part of a relatively large number of people to bring about or resist change.

social revolution The overthrow of a society's state and class structures and the fashioning of new social arrangements.

structural conduciveness Social conditions that permit a particular variety of collective behavior to occur.

structural strain A condition in which important aspects of a social system are "out of joint."

terrorism The use of force or violence against persons or property to intimidate or coerce a government, a formal organization, or a civilian population in furtherance of political, religious, or social objectives.

value-added The idea that each step in the production process—from raw materials to the finished product—increases the economic value of manufactured goods.

world system An approach that views development as involving an unequal exchange between core and periphery nations, with development at the former end of the chain coming at the cost of underdevelopment at the other end.

References

ABERNATHY, WILLIAM J., KIM B. CLARK, and ALAN M. KANTROW. 1983. *Industrial renaissance.* New York: Basic Books.

ABRAHAMSON, MARK. 1978. *Functionalism.* Englewood Cliffs, N.J.: Prentice-Hall.

ACKERMAN, NATHAN W., and MARIE JAHODA. 1950. *Anti-Semitism and emotional disorder.* New York: Harper & Row.

ADELSON, JOSEPH. 1979. Adolescence and the generation gap. *Psychology Today*, 12 (February): 33–37.

ADORNO, T. W., ELSE FRENKEL-BRUNSWIK, DANIEL J. LEVINSON, and R. NEVITT SANFORD 1950. *The authoritarian personality.* New York: Harper & Row.

AGNEW, ROBERT. 1981. The individual and values in human ecology: An examination of the adaptive processes. *The Sociological Quarterly*, 22: 105–117.

AKHAVI, SHAHROUGH. 1980. *Religion and politics in contemporary Iran: Clergy–state relations in the Pahlavi period.* Albany: State University of New York Press.

ALLPORT, GORDON W. 1954. *The nature of prejudice.* Boston: Beacon Press.

ALM, RICHARD and ROBERT J. MORSE. 1984. Growing furor over pay of top executives. *U.S. News & World Report* (May 21): 79–82.

AMERICAN PSYCHIATRIC ASSOCIATION. 1980. *Diagnostic and statistical manual of mental disorders*, 3rd ed. Washington, D.C.: American Psychiatric Association.

AMERICAN SOCIOLOGICAL ASSOCIATION. 1980. Revised ASA code of ethics. *ASA Footnotes* (August): 12–13.

ANDERSON, CHARLES H. 1971. *Toward a new sociology.* Homewood, Ill.: Dorsey Press.

ANDERSON, CHARLES H. 1974. *The political economy of social class.* Englewood Cliffs, N.J.: Prentice-Hall.

ANDERSON, HARRY. 1984. Carving up the car buyer. *Newsweek* (March 5): 72–73.

ANDERSON, L. S., THEODORE G. CHIRICOS, and GORDON P. WALDO. 1977. Formal and informal sanctions: A comparison of deterrent effects. *Social Problems*: 25: 103–114.

ANDERSON, NELS. 1923. *The hobo.* Chicago: The University of Chicago Press.

ANDREW, JOHN. 1983. As computers change the nature of work, some jobs lose savor. *Wall Street Journal* (May 6): 1, 16.

APPLE, MICHAEL W. 1982. *Education and power.* London: Routledge & Kegan Paul.

APPLE, MICHAEL W., and LOIS WEIS. 1983. *Ideology and practice in schooling.* Philadelphia: Temple University Press.

ARIÈS, PHILIPPE. 1962. *Centuries of Childhood.* Trans. R. Baldick. New York: Random House.

ARIÈS, PHILIPPE. 1981. *The hour of our death.* New York: Knopf.

ASCH, SOLOMON. 1952. *Social psychology.* Englewood Cliffs, N.J.: Prentice-Hall.

BALES, ROBERT F. 1970. *Personality and interpersonal behavior.* New York: Holt, Rinehart and Winston.

BALES, ROBERT F., and EDGAR F. BORGATTA. 1955. Size of group as a factor in the interaction profile. In A. P. Hare, E. F. Borgatta, and R. F. Bales, eds., *Small groups: Studies in social interaction.* New York: Knopf.

BALKWELL, CAROLYN. 1981. Transition to widowhood: A review of the literature. *Family Relations*, 30: 117–127.

BANDURA, ALBERT. 1971. *Psychological modeling: Conflicting theories.* Chicago: Aldine-Atherton.

BANDURA, ALBERT. 1973. *Aggression: A social learning analysis.* Englewood Cliffs, N.J.: Prentice-Hall.

BANE, MARY JO. 1976. *Here to stay: American families in the twentieth century.* New York: Basic Books.

BARAN, PAUL, and PAUL M. SWEEZY. 1966. *Monopoly capital: An essay on the American economic and social order.* New York: Monthly Review Press.

BARCLAY, A. M. and R. N. HABER. 1965. The relation of aggression to sexual motivation. *Journal of Personality*, 33: 462–475.

BARKOW, J. H. 1978. Culture and sociobiology. *American Anthropologist*, 80: 5–20.

BARRON, D. SUSAN. 1984. Reviving the rituals of the debutante. *New York Times Magazine* (January 15): 26–37.

BARUCH, GRACE, and ROSALIND C. BARNETT. 1983. Adult daughters' relationships with their mothers. *Journal of Marriage and the Family*, 45: 601–606.

BASS, BERNARD M. 1960. *Leadership, psychology, and organizational behavior.* New York: Harper & Row.

BAUM, ANDREW, and GLENN E. DAVIS. 1980. Reducing the stress of high-density living: An architectural intervention. *Journal of Personality and Social Psychology*, 38: 471–481.

BAUMEISTER, ROY F. 1984. Choking under pressure: Self-consciousness and paradoxical effects of incentives on skillful performance. *Journal of Personality and Social Psychology*, 46: 610–620.

BAUMEISTER, ROY F. and ANDREW STEINHILBER. 1984. Paradoxical effects of supportive audiences on performance under pressure: The home field disadvantage in sports championships. *Journal of Personality and Social Psychology*, 47: 85–93.

BECK, E. M., PATRICK HORAN, and CHARLES TOLBERT. 1978. Stratification in a dual economy: A structural model of earnings determination. *American Sociological Review*, 43: 704–720.

BECK, E. M., PATRICK HORAN, and CHARLES TOLBERT. 1980. Social stratification in industrial society: Further evidence for a structural alternative. *American Sociological Review*, 45: 712–719.

BECK, MELINDA. 1982. The decaying of America. *Newsweek* (August 2): 12–18.

BECK, SCOTT H. 1982. Adjustment to and satisfaction with retirement. *Journal of Gerontology*, 37: 616–624.

BECKER, HOWARD S. 1963. *Outsiders: Studies in the sociology of deviance.* New York: Free Press.

BEIRNE, PIERS. 1979. Empiricism and the critique of

Marxism on law and crime. *Social Problems*, 26: 373–385.

BELKIN, LISA. 1984. In politics, women run by a different set of rules. *New York Times* (September 9): 2E.

BELL, ALAN P. and MARTIN S. WEINBERG. 1978. *Homosexualities: A study of diversity among men and women*. New York: Simon and Schuster.

BELL, ALAN P. MARTIN S. WEINBERG, and SUE K. HAMMERSMITH. 1981. *Sexual preference: Its development in men and women*. Bloomington: Indiana University Press.

BELL, DANIEL. 1973. *The coming of the post-industiral society*. New York: Basic Books.

BELL, T. H. 1985. Bell criticizes "assault on the private colleges." *The New York Times Education Survey* (Spring 1985): 71–72.

BELLAH, ROBERT N. *Beyond belief*. New York: Harper & Row.

BELLAH, ROBERT N., and PHILLIP E. HAMMOND. 1980. *Varieties of civil religions*. New York: Harper & Row.

BELSKY, JAY, GRAHAM B. SPANIER, and MICHAEL ROVINE. 1983. Stability and change in marriage across the transition to parenthood. *Journal of Marriage and the Family*, 45: 567–577.

BELSKY, JAY, and LAURENCE D. STEINBERG. 1978. The effects of day care: A critical review. *Child Development*, 49: 929–949.

BENDIX, REINHARD. 1977. Bureaucracy. *International Encyclopedia of the Social Sciences*. New York: Free Press.

BENEDETTO, RICHARD. 1984. Military ousting more homosexuals. *USA Today* (October 25): 6A.

BENOIT-SMULLYAN, EMILE. 1948. The sociologism of Emile Durkheim and his school. In Harry Elmer Barnes, ed., *An introduction to the history of sociology*. Chicago: University of Chicago Press.

BENSON, J. KENNETH. 1977. Organizations: A dialectical view. *Administrative Science Quarterly*, 22: 1–21.

BEN-YEHUDA, NACHMAN. 1980. The European witch craze of the 14th and 17th centuries. *American Journal of Sociology*, 86: 1–31.

BEQUAI, AUGUST. 1984. Crime that pays. *New York Times* (May 9): 27.

BERGER, BRIGITTE, and PETER L. BERGER. 1983. *The war over the family: Capturing the middle ground*. Garden City, N.Y.: Anchor Books.

BERGER, PETER L. 1963. *Invitation to sociology*. Garden City, N.Y.: Anchor Books.

BERGER, PETER L. 1967. *The sacred canopy: Elements of a sociological theory of religion*. Garden City, N.Y.: Doubleday.

BERGER, PETER L. 1979. *The heretical imperative: Contemporary possibilities of religious affirmation*. Garden City, N.Y.: Doubleday.

BERK, RICHARD, and SARAH F. BERK. 1979. *Labor and leisure at home*. Beverly Hills, Calif.: Sage.

BERLE, ADOLPH, JR., and GARDINER C. MEANS. 1932. *The modern corporation and private property*. New York: Harcourt, Brace and World.

BERNSTEIN, ILENE N., WILLIAM R. KELLY, and PATRICIA A. DOYLE. 1977. Societal reactions to deviants: The case of criminal defendants. *American Sociological Review*, 42: 743–755.

BERREMAN, GERALD. 1960. Caste in India and the United States. *American Journal of Sociology*, 66: 120–127.

BETTELHEIM, BRUNO, and MORRIS JANOWITZ. 1950. *Dynamics of prejudice*. New York: Harper & Row.

BIANCHI, SUZANNE M. 1984a. Children's progress through school: A research note. *Sociology of Education*, 57:184–192.

BIANCHI, SUZANNE M. 1984b. Wives who earn more than their husbands. *American Demographics*, 6 (July): 19–23 + .

BIERSTEDT, ROBERT. 1950. An analysis of social power. *American Sociological Review*. 15: 730–738.

BIRD, GLORIA W., GERALD A. BIRD, and MARGUERITE SCRUGGS. 1984. Determinants of family task sharing: A study of husbands and wives. *Journal of Marriage and the Family*, 46: 345–355.

BIRDWHISTELL, RAYMOND L. 1970. *Kinesics and context*. Philadelphia: University of Pennsylvania Press.

BLACKBURN, McKINLEY L., and DAVID E. BLOOM. 1985. What is happening to the middle class? *American Demographics*, 7 (January): 19–25.

BLAU, PETER M. 1964. *Exchange and power in social life*. New York: Wiley.

BLAU, PETER M. and OTIS DUDLEY DUNCAN. 1972. *The American occupational structure*, 2nd ed. New York: Wiley.

BLAU, PETER M., and RICHARD A. SCHOENHERR. 1971. *The structure of organizations*. New York: Basic Books.

BLAU, PETER, and RICHARD SCOTT. 1962. *Formal organizations*. San Francisco: Chandler.

BLAU, ZENA SMITH. 1973. *Old age in a changing society*. New York: New Viewpoints.

BLAUNER, ROBERT. 1969. Work satisfaction and industrial trends. In A. Etzioni, ed., *A Sociological Reader on Complex Organizations*. New York: Holt, Rinehart and Winston.

BLOCK, FRED. 1977. The ruling class does not rule: Notes on the Marxist theory of the state. *Socialist Revolution*. 7: 6–28.

BLOOM, DAVID E. 1984. Putting off children. *American Demographics*, 6 (September): 30–33 + .

BLUESTONE, BARRY, and BENNETT HARRISON. 1982. *The deindustrialization of America*. New York: Basic Books.

BLUMBERG, PAUL. 1980. *Inequality in the age of decline*. New York: Oxford University Press.

BLUMER, HERBERT. 1946. Collective behavior. In A. M. Lee, ed., *New outline of the principles of sociology*. New York: Barnes & Noble.

BLUMER, HERBERT. 1961. Race prejudice as a sense of group position. In J. Masuoka and P. Valien, eds., *Race relations*. Chapel Hill: University of North Carolina Press.

BLUMER, HERBERT. 1969. *Symbolic interaction: Perspective and method*. Englewood Cliffs, N.J.: Prentice-Hall.

BLUMSTEIN, PHILIP, and PEPPER SCHWARTZ. 1983. *American couples*. New York: William Morrow.

BLYTH, DALE A., and CAROL M. TRAEGER. 1983. The self-concept and self-esteem of early adolescents. *Theory into Practice*, 22: 91–97.

BOHANNON, PAUL, and ROSEMARY ERICKSON. 1978. Stepping in. *Psychology Today*, 11 (January): 53–59.

BONACHICH, EDNA. 1972. A theory of ethnic antagonism: A split-labor market. *American Sociological Review*, 37: 547–559.

BONACICH, EDNA. 1975. Abolition, the extension of slavery, and the position of free blacks: A study of split-labor markets in the United States, 1830–1863. *American Journal of Sociology*, 81: 601–628.

BONGER, WILLIAM A. 1936. *An introduction to criminology/* London: Methuen.

BORNSCHIER, VOLKER, CHRISTOPHER CHASE-DUNN, and RICHARD RUBINSON. 1978. Cross-national evidence of the effects of foreign investment and aid on economic growth and inequality. *American Journal of Sociology*, 84: 651–683.

BORNSCHIER, VOLKER, and JEAN-PIERRE HOBY. 1981. Economic policy and multinational corporations in development. *Social Problems*, 28: 363–377.

BOSERUP, ESTER. 1965. *The conditions of agricultural growth: The economics of agrarian change under population pressures.* Chicago: Aldine.

BOTTOMORE, THOMAS B. 1966. *Classes in modern society.* New York: Pantheon.

BOTTOMORE, THOMAS B. 1981. A Marxist consideration of Durkheim. *Social Forces*, 59: 902–917.

BOWLES, SAMUEL, and HERBERT GINTIS. 1976. *Schooling and capitalist America.* New York: Basic Books.

BRADBURY, KATHARINE L., ANTHONY DOWNS, and KENNETH A. SMALL. 1982. *Urban decline and the future of American cities.* Washington, D.C.: Brookings Institution.

BREINES, WINI. 1980. Community and organization: The New Left and Michels' "iron law." *Social Problems*, 27: 419–429.

BRIDGWATER, CAROL AUSTIN. 1982. Consumer psychology. *Psychology Today*, 16 (May): 16–20.

BRIGGS, KENNETH A. 1984a. Methodist church foresees renewal. *New York Times* (May 7): 1, 15.

BRIGGS, KENNETH A. 1984b. Methodists' conference: Some signs of a rebirth. *New York Times* (May 14): 8.

BRIGGS, KENNETH A. 1984c. America's return to prayer. *New York Times Magazine* (November 18): 106+.

BRIGGS, KENNETH A. 1984d. Catholics aren't collaring enough priests. *New York Times* (February 26): 18E.

BRIM, ORVILLE G., JR. 1980. Types of life events. *Journal of Social Issues*, 36: 148–157.

BRINTON, CRANE. 1938. *The anatomy of revolution.* New York: Vintage Books.

BRODY, ELAINE M., PAULINE T. JOHNSEN, MARK C. FULCOMER, and ABIGAIL M. LANG. 1983. Women's changing roles and help to elderly parents. *Journal of Gerontology*, 38:597–607.

BRODY, JANE E. 1981. Effects of beauty found to run surprisingly deep. *New York Times* (September 1): 15–16.

BRODY, JANE E. 1982. Examining the causes, symptoms and treatment of burnout. *New York Times* (October 6): 19.

BRODY, JANE E. 1983. Divorce's stress exacts long-term health toll. *New York Times* (December 13): 17+.

BRONFENBRENNER, URIE. 1977. Nobody home: The erosion of the American family. *Psychology Today*, 10 (May): 40–47.

BROOKS, ANDREE. 1984. Birth rank: Effects on personality. *New York Times* (March 26): 17.

BROPHY, BETH. 1984 More women work full time; men retire. *USA Today* (June 27): 1A.

BROWN, DON W. 1978. Arrest rates and crime rates: When does a tipping effect occur? *Social Forces*, 57: 671–682.

BROZAN, NADINE. 1984. Helping to heal the scars left by incest. *New York Times* (January 9): 15.

BURAWOY, MICHAEL. 1979. *Manufacturing consent.* Chicago: University of Chicago Press.

BURAWOY, MICHAEL. 1983. Factory regimes under advanced capitalism. *American Sociological Review*, 48: 587–605.

BURGESS, R. L., and T. L. HUSTON. 1979. *Social exchange in developing relationships.* New York: Academic Press.

BURNHAM, JAMES. 1941. *The Managerial Revolution.* New York: John Day.

BURT, MARTHA R. 1980. Cultural myths and supports for rape. *Journal of Personality and Social Psychology*, 38: 217–230.

BUSS, TERRY F., and F. STEVENS REDBURN. 1983. *Shutdown at Youngstown: Public policy for mass unemployment.* Albany: State University of New York Press.

BUTTERFIELD, FOX. 1984. Sect members assert they are misunderstood. *New York Times* (June 24): 12.

BYRNE, JOHN A. 1984. Worth his weight. *Forbes* (June 4): 96–146.

CALHOUN, JOHN. 1962. Population density and social pathology. *Scientific American*, 206: 139–146.

CANN, ARNIE, LAWRENCE G. CALHOUN, JAMES W. SELBY, and H. ELIZABETH KING. 1981. Rape: A contemporary overview and analysis. *The Journal of Social Issues*, 37: 1–4.

CANTRIL, HADLEY. 1940. *The Invasion from Mars: A study in the psychology of panic.* Princeton, N.J.: Princeton University Press.

CANTRIL, HADLEY. 1941. *The psychology of social movements.* New York: Wiley.

CAPLOW, THEODORE, HOWARD M. BAHR, BRUCE A. CHADWICK, REUBEN HILL, and MARGARET H. WILLIAMSON. 1982. *Middletown families: Fifty years of change and continuity.* Minneapolis: University of Minnesota Press.

CARGAN, LEONARD, and MATTHEW MELKO. 1982. *Singles: Myths and realities.* Beverly Hills, Calif.: Sage.

CARMICHAEL, STOKELY, and CHARLES HAMILTON. 1967. *Black power.* New York: Random House.

CARNEGIE CORPORATION OF NEW YORK. 1983. *Education and economic progress: Toward a national educational policy.* New York: Carnegie Corporation.

CARRINGTON, TIM. 1984. U.S. won't let 11 biggest banks in nation fail. *Wall Street Journal* (September 20): 2.

CARVER, CHARLES S., and CHARLENE HUMPHRIES. 1981. Havana day-dreaming: A study of self-consciousness and the negative reference group among Cuban Americans. *Journal of Personality and Social Psychology*, 40: 545–552.

CATTON, WILLIAM R., JR. 1980. *Overshoot: The ecological basis of revolutionary change.* Urbana: University of Illinois Press.

CENSUS BUREAU. 1983. *Fertility of American women: July 1982.* Washington, D.C.: U.S. Government Printing Office.

CENSUS BUREAU. 1984a. *Child care arrangements of working mothers: June 1982.* Series P-23, Number 129. Washington, D.C.: U.S. Government Printing Office.

CENSUS BUREAU. 1984b. *Conditions of Hispanics in America today.* Washington, D.C.: U.S. Government Printing Office.

CENSUS BUREAU. 1984c. *Labor force status and other characteristics of persons with work disability: 1982.* Washington, D.C.: U.S. Government Printing Office.

CENSUS BUREAU. 1984d. Marital status and living arrangements: March 1983. *Current Population Reports,* P-20, No. 389. Washington, D.C.: U.S. Government Printing Office.

CHAIKEN, JAN M., and MARCIA R. CHAIKEN. 1982. *Varieties of criminal behavior.* Santa Monica, Calif.: Rand Corporation.

CHALL, DANIEL E. 1984. Neighborhood changes in New York City. *American Demographics,* 6 (October): 19–23+.

CHAMBLISS, WILLIAM J. 1973. The Saints and the Roughnecks. *Society,* 2 (November): 24–31.

CHAMBLISS, WILLIAM J., and ROBERT B. SEIDMAN. 1971. *Law, order and power.* Reading, Mass: Addison-Wesley.

CHEEK, JONATHAN. 1983. Shyness: How it hurts careers and social life. *U.S. News & World Report* (October 31): 71–72.

CHERLIN, ANDREW. 1978. Remarriage as an incomplete institution. *American Journal of Sociology,* 86: 636–650.

CHILDE, V. GORDON. 1941. *Man makes himself.* London: Watts & Co., Ltd.

CHILDE, V. GORDON. 1942. *What happened in history.* Middlesex, Eng.: Penguin Books, Ltd.

CHIRICOS, THEODORE, and GORDON WALDO. 1975. Socioeconomic status and criminal sentencing: An empirical assessment of a conflict proposition. *American Sociological Review,* 40: 753–772.

CHITTISTER, JOAN D., and MARTIN E. MARTY. 1983. *Faith and Ferment.* Minneapolis: Augsburg Publishing House.

CHOLDIN, HARVEY M. 1978. Urban density and pathology. In R. H. Turner, J. Coleman, and R. C. Fox, eds., *Annual Review of Sociology.* Palo Alto, Calif.: Annual Reviews.

CHOMSKY, NOAM. 1957. *Syntactic structures.* The Hague: Mouton.

CHOMSKY, NOAM. 1965. *Aspects of a theory of syntax.* Cambridge, Mass.: MIT Press.

CHOMSKY, NOAM. 1968. *Language and mind.* New York: Harcourt Brace Jovanovich.

CHOMSKY, NOAM. 1975. *Reflections on language.* New York: Pantheon.

CHRISTIAN, J. J. 1963. The pathology of overpopulation. *Military Medicine,* 128: 571–603.

CICIRELLI, VICTOR G. 1978. The relationship of sibling structure to intellectual abilities and achievement. *Review of Educational Research,* 48: 365–379.

CICIRELLI, VICTOR G. 1981. *Helping elderly parents: The role of adult children.* Boston: Auburn House.

CICIRELLI, VICTOR G. 1983. Adult children's attachment and helping behavior to elderly parents: A path model. *Journal of Marriage and the Family,* 45: 815–825.

CLARK, DAVID L., LINDA S. LOTTO, and MARTHA M. MCCARTHY. 1980. Factors associated with success in urban elementary schools. *Phi Delta Kappan,* 61: 467–470.

CLARK, R. A. 1952. The projective measurement of experimentally induced levels of sexual motivation. *Journal of Experimental Psychology,* 44: 391–399.

CLARK, REGINALD M. 1983. *Family life and school achievement: Why poor black children succeed or fail.* Chicago: University of Chicago Press.

CLENDINEN, DUDLEY. 1984. Two views at odds on Vermont sect. *New York Times* (June 30): 16.

CLINARD, MARSHALL B., and PETER C. YEAGER. 1980. *Corporate crime.* New York: Free Press.

CLINGEMPEEL, W. GLEN. 1981. Quasi-kin relationships and marital quality in stepfather families. *Journal of Personality and Social Psychology,* 41: 890–901.

COHEN, ALBERT K. 1955. *Delinquent boys.* New York: Free Press.

COHEN, ALBERT K. 1965. The sociology of the deviant act: Anomie theory and beyond. *American Sociological Review,* 30: 5–14.

COHEN, ALBERT K. 1966. *Deviance and control.* Englewood Cliffs, N.J.: Prentice-Hall.

COHEN, JERE. 1980. Rational capitalism in Renaissance Italy. *American Journal of Sociology,* 85: 1340–1355.

COHEN, JERE. 1983. Peer influences on college aspirations. *American Sociological Review,* 48: 728–734.

COHEN, MARK N. 1977. *The food crisis in prehistory: Overpopulation and the origins of agriculture.* New Haven, Conn.: Yale University Press.

COLE, STEPHEN. 1972. *The sociological method.* Chicago: Markham.

COLEMAN, JAMES S., THOMAS HOFFER, and SALLY KILGORE. 1982a. *High school achievement: Public, Catholic, and other private schools compared.* New York: Basic Books.

COLEMAN, JAMES S., THOMAS HOFFER, and SALLY KILGORE. 1982b. Cognitive outcomes in public and private schools. *Sociology of Education,* 55: 65–76.

COLEMAN, JAMES S., and LEE RAINWATER. 1978. *Social standing in America.* New York: Basic Books.

COLGAN, PATRICK. 1983. *Comparative social recognition.* New York: Wiley.

COLLIGAN, MICHAEL J., JAMES W. PENNEBAKER, and LAWRENCE R. MURPHY, EDS. 1982. *Mass psychogenic illness: A social psychological analysis.* Hillsdale, N.J.: Erlbaum.

COLLINS, RANDALL. 1975. *Conflict sociology.* New York: Academic Press.

COLLINS, RANDALL. 1976. Review of "Schooling in Capitalist America." *Harvard Educational Review,* 46: 246–251.

COLLINS, RANDALL. 1977. Some comparative principles of educational stratification. *Harvard Educational Review,* 47: 1–27.

COLLINS, RANDALL. 1979. *Credential society.* New York: Academic Press.

COLLINS, RANDALL. 1980. Weber's last theory of capitalism: A systematization. *American Sociological Review*, 45: 925–942.

COLLINS, RANDALL. 1981. *Sociology since midcentury: Essays in theory cumulation.* New York: Academic Press.

COLLINS, RANDALL, and MICHAEL MAKOWSKY. 1984. *The discovery of society*, 3rd ed. New York: Random House.

Columbus *Dispatch*. 1980. Income affects health feelings. Columbus (Ohio) *Dispatch* (June 1): A–8.

Columbus *Dispatch*. 1984a. The rich are different—they have lots of money. Columbus (Ohio) *Dispatch* (October 9): A2.

Columbus *Dispatch*. 1984b. More people will live to 100, but they may not like it. Columbus (Ohio) *Dispatch* (December 26): 1.

CONNOR, WALTER D. 1979. *Socialism, politics, and equality.* New York: Columbia University Press.

CONGER, RAND D., ROBERT L. BURGESS, and CAROL BARRETT. 1979. Child abuse related to life change and perceptions of illness: Some preliminary findings. *Family Coordinator*, 28: 73–78.

COOLEY, CHARLES HORTON. 1902. *Human nature and the social order.* New York: Scribner's.

COOLEY, CHARLES HORTON. 1909. *Social organization.* New York: Scribner's.

CORDES, COLLEEN. 1984. Behavior therapists examine how emotion, cognition relate. *Monitor* (February): 18.

CORNFIELD, NOREEN. 1983. The success of urban communes. *Journal of Marriage and the Family*, 45: 115–126.

COSER, LEWIS A. 1956. *The functions of social conflict.* New York: Free Press.

COSER, LEWIS A. 1957. Social conflict and the theory of social change. *British Journal of Sociology*, 8: 170–183.

COSER, LEWIS A. 1962. Some functions of deviant behavior and normative flexibility. *American Journal of Sociology*, 68: 172–181.

COSER, LEWIS A. 1975. Presidential address: Two methods in search of a substance. *American Sociological Review*, 40: 691–700.

COUNCIL ON ENVIRONMENTAL QUALITY. 1980. *The Global 2000 report to the president.* Washington, D.C.: U. S. Government Printing Office.

COWELL, ALAN. 1984a. African famine battle: Aid has been a villain. *New York Times* (November 29): 1, 6.

COWELL, ALAN. 1984b. South of Sahara, the intrusive politics of hunger. *New York Times* (December 3): 1, 4.

COX, OLIVER C. 1948. *Caste, class, and race.* Garden City, N.Y.: Doubleday.

CRESSEY, DONALD R. 1969. *Theft of the nation: The structure and operations of organized crime in America.* New York: Harper & Row.

CREWDSON, JOHN. 1983. *The tarnished door.* New York Times Books.

CRITCHFIELD, RICHARD. 1978. The culture of poverty. *Human Behavior*, 7 (January): 65–69.

CRITCHFIELD, RICHARD. 1984. Modern farming sows turmoil among India's Sikhs. *Wall Street Journal* (July 16): 15.

CROMER, JANIS. 1984. *The mood of American youth.* Washington, D.C.: National Association of Secondary School Principals.

CROSBY, FAYE, STEPHANIE BROMLEY, and LEONARD SAXE. 1980. Recent unobtrusive studies of black and white discrimination and prejudice: A literature review. *Psychological Bulletin*, 87: 546–563.

CUNNINGHAM, SUSAN. 1984. The new terrorism: Devotion or deviancy? *APA Monitor*, 15 (March): 1, 14.

CURTISS, SUSAN. 1977. *Genie: A psycholinguistic study of a modern-day "wild child."* New York: Academic Press.

DAHL, ROBERT. 1961. *Who governs? Democracy and power in an American city.* New Haven, Conn.: Yale University Press.

DAHL, ROBERT A. 1971. *Polyarchy: Participation and opposition.* New Haven, Conn.: Yale University Press.

DAHRENDORF, RALF. 1958. Toward a theory of social conflict. *Journal of Conflict Revolution*, 2: 170–183.

DAHRENDORF, RALF. 1959. *Class and class conflict in industrial society.* Stanford, Calif.: Stanford University Press.

DAHRENDORF, RALF. 1965. *Gesellshaft Und demokratie in Deutschland.* Munich. Piper Verlag.

DAHRENDORF, RALF. 1968. *Essays in the theory of society.* Stanford, Calif.: Stanford University Press.

DALE, PHILIP S. 1976. *Language development: Structure and function*, 2nd ed. New York: Holt, Reinhart and Winston.

DAMON, WILLIAM and DANIEL HART. 1982. The development of self-understanding from infancy through adolescence. *Child Development*, 53: 841–864.

DATAN, NANCY. 1977. After the apple: Post-Newtonian metatheory for jaded psychologists. In N. Datan and H. W. Reese, eds., *Life-span developmental psychology: Dialectical perspectives on experimental research.* New York: Academic Press.

DAVIE, MAURICE R. 1937. The patterns of urban growth. In George P. Murdock, ed., *Studies in the science of society.* New Haven Conn.: Yale University Press.

DAVIES, JAMES. 1962. Toward a theory of revolution. *American Sociological Review*, 27: 5–19.

DAVIES, JAMES. 1969. The J-curve of rising and declining satisfactions as a cause of some great revolutions and a contained revolution. In H. D. Graham and T. R. Gurr, eds., *The history of violence in America.* New York: Bantam.

DAVIES, JAMES. 1974. The J-curve and power struggle theories of collective violence. *American Sociological Review*, 39: 607–610.

DAVIES, MARK, and DENISE B. KANDEL. 1981. Parental and peer influences on adolescents' educational plans: Some further evidence. *American Journal of Sociology*, 87: 363–387.

DAVIES, ALLISON, B. B. GARDNER, and M. R. GARDNER. 1941. *Deep South.* Chicago: University of Chicago Press.

DAVIES, JAMES. 1982. Up and down opportunity's ladder. *Public Opinion*, 5 (June–July) : 11–15+.

DAVIS, KINGSLEY. 1945. The world demographic transition. *Annals of the American Academy of Political and Social Science*, 237: 1–11.

DAVIS, KINGSLEY. 1948. *Human society*. New York: Macmillan.

DAVIS, KINGSLEY. 1951. Introduction. In William J. Goode, *Religion among the primitives*. New York: Free Press.

DAVIS, KINGSLEY. 1955. The orgin and growth of urbanization in the world. *American Journal of Sociology*, 60: 429–437.

DAVIS, KINGSLEY. 1959. The myth of functional analysis as a special method in sociology and anthropology. *American Sociological Review*, 24: 757–772.

DAVIS, KINGLEY. 1960. Legitimacy and the incest taboo. In Norman W. Bell and Ezra F. Vogel, eds., *A modern introduction to the family*. New York: Free Press.

DAVIS, KINGSLEY. 1967. The urbanization of the human population. In *Cities*. New York: Knopf.

DAVIS, KINGSLEY. 1971. The world's population crisis. In Robert K. Merton and Robert A. Nisbet, eds., *Contemporary social problems*, 3rd ed. New York: Harcourt Brace Jovanovich.

DAVIS, KINGSLEY, and WILBERT MOORE. 1945. Some principles of stratification. *American Sociological Review*, 10: 242–249.

DEAUX, KAY, and LAWRENCE S. WRIGHTSMAN. 1984. *Social psychology in the 80s*, 4th ed. Monterey, Calif.: Brooks/Cole.

DEGLER, CARL. 1980. *At odds: Women and the family in America from the Revolution to the present*. New York: Oxford University Press.

DELACROIX, JACQUES, and CHARLES C. RAGIN. 1981. Structural blockage: A cross-national study of economic dependency, state efficacy, and underdevelopment. *American Journal of Sociology*, 86: 1311–1347.

DE LUCE, JUDITH, and HUGH T. WILDER. 1983. *Language in primates*. New York: Springer-Verlag.

DEMOS, J., and V. DEMOS. 1969. Adolescence in historical perspective. *Journal of Marriage and the Family*, 31: 632–638.

DEPARTMENT OF JUSTICE. 1981. *Criminal victimization in the United States*. Washington, D.C.: U.S. Government Printing Office.

DE VRIES, RAYMOND G. 1981. Birth and death: Social construction of the poles of existence. *Social Forces*, 59: 1074–1093.

DIBOLD, JOHN. 1983. Innovation and new institutional structures. In Howard F. Didsbury, Jr., ed., *The world of work*. Bethesda, Md.: World Future Society.

DiMAGGIO, PAUL. 1982. Cultural capital and school success: The impact of status culture participation on the grades of U.S. high school students. *American Sociological Review*, 47: 189–201.

DION, KAREN. 1972. Physical attractiveness and evaluations of children's transgressions. *Journal of Personality and Social Psychology*, 24: 207–213.

DION, KAREN, ELLEN BERSCHEID, and ELAINE WALSTER. 1972. What is beautiful is good. *Journal of Personality and Social Psychology*, 24: 285–290.

DIONNE, E. J., JR. 1980. Abortion poll: Not clear-cut. *New York Times* (August 10): A-15.

DIONNE, E. J., JR. 1985. Vatican criticizes Brazilian backer of new theology. *New York Times* (March 21): 1, 6.

DIPBOY. ROBERT L. 1977. Alternative approaches to deindividualization. *Psychological Bulletin*, 84: 1057–1075.

DJILAS, MILOVAN. 1957. *The new class*. New York: Praeger.

DOAN, MICHAEL. 1984. The "electronic church" spreads the word. *U.S. News & World Report* (April 23): 68–69.

DOMHOFF, G. WILLIAM. 1970. *The higher circles*. New York: Random House.

DOWD, MAUREEN. 1983a. Many women in poll equate values of job and family life. *New York Times* (December 4): 1, 36.

DOWD, MAUREEN. 1983b. Poll reports many men are shifting views on housework. *New York Times* (December 11): 13.

DOYLE, SIR ARTHUR CONAN. 1927. *The complete Sherlock Holmes*. Garden City, N.Y.: Doubleday.

DRAGASTIN, SIGMUND E., and GLEN H. ELDER, JR. 1975. *Adolescence in the life cycle*. New York: Wiley.

DRUCKER, PETER F. 1985. Depression cycle. *Wall Street Journal* (January 9): 24.

DUBIN, ROBERT. 1976. Work in modern society. In Robert Dubin, ed., *Handbook of work, organization, and society*. Chicago: Rand McNally.

DULLEA, GEORGIA. 1979. Artificial insemination of single women poses difficult questions. *New York Times* (March 9): A18.

DUMONT, L. 1970. *Homo hierarchicus. The caste system and its implications*. London: Weidenfeld and Nicolson.

DUNCAN, GREG. 1984. *Years of poverty, years of plenty*. Ann Arbor: Institute for Social Research, University of Michigan.

DUNCAN, OTIS DUDLEY. 1959. Human ecology and population studies. In Philip Hauser and Otis D. Duncan, eds., *The study of population*. Chicago: The University of Chicago Press.

DUNCAN, OTIS DUDLEY. 1961. From social system to ecosystem. *Sociological Inquiry*, 31: 140–149.

DUNN, WILLIAM. 1984. The growing political power of blacks and Hispanics. *American Demographics*, 6 (September): 26–29.

DUPAQUIER, J., A. FAUVE-CHAMOUX, and E. GREBENIK. eds. 1983. *Maltus past and present*. Orlando, Fla.: Academic Press.

DURKHEIM, EMILE. 1893/1964. *The division of labor in society*. New York: Free Press.

DURKHEIM, EMILE. 1897/1951. *Suicide*. New York: Free Press.

DURKHEIM, EMILE. 1912/1965. *The elementary forms of religious life*. New York: Free Press.

DUSEK, JEROME B., and JOHN F. FLAHERTY. 1981. The development of the self-concept during the adolescent years. *Monographs of the Society for Research in Child Development*, 46 (No. 191).

DUTTON, DONALD G., and ARTHUR P. ARON. 1974. Some evidence for heightened sexual attraction under conditions of high anxiety. *Journal of Personality and Social Psychology*, 30: 510–517.

DYERT, RICHARD M. 1984. Easing labor's transition trauma. *New York Times* (July 22): F-3.

DYNES, RUSSELL, and ENRICO QUARANTELLI. 1968. Looting in American cities: A new explanation. *Transaction* (May): 14.

EBAUGH, HELEN R. F., KATHE RICHMAN, and JANET SALTZMAN CHAFETZ. 1984. Life crises among the religiously committed: Do sectarian differences matter? *Journal for the Scientific Study of Religion*, 23: 19–31.

EBERSTADT, NICK, ed. 1981. *Fertility decline in the less developed countries*. New York: Praeger.

ECKHOLM, ERIK. 1984. Computers on job may improve life. *New York Times* (September 30): 31.

EDWARDS, L. P. 1927. *The natural history of revolution*. Chicago: University of Chicago Press.

EDWARDS, RICHARD. 1978. The social relations of production at the point of production. The Insurgent Sociologist, 8: 109–125.

EDWARDS, RICHARD. 1979. *Contested terrain*. New York: Basic Books.

EHRHARDT, ANKE A., and H. F. L. MEYER-BAHLBURG. 1981. Effects of prenatal sex hormones on gender-related behavior. *Science*, 176: 123–128.

EKMAN, PAUL. 1980. *The face of man: Expressions of universal emotions in a New Guinea village*. New York: Garland STPM Press.

EKMAN, PAUL, WALLACE V. FRIESEN, and JOHN BEAR. 1984. The international language of gestures. *Psychology Today*, 18 (May): 64–67.

EKMAN, PAUL, WALLACE V. FRIESEN, and P. ELLSWORTH. 1972. *Emotion in the human face: Guidelines for research and an integration of findings*. Elmsford, N.Y.: Pergamon Press.

ELKIND, DAVID. 1979. Growing up faster. *Psychology Today*, 12 (February): 38–45.

ELLIOTT, DELBERT S. 1966. Delinquency, school attendance and dropout. *Social Problems*, 13: 307–314.

ELLIOTT, GREGORY C., MORRIS ROSENBERG, and MICHAEL WAGNER. 1984. Transient depersonalization in youth. *Social Psychology Quarterly*, 47: 115–128.

ELLYSON, STEVE L., JOHN F. DOVIDIO, RANDI L. CORSON, and DEBBIE L. VINICUR. 1980. Visual dominance behavior in female dyads. *Social Psychology Quarterly*, 43: 328–336.

ELMENDORF, EDWARD. 1985. Cut federal aid to college students? *U.S. News & World Report* (April 29): 67.

EMSLIE, GRAHAM J., and ALVIN ROSENFELD. 1983. Incest reported by children and adolescents hospitalized for severe psychiatric problems. *American Journal of Psychiatry*, 140: 708–711.

ENGELGAU, DONNA. 1985. Bennett says 13,000 students with family incomes of $100,000 get loans, but experts dispute data. *Chronicle of Higher Education* (March 13): 19, 22.

ENGELS, FRIEDRICH. 1884/1902. *The origin of the family, private property, and the state*. Chicago: Kerr.

ENGLISH, CAREY W. 1983. When workers take over the plant. *U.S. News & World Report* (April 18): 89–90.

EPSTEIN, SUE HOOVER. 1983. Why do women live longer than men? *Science 83*, 4 (OCTOBER): 30–31.

ERICKSON, FREDERICK. 1975. Gatekeeping and the melting pot. *Harvard Educational Review*, 45: 44–70.

ERICKSON, MAYNARD L., and LAMAR T. EMPEY. 1963. Court records, undetected delinquency and decision-making. *Journal of Criminal Law, Criminology and Police Science*, 54: 456–469.

ERICKSON, MAYNARD L., and JACK P. GIBBS. 1978. Objective and perceptual properties of legal punishment and the deterrence doctrine. *Social Problems*, 25: 253–264.

ERIKSON, ERIK. 1963. *Childhood and society*. New York: Norton.

ERIKSON, ERIK. 1968. *Identity: Youth and crisis*. New York: Norton.

ERIKSON, KAI T. 1962. Notes on the sociology of deviance. *Social Problems*, 9: 307–314.

ERIKSON, KAI T. 1966. *Wayward Puritans: A study in the sociology of deviance*. New York: Wiley.

ETAUGH, CLAIRE. 1980. Effects of nonmaternal care on children. *American Psychologist*, 35: 309–319.

ETZIONI, AMITAI. 1964. *Modern organizations*. Englewood Cliffs, N.J.: Prentice-Hall.

ETZIONI, AMITAI. 1975. *A comparative analysis of complex organizations*. New York: Free Press.

EVANGELAUF, JEAN. 1984. Women's average pay trails men's by 19 percent in 3 top professional ranks. *Chronicle of Higher Education* (January 18): 20.

EVANS, PETER B. 1981. Recent research on multinational corporations. *Annual Review of Sociology*, 7: 199–223.

FARBER, B. A. 1983. *Stress and burnout in the human service professions*. Elmsford, N.Y.: Pergamon Press.

FAREL, ANITA M. 1980. Effects of preferred maternal roles, maternal employment, and sociodemographic status on school adjustment and competence. *Child Development*, 51: 1179–1186.

FEATHERMAN, DAVID L., and ROBERT M. HAUSER. 1978a. Sexual inequalities and socioeconomic achievement in the U.S., 1962–1973. *American Sociological Review*, 41: 462–483.

FEATHERMAN, DAVID L., and ROBERT M. HAUSER. 1978b. *Opportunity and change*. New York: Academic Press.

FEIGENBAUM, EDWARD A., and PAMELA McCORDUCK. 1983. *The fifth generation*. Reading, Mass.: Addison-Wesley.

FELDMAN, RONALD A., TIMOTHY E. CAPLINGER, and JOHN S. WODARSKI. 1983. *The St. Louis conundrum: The effective treatment of antisocial youth*. Englewood Cliffs, N.J.: Prentice-Hall.

FENIGSTEIN, ALAN. 1984. Self-consciousness and the overperception of self as a target. *Journal of Personality and Social Psychology*, 47: 860–870.

FENNEMA, MEINHERT. 1982. *International networks of banks and industry*. Boston: Martinius Nijhoff.

FINE, MARK A., JOHN R. MORELAND, and ANDREW I. SCHWEBEL. 1983. Long-term effects of divorce on parent–child relationships. *Developmental Psychology*, 19: 703–713.

FINKELHOR, DAVID. 1979. *Sexually victimized children*. New York: Free Press.

FIREY, WALTER. 1947. *Land use in central Boston*. Cambridge, Mass.: Harvard University Press.

FISCHER, MICHAEL M. J. 1980. *Iran: From religious dispute to revolution*. Cambridge, Mass.: Harvard University Press.

FISHER, ANNE B. 1984. Can Detroit live without quotas? *Fortune* (June 25): 20–25.

FISKE, EDWARD B. 1984. U.S. pupils lag from grade 1, study finds. *New York Times* (June 17): 1, 21.

FLANDRIN, J. F. 1979. *Families in former times: Kinship, household, and sexuality*. New York: Cambridge University Press.

FOLEY, THOMAS J. 1984. Behind all the fuss over election money. *U.S. News & World Report* (October 8): 72–75.

FORD, C. S. and F. A. BEACH. 1951. *Patterns of sexual behavior*. New York: Harper & Row.

FOSTER, THOMAS W. 1980. Amish simply prosper. Columbus (Ohio) *Dispatch* (December 3): B-3.

FRAKER, SUSAN. 1984. Why women aren't getting to the top. *Fortune* (April 16): 40–45.

FREEMAN, JO. 1973. The origins of the women's liberation movement. *American Journal of Sociology*, 78: 792–811.

FREEDMAN, J. L. 1975. *Crowding and behavior: The psychology of high-density living*. New York: Viking.

FREITAG, PETER J. 1975. The cabinet and big business: A study of interlocks. *Social Problems*, 23: 137–152.

FREUD, SIGMUND. 1930/1961. *Civilization and its discontents*. London: Hogarth.

FREUD, SIGMUND. 1938. *The basic writings of Sigmund Freud*. Trans. A. A. Brill. New York: Modern Library.

FRIEDMAN, ANDREW. 1977. *Industry and labor: Class struggle at work and monopoly capitalism*. New York: Macmillan.

FRIEDMAN, THOMAS L. 1984. Lebanese identity is lost in a retreat into factions. *New York Times* (May 31): 1, 6.

FUCHS, VICTOR R. 1983. *How we live: An economic perspective on Americans from birth to death*. Cambridge, Mass.: Harvard University Press.

FULLER, C. J. 1976. *The Nayars today*. Cambridge, Mass.: Cambridge University Press.

FURSTENBERG, FRANK F., JR., and GRAHAM B. SPANIER. 1984. The risk of dissolution in remarriage: An examination of Cherlin's hypothesis of incomplete institutionalization. *Family Relations*, 33: 433–441.

GALBRAITH, JOHN K. 1971. *The new industrial state*, 2nd ed. New York: Mentor.

GALE, DENNIS E. 1984. *Neighborhood revitalization and the postindustrial city*. Lexington, Mass.: Lexington Books.

GANONG, LAWRENCE H., and MARILYN COLEMAN. 1984. The effects of remarriage on children: A review of the empirical literature. *Family Relations*, 33: 389–406.

GANS, HERBERT J. 1972. The positive functions of poverty. *American Journal of Sociology*, 78: 275–289.

GAPPA, JUDITH M., JEAN F. O'BARR, and DONALD ST. JOHN-PARSONS. 1980. The dual-career couple and academe: Can both prosper? *Anthropology Newsletter*, 21 (April): 12–16.

GARBARINO, JAMES, and DEBORAH SHERMAN. 1980. High-risk neighborhoods and high-risk families: The human ecology of child maltreatment. *Child Development*, 51: 188–198.

GARFINKEL, HAROLD. 1974. The origins of the term "ethnomethodology." In R. Turner, ed., *Ethnomethodology*. Middlesex, Eng.: Penguin Books.

GARRETT, G. J. 1968. The tragedy of the commons. *Science*, 162: 1243–1248.

GEERTZ, CLIFFORD. 1963. *Old societies and new states*. New York: Free Press.

GENERAL MILLS. 1981. *The General Mills American family report, 1980–1981: Families: Strengths and strains at work*. Minneapolis: General Mills.

GEORGE, LINDA K., and GEORGE L. MADDOX. 1977. Subjective adaptation to loss of the work role: A longitudinal study. *Journal of Gerontology*, 32: 456–462.

GERSON, MENACHEM. 1978. *Family, women, and socialization in the kibbutz*. Lexington, Mass.: D. C. Heath.

GESCHWENDER, JAMES A. 1964. Social structure and the Negro revolt: An examination of some hypotheses. *Social Forces*, 43: 248–256.

GESCHWENDER, JAMES A. 1978. *Racial stratification in America*. Dubuque, Iowa: William C. Brown.

GEST, TED. 1984. Bulging prisons. *U.S. News & World Report* (April 23): 42–46.

GIBBS, JACK P. 1975. *Crime, punishment, and deterrence*. New York: Elsevier.

GIDDENS, ANTHONY. 1973. *The class structure of the advanced societies*. New York: Harper & Row.

GILBERT, C. 1967. When did a man in the Renaissance grow old? *Studies in the Renaissance*, 14: 7–32.

GINZBERG, ELI. 1982. The mechanization of work. *Scientific American*, 247 (September): 67–75.

GLAMSER, F. D. 1976. Determinants of a positive attitude toward retirement. *Journal of Gerontology*, 31: 104–107.

GLASBERG, DAVITA S., and MICHAEL SCHWARTZ. 1983. Ownership and control of corporations. *Annual Review of Sociology*, 9: 311–332.

GLASS, DAVID, PEVERILL SQUIRE, and RAYMOND WOLFINGER. 1984. Voter turnout: an international comparison. *Public Opinion*, 6 (January): 49–55.

GLENN, NORVAL, and C. N. WEAVER. 1981. The contribution of marital happiness to global happiness. *Journal of Marriage and the Family*, 43: 161–168.

GLICK, CLARENCE. 1980. *Sojourners and settlers: Chinese migrants in Hawaii*. Honolulu: University of Hawaii Press.

GLICK, PAUL C. 1984. How American families are changing. *American Demographics*, 6 (January): 21–25.

GLOCK, CHARLES Y., BENJAMIN B. RINGER, and EARL R. BABBIE. 1967. *To comfort and challenge: A dilemma of the contemporary church*. Berkeley: University of California Press.

GLUCKMAN, MAX. 1955. *Custom and conflict in Africa*. Oxford: Blackwell.

GOFFMAN, ERVING. 1959. *The presentation of self in everyday life*. Garden City, N.Y.: Doubleday.

GOFFMAN, ERVING. 1961a. *Encounters*. Indianapolis: Bobbs-Merrill.

GOFFMAN, ERVING. 1961b. *Asylums: Essays on the social situation of mental patients and other inmates*. Chicago: Aldine.

GOFFMAN, ERVING. 1974. *Frame analysis: An essay on the*

organization of experience. Cambridge, Mass.: Harvard University Press.

GOLD, DOLORES, and DAVID ANDRES. 1978. Developmental comparisons between ten-year-old children with employed and nonemployed mothers. *Child Development,* 49: 75–84.

GOLDIN-MEADOW, SUSAN. 1983. Gestural communication in deaf children: Noneffect of parental input on language development. *Science,* 221: 372–373.

GOLDSTONE, JACK A. 1982. The comparative and historical study of revolutions. *Annual Review of Sociology,* 8: 187–207.

GOLEMAN, DANIEL. 1984. A bias puts self at center of events *New York Times* (June 12): 19, 23.

GONOS, GEORGE. 1977. "Situation" versus "frame": The "interactionist" and the "structuralist" analyses of everyday life. *American Sociological Review,* 42: 854–867.

GOODE, WILLIAM J. 1959. The theoretical importance of love. *American Sociological Review,* 24: 38–47.

GOODE, WILLIAM J. 1960. Illegitimacy in Caribbean social structure. *American Sociological Review,* 25: 21–31.

GOODE, WILLIAM J. 1963. *World revolution and family patterns.* New York: Basic Books.

GOODE, WILLIAM J. 1972. The place of force in human society. *American Sociological Review,* 37: 507–519.

GOODMAN, ANN B., CAROLE SIEGEL, THOMAS J. CRAIG, and SHANG P. LIN. 1983. The relationship between socioeconomic class and prevalence of schizophrenia, alcoholism, and affective disorders treated by inpatient care in a suburban area. *American Journal of Psychiatry,* 140: 166–170.

GORDON, LINDA, and PAUL O'KEEFE. 1984. Incest as a form of family violence: Evidence from historical case records. *Journal of Marriage and the Family,* 46: 27–34.

GORNICK, VIVIAN, and B. K. MORAN. 1971. *Women in sexist society.* New York: New American Library.

GOUGH, E. KATHLEEN. 1959. The Nayars and the definition of marriage. *Journal of the Royal Anthropological Institute,* 89: 23–24.

GOULD, ROGER L. 1978. *Transformations.* New York: Simon and Schuster.

GOULDNER, ALVIN. 1970. *The coming crisis of Western sociology.* New York: Basic Books.

GOVE, WALTER R. 1970. Societal reaction as an explanation of mental illness: An evaluation. *American Sociological Review,* 35: 873–884.

GOVE, WALTER R., and MICHAEL HUGHES. 1980. Reexamining the ecological fallacy: A study in which aggregate data are critical in investigating the pathological effects of living alone. *Social Forces,* 58: 1157–1177.

GRASMICK, HAROLD G., and GEORGE J. BRYJAK. 1980. The deterrent effect of perceived severity of punishment. *Social Forces,* 59: 471–491.

GRASSIAN, STUART. 1983. Psychopathological effects of solitary confinement. *American Journal of Psychiatry,* 140: 1450–1454.

GREELEY, ANDREW M. 1982. American Catholics: Going their own way. *The New York Times Magazine* (October 10): 28+.

GREELEY, ANDREW M. 1985. Who leads Catholics? *New York Times* (March 8): 31.

GREEN, JOHN C., and JAMES L. GUTH. 1984. The party irregulars. *Psychology Today* (October): 46–52.

GREENWALD, A. G. 1980. The totalitarian ego: Fabrication and revision of personal history. *American Psychologist,* 35: 608–616.

GREENWALD, A. G., and A. R. PRATKANIS. 1984. The self. In R. S. Wyer and T. K. Srull, eds., *Handbook of social cognition.* Hillsdale, N.J.: Erlbaum.

GREENWOOD, PETER W. 1982. *Selective incapacitation.* Santa Monica, Calif.: Rand Corporation.

GREER, COLIN. 1979. Once again, the "family question." *New York Times* (October 14): 19E.

GRIMSHAW, ALLEN D. 1980. Social interactional and sociolinguistic rules. *Social Forces,* 58: 789–810.

GRIMSHAW, ALLAN D. 1981. *Language as social resource.* Stanford Calif.: Stanford University Press.

GROSS, A. 1977. Marriage counseling for unwed couples. *New York Times Magazine* (April 24): 52+.

GRUENBERG, BARRY. 1980. The happy worker: An analysis of educational and occupational differences in determining job satisfaction. *American Journal of Sociology,* 86: 247–271.

GRUNDSTAFF, CARL F. 1981. *Population and society: A sociological perspective.* West Hanover, Mass.: Christopher Publishing House.

GRUSKY, DAVID, and ROBERT M. HAUSER. 1984. Comparative social mobility revisited: Models of convergence and divergence in 16 countries. *American Sociological Review,* 49: 19–38.

GURNEY, PATRICK J. 1981. Historical origins of ideological denial: The case of Marx in American sociology. *The American Sociologist,* 16: 196–201.

GURR, TED R. 1970. *Why men rebel.* Princeton, N.J.: Princeton University Press.

GUSFIELD, JOSEPH. 1962. Mass society and extremist politics. *American Sociological Review,* 27: 19–30.

GUTH, JAMES L. 1983. The new Christian right. In Robert C. Liebman and Robert Wuthnow, eds., *The new Christian right.* Chicago: Aldine.

HACKER, HELEN MAYER. 1951. Women as a minority group. *Social Forces,* 30: 60–69.

HACKER, HELEN MAYER. 1974. Women as a minority group: Twenty years later. In Florence Denmark, ed., *Who discriminates against women.* Beverly Hills, Calif.: Sage.

HADDEN, JEFFREY K., and CHARLES E. SWANN. 1981. *Prime-time preachers: The rising power of televangelism.* Reading, Mass.: Addison-Wesley.

HADLEY, ARTHUR T. 1978. *The empty polling booth.* Englewood Cliffs, N.J.: Prentice-Hall.

HAGAN, JOHN. 1980. The legislation of crime and delinquency: A review of theory, method, and research. *Law and Society Review,* 14: 603–628.

HAGAN, JOHN, ILENE N. BERNSTEIN, and CELESTA ALBONETTI. 1980. The differential sentencing of white-collar offenders. *American Sociological Review,* 42: 587–598.

HAGAN, JOHN, and JEFFREY LEON. 1977. Rediscovering

delinquency: Social history, political ideology, and the sociology of law. *American Sociological Review*, 42: 587–598.

HALE, ELLEN. 1984. Menopause: Few feel ill effects. *USA Today* (June 20): D-1.

HALL, EDWARD T. 1966. *The hidden dimension*. Garden City, N.Y.: Doubleday.

HALL, TRISH. 1984. Many women decide they want their careers rather than children. *Wall Street Journal* (October 10): 35.

HALLBLADE, SHIRLEY, and WALTER M. MATHEWS. 1980. Computers and society: Today and tomorrow. In Walter M. Mathews, ed., *Monster or messiah? The computer's impact on society*. Jackson: University Press of Mississippi.

HARE, A. PAUL. 1976. *Handbook of small group research*, 2nd ed. New York: Free Press.

HAREVEN, TAMARA K. 1982. *Family time and industrial time*. New York: Cambridge University Press.

HARRINGTON, MICHAEL. 1976. *The twilight of capitalism*. New York: Simon and Schuster.

HARRIS, CHAUNCEY D., and EDWARD L. ULLMAN. 1945. The nature of cities. *The Annals of the American Academy of Political and Social Science*, 242: 7–17.

HARRISON, MICHAEL I., and BERNARD LAZERWITZ. 1982. Do denominations matter? *American Journal of Sociology*, 88: 356–377.

HARSANYI, ZSOLT, and RICHARD HUTTON. 1979. Those genes that tell the future. *New York Times Magazine* (November 18): 194–205.

HAUSER, ROBERT, and DAVID FEATHERMAN. 1977. *The process of stratification*. New York: Academic Press.

HAWLEY, AMOS H. 1950. *Human ecology: A theory of community structure*. New York: Ronald Press.

HAWLEY, AMOS H. 1963. Community power and urban-renewal success. *American Journal of Sociology*, 68: 422–431.

HAWLEY, AMOS H. 1984. Human ecological and Marxian theories. *American Journal of Sociology*, 89: 904–917.

HAYS, CHARLOTTE. 1984. The evolution of Ann Landers: From prim to progressive. *Public Opinion*, 6 (January): 11–13.

HEARST, PATRICIA CAMPBELL. 1981. *Every secret thing*. Garden City, N.Y.: Doubleday.

HEATH, DWIGHT B. 1958. Sexual division of labor and cross-cultural research. *Social Forces*, 37: 77–79.

HERBERS, JOHN. 1984a. Catholic activism: Reasons and risks. *New York Times* (September 23): E-2.

HERBERS, JOHN. 1984b. Political and religious shifts rekindle church–state issues. *New York Times* (September 2): 1, 20.

HERDT, GILBERT. 1982. *Rituals of manhood: Male initiation in Papua New Guinea*. Berkeley: University of California Press.

HERMAN, EDWARD S. 1981. *Corporate control, corporate power*. Cambridge, Eng.: Cambridge University Press.

HERMAN, JUDITH, and LISA HIRSCHMAN. 1981. Families at risk for father–daughter incest. *American Journal of Psychiatry*, 138: 967–970.

HERSKOVITS, MELVILLE J. 1945. The processes of cultural change. In Ralph Linton, ed., *The science of man in the world crisis*. New York: Columbia University Press.

HESS, BETH B., and JOAN M. WARING. 1978. Parent and child in later life: Rethinking the relationship. In R. M. Lerner and G. B. Spanier, eds., *Child influences on marital and family interaction*. New York: Academic Press.

HETHERINGTON, E. MAVIS. 1979. Divorce. *American Psychologist*, 34: 851–858.

HETHERINGTON, E. MAVIS, MARTHA COX, and ROGER COX. 1982. Effects of divorce on parents and children. In M. E. Lamb, ed., *Nontraditional families: Parenting and child development*. Hillsdale, N.J.: Erlbaum.

HEWITT, JOHN P. 1979. *Self and society*, 2nd ed. Boston: Allyn and Bacon.

HILL, REUBEN. 1964. Methodological issues in family development research. *Family Process*, 3: 186–206.

HILLER, E. T. 1933. *Principles of sociology*. New York: Harper & Row.

HILTZ, STARR ROXANNE, and MURRAY TUROFF. 1978. *The network nation*. Reading, Mass.: Addison-Wesley.

HIMES, JOSEPH. 1973. *Racial conflict in American society*. Columbus, Ohio: Charles E. Merrill.

HIMMELFARB, GERTRUDE. 1984. *The idea of poverty: England in the early industrial age*. New York: Knopf.

HIMMELSTEIN, JEROME L. 1983. The new right. In Robert C. Liebman and Robert Wuthnow, eds., *The new Christian right*. Chicago: Aldine.

HINDELANG, MICHAEL J., TRAVIS HIRSCHI, and JOSEPH WEIS. 1981. *Measuring delinquency*. Beverly Hills, Calif.: Sage.

HINDS, MICHAEL. 1981. The child victim of incest. *New York Times* (June 15): 22.

HINKLE, ROSCOE. 1980. *Founding theory of American sociology: 1881–1915*. London: Routledge & Kegan Paul.

HODGE, ROBERT, and DONALD TREIMAN. 1968. Class identification in the United States. *American Journal of Sociology*, 73: 535–547.

HOEBEL, E. A. 1958. *Man in the primitive world*, 2nd ed. New York: McGraw-Hill.

HOFFMAN, LOIS W., and F. IVAN NYE. 1974. *Working mothers*. San Francisco: Jossey-Bass.

HOLDEN, CONSTANCE. 1983. Can smoking explain ultimate gender gap? *Science*, 221: 1034.

HOLLAND, EARLE. 1983. Science. Columbus (Ohio) *Dispatch* (November 13): E6.

HOLUSHA, JOHN. 1985. Big bonuses at the big 3 again. *New York Times* (April 13): 19.

HORAN, PATRICK. 1978. Is status attainment research atheoretical? *American Sociological Review*, 43: 534–541.

HORNING, DONALD. 1970. Blue-collar theft: Conceptions of property, attitudes toward pilfering, and work-group norms in a modern industrial plant. In Erwin O. Smigel and H. Laurence Ross, eds., *Crimes against bureaucracy*. New York: Van Nostrand/Reinhold.

HOSTETLER, JOHN A. 1980. *Amish society*. Baltimore: Johns Hopkins University Press.

HOYT, HOMER. 1939. *The structure and growth of residential neighborhoods in American Cities*. Washington, D.C.: Federal Housing Administration.

HSU, FRANCIS L. K. 1943. Incentives to work in primitive communities. *American Sociological Review*, 8: 638–642.

HUBER, JOAN and GLENNA SPITZE. 1983. *Sex stratification: Children, housework, and jobs*. New York: Academic Press.

HULTSCH, DAVID F., and J. K. PLEMMONS. 1979. Life events and life span development. In Paul B. Baltes and Orville G. Brim, Jr., eds., *Life-span development and behavior*, Vol. 2. New York: Academic Press.

HUNTLEY, STEVE. 1983. America's Indians: "Beggars in our own land." *U.S. News & World Report* (May 23): 70–72.

HUSAIN, ARSHAD, and JAMES L. CHAPEL. 1983. History of incest in girls admitted to a psychiatric hospital. *American Journal of Psychiatry*, 140: 591–593.

HYDE, JANET SHIBLEY. 1981. How large are cognitive gender differences? *American Psychologist*, 36: 892–901.

HYMAN, HERBERT H., and ELEANOR SINGER. 1968. Introduction. In H. H. Hyman and E. Singer, eds., *Readings in reference group theory and research*. New York: Free Press.

IBRAHIM, YOUSSEF M., 1984. Iranian middle class adjusts to a world hemmed in by fear. *Wall Street Journal* (January 17): 1, 27.

ICHILOV, ORIT, and SHMUEL BAR. 1980. Extended family ties and the allocation of social rewards in veteran kibbutzim in Israel. *Journal of Marriage and the Family*, 42: 421–426.

IMPERATO-MCGINLEY, J., R. E. PETERSON, E. GAUTIER, and N. STURLA. 1979. Androgens and the evolution of male-gender identity among male pseudohermaphrodites with 5a-reductase deficiency. *New England Journal of Medicine*, 300: 1233–1237.

IM THURN, E. F. 1883. *Among the Indians of Guiana*. London: Kegan Paul, Trench & Trubner.

INGHAM, ALAN G. 1974. The Ringelmann effect: Studies of group size and group performance. *Journal of Experimental Social Psychology*, 10: 371–384.

ISAAC, LARRY, and WILLIAM R. KELLY. 1981. Racial insurgency, the state, and welfare expansion: Local and national level evidence from the postwar United States. *American Journal of Sociology*, 86: 1348–1386.

IYER, PICO. 1984. A fever bordering on hysteria. *Time* (March 12): 36–39.

JACKSON, BROOKS. 1984. Loopholes allow flood of campaign giving by businesses, fat cats. *Wall Street Journal* (July 5): 1, 6.

JAMES, DAVID R., and MICHAEL SOREF. 1981. Profit constraints on managerial autonomy: Managerial theory and the unmaking of the corporation president. *American Sociological Review*, 46: 1–18.

JAMES, JOHN. 1951. A preliminary study of the size determinant in small group interaction. *American Sociological Review*, 16: 474–477.

JANIS, IRVING. 1972. *Victims of groupthink*. Boston: Houghton Mifflin.

JENCKS, CHRISTOPHER. 1982. Divorced mothers, unite! *Psychology Today*, 16 (November): 73–75.

JENCKS, CHRISTOPHER, et. al. 1979. *Who gets ahead? The determinants of economic success in America*. New York: Basic Books.

JENKINS, J. CRAIG. 1983. Resource mobilization theory and the study of social movements. *Annual Review of Sociology*, 9: 527–553.

JENKINS, J. CRAIG, and CHARLES PERROW. 1977. Insurgency of the powerless: Farm worker movements (1946–1972). *American Sociological Review*, 42: 249–268.

JENNESS, DIAMOND. 1922. The life of the Copper Eskimo. *Report of the Canadian Arctic Expedition, 1913–1918*, Vol. 12.

JOHNSTONE, RONALD L. 1975. *Religion and society in interaction: The sociology of religion*. Englewood Cliffs, N.J.: Prentice-Hall.

JOSEPH, RAYMOND A. 1983. Repelling repeaters. *Wall Street Journal* (August 10): 42.

KAGAN, JEROME, RICHARD B. KEARSLEY, and PHILIP R. ZELAZO. 1978. *Infancy: Its place in human development*. Cambridge, Mass.: Harvard University Press.

KAIN, EDWARD L. 1984. Surprising singles. *American Demographics*, 6 (August): 16–19+.

KALLEBERG, ARNE L. 1977. Work values and job rewards: Explaining age differences in job satisfaction. *American Sociological Review*, 42: 124–143.

KALMUSS, DEBRA. 1984. The intergenerational transmission of marital aggression. *Journal of Marriage and the Family*, 46: 11–19.

KANTER, ROSABETH MOSS. 1973. *Communes: Creating and managing the collective life*. New York: Harper & Row.

KAPLAN, H. ROY, and CURT TAUSKY. 1972. Work and the welfare Cadillac: The function of and commitment to work among the hard-core unemployed. *Social Problems*, 19: 469–483.

KARABEL, JEROME. 1977. Community colleges and social stratification: Submerged class conflict in American higher education. In Jerome Karabel and A. H. Halsey, eds., *Power and ideology in education*. New York: Oxford University Press.

KASINDORF, MARTIN. 1982. Asian-Americans: A "model minority." *Newsweek* (December 6): 39–51.

KATZ, SIDNEY. 1983. Active life expectancy. *The New England Journal of Medicine*, 309: 1218–1224.

KAUFMAN, MICHAEL T. 1979. Abandoned effort after the Gandhi era. *New York Times* (November 11): E-7.

KELLER, BILL. 1984. Experts describe "Third World" health conditions of farm workers in U.S. *New York Times* (May 24): 15.

KELLER, HELEN. 1904. *The story of my life*. Garden City, N.Y.: Doubleday.

KELLER, SUZANNE. 1963. *Beyond the ruling class*. New York: Random House.

KELLY, ORR. 1982. Corporate crime: The untold story. *U.S. News & World Report* (September 6): 25–30.

KENDLER, KENNETH S. 1983. Overview: A current perspective on twin studies of schizophrenia. *American Journal of Psychiatry*, 140: 1413–1425.

KENISTON, KENNETH. 1970. Youth: A "new" stage in life. *American Scholar* (Autumn): 586–595.

KENNEDY, EUGENE. 1984. America's activist bishops. *New York Times Magazine* (August 12): 14-30.

KENNY, TIMONY. 1984. 73% polled back right to die. *USA Today* (January 3): 3A.

KERBO, HAROLD R. 1983. *Social stratification and inequality*. New York: McGraw-Hill.

KERBO, HAROLD R., and L. RICHARD DELLA FAVE. 1984. Further notes on the evolution of corporate control and institutional investors: A response to Niemonen. *Sociological Quarterly*, 25: 279–283.

KESSLER, RONALD C. and JAMES A. MCRAE, JR. 1981. Trends in sex and psychological distress. *American Sociological Review*, 46: 443–452.

KETT, J. F. 1977. *Rites of passage: Adolescence in America, 1870 to the present*. New York: Basic Books.

KIDD, ROBERT F., and ELLEN F. CHAYET. 1984. Why do victims fail to report? The psychology of criminal victimization. *Journal of Social Issues*, 40: 39–50.

KIFNER, JOHN. 1984. Khomeini's grip in Iran appears unshakable. *New York Times* (November 16): 1, 6.

KIMMEL, D. C. 1980. *Adulthood and aging*. New York: Wiley.

KINDER, DONALD R., and DAVID O. SEARS. 1981. Prejudice and politics: Symbolic racism versus racial threats to the good life. *Journal of Personality and Social Psychology*, 40: 414–431.

KLEIN, FREDERICK C. 1980a. Big old cities of East, Midwest are reviving after years of decline. *Wall Street Journal* (May 19): 1, 20.

KLEIN, FREDERICK C. 1980b. The pot trade. *Wall Street Journal* (August 8): 1, 7.

KLEMESRUD, JUDY. 1983. Americans assess 15 years of feminism. *New York Times* (December 19): 24.

KLUCKHOHN, CLYDE. 1960. *Mirror for man*. Greenwich, Conn.: Fawcett.

KLUEGEL, JAMES R., and ELIOT R. SMITH. 1982. Whites' beliefs about blacks' opportunity. *American Sociological Review*, 47: 518–532.

KOENIG, FREDERICK. 1982. Today's conditions make U.S. "ripe for the rumor mill." *U.S. News & World Report* (December 6): 40.

KOESTLER, ARTHUR. 1949. The god that failed. In R. Crossman, ed., *The god that failed*. New York: Harper & Row.

KOHLBERG, LAWRENCE. 1966. A cognitive-developmental analysis of children's sex-role concepts and attitudes. In Eleanor E. Maccoby, ed. *The development of sex differences*. Stanford, Calif.: Stanford University Press.

KOHLBERG, LAWRENCE. 1969. Stage and sequence: The cognitive-developmental approach to socialization. In D. A. Goslin, ed., *Handbook of socialization theory and research*. Chicago: Rand McNally.

KOHLBERG, LAWRENCE, and D. Z. ULLIAN. 1974. Stages in the development of psychosexual concepts and attitudes. In R. C. Friedman, R. N. Richart, and R. L. Vande Wiele, eds., *Sex differences in behavior*. New York: Wiley.

KOHN, MELVIN L., and CARMI SCHOOLER. 1973. Occupational experience and psychological functioning: An assessment of reciprocal effects. *American Sociological Review*, 38:97–118.

KOHN, MELVIN L., and CARMI SCHOOLER. 1982. Job conditions and personality: A longitudinal assessment of their reciprocal effects. *American Journal of Sociology*, 87: 1257–1286.

KOLKO, GABRIEL. 1962. *Wealth and power in America*. New York: Praeger.

KOMORITA, SAMUEL S., and JOAN M. BARTH. 1985. Components of reward in social dilemmas. *Journal of Personality and Social Psychology*, 48: 364–373.

KORNHAUSER, WILLIAM. 1959. *The politics of mass society*. New York: Free Press.

KRAMER, RODERICK M., and MARILYNN B. BREWER. 1984. Effects of group identity on resource use in a simulated commons dilemma. *Journal of Personality and Social Psychology*, 46: 1044–1057.

KROSNICK, JON A., and CHARLIES M. JUDD. 1982. Traditions in social influence at adolescence: Who induces cigarette smoking? *Developmental Psychology*, 18: 359–368.

KÜBLER-ROSS, ELISABETH. 1969. *On death and dying*. New York: Macmillan.

KÜBLER-ROSS, ELISABETH. 1981. *Living with death and dying*. New York: Macmillan.

KUHN, MANFORD. 1964. Major trends in symbolic interaction theory in the past twenty-five years. *The Sociological Quarterly*, 5: 61–84.

LAMB, MICHAEL E. 1978. Influence of the child on marital quality and family interaction during the prenatal, perinatal, and infancy periods. In Richard M. Lerner and Graham B. Spanier, eds., *Child influences on marital and family interaction: A life-span perspective*. New York: Academic Press.

LANG, ABIGAIL M. and ELAINE M. BRODY. 1983. Characteristics of middle-aged daughters and help to their elderly parents. *Journal of Marriage and the Family*, 45: 193–202.

LANG, O. 1946. *Chinese family and society*. New Haven Conn.: Yale University Press.

LANGLEY, MONICA. 1984. AT&T has call for a new corporate culture. *Wall Street Journal* (February 28): 32.

LANGWAY, LYNN. 1981. At long last motherhood. *Newsweek* (March 16): 86–87.

LARSON, ERIK, and CARRIE DOLAN. 1983. Large computer firms sprout little divisions for good, fast, work. *Wall Street Journal* (August 19): 1, 12.

LASLETT, PETER. 1974. *Household and family in past time*. New York: Cambridge University Press.

LASLETT, PETER. 1976. Societal development and aging. In R. Binstock and E. Shanas, eds., *Handbook of aging and the social sciences*. New York: Van Nostrand/Reinhold.

LASSWELL, HAROLD. 1936. *Politics: Who gets what, when and how*. New York: McGraw-Hill.

LATANÉ, BIBB, KIPLING WILLIAMS, and STEPHEN HARKINS. 1979. Many hands make light the work: The causes and consequences of social loafing. *Journal of Personality and Social Psychology*, 37: 822–832.

LAUER, ROBERT H. and WARREN H. HANDEL. 1983. *Social psychology*, 2nd ed. Englewood Cliffs, N.J.: Prentice-Hall.

LE BON, GUSTAV. 1896. *The crowd: A study of the popular mind*. London: Ernest Benn.

LEE, FELICIA. 1984. Housework and men still don't mix. *USA Today* (August 31): 1D.

LEE, GARY R. 1977. *Family structure and interaction: A comparative analysis*. Philadelphia: Lippincott.

LEMERT, EDWIN M. 1951. *Social pathology: A systematic approach to the theory of sociopathic behavior*. New York: McGraw-Hill.

LEMERT, EDWIN M. 1972. *Human deviance, social problems and social control*, 2nd ed. Englewood Cliffs, N.J.: Prentice-Hall.

LENNEBERG, ERIC H. 1969. *Biological foundations of language*. New York: Wiley.

LENSKI, GERHARD, E. 1966. *Power and privilege*. New York: McGraw-Hill.

LENSKI, GERHARD, and JEAN LENSKI. 1982. *Human societies: An introduction to macrosociology*, 4th ed. New York: McGraw-Hill.

LEUNG, ELEANOR H. L. and HARRIET L. RHEINGOLD. 1981. Development of pointing as a social gesture. *Developmental Psychology*, 17: 215–220.

LEVINSON, DANIEL J., et al. 1978. *The seasons of a man's life*. New York: Knopf.

LEVINSON, HARRY. 1964. Money aside, why spend life working? *National Observer* (March 9): 20.

LEVI-STRAUSS, CLAUDE. 1956. The family. In Harry L. Shapiro, ed., *Man, culture and society*. New York: Oxford University Press.

LEWIN, KURT, RONALD LIPPITT, and RALPH K. WHITE. 1939. Patterns of aggressive behavior in experimentally created "social climates." *Journal of Social Psychology*, 10: 271–299.

LEWIS, MICHAEL, and JEANNE BROOKS-GUNN. 1979. Toward a theory of social cognition: The development of the self. *New Directions for Child Development*, 4: 1–20.

LEWIS, OSCAR. 1959. *Five families: Mexican case studies in the culture of poverty*. New York: Basic Books.

LEWIS, OSCAR. 1961. *The children of Sanchez*. New York: Random House.

LEWIS, OSCAR. 1966. *La vida: A Puerto Rican family in the culture of poverty, San Juan and New York*. New York: Random House.

LEWONTIN, R. C., STEVEN ROSE, and LEON J. KAMIN. 1984. *Not in our genes*. New York: Pantheon.

LIBBY, ROGER W. 1977. Creative singlehood as a sexual lifestyle: Beyond marriage as a rite of passage. In R. W. Libby and R. N. Whitehurst, eds., *Marriage and alternatives*. Glenview, Ill.: Scott, Foresman.

LIEBERSON, STANLEY. 1970. Stratification and ethnic groups. *Sociological Inquiry*, 40: 172–181.

LIEBOW, ELLIOT. 1967. *Tally's corner*. Boston: Little, Brown.

LIMBER, JOHN. 1977. Language in child and chimp? *American Psychologist*, 32: 280–295.

LINDEN, FABIAN. 1984. Myth of the disappearing middle class. *Wall Street Journal* (January 23): 18.

LINDSEY, ROBERT. 1985. Lack of students and money besets California 2-year colleges. *New York Times* (April 29): 8.

LINTON, RALPH. 1936. *The study of man*. New York: Appleton-Century-Crofts.

LINTON, RALPH. 1937. One hundred per cent American. *American Mercury*, 40 (April): 427–429.

LINTON, RALPH. 1945. *The cultural background of personality*. New York: Appleton-Century-Crofts.

LIPSET, SEYMOUR MARTIN. 1963. *Political man*. Garden City, N.Y.: Doubleday.

LIPSET, SEYMOUR MARTIN. 1982. Social mobility in industrial societies. *Public Opinion*, 5 (June–July): 41–44.

LIPSET, SEYMOUR M., and REINHARD BENDIX. 1951. Social status and social structure. *British Journal of Sociology*, 2: 150–160.

LIPSET, SEYMOUR MARTIN, MARTIN A. TROW, and JAMES S. COLEMAN. 1956. *Union democracy*. New York: Free Press.

LIPTON, DOUGLAS, ROBERT MARTINSON, and JUDITH WILKS. 1975. *The effectiveness of correctional treatment: A survey of treatment evaluation studies*. New York: Praeger.

LIVESLEY, W. J. and D. B. BROMLEY. 1973. *Person perception in childhood and adolescence*. New York: Wiley.

LIZOTTE, ALAN J. 1978. Extra-legal factors in Chicago's criminal courts: Testing the conflict model of criminal justice. *Social Problems*, 25: 564–580.

LOFLAND, LYN. 1978. *The craft of dying*. Beverly Hills, Calif.: Sage.

LONG, LARRY, and DIANA DeARE. 1983. The slowing of urbanization in the U.S. *Scientific American*, 249 (July): 33–41.

LOPATA, HELENA ZNANIECKI. 1973. *Widowhood in an American city*. Cambridge, Mass.: Schenkman.

Los Angeles Times. 1984. Women still place family above job, survey finds. *Los Angeles Times* (September 9): 1.

LOWENTHAL, MARJORIE F. 1964. Social isolation and mental illness in old age. *American Sociological Review*, 29: 20–30.

LOWIE, ROBERT H. 1935. *The Crow Indians*. New York: Farrar & Rinehart.

LUKACS, GEORGE. 1922/1968. *History and class consciousness*. Cambridge, Mass.: MIT Press.

LUKES, STEVEN. 1977. Alienation and anomie. In *Essays in social theory*. New York: Columbia University Press.

LUMSDEN, CHARLES J. and EDWARD O. WILSON. 1981. *Genes, mind, and culture*. Cambridge, Mass.: Harvard University Press.

LYND, ROBERT S., and HELEN MERRILL LYND. 1929. *Middletown: A study in American culture*. New York: Harcourt, Brace & World.

LYND, ROBERT S. and HELEN MERRILL LYND. 1937. *Middletown in transition: A study in cultural conflicts*. New York: Harcourt, Brace & World.

LYONS, RICHARD D. 1983. Sex in America: Conservative attitudes prevail. *New York Times* (October 4): 17, 19.

MCBEE, SUSANNA. 1984. Asian-Americans: Are they making the grade? *U.S. News & World Report* (April 2): 41–47.

McCARTHY, JOHN D., and DEAN R. HOGE. 1982. Analysis of age effects in longitudinal studies of adolescent self-esteem. *Developmental Psychology*, 18: 372–379.

MACCOBY, ELEANOR E., and CAROL N. JACKLIN. 1974. *The psychology of sex differences*. Stanford, Calif.: Stanford University Press.

MACCOBY, ELEANOR E., and CAROL N. JACKLIN. 1980. Sex differences in aggression: A rejoinder and reprise. *Child Development*, 51: 964–980.

McCONAHAY, JOHN B. and JOSEPH C. HOUGH, JR. 1976. Symbolic racism. *Journal of Social Issues*, 32: 23–45.

McGEE, REECE. 1975. *Points of departure*. Hinsdale, Ill.: Dryden Press.

McGUIRE, MEREDITH B. 1981. *Religion: The social context*. Belmont, Calif.: Wadsworth.

MACKLIN, ELEANOR D. 1974. Going very steady. *Psychology Today*, 8 (November): 53–59.

MACKLIN. ELEANOR D. 1978., Nonmarital heterosexual cohabitation. *Marriage and the Family Review*, 1: 2–10.

McLANAHAN, SARA S. 1983. Family structure and stress: A longitudinal comparison of two-parent and female-headed families. *Journal of Marriage and Family Living*, 45: 347–357.

McLAUGHLIN, STEVEN D., and MICHAEL MICKLIN. 1983. The timing of the first birth and changes in personal efficacy. *Journal of Marriage and the Family*, 45: 47–55.

McQUILLAN, KEVIN. 1984. Modes of production and demographic patterns in nineteenth-century France. *American Journal of Sociology*, 89: 1324–1346.

McROBERTS, HUGH A., and KEVIN SELBEE. 1981. Trends in occupational mobility in Canada and the United States: A comparison. *American Sociological Review*, 46: 406–421.

MADDOX, GEORGE L., and JAMES WILEY. 1976. Scope, concepts and methods in the study of aging. In R. H. Binstock and E. Shanas, eds., *Handbook of aging and the social sciences*. New York: Van Nostrand.

MADRICK, JEFFREY. 1983. Cutting loose: The drive to divest. *New York Times* (July 3): 1F.

MAEROFF, GENE I. 1984. The class of '84 is another disappointment for blacks. *New York Times* (June 10): 8E.

MAIN, JEREMY. 1984. The trouble with managing Japanese-style. *Fortune* (April 2): 50–56.

MAITAL. SHLOMO. 1982. Kumquats to computers. *Barron's* (July 19): 24–26.

MALAMUTH, NEIL M. 1981. Rape proclivity among males. *Journal of Social Issues*, 37: 138–157.

MALINOWSKI, BRONISLAW. 1929. *The sexual life of savages in northwestern Melanesia*. New York: Eugenics Press.

MALINOWSKI, BRONISLAW. 1964. Parenthood—the basis of social structure. In Rose Coser, ed., *The family: Its structure and functions*. New York: St. Martin's Press.

MANN, JAMES. 1983. One-parent family: The troubles and the joys. *Newsweek* (November 28): 57–62.

MANN, JAMES. 1984. A revival of religion on campus. *U.S. News & World Report* (January 9): 44.

MANN, LEON, JAMES W. NEWTON, and J. M. INNES. 1982. A test between deindividuation and emergent norm theories of crowd aggression. *Journal of Personality and Social Psychology*, 42: 260–272.

MARCUS, REBECCA. 1975. *Survivors of the Stone Age*. New York: Hastings House.

MARGLIN, STEPHEN. 1974. What the bosses do: The origins and functions of hierarchy in capitalist production. *Review of Radical Political Economics*, 6: 60–112.

MARKS, GARY, NORMAN MILLER, and GEOFFREY MARUYAMA. 1981. Effect of targets' physical attractiveness on assumptions of similarity. *Journal of Personality and Social Psychology*, 41: 198–206.

MARS, GERALD. 1974. Dock pilferage: A case study in occupational theft. In *Deviance and social control*. London: Tavistock.

MARTINSON, ROBERT. 1974. What works?—Questions and answers about prison reform *The Public Interest*, 35: 22–54.

MARX, GARY T., and JAMES L. WOODS. 1975. Strands of theory and research in collective behavior. *Annual Review of Sociology*, 1: 363–428.

MARX, KARL. 1844/1960. Estranged labour—Economic and philosophic manuscripts of 1844. In C. W. Mills, ed., *Images of man*. New York: Braziller.

MARX, KARL. 1844/1964. *Critique of the Hegelian philosophy of the right*. Reprinted in Tom B. Bottomore, *Karl Marx*. New York: McGraw-Hill.

MARX, KARL, and FRIEDRICH ENGELS. 1848/1955 *The Communist Manifesto*. S. H. Beer, ed. New York: Appleton-Century-Crofts.

MARX, KARL. 1867/1906. *Capital*. Vol. 1. New York: Modern Library.

MARX, KARL. 1966. *The civil war in France*. Peking: Foreign Languages Press.

MARX, KARL. 1970. *Critique of Hegel's "philosophy of right."* Trans. A. O'Malley and J. O'Malley. London: Cambridge University Press.

MASHEK, JOHN W. 1984. Winds of change are transforming the system *U.S. News & World Report* (October 8): 66–68.

MASTERSON, JOHN. 1984. Divorce as health hazard. *Psychology Today*, 18 (October): 24.

MAZUR, ALLAN, EURGENE ROSA, MARK FAUPEL, JOSHUA HELLER, RUSSELL LEEN, and BLAKE THURMAN. 1980. Physiological aspects of communication via mutual gaze. *American Journal of Sociology*, 86: 50–74.

MEAD, GEORGE HERBERT. 1934. *Mind, self, and other*. Chicago: University of Chicago Press.

MEHRABIAN, ALBERT. 1968. Communication without words. *Psychology Today*, 2 (September): 53–55.

MEIER, ROBERT F., and WELDON J. JOHNSON. 1977. Deterrence as social control: The legal and extralegal production of conformity. *American Sociological Review*, 42: 292–304.

MELMAN, SEYMOUR. 1983. Managers' debacle. *New York Times* (November 4): 29.

MELTZER, BERNARD, JAMES PETRAS, and LARRY REYNOLDS. 1975. *Symbolic interactionism: Genesis, varieties, and criticisms*. London: Routledge & Kegan Paul.

MENDES, H. A. 1976. Single fathers. *Family Coordinator*, 25: 439–444.

MERTON, ROBERT K. 1968. *Social theory and social structure*, rev. ed. New York: Free Press.

MESSICK, DAVID M., HENK WILKE, MARILYNN B. BREWER, RODERICK M. KRAMER, PATRICIA E. ZEMKE, and LAYTON LUI. 1983. Individual adaptations and structural change as solutions to social dilemmas. *Journal of Personality and Social Psychology*, 44: 294–309.

MICHALOWSKI, RAYMOND J., and EDWARD W. BOHLANDER. 1976. Repression and criminal justice in capitalist America. *Sociological Inquiry*, 46: 96–106.

MICHELS, ROBERT. 1911/1966. *Political parties*. New York: Free Press.

MICKLIN, MICHAEL, and HARVEY M. CHOLDIN. 1984. *Sociological human ecology: Contemporary issues and applications*. Boulder, Colo.: Westview.

MIDDLETON, RUSSELL. 1962. A deviant case: Brother–sister and father–daughter marriage in ancient Egypt. *American Sociological Review*, 27: 603–611.

MILGRAM, STANLEY. 1977. *The individual in a social world*. Reading, Mass.: Addison-Wesley.

MILGRAM, STANLEY, and HANS TOCH. 1969. Collective behavior: Crowds and social movements. In G. Lindzey and E. Aronson, eds., *The Handbook of Social Psychology*, 2nd ed. Vol. 2. Reading, Mass.: Addison-Wesley.

MILIBAND, RALPH. 1969. *The state in capitalist society*. New York: Basic Books.

MILLER, WALTER B. 1958. Lower-class culture as a generating milieu of gang delinquency. *Journal of Social Issues*, 14: 5–19.

MILLER, WALTER B. 1975. *Violence by youth gangs and youth groups as a crime problem in major American cities*. Washington, D.C.: U.S. Government Printing Office.

MILLS, C. WRIGHT. 1959. *The sociological imagination*. New York: Oxford University Press.

MILLS, C. WRIGHT. 1962. *The Marxists*. New York: Dell.

MILLS, DAVID M. 1984. A model for stepfamily development. *Family Relations*, 33: 365–372.

MILNE, L. 1924. *The home of an eastern clan*. Oxford: Clarendon Press.

MINTZ, BETH, and MICHAEL SCHWARTZ. 1981a. The structure of intercorporate unity in American business. *Social Problems*, 29: 87–103.

MINTZ, BETH, and MICHAEL SCHWARTZ. 1981b. Interlocking directorates and interest group formation. *American Sociological Review*, 46: 851–869.

MIROWSKY, JOHN, and and CATHERINE E. ROSS. 1984. Working couples. Paper read to the American Association for the Advancement of Science, May 25, 1984.

MISCHEL, WALTER. 1970. Sex-typing and socialization. In P. H. Mussen, ed., *Carmichael's manual of child psychology*, 3rd ed. Vol. 2. New York: Wiley.

MOLLENKOPF, JOHN. 1975. Theories of the state and power structure research. *Insurgent Sociologist*, 5: 245–264.

MONEY, JOHN, and ANKE A. EHRHARDT. 1972. *Man & woman, boy & girl*. Baltimore: Johns Hopkins University Press.

MONEY, JOHN, and P. TUCKER. 1975. *Sexual signatures: On being a man or a woman*. Boston: Little, Brown.

MOORE, DIDI. 1984. It's either me or your job! *Working Woman* (April): 108–111.

MORAN, RICHARD. 1984. More crime and less punishment. *Newsweek* (May 7): 22.

MORRIS, JULIE. 1984. Plans for nudist apartment bared. *USA Today* (January 19): 3A.

MORSE, NANCY C., and ROBERT S. WEISS. 1955. The function and meaning of work and the job. *American Sociological Review*, 20: 191–198.

MORTIMER, JEYLAN T., and ROBERTA G. SIMMONS. 1978. Adult socialization. *Annual Review of Sociology*, 4: 421–454.

MOSKOWITZ, BREYNE ARLENE. 1978. The acquisition of language. *Scientific American*, 239 (November): 92–108.

MOTTL, TAHI L. 1980. The analysis of countermovements. *Social Problems*, 27: 620–635.

MURDOCK, GEORGE P. 1935. Comparative data on the division of labor by sex. *Social Forces*, 15: 551–553.

MURDOCK, GEORGE P. 1943. *Our primitive contemporaries*. New York: Macmillan.

MURDOCK, GEORGE PETER. 1949. *Social structure*. New York: Macmillan.

MURDOCK, GEORGE P. 1950a. Feasibility and implementation of comparative community research. *American Sociological Review*, 15: 713–720.

MURDOCK, GEORGE P. 1950b. *Outline of cultural materials*, 3rd ed. New Haven, Conn.: Yale University Press.

MURDOCK, GEORGE PETER. 1967. *Ethnographic atlas*. Pittsburgh: University of Pittsburgh Press.

MURSTEIN, BERNARD I. 1972. Physical attractiveness and marital choice. *Journal of Personality and Social Psychology*, 22: 8–12.

MURSTEIN. BERNARD I. 1976. *Who will marry whom?* New York: Springer.

MYERS, HENRY F. 1984. Is U.S. industry dying? A rosy minority view. *Wall Street Journal* (December 31): 1.

MYERS, J. K. and L. L. BEAN. 1968. *A decade later: A follow-up of "Social class and mental illness."* New York: Wiley.

MYRDAL, GUNNAR. 1944. *An American dilemma*. New York: Harper.

NANCE, JOHN. 1975. *The gentle Tasaday*. New York: Harcourt Brace Jovanovich.

NAISBITT, JOHN. 1982. *Megatrends*. New York: Warner Books.

NATIONAL COMMISSION ON EXCELLENCE IN EDUCATION. 1983. *A nation at risk: The imperative for educational reform*. Washington, D.C.: U.S. Department of Education.

NATIONAL INSTITUTE OF MENTAL HEALTH. 1980. *Special report: Schizophrenia*. Washington, D.C.: U.S. Government Printing Office.

NATIONAL TASK FORCE ON EDUCATION FOR ECONOMIC GROWTH. 1983. *Action for excellence: A comprehensive plan to improve our nation's schools*. Denver: Education Commission of the States.

NELSON, KEITH E. 1977. Facilitating children's syntax acquisition. *Developmental Psychology*, 13: 101–107.

NEUGARTEN, BERNICE L. 1963. Women's attitudes toward the menopause. *Vita Humana*, 6: 140–151.

NEUGARTEN, BERNICE L. 1968. Adult personality. In E. Vinacke, ed., *Readings in general psychology*. New York: American Book.

NEUGARTEN, BERNICE L. 1977. Personality and aging. In J. E. Birren and K. W. Schaie, eds., *Handbook of aging and the social sciences*. New York: Van Nostrand.

NEUGARTEN, BERNICE L. 1979. Time, age, and the life cycle. *American Journal of Psychiatry*, 136: 887–894.

NEUGARTEN, BERNICE L. 1982. Age or need? *National Forum*, 62: 25–27.

NEWCOMB, THEODORE M. 1950. *Social psychology*. New York: Holt, Rinehart and Winston.

NEWMAN, BARRY. 1979. Do multinationals really create jobs in the Third World? *Wall Street Journal* (September 25): 1, 16.

NEWMAN, BARRY. 1983. Single-country unions of Europe try to cope with multinationals. *Wall Street Journal* (November 30): 1, 31.

NEW YORK TIMES. 1977. "Time theft" said to cause the economy of Canada loss of $8 billion a year. *New York Times* (November 25): 5.

NIEBUHR, H. RICHARD. 1929. *The social sources of denominationalism*. New York: Holt, Rinehart and Winston.

NILSON, N. B. 1978. The social standing of a housewife. *Journal of Marriage and the Family*, 40: 541–548.

NISBET, ROBERT. 1962. *Community and power*. New York: Oxford University Press.

NISBET, ROBERT A. 1970. *The social bond*. New York: Knopf.

NOCK, STEVEN L. 1979. The family life cycle: Empirical or conceptual tool? *Journal of Marriage and Family*, 41: 15–26.

NOEL, DONALD M. 1972. *The origins of American slavery and racism*. Columbus, Ohio: Charles E. Merrill.

NOTESTEIN, FRANK W. 1945. Population—The long view. In Theodore W. Schultz, ed., *Food for the world*. Chicago: University of Chicago Press.

NYE, F. IVAN 1978. Is choice and exchange theory the key? *Journal of Marriage and the Family*, 40: 219–233.

O'BARR, JEAN F. 1979. *Conflict of interest: A growing challenge for working couples*. Durham, N.C.: Duke University, Office of Continuing Education.

O'CONNOR, JAMES. 1973. *The fiscal crisis of the state*. New York: St. Martin's Press.

O'DELL, JERRY W. 1968. Group size and emotional interaction. *Journal of Personality and Social Psychology*, 8: 75–78.

O'DRISCOLL, PATRICK. 1984. USA talks of "a spiritual reawakening." *USA Today* (March 26): 1–2.

OFFER, DANIEL, and JUDITH B. OFFER. 1975. *From teenage to young manhood*. New York: Basic Books.

OGBURN, WILLIAM F. 1922. *Social change*. New York: B. W. Huebsch.

OLSON, DAVID J., and PHILIP MEYER. 1975. *To keep the republic*. New York: McGraw-Hill.

OLSEN, MARVIN E. 1970. *Power in societies*. New York: Macmillan.

OLSEN, MARVIN E. 1978. *The process of social organization*, 2nd ed. New York: Holt, Rinehart and Winston.

O'MALLEY, PATRICK M., and AND GERALD G. BACHMAN. 1983. Self-esteem: Change and stability between 13 and 23. *Developmental Psychology*, 19: 257–268.

OPINION ROUNDUP. 1980. Work in the 70's. *Public Opinion*, 3 (December/January): 36.

OPINION ROUNDUP. 1982. Race: A decade of progress. *Public Opinion*, 5 (October): 34.

OPINION ROUNDUP. 1983. A look at the afterlife. *Public Opinion*, 5 (January): 40.

ORDOVENSKY, PAT. 1985. Lack of aid shuts door on minority grads. *USA Today* (March 21): 1A.

ORDOVENSKY, PAT, and PETER JOHNSON. 1984. Youths fall more in line with their parents. *USA Today* (March 28): 1–2.

O'REILLY, JANE. 1983. Wife beating. The silent crime. *Time* (September 5): 23–26.

PAERNOW, PATRICIA L. 1984. The stepfamily cycle: An experiential model of stepfamily development. *Family Relations*, 33: 355–363.

PALMER, BARBARA. 1984. Putting more care into child care. *USA Today* (April 19): 1.

PARK, ROBERT E., ERNEST W. BURGESS, and RODERICK D. McKENZIE. 1925. *The city*. Chicago: University of Chicago Press.

PARKINSON, C. NORTHCOTE. 1962. *Parkinson's Law*. Boston: Houghton Mifflin.

PARNES, H. S. 1981. *Work and retirement—A longitudinal study of men*. Cambridge, Mass.: MIT Press.

PARSONS, TALCOTT. 1949. *The structure of social action*, 2nd ed. New York: McGraw-Hill.

PARSONS, TALCOTT. 1951. *The social system*. New York: Free Press.

PARSONS, TALCOTT. 1966. *Societies: Evolutionary and comparative perspectives*. Englewood Cliffs, N.J.: Prentice-Hall.

PARSONS, TALCOTT. 1977. On building social system theory: A personal history. In Talcott Parsons, ed., *Social systems and evolution of action theory*. New York: Free Press.

PARSONS, TALCOTT, and ROBERT F. BALES . 1955. *Family socialization and interaction process*. New York: Free Press.

PEAR, ROBERT. 1983. Stockman doubts U.S. poverty rate. *New York Times* (November 4): 13.

PEAR, ROBERT. 1983. $1.5 billion is proposed for interned U.S. Japanese. *New York Times* (June 17): 1, 66.

PEAR, ROBERT. 1984a. Rise in poverty from '79 to '82 is found in U.S. *New York Times* (February 24): 1, 8.

PEAR, ROBERT. 1984b. Rate of poverty found to persist in face of gains. *New York Times* (August 3): 1, 28.

PEAR, ROBERT. 1984c. With U.S. crime rates declining, a record 454,136 are in prisons. *New York Times* (August 28): 1, 9.

PEBLEY, ANNE R., and DAVID E. BLOOM. 1982. Childless Americans. *American Demography*, 4 (January): 18–21.

PENTELLA, CHERYL. 1983. More students say good night at the front door. *On Campus* (January): 16.

PERROW, CHARLES. 1979. *Complex organizations*, rev. ed. Glenview, Ill.: Scott, Foresman.

PERROW, CHARLES. 1982. Disintegrating social sciences. *Phi Delta Kappan*, 63: 684–688.

PETER, LAWRENCE J., and RAYMOND HULL. 1969. *The Peter Principle*. New York: Morrow.

PETERSEN, WILLIAM. 1960. The demographic transition in the Netherlands. *American Sociological Review*, 25: 334–347.

PETERSON, KAREN S. 1984. Child-care benefits in infancy. *USA Today* (September 25): B-1.

POPE, LISTON. 1942. *Millhands and preachers*. New Haven, Conn.: Yale University Press.

POPULATION REFERENCE BUREAU. 1983. *U.S. Hispanics: Changing the face of America*. Washington, D.C.: Population Reference Bureau.

POPULATION REFERENCE BUREAU. 1984. *World development report*. Washington, D.C.: World Bank.

PORTER, BRUCE D. 1980. Parkinson's Law revisited: War and the growth of American government. *The Public Interest*, 60: 50–68.

POULANTZAS, NICOS. 1973. *Political power and social classes*. London: New Left Review.

PRESS, ARIC. 1981. How the mob really works. *Newsweek* (January 5): 34–43.

PRESTHUS, ROBERT. 1978. *The organizational society*, rev. ed. New York: St. Martin's Press.

PREWITT, KENNETH. 1982. Informed choices. *Society*, 20 (November–December): 18–21.

QUADAGNO, JILL S. 1982. *Aging in early industrial society*. New York: Academic Press.

QUADAGNO, JILL S. 1984. Welfare capitalism and the Social Security Act of 1935. *American Sociological Review*, 49: 632–647.

QUINNEY, RICHARD. 1974. *Criminal justice in America*. Boston: Little, Brown.

QUINNEY, RICHARD. 1980. *Class, state, and crime*. New York: Longman.

RAAB, SELWYN. 1984. Asia crime groups spreading in U.S., Smith tells panel. *New York Times* (October 24): 1, 16.

RANGEL, JESUS. 1984. Survey finds Hispanic groups are more unified. *New York Times* (September 8): 5.

RAPOPORT, R., R. N. RAPOPORT, and Z. STRELITZ. 1976. *Fathers, mothers and society: Towards new alliances*. New York: Basic Books.

REDFIELD, ROBERT. 1947. The folk society. *American Journal of Sociology*, 52: 293–308.

REICH, WALTER. 1983. The world of Soviet psychiatry. *New York Times Magazine* (January 30): 21–25, 50.

REIS, HARRY T., JOHN NEZLEK, and LADD WHEELER. 1980. Physical attractiveness in social interaction. *Journal of Personality and Social Psychology*, 38: 604–617.

RHEINGOLD, HARRIET L., and K. V. COOK. 1975. The contents of boys' and girls' rooms as an index of parents' behavior. *Child Development*, 46: 459–463.

RHEINGOLD, HARRIET L., DALE F. HAY, and MEREDITH J. WEST. 1976. Sharing in the second year of life. *Child Development*, 47: 1148–1158.

RICHE, MARTHA FARNSWORTH. 1982. The fall and rise of religion. *American Demographics*, 4 (May): 14–19 + .

RICKS, THOMAS E. 1984. Researchers say day-care centers are implicated in spread of disease. *Wall Street Journal* (September 5): 15.

RIDGEWAY, CECILIA L., JOSEPH BERGER, and LeRoy SMITH. 1985. Nonverbal cues and status: An expectation states approach. *American Journal of Sociology*, 90: 955–978.

RIDING, ALAN. 1984. Brazilians turn to lynchings to fight soaring crime rate *New York Times* (April 15): 1, 8.

RIESMAN, DAVID. 1953. *The Lonely Crowd*. Garden City, N.Y.: Doubleday.

RIGER, STEPHANIE, and MARGARET T. GORDON. 1981. The fear of rape: A study in social control. *Journal of Social Issues*, 37: 71–92.

RISMAN, BARBARA J., CHARLES T. HILL, ZICK RUBIN, and LETITIA ANNE PEPLAU. 1981. Living together in college: Implications for courtship. *Journal of Marriage and the Family*, 43: 77–83.

RITZER, GEORGE. 1983. *Sociological Theory*. New York: Knopf.

RIVERS, W. H. R. 1906. *The Toda*. New York: Macmillan.

ROBERTS, SAM. 1984. A profile of the American Mafia. *New York Times* (October 4): 1, 18.

ROBERTSON, HECTOR M. 1933. *Aspects of the rise of economic individualism*. London: Cambridge University Press.

ROBINSON, BRYAN E. 1984. The contemporary American stepfather. *Family Relations*, 33: 381–388.

ROBEY, BRYANT. 1984. Black votes, black money. *American Demographics*, 6 (May): 4–6.

RODMAN, HYMAN. 1968. Class culture. In D. L. Sills, ed., *International encyclopedia of the social sciences*. Vol. 15. New York: Macmillan.

ROONEY, JAMES F. 1980. Organizational success through program failure: Skid Row rescue missions. *Social Forces*, 58: 904–924.

ROSE, ARNOLD M. 1962. A systematic summary of symbolic interactionist theory. In Arnold M. Rose, ed., *Human behavior and social processes*. Boston: Houghton Mifflin.

ROSENFELD, EVA. 1951. Social stratification in a "classless society." *American Sociological Review*, 16: 766–774.

ROSNOW, RALPH, and GARY ALAN FINE. 1976. *Rumor and gossip: The social psychology of hearsay*. New York: Elsevier.

ROSNOW, RALPH, and ALLAN J. KIMMEL. 1979. Lives of a rumor. *Psychology Today*, 13 (June): 88–92.

ROSOW, IRVING. 1974. *Socialization to old age*. Berkeley: University of California Press.

ROSSI, ALICE S. 1984. Gender and parenthood. *American Sociological Review*, 49: 1–19.

RUBENSTEIN, CARIN. 1982. Real men don't earn less than their wives. *Psychology Today*, 16 (November): 36–41.

RUBINSON, RICHARD. 1976. The world-economy and the distribution of income within states: A cross-national study. *American Sociological Review*, 41: 638–659.

RUSSELL, CHERYL. 1983. The news about Hispanics. *American Demographics*, 5 (March): 15–25.

RUTTER, MICHAEL. 1979. *Fifteen thousand hours: Secondary schools and their effects on children*. Cambridge, Mass.: Harvard University Press.

RYDER, ROBERT G. 1973. Longitudinal data relating marriage satisfaction and having a child. *Journal of Marriage and the Family*, 35: 604–606.

SAGARIN, EDWARD. 1975. *Deviants and deviance*. New York: Praeger.

SALMANS, SANDRA. 1985. Man in the moon loses job at P&G. *New York Times* (April 25): 31, 36.

SAMUELSON, ROBERT J. 1984. The economics of self-pity. *Newsweek* (March 5): 78.

SAMUELSSON, KURT. 1961. *Religion and economic action: A critique of Max Weber*. Trans. E. G. French. New York: Harper Torchbooks.

SANDERS, WILLIAM B. 1974. *The sociologist as detective*. New York: Praeger.

SANOFF, ALVIN P. 1983. Jews find new solace in the old traditions. *U.S. News & World Report* (April 4): 43–44.

SAPIR, EDWARD. 1949. *Selected writings in language, culture, and personality*. Berkeley: University of California Press.

SCARF, MAGGIE. 1976. *Body, mind, behavior*. Washington, D.C.: New Republic Book Company.

SCHACHTER, FRANCES F. 1981. Toddlers with employed mothers. *Child Development*, 52: 958–964.

SCHELLHARDT, TIMOTHY D. 1983. Census unit predicts 60% of Americans will be living in the South or West by 2000. *Wall Street Journal* (September 8): 4.

SCHILL, MICHAEL H., and RICHARD P. NATHAN. 1983. *Revitalizing America's cities: Neighborhood reinvestment and displacement*. Albany: State University of New York Press.

SCHNEIDER, WILLIAM, and I. A. LEWIS. 1984. The straight story on homosexuality and gay rights. *Public Opinion*, 7 (February–March): 16–20 + .

SCHORR, ALVIN L. 1984. Redefining poverty levels. *New York Times* (May 9): 27.

SCHREINER, TIM. 1983. Poverty plagues farmers, study says. *USA Today* (December 22): 3A.

SCHUMAN, FREDERICK L. 1933. *International politics*. New York: McGraw-Hill.

SCHUMER, FRAN. 1984. A return to religion. *New York Times Magazine* (April 15): 90–98.

SCHUR, EDWIN. 1965. *Crimes without victims*. Englewood Cliffs, N.J.: Prentice-Hall.

SCHUTZ, ALFRED. 1971. *Collected papers*. The Hague: Martinius Nijhoff.

SCHWARTZ, HARRY. 1984. Narrowing the black–white health gap. *Wall Street Journal* (February 17): 20.

SCHWARTZ, MICHAEL, NAOMI ROSENTHAL, and LAURA SCHWARTZ. 1981. Leader–member conflict in protest organizations: The case of the Southern Farmers' Alliance. *Social Problems*, 29: 22–36.

SCHWARTZ, WILLIAM B. 1984. The most painful prescription. *Newsweek* (November 12): 24.

SCIOLINO, ELAINE. 1984. American Catholics: A time for challenge. *New York Times Magazine* (November 4): 40 + .

SCOTT, JOAN WALLACH. 1982. The mechanization of women's work. *Scientific American*, 247 (September): 167–187.

SEARS, F. W., M. W. ZEMANSKY, and H. D. YOUNG. 1982. *University physics*, 6th ed. Reading, Mass.: Addison-Wesley.

SEBOLD, HANS. 1977. *Adolescence: A social psychological analysis*, 2nd ed. Englewood Cliffs, N.J.: Prentice-Hall.

SEEMAN, MELVIN. 1959. On the meaning of alienation. *American Sociological Review*, 24: 783–791.

SELLTIZ, CLAIRE, LAWRENCE S. WRIGHTSMAN, and STUART W. COOK. 1976. *Research methods in social relations*, 3rd ed. New York: Holt, Rinehart and Winston.

SELMAN, R. L. 1980. *The growth of interpersonal understanding: Developmental and clinical analyses*. New York: Academic Press.

SERRIN, WILLIAM. 1984a. Companies widen worker role in decisions. *New York Times* (January 15): 1, 12.

SERRIN, WILLIAM. 1984b. Electronic office conjuring wonders, loneliness and tedium. *New York Times* (March 28): 10.

SERVICE, ELMAN. 1971. *Primitive social organization: An evolutionary perspective*. New York: Random House.

SERVICE, ELMAN. 1973. The ghost of our ancestors. In *Primitive worlds*. Washington, D.C.: National Geographic Society.

SEWELL, WILLIAM, and ROBERT HAUSER. 1975. *Education, occupation, and earnings: Achievement in the early career*. New York: Academic Press.

SHABECOFF, PHILIP. 1984. Pesticide is found in food samplings. *New York Times* (January 6): 1, 9.

SHABECOFF, PHILIP. 1985. Toxic waste threat termed far greater than U.S. estimates. *New York Times* (March 10): 1, 15.

SHANAS, ELEANOR. 1972. Adjustment of retirement: Substitution or accommodation? In F. Carp, ed., *Retirement*. New York: Behavioral Publications.

SHANAS, ELEANOR. 1982. The family relations of old people. *National Forum*, 62: 9–11.

SHAW, CLIFFORD R. 1930. *Natural history of a juvenile career*. Chicago: University of Chicago Press.

SHAW, CLIFFORD R., and HENRY McKAY. 1942. *Juvenile delinquency in urban areas*. Chicago: University of Chicago Press.

SHEA, JOHN C. 1984. *American government: The great game of politics*. New York: St. Martin's Press.

SHEEHY, GAIL. 1976. *Passages*. New York: Dutton.

SHEETS, KENNETH R. 1983. War over water. *U.S. News & World Report* (October 31): 57–62.

SHELDON, WILMON HENRY. 1954. *God and polarity*. New Haven, Conn.: Yale University Press.

SHERIF, MUZAFER. 1936. *The psychology of social norms*. New York: Harper & Row.

SHERIF, MUZAFER, O. J. HARVEY, B. JACK WHITE, WILLIAM R. HOOD, and CAROLYN W. SHERIF. 1961. *Intergroup conflict and cooperation: The Robbers' Cave experiment*. Norman: University of Oklahoma Book Exchange.

SHERMAN, JULIA. 1978. *Sex-related cognitive differences*. Springfield, Ill.: Thomas.

SHEVKY, ESHREF, and MARILYN WILLIAMS. 1949. *The social areas of Los Angeles*. Berkeley: University of California Press.

SHIBUTANI, TAMOTSU. 1966. *Improvised news: A sociological study of rumor.* Indianapolis: Bobbs-Merrill.

SHILLS, DAVID. 1957. *The volunteers.* New York: Free Press.

SHILS, EDWARD A., and MORRIS JANOWITZ. 1948. Cohesion and disintegration in the Wehrmacht in World War II. *Public Opinion Quarterly,* 12: 280–315.

SHIPLER, DAVID K. 1984. Israel's kibbutzim turn from communal ideals to needs of the individual. *New York Times* (June 27): 4.

SHORTER, EDWARD. 1975. *The making of the modern family.* New York: Basic Books.

SHREVE, ANITA. 1984. The working mother as role model. *New York Times Magazine* (September 9): 39–43 + .

SHRIBMAN, DAVID. 1984. The textbook approach to terrorism. *New York Times* (April 22): 16E.

SILK, LEONARD. 1982. Economic scene. *New York Times* (December 31): 28.

SIMMEL, GEORG. 1908/1955. *Conflict and the web of group affiliations.* New York: Free Press.

SIMMEL, GEORG. 1908/1959. How is society possible? In Kurt Wolff, ed., *Essays in sociology, philosophy, and aesthetics.* New York: Harper Torchbooks.

SIMMEL, GEORG. 1950. *The sociology of Georg Simmel.* Ed. and trans. Kurt Wolff. New York: Free Press.

SIMMONS, ROBERTA G., DALE A. BLYTH, EDWARD F. VAN CLEAVE, and DIANE MITSCH BUSH. 1979. Entry into early adolescence. *American Sociological Review,* 44: 948–967.

SIMMONS, ROBERTA G., and FLORENCE ROSENBERG. 1973. Disturbance in the self-image at adolescence. *American Sociological Review,* 38: 553–568.

SIMON, JULIAN L. 1981. *The ultimate resource.* Princeton, N.J.: Princeton University Press.

SIMON, JULIAN L., and HERMAN KAHN. 1984. *The resourceful earth: A response to Global 2000.* New York: Blackwell.

SIMPSON, GEORGE EATON, and J. MILTON YINGER. 1972. *Racial and cultural minorities,* 4th ed. New York: Harper & Row.

SINGER, ELEANOR. 1981. Reference groups and social evaluations. In Morris Rosenberg and Ralph H. Turner, eds., *Social psychology.* New York: Basic Books.

SIZER, THEODORE R. 1984. *Horace's compromise: The dilemma of the American high school.* Boston: Houghton Mifflin.

SJOBERG, GIDEON. 1960. *The preindustrial city.* New York: Free Press.

SKINNER, DENISE A. 1983. Dual-career family stress and coping: A literature review. In David H. Olson and Brent C. Miller, eds., *Family studies review yearbook.* Beverly Hills, Calif.: Sage.

SKOCPOL, THEDA. 1979. *States and social revolution.* Cambridge, Eng.: Cambridge University Press.

SKOCPOL, THEDA. 1980. Political response to capitalist crisis: Neo-Marxist theories of the state and the case of the New Deal. *Politics and Society,* 10: 155–201.

SKOLNICK, ARLENE. 1981. The family and its discontents. *Society,* 18 (January): 42–47.

SLOTKIN, JAMES S. 1955. Culture and psychopathology. *Journal of Abnormal and Social Psychology,* 51: 269–275.

SMELSER, NEIL J. 1959. *Social change in the Industrial Revolution.* Chicago: University of Chicago Press.

SMELSER, NEIL J. 1963. *Theory of collective behavior.* New York: Free Press.

SMITH, ALTHEA, and ABIGAIL J. STEWARD. 1983. Approaches to studying racism and sexism in black women's lives. *Journal of Social Issues,* 39: 1–15.

SMITH, KEVIN B. 1981. Class structure and intergenerational mobility from a Marxian perspective. *Sociological Quarterly,* 22: 385–401.

SMITH, RICHARD M., and CRAIG W. SMITH. 1981. Child rearing and single-parent fathers. *Family Relations,* 30: 411–417.

SMITH, TERENCE. 1984. Iran: Five years of fanaticism. *New York Times Magazine* (February 12): 21 + .

SMITH, TOM W. 1984. America's religious mosaic. *American Demographics,* 6 (June): 19–23.

SNOWDEN, FRANK M., JR. 1983. *Before color prejudice: The ancient view of blacks.* Cambridge, Mass.: Harvard University Press.

SOLOMON, JOLIE B. 1984. Procter & Gamble fights new rumors of link to Satanism. *Wall Street Journal* (November 8): 1, 21.

SOMMER, ROBERT. 1969. *Personal space.* Englewood Cliffs, N.J.: Prentice-Hall.

SORENSEN, AAGE B. 1975. The structure of intragenerational mobility. *American Sociological Review,* 40: 456–471.

SOROKIN, PITIRIM. 1959. *Social and cultural mobility.* New York: Free Press.

SOUTHERN SCHOOL NEWS. 1954. Segregation. *Southern School News,* 1 (November): 3.

SPANIER, GRAHAM B. 1983. Married and unmarried: Cohabitation in the United States: 1980. *Journal of Marriage and the Family,* 45: 277–288.

SPENGLER, OSWALD. 1918/1926. *The decline of the West.* New York: Knopf.

SPREY, JETSE. 1979. Conflict theory and the study of marriage and the family. In Wesley R. Burr, Reuben Hill, F. Ivan Nye, and Ira L. Reiss, eds., *Contemporary theories about the family.* Vol. 2. New York: Free Press.

STAGNER, R. 1975. Boredom on the assembly line: Age and personality variables. *Industrial Gerontology,* 2: 23–44.

STANLEY, THOMAS J., and GEORGE P. MOSCHIS. 1984. America's affluent. *American Demographics,* 6 (March): 28–33.

STARK, ELIZABETH. 1984. The unspeakable family secret. *Psychology Today,* 18 (May): 38–46.

STARK, RODNEY, and WILLIAM S. BAINBRIDGE. 1979. Of churches, sects, and cults: Preliminary concepts for a theory of religious movements. *Journal for the Scientific Study of Religion,* 18: 117–133.

STARK, RODNEY, and WILLIAM S. BAINBRIDGE. 1981. American-born sects: Initial findings. *Journal for the Scientific Study of Religion,* 20: 130–149.

STARR, PAUL. 1982. *The social transformation of American medicine.* New York: Basic Books.

STEARNS, PETER N. 1977. *Old age in European society.* London: Croom Helm.

STEINBERG, BRUCE. 1983. The mass market is splitting apart. *Fortune* (November 28): 76–82.

STEINBERG, LAURENCE D., RALPH CATALANO, and DAVID

DOOLEY. 1981. Economic antecedents of child abuse and neglect. *Child Development*, 52: 975–985.

STEPHENS, WILLIAM N. 1963. *The family in cross-cultural perspective.* New York: Holt, Rinehart and Winston.

STERBA, JAMES P. 1982. New study defends the social sciences. *New York Times* (June 22): 20.

STERNLIEB, GEORGE, and JAMES W. HUGHES. 1980. The changing demography of the central city. *Scientific American*, 243 (August): 48–53.

STEVENS, CHARLES W. 1983. European luxury cars capturing a growing share of the U.S. market. *Wall Street Journal* (May 6): 21.

STEWARD, JULIAN H. 1955. *Theory of culture change.* Urbana: University of Illinois Press.

STINCHCOMBE, ARTHUR L. 1983. *Economic sociology.* New York: Academic Press.

STITH, SANDRA M., and ALBERT J. DAVIS. 1984. Employed mothers and family day-care substitute caregivers: A comparative analysis of infant care. *Child Development*, 55: 1340–1348.

STOKES, RANDALL G. 1975. Afrikaner Calvinism and economic action: The Weberian thesis in South Africa. *American Journal of Sociology*, 81: 62–81.

STOKES, RANDALL G., and JOHN P. HEWITT. 1976. Aligning actions. *American Sociological Review*, 41: 838–849.

STOKES, RANDALL, and DAVID JAFFEE. 1982. Another look at the export of raw materials and economic growth. *American Sociological Review*, 47: 402–407.

STOLLER, ELEANOR PALO. 1983. Parental caregiving by adult children. *Journal of Marriage and the Family*, 45: 851–858.

STONE, KATHERINE. 1974. The origins of job structures in the steel industry. *The Review of Radical Economics*, 6: 61–97.

STRAUS, MURRAY A., RICHARD J. GELLES, and SUZANNE K. STEINMETZ. 1980. *Behind closed doors: Violence in the American family.* Garden City, N.Y.: Doubleday.

STRAUSS, ANSELM, and BARNEY GLASER. 1970. *Anguish.* San Francisco: Sociology Press.

STRAUSS, ANSELM, LEONARD SCHATZMAN, RUE BUCHER, DANUTA EHRLICH and MELVIN SABSHIN. 1964. *Psychiatric ideologies and institutions.* New York: Free Press.

STRUBE, MICHAEL J., and LINDA S. BARBOUR. 1983. The decision to leave an abusive relationship: Economic dependence and psychological commitment. *Journal of Marriage and the Family*, 45: 785–793.

STRYKER, SHELDON. 1980. *Symbolic interactionism: A social structural version.* Menlo Park, Calif.: Benjamin/Cummings.

STUCKEY, M. FRANCINE, PAUL E. McGHEE, and NANCY J. BELL. 1982. Parent–child interaction: The influence of maternal employment. *Developmental Psychology*, 18: 635–644.

SUDNOW, DAVID. 1967. *Passing on: The social organization of dying.* Englewood Cliffs, N.J.: Prentice-Hall.

SUMNER, WILLIAM GRAHAM. 1906. *Folkways.* Boston: Ginn.

SUNDSTROM, ERIC. 1978. Crowding as a sequential process: Review of research on the effects of population density on humans. In A. Baum and Y. M. Epstein, eds., *Human responses to crowding.* Hillsdale, N.J.: Erlbaum.

SUTHERLAND, EDWIN H. 1939. *Principles of criminology.* Philadelphia: Lippincott.

SUTHERLAND, EDWIN H. 1949. *White-collar crime.* New York: Dryden Press.

SWANN, WILLIAM B., JR., and CRAIG A. HILL. 1982. When our identities are mistaken: Reaffirming self-conceptions through social interaction. *Journal of Personality and Social Psychology*, 43: 59–66.

SWEENEY, JOAN. 1982. All moms spend about same time with kids. Columbus (Ohio) *Dispatch* (October 21): 11.

SZYMANSKI, ALBERT. 1976. Racial discrimination and white gain. *American Sociological Review*, 41: 403–414.

SZYMANSKI, ALBERT. 1978. White workers' loss from racial discrimination. *American Sociological Review*, 43: 776–782

SZYMANSKI, ALBERT. 1981. *The logic of imperialism.* New York: Praeger.

TAWNEY, R. H. 1926. *Religion and the rise of capitalism.* New York: Harcourt Brace Jovanovich.

TAYLOR, D. GARTH, PAUL B. SHEATSLEY, and ANDREW M. GREELEY. 1978. Attitudes toward racial integration. *Scientific American*, 238 (June): 42–49.

TAYLOR, ROBERT. 1984. White-collar crime getting less attention. *Wall Street Journal* (February 1): 25.

TAYLOR, RONALD A. 1984. The plague that's killing America's trees. *U.S. News & World Report* (April 23): 58–59.

TERRACE, HERBERT S. 1979. How Nim Chimpsky changed my mind. *Psychology Today*, 13 (November): 65–76.

THOMAS, W. I. 1923. *The unadjusted girl.* Boston: Little, Brown.

THOMAS, WILLIAM I., and DOROTHY S. THOMAS. 1928. *The child in America: Behavior problems and programs.* New York: Knopf.

THORNBERRY, TERENCE P., and MARGARET FARNWORTH. 1982. Social correlates of criminal involvement. *American Sociological Review*, 47: 505–518.

THORNBURG, HERSHEL D. 1983. Is early adolescence really a stage of development? *Theory into Practice*, 22: 79–84.

THRASHER, FREDERIC M. 1927. *The gang.* Chicago: University of Chicago Press.

THUROW, LESTER C. 1981. Why women are paid less than men. *New York Times* (March 8): F-2.

THUROW, LESTER C. 1984a. The leverage of our wealthiest 400. *New York Times* (October 11): 27.

THUROW, LESTER C. 1984b. The disappearance of the middle class. *New York Times* (February 5): F-3.

THUROW, LESTER C. 1984c. Learning to say "no." *New England Journal of Medicine*, 311: 1569–1572.

TIEGER, TODD. 1980. On the biological basis of sex differences in aggression. *Child Development*, 51: 943–963.

TILLY, CHARLES. 1978a. *From mobilization to revolution.* Reading, Mass.: Addison-Wesley.

TILLY, CHARLES, ed. 1978b. *Historical studies of changing fertility.* Princeton, N.J.: Princeton University Press.

TINBERGEN, NIKO. 1954. The origin and evolution of courtship and threat display. In J. S. Huxley, A. C.

Hardy, and E. B. Ford, eds., *Evolution as a process.* London: Allen & Unwin.

TITTLE, CHARLES R., and C. H. LOGAN. 1973. Sanction and deviance: Evidence and reexamining questions. *Law and Society Review,* 7: 372–392.

TITTLE, CHARLES R., and ALAN R. ROWE. 1974. Certainty of arrest and crime rates: A further test of the deterrence hypothesis. *Social Forces,* 52: 455–462.

TOENNIES, FERDINAND. 1887/1957. *Community and society.* Trans. Charles P. Loomis. East Lansing: Michigan State University Press.

TOFFLER, ALVIN. 1980. *The third wave.* New York: Morrow.

TOYNBEE, ARNOLD J. 1934/1954. *A study of history.* 10 volumes. New York: Oxford University Press.

TRAFFORD, ABIGAIL, PATRICIA A. AVERY, JEANNYE THORNTON, JOSEPH CAREY, JOSEPH L. GALLOWAY, and ALVIN P. SANOFF. 1984. She's come a long way—or has she? *U.S. News & World Report* (August 6): 44–51.

TRAUGOTT, MARK. 1978. Reconceiving social movements. *Social Problems,* 26: 38–49.

TROELTSCH, ERNST. 1931. *The social teachings of the Christian churches.* 2 vols. Trans. Olive Wyon. New York: Macmillan.

TUMIN, MELVIN. 1953. Some principles of stratification: A critical analysis. *American Sociological Review,* 18: 387–394.

TURCO, RICHARD P., OWEN B. TOON, THOMAS P. ACKERMAN, JAMES B. POLLACK, and CARL SAGAN. 1984. The climatic effects of nuclear war. *Scientific American,* 251 (August): 33–43.

TURKLE, SHERRY. 1984. *The second self: Computers and the human spirit.* New York: Simon and Schuster.

TURNER, JONATHAN H. 1982. *The structure of sociological theory.* Homewood, Ill.: Dorsey Press.

TURNER, PAULINE H., and RICHARD M. SMITH. 1983. Single parents and day care. *Family Relations,* 32: 215–226.

TURNER, RALPH H. 1964. Collective behavior. In R. E. L. Faris, ed., *Handbook of modern sociology.* Chicago: Rand McNally.

TURNER, RALPH H. 1968. The self-conception in social interaction. In C. Gordon and K. J. Gergen, eds., *The self in social interaction.* New York: Wiley.

TURNER, RALPH H., and LEWIS M. KILLIAN. 1972. *Collective behavior,* 2nd ed. Englewood Cliffs, N.J.: Prentice-Hall.

TYREE, ANDREA, MOSHE SEMYONOV and ROBERT W. HODGE. 1979. Gaps and glissandos: Inequality, economic development and social mobility. *American Sociological Review,* 44: 410–424.

UDRY, J. RICHARD. 1965. Structural correlates of feminine beauty in Britain and the United States. *Sociology and Social Research,* 49: 330–342.

U.S. NEWS & WORLD REPORT. 1979. In hot pursuit of business criminals. *U.S. News & World Report* (July 23): 59–60.

U.S. NEWS & WORLD REPORT. 1984. As past events fade in memory. *U.S. News & World Report* (January 23): 50–51.

USEEM, BERT. 1980. Solidarity model, breakdown model, and the Boston anti-busing movement. *American Sociological Review,* 45: 357–369.

USEEM, MICHAEL. 1983. *The inner circle.* New York: Oxford University Press.

VALENTINE, CHARLES. 1968. *Culture and poverty.* Chicago: University of Chicago Press.

VANCE, N. SCOTT. 1984. Sport is a religion in America, controversial professor argues. *Chronicle of Higher Education* (May 16): 25–29.

VAN CREVELD, MARTIN. 1982. *Fighting power: German and U.S. Army performance, 1939–1945.* Westport, Conn.: Greenwood Press.

VAN DEN BERGHE, PIERRE. 1963. Dialectic and functionalism: Toward a theoretical synthesis. *American Sociological Review,* 28: 695–705.

VANDER ZANDEN, JAMES W. 1965. *Race relations in transition.* New York: Random House.

VANDER ZANDEN, JAMES W. 1979. *Sociology,* 4th ed. New York: Wiley.

VANDER ZANDEN, JAMES W. 1983. *American minority relations,* 4th ed. New York: Knopf.

VANDER ZANDEN, JAMES W. 1984. *Social psychology,* 3rd ed. New York: Random House.

VANDER ZANDEN, JAMES W. 1985. *Human development,* 3rd ed. New York: Knopf.

VANNEMAN, REEVE, and FRED C. PAMPEL. 1977. The American perception of class and status. *American Sociological Review,* 42: 422–437.

VAN VELSOR, ELLEN, and ANGELA M. O'RAND. 1984. Family life cycle, work career patterns, and women's wages at midlife. *Journal of Marriage and the Family,* 46: 365–373.

VEBLEN, THORSTEIN. 1899. *The theory of the leisure class.* New York: Viking.

VEBLEN, THORSTEIN. 1921. *Engineers and the price system.* New York: Viking.

VERBA, SIDNEY, NORMAN H. NIE, and JAE-ON KIM. 1978. *Participation and political equality: A seven-nation comparison.* New York: Cambridge University Press.

VINING, DANIEL R., JR. 1982. Migration between the core and the periphery. *Scientific American,* 247: 45–53.

VISCUSI, W. K. 1983. Do economic incentives affect crime? *Chronicle of Higher Education* (January 18): 8.

VOGEL, LISE. 1983. *Marxism and the oppression of women.* New Brunswick, N.J.: Rutgers University Press.

WAGLEY, CHARLES, and MARVIN HARRIS. 1964. *Minorities in the New World.* New York: Columbia University Press.

WALDO, GORDON P., and THEODORE G. CHIRICOS. 1972. Perceived penal sanction and self-reported criminality: A neglected approach to deterrence research. *Social Problems,* 19: 522–540.

WALLERSTEIN, IMMANUEL. 1974. *The modern world-system: Capitalist agriculture and the origins of the European world economy in the 16th century.* New York: Academic Press.

WALLERSTEIN, IMMANUEL. 1980. *The modern world-system II: Mercantilism and the consolidation of the European world-economy, 1600–1775*. New York: Academic Press.

WALLERSTEIN, JUDITH S. 1984. Children of divorce. Paper presented at the sixty-first annual meeting of the American Orthopsychiatric Association, Toronto, April 8, 1984.

WALLERSTEIN, JUDITH S., and JOAN B. KELLY. 1980. *Surviving the breakup: How children and parents cope with divorce*. New York: Basic Books.

WALLIS, ROY. 1975. *Sectarianism: Analyses of religious and non-religious sects*. New York: Wiley.

WALSH, EDWARD J. 1981. Resource mobilization and citizen protest in communities around Three Mile Island. *Social Problems*, 29: 1–21.

WALSH, KENNETH T. 1984. Picking a winner: How candidates are chosen. *U.S. News & World Report* (October 8): 68–72.

WALTERS, PAMELA B. 1984. Occupational and labor market effects on secondary and postsecondary educational expansion in the United States: 1922 to 1979. *American Sociological Review*, 49: 659–671.

WARNER, W. LLOYD, 1949. *Democracy in Jonesville*. New York: Harper & Row.

WARNER, W. LLOYD, and PAUL S. LUNT. 1941. *The social life of the modern community*. New Haven, Conn.: Yale University Press.

WARNER, W. LLOYD, and PAUL S. LUNT. 1942. *The status system of a modern community*. New Haven Conn.: Yale University Press.

WATERMAN, ALAN S. 1982. Identity development from adolescence to adulthood. *Developmental Psychology*, 18: 341–358.

WATSON, RUSSELL. 1984. What price day care? *Newsweek* (September 10): 14–21.

WAYNE, LESLIE. 1982. Management gospel gone wrong. *New York Times* (May 30): F1, F21.

WAYNE, LESLIE. 1984. The irony and impact of auto quotas. *New York Times* (April 8): 14.

WEBER, MAX. 1904/1958. *The Protestant Ethic and the spirit of capitalism*. New York: Scribner's.

WEBER, MAX. 1916/1964. *The religion of China: Confucianism and Taoism*. New York: Macmillan.

WEBER, MAX. 1917/1958. *The religion of India: The sociology of Hinduism and Buddhism*. New York: Free Press.

WEBER, MAX. 1921/1968. *Economy and society*. 3 vols. Totowa, N.J.: Bedminster Press.

WEBER, MAX. 1946. *The theory of social and economic organization*. Ed. and trans. A. M. Henderson and Talcott Parsons. New York: Macmillan.

WEBER, MAX. 1947. *From Max Weber: Essays in sociology*. Ed. and trans. Hans. H. Gerth and C. Wright Mills. New York: Oxford University Press.

WEINBERG, MARTIN S., and COLIN J. WILLIAMS. 1980. Sexual embourgeoisment? Social class and sexual activity: 1938–1970. *American Sociological Review*, 45: 33–48.

WEINSTEIN, EUGENE, and JUDITH M. TANUR. 1976. Meanings, purposes and structural resources in social interaction. *Cornell Journal of Social Relations*, 11: 105–110.

WEISS, ROBERT S. 1984. The impact of marital dissolution on income and consumption in single-parent households. *Journal of Marriage and the Family*, 46: 115–127.

WELLS, GRADY. 1984. Healthy growth for HMOs. *American, Demographics* (March): 34–37 + .

WHEELER, STANTON. 1976. Trends and problems in the sociological study of crime. *Social Problems*, 23: 525–534.

WHITE, GREGORY L. 1980. Physical attractiveness and courtship progress. *Journal of Personality and Social Psychology*, 39: 660–668.

WHITE, LESLIE. 1959. *The evolution of culture*. New York: McGraw-Hill.

WHITE, RALPH K., and RONALD O. LIPPITT. 1960. *Autocracy and democracy*. New York: Harper & Row.

WHITE, THEODORE H. 1961. *The making of the president, 1960*. New York: Atheneum.

WHITEHEAD, ALFRED NORTH. 1929. *Process and reality*. New York: Macmillan.

WHITT, J. ALLEN. 1979. Toward a class-dialectical model of power: An empirical assessment of three competing models of political power. *American Sociological Review*, 44: 81–100.

WHITT, J. ALLEN. 1982. *Urban elites and mass transportation: The dialectics of power*. Princeton, N.J.: Princeton University Press.

WHORF, BENJAMIN L. 1956. *Language, thought, and reality*. Cambridge, Mass.: MIT Press.

WICKS, JERRY W., and EDWARD G. STOCKWELL. 1984. A comment on the neonatal mortality–socioeconomic status relationship. *Social Forces*, 62: 1035–1039.

WIENER, LEONARD, and ROBERT J. MORSE. 1985. The swelling ranks of U.S. millionaires. *U.S. News & World Report* (March 18): 53.

WILFORD, JOHN NOBLE. 1981. Nine percent of everyone who ever lived is alive now. *New York Times* (October 6): 13.

WILLIAMS, DENNIS A. 1985. Is college worth it? *Newsweek* (April 29): 66–68.

WILLIAMS, KIPLING, STEPHEN HARKINS, AND BIBB LATANÉ. 1981. Identifiability as a deterrent to social loafing: Two cheering experiments. *Journal of Personality and Social Psychology*, 40: 303–311.

WILLIAMS, ROBIN M., JR. 1964. *Strangers next door*. Englewood Cliffs, N.J.: Prentice-Hall.

WILLIAMS, ROBIN M., JR. 1970. *American society*, 3rd ed. New York: Knopf.

WILLIAMS, WINSTON. 1984. The shrinking of the steel industry. *New York Times* (September 23): 4F.

WILSON, EDWARD O. 1975. *Sociobiology: The new synthesis*. Cambridge, Mass.: Harvard University Press.

WILSON, JAMES Q. 1967. The bureaucracy problem. *The Public Interest*, 6: 3–9.

WILSON, JAMES Q. 1975. *Thinking about crime*. New York: Basic Books.

WILSON, JAMES Q. 1983. Thinking about crime. *The Atlantic Monthly* (September): 72–88.

WINCH, ROBERT F. 1958. *Mate selection: A study of complementary needs*. New York: Harper & Row.

WINN, EDWARD A. 1981. Looking at good schools. *Phi Delta Kappan*, 62: 377–381.

WINNER, LANGDON. 1984. Mythinformation in the high-tech era. *IEEE Spectrum*, 21: 90–96.

WOLF, ERIC R. 1982. *Europe and the people without history*. Berkeley: University of California Press.

WOLFGANG, MARVIN E., ROBERT M. FIGLIO, and THORSTEN SELLIN. 1972. *Delinquency in a birth cohort*. Chicago: University of Chicago Press.

WOODWARD, C. VANN. 1966. *The strange career of Jim Crow*, 2nd rev. ed. New York: Oxford University Press.

WOODWARD, KENNETH L. 1984. Vows of defiance. *Newsweek* (March 19): 97–100.

WORK, CLEMENS P., and ROBERT J. MORSE. 1985. Earnings of 100 highest-paid executives in 1984. *U.S. News & World Report* (April 29): 64.

WORK, CLEMENS P., and RONALD A. TAYLOR. 1984. Toxic chemicals: Just how real a danger? *U.S. News & World Report* (May 21): 64–67.

WREN, CHRISTOPHER S. 1984. China defends abortion in birth control efforts. *New York Times* (July 4): 4.

WRIGHT, ERIK OLIN. 1978a. *Class, crisis, and the state*. New York: Schocken Books.

WRIGHT, ERIK OLIN. 1978b. Race, class, and income inequality. *American Journal of Sociology*, 83: 1368–1388.

WRIGHT, ERIK OLIN. 1979. *Class structure and income determination*. New York: Academic Press.

YINGER, J. MILTON. 1957. *Religion, society, and the individual*. New York: Macmillan.

YINGER, J. MILTON. 1965. *Toward a field theory of behavior*. New York: Macmillan.

YLLO, KERSTI, and MURRAY A. STRAUS. 1981. Interpersonal violence among married and cohabiting couples. *Family Relations*, 30: 339–347.

ZABLOCKI, BENJAMIN. 1980. *Alienation and charisma: A study of contemporary American communes*. New York: Free Press.

ZALD, MAYER N., and JOHN D. McCARTHY. 1979. *The dynamics of social movements*. Cambridge, Mass.: Winthrop.

ZEY-FERRELL, MARY. 1981. Criticisms of the dominant perspective on organizations. *The Sociological Quarterly*, 22: 181–205.

ZIGLI, BARBARA. 1984. Asian-Americans beat others in academic drive. *USA Today* (April 25): 1D.

ZIMBARDO, PHILIP G. 1969. The human choice: Individuation, reason, and order versus deindividualization, impulse, and chaos. In W. Arnold and D. Levine, eds., *Nebraska Symposium on Motivation*, 17: 237–307.

ZIMBARDO, PHILIP G. 1978. Misunderstanding shyness: The counterattack. *Psychology Today*, 12 (June): 17–18+.

ZIMMER, JUDITH. 1984. Courting the gods of sport. *Psychology Today*, 18 (July): 36–39.

ZIMMERMAN, DON H. 1971. The practicalities of rule use. In Jack D. Douglas, ed. *Understanding everyday life*. Chicago: Aldine.

ZIPP, JOHN F., RICHARD LANDERMAN, and PAUL LUEBKE. 1982. Political parties and political participation. *Social Forces*, 60: 1140–1153.

ZONANA, VICTOR F. 1984. Is the U.S. middle class shrinking alarmingly? Economists are split. *Wall Street Journal* (June 20): 1, 16.

ZUBIN, J., and B. SPRING. 1977. Vulnerability—A new view of schizophrenia. *Journal of Abnormal Psychology*, 86: 103–126.

ZUEKERMAN, MIRON, M. H. KERNIS, S. M. GUARNERA, J. F. MURPHY, and L. RAPPOPORT. 1983. The egocentric bias: Seeing oneself as cause and target of others' behavior. *Journal of Personality*, 51: 621–630.

Name Index

Abernathy, William J., 230, 234
Abrahamson, Mark, 49
Ackerman, Nathan W., 196
Adelson, Joseph, 76
Adorno, T. W., 196
Agnew, Robert, 326
Akhavi, Shahrough, 300
Albonetti, Celesta, 135
Alexander, Herbert, 246
Alger, Horatio, 179
Allport, Gordon W., 191
Anderson, Charles H., 162, 168, 392
Anderson, Harry, 230
Anderson, L. S., 147
Anderson, Nels, 22
Andres, David, 271
Andrew, John, 376
Apple, Michael W., 313, 315
Aries, Philippe, 74
Aron, Arthur P., 17–20
Asch, Solomon, 99, 386

Babbie, Earl R., 298
Bachman, Herold G., 76
Bainbridge, William S., 292–293
Bales, Robert F., 96, 209
Balkwell, Carolyn, 84
Bandura, Albert, 208
Bane, Mary Jo, 254
Bar, Shmuel, 162
Baran, Paul, 233
Barbour, Linda S., 272
Barclay, A. M., 18
Barkow, J. H., 34
Barnett, Rosalinda C., 275
Barrett, Carol, 273
Barron, D. Susan, 160
Barth, Joan M., 97–98
Baruch, Grace, 275
Bass, Bernard M., 96
Baum, Andrew, 335
Baumeister, Roy F., 69
Beach, F. A., 205
Bean, L. L., 174
Bear, John, 65

Beck, E. M., 183
Beck, Melinda, 358
Beck, Scott, 83
Becker, Howard S., 120, 136
Beirne, Piers, 224
Belkin, Lisa, 212
Bell, Alan P., 282
Bell, Daniel, 46
Bell, Nancy J., 270
Bell, T. H., 321
Bellah, Robert N., 309
Belsky, Jay, 269
Bendix, Reinhard, 101
Bendix, Richard, 168
Benedetto, Richard, 282
Benoit-Smullyan, Emile, 12
Benson, J. Kenneth, 108
Ben-Yehuda, Nachman, 124
Bequai, August, 140
Berger, Brigitte, 263
Berger, Joseph, 64
Berger, Peter L., 3, 263, 288, 299
Berk, Richard, 271
Berk, Sarah F., 271
Berle, Adolph, Jr., 234
Bernard, Jessie, 204
Bernstein, Ilene N., 135
Berreman, Gerald, 155
Berscheid, Karen, 264
Bettelheim, Bruno, 196
Bianchi, Suzanne M., 272, 281
Bierstedt, Robert, 220
Bird, Gerald A., 272
Bird, Gloria W., 272
Birdwhistell, Raymond L., 64
Blackburn, McKinley L., 174
Blau, Peter M., 104, 108, 162, 180–182, 265
Blau, Zena Smith, 83
Blauner, Robert, 237
Block, Fred, 224
Bloom, David E., 174, 260, 279, 280
Bluestone, Barry, 175
Blumberg, Paul, 173, 177
Blumer, Herbert, 51–52, 109, 191

Blumstein, Philip, 210, 265, 267, 279, 282
Blyth, Dale A., 76
Bohannan, Paul, 275
Bohlander, Edward W., 135
Bonacich, Edna, 197
Bonger, William A., 134
Bornschier, Volker, 231, 233
Boserup, Ester, 345
Bottomore, Thomas B., 11, 169
Bowles, Samuel, 313
Bradbury, Katharine L., 357
Brewer, Marilyn B., 98
Bridgewater, Carol Austin, 174
Briggs, Kenneth A., 302, 307
Brim, Orville G., 81
Brinton, Crane, 389
Brody, Elaine M., 276
Brody, Jane E., 237, 264, 274
Bromley, D. B., 75, 192
Bronfenbrenner, Urie, 254
Brooks-Gunn, Jeanne, 75
Brophy, Beth, 83
Brown, Don W., 146–147
Brown, Kennedy M., 376
Brozan, Nadine, 273
Bryjak, George J., 146
Burawoy, Michael, 236
Burgess, R. L., 265, 273
Burke, Edmund, 225
Burnham, James, 234
Buss, Terry F., 2
Butterfield, Fox, 292

Calhoun, John, 334
Calvin, John, 299, 301
Cann, Arnie, 142
Cantril, Hadley, 386
Caplow, Theodore, 267–268
Cargan, Leonard, 278
Carrington, Tim, 231
Carter, Jimmy, 246–247
Carver, Charles S., 94
Catalano, Ralph, 283
Catton, William R., Jr., 331–333
Chafetz, Janet Saltzman, 294

Chaiken, Jan M., 147
Chaiken, Marcia R., 147
Chall, Daniel E., 356
Chambliss, William J., 135, 137–138
Chapel, James L., 273
Chase-Dunn, Christopher, 231
Chayet, Ellen F., 144
Cheek, Jonathan, 69
Cherlin, Andrew, 274
Childe, V. Gordon, 45, 350
Chiricos, Theodore G., 135, 146
Chittister, Joan D., 307
Choldin, Harvey M., 326, 334
Chomsky, Noam, 63
Christian, J. J., 334
Cicirelli, Victor G., 275
Clark, David L., 319
Clark, R. A., 18
Clark, Reginald M., 181, 230
Clendinen, Dudley, 292
Clinard, Marshall B., 135
Clingempeel, W. Glen, 275
Cohen, Albert K., 120, 125, 130–131
Cohen, Jere, 77, 302
Cohen, Mark N., 345
Cole, Stephen, 16
Coleman, James S., 106, 160, 275, 319
Coleman, Richard D., 165
Colgan, Patrick, 33
Colligan, Michael J., 381
Collins, Randall, 3, 31, 49, 108, 168–169, 209, 223, 261–262, 288, 299, 302, 313, 315
Comte, Auguste, 7–8, 268
Conger, Rand D., 273
Connor, Walter D., 182
Cook, R. V., 208
Cook Stuart W., 22
Cooley, Charles Horton, 51, 68–69
Cordes, Colleen, 92
Cornfield, Noreen, 283
Coser, Lewis A., 50, 125, 183, 371
Cowell, Alan, 327–328
Cox, Martha, 273
Cox, Oliver C., 197

Cox, Roger, 273
Cressey, Donald R., 141
Crewdson, John, 200
Critchfield, Richard, 155, 177
Cromer, Janis, 77
Crosby, Faye, 192
Cunningham, Susan, 390–391
Curtiss, Susan, 60–61
Cyert, Richard M., 175

Dahl, Robert, 49–50, 167, 171–172, 247, 263, 370–371, 377
Dale, Philip S., 63
Damon, William, 75
Datan, Nancy, 73
Davie, Maurice, 354
Davies, James, 181, 392
Davies, Mark, 77
Davis, Albert J., 270–271
Davis, Allison, 164
Davis, Glen E., 335
Davis, Kingsley, 14, 47, 60, 73, 155, 168–169, 222, 258, 293, 345, 347–348, 379
DeAre, Diana, 357
Deaux, Kay 20–21, 23
Degler, Carl, 254
Delacroix, Jacques, 377
de Luce, Judith, 34
Demos, J., 75
Demos, V., 75
De Vries, Raymond G., 84
Diebold, John, 372
DiMaggio, Paul, 173
Dion, Karen, 264
Dionne, E. J., Jr., 21, 291
Dipboye, Robert L., 382
Djilas, Milovan, 109, 171
Doan, Michael, 304
Dolan, Carrie, 113
Domhoff, G. William, 224, 247
Donne, John, 2
Dooley, David, 273
Dowd, Maureen, 210, 214
Downs, Anthony, 357
Doyle, Patricia, 135
Dragastin, Sigmund E., 76
Driggs, Michael, 230
Drucker, Peter F., 394
Dubin, Robert, 236

Dullea, Georgia, 261
Dumont, L., 256
Duncan, Greg, 177, 180
Duncan, Otis Dudley, 162, 180–182
Dupaquier, J., 345
Durkheim, Emile, 11–13, 126, 129, 237–238, 288, 293–294
Dusek, Jerome B., 76
Dutton, Donald G., 17–20
Dynes, Russell, 171

Ebaugh, Helen R. F., 294
Eberstadt, Nick, 346
Eckholm, Erik, 374
Edwards, L. P., 389
Edwards, Richard, 109
Ehrhardt, Anke A., 206
Ekman, Paul, 65–66
Elder, Glen H., 76
Elkind, David, 76
Elliott, Delbert S., 131
Elliott, Gregory C., 67
Ellyson, Steve L., 160
Elmendorf, Edward, 321
Empey, Lamar T., 144
Emslie, Graham J., 273
Engelgau, Donna, 319
Engels, Friedrich, 162, 261
English, Carey W., 113
Epstein, Sue Hoover, 338
Erickson, Frederick, 194
Erickson, Maynard L., 144, 147
Erickson, Rosemary, 275
Erikson, Erik, 76, 77, 78–79, 379–380
Erikson, Kai T., 120, 126–127, 136
Etaugh, Claire, 271
Etzioni, Amitai, 100
Evangelauf, Jean, 211
Evans, Peter B., 233

Farber, B. A., 237
Farel, Anita M., 269
Farnworth, Margaret, 144
Fauve-Chamoux, A., 345
Fava, L. Richard Della, 235
Featherman, David L., 180–181, 211, 315

Feigenbaum, Edward A., 373–374
Feldman, Ronald A., 2
Fenigstein, Alan, 67
Figlio, Robert M., 146
Fine, Mark A., 274, 378
Finkelhor, David, 273
Fischer, Michael M. J., 300
Fisher, Anne B., 230
Fiske, Edward B., 318
Flaherty, John F., 76
Flandrin, J. F., 254
Ford, G. S., 205
Freedman, J. L., 335
Freeman, Jo, 212
Freud, Sigmund, 77, 207–208, 262
Friedman, Andrew, 109
Friedman, Thomas L., 50
Friesen, Wallace V., 65
Fuchs, Victor R., 254
Fuller, C. J., 256
Furstenberg, Frank F., 274

Galbraith, John Kenneth, 234–235
Gale, Dennis E., 356
Ganong, Lawrence H., 275
Gans, Herbert J., 48
Gappa, Judith M., 271
Garbarino, James, 273
Gardner, B. B., 164
Gardner, M. R., 164
Garfinkel, Harold, 110
Geertz, Clifford, 189
Gelles, Richard J., 272–273
George, Linda K., 83
Gerson, Menachem, 161
Geschwender, James A., 208, 392
Gest, Ted, 140
Gibbs, Jack P., 146–147
Giddens, Anthony, 392
Gilbert, C., 82
Gintis, Herbert, 313
Ginzberg, Eli, 236
Glamser, F. D., 83
Glasberg, Davita S., 235
Glaser, Barney, 84
Glass, David, 243

Glenn, Norval, 268
Glick, Clarence, 191, 274
Glock, Charles Y., 298
Gluckman, Max, 263
Goffman, Erving, 42, 72, 100, 317
Gold, Dolores, 271
Goldin-Meadow, Susan, 63
Goldstone, Jack A., 389
Goleman, Daniel, 68
Gonos, George, 72
Goode, William J., 222, 256, 261, 263
Goodman, Ann B., 174
Gordon, Linda, 273
Gough, E. Kathleen, 256
Gould, Roger L., 77
Gouldner, Alvin, 49
Gove, Walter R., 90, 138
Grasmick, Harold G., 146
Grassian, Stuart, 90
Grebenik, E., 345
Greeley, Andrew M., 192, 307
Green, John C., 245
Greenwald, A. G., 67–68
Greenwood, Peter W., 147
Greer, Colin, 254
Grimshaw, Allen D., 62, 64
Gruenberg, Barry, 237
Grundstaff, Carol F., 347
Grusky, David, 182
Gurney, Patrick J., 10
Gurr, Ted R., 392
Gusfield, Joseph, 240
Guth, James L., 245, 304

Haber, R. N., 18
Hacker, Helen Mayer, 188
Hadden, Jeffrey K., 304
Hadley, Arthur T., 243
Hagan, John, 135
Hale, Ellen, 82
Hall, Trish, 34, 280
Hallblade, Shirley, 373
Hamilton, Alexander, 174, 220
Hamilton, Charles, 192
Hammersmith, Sue K., 282
Hammond, Phillip E., 309
Handel, Warren, 110
Hardin, Garrett J., 97–98

Hare, A. Paul, 95
Hareven, Tamara K., 256
Harkins, Stephen, 97
Harrington, Michael, 392
Harris, Chauncey, 355
Harris, Marvin, 190, 223–224
Harrison, Bennett, 175
Harrison, Michael I., 308
Harsanyi, Zsolt, 61
Hart, David, 75
Hauser, Robert M., 180–182, 211, 315
Hawley Amos H., 160, 326
Hay, Dale F., 75
Hays, Charlotte, 31
Hays, Robert H., 234
Hearst, Patricia, 99
Heath, Dwight B., 259
Hegel, Georg, 10
Herbers, John, 304, 308
Herdt, Gilbert, 76
Herman, Edward S., 235
Herman, Judith, 273
Herskovits, Melville J., 367
Hess, Beth, 276
Hetherington, E. Mavis, 273
Hewitt, John P., 30, 32
Hill, Charles T., 68
Hiltz, Starr Roxanne, 374
Himes, Joseph, 50
Himmelfarb, Gertrude, 178
Himmelstein, Jerome L., 304
Hindelang, Michael J., 144
Hinds, Michael, 273
Hinkle, Roscoe, 14
Hirschi, Travis, 144
Hirschman, Lisa, 273
Hobbes, Thomas, 221
Hoby, Jean Pierre, 232
Hodge, Robert, 182
Hoebel, E. A., 31
Hoffman, Lois W., 270
Hoge, Dean R., 76
Holden, Constance, 338
Holusha, John, 235
Horan, Patrick, 183
Horning, Donald, 108
Hostetler, John A., 38
Hough, Joseph C., Jr., 191
Hoyt, Homer, 354

Hsu, Francis L. K., 237
Huber, Joan, 272
Hughes, Michael, 90
Hughes, Raymond, 357
Hull, Raymond, 105
Hultsch, David F., 81
Humphries, Charlene, 94
Huntley, Steve, 202
Husain, Arshad, 273
Huston, T. L., 265
Hutton, Richard, 61
Hyde, Janet Shibley, 207
Hyman, Herbert, 94

Ibrahim, Youssef M., 300
Ichilov, Orit, 162
Imperato-McGinley, J., 207
Im Thurn, E. F., 82
Ingham, Alan G., 97
Innes, J. M., 382
Isaac, Larry, 179
Iyer, Pico, 300

Jacklin, Carol N., 207–208
Jaffee, David, 378
Jahoda, Marie, 196
James, John, 95
Janis, Irving, 98
Janowitz, Morris, 92, 196
Jencks, Christopher, 274, 315
Jenkins, J. Craig, 392–393
Jenness, Diamond, 311
Johnson, Lyndon B., 192
Johnson, Peter, 77
Johnson, Weldon, 147
Johnstone, Ronald L., 290
Judd, Charles M., 77

Kagan, Jerome, 271
Kahn, Herma, 333
Kain, Edward L., 277
Kalleberg, Arne L., 237
Kamin, Leon J., 9, 34, 62
Kandel, Denise B., 77
Kantrow, Alan, 230
Kaplan, H. Roy, 237
Karabel, Jerome, 315
Kasindorf, Martin, 203
Katz, Sidney, 173

Kaufman, Michael T., 348
Kearsley, Richard B., 271
Keller, Bill, 177
Keller, Helen, 32–33
Keller, Suzanne, 238
Kelly, Joan B., 274
Kelly, Orr, 135
Kelly, William R., 179
Kendler, Kenneth S., 128
Keniston, Kenneth, 77
Kennedy, Eugene, 308
Kenny, Timony, 84
Kerbo, Harold R., 162, 166, 172,
    178–179, 235
Kerr, N. L., 97
Kessler, Ronald C., 272
Kett, J. F., 75
Khomeini Ayatollah, 299
Kidd, Robert F., 144
Kifner, John, 300
Killian, Lewis M., 386
Kim, Jae-On, 174
Kimmel, D. C., 78, 378
Kinder, Donald R., 191
Klein, Frederick C., 357
Klemesrud, Judy, 212–213
Kluckhohn, Clyde, 30, 35
Kluegel, James R., 191
Koenig, Frederick, 378–379
Koestler, Arthur, 296–297
Kohlberg, Lawrence, 208
Kohn, Melvin L., 81, 237
Kolko, Gabriel, 224
Komorita, Samuel S., 97–98
Kornhauser, William, 240
Kramer, Roderick M., 98
Krosnick, Jon A., 77
Kübler-Ross, Elisabeth, 85

Lamb, Michael, E., 269
Landerman, Richard, 174
Landers, Ann, 31–32
Lang, Abigail M., 276
Lang, O., 82
Langley, Monica, 38
Langway, Lynn, 280
Larsen, Erik, 113
Laslett, Peter, 256
Lasswell, Harold, 49

Latané, Bibb, 97
Lauer, Robert H., 110
Lazarsfeld, Paul L., 14
Lazerwitz, Bernard, 308
Le Bon, Gustave, 385–386
Lee, Felicia, 210
Lee, Gary R., 257
Lemert, Edwin M., 120, 136
Lenneberg, Eric H., 64
Lenski, Gerhard E., 45, 49, 50,
    152, 167, 172, 220, 225, 368–
    369
Lenski, Jean, 45
Leon, Jeffrey, 135
Leung, Eleanor H. L., 75
Levinson, Daniel J., 77, 80–82
Levinson, Harry, 237
Lévi-Strauss, Claude, 258
Lewin, Kurt, 96
Lewis, I. A., 282
Lewis, Michael, 75
Lewis, Oscar, 177
Lewontin, R. C., 9, 34, 62
Libby, Roger W., 277–278
Lieberson, Stanley, 189
Liebow, Elliot, 3–6, 22, 177
Linden, Fabian, 175
Lindsey, Robert, 316
Linton, Ralph, 36, 41, 73, 258,
    367–368
Lippitt, Ronald, 96
Lipset, Seymour Martin, 106,
    181, 240
Lipton, Douglas, 146
Livesley, W. J., 75
Lizotte, Alan J., 135
Loeb, Leonard, 261
Lofland, Lyn, 84
Logan, C. H., 146
Long, Larry, 357
Lopata, Helena Znaniecki, 84
Lotto, Linda S., 319
Lowenthal, Marjorie F., 238
Lowie, Robert H., 30
Luebke, Paul, 174
Lukacs, George, 171
Lukes, Steven, 237
Lumsden, Charles J., 158
Lung, Chien, 36

Lunt, Paul S., 164
Lynd, Helen Merrill, 267
Lynd, Robert S., 267
Lyons, Richard D., 278

Maccoby, Eleanor E., 207–208
Maddox, George L., 83, 182
Madrick, Jeffrey, 234
Main, Jeremy, 112
Maital, Shlomo, 162
Makowsky, Michael, 3
Malinowski, Bronislaw, 208, 261
Malthus, Thomas Robert, 344
Mann, James, 281, 303
Mann, Leon, 382
Marglin, Stephen, 109
Mars, Gerald, 108
Martinson, Robert, 146, 148
Marty, Martin E., 307
Maruyama, Geoffrey, 264
Marx, Gary, 264, 385
Marx, Karl, 7, 9–11, 109, 155, 161, 162, 169–171, 237–238, 297–298, 371, 385, 391–392
Maschek, John, W., 246
Masterson, John, 274
Mathews, Walter M., 373
Mazur, Allan, 64
McBee, Susanna, 203
McCarthy, John D., 76, 392
McCarthy, Martha M., 319
McConahay, John B., 191
McCorduck, Pamela, 373–374
McGee, Reece, 288
McGhee, Paul E., 270
McGuire, Meredith B., 298–299
McKay, Henry, 131
McKinley, William, 298–299
McLanahan, Sara S., 280
McLaughlin, Steven D., 269
McLuhan, Marshall, 352
McQuillan, Kevin, 347
McRae, James A., 272
McRoberts, Hugh, A., 182
Mead, George Herbert, 51, 69–70, 72
Means, Gardiner C., 234
Mehrabian, Albert, 64
Meier, Robert F., 147

Melko, Matthew, 278
Melman, Seymour, 234
Merton, Robert K., 14, 47–48, 124, 129–131
Messick, David M., 98
Meyer-Bahlberg, H. F. L., 206
Michalowski, Raymond J., 135
Michels, Robert, 105–106
Micklin, Michael, 269, 326
Middleton, Russell, 258
Milgram, Stanley, 385–386
Miliband, Ralph, 224
Miller, Norman, 264
Miller, Walter B., 133
Mills, C. Wright, 6–7, 10, 14, 49, 241, 247
Mills, David M., 275
Milne, L., 82–83
Mintz, Beth, 235
Mirowsky, John, 210
Mischel, Walter, 208
Mollenkopf, John, 224
Money, John, 206–207
Moore, Didi, 272
Moore, Wilbert, 168–169
Moran, Richard, 139
Moreland, John R., 274
Morris, Julie, 121
Morse, Nancy C., 237
Morse, Robert J., 156, 158
Mortimer, Jeylan T., 73, 82
Moschis, George P., 157
Moskowitz, Breyne Arlene, 63
Mottl, Tahil, 394
Murdock, George Peter, 35, 37, 73, 204–205, 212, 258
Murphy, Lawrence R., 381
Murstein, Bernard I., 265
Myers, Henry F., 376
Myers, J. K., 174
Myrdal, Gunner, 188

Nader, Ralph, 271
Naisbitt, John, 46, 394
Nathan, Richard P., 356
Nelson, Keith E., 64
Neugarten, Bernice L., 78, 82, 275
Newcomb, Theodore M., 40

Newman Barry, 233
Newton, James W., 382
Nezlek, John, 264
Nie, Norman H., 174
Niebuhr, H. Richard, 290, 292
Nilson, L. B., 209
Nisbet, Robert, 162, 239–240
Nock, Steven, 268
Noel, Donald M., 196–197
Notestein, Frank W., 345
Nye, F. Ivan, 270

O'Barr, Jean F., 271
O'Connor, James, 224
O'Driscoll, Patrick, 302
Offer, Daniel, 76
Offer, Judith B., 76
Ogburn, William F., 307–371
O'Keefe, Paul, 273
Olsen, Marvin E., 49, 239, 247, 364
O'Malley, Patrick M., 76
O'Rand, M. O., 211
Ordovensky, Pat, 77, 321
O'Reilly, Jane, 272
Ovid, 17–18

Palmer, Barbara, 271
Pampel, Fred C., 162
Papernow, Patricia, 275
Parkinson, C. Northcote, 104–105
Parnes, H. S., 83
Parsons, Talcott, 14, 47, 209, 369–370
Pear, Robert, 140, 158, 176–177
Pebley, Anne R., 260, 280
Pennebaker, James W., 381
Pentalla, Cheryl, 279
Perrow, Charles, 104, 111–112, 392–393
Peter, Lawrence J., 105
Petersen, William, 346
Peterson, Karen S., 80, 271, 280
Petras, James, 54
Plemmons, J. K., 81
Plumb, J. H., 74
Pope, Liston, 290
Porter, Bruce D., 105

Poulantzas, Nicos, 224
Pratkanis, A. R., 68
Press, Aric, 141
Presthus, Robert, 100
Prewitt, Kenneth, 2, 223

Quadagno, Jill S., 224, 256
Quarantilli, Enrico, 171
Quinney, Richard, 134

Raab, Selwyn, 141
Ragin, Charles C., 377
Rainach, W. M., 298
Rainwater, Lee, 160, 165
Rangel, Jesus, 201
Rapoport, R., 268
Rapoport, R. N., 268
Redburn, F. Stevens, 2
Reich, Walter, 121
Reis, Harry T., 264
Reynolds, Larry, 54
Rheingold, Harriet L., 75, 208
Riche, Martha Farnsworth, 307
Richman, Kathe, 294
Ricks, Thomas E., 271
Ridgeway, Cecilia L., 64
Riesman, David, 247
Ringer, Benjamin B., 298
Risman, Barbara J., 279
Ritzer, George, 7, 14, 47, 49, 104, 225
Rivers, W. H. R., 259
Roberts, Sam, 141
Robertson, Hector M., 302
Robey, Bryant, 199
Robinson, Bryan E., 275
Rockefeller, John D., 9
Rodman, Hyman, 162
Rooney, James F., 100
Rose, Arnold, 66
Rose, Steven R., 9, 34, 62
Rosenberg, Morris, 67, 77
Rosenfeld, Eva, 161
Rosnow, Ralph, 378
Rosow, Irving, 83
Ross, Katherine E., 210
Rossi, Alice S., 62
Rousseau, Jean Jacques, 221
Rovine, Michael, 269
Rubenstein, Carin, 272

Rubinson, Richard, 231, 233, 378
Russell, Cheryl, 201
Rutter, Michael, 318
Ryder, Robert G., 269

Sagan, Carl, 330
Sagarin, Edward, 120, 125–127, 131
Salmans, Sandra, 379
Samuelson, Robert J., 230
Samuelsson, Kurt, 302
Sanders, William B., 15
Sanoff, Alvin P., 308–309
Sapir, Edward, 34
Saxe, Leonard, 192
Scarf, Maggie, 207
Schacter, Francis F., 269
Schellhardt, Timothy D., 341
Schill, Michael P., 356
Schneider, William, 282
Schoenherr, Richard A., 108
Schooler, Carmi, 81, 237
Schorr, Alvin L., 176
Schreiner, Tim, 177
Schroeder, Patricia, 212
Schuman, Frederick L., 297
Schumer, Fran, 302–303
Schur, Edwin, 142
Schutz, Alfred, 51
Schwartz, Harry, 199, 349
Schwartz, Michael, 235
Schwartz, Pepper, 210, 265, 267, 279, 282
Schweiker, Richard S., 330
Sciolino, Elaine, 307
Scott, Joan Wallach, 210
Scott, Richard, 104
Scruggs, Marguerite, 272
Sears, F. W., 364
Sears, O., 191
Sebald, Hans, 76
Seeman, Melvin, 237
Seidman, Robert, 135
Selbee, Kevin, 182
Sellin, Thorsten, 146
Selltiz, Claire, 22
Selman, R. L., 75
Semyonov, Moshe, 182
Serrin, William, 112–113, 376
Service, Elman, 37, 368

Sewell, William, 182
Shabecoff, Philip, 329, 331
Shakespeare, William, 41
Shanas, Eleanor, 83
Shaw, Clifford, R., 131
Shea, John C., 245, 248
Sheatsley, Paul B., 192
Sheehy, Gail, 79–80
Sheets, Kenneth, 330
Sheldon, Wilmon Henry, 364
Sherif, Muzafer, 93–94, 98–99, 197, 386
Sherman, Deborah, 273
Sherman, Julia, 207
Shevky, Eshref, 355
Shibutani, Tamotsu, 378
Shils, Edward A., 92
Shipler, David, 162
Shorter, Edward, 254
Shreve, Anita, 271
Silk, Leonard, 375
Sills, David, 100
Simmel, Georg, 49, 262
Simmons, Roberta G., 73, 77, 82
Simon, Julian L., 333–334
Simpson, George Eaton, 194
Singer, Eleanor, 94
Sizer, Theodore R., 317
Skinner, Denise A., 271
Skocpol, Theda, 23, 224, 389
Skolnick, Arlene, 255, 273–274
Slotkin, James S., 128
Small, Kenneth A., 357
Smelser, Neil J., 256, 382–385
Smith, Althea, 188
Smith, Craig W., 281
Smith, Kevin B., 183
Smith, LeRoy, 64
Smith, Richard M., 281
Smith, Terence, 300
Smith, Tom W., 174, 305, 308
Snowden, Frank M., Jr., 191
Solomon, Jolie B., 379
Sorenson, Aage B., 180
Soroken, Pitirim, 172
Spanier, Graham B., 269, 274, 278–279
Spencer, Herbert, 8–9, 368
Spengler, Oswald, 360
Spitze, Glenna, 272

Sprey, Jetse, 50, 262
Spring, B., 128
Squire, Peverill, 243
St. John–Parsons, Donald, 271
Stagner, R., 238
Stanley, Thomas, J., 157
Stark, Elizabeth, 273
Stark, Rodney, 292–293
Starr, Paul, 348
Stearns, Peter N., 256
Steinberg, Bruce, 174–175
Steinberg, Laurence D., 271, 273
Steinhilber, Andrew, 69
Steinmetz, Suzanne K., 272–273
Stephens, William N., 254, 259
Sterba, James P., 2
Sternlieb, George, 357
Stevens, Charles, 159
Steward, Abigail J., 188
Steward, Julian, 368
Stinchcombe, Arthur, 236
Stith, Sandra M., 270–271
Stockwell, Edward G., 173
Stokes, Randall G., 30, 302, 378
Stoller, Eleanor Palo, 276
Stone, Alan, 223
Stone, Katherine, 109
Straus, Murray A., 272–273, 279
Strauss, Anselm, 84, 110
Strelitz, Z., 268
Strube, Michael J., 272
Stryker, Sheldon, 52–53
Stuckey, Francine, 270
Sudnow, David, 84
Sullivan, Anne Mansfield, 32–33
Sumner, William Graham, 30, 35
Sundstrom, Eric, 334–335
Sutherland, Edwin H., 132–133, 135
Swann, Charles E., 304
Swann, William B., 68
Sweeney, Joan, 270
Sweezy, Paul M., 233
Szymanski, Albert, 197, 231, 233

Tanur, Judith M., 54
Tarde, Gabriel, 131
Tausky, Curt, 237
Tawney, R. H., 302

Taylor, D. Garth, 192
Taylor, Robert, 141
Taylor, Ronald A., 328–329
Taylor, Frederick Winslow, 113
Terrace, Herbert S., 34
Thomas, Dorothy S., 66–67
Thomas, William I., 22, 66–67
Thoreau, Henry David, 94
Thornberry, Terence P., 144
Thornburg, Hershel, D., 75
Thrasher, Frederic M., 22, 131
Thurow, Lester C., 157–158, 174, 211, 348
Tieger, Todd, 207
Tilly, Charles, 346–347, 392, 394
Tinbergen, Niko, 18
Tittle, Charles R., 146–147
Toch, Hans, 386
Tocqueville, Count Alexis de, 100
Toffler, Alvin, 46, 394
Tolbert, Charles, 183
Toynbee, Arnold J., 369–370
Traeger, Carol M., 76
Trafford, Abigail, 210
Traugott, Mark, 386
Troeltsch, Ernst, 290
Trotsky, Leon, 298
Trow, Martin A., 106
Tucker, 206–207
Tumin, Melvin, 168
Turco, Richard P., 330
Turkle, Sherry, 374
Turner, Jonathan H., 7
Turner, Pauline H., 281
Turner, Ralph H., 68, 70, 386
Turoff, Murray, 374
Tyree, Andrea, 182

Ullian, D. Z., 208
Ullman, Edward I., 355
Urdy, J. Richard, 264
Useem, Bert, 394
Useem, Michael, 247

Valentine, Charles, 177
Vance, N. Scott, 297
Van Creveld, Martin, 92
van den Berghe, Pierre, 50, 172

Vander Zanden, James W., 2, 47, 51, 62, 67, 90, 189–190, 196, 273, 356, 388, 392, 394
Vanneman, Reeve, 162
Van Velsor, Ellen, 211
Veblen, Thorstein, 159–160, 194
Verba, Sidney, 174
Vining, Daniel R., Jr., 340
Viscusi, W. K., 138
Vogel, Lisa, 209

Wagley, Charles, 190, 223–224
Wagner, Michael, 67
Waldo, Gordon P., 135, 146–147
Wallerstein, Immanuel, 231, 233
Wallerstein, Judith S., 274
Wallis, Roy, 290
Walsh, Edward J., 394
Walsh, Kenneth T., 245
Walster, Elaine, 264
Walters, Pamela, 313
Ward, Lester F., 14
Waring, Joan M., 276
Warner, Lloyd W., 164–165
Watson, Russell, 271
Wayne, Leslie, 230, 235
Weaver, C. N., 268
Weber, Max, 13–14, 101–104, 155, 225–226, 300–301
Weinberg, Martin S., 174, 282
Weinstein, Eugene, 54
Weis, Joseph, 144
Weis, Lois, 313
Weiss, Robert S., 237
Wells, H. G., 381, 383–384
West, Meredith J., 75
Wheeler, Ladd, 264
Wheeler, Stanton, 135
White, Gregory, 265
White, Leslie, 368
White, Ralph K., 96
White, Theodore H., 158–159
Whitehead, Alfred North, 364
Whitt, J. Allen, 246
Whorf, Benjamin L., 34
Wicks, Jerry W., 173
Wiener, Leonard, 156
Wilder, Hugh T., 34
Wiley, James, 182
Wilford, John Noble, 336

Wilks, Judith, 146
Williams, Colin J., 174
Williams, Dennis A., 320
Williams, Kipling, 97
Williams, Marilyn, 355
Williams, Robin M., 31, 124
Williams, Winston, 230
Wilson, Edward O., 258
Wilson, James Q., 106, 146, 258
Winch, Robert F., 265
Winn, Edward A., 319
Winner, Langdon, 374–376
Wolf, Eric R., 377
Wolfgang, Marvin E., 146–147
Wolfinger, Raymond, 243

Woods, James I., 385
Woodward, C. Vann, 198
Woodward, Kenneth L., 308
Work, Clemens P., 158, 328
Wren, Christopher S., 348
Wright, Erik Olin, 156, 162, 171, 172, 181, 183
Wrightsman, Lawrence, 20–21, 23

Yeager, Peter C., 135
Yinger, J. Milton, 67, 194, 298
Yllo, Kersti, 279
Young, H. D., 364

Zablocki, Benjamin, 282–283
Zald, Mayer N., 392
Zelazo, Philip R., 271
Zemansky, M. W., 364
Zey-Ferrell, Mary, 108–109
Zigli-Barbara, 203
Zimbardo, Philip G., 69
Zimmer, Judith, 298
Zimmerman, Don H., 111
Zipp, John F., 174
Zonana, Victor F., 174
Zubin, J., 128
Zuckerman, Miron, 67

Subject Index

achieved statuses, 41
acting crowd, 382
adolescence, 75–77
adulthood:
later, 82–84
middle, 81–82
young, 77–81
age norms, 77–78
age-specific death rate, 337
age-specific fertility, 336
aggregate, 43
alienation, in work, 237–238
American Sign Language, 32–33, 63
American Sociological Association, 23–24
Amish, 37–38
animism, 289
anomie, 128
anomie perspective:
applying, 130–131
and Durkheim, 129
evaluating, 130–131
and Merton, 129–131
anticipatory socialization, 73
apartheid, 195; *see also* discrimination
arbitration, 222
archival research, 23
artifacts, 65
asceticism, 301
ascribed statuses, 41
Asian-Americans, 202–204
assimilation, 194
authority:
definition of, 225
in family, 257
and legitimacy, 224–226
See also power; state

baby boom generation, 342
Bay of Pigs invasion, 98
behavior:
choking, 69
conformity, 129–130
fashioning, 52
innovation, 130
rebellion, 130
retreatism, 130
ritualism, 130
self-awareness, 68
sexual, 260–261
shyness, 68–69
See also collective behavior
bilineal descent, 256
blacks, 198–199
body language, 64; *see also* nonverbal communication
bureaucracy:
definition of, 101
disadvantages of, 104–106
in education, 316–317
humanizing, 112–114
Weber's analysis of, 101–104
burnout, 238

campus religious revival, 303
capitalism, *see* corporate capitalism
capitalist economies, 227
capitalists, 224
casual crowd, 381
category, 43–44
Catholics, 307–308
charismatic authority, 226
child abuse, 272–273
childhood, 74–75
choking, 69
Christian right, 304–305
church, 290–292
circular reaction, 385
city:
definition of, 350
and ecological processes, 355–356
future of, 356–358
growth of, 352–355
industrial-urban, 351
metropolitan, 351–352
preindustrial, 350–351
social area analysis of, 355
civil religion, 309

class conflict, 10, 371
closed system, 153, 155
coercive organizations, 100–101
cognitive-developmental theory, *see* labeling perspective
cohabitation, 278–279
Coleman-Rainwater divisions, 165–166
collective behavior:
definition of, 378
explanations of, 385–387
preconditions for, 382–385
varieties of, 378–382
See also behavior
communes, 282–283; *see also* kibbutzim
communication, 62–66
complementary needs, 265
computer revolution, 372–374;
see also technology
concentric-circle model, of urban structure, 352–354
conflict perspective:
on deviance, 133–135
diversity of approaches in, 49
on education, 313, 315–316
on environment, 328
evaluating, 50, 54
on family, 261–262
on formal organization, 108–109
on gender stratification, 208–209
on racial and ethnic stratification, 196–198
on religion, 297–299
on social change, 371
on social stratification, 169–172
of society, 50
and sources of conflict, 49–50
on state, 223–224
theorists of, 49

conformity, 99, 129–130
conglomerates, 235
consensus, social, 48
constraints, 160
constructed reality, 51–52
contagion theory, 385–386
control group, 19
conventional crowd, 381–382
convergence theory, 386
Copper Eskimos, 311
core regions, 231, 233
corporate capitalsim:
    concept of, 228
    and control of corporations, 234–236
    and multinational corporations, 231, 233–234
    and national corporations, 228, 230–231
correlation, 16
correspondence principle, 313
Cosa Nostra, 141
countercultures, 38–39
courts, 139–140
crazes, 380
credentialism, 315–316
crime:
    definition of, 138
    deterrence from, 146–147
    index, 141
    measure of, 143–144
    organized, 141
    punishment for, 145
    rehabilitation after, 145–146
    and selective confinement, 147–148
    victimless, 142–143
    violent, 141–142
    white-collar, 140–141
    See also criminal justice system
criminal justice system:
    and courts, 139–140
    definition of, 138–139
    and police, 139
    and prisons, 140
    See also crime
criminology; see crime; criminal justice system; penology
crowd behavior; see collective behavior

crowding, 334–335
crowds, 381–382
crude birth rate, 336
crude death rate, 337
cult, 293
cultural integration, 35–36
cultural lag, 370
cultural relativism, 37
cultural transmission perspective:
    applying, 133
    evaluating, 133
    and gender identities, 208
    Sutherland and, 131–132
    Tarde and, 131
cultural universals, 35
culture:
    components of, 29–30
    and countercultures, 38–39
    and cultural integration, 35–36
    and cultural relativism, 37
    and cultural universals, 35
    definition of, 29
    and ethnocentrism, 36–37
    and gender roles, 204–206
    and groups, 43–44
    and institutions, 44
    and language, 32–34
    and norms, 30–31
    and roles, 41–43
    and societies, 44–46
    and statuses, 40–41
    and subcultures, 37–38
    and symbols, 32–34
    and values, 31–32
    See also society
culture of poverty, 177
cyclical perspectives, 369–370

death, 84–85
defense, 222
definition of situation, 66–67
deindividualization, 382
democracy, 240–241
demographic transition, 345–347
demography, 336; see also population
denomination:
    definition of, 293
    types of, 305–309

density, 344–345
dependency; see world-system
dependent variable, 16, 19
deprivation approaches, 391–392
descent, 256–257
deterrence, 146–147
deviance:
    anomie perspective on, 129–131
    conflict perspective on, 133–135
    cultural transmission perspective on, 131–133
    definition of, 120
    effects of, social, 125–127
    labeling perspective on, 135–138
    nature of, social, 122
    primary, 136
    properties of, social, 120–121, 123–124
    relativity of, 120–121
    secondary, 136
    and social control, 124–125
    sociological perspective on, 127–129
    See also crime; criminal justice system
dialectic, 10
dialectical materialism, 10–11
differential association, 132–133
diffusion, 367–368
discovery, 367
discrimination, 191–194
displaced homemakers, 274
divorce, 273–274
dominant group policies, 194–195
donut structure, 297
dramaturgical approach, 72
dual labor market, 183
duties, 42
dyads, 95
dying; see death
dysfunctions, 47–48, 104, 125–126

ecological environment:
    and carcinogens, 330–331
    conflict perspective on, 328

and crowding, 334–335
definition of, 326–327
functionalist perspective on,
327–328
optimistic view of, 333–334
pessimistic view of, 331–333
and population, 329–330
and resources, 328–329
and toxic sites, 328–329
economic power:
and comparative economic
systems, 227–228
concepts of, 226–227
and corporate capitalism,
228–236
and workplace, 236–239
economic standing, 156–158
See also social class
economic systems, 227–228
economies of scale, 340
ecosystem, 326
education:
availability of, 319–321
and bureaucracy in schools,
316–317
conflict perspective on, 313,
315–316
definition of, 310
and effectiveness of schools,
317–319
functionalist perspective on,
310–313
and population changes, 344
egalitarian authority, 257
egocentric bias, 67
elderly; see old age
elections, 243–244
electronic church, 303–304
elitist perspective, on political
power, 247–248
emergent-norm theory, of collective behavior, 386
employee-ownership plans,
113–114
employee participation, 112–113
endogamy, 257–258
enforcement of norms, 221–222
environment, 326; see also ecological environment; pop-
ulation; urban environ-
ment

ethic, 301
ethnic groups, 190
ethnic stratification; see racial
and ethnic stratification
ethnocentrism, 36–37, 196–197
ethnomethodological perspective, 110–111
ethnomethodology, 110–111
evolution, 368–369
evolutionary perspectives, 368–
369
exchange theory, 265
exogamy, 257–258
experimental group, 19
experiments, 19–20; see also research
expressive crowd, 382
expressive movements, 388–389
expressive ties, 91
extended family, 255–256
extermination, 195

fads, 379–380
family:
authority in, 257
and childless marriages,
279–280
and cohabitation, 278–279
and communes, 282–283
composition of, 255–256
concept of, 254–255
conflict perspective on, 261–
262
and descent, 256–257
divorce in, 273–274
elderly in, 275–276
employed mothers in, 269–
271
functionalist perspective on,
259–261
and gay couples, 281–282
gender roles in, 209–210
interactionist perspective on,
262–263
parenthood in, 268–269
residence of, 257
and singlehood, 276–278
and single parenthood, 280–
281
and stepfamilies, 274–275

two-income couples in, 271–
272
violence in, 272–273
See also marriage
family life cycle, 268
family of orientation, 256
family of procreation, 256
fashions, 379
fecundity, 336
feminism, see women's movement
folkways, 30
force, 220; see also power
formal organizations:
alternative perspectives,
108–112
definition of, 99–100
types of, 100–101
See also bureaucracy; education; groups; informal organizations; religion
fraternities, 53
functionalist perspective:
and consensus, social, 48
on education, 310–313
on environment, 327–328
evaluating, 48–49, 54
on family, 259–261
and functions, 47–48
on gender stratification, 208–
209
on racial and ethnic stratification, 195–196
on religion, 293–297
on social change, 370–371
on social stratification, 168–
169
on state, 221–223
and system, social, 47
theorists of, 47
functions, 47–48, 125–127
fundamentalist revival, 302–305
futurists, 394

gatekeeping, 192, 194
gay couples, 281–282
gender identities, 207–208
gender roles, 204–207
gender stratification:
and biology, 206–207
changes in, 213–214

gender stratification (continued)
    conflict perspective on, 208–
        209
    and culture, 204–206
    definition of, 204
    in family, 209–210
    functionalist perspective on,
        208–209
    and gender identities, 207–
        208
    in politics, 211–212
    and women's movement,
        212–213
    in workplace, 210–211
    See also racial and ethnic
        stratification; social strati-
        fication
general fertility rate, 336
generalized belief, 383
generalized other, 70, 72
genocide, 195
government:
    concept of, 239–240
    democracy, 241–242
    gender roles in, 211–213
    and religion, 309–310
    totalitarianism, 240–241
    See also political power
Great Society, 178–179
group marriage, 258–259
groups:
    and conformity, 99
    definition of, 90
    ethnic, 190
    and groupthink, 98–99
    in-groups versus out-groups,
        93–94
    interest, 244
    leadership in, 96
    minority, 190–191
    primary versus secondary,
        91–93
    reference, 94–95
    and relationships, 91
    role of, 90
    size of, 95–96
    and social dilemmas, 97–98
    and social loafing, 97
    social structure of, 43–44
    See also formal organization;
        informal organizations

groupthink, 98–99
growth rate, 340–341

health care system, American,
        348–349
health maintenance organiza-
        tions (HMOs), 348-349
hermaphrodites, 206
hidden curriculum, 313
Hindu caste system, 155
Hispanics, 199–201
HMOs, 348–349
homogamy, 264
homosexuality, 282
horizontal mobility, 180
hospice, 85
hypothesis, 16, 18

ideal type, 13
ideology, 387
imitation, 385
impression management, 72
imprisonment, see penology
incest taboos, 258, 272–273
income, 156
independent variable, 16
index crimes, 141
Indians, American, 201–202
inducements, 160
Industrial Revolution, 7, 14, 45–
        46
infant mortality rate, 337–338
informal organizations, 106–
        108; see also formal orga-
        nizations; groups
in-group, 93–94
innovations, 130, 367
institutional discrimination,
        192–194
institutions, 44; see also educa-
        tion; formal organiza-
        tions; religion
instrumental ties, 91
integration, in education, 311
interactionist perspective:
    and behavior, 52
    evaluating, 52, 54
    on family, 262–263
    on formal organizations, 109
    on meaning, 51–52
    theorists of, 51

interest groups, 244
interests, 244
intergenerational mobility, 180
internalization, 125
internal migration, 339
international migration, 339
intimacy, 266; see also marriage
invasion, 356
invention, 367
invulnerability, 382
iron law of oligarchy, 105
Islamic Revolution, Iranian,
        299–300

Jews, 308–309

kibbutzim, 161–162, 258; see also
        communes
kinship, 45

labeling perspective:
    applying, 137–138
    Becker and, 136–137
    Erikson and, 136–137
    evaluating, 138
        and gender identities, 208
    Lennert and, 136–137
language, 32–34
language acquisition device, 63
latent functions, 48, 312–313
laws, 31, 120, 222
leadership, 96
learning, 310; see also education
legal-relational authority, 225–
        226
legitimacy, 224–226
life chances, 173
life events, 81
life style, 276
linguistic relativity hypothesis,
        34
lobbying, 244, 246
looking-glass self, 68
love; see marriage; romantic
        love

Mafia, 141
mana, 288
manifest functions, 48
marriage:
    childless, 279–280

and cohabitation, 278–279
and communes, 282–283
definition of, 257
and divorce, 273–274
and elderly, 275–276
and employed mothers, 269–271
exogamy and endogamy, 257
and gay couples, 281–282
group, 258–259
and married couples, 265, 267–268
and parenthood, 268–269
partners, choice of, 263–265
and singlehood, 276–278
and single parenthood, 280–281
and stepfamilies, 274–275
and two-income couples, 271–272
types of, 258–259
violence in, 272–273
See also family
Marxism, 224, 227, 246
mass hysteria, 380–381
mass media, 245–246
mass psychogenic illness, 380
master statuses, 41
matching hypothesis, 265
material culture, 29
matriarchal authority, 257
matrilineal descent, 256
matrilocal residence, 257
mechanical solidarity, 12
megalopolis, 352
menopause, 82
Mexican-Americans, 200
middle class, 174–175
minority groups:
    and ethnic groups, 190
    legal protection of, 195
    properties of, 190–191
    and races, 189–190
mobilization, 384, 389
modernization, 377
monogamy, 258
monotheism, 289
mores, 30–31
mortification, 101
multinational corporations, 231, 233–234

multiple nuclei model, 354–355

national corporations, 228, 230–231
Native Americans, 201–202
Nazism, 239–241
natural areas, 355
natural history of revolution, 389
natural selection, 9
nature/nurture controversy, 61–62
negotiated order, 110
neolocal residence, 257
net migration rate, 338–339
nonmaterial culture, 29
nonverbal communication, 64–66
norm of legitimacy, 260–261
norms, 30–31
nuclear family, 255–256
nurture/nature controversy, 61–62

objective method, 163–164
observations, 22–23
Oedipus conflict, 207–208
old age, 82–84, 275–276
oligarchy, 105–106
oligopoly, 228, 230
open system, 153, 155
operational definition, 18
organic solidarity, 12
organized crime, 141
out-group, 93–94

PACs, 244, 246
panic, 381
paralanguage, 64
parenthood:
    and divorce, 273–274
    and employed mothers, 269–271
    in nuclear families, 268–269
    single, 280–281
    and stepfamilies, 274–275
    in two-income couples, 271–272
    and violence, 272–273
Parkinson's law, 104–105
participant observation, 22

patriarchal authority, 257
patrilineal descent, 256–257
patrilocal residence, 257
penology:
    deterrence, 146–147
    punishment, 145
    rehabilitation, 145–146
    selective confinement, 147–148
periphery regions, 232
persuasion, 160
Peter principle, 105
Pitcairn Islanders, 28–29
pluralism, 194
pluralist perspective, on political power, 248
POET complex, 326–327
police, 139
political-action committees (PACs), 244, 246
political parties, 242–243
political power:
    concept of, 238–239
    elitist perspective on, 246–248
    gender roles in, 211–212
    Marxist perspective on, 246
    pluralist perspective on, 247–248
    in U.S., 242–244, 246–247
    See also government
pollution, 329–330
polyandry, 258–259
polygyny, 258–259
polytheism, 289
population:
    change in, 336–341
    composition of, 341–342, 344
    and demographic transition, 345–347
    and ecological environment, 329–330
    and education, 344
    and health care system in U.S., 348–349
    Malthus and, 344–345
    Marx and, 345
    policies, 347–348
    and social change, 366
population pyramid, 342
population transfer, 195

poverty:
    definition of, 175–176
    programs for, 178–179
    properties of, 48
    theories of, 176–178
    victims of, 176
power:
    and conflict, 40
    definition of, 160, 220
    and social stratification, 160–
        161
    See also state
predestination, doctrine of, 301
prejudice, 191
prestige, 158–160
primary deviance, 136
primary group, 91–93
prisons, 140
profane, 288
Protestant ethic, 300–302
Protestants, 306–307
proxemics, 64–65
puberty rites, 76
public-interest groups, 244
public opinion pollsters, 21
punishment, 145

races:
    Asian-Americans, 202–204
    blacks, 198–199
    concept of, 189–190
    Hispanics, 199–201
    Native Americans, 201–202
racial and ethnic stratification:
    and Asian-Americans, 202–
        204
    and blacks, 198–199
    conflict perspective on, 196–
        198
    definition of, 188–189
    and dominant-group poli-
        cies, 194–195
    functionalist perspective on,
        195–196
    and Hispanics, 199–201
    and minorities, 189–191
    and Native Americans, 201–
        202
    and prejudice and discrimi-
        nation, 191–192, 194

    See also gender stratification;
        social stratification
random sample, 21
rape, 142
rebellion, 130
recidivism, 146
reference groups, 94–95
reform movements, 387–388
rehabilitation, 145–146
relationships, 91
relative deprivation, 94, 392
religion:
    conflict perspective on, 297–
        299
    definition of, 288
    functionalist perspective on,
        293–297
    and fundamentalist revival,
        302–305
    and Islamic Revolution, 299–
        300
    mainline groups of, 305–309
    organizations of, 290–293
    and Protestant ethic, 300–302
    and state–church issues,
        309–310
    types of, 288–290
reproduction, 259–260
reputational method, 164–165
research:
    ethics, 23–24
    and logic of science, 15–16
    methods, 19–23
    and scientific method, 16
residence, family, 257
resistance movements, 388
resource mobilization ap-
        proaches, 392–393
resources, 328–329, 366
retirement, 83
retreatism, 130
revolutionary movements, 387–
        388
rights, 42
ritualism, 130
rituals, 288
rivalries, 295
role conflict, 42–43
role performance, 42
roles, 41–43

role set, 42
role strain, 43
romantic love, 263
rumors, 378–379

sacred, 288
Sardinians, 61–62
satisfaction, in work, 237–238
schools; *see* education
secondary deviance, 136
secondary group, 91–93
sect, 292–293
sector model, 354
segregation, 2, 355
selective confinement, 147–148
self:
    Cooley and, 68–69
    definitions of, 67–68
    Goffman and, 72
    Mead and, 69–70, 72
self-awareness, 68
self-conception, 68; *see also* self
selfhood process, 71
self-image, 68; *see also* self
self-placement method, 164
sexism; *see* gender stratification
sex ratio, 341–342
shyness, 68–69
significant other, 70
singlehood, 276–278
small work groups, 113
social area analysis, 355
social change:
    definition of, 364–365
    and future, 394–395
    patterns of, 372–373
    perspectives on, 368–371
    sources of, 365–368
    in third world nations, 377–
        378
    in U.S., 371–377
    See also collective behavior; so-
        cial movements
social class:
    combined method of identi-
        fying, 165–167
    divisions in, 162
    and middle class, 174–175
    objective method of identify-
        ing, 163–164

and poverty, 175–179
reputational method of identifying, 164–165
self-placement method of identifying, 164
significance of, 173–174
See also social mobility; social stratification
social clock, 78
social control, 124–125, 384–385
social differentiation, 153
social dilemmas, 97–98
social dynamics, 8
social-emotional specialist, 96
social facts, 12, 40, 90
socialist economies, 227
socialism; *see* Marxism
socialization:
    in adolescence, 75–77
    in childhood, 74–75
    and communication, 62–66
    in death, 84–85
    definition of, 60
    and definition of situation, 66–67
    in education, 311
    in family, 260
    in later adulthood, 82–84
    in middle adulthood, 81–82
    and nature versus nurture, 61–62
    process of, 73–74
    in young adulthood, 77–81
    See also self
social loafing, 97
social mobility:
    definition of, 179–180
    forms of, 180
    in industrialized societies, 181–182
    and status attainment process, 182–183
    in U.S., 180–181
    See also social class; social stratification
social movements:
    causes of, 391–394
    definition of, 381
    and social revolution, 389–390

and terrorism, 390–391
types of, 387–389
See also social change
social revolution, 389–390
social statics, 8
social stratification:
    conflict perspective on, 169–172
    definition of, 152
    dimensions of, 155
    and economic standing, 156–158
    explanations of, 167–168
    functionalist perspective on, 168–169
    and kibbutzim, 161–162
    open versus closed systems of, 152–153, 155
    and power, 160–161
    and prestige, 158–160
    and social differentiation, 152
    synthesis of perspectives on, 172
    See also gender stratification; social and ethnic stratification; social class; social mobility
social structure:
    definition of, 39–40
    and groups, 43–44
    and institutions, 44
    and roles, 41–43
    and societies, 44–46
    and statuses, 40–41
society:
    conflict perspective on, 50
    definition of, 29
    social structure of, 44–46
    and sociology, 2
    superstructure of, 11
    See also culture
socioeconomic life cycle, 182
sociological imagination, 6–7, 14
sociology:
    American, 14–15
    and Comte, 7–8
    definition of, 2
    and deviance, 122

and discrimination, 193
and Durkheim, 11–13
and fraternities and sororities, 53
and informal organizations, 107
and intimacy, 266
and Liebow study, 3–6
and Marx, 9–11
and rivalries, 295
and selfhood process, 71
and social change, 372–373
and society, 2
and sociological imagination, 6–7
and Spencer, 8–9
and stratification, 154
and technology, 375
value-free, 13
and walkways, 4–5
and Weber, 13–14
See also conflict perspective; functionalist perspective; interactionist perspective; research
sororities, 53
special-interest groups, 244
split labor market, 197
state:
    conflict perspective on, 223
    definition of, 220–221
    functionalist perspective on, 221–223
    See also authority; power; political power
statuses, 40–41, 260
stepfamilies, 274–275
strategic elites, 230
stratification, *see* social stratification
stratified random sample, 21
structural conduciveness, 383
structural strain, 383
style of life, 174
subcultures, 37–38
subjugation, 195
succession, 356
suggestibility, 382, 385
suicide, 12
superstructure, 11

superwoman syndrome, 271
surveys, 20–22
symbolic racism, 191
symbols, 32–34, 51
system, 47

task specialist, 96
TAT, 18
technology, 374–377; *see also*
    computer revolution
terrorism, 390–391
theism, 289
Thematic Apperception Test
    (TAT), 18
Thomas theorem, 66–67
total institution, 317
totalitarianism, 239–240
totemism, 293–294
touch, 65
toxic waste sites, 329, 331
traditional authority, 225
trained incapacity, 104

triads, 95
trigger, 383–384

unobtrusive observation, 22
urban environment:
    and ecological processes,
        355–356
    and evolution of cities, 350–352
    and future of cities, 356–358
    and growth of cities, 352–355
urban gentrification, 356
utilitarian organizations, 101

value-added model, 382–385
value-free sociology, 13
values, 31–32, 366–367
variable, 15–16
verbal communication, 63–64
verstehen, 13, 52
vertical mobility, 180
victimless crime, 142–143
violent crime, 141–142
voluntary organizations, 100

walking, 4–5
Watergate, 125, 226
wealth, 156
white-collar crime, 140–141
women's movement, 212–213
work:
    alienation in, 237–238
    satisfaction in, 237–238
    significance of, 237
    See also workplace
workplace:
    and economic power, 236–
        239
    gender roles in, 210–211
    See also work
world-system, 377–378

youth culture, 38

zero population growth (ZPG),
    337

About the Author

James W. Vander Zanden is a professor of sociology at Ohio State University and previously taught at Duke University. His Ph.D. is from the University of North Carolina. Professor Vander Zanden's published works include more than twenty professional papers and eight books, including *Human Development*, Third Edition; *American Minority Relations*, Fourth Edition; and *Social Psychology*, Third Edition, which are published by Random House/Alfred A. Knopf.